THE LIFE OF
ANDREW JACKSON

THE MACMILLAN COMPANY
NEW YORK · BOSTON · CHICAGO · DALLAS
ATLANTA · SAN FRANCISCO

MACMILLAN & CO., Limited
LONDON · BOMBAY · CALCUTTA
MELBOURNE

THE MACMILLAN CO. OF CANADA, Ltd.
TORONTO

ANDREW JACKSON IN 1829. AGE 62

From a portrait by Thomas Sully owned by the Historical Society of Pennsylvania. Sully's
portraits of Jackson are probably the best. For a list see Hart, C. H.,
Thomas Sully's Register of Portraits, page 89

THE LIFE

OF

ANDREW JACKSON

BY

JOHN SPENCER BASSETT, PH.D.

*Professor of American History in Smith College on the
Sydenham Clark Parsons Foundation*

VOLUME ONE

Illustrated

NEW EDITION

" *If you would preserve your reputation, or that of
the state over which you preside, you must take a
straightforward determined course; regardless of the
applause or censure of the populace, and of the forebodings of that dastardly and designing crew who,
at a time like this, may be expected to clamor
continually in your ears.*" — *Jackson to Governor
Blount, 1813.*

New York

THE MACMILLAN COMPANY

1916

PREFACE

PROBABLY the first person to take thought of a life of Andrew Jackson was Jackson himself. His letters show that he began to preserve material for his biographer from the time he became a public personage. The drafts of the letters he wrote, the letters he received, and his simplest public papers were carefully filed away in boxes. Some of the papers were endorsed, "To be kept for the historian." They became numerous with the wars against the Creeks and the British, his first great achievements; and out of that phase of life came his first biography. To Major John Reid, military aide, faithful companion in the darkest hours of trial, author of many of Jackson's military papers, and a man of real ability — as his book shows — was entrusted the task of preparing this story. He carried the narrative through the Creek war before it was interrupted by death in 1816. Jackson was concerned to find a man to complete the work, and at last hit upon John H. Eaton, then a promising young lawyer whose industry was so great that the book was placed before the public in 1817. Its origin, progress, and completion were all under the direct oversight of Jackson himself. Eaton brought out a second edition in 1828, with chapters bringing the story down to date. It was not a critical work, but the parts which had no bearing on the political campaigns of 1824 and 1828 were well written. Reid particularly recommends himself as a straightforward historian.

Jackson's political career brought forth a plentiful crop of biographies, all of which are mentioned in the exhaustive preface to Parton's "Life of Jackson." Some praised him and some condemned, but none were satisfactory. Meantime, the collection of letters and official documents was ever growing, and other men, ambitious of renown or of Jackson's favor, aspired to write a comprehensive biography. First it was James Gadsden, who was assured in 1822 that he should have the coveted opportunity. Why he gave it up does not appear. He was from South Carolina, a friend of Calhoun, and went into occultation when that statesman ceased to be chief lieutenant of the democratic leader. That of itself would have made his literary hopes impossible. Next, Major Henry Lee, of eminent Viriginia lineage, and a ready political writer, got the promise. He actually began the task, but fell from favor in 1829 when charged with such grave personal immorality that he could no longer be countenanced. He was rejected by the senate for an unimportant consulate, and turned against Jackson. It was with some difficulty that he was induced to give up the forty pages he had finished of the proposed book.

Other aspirants were Roger B. Taney, George Bancroft, and Amos Kendall. The last was given the promise of the papers. He began to write in 1842, when he had lost the auditorship to which his patron appointed him. He was then poor financially and expected large returns from his venture. He began to publish it in parts, announcing that fifteen would complete the enterprise. Jackson placed the entire collection of papers at his disposal, and two visits to the "Hermitage" gave fair opportunity to get all it contained. He carried away to Washington many of the most important papers and had not returned them when Jackson died in 1845. His work was interrupted when seven instalments had appeared, and it was not completed. Jackson was not pleased with the numbers which he saw, but did not withdraw the papers. There was a plan on foot to build a Jackson memorial in Washington, and he desired them to be handed over by Kendall, when he had finished with them, to Frank P.

Blair to hold until the memorial was completed, when they were to be deposited there. The least valuable of the collection were not taken to Washington by Kendall, and these went to Blair from Jackson himself. Later Kendall turned over a part of those in hand to Blair, but the latter complained that the most valuable were not delivered. Blair also said that Kendall would yet publish a life of Jackson, written to glorify the writer of it; and he intended to charge his sons to write a true biography which would counteract the errors he expected to be in Kendall's. This, so far as the letters show, is all the basis that existed for the assertion that Blair was to write the life.

Kendall died in 1869 and Blair in 1876. They had long been estranged, and neither had the impulse to write the authentic book which Jackson contemplated. Meanwhile, James Parton, the most successful American biographer of his day, undertook the task. Blair gave him all encouragement, but he seems to have had none from Kendall. His first volume appeared in 1859 and was followed by the second and third in 1860. It had the failings and the good qualities of its author. It dwelt on the personality of Jackson, emphasized the striking traits of his character, and paid little attention to the general history of the period. It gained much in interest by this process, and the interest was not abated by the large number of letters which Parton included. And as long as he was concerned with the early life of the subject, in which the action was chiefly personal, the result was mostly good. But in regard to Jackson's political career, the most important phase of the book for the historical student, the treatment was wholly unsatisfactory. Parton had no sympathy for Jackson's political ideal. He had, to begin with, little sense of the historic forces of the period. Jackson, the party builder and the centre of as tense a group of political agents as we have had, made a slight impression on him. And, failing to get this point of view, Parton ceased to have a correct view of the personality of his subject. Long accustomed to the denunciations and ridicule which educated men of the day cast at Jackson, his mind seems to have had a singular reaction. He would not accept them as applicable to the motives of his subject, but he accepted charges as facts and disposed of them with a smile. Under his touch President Jackson became the great, blustering, ignorant, well-intentioned, and always amusing doer of most of the politically bad things of the day. In this sense his biography did not meet the need; and the work remained to be done by another.

Several excellent writers have undertaken the same task in later years. I have not the hardihood to criticize any of them. But I cannot fail to express admiration for the succinct and calm treatment in Professor Sumner's book and for the remarkably clear and balanced portrait in the small volume by Mr. William Garrott Brown. Neither was meant for a comprehensive presentation of Jackson's career, and the recent disclosure of much manuscript material made it possible to write a more intimate and complete biography than either undertook to produce. My own task has been to examine these newer sources with an eye to a larger treatment, and to give the story its legitimate setting in the general history of the country. These sources exist in several collections of manuscripts.

The first is what remains of Jackson's own collection. After the death of Frank P. Blair, sr., it went to his son, Montgomery Blair, a member of Lincoln's and Johnson's cabinets, and after his death in 1883 passed into the hands of his children, Mrs. Minna Blair Richey, and Messrs. Montgomery, jr., Gist, and Woodbury Blair. It remained for many years at the home of Montgomery Blair, sr., at Silver Springs, Maryland, and in 1903 was presented by the owners to the Library of Congress, with the stipulation that it be classified, filed, and preserved for the use of historical students. As an expression of appreciation of the generosity of the donors the Library has called it "The Montgomery Blair Collection." Historians have cited it by the briefer title of "Jackson Mss." and that term has been used in the foot-notes in the present work. I cannot refrain from acknowledging my indebtedness to Mr. Montgomery Blair, jr., and his wife for many courtesies in connection with the use of the papers, and for much help which I have been permitted to receive from their intelligent knowledge of the contents. Their interest in preserving them and making them accessible to historians demands the gratitude of every student of the Jacksonian period.

It is not possible to say how much was withheld from the collection by Kendall, since the destruction of his papers by fire about twenty years ago disposed of most of those in his possession. The collection is not full for the two presidential terms of Jackson. It is a fair inference that Jackson had many papers for that period, and since they are not found it is probable these were retained. But on this phase of his career contemporary criticism was so fierce that the light has been fairly abundant. Here, too, we have much information in the papers of contemporary politicians, particularly in those of Van Buren, who was closely associated with the minor leaders of his party.

Before fire destroyed the Kendall papers a portion of them, it is not possible to say how many, came into the hands of W. G. Terrell, a Washington newspaper man, who disposed of them in various ways. Some were published in the Cincinnati *Commercial*, February 4, 5, and 10, 1879. These were sixty-nine letters from Jackson to Kendall and cover the period from September 4, 1827, to May 20, 1845, the entire acquaintance of the two men. They are most complete from 1832 to 1835. It is possible that some of these letters were from the Jackson collection, although all were conceivably the property of Kendall. In 1909 Hon. John Wesley Gaines, member of congress from

Tennessee, purchased other papers which had been in Terrell's possession and came from Kendall. Mr. Gaines presented them to Mrs. Rachael J. Lawrence, daughter of Andrew Jackson, jr. Among them were several which must have been secured by Kendall from Jackson. The most important were published in the Nashville *Tennesseean*, April 18 and 25, 1909.

Some other smaller collections of Jackson letters exist. The Tennessee Historical Society owns one collection, and a complete list of its contents is published in the *American Magazine of History* (Nashville), volume vi., pp. 330-334. The most important pieces are published in full in the same journal. Many letters from Jackson to W. B. Lewis are in the Ford collection in the New York Public Library, some of which have been published in the *Bulletin* of the library. Through the courtesy of Mr. Worthington C. Ford and Mr. Gaillard Hunt, his successor as chief of the manuscripts division of the Library of Congress, I have been able to satisfy myself of the value of other smaller and more personal collections.

Of the papers not primarily Jackson's the most important are in the Van Buren collection in the Library of Congress. It contains few letters by Van Buren, for it was not his habit to leave an exact record of transactions. Late in life he asked Jackson to return his letters, and the master of the "Hermitage" complied. Van Buren gave as his reason the desire to use them in an autobiography he was preparing. The missives in question were doubtless destroyed, since they do not appear in the Van Buren collection, nor are there traces of them or the use of them in the unpublished autobiography which survives. A few remain in the Jackson papers, probably overlooked when the rest went back to the writer of them. On the other hand, Van Buren did not mind keeping the correspondence of his friends. A large collection survives in which are many letters from the leading politicians of the day. Men who were in awe of Jackson, or who represented other factions than his, were in communication with the cool and shrewd New Yorker, whose philosophy was to keep on personal terms with any man whom he might some day need for a friend. Another valuable series is the W. B. Lewis letters in the Ford collection in the New York Public Library.

It was Jackson's habit to write his letters in draft, leaving his secretaries to make the fair copies which were actually sent to correspondents. The originals were carefully filed and are numerously preserved. The Blair heirs placed in the collection before it went to the Library of Congress many originals from him to their grandfather, of which no drafts or copies were made. Besides these, the Jackson papers contain many unimportant documents. Business letters, formal notes from strangers, dinner invitations, morning reports of regiments at New Orleans, and letters from admirers begging for locks of his hair were treasured with as much care as the correspondence of his most prominent party associates. This lack of discernment in reference to the source of information of the future biography witnesses how seriously he considered the task he was leaving to the historian. Van Buren and Lewis showed more discrimination and weeded out unimportant matter. In the *Atlantic Monthly*, volume 95, page 217, there is a valuable description of "The Jackson and Van Buren Papers" from the pen of Mr. James Schouler, the historian.

These manuscripts are the best portrayers of Jackson. They reveal faithfully a man who was great, spite of many limitations. He was badly educated, he was provincial, his passions frequently overcast judgment, he had a poor concept of a proper adjustment of the administrative machine, and he clung tenaciously to some of the worst political ideals of the past; yet he was so well endowed by nature that he broke over these impediments and became a man of distinction. He belonged to the class of strong personalities in which are Bismarck, Wellington, Wallenstein, and Julius Cæsar. He was untaught in books and to a large extent unteachable, but through native ability he solved the greatest problems from the standpoint of the light within him. His ideals were absorbed from the frontier environment: had he been placed by nature in other surroundings, for example, the society of some older community, he must still have been a marked man, possibly a leader equally effective in the life around him. But it was his to represent a new community which reckoned little with the finer points of intelligent experience. He voiced the best thought of the frontier, which happened to be the average thought of the older parts of America of his day. His Western ideals were for him the only ideals. They gave him his battle-cry, which, when once uttered, found support in the hearts of average Americans everywhere; and this was the secret of the Jacksonian movement.

Nor was he altogether dependent for position on his military renown, which only served to call attention to qualities which on the battlefield or in the political arena were the real Jackson. He persisted as a politician quite independently of the admiration men had for his achievements as a warrior. Taylor, Scott, and Grant were also military heroes whose soldierly qualities thrust them into the political field, where their well-earned laurels faded. In Jackson's case the soldier's wreath blossomed and grew until political achievement became the chief part of his glory.

It has been my object to show in the faithful story of his life the exact trace he left in the nation's history. I have not slighted his failings or his virtues; and I have tried to refrain from warping the judgment of the reader by passing upon his actions. I have sought, also, to present a true picture of the political manipulations which surrounded him and in which he was an important factor. I can hardly hope to have performed either task with universal satisfaction. I am conscious that errors of judgment and misapprehension of facts may have clouded the effort on either or both sides; but as each little may serve to lead the human mind to a clearer realization of truth, so I venture to hope that this life may be a contribution to a better knowledge of the complex period with which it deals. For the errors of either kind I beg the reader's generous indulgence.

I must add an expression of my gratitude to many friends of learning for abundant aid in the work I have done. To Messrs. Herbert Putnam, Worthington C. Ford, and Gaillard Hunt, of the Library of Congress, I am especially indebted for kindnesses which went far beyond the requirements of professional service. I have received valuable aid from Mr. Wilberforce Eames, of the New York Public Library; Mr. and Mrs. Montgomery Blair, of Silver Springs, Maryland; Miss E. Estella Davies, of Nashville; Mr. Edward Biddle, of Philadelphia; Mr. George W. Cable, Dr. John C. Hildt, and Mr. Henry B. Hinckley, of Northampton, Massachusetts; Professor R. C. H. Catterall, of Cornell University; Mrs. J. Lindsay Patterson, of Winston-Salem, North Carolina; Mr. William Beer, of New Orleans; Professor Frederic W. Moore, of Vanderbilt University; and many others whose interest and encouragement have been as valuable as more material assistance. I save for my last mentioned and best gratitude the personal help of my wife, Jessie Lewellin Bassett, through the tedious years of labor which my task has demanded.

Northampton, Massachusetts,　　　　　　　　　　J. S. B.
　September 23, 1910.

PREFACE TO THE SECOND EDITION

A NEW edition enables me to notice a criticism made when the first edition appeared. An otherwise friendly reviewer thought that it was a pity that the book was not a "life and times" of Jackson. In an equally friendly spirit I wish to say that it was not meant to be such a book. History is one thing and biography is another: this is biography, unless it fails of its purpose. To try to make one treatment combine the two mars the unity which ought to characterize any well-written book. The subject of a biography is entitled to the chief place in his own life: when he ceases to have it he becomes a mere peg upon which to hang other men's deeds. I have sought to keep Jackson in the foreground and to treat the political history of his time as an important background. Of course, it is agreed that the background is a part of the picture.

Jackson was the centre of a web of political intrigue that cannot be ignored by the student of the history. The actual course of events was directed by the circle around him. It is vain that the academic historian is satisfied to deal with the results of the intrigues, without wishing to observe the process by which they worked. The citizen wishes to know the manipulations of the politicians in the past, because knowing them enables him to understand the process and better to give value to the actions of present-day leaders. The politician of to-day has equal interest in knowing what really happened in the inner circles, because knowing it enables him better to play the part he has to play in present activities. We cannot understand the Jacksonian period without understanding Jackson. It is to understand him, and through him the work he did, and not because gossip is attractive, that I have tried to raise the curtain of the inner-most party stage.

This edition differs from the first in two respects: the one-volume form places it more easily within the reach of persons who may desire to know something about Jackson; and various minor changes have been made in the text, many of them in accordance with the suggestions of friends who have kindly offered their aid. The most notable alteration is in the extract from Biddle's memorandum, page 599. It is based on a more careful reading of the original, in which I have had the generous aid of Mr. Edward Biddle of Philadel-phia. It may not be improper to add that Professor Cat-terall, before he died, expressed his satisfaction with my interpretation of this paper, so different from his own.

JOHN SPENCER BASSETT.

SMITH COLLEGE,
NORTHAMPTON, MASS.,
    December 26, 1915.

CONTENTS

ILLUSTRATIONS

MAPS

THE LIFE OF
ANDREW JACKSON

CHAPTER I

EARLY YEARS

IN THE years immediately following the Treaty of Paris, 1763, the western parts of Virginia and the Carolinas were filled with vast pioneer enterprises. Along the roads which ran southward from the Potomac to the Dan, Yadkin, and Catawba, toiled many trains of immigrant wagons, and from Charleston to the upper valley region of South Carolina another throng of settlers was ever traveling. They all sought the red uplands, where rich meadows bordered a thousand creeks and brooks. Before this host primitive nature quickly gave way. Their axes soon sang triumphantly through many square miles of oak and pine land, their cattle drove the deer from the rich canebrakes, their corn fields began to nod saucily at the retreating forests, and homesteads and orchards announced the advent of the white man's civilization.

The people came from several sources. Scotch-Irish predominated, but Germans were numerous, and there were many who belonged to that roving frontier class which, already separated from their Old-World moorings, had acquired the right to be called "American." It is convenient to classify them by their religious association, since religion was one of their earliest concerns. The Scotch-Irish were Presbyterians almost to a man; and their arrival was quickly followed by itinerant preachers, meeting-houses, and organized congregations. The Germans were Moravians, Lutherans, and German Reformers. Of the others many were Baptists, some were Quakers, and many more were of the class who care little for creed or parson.

3

Some of the best land in all this region was that which the Catawba Indians had occupied from the days of early colonial settlement. It lay on the Catawba River at the point where it crosses the North Carolina boundary line and south of Mecklenburg County in the upper province. By the middle of the eighteenth century this land was open for settlement. It passed the ordinary course with good land, first into the hands of speculators, then into the possession of small holders, and finally after many transfers among these purchasers into the hands of a permanent body of prosperous settlers.

A little north of the point where the state line turns to pass around the old Indian reservation it is cut by Waxhaw Creek, which rises in North Carolina and flows westward to the Catawba. Its adjacent lands are particularly desirable, and they attracted a thrifty and valuable class of immigrants. Most of them were from the North of Ireland, and the Waxhaw Meeting-House, which they built soon after their arrival, was one of the most noted early landmarks of the Catawba Valley.

Among the people whom the wagon trains from Charleston brought to this place in 1765 were Andrew Jackson, Elizabeth, his wife, and their two sons, Hugh and Robert. They were poor people from the neighborhood of Carrickfergus. The husband was probably of the Irish tenant class, and the wife is said to have been a weaver both before and after her marriage.[1] With

---

[1] "A memorandum preserved by Jackson among his papers and without evidence of its reliability asserts that there were four brothers in Ireland by the name of Jackson each of whom occupied as freeholder "a large farm." Andrew, the youngest, lived near Castlereagh and sold his property in 1765, and went to America where he landed at Charleston, S. C., and removed to the back country. All of these Jacksons, it declared, were devoted to the Established Kirk of Scotland and were noted for their hospitality. Castlereagh is about one hundred and twenty-five miles from Carrickfergus whence Jackson and Crawford sailed for America. One brother — his name is not given — lived at Ballynisca, in the parish of Car-Donnell and was father of Samuel Jackson, who became senior partner in the Philadelphia firm of Jackson and Bayard, with whom William Patterson, of Baltimore, lived when a youth. Another brother, name not given, lived at Knocknagoney, parish of Holywood, and his daughter married James Suffern, of New York, a brother of John Suffern, a prominent state politician. The fourth brother, whose name is not mentioned, lived at Bally Willy, parish of Bangor, and was called "Laird Jackson." This memorandum could have been prepared after the appearance of Reid's book, and there is an evident purpose to enhance Jackson's social standing. He endorsed most of his papers, but nothing appears on this.

them came James Crawford and his wife, a sister of Elizabeth Jackson. Another sister had already come to the neighborhood, and her husband, George McKemy, bought land on the North Carolina side of the boundary line. Several other sisters were settled in the same community, two of whom were married to brothers by the name of Leslie. Crawford had some money and was able to buy a good farm on the lower part of the creek and in the southern province, but Jackson, being very poor, contented himself with a tract of land on Twelve Mile Creek, about five miles east of the line. The place was in North Carolina, near the present railroad station of Potter, and it lies now, though not definitely pointed out, in a township and county which are called respectively Jackson and Union in honor of the son of this impecunious immigrant. Two years of labor were enough to break the body of the unfortunate man, and early in March, 1767, he rested from all his anxieties. His loyal friends, after giving his spirit the honor of a true Irish wake, placed his remains in the Waxhaw churchyard. The widow abandoned the farm, the title to which the husband seems never to have acquired, and was received with her children into the home of her sister Crawford. A few days later, March 15, she was delivered of a third son whom she called Andrew in token of his father. In the house of her sister she took the place of housekeeper — for Mrs. Crawford was an invalid — and her children were given the usual advantages of a well-to-do frontier home.

The exact spot at which Jackson was born has become a subject of controversy. By a tradition which lingered in the Leslie branch of the family the event was said to have occurred at the house of George McKemy. When the mother, so the story runs, journeyed from her stricken abode to her sister's home, she stopped for a visit at the home of McKemy, and here labor came upon her. But when she was able to travel she continued her journey; and thus it came about that people thought the Crawford home welcomed into the world the future President.

The Leslie tradition was reduced to writing in 1858, by General Walkup, a citizen of North Carolina, who was enthusiastically convinced that to his own state belonged the honor of having the birthplace of so distinguished a man. The evidence is chiefly traceable to the statement of Sarah Lathen, whose mother, Mrs. Leslie, was a sister of Mrs. Jackson. Sarah Lathen, in 1767, was a girl of seven years, and in her old age she was accustomed to tell her family and friends that she remembered going with her mother across the fields at night to the house of George McKemy to attend Mrs. Jackson when Andrew was born, and that her mother, who was a midwife, was summoned for that purpose. Some thirty years after her death the story was collected from those who remembered that she told it and reduced to written affidavits. Parton has reproduced it at length and accepted it as true in his *Life of Jackson*[1].

On the other side is the general story accepted in the community and not openly contradicted in the life of Jackson, although several biographies of him were written in that period, two of them under the immediate supervision of their subject. Jackson himself was, in fact, very clear in his idea of his birthplace. "I was born," said he on August 11, 1824, "in South Carolina, as I have been told, at the plantation whereon James Crawford lived, about one mile from the Carolina Road and of the Waxhaw Creek; left that state in 1784."[2] This idea was confirmed in many of his important state papers and private letters. In the nullification proclamation and in his will he referred to South Carolina as "my native state."

In later years a spirited controversy, has grown up on this

---

[1] Vol. I., 53-57.

[2] Jackson to James H. Weatherspoon, of South Carolina, Aug. 11,1824, Jackson Mss. See also F. P. Blair to Lewis, Oct. 25, 1859, Mss.N. Y. Pub. Library; and Jackson, to Kendall, Nov. 2, 1843, (*Cincinnati Commercial*, Feb. 10, 1879) in which he speaks of South Carolina as "my birthplace and of which I am proud."

point between citizens of the two states. Enthusiasm has abounded, and the argument has followed state lines till much confusion has resulted. Aside from such puzzling factors, each contention presents some elements of probability. To the writer the weight of evidence seems to favor the South Carolinians. The Leslie tradition rests on an old woman's account of an event which happened when she was a child of seven, an event, too, about which a child could not be well informed. It was weakly corroborated by a statement of Thomas Faulkner, aged seventy; by another man, also a Leslie descendant, who relied on information which he said he had from Sarah Lathen's mother fifty years earlier: and by James D. Craig's statement that he had heard — evidently much earlier than his statement — "a very aged lady," Mrs. Cousar, say that she assisted at the birth at McKemy's house.

The weakness of this evidence lies in the long time which elapsed between the event and the time of its recording. All of it must have been carried many years in the minds of two people, one passing it on when she was very old to another who told it when he was very old. Add to this the enthusiasm which the narrators had for their story and the lack of critical examination of it when it came from their lips, place against it the clear statement of Jackson made in response to a question which this controversy aroused, that he was born in the house of James Crawford, in South Carolina, and to most men the story will probably appear doubtful. Somewhat more trustworthy is the explicit statement of General Jackson.[1]

Mrs. Jackson was a pious woman and is said to have fixed in her heart that her youngest son should become a minister, which leads to the suggestion that he must in early life have shown some leaning toward a life of public activity. But in his

---

[1]The evidence favoring the South Carolina side has been collected by A. S. Salley, jr., and published in the Charleston *Sunday News*, July 31, 1904. Later contention on the opposite side has added little to Parton; but see Tompkins's *History of Mecklenburg County, North Carolina*, II., Chap. V.

earliest habits there was little to confirm her hopes. Of all the wild youths of the neighborhood he was the wildest. The rough sports, passions, and habits of the North Ireland tenantry were planted in the new community, although ideals were being elevated by the development of property and new obligations. The boy had a sensitive, quick-tempered, persistent, independent, and rather violent disposition; and there was little in the life around him to soften these traits. He had an absorbing passion for excelling among a people whose ideals of excellence expressed themselves in horse-racing, cock-fighting, readiness to fight in defense of what they considered their honor, and in the rather stilted but genuine habits of the frontier gentleman. As he came into the teens he was proficient in the use of heavy oaths, proverbially ready for a quarrel, fond of cock-fighting, already precocious in the knowledge of a horse, and in many other ways developed in waywardness. A moralist might have seen in this no good results for the boy's future, and for most youths the forecast would have been a good one; but Jackson differed from most people. He was ever filled with a purpose to attain eminence. Vice was not an absorbing trait with him, even when he set at defiance the canons of decorum. He was not addicted to the more animal faults, and his errancy grew out of intellectual qualities rather than appetite. He was destined to shake it off with the advent of serious things, as many another strong-spirited man has done.

The ideals of the Waxhaw settlement did not demand much schooling for the boys. Ability to read and understand indifferent English, to write a legible hand, and to make ordinary business calculations were then the chief features of our rural education everywhere. It was enough for the ordinary purposes of the mass of American farmers, but it was too little for a man who was to play a part in the government of the state or nation. Of such instruction a modicum was offered in the upper parts of the Carolinas and of that Andrew got his share, or something less. He was neither studious nor teachable, and what he got came through sheer contact with the process of education. He was mentally an egoist; that is to say, one who relied on himself. There was no time in his life when he was willing to learn of others. Ideas came to him originally, and in obedience to a strong natural aptness for knowing what he wanted: it was not his nature to take them from others.

To the day of his death Jackson's attainments in scholarship were very meagre. He knew no more Latin than he could pick up in the practice of his profession of lawyer; his spelling and grammar were devoid of regularity and showed the utmost indifference to the rules by which they were determined for other people; and his acquaintance with literature is a negligible quantity in an estimate of his life. Occasionally one finds in his papers some oft-quoted phrase, as, *Carthago delenda est*, but it is always one which he must have heard on a hundred stumps in Tennessee. Of all his prominent contemporaries his utterances are most barren of allusions which show an acquaintance with poetry, history, or literature; and in comparison with him the grandiose Benton seems a pedant.

His education was interrupted by the call for soldiers to resist the British invasion, an appeal most in keeping with his spirit. In the spring of 1780, all the American troops in South Carolina were carefully gathered into the city of Charleston, and when the place was taken with all its defenders on May 12, the state was at the mercy of its foes. Bands of red-coats and tories began to ravage the state wherever the patriots made a stand. One of them, the remorseless Tarleton riding at its head, fell on the Waxhaw community like an angry spirit, butchering a band of soldiers and ravaging the homes of the people. Hard after this attack came Rawdon for another blow, but the people, unwilling to face him, fled into the north till the invader turned back. Then the whigs rallied for vengeance. Down from North Carolina came Davie and Sumter, two of the best light-horse leaders of the whole war, and at the battle of Hanging Rock, on August 1, 1780, they almost took revenge for the wrongs of their compatriots. In this battle was Andrew Jackson, then but thirteen years old, and his brother Robert rode in the army of Davie. Hugh, the eldest of their mother's sons, had given up his life some months earlier at the battle of Stono.

From Hanging Rock the boy troopers returned safely to their home, but the expedition gave them a taste for war, and in the following year they joined with their neighbors in trying to capture a body of British troops at Waxhaw Church. The attempt was a failure, the enemy turned and defeated them, and scouring the country for fugitives took the two boys prisoners. The commanding officer — it was not Tarleton — ordered Andrew to black his boots. The boy remonstrated, we may guess in what tone, that he was a prisoner-of-war and not a servant. The reply was a saber-blow aimed at the head of the young prisoner: it was warded by the arm of the recipient, but hand and head carried the mark of it to the grave. Robert was also ordered to do the same service and on refusing received a more serious wound than his younger brother. In this plight they were placed in Camden jail with a number of other prisoners. They received little attention here and were exposed to small-pox. From such a situation they were rescued by the efforts of their mother who induced the British to include them in an exchange of prisoners arranged between the two sides. Robert soon died, either of small-pox or of his neglected wounds, but Andrew escaped further danger. Thus the widowed mother gave two of her sons, both of whom were under age, to the cause of the Revolution. One other sacrifice, her own life, remained to her. Word came up from the seacoast that the Waxhaw prisoners on the British ships in Charleston Harbor were ill and needed attention. She joined a party of volunteers who went down to the city to nurse the sufferers, took prison fever from her patients, and died from the effects of it.[1]

The end of the Revolution thus found Jackson alone in the world at the age of fourteen, a strong and self-reliant boy, who was likely to take care of himself, although it was not quite certain that he would do it in the best way. He thought first, so we are told, of completing his education; but there was not much that a boy of his experience and disposition could learn in the schools of the vicinity. Then he thought of becoming a saddler, but a few weeks were enough to satisfy him that he was not fitted for so monotonous a life. Next he tried school-teaching, but neither his attainments nor his temper suited such a calling. If his mother left any property at all it was inconsiderable, and to begin life as a planter was, therefore, out of the question. In his dilemma he turned to Charleston, which meant to the frontiersman the great world beyond the forest; and there he would try his fortune. In what line he sought to establish himself we are not informed, but he was not long in finding his way to the race-track, where he soon bet and swaggered himself into notice. Tradition affirms that he thus came to know some of the prominent young blades of the city and that it was here he developed the manner of a fine gentleman which impressed those who met him in later years. A dignified bearing and exact conduct on state occasions were natural to him, and it is not improbable that during this visit to Charleston he first saw these qualities exemplified and felt an impulse to act accordingly.

The next we hear of him he has decided to become a lawyer. It is pleasant to fancy that a sight of the great men of the city had given him the idea that there was something greater in

[1] Some details of her burial in a letter from J. H. Weatherspoon to Jackson, April 16, 1825 (Jackson] Mss.), indicate that she was buried "in and about the forks of the Meeting and Kingstreet Roads," then in the suburbs of Charleston.

life than being the leading backwoodsman of his vicinity, and that he determined to attain it. He was conscious that it was the frontier, however, that offered most opportunities to a man without fortune or family, and he turned back to the red-hill country of his childhood. There were lawyers in Charleston under whom he might read law, but it was not to them that he went. In Morganton, N. C., lived Waightstill Avery, the most influential attorney in all the upper country, and to him he first applied, but his request was not granted. Then he went to Salisbury, where he joined a class of students under Spruce Macay,[1] a lawyer of local note. Thus it was that in the year 1784, in the old colonial town of Salisbury, when he was seventeen years old, that Andrew Jackson found a profession and sat down to master as much of it as the people of the backwoods thought necessary.

It was not a very great deal of time that he gave to his lawbooks. Tradition is our only guide for this period,[2] and it speaks chiefly of wild escapades; of horse-racing, cock-fighting, and gambling for board-bills with his landlord. "He was," said an old resident after the former student had become famous, "the most roaring, rollicking, game-cocking, card-playing, mischievous fellow that ever lived in Salisbury." Macay's instruction was pieced out, just why does not appear, by that of John Stokes, and in spite of the time given to carousing, the law course was at length completed. He finally settled at Martinsville, in Guilford County, North Carolina, and awaited clients. November 12, 1787, he was at the court in the neighboring county of Surry as the following entry in the court's records shows:

"William Cupples and Andrew Jackson, Esquires, each produced a license from the Hon. Samuel Ashe and John Williams,

---

[1] This spelling is justified by Macay's own signature.

[2] In 1844 Jackson said in his early years he knew the Polks intimately. Now this was the most prominent family in Mecklenburg County and the adjoining region; and the inference is that his early position must have been as good as the North Carolina frontier afforded. See *Am. Histl. Mag.* (Nashville), III., 188.

Esquires, two of the Judges of the Superior Court of Law and Equity, authorizing and empowering them to practice as attorneys in the several County Courts of Pleas and Quarter Sessions, within this State, with testimonials of their having hitherto taken the necessary oaths, and are admitted to practice in this Court."[1]

With this our young gentleman was launched in a professional career. Clients were none too abundant, and tradition says that he served a while as constable in lack of some more remunerative employment. At Martinsville were two of his friends, Searcy and Henderson, united in a mercantile partnership, and he was thrown into close relations with them. It is even possible that he gave certain assistance in the business. The court-house of Surry was then at a place called Richmond, and two facts in connection with Jackson's visits there have come down to us in a reliable way: Once he stopped at a tavern kept by Jesse Lister, who claimed later that Jackson did not pay his board-bill, and it has long been a tradition that Lister, in 1815, wrote against the account, "Paid at the battle of New Orleans." It is certain that after the inn-keeper's death his daughter presented the bill to Jackson, who was then President and who refused to pay it on the ground that he did not owe it. He based his opinion on the fact that it had ever been his custom to pay such bills promptly, and he asked why Lister had not presented it in his life-time, saying that it might have been done easily in 1788, when he passed Lister's house on his way to Tennessee.[2] The other slight view of his life here is in a statement from Cupples himself, who in 1795, wrote to Jackson in regard to a note which was given, presumably by Jackson, to settle the balance of a gambling debt at Richmond.[3] Thus we see that Jackson began life quite like himself in the law courts of North Carolina.

[1] Surry Court Records, 1787.
[2] Lewis Williams to Jackson, February 2, and endorsement, 1832, Jackson Mss.
[3] William Cupples to Jackson, Aug. 19, 1795, Jackson Mss.

It is impossible to say how much practice these early months brought him; for no record of his practice survives. If it were nothing at all, it was still as much as could have been expected of a boy, still less than twenty-one years old, who had no friends but those he made. He doubtless knew little law; but many a lawyer who was not versed in legal principles has succeeded through successful personality, and in this respect Jackson was strong. Gamble as he might, he had a straightforward way of dealing which ever made him friends; he was bold, he had the faculty of leading, he was just to a fault, he did not countenance double-dealing, and he spoke his mind frankly. These qualities made him friends in this first year of waiting in North Carolina, and out of this initial success grew the confidence which gave him the second advance in his career, his Tennessee appointment.

CHAPTER II

EARLY CAREER IN TENNESSEE

WHEN Jackson began to practise law, the portion of North Carolina which lay west of the Alleghanies was being settled in two communities. In its eastern part many people were living on the Watauga, Holston, Nollichucky, and French Broad Rivers as far westward as the neighborhood of Knoxville. Two hundred miles beyond them, in the rich Cumberland Valley, was another group of adventurers, whose centre was Nashville, but it extended up and down the river for nearly eighty-five miles. In 1790 its population was five thousand and it was organized into three counties, Davidson — with Nashville for the county-seat— Sumner, and Tennessee. The region between these two settlements was a wilderness, so infested by hostile Indians that when the national government in 1788 opened a road through it, a guard was established to go its entire length twice a month for the protection of travelers. The soil along the Cumberland was more fertile than that of the mountains, and it was destined to support after a time a more prosperous and influential society. Tennessee was thus divided into two sections, each of which was apt to be suspicious of the motives of the other; and the ability of the future political leaders was frequently taxed to secure harmonious action between them.

The Cumberland colony was established in 1779, under the leadership of two remarkable men, James Robertson and John Donelson; and in spite of many difficulties it grew rapidly. The chief danger was Indians, whom the British, before the treaty of

15

peace in 1783, and the Spanish, after that time, incited to attack the exposed American frontier. The whites retaliated with true Western spirit. The national government was then pressing Spain for a treaty and gave orders that peace should be preserved on the Spanish borders. But the Tennesseeans were not willing to see their homes devastated. Bands from the east marching under John Sevier in 1793, and bands from the west marching under James Robertson in 1794, delivered two blows which reduced the savages to a respectful state of mind. In 1795 Spain yielded the long desired treaty and opened the Mississippi to the Americans. Great results came from these events, but the people could not forget the perils through which they had passed, and it was many a day before they ceased to hate both Spaniards and Indians.

In 1788, when the first struggle for existence was won, but before complete safety was secured, the assembly of North Carolina erected a superior court district out of the three counties on the Cumberland and called it "Mero."[1] Over this district John McNairy, one of Jackson's fellow law-students at Salisbury, was appointed judge. The new tribunal was a court of law and equity, with jurisdiction above that of the county court, and it was to meet at regular intervals in each of the counties. McNairy set out for Tennessee in the spring of 1788, and induced Jackson to accompany him in order to see the country. They proceeded leisurely, reached the settlements on the Holston in a few weeks, loitered there till autumn, and then passed over the new road to Nashville. Although Jackson had not come as a settler, profitable business was immediately thrust upon him. The one established lawyer whom he found in the place was retained by a combination of debtors who were thus able to

---

[1] *Laws of North Carolina*, 1785, Chap. 47, and 1788, Chaps. 28 and 31: they may be found in the *State Records of North Carolina*, XXIV, 973 and 975. " Mero " is an incorrect spelling for "Miro," the name of the governor of New Orleans.

laugh at their creditors. The latter turned gladly to Jackson, who prosecuted boldly and successfully. His clients, most of them merchants, were from that time his warm friends and supporters.[1] To this success was added, in 1789, the solicitorship in McNairy's jurisdiction with a salary of forty pounds for each court he attended.[2] Thus it happened that he determined to throw in his fortune definitely with the new community. Prosperity followed the decision. Fees and salary were soon converted into land whose value rose with the settlement of the country, and eight years after his arrival he was one of the wealthy men of that region.

When Jackson arrived at Nashville, John Donelson, one of the two leaders of the first colony, was already dead, a sacrifice to the red man's vengeance, and his widow was taking boarders. The new lawyer became one of her household and eventually her son-in-law. So much was afterward said about this marriage that its history must be presented here with some detail.

Rachael Donelson, daughter of the pioneer, was married to Lewis Robards, of Kentucky, a man of dark and jealous disposition who succeeded in making her life miserable. She is described as a woman of a lively disposition, by which is meant that she was not that obedient, demure, and silent wife which some husbands of the day thought desirable. By common report she was entirely innocent of wrong-doing and finally was forced by the cruelty of her husband to return to Nashville, where she lived with her mother when

---

[1] This story follows Parton (I, 135). When Gov. Blount organized the territory in 1790, he licensed the lawyers anew. Those mentioned in Davidson County are given in the following order: Josiah Love, John Overton, A. Jackson, D. Allison, H. Tatum, J. C. Mountflorence, and James White. These were probably named by seniority of residence. We know that Overton arrived about the same time as Jackson. Josiah Love, therefore, must have been the protector of the creditors. See *Am. Histl. Mag.* (Nashville), II, 232.

[2] Reid and Eaton, *Jackson* 15: Parton, *Jackson*, I., Chaps, 10, 11, and 12; also Jackson's petition to the Tennessee legislature, Apr. 11, 1796, *Jackson*, Mss.

Jackson appeared in the town. A short time later friends intervened and succeeded in reconciling the couple, so that Robards came to Nashville and also became an inmate of the Donelson home.

For a time all went well, but at length the old suspicions returned. All Nashville was singing the praises of the young solicitor, Mrs. Robards included, and the jealous husband chose to make this the ground of new charges. So open were his reproaches that the boarders soon learned the situation as thoroughly as the unhappy wife herself. Thus the knowledge of it came to Jackson, whose habit ever was to settle difficulties face to face with his opponents. He had an interview with Robards and sought to convince him that the suspicions against Mrs. Robards were unfounded. But the husband took an injured air and refused to be convinced. Jackson became angry, and the affair assumed a worse state than ever. Robards stormed at his wife, swore at Jackson, and rode away to Kentucky never to return, vowing that he would have a divorce.

The solicitor was now in genuine distress. He was by nature exceedingly chivalrous and bore himself toward women with a protecting deference which made them all, even the fine ladies of New Orleans and Washington, his warm friends. For such a man the situation in which he found himself was calculated to create within him the feeling which he had just been falsely accused of having. The state of his emotions reached a crisis in the following autumn, the year was 1790, when a report came that Robards was coming to claim his wife. At this Jackson confessed to his friend Overton that he was a most unhappy man and that he loved Mrs. Robards. She returned his affections, and when later in the year she set out for Natchez in company with a family friend, in order to escape the threatened force of her husband, Jackson went along as a protector through the wilderness. In the following summer news came to Nashville that the legislature of Virginia had granted a divorce to Robards, Kentucky not yet being a state. The news went rapidly down the river to Natchez, and in the same summer the solicitor followed it. A few weeks later he returned bringing Rachael Robards as his wife. They settled thirteen miles from Nashville on a beautiful plantation called "Hunter's Hill," and for two years life went smoothly. But in December, 1793, came news that Robards was suing in a Kentucky court for divorce on the ground that his wife had lived for two years in adultery with Andrew Jackson. It then transpired that no divorce had been granted in 1791, but that the Virginia legislature merely gave Robards the right to sue for a divorce in a Kentucky court. Up till a recent time no suit was instituted, Jackson had acted precipitately, and the charge that Mrs. Robards was living in adultery was technically true. On this state of facts the court readily gave Robards the liberty he sought. Nothing remained for the surprised couple at "Hunter's Hill" but to have a second ceremony.[1]

Years later it was the habit of his political enemies to say that Jackson ran away with another man's wife. During the presidential campaign of 1828 this charge was freely circulated, and Jackson's friends in Nashville published the refutation in full with affidavits. It is from this source that later biographers have drawn their story. By this means their subject is relieved from the imputation of wicked intent but not from that of professional inefficiency. As a lawyer he should have known that it was not usual at that time for either the Virginia or North Carolina legislature to grant a divorce outright, but that the law provided just that course which Robards had followed. Had Jackson been acting only as a lawyer for a client, he would at least have read the Virginia statute before setting out for

---

[1] For the story as told by Overton see Parton, *Jackson*, 1, 148-155.

Natchez, and the casual perusal of it would have shown him the true state of the case.[1]

Never was divorce better justified by the results. His devotion to his wife was the gentlest thing in the turbulent life of the husband: her pathetic affection for him in return for his loyalty raised the rather prosaic life of the wife quite to the level of the poetic. She was a woman of great goodness of heart, benevolence, and religious fervor; but she was by endowment and by training the intellectual inferior of her husband. Her strongest quality was her religion, which in her case was pervasive, effusive, and serious. Although Jackson was irreligious in early life, her piety made a deep impression on him; and in her old age it consoled her much to know that he was a believer in the doctrines of the Presbyterian church. She herself was highly esteemed for her good intentions, and her husband's friends, knowing his tenderness for her, frequently closed their letters to him by commending themselves to her favor.

Jackson's marriage identified him with an influential family connection; for John Donelson was a leading citizen in his day, and his many sons and daughters shared his popularity. Among them our strong-willed solicitor took place as a leader.

---

[1]It was not till 1827 that Virginia passed a general law to regulate granting divorces. It then authorized divorce *a vinculo* for impotency, idiocy, and other natural incapacity, and divorce *a mensa et thoro* for adultery, etc., both to be granted in the court of chancery. Divorces might still be had for other grounds from the assembly, and the law provided that investigations should be had beforehand in the county court and the verdict should be referred to the legislature, where the divorce might be granted. (Act of February 17, 1827.) The first general law of divorce in North Carolina was enacted in 1816. By it, the court could grant divorce for natural incapacity, but for other causes there must be a prior investigation in the nature of a suit in the courts, and the matter must be referred to the assembly before the court decision was final. Laws of 1816, Chapter 928; 1818, Chapter 968; and 1819, Chapter 1007. Before the adoption of these general laws, the method was by appeal to the legislature only, and the custom was general for the case to be referred to a court for ascertaining the facts. All the presumption, both from Jackson's experience under North Carolina law and from what he ought to have known about Virginia custom, was against the supposition that a divorce outright was given in Virginia. The Virginia assembly acted on Robards's petition on December 20 1790. It authorized "Roberts" to have a divorce from his wife "Rachel," by suit in the supreme court of Kentucky, the writ to be published for eight weeks successively in the *Kentucky Gazette*, and "if defendant does not appear within two months after publication, the case may be set for trial but postponed for cause, and if the court finds that the wife has deserted her husband or is living in adultery, the marriage is to be dissolved." See Henning, *Statutes*, XIII., 227.

He gave them in time as much as they gave him. The Donelsons were but easy-going English people and dropped behind in the strenuous struggle of the day; while Jackson's Scotch-Irish spirit ever drove him forward. He was the soul of generosity, and denied them no favor or service. Some he took into business partnerships; to some he gave military, and to others civil, office; some he sent to school; for others he acted as guardian during their minority; and one he adopted, giving him his name, but, unfortunately, not his capacity.[1]

A sister of Mrs. Jackson married Colonel Robert Hays, who was a revolutionary soldier and became one of the most reliable men of the community. He was till the end of a long life a firm friend of General Jackson, and many letters which survive show that he was a useful counselor and a worthy gentleman. A niece of Mrs. Jackson married John Coffee, a man great of body and of heart, and a splendid frontier soldier who served Jackson and his country well in the Creek and New Orleans campaigns.

Jackson had now encountered three interesting stages of American society. In Charleston he met the most formal phase and knew that it had no welcome for a man like him: in Salisbury he found the settled and regular life of the up-country farmers and saw that its welcome was strained: in Nashville's newly formed society he met the charity of the frontier which receives talent without questions. He accepted its confidence and became a leading citizen. New responsibilities sobered him to an extent, and something of the old rollicking manner was laid aside. But Nashville was not very exacting in this respect. It allowed him to retain, it even approved of, many habits which to-day it pronounces uncouth. He fought cocks, raced horses, gamed if he felt like it, quarrelled frequently, held himself ready to fight

---

[1] In 1845, a correspondent sent Jackson a letter from Mrs. Jackson's mother, Rachael Donelson. From it, we see that the writer was the youngest of eleven children, that she was from Accomac County, Virginia, and that her family were people of moderate circumstances. See A. T. Gray to Jackson, March 19, 1845, Jackson Mss.

duels, and, when the occasion arose, indulged in oaths which were the acme of profanity. None of these things by the standards of the place made a man less a gentleman. They rather added to his standing; and inasmuch as Jackson excelled in all of them his standing was secure. His horses were the fastest, his cocks were the most noted, he would quarrel with none but men of distinction, and his great oaths became the despair of the young braggarts of the valley.

In appearance he was tall, slender, and very erect. His face was pale; his eyes, which were very blue, were also very intense; and above a high and narrow forehead rose a mass of stiff hair which was too brown to be sandy and too light to be auburn. His chin was clear-cut and square, but without heaviness, his mouth, always his best feature, was large, and his lips were of that flexible kind which emphatically express on occasion extremes of benevolence or anger. He bore himself with the air of a man who was his own master. In a trade he would announce his terms without hesitation, and the other party might accept or reject at once. His opinions were formed and expressed with the same celerity.

In the courts of the day such a man appeared to advantage. Offenders were apt to be turbulent and often they were supported by bands of associates who made the life of a prosecuting attorney both unpleasant and perilous. Jackson's physical courage was equal to his moral courage, and he loved justice. He loved also to feel that no one thwarted his purpose, and in the courts his purpose was to be a good solicitor. His speeches were brief and not much interrupted by taking up law-books; but they were filled with feeling and common sense. Bad grammar, bad pronunciation, and violent denunciation did not shock judge or jury nor divert their minds from the truth. His cases were rarely postponed to suit the convenience of lawyers. When he left the court, his docket was apt to be clean, and he was likely to carry with him the esteem of the law-abiding and the respect of evil-doers.

Many years later this vigorous young lawyer became a national figure. The qualities which in the beginning of his career gave him preëminence in the backwoods now seemed eccentricities to the more cultured East. They became the basis of a thousand anecdotes which were told by his enemies and friends. Parton, his best biographer, has repeated many of them, led on, as it seems, by the tendency to write things which only amuse. Other writers have followed Parton, and thus it happens that Jackson's shadow falls across written history as a grotesque embodiment of violence, prejudice, and political inefficiency. But history is not to be written from caricature; and, if we are to understand the personality before us, we must look beyond the entertaining stories told about him, stories which are sometimes exaggerations and sometimes made to take a meaning more peculiar to the mind of the narrator than to that of him about whom they were told. Probably the best means of knowing the man, aside from his eccentricities, is to remember always his manner of meeting his problems in the early and simple days of the Cumberland frontier. The foundation of his career was laid in those days when he rode from court to court in West Tennessee as public prosecutor. It was then that the people came to have confidence in him and he learned the art of leading them. When he secured promotion it came from the hands of as democratic a people as ever lived. Solicitor under state authority at twenty-two, United States attorney at twenty-three, member of congress at twenty-nine, United States senator at thirty, justice of the supreme court of Tennessee at thirty-one, and major-general of militia on a dangerous frontier at thirty-five — accident or personal favoritism could not have been responsible for such a career among such a people.

While Jackson was judge occurred the incident of the arrest of the felon, Bean. It was often told by his friends and acquired such embellishment from their hands that Jackson in his old age thought proper to write a correct account, possibly for Kendall's biography. From that it appears that Jackson on the bench learned that Bean was resisting authority and ordered his arrest. The sheriff tried but reported that he was defied. The judge ordered him to summon a posse. In a short time he reported that the posse was defied. Then Jackson rebuked him asking how he would account to the country, but did not, as has been said, ask the sheriff to summon him. Shortly afterward court adjourned, and the three judges were walking to their dinners when the sheriff, smarting from his rebuke, summoned them as a posse. Two of them, Campbell and Roane, put themselves on their dignity and refused, but Jackson agreed to act. He armed himself, approached Bean, and said he would shoot him down if he did not surrender. The latter said he would submit but was afraid of the people, but when assured he should have no harm from that source he surrendered to Jackson, who handed him over to the sheriff. The incident shows Jackson at his best, in enforcing order against violent men.[1]

---

[1]The statement is in the Jackson Mss. without signature or date and in the hand of a copyist. It has an endorsement in Kendall's hand.

CHAPTER III

EARLY PUBLIC SERVICE

By an act of May 26, 1790, congress organized the country between Kentucky and the present states of Alabama and Mississippi as "The Territory of the United States Southwest of the Ohio River," and in September, 1790, William Blount, of North Carolina, became its governor. The name was too long for ordinary use and the people shortened it into "Southwest Territory," by which it was in the future generally called. In 1791 the northern half of the territory became the state of Kentucky, and Blount's jurisdiction was limited to the southern half. The government of this region was modeled after that of the Northwest Territory, by which it might expect to have a territorial legislature when it contained five thousand adult male inhabitants and to become a state when its total population was sixty thousand.

Governor Blount sought to substitute his authority for that of North Carolina with as little friction as possible, and for that reason he continued in office as many as possible of the old officials. He recognized the dual nature of the territory by organizing anew Washington District in the east and Mero in the west; and these subdivisions served for the bases of judicial and military organization. John McNairy, Jackson's old friend, was continued territorial judge, and James Robertson was made commander of the militia with the rank of brigadier-general. Jackson was appointed attorney-general for Mero with duties like those he discharged under the old authority. For

25

emergency service a cavalry regiment was organized in each
district, and over the Mero regiment Robert Hays was placed
with the rank of lieutenant-colonel. Thus the power of the
United States was established in what was destined to be the
state of Tennessee. A year later, September 10, 1792, Jackson
received his first military office when Blount made him "judge-
advocate for the Davidson Regiment." It was not a prominent
place, and it was no doubt conferred chiefly because he was a
lawyer; but it identified him with a calling for which he was by
nature eminently fitted and in which he was to perform his most
signal services.

In 1793 the "Southwest Territory" took its first step toward
statehood by establishing a territorial legislature. Two years
later it opened the way for the second step by ordering that a
census of the population should be taken, and, if the returns
should show sixty thousand inhabitants, directing the governor to
call a constitutional convention. The enumeration indicated a
population of seventy-six thousand, blacks and whites; and
January 11, 1796, five delegates met from each of the eleven
counties to prepare a frame of government. For such a purpose
the community put forward its best men; and among those who
went from Davidson County were Jackson, McNairy, and General
Robertson. In the convention the burden of the business was
entrusted to a committee of two from each county, who were
appointed to prepare the scheme of a constitution. The two
members of this committee from Davidson were Jackson and
McNairy, whom we must regard as the intellectual men of the
delegation. McNairy took prominent part in the debates, but
Jackson, who was never a debater, said but little. Tradition
declares that he suggested the name Tennessee for the proposed
state, and he seconded an amendment by which ministers of the
gospel were allowed to hold any office except member of assembly.
The convention soon completed its labors and adjourned leaving

the assembly which it created to put the new state government into operation. It fixed March 28, 1796, as the day for the expiration of the territorial government, and it declared that if congress did not accept the state as an equal member of the sisterhood, Tennessee should continue to exist as an independent state.

In this the people of Tennessee were acting on the basis of a supposed right to statehood, which they thought was implied in the act by which congress received North Carolina's cession of the whole region. In the absence of precedents for the creation of states out of territories their view was probably not unnatural; but it is impossible to doubt that it originated partly in that spirit of defiance to national authority which had long been strong in the West, and which did not entirely disappear till the collapse of Burr's projects.

But congress was not inclined to admit the contention of the Tennesseeans. To allow the people of a territory to meet of themselves and set aside the authority which ruled them was a loose way of exercising the function of government. It is not, therefore, surprising that when the newly elected senators presented themselves in Philadelphia in the spring of 1796, while party feeling over the execution of the Jay treaty ran high, they should have received cold welcome. Tennessee was strongly republican, the country was about to elect a President, and it was natural for the question of right to be viewed through partisan spectacles. The republicans argued that the senators from the new state ought to be admitted, but the federalists declared that they could have no recognition until congress authorized the territory to change itself into a state. The house was carried by the republicans in favor of admission, but the senate went with the federalists and refused to concur. Finally, on June 1, 1796, as congress was about to adjourn, the federalists relented and recognized Tennessee as a state. The delay produced bad feeling among the people of the new state, who attributed the action of the federalists to the worst motives.

In the change into statehood there were many offices to be filled, most of them by the legislature. It was thus that senators and high state officials were chosen. Besides the governorship there was a single office depending upon the suffrages of all the people, and in the nomination of various persons to various posts the leaders reserved it for Jackson, probably because he was strong with the people: this was the one member of the national house of representatives. To this office Jackson was triumphantly elected, and on December 5, 1796, he took his seat in the congress at Philadelphia.

The contrast of life between Nashville and the Pennsylvania city was a sharp one. In the former Jackson was easily a leader: in the latter he was less at home. Unfortunately, no friend has told us of the impression he made on his associates, but his opponents had better memories. From one of them we learn that he was regarded as a grave backwoodsman, his hair done up in queue with an eel skin, and his clothes fitting badly on his long body. Another — it was Jefferson himself — said that he had violent passions and that when he attempted to make a speech he was unable to go on with it because he "choked with rage."[1] With certain allowances for the exaggerations of an enemy, the charge was probably well founded. Jackson felt too strongly to express himself in extempore speeches; but ready speech-making is not essential to political success. Jefferson himself did not have it, but by political management he was the controlling power of a great party. Jackson also ruled a great party, not by speech-making nor by political management, as Jefferson, but by the force of his personality.

In congress he gravitated toward that group of extreme repub-

---

[1]The informant was Gallatin. See Hildreth, *History of the United States*, IV., 692. See also Webster *Private Correspondence*, I., 371.

licans which was led by Macon and Randolph. Letters are preserved indicating that he was on intimate terms with its leading members.

The draft of a letter dated October 4, 1795, and probably written to Macon, shows what his political views then were. "What an alarming situation," he said, "was the late negotiation of Mr. Jay with Lord Granville, and that negotiation (for a Treaty of Commerce it cannot be called, as it wants reciprocity) being ratified by the Two thirds of the Senate and president has plunged our country in; will it end in a Civil war; or will our country be retrieved from this present |situation| by the firmness of our representatives in Congress (by impeachments for the daring infringements of our Constitutional rights) have the insulting cringing and ignominious Child of aristocratic Secracy; removed Erased and obliterated from the archives of the Grand republic of the United States. I say unconstitutional; because the Constitution says that the president by and with the advice and consent of the senate are authorized to make Treaties, but in the present Treaty the advice of the senate was not required by the president previous to the Formation of the Treaty; nor the Outlines of the said Treaty made known to the senate until after made and their Consent wanting to make it the supreme law of the land (therefore made without the advice of the senate and unconstitutional) and erecting courts not heard of in the constitution, &c. all bills for raising a revenue to originate in the house of representatives by treaty.

" It is not only unconstitutional but inconsistent with the law of Nations, Vattel B2, P242, S325 says that the rights of Nations are benefits, of which the soveriegn is only the administrators, and he ought to Dispose of them no farther than he has reason to presume that the Nation would dispose of them therefore the president (from the remonstrance from all parts of the Union) had reason to presume that the Nation of America would not have ratified the Treaty, notwithstanding the 20 aristocratic Neebobs of the Senate had consented to it."[1] Crude as this draft is, the reader and not the biographer ought to determine how much allowance should be made for the carelessness of its preparation. After all proper deductions are made on this score it must still mark the author of it as a man of ill-formed and untutored political judgment.

Two days after Jackson took his seat in congress Washington made before that body his last annual address, the tone of which was mildly partisan. The committee of the house which prepared an answer went a little further in the same spirit, and the submission of their report to the house was the signal for criticisms from the republicans. They objected to being made to declare that they approved of the measures of Washington's administration, and they strove hard to secure an amendment which would soften the words of the report into a form more nearly non-committal. In this they failed: some of them had not the courage to vote at last against the commendation of Washington, but twelve extreme republicans held out to the last, voting against the resolutions. One of them was Andrew Jackson and another Edward Livingston, then of New York. It demands some explanation to show why the well-born New Yorker remained obdurate against what he considered the aristocratic tendencies of Washington, but none is needed to show why the fierce Westerner resented the popular idea that the Father of his Country was too sacred to be attacked in any of his opinions. Livingston was a republican by theory, but Jackson was one by environment and by every instinct of his nature.

In his short stay in Philadelphia Jackson made a good impression on the leading republicans. From the few letters of this

---

[1] See the Jackson Mss. See also Jackson to Overton, January 22, February 3, 23, March 6, 1798; Copy in Library of Congress.

period which have been preserved we see that he continued after he retired from congress to correspond in familiar terms with such men as Stevens Thomson Mason and Henry Tazewell, of Virginia, and Nathaniel Macon, of North Carolina. "We often wish you back," wrote Mason in 1798,[1] and from Macon several very friendly letters are preserved, some of them written before Jackson was a congressman.[2] This confidence must have been based on his strong personality as much as on the fact that he represented the opinion of West Tennessee.

Although he did not distinguish himself on the floor of congress, Jackson secured the passage of two measures which made him popular in Tennessee. One was a bill to place a regiment on the southern border of the state for protection against indians: the other was a bill to pay those who took part in Sevier's unauthorized Nickajack expedition of 1793. As to the latter, the executive refused to pay the claim on the ground that it would require special authority from congress to do so. Jackson promptly introduced the necessary resolution, and the debate on it became sharp. His own speech, in the contracted form used in the "Annals of Congress," appears respectable. One point in it was characteristic of the speaker. If this vote was refused, said he, the discipline of the militia would be destroyed: the private soldier ought not to have to determine the authority of the officer who called him into the field: it was his to obey, and if the call was illegal the soldier should not have to suffer for the error of his superior by losing his pay. In this debate Jackson was on his feet four times, and no less a leader than Madison rose in his behalf. Finally the resolution was referred to a select committee, of which Jackson was chairman. The

---

[1]Mason to Jackson, April 27, and May 25, 1798, Jackson Mss. Tazewell to Jackson, July 20, 1798; *Ibid;* Macon to Jackson, January 17, 1796, February 14, 1800, January 12, 1801, *Ibid;* John McDowell to Jackson, April 26, 1798, *Ibid.*

[2]When Jackson began to win victories in the Creek campaign, Macon stood sponsor for him in Washington and told the world who he was. Benton, *View,* I., 116.

report was in favor of paying the claim, and congress gave its approval without a division.[1] For a new member who had no special gifts in speaking the achievement was respectable.

The wave of popularity which followed his first session in congress brought him in 1797 an election to the United States senate.[2] To the floor of the more dignified house he went with personal reluctance, for he was little suited to the formal methods of that body. One session was all he could bring himself to endure. He was, in fact, fitted neither by talents nor inclination for a legislative body. Moreover, his private business demanded his attention, and in the spring of 1798 he resigned the office to which he had been elected and accepted a judgeship of the state supreme court. The latter position suited his tastes better than the former, and he held it for six years. The manner of life which it entailed was much like that which the attorney-generalship involved: there were the same riding of circuit, the same variety of experience, the familiar faces of old lawyer friends, and the ever recurring excitement of settling the perplexing affairs of the community. Into the life Jackson fitted easily and happily. He had many of the qualifications of a good judge. He was, no doubt, but little versed in the law; but he had common sense, integrity, courage, and impartiality. Only one of his decisions has been preserved, and that is an unimportant one. Tradition asserts, says Parton[3] that they were "short, untechnical, unlearned, sometimes ungrammatical, and generally right." So highly was he esteemed as a lawyer that one of the prominent business men of west Tennessee, on hearing the rumor that he would retire from the bench, wrote at once to retain him for all his business and expressed the hope that he might succeed to

---

[1] Annals of 4th congress, 2nd session, 1738, 1742, 1746.

[2] For the desire to combine the East and the West, Cocke and Jackson, in this canvass, see Robertson to Cocke August 1, 1797, *American Historical Magazine*, (Nashville), IV., 344. He succeeded Cocke and not Blount, as is sometimes said. See Garrett and Goodpasture, *Tennessee*, 338.

[3] Parton, *Jackson*, I., 227.

all the practice of G. W. Campwell, a good lawyer who was just
elected to congress.[1] The news that he was finally to resign
brought protests from many prominent people, among them
General Robertson; and a petition is preserved to the same effect
with the signature of forty-three prominent citizens attached.
Further evidence of his success on the bench is found in the
general apprehension that if he left it Judge Hugh L. White,
the only other member of the court, in whom the state had high
confidence, would also feel impelled to leave. These points
are mentioned to show with what acceptability he filled the
office of judge. It was July 24, 1804, that his resignation of
the judgeship was accepted by the Tennesse legislature.[2]

It happened that at this time a governor was to be appointed
for the newly established Orleans Territory. The Tennessee
senators and representatives signed a request that Jackson
have the place, and Matthew Lyon, whose troubles in 1798
distressed Jackson greatly, added his name to the petition.
The appointment went to W. C. C. Claiborne, but Jackson's
endorsement by the entire state delegation shows how great
was his influence at the time. Among the papers preserved in
regard to the affair is a letter from one Henderson who declared
that the applicant was a contentious man, that he was indicted
for assault and about to be arrested for breach of the peace.
In view of other endorsements this must be taken as the outburst of personal pique. Jackson was then an admirer of Macon
and Randolph and his failure to get the office he sought confirmed his opposition to Jefferson. In 1809 he was the leader of
Monroe's cause in Tennessee.[3]

Six years on the bench was calculated to withdraw him from

---

[1]Mark Armstrong to Jackson, August 19, 1803, Jackson Mss.

[2]In the first published volume of *Tennessee Reports*, 1813, only eight cases are reported for the period before September, 1804, when Jackson was on the bench. He wrote the opinion in none of them. They are all very meager reports of cases from Mero district and seem to have been made originally by the reporter Overton for his private use.

[3]See *American Historical Review*, III., 285-7.

active participation in politics, but another cause operating more powerfully to the same end was his quarrel with John Sevier, the popular hero of East Tennessee. This affair will be discussed in another chapter: here it will be proper to remark that it made Jackson unpopular with Sevier's many friends and seriously lessened his political strength in the whole state. Even in the days of his greatest fame he had many enemies in the eastern part of the state.

When Jackson retired from the bench his private affairs were in a serious condition. For several years he had been struggling beneath a heavy financial load from which he was resolved at last to rid himself. Like all the men of means of his community he bought much of the cheap public land of the first days of settlement. In 1795 he owned jointly with his friend, John Overton, as much as twenty-five thousand acres. In that year he went to Philadelphia and sold this land to a wealthy man named David Allison, receiving for his own share notes which he endorsed and exchanged for a stock of goods preparatory to opening a general merchandise store in Nashville. He was hardly at home before news came that Allison had yielded to the panic which was then sweeping over the country and that the notes which Jackson had endorsed were held against him. To save himself from a swarm of hungry creditors required prompt action, and he knew it. He at once closed out his store for thirty-three thousand acres of land, which he soon sold for twenty-five cents an acre, taking for it a draft on William Blount, then United States senator from Tennessee, who was generally esteemed a very rich man. He hurried to Philadelphia to cash the draft and pay his creditors, only to find that Blount himself was embarrassed through Allison's failure. By the greatest exertion he managed to pay his notes as they became due, but in doing so he sacrificed much of his property; and he came out of this experience much shorn of financial strength.

His rallying power was great, and he quickly adapted himself to the new situation. The fine estate of "Hunter's Hill," on which he lived, was absorbed in the general disaster; but he gave it up readily and moved to a smaller plantation eight miles from Nashville. It was then mostly unimproved and in size it was a modest square mile. The dwelling on it was built of logs and so many of his slaves were sold for debts that it was difficult to work it; but the struggle was taken up bravely. It was not many years before the farm was brought into excellent condition, a handsome brick house was built, and the estate — for it was the "Hermitage" — became one of the most famous in America.

His affairs settled on a new basis, Jackson returned to his plan to establish a store. At Clover Bottom, on Stone River, four miles from the "Hermitage," he opened a general merchandise business. He took two partners, neither of whom proved an efficient trader. One was John Coffee, not yet married to Mrs. Jackson's niece; and the other was John Hutchings, himself a relative of Mrs. Jackson. The firm dealt in all kinds of goods, buying of the inhabitants their produce, their lumber, their horses, and even their slaves, all of which were sent down the river to whatever profit Natchez or New Orleans could offer.[1] His partners looked regularly after the business, and Jackson, when he was home from his courts, rode over daily and served customers as though he were not a member of the highest court in Tennessee. During this period Mrs. Jackson, with the resourcefulness of the women of the frontier, took chief part in the supervision of the farm, and the tradition long survived that she did it exceedingly well.

Jackson was a good trader in large transactions. He could with his frank abruptness sell or buy lands, slaves, or horses to advantage. But he was not so successful in small affairs. In the petty bargaining of a general merchandise store, in keep-

---

[1] Jackson to James Jackson, August 25, 1819, Jackson Mss.

ing up an attractive stock of goods, and in the little tricks by which the successful merchant humors the foibles of a trading public he was not proficient. Thus it happened that the enterprise at Clover Bottom languished for a while, then began to be unprofitable, and finally was so unremunerative that he was glad to sell his share to his partners for notes-in-hand which he could hardly expect them to pay. This occurred after he was off the bench. From that time till the war of 1812 he occupied himself with farming; and in that respect he was successful. General Jackson was never a very rich man. He was only a prosperous planter and slave-owner, probably a little too prone to make business ventures which he was not careful enough manager to bring to a successful issue. Of such a nature was the venture in merchandising and his later venture in Mississippi lands. A man of more reliable and less erratic business habits might have made either affair a success.

CHAPTER IV

JACKSON AND BURR

WHILE Jackson was merchant and planter the incident occurred which posterity has insisted on calling Burr's Conspiracy. His connection with it is important, because it shows with what group of national politicians he was now in sympathy and because it reveals his complete identity with that new and self-asserting West which burned to drive Spain from the northern shores of the Gulf of Mexico.

Until the summer of 1804, Aaron Burr was the leader of a respectable faction of New York republicans, and he had friends in many other states. He was opposed to Jefferson on personal grounds, and this brought him into touch with the group of extreme republican theorists who were dissatisfied with the more practical policy of the President. He had ability, daring, and personal magnetism, but those who knew him well felt that he lacked sincerity and was far too anxious to triumph. His duel with Hamilton, July 11, 1804, ended for the East a career which was already desperate; and he turned to the West to repair his fortunes. A good lawyer and still in his prime, he might have won professional success and finally political promotion in New Orleans or in any other promising Western city, had he been content to follow a steady life. But he was not a quiet man. He was by temperament an adventurer, and the West was to him a theatre in which he could by dash and sagacity carry through the greatest schemes. He would test its possibilities and win political control of some new colony, state, or empire.

37

For such an undertaking money and men were necessary, and he had neither. His son-in-law, Governor Alston, of South Carolina, though rich, was not rich enough for so vast an enterprise. But the Western situation was such that Burr thought he could make it contribute to his ends. Louisiana had recently come into American hands, much to the disappointment of England, Spain, and its own ancient inhabitants; and he believed that the people of Kentucky and Tennessee were hostile to the government of the United States.[1] He thought, therefore, that England would lend money, arms, and probably ships to check the westward expansion of the United States; that Spain would give aid to any plan which would stay our approach to her Mexican border, and that the foreign-born people of Louisiana, not yet reconciled to American dominion, and the dissatisfied population of the upper valley, would furnish men to overthrow an authority which they were believed to disdain. It was, moreover, impossible for him to win the support of either party to the plot without concealing his purpose from the other parties to it. As a result, so many stories of his plans were put into circulation that posterity has had difficulty in determining what was his real object.

Burr's first move was to appeal to England, He won over Anthony Merry, the British minister in Washington. Then he sent an agent to London where a fair hope of success was unexpectedly defeated by changes in the ministry which brought into the foreign office Charles James Fox, ever a good friend to the United States. Next he turned to Spain, whose American representative he also fascinated; but the government in Madrid would not adopt

[1]For the reluctance with which the people of the Cumberland approved of statehood in 1796, see Ramsay, *Annals of Tennessee*, 648, also 634.

the enterprise nor let it fail entirely. They offered Burr a small sum, enough to keep up his scheming, but not enough to carry the project to success.

While this phase of the scheme was progressing, its master mind turned to the West, where he was generally popular. Ten years earlier Kentucky and Tennessee were full of the spirit of revolt, but the Spanish treaty in 1795, and the acquisition of Louisiana in 1803, dispelled most of it. In 1805, the country was loyal, although some restless leaders of the old movement remained in the region. One of them was James Wilkinson, commander of the regular troops in the lower Mississippi Valley. He was tainted with nearly all the treason which crossed his path during a long life, he was long a pensioner of Spain while an officer of the United States, and he yielded ready consent to Burr's propositions. He was more experienced in sedition than his confederate, and the future was to show that he knew better the proper moment for abandoning a perilous adventure.

In the West Burr talked openly of a plan to settle a colony on a tract of land which he owned on the Red River. To the leading Westerners he confided that at the first declaration of war between the United States and Spain — an event which was generally considered more than probable — he would move on Mexico and wrest it from the hands of Spain. Most of his defenders contend that this was his real purpose and that it did not differ from many other filibustering plans against Mexico.

Another theory is that Burr conspired with Wilkinson to the end that they should unite the Western adventurers which the one should raise with the regulars under the command of the other, and by coöperating with disaffected persons in Louisiana set on foot a revolution in the territory

---

[1]William Dickson to Jackson, March 4, 1802, Jackson Mss.

newly acquired from France. It was on the ground that this was his real purpose that Burr was later tried for treason. Although he was acquitted because of the ruling of the court that treason must be an overt act testified to by two witnesses — which the prosecution could not substantiate — posterity and most of the people of the day believed that the charge was just.

In all his negotiations Burr lied so much that it is useless for the historian to try to discover which of the schemes was the true one. He lied to the British minister about his support in the West; he lied to the Spanish minister about his failure with the British minister; and he lied to the people of the West as it suited his convenience.[1] He told the West that England was supporting him: when he observed their hostility to Spain he talked about taking Mexico: and when they expressed a desire for Mobile he dropped hints of taking Florida. At the same time he told Yrujo, Spanish minister, not to be alarmed at rumors of an attack on Mexico or Florida, since such reports were only a part of the game. To the politicians of the West he said that the government in the East was sure to dissolve. To a small group of intimates he said that he would join a body of Mexican patriots, overthrow the Spanish authority, and make himself king of Mexico. His beautiful daughter, Theodosia, dreamed of being a princess, while his lieutenant, the enthusiastic Blennerhassett, exulted in the prospect of representing the new state in England. Burr is supposed to have given his best confidence to Wilkinson, but for all their correspondence was in cipher, it is evident that he did not reveal to his confederate the failure to get money in England. Thus the arch-schemer kept the centre of the plot in his own hands, communicating

[1]Senator Smith, of Tennessee, wrote to Jackson from Washington, January 3, 1807 (Jackson Mss), that he had seen a letter from Burr to Clay, stating that he, Burr, did not "own a single boat, musket, or bayonette, and that the executive of the United States are acquainted with his object and view it with complaisance." Smith added that Jefferson denied this utterly.

to none of his associates more than was necessary to forward the project.[1]

Burr made a preliminary visit to the Mississippi as far as New Orleans in the summer of 1805 and found everything to his liking. He gave the following winter and spring to efforts to obtain foreign aid. The failure to get it was a severe blow and was the real crisis of the affair. Wilkinson, more experienced in treason, recognized it and prepared to withdraw; but Burr decided to take the gambler's last chance. He believed that an initial success would rally the West and that victory would follow. According to the story usually accepted, he planned to go down the river on November 15, 1806, with one thousand men, join Wilkinson at Natchez, wait there until the legislature of Louisiana under the influence of the Creoles, should declare independence, and then occupy New Orleans in the name of the revolutionists.

As November 15 approached, difficulties accumulated. A group of federalists in Louisville began to attack him in a newspaper, and he was tried for treason but acquitted through the efforts

---

[1]Burr's correspondence with English and Spanish officials, which was brought to light by Mr. Henry Adams, is considered evidence that he intended to revolutionize Louisiana, and in this view the Mexican part of the scheme is pronounced a subterfuge. But Mr. W. F. McCaleb (*The Burr Conspiracy*, 1903), thinks that the Mexican project was the real one and that the foreign negotiations were a subterfuge. The historian's problem is not that of the court at Richmond. He is concerned to know if Burr had a treasonable intent, while the trial rested on the commission of an overt act. To prove such an intent, we have the foreign negotiations and particularly the request that England would send a ship to the mouth of the Mississippi to keep off any American naval force, which might be sent against Burr, the charges of Wilkinson after he turned state's evidence, and the general rumor in the West, that Burr was going against New Orleans. On the other side we have the apparent sincerity with which many of his supporters held to the Mexican plan. Most of the evidence on each side can be explained away on the ground that Burr was duping somebody, and his character is so doubtful that we must admit that he was capable of duping everybody. Thus, we are almost justified in saying that it is impossible to determine the real purpose of the conspirators. But one piece of evidence will not be so easily disposed of, and that is Wilkinson's attitude, not his assertion, which was certainly unreliable. If any persons besides Burr knew his real purpose, Wilkinson must have been one of them. If, therefore, Wilkinson knew that the expedition was intended against Mexico, which was legally a misdemeanor, why should he have alleged that it was intended against Louisiana, which was legally treason, a more serious offence? If he were going to turn state's evidence to save himself, why should he allege a more serious offence than was necessary, one which he knew to be untrue and out of which he must manufacture supporting evidence out of the whole cloth? He was not an imbecile; his many successful intrigues required a certain amount of mental ability. It is inexplicable that he should have placed himself in an attitude, which was unnecessarily perilous to himself.

of his attorney, Henry Clay. Moreover, supplies and boats were hard to obtain, men did not enlist freely where so much was unexplained, and the date set for departure passed without a movement. In the meantime, President Jefferson was aroused to the gravity of the situation. He sent agents to the West to investigate the situation and to use their efforts to check the plotters.[1]

In October Wilkinson decided to desert the conspiracy. He knew that Burr's promises to take an equal share in the enterprise were futile. If it succeeded, it must be through the aid which it would derive from the regular troops. He would not scorch his fingers for Burr's chestnuts; and in his code of morals he was justified in renouncing a partner whose promises were broken. He accordingly sent Jefferson a full account of a treasonable plot which he said he had discovered. It was ingeniously written to cast suspicions on Burr, while it concealed his own complicity.[2] Up to this time Jefferson refused to treat seriously the rumors from the West, but he was either convinced by Wilkinson's letter or considered it good grounds for arresting the adventurer. He sent out a proclamation for the apprehension of all plotters of treason, but without calling names, and a short time later sent orders to seize the members of the expedition.

When this proclamation reached the Cumberland, Burr was in Nashville, where the mercantile firm with which Jackson was connected was preparing for him boats and supplies and where Patten Anderson, one of Jackson's faithful friends, was enlisting men. Bending every effort he could to get away, he was able to depart at the first intimation that he was about to be arrested. He reached the Ohio with but a handful of men only to find that the states of Kentucky and Ohio were also aroused and that

[1] One of the agents was Seth Pease dispatched in December with a confidential letter from Senator Smith of Tennessee. See Smith to Jackson, December 19, 1806, Jackson Mss.

[2] A year later Governor Claiborne thought Wilkinson innocent. See Claiborne to Jackson, December 3, 1807, Jackson Mss.

he must flee still farther. Gathering all the strength possible he began at once the long expected voyage. During the last week of the year he passed from the Ohio to the Mississippi and to the fate which awaited him. He had thirteen boats and sixty men, a small force for such an undertaking, but he counted on Wilkinson. Near Natchez he learned that this was a false hope and attempted to escape while he could. He was arrested at Fort Stoddart and subsequently tried for treason at Richmond, in Virginia.[1]

While he was in the West, Burr made four visits to Nashville, the first beginning on May 29, 1805. He was popular there because in 1796 he worked effectively to keep the federalists from delaying the admission of Tennessee into the union. He must have met Jackson while the latter was a member of congress from 1796 until 1798, but there is no evidence that they knew much of each other at that time. The backwoodsman, with his hair done in queue with an eel skin was not apt to impress the trained New York lawyer. When the two men met on the Cumberland the case was different. The major-general of militia fitted the Tennessee environment better than that of Philadelphia, and Burr now found him, what he really was, a man of distinction among his fellows. During this visit to Nashville the traveler spent five days at the "Hermitage" before he continued his journey to New Orleans. Returning northward he came on August 6 for a second visit under the same roof. The people of Nashville gave him a public dinner on the twelfth. It was a notable occasion, and the prominent people of the neighborhood gathered in their bravest clothes to do honor to the recent vice-president and friend of Tennessee.

Burr was pleased, as most other people who knew him were pleased, at Jackson's qualities. He found him, as he said in a

---

[1]For fuller accounts of Burr's project, see Adams, *History of the United States*, III., 219-343, and 441-471; and McCaleb, *Aaron Burr's Conspiracy*.

letter to his daughter, Theodosia, "a man of intelligence, and one of those prompt, frank, ardent souls whom I love to meet." When the two men parted, their relations were cordial. No evidence was produced, even in the heat of political controversy, to show that they plotted treason. It is more than probable that Burr spoke to Jackson of an impending war with Spain during which an attempt would be made to wrench from her grasp a vast territory west of Louisiana. Although Jackson was very careful to preserve the most trivial papers for the use of his biographer, he has given us no other intimation of what Burr said to him than that it was not treasonable. His strict sense of honor would explain this silence.

Burr was good enough judge of a man to recognize Jackson's military capacity. He knew that the commander of the militia in West Tennessee, the frontier nearest the scene of future action, held a position only less important than that of Wilkinson and sought by every possible means to conciliate him. After his departure from the "Hermitage" he sent several letters to his host. In one he said that war was imminent on account of the Miranda incident, and he urged his correspondent to prepare to act promptly. New Orleans, he suggested, would be the objective of such a war, and if Jackson would send a list of suitable officers for two regiments he would in case of hostilities be able to get them accepted and commissioned by the secretary of war. The request met a ready acceptance. This gave Burr valuable information for the organization of a future expedition, and it had the promise of added local influence for Jackson.

In September, 1806, the "Hermitage" again received its illustrious guest, and again the people of Nashville were called together to do him honor in a public dinner. The repetition of this demonstration suggests the purpose to establish the visitor in the good opinion of the people. Unusual care seems to have been given to the dinner. At the proper moment the doors

THE HERMITAGE

Drawn and engraved by H. B. Hall

opened and Burr and Jackson entered together, the latter in full militia uniform. Bowing in stately manner they made the round of the room, the natives looking on in admiration. It was long remembered in Nashville that the dignified bearing of their own general equaled that of his companion, who was usually pronounced one of the most correct men of fashion of his day.

From this reception Burr had reason to think that his affairs went well on the Cumberland, and a few days later he returned to the Ohio. November 3d, he sent the firm of which Jackson was a member an order for five boats and a quantity of provisions. Money in advance accompanied the order and the firm, which was accustomed to fit out boats for the river, accepted the commission.

November 10, 1806, as Jackson himself relates, a friend came to the "Hermitage" and revealed the outlines of a scheme to divide the union, and they both recognized the proposals of his recent guest. Until that time, says Jackson, he did not question the statement that Burr intended to settle a colony on his Red River lands and, in case of war with Spain, to move against Mexico. But he was now alarmed and wrote letters of warning to the governors of Tennessee and Louisiana and to his friends, Dickson and Smith, in Washington.[1] He took the further precaution to order the militia to be ready for duty, and he tendered his and their services to the President of the United States.

He wrote also to Burr demanding the truth about the rumors in circulation and received such a positive and prompt denial that he suspended his judgment, saying that he was not willing to condemn a friend on mere rumor. Consulting with his partners he decided that the contract for boats and provisions must be executed, but that no other help should be given. It finally

---

[1] Jackson to Claiborne, November 12, 1806; Jackson to Dickson, November 17, 1806; Claiborne to Jackson, December 3, 1807; Jackson Mss. The first is in Parton, *Jackson*, I., 319.

happened that Burr needed but two of the boats, and the money advanced for the others was returned to him.

December 14, Burr made his fourth visit to the Cumberland, staying now at a tavern at Clover Bottom, where the store which Jackson and his partners owned was located. He called at the "Hermitage" in the absence of its owner, but Mrs. Jackson received him coldly. When her husband returned, he called at the tavern in company with his friend, Overton, and again demanded the full nature of Burr's plans. Again he received explicit assurances that disloyalty to the union was not contemplated.

Jackson's fears were thus quieted, but the course of the adventurer was nearly run. Already his establishment on the Ohio was broken up and the President's proclamation against him was approaching Nashville. He seems to have had some intimation of his danger; for one day he stole away in his two boats, leaving behind him seven hundred dollars to pay Patten Anderson for services in getting recruits. A few hours after he was gone Jefferson's orders were received. The people were thunderstruck when they learned that he whom they were recently covering with honor was suspected as a lawbreaker. Public opinion now rose against the fugitive. He was generally denounced and the more excitable part of the town burned him in effigy.

January 1, 1807, Jackson received orders from the President and the secretary of war to hold his command ready to march and to arrest Burr if possible. He called out the militia at once and sent off letters of warning to various persons. Visions of a great expedition down the river began to float before him. To Patten Anderson he revealed himself rather fully in a letter of the fourth.[1] He wrote:

I received your note: its contents duly observed. The

---

[1] Parton, *Jackson*, I., 328.

receipts as directed I have retained. The negro girl named, if likely, at a fair price, I will receive.

I received some communications from the President and Secretary of War; and your presence is required at my house to-morrow evening, or early Monday morning, to consult on means and measures, and to determine the latitude of the authority. It is the merest old woman letter from the Secretary that you ever saw. Your presence on Sunday evening will be expected, and your presence on Monday morning at nine o'clock can not be dispensed with, you must attend. I have sent an express to the mouth of the Cumberland and to Massac to see and hear and make observations. I have wrote to Captain Bissle; from information received at the moment the messenger was starting gives me reason to believe that Bissle is the host of Aaron Burr. Wilkinson has denounced Burr as a traitor, after he found that he was implicated. This is deep policy. He has obtained thereby the command of New Orleans, the gun boats armed; and his plan can now be executed without resistance. But we must be there in due time, before fortifications can be erected, and restore to our government New Orleans and the Western commerce. You must attend. Give to those officers that you see assurances that all volunteer companies will be gratefully accepted of. We must have thirty, thirty-five, or forty companies into the field in fifteen or twenty days; ten or twelve in four. I have it from the President, I have it from Dixon, that all volunteers will be gratefully accepted. To-morrow night Winchester will be with me; I wish you there. The Secretary of War is not fit for a granny. I fear John Randolph's ideas were too correct; but dubious as he has wrote, there are sufficient authority to act? Act I will, and by the next mail I will give him a letter that will instruct him in his duty, and convince him that I know mine. If convenient, bring the girl with you; and health and respect.

A. JACKSON.

Compliments to Mrs. Anderson. I must tell you that Bonaparte has destroyed the Prussian army. We ought to have a little of the emperor's energy.

The Napoleonic energy to which this letter referred was distinctly a characteristic of Jackson, as later events were to prove. But in this case it turned out to be unnecessary. In a week came a letter from Captain Bissell, whose name Jackson misspelled, at Fort Massac on the Ohio, saying in a tone of fine irony:

There has not, to my knowledge, been any assembling of men and boats at this, or any other place, unauthorized by law or presidency, but should anything of the kind make its appearance which carries with it the least mark of suspicion as having illegal enterprises or projects in view hostile to the peace and good order of government, I shall, with as much ardor and energy as the case will admit, endeavor to bring to justice all such offenders. For more than two weeks past I have made it a point to make myself acquainted with the loading and situation of all boats descending the river; as yet there has nothing the least alarming appeared. On or about the 31st ult., Colonel Burr, the late Vice President of the United States, passed with about ten boats, of different descriptions, navigated by about six men each, having nothing on board that would suffer a conjecture more than a man bound to a market; he has descended the river towards Orleans. Should anything to my knowledge transpire interesting to government, I will give the most early notice in my power.[1]

From this as well as from the report of his special messenger, Jackson concluded that the game was beyond his reach and sent the militia, who had responded to his call in a most generous manner, to their homes again, first making them a ringing addresss which officers thought it advisable to have published. With this the Burr incident, so far as Tennessee was concerned, was passed.

The quick and strong response of the militia shows how completely Jackson was already master of the fighting spirit of the frontier. He had then, as in his later military and political

---

[1] Parton, *Jackson*, I., 323. Jackson replied in a more moderate tone, January 9, 1807, Jackson Mss.

career, a group of lieutenants who believed in him. They imbibed his energy and accepted his authority. And he was always their master, justifying his domination by his power to maintain their confidence and by utilizing it to accomplish the most important objects.

This phase of the Burr incident also brings into view that turbulent egotism which for Jackson in many critical periods was a source of weakness as well as of strength. In this case it shows a man who could seize and rule a complex situation without authority to do so, but with the approval of the community. As a militia officer he had no power to give orders to Bissell, but he thought it necessary and did not hesitate to assume the power needed. In whatever position he was thrown he was apt to take the place of leader, both by reason of his own pretension and through the acquiescence of others.

A still better illustration in point is his attitude toward the secretary of war, the incompetent Henry Dearborn. "By the next mail," said he in the letter to Patten Anderson given above, "I will instruct him in his duty and convince him that I know mine." and he was as good as his word. At this time war with England and Spain was generally expected and from it Jackson fervently hoped he would get the opportunity to begin a military career. His thrust at Dearborn was, therefore, most incautious; for no ordinary man under such circumstances would dare the wrath of the superior who must sign his first commission in the regular army.

The beginning of the quarrel was as follows: One of the stories which Burr told to secure aid was that he had the support of Jackson and the Tennessee militia. Rumor magnified it till in Washington it was asserted that Jackson and the west Tennessee militia were going to support Burr. The secretary gave too ready an ear to the report, and in the letter which reached Jackson on January 1, 1807 he said: "It is industriously reported among the adventurers that they were to be joined at the mouth of the Cumberland by two regiments under the command of General Jackson." The thrust reached the Tennesseean in a tender part, his sense of honor.

Morever, this was not Jackson's first quarrel with Dearborn.[1] In 1803, Colonel Thomas Butler, a revolutionary soldier then serving under Wilkinson in New Orleans, was arrested on a charge of disobedience and neglect of duty. He had many friends in Nashville who came to his defense, alleging that the real cause of the arrest was Wilkinson's desire to rid himself of an honest subordinate who would not tolerate his superior's treasonable dealings with the Spaniards. The leading man of these defenders was Jackson. He wrote a letter of protest to President Jefferson and later forwarded to him a petition from citizens of Nashville in behalf of Butler.[2] None of his efforts were successful, but the affair convinced him that Wilkinson was a scoundrel. Jefferson replied that Butler was arrested for absence from duty.[3] When, therefore, Jackson learned the prominent part Wilkinson was taking in the revelations of Burr's evil doing, his mind reacted against the whole affair. It angered him to see that hypocrite supported by the secretary of war and the President, and the imputations now received from the former gave him an opportunity which he was more than willing to accept.

Writing to the secretary on January 8, 1807,[3] he sent a full account of the steps he had taken to arrest the conspiracy, with copies of his letters to Bissell and others, and added:

The first duty of a soldier or good citizen is to attend to the safety and interest of his country: the next to attend to his

---

[1] Jackson himself thought the part he took in support of Butler aroused the hostility of Dearborn. Jackson to Dearborn, January 8, 1807, "Supplement," Jackson Mss.

[2] Jackson to Jefferson August 7, 1803; Jackson and others to Jefferson, December ——, 1804 ; Jefferson to Jackson, September 19, 1803; Jefferson Mss., Library of Congress.

[3] Jackson Mss.

own feelings whenever they are rudely or wantonly assailed. The tenor of your letter is such and the insinuations so grating, the ideas and tenor so unmilitary, stories allude to, and intimations of a conduct, to stoop, from the character, of a general to that of a snarling assassin. (Then hereafter) I will sir enclose you, a copy of a letter from Governor Claiborne, that will shew you I never depart, from the true sense of duty to my country, whenever I am even suspicious of its injury.

Health and respect,
ANDREW JACKSON.

Through the broken sentences of this extract one sees clearly the strong emotion with which it was written. In what he called a "supplement" to the letter of January 8th, he found a more fluent tongue, saying:

Col. B. received, sir, at my house all that hospitality that a banished patriot from his home was entitled to. I then thought him a patriot in exile for a cause that every man of honor must regret, the violence with which he was pursued, all his language to me covered with a love of country, and obedience to the laws and your orders. Under these declarations and after his acquittal by a respectable grand jury of Kentucky, my suspicions of him vanished, and I did furnish him with two boats, and had he wanted two more on the same terms and under the same impressions I then had he should have had them. But sir when prooff shews him to be a treator, I would cut his throat with as much pleasure as I would cut yours on equal testimony.[1]

This spirited protest was more than Dearborn expected from a general of militia, but others interfered and the quarrel went no farther.[2]

But friends were not able restore to Jackson his former equa-

---

[1] Jackson Mss. The "Supplement" is in Jackson's hand, but crossed over in such a way as to suggest that it was not sent.
[2] G. W. Campbell to Jackson, February 6, 1807, Jackson Mss.

nimity. The safe refuge which Wilkinson, equally guilty with Burr, found under the wing of the administration was enough to convince his suspicious mind that Dearborn and probably Jefferson had collusive knowledge of the exploded conspiracy. He never forgave either of them; and when he was summoned to Richmond as a witness for the prosecution he came so full of wrath that the attorneys' for the government did not dare put him on the witness stand.[1] This was a disappointment; for he expected to testify to things which would put Wilkinson in a very uncomfortable position. With characteristic impetuosity he assembled a crowd on the public square and harangued them against Jefferson to his heart's content.

From that time he was entirely out of sympathy with the administration. "I have loved Mr. Jefferson as a man," he said, "and adored him as a president. Could I see him attempt to support such a base man with his present knowledge of his corruption and infamy I would withdraw that confidence I once reposed in him and regret that I had been deceived in his virtues. . . . My own pride is, if our country is involved in war in the station I fill, I will do my duty. My pride is that my soldiers has confidence in me, and on the event of war I will lead them on to victory and conquest."[2] A month later John Randolph introduced into congress a resolution to inquire into the alleged treasonable conduct of Wilkinson, and a resultless investigation was made. Randolph was not, in fact, proceeding in good faith. He sought to embarrass Jefferson and hoped that the revelation of a plot between Spanish officials and Wilkinson would produce such a popular outburst that war would be inevitable and that this would be accompanied by the fall of the advocates of peace who then controlled Jefferson's council.[3]

[1]Jackson was sworn and ordered before the grand jury, but here the record fails us. See Robertson, *Report of Trial of Burr*, I., 312.
[2]Jackson to Daniel Smith, Hermitage, November 28, 1807, Jackson Mss.
[3]McCaleb, *Burr Conspiracy*, 334; *Annals of 10th Congress*, 1st session, Volume I., 1257-68, 1296-1328.

But Jackson's purpose was simpler. He believed that Wilkinson was a scoundrel and that the recognition he received was a disgrace to the government. He lost no opportunity to uncover the treachery which he, with many others, believed was concealed within the records of the general's tortuous career. In January, 1810, he learned that an incriminating correspondence between Wilkinson and Michael Lacassonge, late postmaster at Louisville, was in St. Louis and could be obtained by the government. He wrote at length to Senator Whitesides, of Tennessee, enclosing necessary papers and urging him to lay the matter before the President. Lest nothing should be done in that quarter he sent duplicates to John Randolph and wrote a letter to him in which he relieved his feelings. He said:

It is to be regretted, that the arm of government has been stretched forth to shield this public villain, from the just publick punishment that he merits. It has appeared to me that the closer the clouds of testimony of his guilt threted around him, the more the respectability of his answers; the more the favors of government were heaped upon him; and by this means enquiry crushed and truth intimidated and from the enclosed you will see, that this object has been attained, for I believe Capt. OAllen a man of firmness, and a patriot; and with what solicitude he writes and expresses himself on the occurrence! The publick mind is now calm; this villain of corruption and iniquity must be draged from his lurking place, and unmasked to the world. The stain that the government of our country has received by having such a character at the head of our army must be washed out by a just and publick punishment; and I fear that there is not a man on the floor of congress that has firmness and independence enough, to bring forward to the bar of justice this once favorite of presidential care but yourself.[1]

But for all the efforts of Jackson, General Wilkinson continued

[1] Jackson to Whitesides, Hermitage, February 10, 1810; Jackson to Randolph, Hermitage, n. d., but apparently of same date; and Capt. Wm. OAllen to Jackson, January 10, 1810,—Jackson Mss.

to enjoy the favor of Madison as he formerly enjoyed that of Jefferson.

The turn which the Burr incident thus took placed Jackson in opposition to Jefferson and Madison. In 1808 he supported Monroe in Tennessee and ceased his efforts only when informed that to continue them was a useless expenditure of money and influence. His course identified him with the opponents of the regular Virginia politicians, men who supported Crawford in the contest which ended in 1824; and the result was that his own election in 1828 involved the complete overthrow of the Virginia influence in the republican-democratic party.

In all the later criticism of political enemies no evidence was produced to show that he was privy to a scheme to divide the union. His clear patriotism is revealed in all his conduct. "I love my country and government," he said to Claiborne at the first suggestion of treason, "I hate the Dons, I would delight to see Mexico reduced, but I would die in the last ditch before I would yield a foot to the Dons or see the union disunited."[1] The words are strong and passionate but they have the ring of sincerity.

Jackson's hostility to Wilkinson was well known in Tennessee. Burr must have heard of it, and knowing it he would hardly have proposed to Jackson a scheme which depended in its essential parts on the coöperation of the general at New Orleans. The fact that Wilkinson was necessary to an attempt against Louisiana goes to show that no plans to that end could have been proposed to Jackson.

---

[1] Jackson to Claiborne, November 12, 1806, copy in Jackson Mss. See also Parton, *Jackson* I, 319.

CHAPTER V

ONE who appreciates the many good qualities of General Jackson's character may well wish that this chapter was omitted; for it deals with matters which were no credit to him, and for which the best apology is that they but reflected the ideals of the community in which he was bred. But, in truth, he went further than the ideals of the community. Duelling was, no doubt, generally approved in his time in the South and West; but his high passions gave it an application which went further than the average ideals, and he carried himself in ordinary quarrels more strenuously than most Southern and Western gentlemen. He was not properly quarrelsome, for he did not practise the small arts of one who stirs up strife; but he was sensitive to criticism and too apt to pay respect to the tattling of busybodies who surrounded him. Most of his "difficulties" would have been avoided by a magnanimous man, even in a community in which the authority of the code was recognized. But here we must recognize that his passions were allied to qualities of mind which sustained him in, if they did not impel him to, many of his most important achievements.

The first notable quarrel[1] of Jackson in Tennessee was that which he had through a number of years with John Sevier. Its origin is uncertain, but facts seem to support the following account: In 1796 came an election for major-general of militia. Under the territorial regime, Sevier held this office, but as he

---

[1] It is impossible to include in this narrative all of Jackson's encounters. It seems necessary to omit the duel with Avery, which most writers describe, but which had but little influence on his career.

was commander-in-chief under the state constitution, he must relinquish the post. Jackson, whose military rank at this time was not higher than judge advocate,[1] desired the place. Sevier favored George Conway, opposing Jackson on the ground of inexperience; and a blazing quarrel occurred between the two men at Jonesborough.[2] In November, 1796, the election was held. The law provided that the brigadier-general and field officers of each of the three districts should assemble at three places and cast their votes for major-general. Those for Mero District were to meet at Nashville. Before the election Sevier sent Brigadier-General Robertson, of the district, some blank commissions with instructions to appoint cavalry officers and wrote a letter to Joel Lewis in which he spoke in favor of Conway. Before the actual voting there was some discussion of candidates at which Jackson remained a silent spectator till Lewis, who was not an officer, rose to speak against him and while doing so read from the governor's private letter. This brought Jackson to the floor. He criticized Sevier for exceeding his constitutional power in delegating Robertson to make appointments for him and for interfering in an election, which ought to be free from executive influence. Busy tongues carried the speech to Sevier, who was as hot-headed as his critic. He took a lofty tone and declared that he cared nothing for what "a poor, pitiful, petty-fogging scurrilous lawyer" might say about him. Of course the lawyer was duly advised of this retort; and the controversy became warm. Jackson was in Philadelphia when he learned that Sevier had replied to his charges: he restrained himself till he returned to Nashville in the spring of 1797, and then there began an angry correspondence between the two men. It threatened an appeal to the code, but that was avoided;

---

[1] See below, I., 75. He was called colonel in 1797.
[2] Narrative of Colonel Isaac T. Avery which, however, is not the best evidence. Parton, *Jackson*. I., 163.

and in the end a peace was patched up.[1]   The controversy reveals that there were in the state two factions in the republican party, one led by Sevier and another in which Jackson was a prominent person.

Sevier was particularly strong in East Tennessee, then the most populous part of the state.   He was chosen governor in 1796 and reëlected till 1801, when by the constitution he was ineligible for further choice to that office till another term was passed.   Archibald Roane, a friend of Jackson, was then elected for one term, after which Sevier was re-elected in 1803 and held the office till 1809.   This magnetic revolutionary hero and Indian fighter was irresistible when he appealed to the Tennesseeans for votes, but he was not able to develop an organization which should live after him.   In 1809 he gave way to his opponents, who then took a continuous control of the affairs of the state.[2]

The peace which was made between Jackson and the East Tennessee hero in 1797 was violated in 1803, when Roane ran against Sevier for governor.   In his canvass Roane charged his opponent with obtaining fraudulently certain lands from the state of North Carolina.   He relied on information furnished by Jackson, who on July 27, 1803, published in *The Tennessee Gazette* a long letter in support of Roane's charge, thus formally assuming responsibility for the quarrel.

In order to understand this dispute even passably it is necessary to go back to 1797.   In the autumn of that year Jackson, then a senator from Tennessee, revealed to Alexander Martin, who was serving in the same capacity from North Carolina, the particulars of a plot, about which he had recently heard, to defraud the latter state of military lands.   Jackson had the

---

[1]See Jackson to Sevier, May 8, 10, and 13, 1797, *American Historical Magazine*, (Nashville,) V., 118, 120, 121. A draft of the first is in the Jackson Mss. See also Sevier to Jackson, May 8 and 13, 1797, Jackson Mss.
[2]Garrett and Goodpasture, *Tennessee*, 161.

story from Charles J. Love and declared that, when he revealed
it, he did not know Stokely Donelson and James Glasgow would
be implicated. The Nashville agents were Tyrrell and W. T.
Lewis.[1] Martin sent the information to the governor of his
state, and he promptly laid the communication, together with a
written statement which Jackson furnished, before the North
Carolina assembly.[2] This was the beginning of an investigation
which revealed extensive forgeries of papers which entitled old
soldiers to lands in the West and under cover of which the state
had been recently cheated of vast tracts. One of the men involved was Stokely Donelson, a brother of Mrs. Jackson, but
this fact did not deter Jackson from exposing the evil-doers.
Another was James Glasgow, secretary of state in North Carolina, a man of brilliant personality, who had aided the plotters
by accepting the forged papers knowing them to be such. He
was forced to resign his secretaryship and, broken in fortune
as well as reputation, was glad to find a refuge in Tennessee
during his old age.

One hundred and sixty-five of the forged warrants found their
way into the hands of John Sevier, by what means is not clearly
explained; but the advantage which the conspirators would
derive from drawing the governor of Tennessee into their scheme
was so evident that many people considered the mere fact that
the fraudulent warrants were found in his hands evidence of
collusion. Their conviction was strengthened by the fact that
in 1795, sixteen years after these warrants were issued, the
entry-book in which one would expect them to be recorded was
destroyed, apparently by design. Moreover, on going through
the papers in Glasgow's office a letter from Sevier to Glasgow
was found in which the writer asked that certain words in the

---

[1] Jackson to Overton, January 22, 1798, Library of Congress. (Copy)

[2] Alexander Martin to Governor Ashe, Philadelphia, December 7, 1797. The records of the Glasgow trial
are preserved in the office of the secretary of state, Raleigh, North Carolina.

fraudulent grants should be changed so as to make them conform
to the words in the warrants issued legally under the act to give
lands to the continental soldiers, and for this trifling service
Sevier asked his correspondent to accept three of the warrants
for six hundred and forty acres each.

To the enemies of Sevier the case seemed a clear one. Why,
they asked, should the entry books be burned by one who had
good warrants? and why should the governor give Glasgow land
worth $960 for a service for which the legal fee was one dollar?
Sevier replied to his critics by saying that he acquired the warrants in a fair way, that he had merely asked Glasgow to con-
solidate them into one warrant for his greater convenience in
disposing of them. In the summer of 1803 there were several
plain communications in *The Tennessee Gazette*, attacking or
defending Sevier. The matter was referred to a committee of
the assembly which reported against Sevier, but his friends in
the assembly were strong enough to amend the report by setting
forth the facts in the case without imputing fault to anybody,
and in that shape the report passed. It has never been definitely
ascertained whether Jackson's charges were well grounded or
not, but he never doubted their truth.[1]

In October, 1803, while the controversy was at its height,
Jackson, on his eastern circuit, came to Knoxville to hold court.
On coming out of the court-house one day, he saw Sevier, who was
then a candidate for governor, haranguing a crowd not far from
the building. Sevier's coming to this place for such a purpose
seems to show that he sought to provoke a conflict, and this
supposition is strengthened by the fact that as soon as he saw
Jackson he began to denounce him. The latter, regardless of
his judicial dignity, replied in a similar strain, and a turbulent

---

[1]Jackson's charges were made in a long communication to *The Tennessee Gazette*, July 27, 1803; reprinted in *American Historical Magazine* (Nashville,) IV., 374-481. Sevier's reply with a counter blast
by "An Elector" appears in the same paper, August 8, 1803. A file of this journal is in the Library
of Congress.

scene occurred, in which Sevier, carried away by his emotions, declared the only public service he ever heard of Jackson performing was to run off with another man's wife. This allusion to a very delicate matter was well calculated to throw the object of the gibe into a furious rage. "Great God!" he exclaimed, "do you mention *her* sacred name?" and a challenge promptly followed.[1] But Sevier declined to fight on the ground that his courage was so well known that he could afford to refuse to risk his life in an encounter. This angered Jackson more than ever. He sought to bring on an encounter at sight, but was not successful; and after some ebullition of feeling, friends interfered and arranged a truce between the two men.[2]

The quarrel with Sevier had an important influence on Jackson's political career. As leader of West Tennessee he was necessary to the republican organization, and up to this time an open rupture was avoided between the two men through the efforts of friends; but in the future no truce could exist. Jackson, as the less popular man, suffered in the estimation of the public. Sevier's election to the governorship for three terms following the land-frauds controversy emphasized his victory and discredited his opponent.

---

[1]This account follows Avery's story, which is confused as to dates, and is given with some degree of reservation. The Knoxville wrangle, to which Avery refers, plainly occurred in 1803. See Parton, *Jackson*, I., 163.

[2]Inasmuch as several accounts of this affair have been given, the author gives here the substance of an affidavit by Andrew Greer, an eyewitness, sworn to on October 23, 1803. It proceeds: On the fifteenth instant, the affiant was riding with Governor Sevier and his son "to go to South-west Point," that in the "hollow that leads down to Kingston" they met Judge Jackson with Dr. Vandyke, both armed with pistols, that Jackson stopped and conversed with Greer, while Dr. Vandyke rode on, that while he and Jackson were talking, he observed Jackson cast his umbrella on the ground, draw one pistol, dismount, draw the other, and advance up the road. Turning, he saw Sevier, dismounted and pistol in hand, advancing on Jackson. Within twenty paces, the two men halted and began to abuse one another Sevier damning Jackson to fire away; but after some words, each replaced his pistol in his holster and began to approach the other, Jackson swearing he would cane his antagonist. Sevier then drew his sword, at which his horse was frightened and ran off with the owner's pistols in the holsters, Jackson then drew his pistols, and advanced. Sevier leapt behind a tree and damned Jackson, and did he mean to fire on a naked man? Whereupon young Sevier drew his pistol and advanced on Jackson, while Dr. Vandyke drew on young Sevier. After some talk, all the pistols were replaced, and the party mounted and rode down the road, Jackson and Sevier within shouting distance and still abusing one another. Jackson thus called to Sevier to fight it out on horseback, and Sevier replied that his opponent knew that he, Sevier, would not fight in the state. See *American Historical Magazine*, (Nashville), V, 208.)

Of a similar influence, but more striking as an incident, was the duel with Charles Dickinson, the particulars of which are as follows: In 1805, Jackson's noted horse, "Truxton," was backed in a race against Captain Joseph Ervin's "Plowboy," and a forfeit of $800, payable in certain specified notes, was agreed upon if the race was not run. Before the day fixed, the race was cancelled by Ervin, and the forfeit was paid without dispute. A short time afterward a report was out that the notes tendered were not those which were specified in the original agreement. Dickinson was Ervin's son-in-law and was concerned with him in behalf of "Plowboy." One of his friends was Thomas Swann, a young spark from Virginia; and he asked Jackson if the report about the notes was true. Swann alleged that the reply to his question was in the affirmative and so informed Dickinson, who saw Jackson and asked if the report which had come to him, Dickinson, were true. The general quickly replied that the author of the report had told a damned lie; and then he was told that it came from Swann, between whom and Jackson a question of veracity was thus raised. It was really the merest word-play; for Jackson claimed that what he had said was that Ervin offered to pay the forfeit in notes not strictly those agreed upon, while the other claimed that Jackson said that *the list of notes* offered, out of which the forfeit was to be paid, was not the list which was specified in the original agreement, and that there was a great deal of difference between notes offered and the list of notes offered. Small as the point was, it was large enough to support a quarrel between men who were already sensitive in their relations to each other.

Swann became noisy and insisted that Jackson give him the satisfaction which a gentleman had the right to claim. His opponent in the affair replied by saying that he would give him a caning, and he followed the threat with actions. If he had done no more, the result would have been eventless; but in his replies to Swann he used rasping expressions about Dickinson, whom he persisted in thinking responsible for the young Virginian's attacks. This gave the controversy a new character. Dickinson was regarded as the best rifle shot of the West, and he probably did not fear an encounter with Jackson. He certainly did not try to avoid one. When he saw in the Nashville paper a letter written by Jackson in which his motives were denounced, he wrote a scathing and contemptuous reply and sent it to the editor. Jackson knew about it before it was published, and he waited not one instant, but sent a challenge naming his friend, General Thomas Overton, as his second.

Whatever we may think of the morality of duelling, it will be conceded by most people that to receive at ten paces the fire of an angry enemy requires no little physical courage. Some men have entered such encounters impetuously or because they shrank from a public opinion which approved duelling as a test of a man's bravery; but in Jackson's duel with Dickinson neither of these causes operated. Each man went into the affair deliberately, and each had determined to kill the other if he could. The conditions were such that each must have realized that one or the other was likely to be slain; yet they went to the meeting without a tremor. In the quarrel which had preceded the challenge each man called the other the most abusive epithets. "A worthless, drunken, blackguard scoundrel" was one of the descriptions which Jackson gave of his opponent, who retaliated in kind; but when the business reached the actual challenge it was conducted with the exact politeness which is demanded between perfect gentlemen; such was the way of duelists.

Jackson's challenge was sent on May 22, 1806, and the date of the meeting was fixed for the thirtieth of the same month. The weapons were to be pistols, and the distance was eight yards. The place of the encounter was in Kentucky just beyond

the state line at a point north of Nashville.   Dickinson rode out
to the grounds with confidence, accompanied by a gay group
of his young companions.   As he passed an inn, so it is said, he
fired at a string by which some object was suspended, his ball
cutting it half through, and he told the inn-keeper to show the
string to General Jackson if he passed that way.

In the meantime Jackson and his second, General Overton,
riding to the duelling grounds were discussing the manner in
which they should meet the antagonist.   It had been agreed
that the two men should stand facing the same direction, and
that at the word they should turn toward each other and fire
as they chose.   Between Overton and his principal all the
chances in such an encounter were gone over: they agreed that
Dickinson should be allowed to fire first.   Like most crack
shots, he was a quick one; and they thought that he would
probably fire first anyway and at least hit his opponent: Jackson was sure to hit in a deliberate shot, but if he fired quickly
and an instant after he was hit by a ball, his aim would probably
be destroyed.

The surmise of the two men proved correct: when all was
ready in the early morning and Overton gave the word "Fire!"
the pistol of Dickinson rose instantly, there was a quick flash
and report, and Jackson was seen to press his hand tightly over
his chest, although his tall figure did not tremble.   Dickinson
was seized with terror.   "Great God!" he cried, "have I missed
him?"   He thought it impossible that he should not hit a man
at twenty-four feet.   For a moment he shrank from the peg
till a stern word from Overton brought him again to an erect
position.

Jackson now had his opponent at his mercy.   He stood glower-
ing at him for an instant, and then his long pistol arm came
slowly to a horizontal position.   Dickinson shuddered and turned
away his head.   Jackson's eye ran along the pistol barrel,

deliberately adjusting the aim, and then he pulled the trigger. But there was no explosion. A hurried consultation by the seconds revealed that the hammer stopped at half-cock, which by the rules agreed upon was not to count as a fire; and Jackson was given another shot. Again he took careful aim at the poor victim who all the time stood awaiting his fate, and this time the pistol fired. The ball cut a large artery, and Dickinson died that night. Jackson walked triumphantly from the field, carefully concealing from his attendants the fact that he was wounded; for he wanted his dying antagonist to think his shot failed. "I should have hit him," Jackson once said, "if he had shot me through the brain."

The coolness he displayed in this duel brought much criticism on Jackson. He did, undoubtedly, fail to show magnanimity, but that was never one of his virtues. If instead of shooting down an unresisting man he had fired into the air and refused to fire again, public opinion would have justified him; for one did not have to face Dickinson's pistol a second time to prove his courage. It is plain enough that he killed the man whom he hated because he wanted to kill him; and it was little less than murder. Dickinson had many friends in West Tennessee, and they denounced bitterly his slayer. The controversy became general and bitter, and the large number of people who took sides against Jackson, added to those who were already his opponents on account of the quarrel with Sevier, materially lessened his influence in the political life of the state.[1]

The natural result of this reversal of sentiment was to fix Jackson in private life. He remained at the "Hermitage," devoting himself to his plantation and his blooded horses, trying in vain to bring his mercantile business out of the confusion into which it was fallen. He retained his position as commander-in-chief of the militia of the western district; and this gave

---

[1]Parton, *Jackson*, I., Chapters 23 to 27.

him no mean station. He was recognized as peculiarly suited for that kind of duty, his officers liked him, and it was his pride that he could call out a full quota of men, if the war which always seemed imminent should at last arrive. But in the annals of the community, and in his own voluminous collection of papers relating to his career, there is almost nothing in this period which makes his course interesting above that of any other well esteemed citizen of West Tennessee. In fact, it is two other quarrels which bridge over the period between the Burr incident in 1806-'07, and the Creek campaign in 1813, which were to make him one of most commanding figures in the country. An honest Indian agent and a faithful supporter were the objects of these angry outbursts.

Silas Dinsmore was United States agent among the Choctaws. He gave satisfaction to the government and won the esteem of the Indians, but became objectionable to many persons living in the Mississippi Territory. His agency-house was on the great road from Nashville to Natchez, and the planters living south of it complained that their slaves were accustomed to run away along this road in company with pretended masters and that it was his duty to arrest them. Whereupon he announced that he would detain every slave traveling with a white man, unless the latter had a certificate that the Negro was his property; and he enforced the rule strictly. There now arose louder complaint than ever. Without knowing of the regulation a master would arrive at the agency to meet an annoying delay till he could get proof of ownership of his slaves, and then he would go on his way with loud complaints against the officious agent who delayed him. Nashville was the next stopping place on the way north and most of their tales of woe were unburdened there. The lamentations reached the ears of the secretary of war, who instructed Dinsmore to use discretion in enforcing his rule; but the agent replied that he could not undertake to decide by appearances the claims of masters who passed him, and he continued to require certificates of all.

Jackson never saw both sides of a subject; and to him Dinsmore was a perverse official who needed to be disciplined. He spoke his mind freely about a man who tried to impede the passage of an American citizen along the public roads, and Dinsmore heard of his threats. In his trading Jackson took all kinds of things which the people bought and sold and thus he frequently got possession of slaves which he sent to the southern country for sale. Such a venture he made about the time the feeling against Dinsmore was at its height; but his Natchez agent mismanaged the affair, and he went to that place in person to bring the slaves home. On his return he must pass the Choctaw agency, and he determined to give Dinsmore what he considered a proper rebuke. He armed two of his trusted Negroes, took a rifle in his own hands, and in this fashion marched on the enemy. He had no certificates that he owned his slaves, and trouble seemed imminent, but the agent proved to be absent, and the cavalcade passed the house without incident.

In Nashville Jackson now became more violent than ever, swearing that if any more slaves were detained he would burn both agent and agency. Soon afterward a lady arrived in the town reporting that her ten slaves were detained for lack of passports. At the same time the town paper contained an announcement from Dinsmore that he would execute the rules of his office. Jackson was already striving to secure the removal of Dinsmore. To G. W. Campbell, congressman from Tennessee, he sent a blazing letter. "My God!" he exclaimed. "Is it come to this? Are we freemen, or are we slaves? Is this real or is it a dream? . . . Can the Secretary of War for one moment retain the idea that we will permit this petty tyrant to sport with our rights secured to us by treaty, and which by the law of nature we do possess, and sport with our feelings by publishing his lawless tyranny exercised over a helpless and unprotected female?"

This fiery appeal effected nothing. Dinsmore kept his place for the time; but in the following year, 1812, he lost it because he happened to be absent when an important crisis occurred in Indian affairs and when a man was needed on the spot immediately. Jackson never forgave him for what he considered usurpation of authority; and he exerted himself after the war, when his influence with the war department was great, to prevent Dinsmore's reappointment to the Choctaw agency. The incident illustrates Jackson's extreme sensitiveness to the restraint of his actions by another and his readiness to take the lead in protesting against what he deemed a wrong;[1] and his side of the contention was, probably, nearer right than Dinsmore's. It was sheer wrong-headedness in the agent to retaliate for criticism, although it was unfounded, by a practice which could in no sense be a public service, and to persist in it in the face of universal opposition. Jackson was not alone in his position; for Governor Blount, Felix Grundy, and Poindexter, of Mississippi, all protested to the secretary of war against Dinsmore.[2]

His other noted quarrel of this period was with the two Bentons, and it occurred in 1813. One of his friends was William Carroll, destined to have an important military and political career in Tennessee. He was then a young man and recently arrived in Nashville; and from a certain superior air which he had he was unpopular with the young gentlemen of the town. Jackson quickly recognized his soldierly qualities and supported him so well that the other militia officers became jealous. A quarrel ensued and from one of them Carroll got

[1]Parton, *Jackson*, I., 349-360.

[2]Blount to Jackson, March 20, 1812; Blount to the secretary of war, March 22, 1812, and Grundy to Jackson, February 12, 1812; Jackson Mss.

a challenge. He declined on the ground that the sender was not a gentleman. Another challenger was found, but the same reply was given. Then the officers induced Jesse, the brother of Thomas Hart Benton, to send a challenge; and this was accepted. Carroll now found that none of the young men of the town would act as his second, and he asked Jackson to do him that service, who at first declined on the ground of his superior age, and because after investigation the grounds of the quarrel did not seem to justify a duel. He sought Jesse Benton and got him to agree that the matter should be dropped; but that young man's friends easily persuaded him into a renewal of his demands. Jackson then became impatient with Benton and agreed to act as Carroll's second.

The duel which followed was a farce. The parties were placed back to back, and at a given word they wheeled and fired. Benton discharged his weapon first, and, in order to expose as small a target as possible, came to a crouching position. His opponent's ball struck the lower part of his back and made a long raking flesh wound in the buttock. The unfortunate man suffered more from ridicule than from the wound.

When this duel was fought, Thomas Hart Benton was in Washington. It was just after Jackson's Natchez expedition and Benton's taste of military life in that undertaking gave him a desire for a permanent career in the army. His business in Washington was to get such a position and he carried with him a recommendation from Jackson. He sought also to get certain accounts of Jackson's allowed by the government, an errand which, however, was rendered of little account by the small disposition of the war department to refuse to pay them.[1] While returning to Nashville, he learned of the duel in which Jackson was second on the opposite side to his brother, Jesse.

[1] See below 86.

That sensitive young man sent him a long account of the affair in which the action of the general was placed in as bad a light as possible. Thereupon, Thomas wrote Jackson a letter, the tone of which was cooler than he was accustomed to use toward his old friend and received a reply in the same key. Officious acquaintances repeated to each man remarks which the other was reported to have used till at last Jackson declared that he would horsewhip Thomas Benton on sight.

Had some quieting spirit interfered at this point, it is possible that the matter could have been checked where it was; but no such spirit existed in the community, and the affair ran rapidly into one of the most disgraceful encounters of the day. Benton neither sought nor avoided it. On reaching home he went to Nashville on business, taking the precaution to put up at a tavern at which Jackson was not in the habit of staying when in town. Busybodies hurried to the "Hermitage" with the news and its owner determined to carry out his threat. He rode into town in the afternoon and stopped at the usual place. Next morning with Coffee he crossed the public square to the post-office and observed Benton standing in the doorway of his own tavern. "Do you see that fellow?" said Coffee. "Oh yes," was the reply, "I have my eye on him." Returning from the post-office the two men passed directly by the doorway in which the enemy was displaying himself. As they reached the spot, Jackson wheeled sharply in front of his foe, raised a riding-whip, and exclaimed, "Now you damned rascal, I am going to punish you! Defend yourself!" Benton, while endeavoring to draw a pistol from his breast pocket, retreated backward down a hallway, his adversary following with a pistol in his hand. As they passed a side door Jesse Benton rushed out of it, and, believing his brother to be in imminent danger, emptied his pistol into the shoulder of Jackson, who had not seen him. The wounded man fell to the floor. Coffee had joined the mêlée and now continued the pursuit of Thomas, who stumbled and fell down a stairway which he had not seen, thus saving himself from the vengeance of the towering figure which pursued him. In the meantime, another friend of Jackson fell on the other of the two brothers, threw him to the floor, and was about to do him serious harm when the bystanders interfered. With this the combat ended. Jackson received a painful flesh wound, the effects of which he long felt; but it did not seriously inconvenience him, while neither of the others was injured.

From being one of Jackson's trusted political allies Benton now found all the general's friends arrayed against him, and his political prospects in Tennessee vanished. At the same time, he got the position in the army which he desired, lieutenant-colonel of the Tenth Regiment of regulars; but the promotion did not bring satisfaction, for the recent turn of military affairs in the Southwest made Jackson supreme there, and under him Benton could hope for no advancement. During the rest of the war, while other Tennesseans won glory in the Creek country and at New Orleans, he was kept on duty with detachments sent to keep the Indians quiet, and the return of peace saw him still a lieutenant-colonel. It was for this reason that he turned his face westward, seeking a place where his course would not be blocked by the hostility of Jackson. In 1815 he settled in Missouri, where his career soon became very brilliant. Later in life he became reconciled to his old enemy and earlier friend; and in the stern struggles of the latter's presidency he was one of the most devoted of his defenders. But Jesse Benton never forgave Jackson, and he signalized his hostility by writing some bitter attacks on him in the presidential campaigns of 1824 and 1828.

On Jackson, himself, the effect of these repeated encounters was little less injurious than on Benton. They not only increased the number of his enemies, but they served to make impartial men think that he was not a man to be trusted in public life. They also increased his irritability, as he himself recognized. He even thought of moving from Tennessee in order to make a new start in life. He turned his eyes to Mississippi, where he thought of getting a judgeship. Two reasons which he gave for this action show the state of his mind in 1810:

"From my pursuits for several years past," he said, "from many unpleasant occurrences that took place during that time it has given my mind such a turn of thought, that I have laboured to get clear off. I have found this impossible, and unless [I have] some new pursuit to employ my mind and thoughts, I find it impossible to divert myself of those habits of gloomy and peevish reflections that the wanton and flagitous conduct, and unremitted reflections of base calumny, heaped upon me has given rise to; and in order to try the experiment how far new scenes might relieve me from this unpleasant tone of thought, I did conclude to accept that appointment in case it was offered me."

His second reason was more in keeping with our usual ideas of his motives. "From a temporizing disposition displayed by congress," he declared, "I am well aware that no act of insult, degradation or contumely offered to our Government will arouse them from their present lethargy and temporizing conduct, until my namesake sets fire to some of our seaport towns and puts his foot aboard a British man-of-war. . . . From all which I conclude that as a military man I shall have no amusement or business, and indolence and inaction would shortly destroy me."[1]

Jackson might well think that the hand of fate was against him. When he left the bench in 1804, he gave up his last connection with civil life. He felt little interest in the career of

---

[1] Jackson to J. Whitesides, February 10, 1810; Jackson Mss.

lawyer, lawmaker, or judge, and his success as a merchant was not reassuring. Tennessee had passed beyond its frontier stage of development: it demanded, in civil matters, a more temperate, intellectual, and self-controlled leader than Jackson, and if in 1810 he had become a judge in Mississippi Territory he would merely have followed the frontier, to whose conditions he was best adapted.

But there was one chance of his reappearance in public life in his own state. In spite of all disappointments, war was at last coming and in its course England would encourage the Indians to attack the Southwestern settlements. Again would the border call for a man of elemental force, one whose will, courage, sagacity, and power of command could organize the rude men around him into an effective fighting machine and direct it for the safety of his country. Just such a man was Jackson. From 1802 he was in command of the militia, always waiting for the chance to distinguish himself in battle. And now, late in 1812, the hour struck.

CHAPTER VI

EARLY MILITARY CAREER

JACKSON's rise into prominence in the militia was due to native soldierly qualities which were early manifested and always evident. The Tennesseans of the day were of necessity much engaged in war and in the preparations for it. Many of them were revolutionary soldiers, men who fought in the continental line and moved west to take the lands which were given them as rewards for that service. These soldiers furnished the officers and some of the privates in what was probably the best body of militia ever seen in America. Such people were apt to know a soldier when they saw him; and one who had the talents to be a revolutionary trooper at thirteen and the hero of New Orleans at forty-eight would hardly fail to impress them.

For Jackson there was much inducement to escape from the law into the soldier's calling. For ten years after his arrival there was constant danger of a separation of the West from the seaboard region: when that subsided all eyes turned to the task of thrusting the Spaniards out of New Orleans: and when the purchase treaty of 1803 solved that problem there remained the growing belief that war must come with England, and probably with her protected ally, Spain, during which Canada and Florida would offer fields for glorious achievement. If war should come from either of these causes the Cumberland district would be a most important part of the situation. Jackson understood this and from an early day in his residence sought military office.

Two groups of politicians controlled affairs in Tennessee at

73

the time with which we are now concerned. One of them was led by the Blounts, William, the first territorial governor, and Willie,[1] his brother: the other was led by John Sevier, through many daring exploits the hero of the people. He was not the equal of either of the Blounts as a politician or as a statesman, but whenever he asked for office, the people gave it. Blount was governor under the territorial régime and retired from the office in 1796 to be United States senator. He was succeeded by Sevier who was reëlected till 1801, when he could not by constitutional limitation be chosen again for two years. But after that interval, during which Archibald Roane, who was friendly with the Blounts, was governor, he again came into office in 1803 and held it for another period of six years.

As a part of the territorial organization Jackson came to be identified with the Blount group, and this brought him into opposition to Sevier.[2] It therefore happened that when Sevier was governor there was no possible appointment for Jackson which depended on the will of the governor, although in those offices which depended on votes of the people or on the assembly, he had abundant success. It was fortunate for Jackson that the two events most critical in his military career, his election as major-general and the outbreak of the war of 1812, came, one during the short interval between his opponent's two periods of office-holding and the other after the expiration of the second period.

When Tennessee became a state in 1796 it was divided into three militia districts, one of which was Mero. The militia of each county constituted a regiment and that of a district made a brigade, with one calvary regiment attached to each brigade. Company and regimental officers were to be elected by persons liable to militia duty, and commissions were to be issued by the

[1]Pronounced Wi-lie.
[2]For the Sevier-Jackson quarrel see above pp. 55-60.

governor. The field officers of each district elected the brigadier-general; and the field officers of all the districts, brigadier-generals included, elected a major-general who commanded the militia of the whole state. If there should be a tie vote in the selection of the major-general, the governor was to cast the deciding vote. These features of the militia system were unchanged during Jackson's major-generalship. The effect was essentially democratic. Personal jealousies sometimes entered into the elections, and the system did not tend to secure military subordination, but it facilitated the rise into power of a really capable man, like Jackson; and under his direction it became a good piece of fighting machinery.[1]

The first suggestion we have of Jackson's interest in the militia system is found in a plan which he sent in 1791 to Governor Blount, who liked it so well that he forwarded it to the secretary of war.[2] A year later, September 10, 1792, he appointed the author judge advocate of the Davidson County regiment.[3] James Robertson, who with John Donelson, Jackson's father-in-law, was joint leader of the original Nashville settlement, and who was now the leading military man on the Cumberland, seems to have urged Jackson's appointment to a line command. The governor was willing and wrote: "Can't you contrive for Hay to resign and I will promote Donelson [now second major] and appoint Jackson second major?"[4] The scheme did not succeed, and in 1796 he was not a field officer, as he himself says.[5] His promotion was probably to colonelcy, for he was spoken of on December 7, 1797, by that title. But his ambition was for major-generalship. At the first election to that office, in 1796, he was a can-

[1]Scott, Laws of Tennessee, I., 559.
[2]Gov. Blount to General Robertson, September 21, 1791, American Historical Magazine (Nashville), I., 193.
[3]See American Historical Magazine (Nashville), II., 231. Nashville is located in Davidson county. Jackson was not one of those commissioned by Blount in 1790 when he created the militia establishment for the newly organized territory.
[4]Blount to Robertson, October 28, 1792, American Historical Magazine (Nashville) II., 84,
[5]Jackson to Sevier, May 8, 1797, Jackson Mss.; also American Historical Magazine (Nashville), V., 118.

didate and had the opposition of Sevier, who in the heat of later controversy asserted that he would not at that time consent to the election of an inexperienced man.[1] The office went to Conway, who died during Roane's term as governor. In the election to fill the vacancy Jackson and Sevier each received seventeen votes and James Winchester had three. Roane cast the deciding vote in favor of the first of the three, who thus arrived at the top of his ambition in February, 1802.[2] But this dignity was shorn of half its strength by the passage, November 5, 1803, of a new militia act by which there were to be two divisions of militia each to be commanded by a major-general. Eleven counties in West Tennessee were to constitute the second division, and over this Jackson retained command; while fourteen counties in East Tennessee made up the first division, over which a major-general was to be elected.[3] In this condition the militia system remained substantially till the beginning of the war.

The ten years following Jackson's election as major-general were years of expectancy. They brought him three calls from the government: one in 1803 when it was feared that Spain would not give up Louisiana without force, one in 1806 in order to defeat Burr's alleged conspiracy, and one in 1809 when the government planned a secret attack against West Florida.[4] In each case his response was decided and was seconded by the enthusiastic support of the militia under his command. "Rest assured," he said, "that should the Tocsin of war be sounded the hardy sons of the west that I have the honor to command will deserve

[1]*American Historical Magazine*, Nashville, V., 116.

[2]See David Campbell to Jackson, January 25, 1802. Jackson Mss.

[3]*Acts of Tennessee*, 1st session, 5th General Assembly, Chapter I., November 5, 1803.

[4]On the first, see G. W. Campbell to Jackson, October 29, 1803; William Dickson to Jackson, October 31 and November 20, 1803; Jackson to the secretary of war, November 12, 1803 and January 13, 1804, Jackson Mss, and Jackson to Jefferson, n. d., in Jefferson Mss., Library of Congress, volume 46, number 46. On the second see above, 46-49. On the third, see Jackson to Winchester, March 15, 1809, and Sevier to Jackson, January 12, 1809, Jackson Mss.

well of their country."[1] The assertion is supported by ample evidence in his unpublished correspondence, and it marks the extent to which his extraordinary leadership was accepted by the people around him.

In 1812 war was declared against England, when there seemed no other excuse for it than to wipe out the disgrace of a long and spiritless inactivity. To the people of West Tennessee it gave peculiar joy: Spain was in such close alliance with England that it seemed inevitable that she would be brought into the struggle; and this would give the long desired opportunity to take vengeance for many wrongs on the frontier. But the cautious congress refused to draw Spain into the conflict, and His Catholic Majesty was not willing to risk his hold on Florida by becoming involved in a war to which he could contribute no armies.

Two years before the war began, the Indians of the West, under the guidance of the British, were planning to form a great combination to protect themselves against the fatal advance of the whites. The movement was led by Tecumseh and his brother, the Prophet, and aimed to unite both the northwestern and the southwestern tribes in a great confederacy. It aroused so much alarm that the Indiana and Kentucky militia under Harrison moved suddenly on the northwestern tribes in 1810 and dealt them a severe blow at Tippecanoe. This expedition was watched with great interest in Tennessee, and when news came that it was involved in difficulties Jackson wrote hurriedly and fervently to Harrison offering on request to come to his assistance with five hundred West Tennesseeans.[2] Correct news from the northward soon dissipated all the hopes which sprang from this situation.

But the war spirit was alive in the West and continued to

---

[1] Jackson to Servier, December 30, 1805, Jackson Mss.
[2] Jackson to Winchester, November 28, 1811, Jackson Mss.

grow. In the winter of 1811-1812 it made itself felt in congress, the western members taking the lead. Long before hostilities were authorized the impetuous Jackson believed that they were at hand. Six months beforehand he was using every avenue of influence open to him to obtain service at the head of his faithful militiamen. To Governor Willie Blount he wrote saying that with ten days' notice he could take the field at the head of four thousand men, and engaging within ninety days to be before Quebec with two thousand five hundred. The governor did not think this an idle boast: he transmitted the information to the secretary of war approvingly and added by way of vouching for Jackson: "He loves his country and his countrymen have full confidence in him. He delights in peace; but does not fear war. He has a peculiar pleasure in treating his enemies as such; with them his first pleasure is to meet them on the field. At the present crisis he feels a holy zeal for the welfare of the United States, and at no period of his life has he been known to feel otherwise. His understanding and integrity may be confided in. He is independent and liberal in mind; easy in his circumstances; generous and open in his habits and manners. He ought to command his volunteers."[1]

February 6, 1812, congress, in anticipation of hostilities, authorized the enlistment of fifty thousand volunteers. The information brought enthusiasm to the Tennesseeans, who for months had petitioned in town meetings and in the legislature for an appeal to arms. March 7, Jackson sent to his division a ringing call for volunteers.[2] The people, he urged, had long demanded war; now let them prove their sincerity by offering their services. The reponse justified his anticipations; June 25, a week after war was declared by congress, he offered the President twenty-five hundred volunteers. In due time the tender

---

[1] Blount to Eustis, January 25, 1812, Jackson Mss.
[2] See Jackson Mss.

was formally accepted,[1] but orders for immediate service did not arrive.

While he waited to hear from Washington he was dreaming of conquering Florida, and on July 21, he expressed his feelings in a passionate proclamation to his division.[2] "You burn with anxiety," he said, "to learn on what theatre your arms will find employment. Then turn your eyes to the South! Behold in the province of West Florida, a territory whose rivers and harbors, are indispensable to the prosperity of the western, and still more so, to the eastern division of our state. Behold there likewise the asylum from which an insiduous hand incites to rapine and bloodshed, the ferocious savages, who have just stained our frontier with blood, and who will renew their outrages the moment an English force shall appear in the Bay of Pensacola. It is here that an employment adapted to your situation awaits your courage and your zeal, and while extending in this quarter the boundaries of the Republic to the Gulf of Mexico, you will experience a peculiar satisfaction in having conferred a signal benefit on that section of the Union to which you yourselves immediately belong." During the next two years Jackson issued many proclamations to his troops: they were usually drafted by himself and finished by an aide. Although the rhetoric was inclined to be turgid, the language was direct and impelling. They suited the people to whom they were addressed.

In the meantime, the President and cabinet decided to occupy the Floridas, if congress would authorize it. They reckoned badly; for Madison's enemies suddenly became warm defenders of the rights of neutrality and rallied enough votes in the senate to defeat the proposed expedition. On February 12, 1813, however, they voted to authorize the occupation of Mobile and the region west of the Perdido, a task

---

[1]See Jackson Mss.
[2]Secretary of War to Governor Blount, July 11, 1812, Jackson Mss.

which was easily performed by the regular troops under Wilkinson.

Madison did not expect this decision and long before it was made was preparing to send an expedition into Florida. Early in November, 1812, the governor of Tennessee received a call for fifteen hundred volunteers for the defense of New Orleans. That place was not threatened, but it was not good policy to reveal the real destination of the force before congress acted in reference to the expedition. To the Tenesseeans the order brought real joy. Governor Blount forwarded it to Jackson as soon as it was received in Knoxvillle and followed in person in order to aid in dispatching the detachment. In a patriotic proclamation of November 12,the major-general called his forces into the field and fixed December 10 as the date of the rendezvous.

The spirit of the militia was excellent. In the preceding spring, in response to Jackson's manifesto of March 7, two thousand seven hundred and fifty of them signified their willingness to volunteer in case there should be war. Now, although the call was for only fifteen hundred, there came to Nashville at the appointed time two thousand and seventy men, and the question was, should all of them be accepted ? After a moment's hesitation Governor Blount authorized the mustering of the whole force, and Jackson hurried forward its equipment. In ordinary experience two months is not too much to muster, organize, and bring into marching condition two thousand militia; but it was more than Jackson would now have. By the end of the year he was ready to march, and on January 7, 1813, the expedition was put into motion. The infantry, fourteen hundred strong, went down the river in flat-bottomed boats, and the cavalry, which numbered six hundred and seventy, proceeded by land under the command of Colonel Coffee. The point of concentration was Natchez.

When Governor Blount submitted to Jackson his orders from

Washington it was seen to be doubtful if the latter would command the detachment. In the first place the numbers in the detachment did not seem to require a major-general for commander; in the second place they were merely to march to New Orleans where they would be under Wilkinson's orders and for this a brigadier-general was ample. Moreover, the secretary in his call on the governor made no reference to Jackson's tender of service in the preceding winter, and the inference was pretty plain that he did not desire to utilize it.[1] If such was the secretary's intention he was perhaps not much to blame; for Jackson's antipathy to the commander at New Orleans was well known in Washington. No good could have been expected from bringing the two men together under the proposed conditions.

Jackson realized the seriousness of this situation and with a moderation unusual for him offered to subordinate his feeling and serve anywhere his country might call him.[2] There is no doubt that he was honest in his intention, but it is nevertheless fortunate that he had no opportunity to test his power of executing his resolve.

Governor Blount took legal advice and decided that, inasmuch as the secretary's orders were not explicit, discretion was given him as governor to appoint the commander of the expedition as seemed best. Accordingly one of the seventy blank commissions which came ready signed from Washington was filled with the name of Andrew Jackson, who thus became major-general of United States volunteers. Under him served no brigadier-general, but there were three colonels, two commanding infantry regiments, and another, the redoubtable Coffee, leading the one cavalry regiment.

Colonel John Coffee deserves a special word of description. He was a tall, broad-shouldered, and honest Westerner, married

---

[1] Secretary of War to Blount, October 21 and 23, 1812, Jackson Mss.
[2] Jackson to Blount, November 11, 1812, Jackson Mss.

to a niece of Mrs. Jackson and thus bound to his superior both by family feeling and by long established friendship. Before this he had been Jackson's business partner; but the qualities which made him a poor merchant did not keep him from being a good soldier. He was brave, energetic, and always loyal; and he was destined to prove an invaluable first assistant to his chief on many a field of battle from 1813 to 1815. Two other subordinates must not be omitted. Thomas Hart Benton, who began the campaign as lieutenant-colonel of one of the two infantry regiments but was soon made aide to the general, was later to be a large figure among those political friends who made the success of the Jacksonian party possible. John Reid, another aide, was a man of real intellectual ability. He served his superior faithfully till the end of the New Orleans campaign, and before his untimely death wrote the larger part of the biography which is usually ascribed to Eaton.

Parton well says that the heart of Western Tennessee went down the river with this Natchez expedition. The militia organization was closely associated with the political organization and the leading persons in the community were at its head. It was they who volunteered to go to New Orleans. If they returned victorious they would have added power over the imagination of the community. Their patriotism, also, was not questioned. Every impulse of this new region sprang spontaneously to the defense of their country. The governor sped them with an outburst of pious confidence which a calmer people might have flouted. Jackson sent for reply a letter in which was an unwonted tone of humility.

"Brought up," he said, "under the tyranny of Britain, altho' young I embarked in the struggle for our liberties, in which I lost everything that was dear to me, *my brothers and my fortune!* for which I have been amply repaid, by living under the mild administration of a republican government. To maintain which and the independent rights of our nation, is a duty I have ever owed to my country, myself and posterity. And when I do all I can for its support, I have only done my duty, and it will be ever grateful to my reflection, if I find my acts and my exertions meet your approbation. I sincerely respond to your Excellency's letter, in praying that the God of battles may be with us, and that high Heaven may bestow its choicest benedictions on all who have engaged in this expedition." [1]

The river trip was uneventful, and on February 15, 1813, the boats arrived at Natchez where they found Coffee's regiment and joined them on the sixteenth. To Jackson's surprise he found, also, a letter from Wilkinson ordering him to halt where he was and await further instructions. Several reasons for the order were given by its author. He had received no commands from Washington in regard to the expedition; he could not furnish it with provisions in New Orleans; and if, as he supposed, the detachment was to be sent against Florida it could best proceed on that service from some point on the river above New Orleans, as from Natchez or Baton Rouge. All these reasons were courteously expressed in several letters to which Jackson replied in similar strain. [2]

Wilkinson may be pardoned if he desired to avoid a possible conflict with Jackson. He had a letter in his possession from Governor Blount, informing him that the Tennessee detachment was a coordinate command. [3] Probably he did not know that the Tennessee commander was bringing with him, in spite of many pacific assertions, the pair of duelling pistols which did service in the affair with Dickinson. It was fortunate that these two men were not to be thrown into close association.

Jackson was greatly disappointed at his enforced idleness

[1]Jackson to Blount, January 4, 1812, Jackson Mss.
[2] Wilkinson to Jackson, January 22 and 25, February 22, and March 1 and 8, 1813. Jackson to Wilkinson February 21, March 15, 1813, Jackson Mss.
[3]Wilkinson to Jackson. February 27, 1813, Jackson Mss.

in Natchez. He placed his army in camp four miles from the place and awaited orders to move. After an exasperating month of inactivity he received on March 15 a still greater disappointment. It came in a brief letter from Armstrong, secretary of war, which ran as follows:

SIR:— The causes of embodying and marching to New Orleans the corps under your command having ceased to exist you will, on the receipt of this letter, consider it as dismissed from the public service, and take measures to have delivered over to Major-General Wilkinson all the articles of public property which may have been put into its possession. You will accept for yourself and the corps the thanks of the President of the United States.[1]

This order was preposterous, and Armstrong, who was only two days in office when it was written, could hardly have understood its full purport. It meant that the volunteers were to be turned adrift in the wilderness, to return to their homes as they could, and with small thanks for their patriotism. March 22, after there was time to hear from Natchez, the secretary explained that he wrote his dismissal in the belief that it would reach the troops before they went far on their journey, and he gave full instructions for paying the expenses of the return to Nashville. His intentions seem to have been good.[2]

But Jackson was hardly expected to see this. All his hopes appeared to be destroyed, and dark suggestions of plotting came into his mind. He restrained himself enough to write temperately a letter to the President in which he said that he considered as a mistake that part of the order which directed him to give up his tents and other equipment and announced that he would disregard it.[3] He pushed forward his arrangements to take the whole column back to Tennessee.

---

[1]Armstrong to Jackson, February 6, 1813, Jackson Mss.
[2]Armstrong to Jackson, March 22, and April 10, 1813, Jackson, Mss.
[3]Jackson to Madison, March 15, 1813, Jackson Mss.

But beneath the surface his anger was boiling. To Governor Blount he wrote as he felt. Armstrong's order, he said, was but a scheme to have the militia stranded far from home in the hope that Wilkinson's enlisting officers, who were already hovering around the camp, might draw them into the regular service,[1] To his officers he expressed himself with equal freedom and swore that not one of his men should be left at Natchez who wanted to go home. To the volunteers he sent a fiery proclamation denouncing the whole situation. It was a question, he said, if they had been treated justly by the government and by their own congressmen, but they might rely on it, not one of them, sick or well, should be left behind when the column marched.[2] These sentiments were cordially endorsed by the men: they were calculated to secure careful consideration from the state's representatives in Washington. They show that he knew the art of appealing to the people long before he was associated with the so-called "Kitchen Cabinet."

Having decided to return, Jackson lost no time to put his army in motion. He drew twenty days' rations from the commissary department at Natchez and urged Blount to forward other supplies to the Tennessee River and thus relieve him from the necessity of taking them from the inhabitants "vie et armis."[3] But the deputy-quartermaster, who was under Wilkinson's authority, did not feel authorized to pay the cost of transporting the sick, and it was necessary for Jackson to pledge his own credit to meet this expense.[4] He did it cheerfully, and the government as willingly relieved him of the responsibility when the matter came to its attention.[5] It was on this return march

---

[1]Jackson to Blount, March 15, 1813, Jackson Mss. He retained this notion even after ample explanation came from the secretary. Jackson to Governor Holmes, April 24, 1813, Jackson Mss.

[2]Jackson Mss., March, 1813.

[3]Jackson to Blount, March 15, 1813, Jackson Mss.

[4]Jackson to R. Andrews, July 12, 1813, Jackson Mss. See also W. B. Lewis to Coffee, April 9, 1813, Jackson Mss., by which it appears that some of Jackson's friends pledged money to aid in assuming the responsibility.

[5]Jackson to Governor Holmes of Mississippi Territory, April 24, 1813, Jackson Mss.

that the soldiers gave him the nickname, "Old Hickory," in admiration for his tenacity and endurance.

Soon after his arrival in Nashville he learned that the Natchez quartermaster refused to pay the wagoners who helped to carry the sick to the Tennessee River.[1] This caused further irritation, but a reference of the matter to Washington removed the difficulties.

Jackson's attitude in this affair was made to do good service in the political campaigns in which he was later concerned. His friends asserted that he assumed the responsibility for all the expenses of the homeward journey; and the imagination of Benton served to put it in such permanent form that it has secured a strong position in the published histories of the expedition. The truth, as shown in the correspondence, is that the general's assumption of responsibility extended no further than to hire thirteen wagons and twenty-six pack-horses to carry the sick, and that he became personally responsible for the forage which the horses consumed. Benton also gives an entertaining account of how he finally persuaded the war department to allow these accounts, but from his own letter to Jackson this part of the narrative assumes the following form:

It happened that Colonel Benton returned from Natchez with decided ambitions of a military nature. It also happened that he knew that the government expected to raise a new regiment of regular troops in Tennessee. He thought this an opportunity to gratify his ambition and went to Washington to apply for a colonel's commission. Jackson readily gave him letters of recommendation to the secretary of war[2] and made him his messenger in regard to the pay of the wagoners. June 15, Benton was able to report success in regard to the claims. The secretary, he said, first inquired if the claims were approved by the deputy-quartermaster-general at New Orleans and was

---

[1] Jackson to the Secretary of War, May 10, 1813, Jackson Mss.
[2] *Ibid.*

told that this officer had no authority in regard to them. It was decided to approve them in the accountant's office in Washington. Benton went away, but realizing how much delay this would occasion he wrote and urged that an agent be allowed to audit the claims in Tennessee. After some delay this request was granted in an order dated June 14, which left nothing to be desired by Jackson. Benton in his later account asserted that he had to threaten the administration with a loss of Tennessee votes in order to get this tardy justice, but there is really nothing in his report to show that the war department was not inclined to pay the claims or that the hesitation was anything more than a mere matter of detail as to the manner of settlement.

Benton's report in regard to his own affairs is interesting. But one regiment, he said, would be raised in Tennessee, and for that John Williams, of whom we shall hear more later, was to be colonel and he, Benton, lieutenant-colonel. He himself, he said, tried in vain to convince the secretary that two regiments ought to be formed in the state; this would, under existing regulations, mean a Tennessee brigade, with a brigadier-general and two colonels. The inference was plain, but he made it plainer still by adding that some congressmen had it in mind to propose Jackson for appointment the first time there should be a vacant brigadier-generalship.[1]

Before the end of the year the new regiment, the thirty-ninth, was organized, and Williams and Benton received their commissions. They saw service in the South, but in September the lieutenant-colonel became the enemy of Jackson through the Benton affair. From that beginning grew a bitter personal enmity and the new regiment saw no conspicuous service in the exciting times just ahead. Williams and Benton are almost the only Tennesseeans of prominence who went through the war without achieving distinction.

[1]Benton to Jackson, June 15, 1813; Jackson to R. Andrews, July 12, 1813, Jackson Mss.

CHAPTER VII

AFFAIRS AT FORT STROTHER

THE Natchez expedition was a success in all but actual fighting. It seasoned officers and privates by four months of campaigning and whetted their appetites for more serious service. When they volunteered it was for one year, and when they were dismissed in March they went home subject to another call for duty. They were hardly there before disquieting information came from the South. The Creek Indians were giving unmistakable signs of hostility. Jackson received his wound from Jesse Benton on September 4; and within two weeks he learned that his services were again needed in the field.

A century ago the region south of the Tennessee River was popularly known as "the Creek Country." By the early inhabitants of that region its settlement was considered essential to the welfare of the Tennesseeans; for the best water communication from the Holston settlements to the outside world was through its borders. Down the Tennessee the traveler may go by boat to the vicinity of Huntsville, Alabama, from which by a portage of fifty miles he may gain the upper Coosa, which unites with the Tallapoosa in the very heart of the old Creek territory to form the Alabama, which in turn becomes the Mobile when it receives the waters of the Tombigbee near the Florida border. It seemed to the transmontane settlers that nature designed this line of communication for their special use. The idea was not less attractive because the Creek lands were exceedingly fertile. In 1813, therefore, both interest and feeling prompted the Amer-

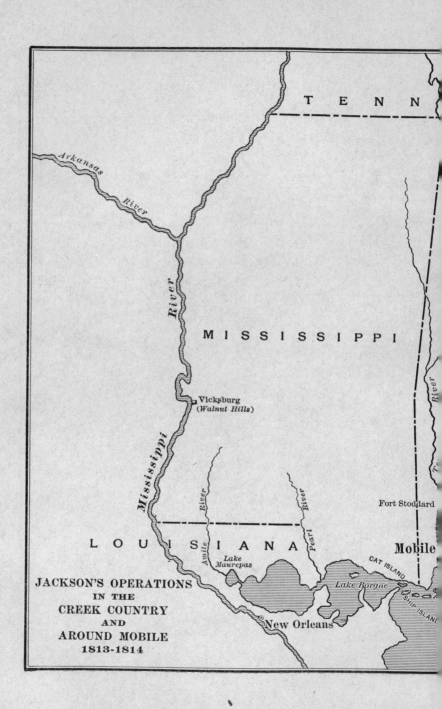

JACKSON'S OPERATIONS
IN THE
CREEK COUNTRY
AND
AROUND MOBILE
1813-1814

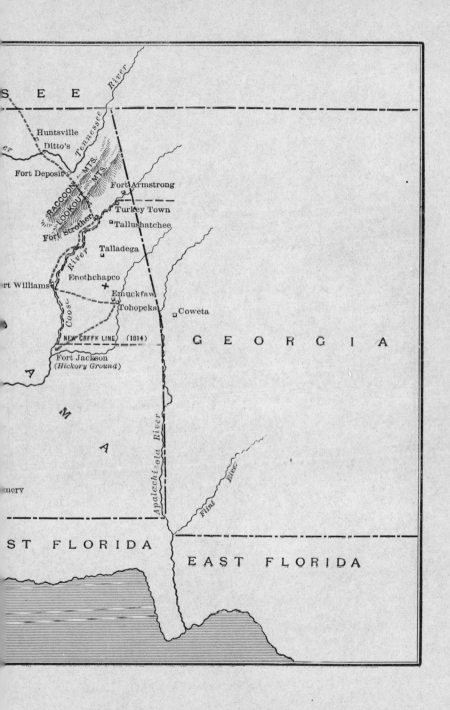

icans to suppress the ancient annoyance they received from the Indians and to spoil them of their inheritance.

The Creeks realized this situation. Their old ally was Spain with whom most Americans of the war party desired a conflict. Spain, however, would not fight, not even when Wilkinson in the spring of 1813 seized Mobile and held it as American territory under the ten-year-old claim which his government asserted to it. To her, in fact, war would have been sheer madness. In Europe her resources were exhausted to the last extremity by the long struggle against Napoleon. In South and Central America her colonies were on the point of revolution. War with America in support of the Creeks meant the loss of Florida, to which she could not send a regiment without great sacrifice. It was her policy to be neutral. But the British were at war, and the Indians turned to them. Agents came with the offer of an alliance, and it was accepted. Arms and ammunition were promised and later some were sent.

More notable was the influence of Tecumseh. This remarkable man appeared in October, 1811, at a Creek council held at the ancient town of Tuckaubatchee, on the upper Tallapoosa, and made one of his effective pleas for a union of all the red men of the West against the extension of the settlements. Standing like a statue in the midst of a silent group of warriors he held aloft his war club in one hand and slowly loosened finger after finger till at last it fell to the ground. This savage pantomine to express the results of disunion made a deep impression on the young braves. When Tecumseh was gone, hostilities did not immediately begin, but there sprang up in his wake a number of prophets who kept his ideas alive and who by magic and the promises of supernatural assistance fired the Creek heart to a great struggle of national self-preservation. Benjamin Hawkins, since 1797 Creek agent and hitherto much loved by the Indians, found that his influence with the younger warriors was gone, and the best he could do for his government was to build up a small party of more conservative chiefs who tried to restrain the others from war.

The information that hostilities with England were actually begun created great excitement in the Indian towns, and a party of warriors set out for the North where they took part in the attack on the Americans at the river Raisin, January 22, 1813. Returning from that engagement, the blood thirst still hot in them, they murdered two white families on the banks of the Ohio. For this outrage the Americans demanded reparation; and the old men, anxious to preserve peace, sent runners through the forests to kill the violators of the law. This was the Indian custom of executing persons adjudged to die. In this case the murderers were all slain, but the war party were only further excited and not awed into submission. Within a short while two thousand warriors from twenty-nine of the thirty-four towns of the Upper Creeks took up arms.

The center of the Creek country was the junction of the Coosa and Tallapoosa Rivers near which was the "Hickory Ground," a sacred meeting place of the tribes, thought to be so well protected by their gods that no white man could tread it and live. Near this, chiefly on the Tallapoosa, were the towns of the Upper Creeks, while farther south was the group of villages known as Lower Creeks. In all they embraced about seven thousand warriors, of whom the hostile party by midsummer, 1813, was about four thousand. Not more than a third of these, it was said, had guns; and ammunition was very scarce. All their supplies must be obtained at this time from Florida, where the Spanish officials refused to sell more than enough for hunting. To this item of weakness add the fact that there were always some friendly Creeks who actually helped the Americans against their brethren, and we may see that the savages were poorly prepared to contend with the soldiers whose vengeance they were rashly inviting.

The probability of a Creek war was understood in Washington and plans were made for opposing it. It was proposed to send three columns into the disaffected region; one from Georgia containing fifteen hundred militia, another from Tennessee of like strength and another — the 3d regiment of regulars — from the southward up the Alabama River. The whole to be under the supervision of Major-General Thomas Pinckney, commander of the district. The success of this plan would depend on exact and active coöperation between the three columns, and in a region as trying as the Creek country this was very difficult. It gave the Indians, if they were alert, the opportunity to attack their foes in detail; and it was likely to leave the severest fighting to one of the three attacking forces. Such, indeed, proved to be the result when the plan was put into execution: the heaviest fighting fell on Jackson with his Tennesseeans. The secretary's plan was submitted to the governor of Tennessee for his opinion on July 13, 1813.[1]

Before a move could be made the Indians began the war by a bloody stroke. The inhabitants of the more exposed section of the frontier were fleeing to block-houses for protection. A large number took refuge in a fortified stockade of Samuel Mims on Lake Tensaw, and the authorities sent Major Beasley with one hundred and seventy-five militia to protect them. In August the place, popularly called Fort Mims, held five hundred and fifty-three persons of all conditions. Beasley was singularly inefficient and in spite of warnings left the gates unguarded. On the thirtieth, when the signal was given for the noonday dinner, one thousand Creeks rushed from the coverts, gained the unfastened gates, and proceeded to destroy the inmates at their pleasure. Most of the Negroes were spared for slaves, twelve of

[1]Armstrong to Blount, July 13, 1813, Jackson Mss.

the whites cut their way to liberty, but the rest, two hundred and fifty in number, were slain. It was a crushing stroke, and from one end of the border to the other rose a cry for vengeance.

Nowhere did the tidings from Fort Mims arouse more horror than in West Tennessee, where the inhabitants daily expected an attack. In fact, it was only through the failure of the British to furnish the Creeks with expected supplies that such a calamity was avoided.[1] To meet this danger the community assumed the offensive without waiting for the authority of the government, and all eyes turned to Jackson. September 18, there was a meeting of leading citizens in Nashville to consider measures of defense. They decided that a strong force ought to be sent at once into the heart of the Creek territory to destroy their villages and force them to make peace. They asked the legislature to authorize such a move, and at their request the governor agreed to call out for immediate service the recently dismissed Natchez volunteers. The assembly was as complaisant as the governor, and a week later called also for three thousand five hundred detached militia for a three months' tour of duty. It was a hearty response to a public necessity and marks a high state of patriotism in Tennessee. If every state in the union had displayed the same kind of war spirit, the story of the national struggle would have been different.

A committee from the meeting on September 18, waited on Jackson to know if he would be able to take the field at the head of the volunteers. They found him in bed from the wound he received on the fourth of the month in the affair with Benton; but he expressed the greatest confidence in his ability to lead his division. He did, in fact, at once assume direction of the movement for defense, calling the volunteers to assemble at Fayetteville, Tennessee, on October 4, arranging for supplies of food and ammunition, and writing many letters on all kinds of similar sub-

---

[1]Governor Blount to Jackson, Oct. 18, 1813. Jackson Mss.

jects. In one of the letters he said: "The late fracture of my left arm will render me for a while less active than formerly. Still I march and before we return, if the general government will only hands off — we will give peace in Israel."[1] Jackson's peace was likely to be a grim one.

Before he could assemble his forces news came that Madison County, in Mississippi Territory, was threatened by the savages. This county embraced a large part of the northern region of the present states of Mississippi and Alabama, and Huntsville, in the latter state, was its most populous center. It was the natural approach to the theatre of his coming exploits. To relieve its danger Jackson sent Coffee forward with three hundred cavalry and mounted riflemen, and hastened the preparations of the main body. On October 4th, his wound was not healed enough for him to take up the march, nor were all the arrangements completed. On the seventh, however, he rode into camp weak and haggard and took personal direction of the army. Immediately came urgent calls from Coffee, who reported that he was about to be attacked. On the tenth, at nine in the morning, camp was broken and at eight in the evening the troops were near Huntsville, having marched thirty-two miles. The general intended to take them into town before stopping, but he learned that Coffee's perils were exaggerated and went into camp where he was. For a commander with a lame shoulder this was a good day's journey. On the next day he reached the Tennessee at Ditto's Landing, a few miles south of Huntsville, and crossing the river united his forces with Coffee's. Here he halted for a few days, seeking a favorable place for a fortified depot of supplies. On October 22d, he moved up the river from Ditto's in a southeasterly direction for twenty-four miles and laid out at the mouth of Thompson's Creek the fortification which he called Fort Deposit. It

---

[1] Jackson to Governor Holmes (Miss.), September 26, 1813, Jackson Mss.

was his base of supplies and looked frowningly upon the wilderness into whose fateful mysteries he longed to plunge.

The Tennessee forces were now organized in two bodies, following the two militia divisions, each containing about two thousand five hundred men. One of them was from the east and was commanded by Major-General John Cocke, regular commander of the second division of militia. The other was from the west and was commanded by Jackson. It included the United States volunteers to the number of two thousand and a supplementary body of militia numbering nearly a thousand. Both divisions were under the command of the governor, but otherwise acted separately. Cocke was ordered southward from Knoxville by way of Chattanooga into what is now northwestern Georgia and northeastern Alabama, with instructions to coöperate with the Georgia militia and with the regulars who were moving on the hostile Indians, and to protect the friendly Creek towns in this region.[1]

The orders to Jackson were to "act in conjunction with the forces relied on for the expedition or separately as your knowledge of the circumstances may teach the propriety of, first making the necessary arrangements for concert with Major-General Cocke and Colonel Meigs."[2] If the two divisions should unite, Jackson as senior officer would have the command. His letters show that he expected a junction, but nothing in the instructions contemplated it.

Jackson's plan of campaign provided for a base of supplies on the Tennessee at its southernmost part, a military road thence for fifty miles to the Ten Islands on the Coosa, where another fortified post would be established for supplies, and thence down the Alabama River system to Fort St. Stephens, always

---

[1]Blount to Cocke, September 25, 1813, Jackson Mss.
[2]Blount to Jackson, October 4, 1813, and November 17, 1813, Jackson Mss. Meigs was agent among the Cherokees.

destroying such armed bands as opposed him and devastating villages as he went. By this plan he would establish a permanent line of communication from East Tennessee to Mobile. It had the advantage, also, of being adjusted to the general plan which was suggested to Blount by the secretary of war, and which its author must have seen before he left Nashville. On the other hand, it was in itself a complete military movement and if made in force would succeed without reference to the success or failure of the coöperating columns. He did not rely greatly on aid from the Georgia militia or from the regulars by way of Mobile. He believed that by uniting with Cocke's division at the friendly village of Turkey Town on the upper Coosa he could make a quick dash southward, wreaking vengeance as he went, until he dictated peace before the end of the year on the Hickory Ground.[1]

This project would necessarily make heavy demands on the newly organized and imperfect commissary department of the army. Provisions were abundant in East Tennessee, and to carry them down the Tennessee River in ordinary times was not a great task. But to gather and convey them in the autumn, when the river was very low, and to convey them from Fort Deposit across the wilderness road, and down the Coosa in the wake of the impetuous general was not an easy task. It demanded a well organized, well equipped, and well experienced commissary; and such a department Jackson did not have.

The first intimation he had of trouble of this kind came at Ditto's Landing when he announced to the contractors that he would soon need rations on the Coosa. To his astonishment the reply was that such a thing was impossible. Jackson stormed, as was his custom, and ended by removing his contractors and employing others. These gave fair promises but did little more than the first. The contractor system of supplying provisions was bad in itself, and caused disappointment in the

---

[1] Jackson to Governor Early (Georgia), October 10, 1813, Jackson Mss.

army till it was abandoned.   Nor is Jackson to be entirely relieved from responsibility for the trouble.   He was, undoubtedly, more eager than cautious.   A calmer man would have hesitated to lead an active winter campaign into the Alabama mountains until assured of an abundance of provisions.

While these difficulties engaged his attention the road to the Coosa was being opened as rapidly as possible.   Within a week it was ready for use, and leading his army over its stumps and rude bridges he came, about November 1st, to the Coosa at the Ten Islands, where he erected another fortified base and called it Fort Strother.   If it was difficult to place supplies at Fort Deposit, it was far more difficult to place them at this new base.   The whole reliance was on contractors, who were expected to have rations deposited for 3,000 men forty days ahead.   This meant the accumulation by them of a large number of wagons and teams, an operation for which they showed little energy.   It was not till Jackson took this part of the work into his own hands, impressing wagons and horses in Madison County, that it was possible to bring up his supplies with any degree of regularity.

The army was now organized in three brigades.   The first was commanded by Brigadier-General William Hall and was composed of two regiments of volunteer infantry under Colonels Bradley and Pillow.   The second was commanded by Brigadier-General Isaac Roberts and was composed of two regiments of militiamen under Colonels Wynne and McCrary.   The third was commanded by Brigadier-General John Coffee and was composed of a regiment of volunteer cavalry under Colonel Alcorn and a regiment of mounted riflemen under Colonel Newton and Lieutenant-Colonel Allen.   The first brigade numbered 1,400, the second was probably something more than six hundred, and the third contained 1,000 men.[1]

---

[1] General Orders, October 10 and 30, 1813, Jackson Mss.

At Fort Strother Jackson came for the first time within striking distance of the foe. Thirteen miles to the eastward was the hostile village of Tallushatchee with nearly two hundred warriors, and Coffee was sent to destroy it. On the morning of November 3d, his men, 1,000 strong, were in line around the village, the inhabitants of which by shouts and other expressions of defiance raised such a commotion that he believed them equal in number to his own troops. By a feint he drew them out of their position, which was strong, surrounded them with all his forces, and steadily cut them to pieces. Not a warrior escaped, and in the confusion some of the women were slain with the men. The Indians did not ask for quarter and the whites did not offer it; for this was a war in which prisoners were rarely taken. Coffee reported that he slew 168 and a few more whose bodies were not found: eighty-four Indian women and children were taken captive. The loss of the whites was five killed and forty-one wounded. This first blow gave courage to the rest of the army at Fort Strother, and strengthened the confidence of the friendly Indians. In the enthusiasm of the moment it was forgotten that it was won with an immense disparity of numbers and equipment. Coffee reported that his opponents first fired with guns and then fought with bows and arrows.[1]

No sooner was the cavalry back at Fort Strother than news came which put the whole army into motion. Thirty miles to the south was the friendly village of Talladega with a population of 154 persons. It was now ascertained that for some days it had been surrounded by more than a thousand hostiles, whose investment was so close that it was extremely difficult to get messengers through to Jackson. But after several days of siege a chieftain disguised in the skin of a hog escaped the vigilance of the besiegers and reached Fort Strother on the seventh.

---

[1]Coffee's report is in Parton, *Jackson*, I., 436. Jackson's report says one warrior escaped.

He reported the extremity of the Talladegas and declared that help to be effective must be speedy.

Before dawn of the following day Jackson was on the march with 1,200 infantry and 800 cavalry. He left his wounded at the fort with a small guard; and for their better protection he urged Brigadier-General White, who, leading Cocke's advance, had approached to the neighborhood, to protect the fort. It was like Jackson to take all his available force on this expedition, although in doing so he had double the number of the enemy. He was never a man to risk a battle without having all the odds possible on his own side.

At sunrise on the ninth he was before Talladega, and the Indians came out to give him battle. He arranged his troops in a crescent with the points thrown forward. On the flanks he placed his cavalry, with orders to fall on the rear of the enemy as soon as the engagement became general. A mounted reserve was behind the main line. In opening the battle he employed the feint which Coffee used so effectively at Tallushatchee. He sent forward some companies who fired four or five rounds and fell back to the main line while the enemy eagerly rushed forward. Immediately the circle of Americans was formed as planned by their leader. The Creeks, hotly engaged on their front, were soon discouraged and turned to fly. To their confusion they found themselves surrounded. Turning hither and thither for an avenue of safety they encountered a circle of relentless marksmen whose rifles claimed victims at every moment. They were in a fair way to be exterminated when an accident offered a door of escape to a large part of them. Early in the battle a portion of the infantry retreated from the front of the enemy. It was now necessary to dismount the reserves and throw them into the breach, and that body was no longer available for an emergency. When, therefore, the hunted fugitives found a slight gap between the cavalry and the infantry and began to pour through it, there was no force which could be quickly sent to check them. Thus it happened that nearly seven hundred slipped out of Jackson's fingers to oppose him another day. Could he have made an end of them here the battle of Tohopeka might have been avoided. As it was, more than three hundred Indians were slain, while the loss of the Tennesseeans was only fifteen killed and eighty-five wounded.[1]

At Talladega Jackson was only eighty miles from the Hickory Ground, where he hoped to end the war. The engagements of the third and ninth left the foe badly shattered, and less than another month of active campaigning must have completed their discomfiture. Brilliant as that prospect was, it was necessary to relinquish it and return to Fort Strother. The arrival of provisions was almost at a standstill, and it was becoming a question, not of further advance, but of holding the position on the Coosa. Furthermore, news came that White's brigade was recalled by Cocke and the fort with its wounded was left undefended. Jackson's retrograde movement at this particular time had a bad effect on both friendly and hostile Indians. Suffering from his wound, ill from other disease, with the whole burden of the expedition on his shoulders, he was very angry with the persons responsible for his embarrassments. He railed at his quartermasters, began a long quarrel with Cocke, and wrote scores of appeals for aid from every promising quarter. The rest of the year was one of military inactivity, beset by starvation and mutiny. Some of his best friends thought he ought to recognize the inevitable and fall back to the frontier till supplies could be accumulated; but he would not hear them. He said he would maintain his advance if he had to live on acorns.[2]

During this period of distress two mutinies occurred in his

---

[1] Jackson's report is in Parton, *Jackson*, I., 442; Coffee's is in *Ibid* I, 443.
[2] Jackson to Lewis, October 24, 1813, Jackson Mss. The story that Jackson was once seen dining on acorns is probably apocryphal.

camp, the first from the lack of supplies and the second from a conflict of opinion in interpreting the laws under which volunteers and militia were serving. In each case agitators were present who fanned the flame. In the accounts of these two mutinies, historians have usually depended upon Reid and Eaton,[1] all of whose information was on Jackson's side. He himself has preserved enough of the petitions and letters of the discontented ones to show that the affair had another phase.

The first protest came from the United States volunteers. On the return from Talladega they petitioned to be led back to the frontier until supplies could be collected. The request was not granted, and November 14th, their field officers and captains held a meeting at which they renewed the request and gave the following reasons: (1) Because supplies were wanting. Not more than ten rations had been issued since the army left Fort Deposit more than two weeks earlier, and "both officers and soldiers have been compelled to subsist for five days on less than two rations." (2) The frontier was now safe and the contractors continued to deceive the soldiers in regard to supplies. (3) The order for their assembling was issued only five days before they left their homes, giving them no time to provide winter clothing, so that they now needed clothes and shoes badly. This address was loyal and respectful and had the air of truthfulness. It shows that the army was in a wretched condition; and any man less inflexible than Jackson would have made some concession to its demands.[2]

The petition of the volunteer officers was reinforced by similar requests from other bodies of troops, but to all Jackson was unyielding. Then the militia mutinied and broke ranks to go

---

[1]Reid and Eaton, *Jackson*, 62.

[2]The address in manuscript is among the Jackson Mss. it is not dated, but the address of the officers of the second regiment on November 15, shows that the omitted date should be the fourteenth. See also the second regiment to Jackson, November 13, and Jackson to Blount, November 14, 1813, Jackson Mss.

home. He threw the volunteers across their path, and the militia, who were probably not deeply in the affair, returned to their places. Next the volunteers themselves announced that they would stay no longer, and were marching away when they were confronted by the now loyal militia and forced back to duty. The quickness with which each yielded indicates that neither was actuated by bad motives and that they feared to commit an action which would stamp them as disloyal citizens throughout Tennessee.

At last Jackson learned that provisions had arrived in sufficient quantities at Fort Deposit. Believing they would reach him immediately he issued a general order announcing the good news and saying that if they did not arrive in two days he would consent to fall back. Two days passed and no provisions came. Then, deeply disappointed and distressed, he kept his promise. He gave the order to march but declared that he would continue to hold Fort Strother if only two men would stay with him. At this a call for a volunteer garrison was circulated, and 109 men offered to remain, but the rest of the army marched joyfully toward the Tennessee.

Before they proceeded more than twelve miles they met a drove of cattle on the way to Fort Strother. It was the supply which was expected on the previous day. Orders were given to kill and feast. After a full meal the command was given to return to the fort. It was received with murmurings, and when the men were ordered to march, one company, in spite of its officers, started homeward. Jackson was now enraged. With a few followers from his staff he threw himself in front of the mutineers and by threatening to fire drove them back to the main body, which with much scowling and muttering refused to resume the march. Going alone among the men he found them on the point of marching homeward in a mass. It was a moment of crisis, and if authority were not now enforced, the whole campaign would be lost. The towering strength of his will enabled him to make it a turning point in his military career. His left arm was still disabled, but he seized a musket in his right hand and using the neck of his horse for a rest stood defiantly before the whole body of troops, his eyes flashing and his shrill voice shouting with many oaths that he would kill the first man who stepped forward. For a few moments he stood alone; then he was joined by Reid and Coffee, each with a musket; and then some loyal companies formed across the road in their rear. Seeing this the mutineers gradually relinquished their defiance and sullenly moved away on the road to Fort Strother. From this time provisions were ample and the first phase of the mutiny was over.

But the spirit of discontent was not destroyed and it appeared in another form. The United States volunteers were mustered into service on December 10, 1812, under a law of congress (February 6, 1812), which provided that they should be "bound to continue in service for the term of twelve months after they should have arrived at the place of rendezvous, unless sooner discharged."[1] It also provided that each infantryman when discharged should receive as a gift the musket with which he had fought and each cavalryman his sword and pistols. When they were dismissed in the following spring the volunteers were anxious for these gifts and Jackson, in order that they might be allowed to keep them, issued formal discharges; but they agreed that they would hold themselves bound to come into the field again when summoned. It is a high tribute to the personal qualities of the men that their general would trust them under such circumstances and that in October, 1813, they did almost to a man redeem their promises.[2] These discharges

---

[1] *United States Statues at Large.*, II, 676.

[2] Jackson to Colonel William Martin, December 4, 1813, Jackson Mss. Jackson said that the secretary of war declared that he, Jackson, had no authority to discharge the troops, but this hardly agreed with Armstrong's orders of February 6 and March 22, 1813.

played an important part in the discussion now about to begin.

As December 10th approached, the discontented volunteers began to speak of it as the day on which their term of service expired. Jackson, alarmed at the prospect of losing four-fifths of his army, replied that the twelve months they were required to serve did not include the time they were at home the preceding summer. The volunteers thought the law declared for a twelve months' tour of duty and that an interruption during which they were at the call of the government was not to be counted against them. They further asserted that they would go home on the 10th, whether Jackson gave his permission or not, and that inasmuch as they already had their discharges such an action could not be held illegal. It was a strong point in their favor, and had Jackson been as logically minded as patriotic he would have thought himself stopped from denying the technical value of his own discharge. But he was not logical, and he replied, in effect, that it was not really a discharge but a dismissal which he gave them the preceding spring, and only the President could order a discharge. He seems to have had no compunction in thus admitting that in his former action he practised a subterfuge on the government in order to enable his men to get their arms without legal warrant. It was natural that the volunteers should not accept Jackson's repudiation of his discharges, and each side remained unconvinced.

After discussing the matter for some time, Jackson referred the whole affair to Governor Blount and the secretary of war, promising to abide by their decision. Such an arrangement, if accepted by the soldiers, would give him at least two months of additional service, and in the meantime he hoped by the strenuous efforts he was making to raise additional volunteers to repair the loss.[1] Blount, as might have been expected,

---

[1] Jackson to Colonel William Martin, December 4, 1813, Jackson Mss.

refused to settle a dispute in which he was sure to displease either the commander or the men, and it was referred to Washington.[1] All this did nothing to quell the spirit of mutiny in the camp of the volunteers.

On December 9th, the affair came to a crisis. The first brigade of the volunteers announced they would march in the night, and prepared to carry out the threat. Jackson acted with promptness. He ordered the brigade to parade on the west side of the fort, placed his two pieces of artillery in position to rake them, and on an adjacent eminence drew up the militia, who were not concerned in this mutiny. He then made a speech to the brigade: He had argued with them, he said, until he was tired; if they were going to desert let them do it now; otherwise let them return to camp quietly and cease to complain: would they obey or not? He waited for an answer. They remained a moment in silence and he ordered the gunners to light their matches. Then he spoke again telling them to go to their places or abide by the results. It is hardly to be doubted that he was prepared to fire if they remained unimpressed; but at this moment there was a hurried conference among the officers, not all of whom were disaffected. In a few minutes they approached the general to say that the men would resume their places in the camp.

The volunteers, however, were not convinced, They declared they would not go home until honorably discharged, but they demanded a release so persistently that even the governor and other friends of the general advised him to send them home,[2] since they were useless as soldiers. This advice at length prevailed, and December 14th, the first brigade, including all the infantry among the United States volunteers, was ordered

---

[1]Blount to Jackson, November 24, December 7, 15, and 26, 1813; Blount to secretary of war, December 10, 1813; Jackson to Blount, December 3, 12, and 26, 1813, all in Jackson Mss.
[2]William Carroll to Jackson, November 22, 1813, Jackson Mss.

under its brigadier-general to march to Nashville and be disbanded pending the decision of the President.[1]

---

[1]March 19, 1814, in the Carthage *Gazette* Brigadier-General Hall and several of his higher officers published a defence of the first brigade, written in a commendable spirit.

An interesting pasquinade appears among the Jackson Mss. It describes the departure of the volunteers and runs as follows:

FIRST BULLETIN OF THE GRAND ARMY OF HOME BOUND PAT-RY-OTS COMMANDED BY PORTER BOTTLE, BUILT, COL. KONSHER & COL. CONSCIENCIOUS, BY MAJORS OUT FLANK-US & UP-TO-THE-10-DECR.

This veteran corps paraded on the night of the 9th Inst., by command and were reviewed in a manner no ways pleasing to them; they were brought to a sense of their duty by the force of eloquence; and returned to their quarters very quietly which presaged future amendment. On the morning of the 10th Lieutenant Sheephead made his appearance (a little after reveille) to complain that his superiors had 'made merry' and 'wondered that men under such circumstances would sing and rejoice at detaining an army 'against their wills.' Colonel Conciencious commenced scribbling and wished to convince others of what he believed or affected to believe, i. e., 'that *soldiers* ought not to be detained in service when they thought their time out, Major Out-Flank-Us 'was of opinion the muster rolls ought to govern, they were dated muster in on the 10th Decr., 1812, and muster out 10th Decr., 1813 and was of opinion that the muster rolls superseded the laws, which says they shall serve 12 mos in a year.' Colonel Konshers opinion 'as how I think, the mens time is up and by God dey most have some meet wen wee meat de waggons you most think wee is beasts and can liv on gras, but by G—d wee is men an hav som feelings.'

This renowned Colonel was concious himself and *brave men* could not like Nebuchadnezzer in days of yore live on grass.

Major Up-the 10th-Decr 'had told his men their time would expire on the 10th-Decr and by making this and such arrangements he had prevailed on his men to turn out and felt himself bound to see them justice done.' Captain Sniveling (this veteran appears as if he had been in the revolution, for he carries Breadsmount upon his back) 'couldn't do anything with his men they can speak for themselves.'

A Bulletin 14th December, 1813

This day the whole corps of *home-bound* Pat-ry-ots obtained a special permit to return to de settlements they marched off amidst the hootings of the militia. Our avocations and inclinations not permitting us to accompany them, wee know not how they will proceed nor can we give a detailed account of all the *marvellous actions and hairbreadth escapes* they may have and make on their march to 'de settlements.' We hear they march in as good order as could be expected and that part who were in command on the morning of the 10th settled some old grudges in the *gentlemanly stile of pugilists, vulgarly called fisty cuffs.* We wish them a safe march to 'de settlements.' We wish the Ladies of that part of Nashville, by the *envious called Scuffle town* to greet their arrival with loud huzzas of long live the Pat-ry-ots and

'Sound the trumpets, beat the drums,
Lo! the conquering heroes come!'

An as Colonel *Konsher* is a man of *modesty* and *extreme gentleness of manners* we would wish the above named *Ladies* to sing or bawl

'He that wants but impudence
To all things has a fair pretence
And place among his wants but shame
To all the world may lay his claim.'

We have been faithful recorders, we nothing have extenuated or ought set down in malice.
Kyelijah Town
Dec. 15, 1813.   Auto-aboy
                                                                      Coosurvatee.

From this document it appears that there was some kind of meeting on the morning of the tenth, a fact which one does not get from Reid's account (Reid and Eaton, *Jackson*, 83–92). It also seems to indicate that when the troops dispersed on the night of the ninth it was because they meant to consider their cause further, and not because they were willing to submit to authority.

At Washington the affair seemed less serious than at Fort Strother, and the secretary of war readily ordered the volunteers to be honorably discharged.[1]

The departure of the first brigade left only the second brigade at Fort Strother. It was composed of militia infantry, while the first was composed of volunteer infantry. The third brigade, commanded by Coffee, was composed of volunteer cavalry and mounted riflemen, and November 14th, it was ordered to Madison County to refresh its jaded horses, and soon afterward in compliance with the request of the men it was allowed to go to Tennessee to secure winter clothing and other necessaries, first giving written pledges through its officers that the men would return when called. Jackson ordered them to return on December 8th, and at that time they were at Huntsville. But they were as much discontented as the volunteer infantry and petitioned Jackson for a discharge. When nine days later the first brigade arrived in Huntsville on their way home the cavalry and mounted riflemen became as deeply anxious as they to disband. Some of them seem to have broken away then; but on the twenty-sixth and twenty-seventh the whole brigade crossed the Tennessee and marched away, save for a few faithful officers and men who were willing to remain. Coffee was just recovering from severe illness, but he mounted his horse and tried to stop their going. They paid little attention to him, and seeing that all their usefulness as soldiers was past he concluded it was as well to let them go.[2] On the twenty-ninth he reported that he had not enough men left to make a camp.[3]

[1]Secretary of war to Blount, January 3, 1814, Jackson Mss.

[2]Coffee to Jackson, December 22, 1813, Jackson Mss.

[3]Coffee's letters to Jackson are not very clear in regard to the details of the defection and departure of his men. They show much discontent before the arrival of the returning infantry. In his letter to Jackson of December 17, he seems to say that more than 500 of his men have gone: December 20, he says he has 850 men, which was his full strength (see Coffee to Jackson, December 10, 1813): December 28, he tells how the whole brigade crossed the river and went off on December 26 and 27: and finally on December 29, he read to

Jackson now had only the second brigade of his first army, composed of militia enlisted under resolution of the Tennessee legislature in the preceding September. They were commanded by Brigadier-General Roberts and numbered 1,000. They constituted Jackson's sole remaining force, except an East Tennessee regiment which was also disaffected. Under the state law a tour of duty was three months, and they volunteered to serve for that time. But after they were in the state's service they were received into the army of the United States under an act of congress which provided that the tour of duty under such conditions should be six months.[1] It is possible that the militia understood little of this change, although Jackson was careful to read to them the law under which they were received. The departure of the volunteers made them think of going home also. They began to assert that their term would be out on January 4, 1814, three months from their enlistment, and to threaten to go if they were restrained. The general thus found he was likely to be left sixty miles beyond the frontier with only a handful of troops to protect himself against a winter attack. The situation was all the more irritating because he had just completed other arrangements for an advance which promised to end the war.

To their request for a discharge he returned a prompt refusal but at last referred the matter to the governor. Blount was probably getting tired of these disputes; he may have felt that Jackson ought not to throw the responsibility on him; and it is possible also that he had some thought of preserving his popularity. At any rate on December 7th, he gave his

his troops Jackson's letter giving consent to their return, whereupon they left him almost to a man. The only plausible way of reconciling these statements is to suppose that the deserting troops did not really go home, but remained for some days in Huntsville, although they repudiated the authority of their commander. All the letters referred to here are from Coffee to Jackson and may be found in the Jackson Mss. under the dates cited.

[1] *United States Statutes at Large*, II., 705.

opinion in favor of a three-months term, but suggested that the matter be referred to the secretary of war. Jackson argued, the militia grumbled, and affairs grew steadily worse. Blount had more discretion, if less military ardor, than the general, and soon saw the uselessness of keeping the discontented militia at Fort Strother. December 22d, he advised Jackson to evacuate the place, fall back to the Tennessee River, and await reinforcements. Four days later he changed his position somewhat and suggested that the militia be sent home pending the decision of the secretary of war; and he added that this opinion ought to be submitted to the men. Jackson was disgusted, but he told the troops what the governor said and left them to decide whether they would leave him alone or stay and finish the campaign. It was the opportunity for which they waited, and they started on the 31st, pleased to leave a place thoroughly hateful to them.[1] They left him raging impotently in what was well-nigh an abandoned fort. He sent his imprecations after them, strongly wishing, as he said, that each one had "a smok-tail in his teeth, with a petticoat as a coat of mail to hand down to posterity."[2] One regiment only remained with him and their term was to expire on January 14th. As this date was so near at hand he foresaw that he could do little with them unless he could persuade them to stay longer than their time. He asked them if they would consent to do as much, and when they refused he sent them off to Tennessee with orders to their officers to recruit new forces for six months' service.

---

[1] Jackson's attitude at this time, is revealed in several letters to Blount, December 12 and 26, 1813; Jackson to Coffee, December 13, 25, 29, and 31 (most likely to Coffee); Blount to Jackson, December 7, 22, 26 1813 and March 13 and 20, 1814; Blount to secretary of war, December 10, 1813, and January 4, 1814. All in Jackson Mss.

[2] Jackson to Coffee, December 31, 1813, Jackson Mss.

CHAPTER VIII

THE CREEKS SUBDUED

WHETHER we think Jackson prudent or imprudent in rushing unprepared into the Creek campaign, or reasonable or unreasonable in holding out against the demands of his troops, we must admire the heroic spirit with which he met the crisis he now faced. He refused to fall back to the frontier, although for one short interval he had no more than one hundred men.

His first care was to bring back the courage of Governor Blount. Privately he described Blount's arguments as "damd. milk and water observations, which is well calculated to arouse mutiny in the minds of the men, keep their good opinion of himself and throw responsibility on me." To the governor, himself, he sent what he described as "a gulger that will make him look and see his own situation."[1] This "gulger" was a long and urgent letter of which the following is a part:

Had your wish that I should discharge a part of my force and retire with the residue into the settlements assumed the form of a positive order, it might have furnished me some apology for pursuing such a course; but by no means a full justification. As you could have no power to give such an order, I could not be inculpable in obeying it. But a bare recommendation, founded, as I am satisfied it must be, on the artful suggestions of those fire-side patriots who seek in a failure of the expedition an excuse for their own supineness, and upon the misrepresentations of the discontented from the army, who wish it to be believed that the difficulties which overcame their patriotism are wholly insurmountable, would afford me but a feeble shield

---

[1] Jackson to Coffee, December 29, 1813, Jackson Mss.

against the reproaches of my country or my conscience. Believe me, my respected friend, the remarks I make proceed from the purest personal regard. If you would preserve your reputation, or that of the state over which you preside, you must take a straightforward determined course; regardless of the applause or censure of the populace, and of the forebodings of that dastardly and designing crew, who, at a time like this, may be expected to clamour continually in your ears . . .

You say that an order to bring the necessary quota of men into the field has been given, and that of course, your power ceases; and although you are made sensible that the order has been wholly neglected, you can take no measure of the omission. Widely different, indeed, is my opinion. I consider it your imperious duty when the men called for by your authority, founded upon that of the government, are known not to be in the field to see that they be brought there; and to take immediate measures with the officer who, charged with the execution of your order, omits or neglects to do it. As the executive of the state, it is your duty to see that the full quota of troops be kept in the field, for the time they have been required. You are responsible to the government; your officers to you. Of what avail it to give an order if it never be executed and may be disobeyed with impunity? Is it by empty mandates that we can hope to conquer our enemies, and save our defenceless frontiers from butchery and devastation? Believe me, my valued friend, there are times when it is highly criminal to shrink from responsibility, or scruple about the exercise of our power.[1]

These sentiments were characteristic of Jackson. They contain the patriotism, energy, readiness to take the initiative, esteem of the national authority above that of the state, and the willingness to lecture his official superior which continually reappear in his career. We find also the disposition to beat a public servant with the club of popular disapproval, which

---

[1]Reid and Eaton, *Jackson*, 110. This letter is given here without date, but it seems undoubtedly to have been the one which Jackson called a "gulger."

in the Natchez proclamation was held over the Tennessee congressmen,[1] and which in later times was to be used against politicians in all parts of the union. To use such a club is an old trick, but it is usually employed with finesse: Jackson's method was fierce, open, and relentless chastisement.

Governor Blount was too sensible to sulk because Jackson railed and tried earnestly to raise a new army. Many of the officers of the disbanded troops were warmly attached to Jackson and went home to raise new companies. From Tennessee the response was encouraging. Best of all, General Pinckney placed the newly raised thirty-ninth regiment, John Williams, colonel, and Thomas H. Benton, lieutenant-colonel, at Jackson's disposal. Thus it happened that by the 14th of March Fort Strother contained 5,000 troops, more than were needed for the work before them, and more than it was possible to support in the Creek country.

Physical suffering, as well as anxiety, marked this period of waiting. Privations, exhaustion, irritation, and the drain of a slowly healing wound produced serious effects on a system which was habitually on the verge of collapse. But Jackson's extraordinary will sustained him, and he not only gave the impulse but supervised most of the details of reorganization. His correspondence was heavy. To Blount, Pinckney, and many others he wrote frequently. The condition of the fort and the roads, the activity of the contractors, the progress of enlistment, all passed under his eye. He was said to be the last to retire and the first to rise in the camp. "We have not slept three hours in four nights," he said. "Reid and myself are worn out."[2]

At such a time his strong nature justified itself. We may forgive many faults of passion, when we remember that they

---

[1] See above, page 85.
[2] Jackson to Coffee, December 31, 1813, Jackson Mss.

were correlative functions of an iron will which on occasion could give direction to the history of his country. They now carried him through what was probably the supreme crisis in his career. There were other times when failure would have forestalled all that came after, but no other period of doubt was so long or so forlorn in appearance, and into which it was necessary to put so much energy and personal sacrifice in order to overcome it.

In the campaign about to begin he was left largely to his own resources. It was he who would not give up Fort Strother, he who put to work the means of gathering reinforcements, and he who gave purpose to troops and contractors. The direction of the movements was also chiefly his, for Pinckney in the Carolinas and Georgia recognized his ability and gave him wide discretion. Nor was he benefited by either of the other expeditions which in the preceding summer had been ordered to move against the Creeks.[1]

While he contended with difficulties at Fort Strother, General Floyd with a body of Georgia militia was marching on the villages on the lower Tallapoosa. At Autosee, sixty miles west of Coweta, he fought on November 29th, a fierce battle in which the Indians were driven from the field with a loss of two hundred warriors, but he himself was wounded and withdrew his force to the settlements.

Throughout January and February Floyd made ineffectual efforts to resume his advance. He had a good road to the Upper Creek towns and Pinckney expected him to carry supplies to Jackson, but one thing after another interfered with his movement and Pinckney finally warned Jackson to expect no assistance from Floyd.[2] At the same time the expedition up

---

[1] See above, page 96.

[2] Pinckney to Jackson, December 12, 1813, February 5 and 20, 1814, Jackson Mss. Also see Floyd to Pinckney, December 4, 1813, in Niles, *Register*, V., 283.

the Alabama, entrusted to General Claiborne, proved a failure.[1] It was evident that the only hope for pacifying the Creeks was Jackson's column: it was also evident that success under the circumstances would make a deep impression on the country.

Soon after New Year's, 1814, new troops began to arrive on the Coosa. By the middle of the month they were ready for a blow. Eighty miles south of the fort was the fortified encampment of Tohopeka where hostile Indians were assembling from many villages. With 900 mounted riflemen, 200 friendly Indians, and one of his six-pounders he marched against it on the seventeenth. Five days later, just before dawn, as he lay encamped on Emuckfau Creek three miles from the fortification, the enemy tried to surprise him. But he was ready for the attack and drove them off in a fierce countercharge. Later in the day it was renewed and again beaten off. Thereupon the savages retired into their encampment which he did not feel strong enough to storm. They lost 45 killed and wounded, while three of the whites were killed and several wounded. Jackson set out at once for Fort Strother followed closely by the foe. On the twenty-fourth, as he was crossing Enotachapco Creek, they fell on his rear so fiercely that for a moment the situation was critical. But Colonel Carroll rallied 25 men and with the aid of the six-pounder held off the enemy till the crossing was completed. This incident ended the pursuit, and on the twenty-ninth the detachment arrived at the fort, having lost in the two engagements 24 killed and 71 wounded, while the Creeks lost considerably more than two hundred.[2]

This was the only stroke Jackson gave the Creeks without routing them completely. It was undertaken with a small and dispirited force against an enemy strongly posted. If the savages had remained in their fortifications and awaited

[1] Adams, *History of the United States*, VII., 243.
[2] Reid and Eaton, *Jackson*, 132-147.

battle, he must have fought at disadvantage or returned without an attack, either of which would have been unfortunate. As it happened, he could report that he drove back two assaults and inflicted more damage than he sustained. "Unless I am greatly mistaken," he said, "it [the expedition] will be found to have hastened the termination of the Creek war more effectually than any measure I could have taken with the troops under my command."[1] Its best results were to give the new troops a taste of war, to restore confidence in Tennessee, and to dash the rising confidence of the enemy. Pinckney gave it his endorsement: referring to Jackson in a letter to the secretary of war he said, "If government think it advisable to elevate to the rank of general other persons than those now in the army, I have heard of none whose military operations so well entitle him to that distinction."[2]

During the Creek war the Indians showed unusual knowledge of civilized warfare. The strength of their encampment near Emuckfau turned Jackson aside. They had some able leaders of mixed blood and understood the advantages of military subordination. After the affair at Enotachapco they gave up a policy of aggression and gathered their strength to meet an attack in the midst of their villages. They had selected the strongest available point on the Tallapoosa, famous in history as Tohopeka, or the Horse-Shoe, and believed it impregnable. While they awaited attack Jackson had leisure to complete the organization of his army.

It was February 6th, when Colonel Williams arrived with the 39th regiment of regulars, six hundred strong. Their coming gave comfort to Jackson who was beginning to discover signs of mutiny in the raw troops. The regulars gave a nucleus of permanent authority independent of the popular agitation

[1]Parton, *Jackson*, I., 495.
[2]Parton, *Jackson*, I., 498.

in the minds of the militia. The commander consequently
stiffened his attitude and announced that he would not pardon
the next man convicted of mutiny. He was determined to
make an example of disobedience. John Woods, a youth,
who was perhaps misled by others, was to fall into the breach
thus opened. He was charged with disobedience and with
threatening to shoot when ordered under arrest. He was only
eighteen and the officer whom he defied was undoubtedly inconsiderate, but the court found him guilty and sentenced him
to death. The case would ordinarily demand commutation
into some milder punishment, but Jackson stood to his purpose
and the boy was executed on March 14th. Long afterward
those who opposed the political ambitions of General Jackson
made the incident support their general charge that he was cruel
and irresponsible. In their hands it was grossly exaggerated
and aroused violent controversy.[1] But whatever we may say
of the wisdom of the execution, its effect on discipline was salutary.

The day Woods met his fate the second advance of the army
began. Three thousand of the newly collected forces were led
southward along the banks of the Coosa. Colonel Williams
and the regulars were ordered to guard the supplies which in
flat boats were sent down the stream. Thirty miles southward
a new fort was begun which Jackson, with no premonition of
a later quarrel, called Fort Williams. It was within easy distance of the Tallapoosa villages and marked the point at which
the Coosa was to be abandoned for overland journeying. For
a moment there was hesitation in the mind of the general on
account of the difficulty of bringing up supplies. "All I want,"
said he, "is supplies for my army. Had I a sufficiency for four
weeks now at this place my mind would be at ease, and the war,
I think, pretty near its termination."[2] But cheering news came

---

[1] Parton, *Jackson*, I., 504, gives the essential facts of this incident.
[2] Jackson to Hickman, March 21, 1814, Jackson Mss.

from Pinckney: 1,500 men with ample provisions were about to move from Fort Stoddart for the Hickory Grounds and these would make the future secure. The long sought opportunity was at hand and Jackson hesitated no longer. Leaving his river base he marched through the forest for that point on the Talla-poosa, sixty miles away, in which the enemy during two months had been preparing for their last stand.[1]

Early in the morning of March 27th, he was before it. In a horse-shoe-like bend of the river lay a thousand warriors and about three hundred women and children, the flower of the hostile Creeks. Across the narrow part of the peninsula within the bend was a zigzag wall of logs from five to eight feet high, 450 yards long, and pierced by a double row of port-holes. The angles of the zigzag enabled the defenders to cover the ground in front of it with a cross fire. The area enclosed was 100 acres. In the part nearest the wall trees were felled so that their inter-laced branches made excellent covert for sharp-shooters. Along the banks were the huts of the inhabitants, with canoes drawn up on the edge of the water. To the unskilled savage this doubt-less seemed an impregnable position; but the trained soldier would have understood that it afforded poor egress, should it have to be abandoned in the face of an enemy.

Jackson's plan of attack was quickly formed. He proposed to surround the foe and make the destruction as complete as possible. He placed his infantry before the unpleasant looking wall to carry it at the right moment. He planted his two small cannon on a hill which at a distance of eighty yards commanded the whole zigzag defense. He ordered Coffee with the cavalry and mounted men and the friendly Indians to cross the river and hold the opposite bank so as to prevent escape in that direction. At 10.30 o'clock, when Coffee was hardly in position, Jackson ordered the artillery to batter down the enemy's fortifi-

---

[1] Pinckney to Jackson, March 8 and 23, 1814, Jackson Mss.

cations. For two hours the six-pounder tried ineffectually to do this, while the infantry kept up a galling fire whenever an Indian showed himself.

While this happened Coffee's friendly Indians made a diversion which soon brought the battle to a close fight. Seeing the canoes of the hostiles they swam across the river, seized them, and rushed among the huts burning them and scattering the women in confusion. The infantry observing the smoke of these fires urged that they be allowed to charge the wall. Permission was given, and the 39th regiment with the East Tennessee militia under Doherty were soon within the enclosure fighting hand to hand with the enemy in the mass of fallen timber and underbrush. It was an unequal contest for the Creeks, but they asked no quarter. They retreated to whatever protection the place afforded and fired at every opportunity. When a flag of truce was sent to a group of them thus placed, it was received with a shower of bullets. By three o'clock the battle was over. No Indians remained in the enclosure except a few who were concealed in clefts in the rocks some of whom by good fortune escaped in the night. Eight hundred were killed and 300, all but four of whom were women, were captured. The reports mention no wounded Indians. Jackson thought that not more than twenty escaped. The Americans lost 45 killed and 145 wounded. Among the former was Major Montgomery, of the Thirty-Ninth; among the latter was Jackson himself whose injury was slight, and Samuel Houston, then hardly more than a boy, whose wounds were at first thought fatal. Three of the Creek prophets, whose harangues did much to bring on the war, were killed. One of them was struck in the mouth by a grape-shot, "as if," said Jackson, "Heaven designed to chastise him by an appropriate punishment."[1]

---

[1] The reports of Jackson, Coffee, and Morgan, who commanded the friendly Cherokees, are in Niles, VI., 146, where Jackson's report to Blount is dated March 31: a copy in the Jackson Mss. is dated April 2, 1814.

To some gentle spirits it seemed unnecessary to kill so many Indians; but to the people of Tennessee, who remembered fifty years of border warfare, it seemed just and appropriate. It was their glory that it came at last under one of their own leaders. When some one asked Governor Blount how it was that Jackson killed so many Indians he replied, "Because he knows how to do it."[1]

The battle of the Horse-Shoe, or Tohopeka, broke the Creek power of resistance. Since the beginning of hostilities in the preceding October they had lost by death in battle, according to the rather indefinite published reports, thirteen hundred and twenty. If we consider that many of the dead were not accounted for and many wounded were incapacitated for further service, we shall see that their fighting strength was now diminished by about twenty-five hundred and was probably not much more than fifteen hundred. This panic-stricken remnant, offering no more resistance, collected in the towns of the lower Tallapoosa, where some believed superhuman power would save their sacred places from desecration.

Jackson left them little time to doubt the issue. Returning to Fort Williams for supplies, he gave his army a needed rest and ten days after the battle of Tohopeka marched for the towns on the lower Tallapoosa. On April 15th he was joined by the Georgia militia, and three days later the combined force reached the junction of the rivers. Going thither they saw many abandoned villages but no warriors. The inhabitants had fled to Florida, where they were safe, and where they kept up their adverse organization without restraint from Spain. The hostile party numbered a thousand and did not cease to plan reprisals on the whites until, in 1818, Jackson entered Florida and convinced them that not even a Spanish fort could protect them from his vengeance.

---

[1] Blount to Jackson, January 15, 1814, Jackson Mss.

Many of the Creeks did not flee, but came into the American camp and submitted. One of them was the chief Weathersford, a half-breed, rich in lands and cattle. Another chief equally prominent, McQueen, escaped with the fugitives. April 20th, General Pinckney arrived and took command. On the twenty-first he ordered Jackson to Fort Williams to erect forts and plant garrisons in the conquered territory. This placed the strong willed Tennesseean in an independent command and removed the possibility of a clash between superior and subordinate. Near the Hickory Ground, a strong fort was built and called Fort Jackson.

When Tennessee fought and won the Creek war, she had a definite purpose: She desired to break the Spanish-Indian Alliance, to bring the Creek trade into American instead of Spanish hands, to gain complete military ascendency over the Creeks, to open and make safe the Coosa-Alabama River communication, to acquire rich lands for settlement, and to plant American power so strongly on the Florida border that the future expulsion of Spain from Florida might be an easy task. When the Creeks were at last broken she felt a great impulse to have all these advantages. With it came the conviction that the national government, from its traditionally mild policy toward the Indians, could not be trusted to demand all that ought to be taken. Especially, she distrusted the benevolent Hawkins, who had long held the position of Creek agent and fulfilled his duties on the theory that he was father and friend of the red men.

The first views of the government were in keeping with its policy of mildness. March 17th, in anticipation of the final outcome of the campaign, Secretary Armstrong told Pinckney that the terms of peace should include an indemnity in lands, relinquishment of Spanish influence among the Creeks, freedom of travel in the Nation, and the surrender of the prophets who

instigated the war.[1] Three days later, possibly in response to
efforts of the Tennessee congressmen who were always in close
touch with the situation, the terms were altered and Pinckney
was instructed to require merely a military capitulation.[2] Jackson, himself, thought that the Indians ought to surrender unconditionally, and Pinckney agreed with him.[3] It was, therefore, on such a basis that the Creeks who did not flee to Florida
submitted to the American military authority. Of those who
thus placed themselves in the hands of the Americans the
majority were friendly in the war and believed that they had
nothing to fear from unconditional submission. It was announced to all that they would be summoned later to a council
in order to conclude a general peace.

The work of the army was now over. Leaving strong garrisons in the forts, Jackson turned his face toward Nashville,
where honors were prepared for him. To his soldiers he sent
a triumphant peal by way of parting. "Your vengeance,"
he said in a proclamation which struck a sympathetic chord
in the whole countryside, "has been glutted. Wherever these
infuriated allies of the arch enemy assembled their forces for
battle, you have seen them overthrown. . . . The bravery
you have displayed on the field of battle, and the uniform good
conduct you have manifested in your encampment, and on your
line of march, will long be cherished in the memory of your
general, and will not be forgotten by the country which you
have so materially benefitted.'"[4]

In Tennessee the rejoicings were tumultuous; for it was the
state's first important historic achievement. When the campaign began, seven months earlier, Jackson had many enemies.
Two months later, when mutiny existed at Fort Strother and

---

[1] *American State Papers, Indian Affairs*, I., 836.
[2] *Ibid*, I, 837.
[3] Pinckney to Jackson, April 14, 1814, Jackson Mss.
[4] April 28, 1814, Jackson Mss.

when some of the sanest heads began to shake at what people said was his obstinacy, these enemies were exultant. Now all opponents were silenced and shamed, and from that time he was the state's military hero.

From these marks of glory he turned gladly to the "Hermitage" where Mrs. Jackson awaited him. She had watched the campaign with anxiety. A number of letters which she wrote him at this period witness her distress from his absence and her joy at his return. They are the only letters from her found in that large collection which tells so much of his life. From their tender sentiment we may think he had not the heart to destroy them. They seem to be the only unedited letters which posterity has from her pen; and one of them is given here as an illustration of the spirit of the woman who had the affection of one of the most strenuous of the world's leaders.

Hermitage, Feb. 10, 1814.

MY DEAREST LIFE:

I received your letter by Express. Never shall I forgit it I have not slept one night since. What a dreadfull scene it was — how did I feel. I never can describe it. I Cryed aloud and praised my god For your safety how thankfull I was — Oh my unfortunate Nephew he is gon how I deplore his Loss his untimely End — My dear pray let me conjur you by every Tie of Love of friendship to let me see you before you go againe I have borne it untill now it has thrown me into feavours I am very unwell — my thoughts is never diverted from that dreadfull scene oh how dreadfull to me & the mercy and goodness of Heaven to me you are spared perils and Dangers so maney troubles — my prayer is unceaseing how long O Lord will I remain so unhappy no rest no Ease. I cannot sleepe all can come home but you I never wanted to see you so mutch in my life had it not have been for Stokel Hayes I should have started oute to Huntsville let me know and I will fly on the wings of the purest affection I must see you pray my Darling never make me so unhappy for aney Country   I hope the Campain will soon end the troops that is now on their way will be sufficient to end the ware in the Creek Country   You have now don more than any other man ever did before   you have served your country long enough   You have gained many Laurels   You have bind them and more gloriously than had your situation have been diferently   and instid of   your enemyes injuring of you as theay intended it has been an advantage to you you have been gon a long time six months   in all that time what has been your trialls daingers and Diffyculties hardeships oh Lorde of heaven   how can I beare it — Colo Hayes waites once more I commend you to god   his providential eye is on you his parental Care is garding you — my prayers my tears is for your safety Day and night farewell   I fell too mutch at this moment   our Dear Little Son is well   he sayes maney things to swet papa which I have not time to mention — the Cohest blessings of Heaven awaite you   Crown your wishes — health and happy Days untill we meete — Let it not be Long   from your Dearest friend and faithfull wife untill Death

Mrs. Jackson was an illiterate woman: probably most of her mental development came through a deeply religious life. Many of her phrases are conventional expressions in the fervid pulpit language of the day. But she had an extremely benevolent nature, and through her emotions she ruled her husband's affection until the day of her death. It was no slight achievement, and whatever her education, it indicates that naturally she was a woman of distinction.

A reward more tangible than popular esteem came in promotion to rank in the regular army. Pinckney suggested it to Armstrong, who on May 20th, offered a brigadier-generalship with a brevet major-generalship, saying it was all he could then do; but he added that Jackson should have the next first-class vacancy.[1] The promise was speedily fulfilled. Major-

---

[1] Campbell to Jackson, May 29, 1814, Jackson Mss.

MRS. RACHAEL DONELSON JACKSON, WIFE OF ANDREW JACKSON

From a miniature on ivory by Anna C. Peale.   The date is given as 1819 and the place as Washington. ˙ But
Mrs. Jackson seems not to have been in Washington with Jackson in that year.   She spent the winter
of 1824-1825 in the capital.   Her husband, it is said, wore this miniature over his
heart from her death in 1828 until his own demise seventeen years later

General Harrison was in the midst of a quarrel with the government and tendered his resignation. It was accepted and on May 28th, the position was offered to Jackson. With it went the command of the seventh military district, including Louisiana and Mississippi Territory. Thus did the frontier soldier, who eighteen months earlier had not commanded an expedition or a detachment, come to occupy the highest rank in the army of his country. No other man in that country's service since the revolution has risen to the top quite so quickly.[1]

With the command of the seventh military district came orders go to Fort Jackson and make a treaty of peace with the Creeks. This pleased the Tennesseeans, who felt that in his eyes their views would find favor. The first announcement from Washington in regard to the treaty was that Pinckney and Hawkins would make it. This disappointed the people of the West. They sent a protest against the proposed appointments signed by nine of Jackson's highest officers, asking that the negotiations be left in the hands of some one who knew the needs of the frontier better. The fact that Jackson was not one of the signers of this paper seems to indicate that it was contemplated that he should have the appointment.[2]

Most of the hostile Creeks were in Florida when the great council met on the date named, August 1, 1814. Those who attended were such as submitted in the preceding spring and a large number of friendly allies.[3] The former expected little consideration, since they surrendered at discretion; but the latter looked for reward rather than punishment.

Neither party was prepared for the terms which Jackson quietly announced as his ultimatum. Without much opportunity of deliberation he presented a treaty and commanded the chiefs to sign it. It conceded to the Americans military

[1]Armstrong to Jackson, May 28, 1814, Jackson Mss.
[2]Jackson Mss.
[3]Jackson to Coffee, July 17, 1814, Jackson Mss.

posts and roads in the Creek Nation, freedom to navigate the rivers, and the relinquishment of trade relations with Spain. To all these the friendly Creeks returned submissive answers; for they desired to see the Nation Americanized. But his demands for land astonished both factions. It went, in fact, beyond reasonable indemnity and took more than half of the old Creek territory. He demanded an L-shaped belt of rich lands lying west and south of the part which would remain to the Nation; and he told the council that the Great Father in Washington wanted this belt to separate his children, the Creeks, from the Choctaws and Chickasaws on the west and from the Spaniards in Florida, so that the Creeks should never again be drawn by those powers into war with the United States. The traditional hostility, added this relentless pacificator, between the Creeks and the Cherokees was guarantee that the latter would never do the Creeks a similar disservice, and for that reason he made no demands for territory on the north.

The friendly Creeks dared not openly refuse but they sought delay. They said that since half the chieftains were in Florida, the council was not competent to cede so large a part of the ancient inheritance, and they proposed to postpone the matter until there was a general peace. Jackson curtly told them to sign the treaty as prepared or join their relatives in Florida. They could not carry on the war, and so on August 9, 1814, the treaty was accepted. The older chiefs protested and warned Jackson that his people would have trouble in taking possession of the land. He knew well that they were right, but he was willing to leave the future to take care of itself. The treaty of Fort Jackson only half ended the Creek War, as the events of the next four years were to show.

The boundary line between the Creek and American territory, as provided in the treaty, was to begin on the Coosa where the river crossed the Cherokee boundary line, thence to run southward with the river to the Great Falls, seven miles north of Fort Jackson, and thence east in an irregular line to the Georgia boundary. If the residence of any friendly chief should fall within the region thus ceded, he was to have, as long as he chose to hold it, a reservation of one square mile lying around the residence.[1]

---

[1] For the text of the treaty see *American State Papers, Indian Affairs,* I., 826: for Correspondence see *Ibid,* 837. The Tennessee view of the treaty is well given in Reid and Eaton, *Jackson,* 196-209.

CHAPTER IX

FROM the completion of the treaty of Fort Jackson, August 9, 1814, until December 1st, Jackson gave himself to the defense of Mobile and the surrounding country, leaving to its own resources the more important position of New Orleans. Several reasons convinced him it was wise to look first after the defenses of Mobile: (1) he wanted to keep the Creeks overawed, so as to retain the conquests already made; (2) the fugitives were receiving aid from the British and were likely to renew the war; (3) like other Tennesseeans he had a high opinion of the value of the Mobile-Alabama-Tennessee line of communication; (4) he longed for an opportunity to strike Spain in Florida; (5) he did not during this period have clear evidence that the British would make a direct attack on New Orleans; and (6) he had, on the contrary, many apparently safe intimations that they would attack Louisiana through Mobile. All these seemed to Jackson reasons justifying a prolonged stay in Mobile. His idea of military policy gave added reasons.

Jackson's strategy was that of the frontier Indian fighter. To move straight and quickly, surround and exterminate the foe summed up his military theory. Few American generals have equaled him in courage, promptness, perseverance, resourcefulness, and the ability to command the confidence of his officers and the obedience of his private soldiers. These were natural qualities, and they are much more than half the making of a great soldier; but they were not all. He lacked — for he had no opportunity to acquire — the trained officer's

knowledge of military technique. Had he risen through the
lower grades of service the deficiency might not have existed,
though this is not entirely certain. The campaign preliminary
to the attack on New Orleans was poorly planned from a military standpoint. It involved the loss of more than two months
given to the invasion of Florida, with no more important result
than to impress the Indians — a result which one regiment
on the frontier might have accomplished equally as well; and
in the meantime the defenses of New Orleans, and even those
of Mobile, were not adequately developed. It was his good
fortune that Pakenham, at the final test of strength, utterly
despised him. The British commander threw aside through
disdain the caution of an experienced officer as effectively as
Jackson lacked it through ignorance of the art of war. So far,
therefore, as his short career witnesses, the "Hero of New
Orleans" was a man who would blunder against his opponent
and then defeat him by sheer fighting. But it is necessary to
remember that there are many generals of whom we cannot
say as much as this.

When Wilkinson left the seventh district in the spring of 1813,
the command devolved on Brigadier-General Flournoy. Later
in the year, General Pinckney was placed in command, in order
to direct the Creek war, but his appointment did not supersede
Flournoy's authority for other purposes. The latter officer,
under the secretary of war, was responsible for the defenses
of that district. In the spring of 1814, he tired of the position and sent his resignation to the secretary, and about July
10th, left New Orleans,[1] so that from this time till the arrival
of Jackson on December 1st, it had no higher officer than a
colonel. The period was one of inactivity, dissension, and
discouragement.

Jackson intended, when he set out from Nashville to meet

---

[1] Major Hughes to R. Butler, July 8, 1814, Jackson Mss.

the Creek council at Fort Jackson, and to return to Tennessee and go to New Orleans by water, where he would open district headquarters. But while journeying to the council he learned that a British expedition was at the mouth of the Apalachicola River, where a fort was being built supplied with 22,000 stands of arms and ammunition for the fugitive Creeks, and where nine British officers were training the savages in the methods of civilized warfare.[1] This event, he thought, threatened a renewal of the Creek war, and he concluded that he was needed near the Florida border. He wrote to the secretary of war for permission to carry his arms into the Spanish province, promising, if the request were granted, "that the war in the South shall have a speedy termination, and English influence be forever destroyed with the savages in this quarter." The secretary replied promptly enlarging on our neutral obligations but saying finally that, if the Spaniards were really aiding the British and Indians, Jackson would be justified in dealing the proposed blow. The letter was indefinite enough to support a disavowal, if one should become necessary, but explicit enough to suit the commander of the seventh district, who awaited only a wink from the eye of the secretary of war. But for some unexplained reason the communication did not reach its destination until January 17, 1815.[2] It was a useless connivance, and the expedition which Jackson conducted against Pensacola was made, in default of this letter, on his own responsibility. It had the hearty approval of the people of the Southwest, whose view may be stated in the words of an anonymous correspondent in Pensacola.   "The neutrality of this province," he wrote, "is no more: it is entirely done away with, and if you do not take advantage of the present opportunity to come on, John Bull will."[3]

---

[1]Jackson to Governor Claiborne, August 22, 1814, also anonymous letter from Pensacola, June 5, 1814, Jackson Mss.

[2]Armstrong afterward said that it was Madison, who delayed the letter, Armstrong's *Notices*, page 16 n. 1.

[3]An anonymous letter dated June 5, 1814, Jackson Mss.

When he wrote to the secretary, Jackson wrote also to the governor of Florida, sending the letter by the sensible and observant Captain Gordon, of the company of spies.[1] The communication was in the nature of a formal demand which precedes an attack. It called for the surrender of the fugitive chiefs, asked why our enemies received aid and comfort in Spanish territory, and made formal complaint of the British proceedings on the Apalachicola. Gordon returned and reported that he saw the hostile Indians hold a council in the public square of Pensacola, that he saw them drive cattle through the town, some of which they avowed were taken from the whites on the Tensas, that he saw them receive provisions from the Spanish authorities; and was told that they would receive ammunition from the same source when he was gone.[2]

The reply of the governor came soon after the arrival of Captain Gordon. The hostile chiefs, he said, could not be given up, because (1) they were not at hand; (2) they could not be rightfully demanded, and he reminded his correspondent that Spain had not demanded Gutierrez, Toledo, or any other revolutionist who was harbored in the United States; (3) Spain was bound by treaty to give hospitality to the Creeks; and (4) it was not denied that the British landed arms and ammunition on the lower Apalachicola, but the action was justified on the ground that the Creeks by an old treaty with England had certain rights on that river. In closing the governor, sent this parting shot: "Turn your eyes to the Isle of Barataria and you will there perceive that in the very territory of the United States, pirates are sheltered and protected with the manifold design of committing hostilities by sea, upon the Merchant vessels of Spain, and with such scandalous notoriety that the cargoes of our vessels taken by these pirates have been sold in Louisiana,

[1] Jackson to Coffee, July 17, 1814, Jackson Mss.
[2] Gordon to Jackson, July [30], 1814, Jackson Mss.

as was the case with the *Pastora* (Shepherdess) and with other vessels."[1] A moment's reflection will probably convince the reader that not all the breaches of neutrality and international comity were on the southern side of the Florida boundary line.

Jackson believed in his own side of the matter, and the reply of the governor thoroughly infuriated him. He forwarded to Pensacola a counterblast which was creditable neither to him nor the government he represented. It breathed the spirit of the backwoods bully. "To sum up the whole," he said, "Justice to my government compels me to remark, if your Excellency had been as industrious in your researches for facts as you have been studious of evasions and unfounded innuendos, you might have long since have acquired a knowledge that Monsieur Le Fete [*sic*] commander of the piratical band has been arrested and confined, and is now under legal trial for the multifarious crimes complained of,[2] and such should be Your Excellency's conduct toward Francis, McQueen, Peter and others forming that matricidal band for whom your Christian bowels seem to sympathize and bleed so freely." He charged the governor with imbecility and falsehood and closed by saying, "In the future I beg you to withhold your insulting charges against my government for one more inclined to listen to slander than I am; nor consider me any more as a diplomatic character, unless so proclaimed to you from the mouths of cannon."

In spite of these turbulent words the governor replied with good effect. He reminded Jackson that the United States could not with good grace complain of violated treaties and pointed to the proceedings at Baton Rouge in 1810, and at Mobile in 1813. He showed that they allowed troops to be raised in their territory for service against a neutral power, as witness the succor of Miranda in his plans against Caracas and of others who

---

[1]Governor Manique to Jackson, July 26, 1814, Jackson Mss.
[2]Jackson was in error about the capture of Lafitte; see below, I., 148-150.

plotted against Mexico. As to the violation of neutrality on the Apalachicola, the governor replied, first, the Indians by treaty had rights on this river, and secondly, even if the region were indubitably Spanish territory he might reply that he had no force with which to enforce neutrality, which was what the United States said about the landing of the Baratarians, who fortified a post in Louisiana and made it, under the French flag, a base of operation against the Spanish commerce. As to Lafitte, the general well knew that he was arrested because he shed American blood and not for his piracies, and that he was still at large continuing to seize Spanish ships. "I have armed the Indians," he continued, "and have taken all the measures that I have been obliged to take, not for the purpose of committing hostilities on the United States nor on their property, but to defend myself from the insults that may be offered. If the United States continue the aggressions they have begun the officers and soldiers subject to my orders will do their duty, and support to the last extremity the great, heroic, and generous character of the Spanish Nation to which they belong." He closed by declaring. "I protest against the act [the treaty of Fort Jackson] and declare the cession void in the name of my king."[1] It is evident that the arrival of the British force in Pensacola gave increased courage to the Spanish governor.

This correspondence was not concluded before Jackson learned that the British were actually at Pensacola. August 5th, Col. Edward Nicholls, with three ships of war and 200 soldiers, landed there, took possession of a fort, and boasted that within fifteen days he would be followed by 10,000 troops and a great fleet, and that within a month afterward Mobile and the surrounding country would be in British and Spanish hands. The news gave Jackson cause for alarm, but he did not

---

[1]The letters from Jackson are in his letter-book, July 12, and August 24, 1814, among the Jackson Mss., where are also the replies of the governor, July 26 and August 30, 1814.

seem afraid. He sent urgent orders for the dispatch of reinforcements and remarked, "There will be bloody noses before
this happens."[1]

Nicholls's purpose in Florida was twofold: He expected to
organize out of the fugitive Creeks and other tribes a strong
body of auxiliary troops to be used against the settlements,
and the marked unrest among all the savages after the treaty
of Fort Jackson made it seem that this was not an idle hope.
That done, Mobile would be seized and with that as a base the
British and their allies would harry the border from Georgia
to Tennessee, cutting the Mississippi at some point above Natchez and isolating New Orleans so that the city would fall easily
into their hands. The plan was not unreasonable; for Flournoy
left Mobile's defenses so weak that the British were justified
in disregarding them, and Mobile taken it was fair to expect
that the Indians would join the victors in strength.

Nicholls was a man of acknowledged bravery, an impetuous
Irishman, described as "warm in the cause of the African race
and the depressed and distressed Indians." He armed the
savages and clothed them in British uniforms. They were
organized in a separate body under "the notorious" Captain
Woodbine and became an object of horror to the settlements,
where people seem to have forgotten that Jackson himself
had Indian allies similarly organized and commanded by white
officers. It was generally believed that Nicholls also planned
to arm the negro slaves against the whites, but the evidence
in support of the allegation is not convincing.[2] Nicholls believed, with some show of truth, that the old inhabitants of
Louisiana were not very loyal to the United States: he sent
out, therefore, a proclamation telling them that the British
were come to relieve them from the hands of the usurper, and

---

[1]Jackson to R. Butler, August 27, 1814, Jackson Mss.
[2]But Monroe gave it credence. See Monroe to Jackson, September 7, 1814, Jackson Mss.

calling on them to take part in the struggle. Mindful of the former defection in Kentucky, he imagined the people of that state could be turned against the government, and he called on them to repudiate its authority. He said nothing to the Tennesseeans.[1]

In 1814 Mobile had 150 houses and most of the population did not speak English. Fort Charlotte, its ancient defense, was a small work so placed that it protected nothing but the ground covered by its guns. The key to the position was thirty miles from the town at the entrance to the bay. Here the channel lies between some islands and Mobile Point, a long sandspit thrust out from the eastern mainland. On the end of this spit Wilkinson in 1813, just before his departure for the North, ordered the erection of a fortification which he called Fort Bowyer. Its walls were of sand, and it was equipped with twenty guns of various sizes. The work was begun, but Flournoy thought little of it and did nothing toward finishing it. In fact, he thought so little of Mobile as a military post that he advised the government to withdraw the garrison. The secretary of war liked the suggestion and sent it to Jackson for his consideration,[2] who was so far from accepting it that immediately after his arrival in the town, he sent down Major Lawrence with 160 men[3] who by working day and night for two weeks placed the fort in a tolerable state of defense.

This was not a moment too soon. September 12th, four British ships commanded by Captain Percy, of the navy, appeared off the fort. They were the *Hermes*, 22 guns; the *Carron*, 20 guns; and the *Sophie* and the *Childers*, 18 each. They came from Pensacola and anchoring six miles east of Fort Bowyer, put ashore 60 marines and 120 Indians,[4] who immediately

<hr />

[1] Monroe to Jackson, September 7, 1814, Jackson Mss. For Nicholls's proclamations see Latour *Historical Memoir*, appendix, page vii., and Gayarre, *Louisiana*, IV., 338.
[2] Armstrong to Jackson, July 2, 1814, Jackson Mss.
[3] Latour says one hundred and thirty. *Historical Memoir*, 34.
[4] The figures follow James, the English historian, *Military Occurrences*, II., 343. Latour says one hundred and twenty marines and six hundred Indians, *Historical Memoir*, 40, and Reid and Eaton make the Indians four hundred. *Jackson*, 234.

constructed some weak earthworks within cannon shot of the fort. The Americans with their long guns drove them back to a respectful distance, and they were useless in the battle of the fifteenth. They seem to have been landed merely to intercept the garrison if it tried to escape by land.

After three days spent in taking soundings and in making other preparations, Percy, on the fifteenth, brought his four ships, the *Hermes* leading, into position for attack. The channel was narrow and only two vessels, the *Hermes* and the *Sophie*, got in easy distance. If all of them could have been brought into action at once, it would still have been hazardous for them unsupported by a strong landing party to try to destroy earthworks, and Percy, who was an able officer, would not have made the attempt if he had not, like Pakenham at New Orleans, felt contempt for the fighting qualities of the Americans.

The battle opened at half past four in the afternoon and was waged fiercely from the first. Lawrence's men served their pieces with precision and at the end of an hour one of the shots cut the cable of the *Hermes*, and in the hot fire the vessel became unmanageable. Drifting directly under the American guns it was raked by a heavy fire, the crew lost control, forsook the deck, and the ship went on a sand bank still within range of the fort. Percy now decided to abandon the ship and accomplished the feat with coolness, first setting her on fire to keep her from falling into the hands of his foe. All his wounded were transferred to the *Sophie*, which was so severely used that it was thought advisable to withdraw her also from the engagement. As the three survivors sailed away, the *Hermes* was burning brightly and at eleven at night blew up with a great report. This beautiful vessel, with 31 men killed and 40 wounded, was the British loss, while Lawrence reported only 4 killed and 5 wounded. Percy embarked his landing party and returned immediately to Pensacola, where hopes of success had been high.

The day before the battle, Jackson, in response to a request from Lawrence, sent reinforcements to Fort Bowyer. They arrived during the bombardment and concluding that it was impossible to reach the garrison returned at once to Mobile. While still on the bay they heard the report of the exploding *Hermes*, construed it as disaster to their friends, and hastened to Jackson with the news that the fort was blown up. For many hours there was a sad state of consternation in the town. It was not until the seventeenth, probably in the afternoon, that the commander knew that the Americans were successful.[1]

The repulse of the British brought to a close all Nicholls's boasted plans for movements into the interior, if, indeed, he seriously entertained them. It produced on the Indians an effect favorable to the Americans. Jackson thought, also, that it was a good time to impress the inhabitants of Louisiana, and he sent forth two proclamations with that purpose. In one he called on the Louisianians to observe how the intruders were driven back and urged them to rally to the support of their government. In the other he made a strong appeal to the free people of color in Louisiana, telling them to organize in corps under the direction of the governor of the state in order to protect their homes and liberty.[2]

For nearly three months after this event the British advance expedition lay quietly in Pensacola, awaiting the arrival of the main body. Jackson, ignorant of what was planned, burned with a desire to get at them. He threw aside all scruples about violating neutrality, as he might well do; for Florida was really not neutral territory. He determined to wait no more for the approval of government, but to make a quick march on Pensacola as soon as he could get reinforcements which he

---

[1] Jackson to Butler, September 17, 1814, Jackson Mss. shows that he did not know of the victory when the letter was written. On the same day, he wrote a letter to Lawrence complimenting him on the victory. Latour, *Historical Memoir*, 42.

[2] For texts of these proclamations see Latour, *Historical Memoir*, Appendix, pages xxix and xxxi.

expected from Tennessee by way of Forts Strother and Jackson. He sent urgent orders northward where Coffee was preparing to march with a strong body of cavalry and mounted riflemen. Meantime, reliable information continually arrived, making it appear that the Indians, spite of their respect for the American successes, were in a dangerous frame of mind. One of Nicholls's first acts was to send agents among the friendly tribes urging them to save their hunting grounds while they could have British assistance and inviting them to send delegates to consult with him in Florida. Many chiefs, particularly of the Creeks, who were disappointed at the treaty of Fort Jackson, accepted the invitation. One of them was the Big Warrior himself, the leading friendly Creek at the council, who signed the treaty with great reluctance. Americans who returned from Pensacola reported that he visited the place and was entertained by the English commander. They also reported that Captain Woodbine was daily drilling his savage recruits and boasting that all the friendly Creeks were about to forsake the Americans.[1] All this made Jackson very anxious to deliver a blow at the centre of mischief.

When he reached Mobile, August 15, he had under his command 2,378 regulars, distributed at various points on the coast and including the 2nd, 3rd, 7th, 39th, and 44th regiments, all of which were much less than regulation size.[2] These were intended for the defense of the department against possible external danger. To fill the forts erected in the newly conquered Creek territory the secretary of war in July, 1814, called for 2,500 Tennessee militia, fixing September 20th, for their assembling. Col. Robert Butler, adjutant-general, was in Nashville supervising the raising of these troops when, on August 27th, news came to Mobile that Nicholls was at Pensacola. Jackson

---

[1] Claiborne to Jackson, August 29, 1814, Jackson Mss.
[2] Adams, *History of the United States*, VIII., 316.

got the information at five o'clock in the afternoon, and before he slept wrote several urgent letters calling out every available man for the defense of the coast. Butler was directed to hasten the march of the militia, the Louisiana and Mississippi militia were summoned, the friendly Indians were called out, and the contractors were ordered to place supplies for 3,000 men along the Coosa-Alabama line of transportation. Fort Jackson was named as the place of rendezvous: it was 100 miles from Pensacola and the road thither was good.

His letters to Butler are as full of details as if he were still major-general of the Tennessee militia. He shows that he understands all the conditions at home, and in one characteristic outburst expresses his deep anxiety at the situation. "I would to God, John Hutchings could come," he exclaims, "I wish you would say to the Irish to drop their race and betake themselves to the defense of their country. If this was not in the way, I know Joney would bring a company of mounted men into the field."[1]

The prospect of a campaign in Florida brought a warm response from the men of Tennessee, and Butler found his task easy. October 5th, Coffee marched southward with 2,000 horsemen from West Tennessee: on the journey he was joined by 500 more from the east and by some irregular companies to the number of 300, so that he arrived at the rendezvous with 2,800 enthusiastic followers. Jackson, aware of his approach, moved out of Mobile on October 25th, and the two bodies were united at Pierce's Stockade, or Mills, on the Alabama River.[2]

Halting here to reorganize his forces, he sent the secretary of war a statement of his motives, saying:

As I act without orders of the government, I deem it important to state to you my reasons for the measure I am about

---

[1]Jackson to R. Butler, August 27 and 28, and September 8, 1814, Jackson Mss.

[2]R. Butler to Coffee, September 10 and 13; Coffee to Dyer, September 11 and October 1; Hayne to Coffee, October 19; Coffee to Governor Blount, October 4, 1814; Jackson Mss.

to adopt. First I conceive the safety of this section of the union depends upon it. The hostility of the Governor of Pensacola in permitting the place to assume the character of British territory by resigning the command of the fortress to them, permitting them to fit an expedition against the United States, and after its failure to return to the town, refit, and make arrangements for a second expedition. At the same time making me a declaration that he (the governor) had armed the Indians and sent them into our territory. Knowing at the same time that these very Indians had under the command of a British officer captured our citizens and destroyed their property within our own territory.[1]

The whole number of men fit for duty at Pierce's Stockade was now about four thousand, but 780 of them were Indians.[2] Lack of forage in Florida made that region difficult for horsemen, and all but 1,000 of Coffee's men were ordered to stay with their horses on the banks of the Alabama. On the afternoon of November 6th, the rest of the force, 3,000 men, were before Pensacola. The commander halted long enough to send in his demands under a flag of truce. His messenger was that Major Peire, of the 44th regiment, who was Wilkinson's messenger when Mobile was seized in 1813,[3] and he was sent to announce to the Spaniard that Jackson came not to make war on Spain, but to insist on the neutrality of Florida. In order that this might be ensured, Jackson demanded that the Barrancas and other fortifications be placed in his hands in one hour and without armed resistance: otherwise, he added, "I will not hold myself responsible for the conduct of my enraged soldiers and warriors."[4] Jackson was thus threatening to use the same methods of distressing the enemy which the

[1]Jackson to secretary of war, October 26, 1814, Jackson Mss. The British officer referred to is Woodbine.
[2]Jackson's morning report for October 30, gives the number as 4117, but its computations seem defective. See Jackson Mss.
[3]Hamilton, *Colonial Mobile*, 559.
[4]A copy is in Jackson Mss. See also Reid and Eaton, *Jackson*, 247.

Americans complained so loudly of the British for using in the Northwest. But the letter was not delivered. The governor, mindful, perhaps, of the American general's letter of the preceding August 30th, fired on the flag of truce, and Major Peire returned to the army. It was then too late in the afternoon to begin an attack, but arrangements were made for one in the early morning.

Pensacola lies on the shore of the bay and the defenses were constructed on the theory that it would be attacked from the west along the beach. The British ships, seven in number, were so placed that their guns could command this approach. East of the town the beach was narrow but undefended, and Jackson determined to attack from this quarter. Early in the morning he sent a column of 500 to make a feint on the west and threw his main body to the opposite side by a rapid detour. He thus entered the streets of the town before the men-of-war could change their position, and before the Spanish authorities realized his tactics. In the streets there was a sharp battle. A battery opened on him with solid shot and grape, while a musketry fire raked his flanks from the houses and garden. Captain Laval, of the 3d regiment, led the advance with his company and two field-pieces. He fell in the streets severely wounded, but his men carried the battery in good style. Other columns penetrated other parts of the city, driving the Spanish soldiers from gardens and houses. A body of Choctaws under Major Blue were also within the town with the army. As soon as the governor realized that these forces held the streets he became terrified and hastened forward with a flag to surrender the town and its fortifications. It was agreed that forts, arsenals, and armaments should be given over to the Americans till a Spanish force should arrive strong enough to enforce the obligations of neutrality, the Americans promising to respect the persons and property of the inhabitants. But when the public property passed into the hands of the Americans, Jackson was careful to order that all arms in the town worth transporting should be sent at once to Fort Montgomery, a new post in Alabama.[1]

One of the places which the governor promised to surrender was the Barrancas, which commanded the entrance of the bay fourteen miles from Pensacola. It had been in the hands of the British since the arrival of Nicholls. Jackson gave himself much pleasure in the thought that he should turn them out and probably make them his prisoners. He was preparing to take the place on the morning of the eighth when it was abandoned and blown up by the occupants, in order that it might not fall into the hands of the Americans.[2] Gathering all their supplies and taking Woodbine and the Indian allies on board the ships, the British sailed away in the early morning, leaving Jackson with a barren victory. He felt some chagrin at losing out of his grasp both garrison and vessels. But the destruction of the Barrancas may have been fortunate for the Americans. It kept their commander from attempting to hold it, which would have been a costly experiment. He at last realized that his work in Pensacola was done and on the ninth set out for his own country. On the thirteenth he arrived on the Tensas.[3]

Admirers of Jackson's courage and honesty have frequently to deplore his crude intellect, and they must feel a little disappointment at the manner in which he swallowed his anger and left Pensacola. To the Spanish governor he wrote: "Finding that the Barrancas and fortifications adjacent to it, have been surrendered to and blown up by the British, contrary to the good faith I was induced to place in your promises, I find it

---

[1] Jackson to Hayne, November 8, 1814, Jackson Mss. A copy of the terms of surrender is in the Jackson Mss.
[2] Latour, *Historical Memoir*, page 50, says that the British persuaded the Spaniards to blow up the fort.
[3] Jackson to Blount, November 14, 1814, Jackson Mss. give the writer's account of this movement.

out of my power to protect your neutrality as I was willing to have done. The Enemy having disappeared from your Town and the hostile Creeks fled to the forest, I retire from your Town, and you are again at liberty to occupy your Fort, as I received it for the protection of your citizens." One of his officers was wounded severely and had to be left behind. Referring to him, Jackson wrote to the governor, forgetful of the obligations of courtesy: "I shall therefore expect from you sir, that attention and security for the person of this officer that is due, and every brave and honorable man would extend to another whose misfortunes had placed him in his power."[1] Jackson was not a generous foe, and the frontiersman's habits of braggadocio and bluster were very deeply fixed in his nature.

The excursion into Florida satisfied the Southwestern feeling against Spain, it improved the *morale* of the army, it impressed the Indians who saw Woodbine and Nicholls for the second time scampering away from the irate victor of Tohopeka, it strengthened the weak knees in Louisiana,[2] and it gave Jackson himself added confidence in the ability of his army. "My pride was never more heightened," said he, "than on viewing the uniform firmness of my troops, and with what undaunted courage they advanced with a strong fort ready to assail them on the right, seven British vessels on the left, strong blockhouses and batteries of cannon on the front, but they still advanced with unshaken firmness, [and] entered the town. . . . The steady firmness of my troops has drew a just respect from our enemies: it has confirmed the red sticks' that they have no stronghold or protection only in the friendship of the United States. The good order and conduct of my troops whilst in Pensacola has convinced the Spaniards of our friendship and our prowess, and has drew from the citizens an

---

[1] Jackson to the governor of Pensacola, November 9, 1814, Jackson Mss. (2 letters).
[2] Governor Claiborne to Jackson, November 19, 1814, Jackson Mss.
[3] The hostile Creeks were called "Red Sticks" because they painted their war clubs red.

expression, that our Choctaws are more civilized than the British."[1]

Before we criticize this expedition it is necessary to consider Jackson's situation. When it was undertaken, the President and cabinet were fugitives from the national capital and he was left for weeks to act on his own judgment. He knew nothing of the great attack which was impending and had before him the simple task of beating off the dangers which seemed to threaten. The visible peril was an attack from the force then in Pensacola, and following his characteristic strategy he struck hard and swiftly at the point at which trouble seemed to be brewing. In the cataclysm at Washington the country got a new secretary of war in the place of the nerveless Armstrong. James Monroe, to whom the place went, qualified on October 1st, after holding the office for a month as an *ad interim* appointee. He had more energy than his predecessor and he and Jackson were old friends. One of his first letters to the general was in reply to the latter's report of September 9th, giving an account of his correspondence with the governor of West Florida. He advised Jackson to leave the insolent language of the governor to the diplomats and ordered him to do nothing which would bring on a war with Spain.[2] When this letter reached its destination the expedition was a thing of the past, and to the diplomats was left the task of soothing the ruffled feelings of the Spanish court, which, indeed, proved no formidable task, so clearly had Spain been in the wrong.

Jackson did not fear the frowns of the government; for he had reassuring information from a private source. September 23d, a friend in the war department to whom he had made application wrote after a two hours' conversation with Monroe: "You will receive all the support in the power of the government,

---

[1]Jackson to Blount, Nov. 14, 1814, Jackson Mss.
[2]Monroe to Jackson, October 21, 1814, Jackson Mss.

relating to the Spaniards, if it should be necessary to notice them in a hostile manner. Colonel Monroe spoke in *strong* terms on the subject, as well as on subjects relating to extensive national policy."[1]

From the Tensas, Jackson hastened to Mobile. Reliable information made it evident that he was needed in New Orleans. During the recent operations, he received many letters from that quarter, urging his immediate presence there, but he considered the work then at hand more important and refused to leave until it was thoroughly finished.

Two things must be done before he could leave the present position: Forces must be provided to defend it against a possible surprise by the British, and steps must be taken to protect the settlements against the hostile Creeks who were still lurking in Florida. To the former task he assigned the 2d, 3d, and 39th regiments' with a body of Georgia militia now approaching through the Creek nation, all to be under the command of Major-General McIntosh, of the Georgia militia. Brigadier-General Winchester was left in command until the arrival of McIntosh.[3] Major Blue of the 39th regiment, was given command of the force intended to operate against the Indians. It was composed of certain companies from West Tennessee, three from East Tennessee, and one from Mississippi Territory, in all 1,000 horsemen, together with the Choctaw, Chickasaw, and friendly Creek allies. Blue was ordered to operate along the Escambia.[4] Having made these arrangements to his satisfaction, Jackson set out on November 21st, for New Orleans, going by land so as to inspect the intervening country.

[1]Charles Cassiday to Jackson, war office, Washington, September 23, 1814, Jackson Mss.
[2]General orders, November 14, 1814, Jackson Mss.
[3]Jackson to Winchester, November 14, 1814, Jackson Mss.
[4]Jackson to secretary of war, November 20, 1814, Jackson Mss.

CHAPTER X

THE DEFENSES OF NEW ORLEANS

NEW ORLEANS is situated 105 miles from the mouth of the Mississippi and has two water approaches, one, by the river and the other by Lakes Borgne and Pontchartrain. The latter opens on Mississippi Sound, which extends as far east as the mouth of Mobile Bay and, separated from the Gulf by a chain of small islands, makes a protected communication between these two important gulf ports. Between the river and the lake is a narrow strip of land on which the city is placed fronting immediately on the river and distant from Lake Pontchartrain about four miles. The roads which lead to it are built through tropical forest and are frequently bordered by swamps impassable for bodies of troops, so that the way may be impeded by fallen timber, and a few hardy defenders may hold it against greatly superior forces. The two lakes are connected by the Rigolets, a narrow channel, commanded in 1814, by a small fort at a place known as Petites Coquilles and later known as Fort Pike. There were six obvious ways of reaching the city described by Jackson's engineers as follows:

1. *The River from Its Mouth* — This was the most usual approach, but it was, nevertheless, very difficult. The waters of the Mississippi reach the Gulf through five comparatively shallow "passes," the best of which, then about twelve feet deep,[1] was defended by an old fort at Belize, which was useless because the river could be entered by one of the other "passes." Fifty miles higher up at a sharp angle in the river was Fort

---

[1] A. P. Hayne to Jackson, November 27, 1814, Jackson Mss.

St. Philip and across the river from it Old Fort Bourbon. The former was an important work, but in the summer of 1814 it was in a state of neglect, and the latter was dismantled. The best defense of the river was 65 miles still higher up at the English Turn. Here the Mississippi makes so decided a turn that for three or four miles it is flowing nearly due north. A breeze which would bring a ship to this point would be nearly dead ahead when the ship rounded the curve and made southward.[1]

2. *Chef Menteur* — Fifteen miles east of the city, on Lake Pontchartrain, was this high district. It was connected with the city by a narrow ridge of dry ground between the swamps. The ridge was known as the Plains of Gentilly. The inhabitants in September thought this the most likely means of approach. It was then unfortified but easily defended.

3. *River aux Chênes and the Bayou Terre aux Bœufs* — East of the mouth of the Mississippi and parallel with the river were a bay, a short river, and a bayou, which together gave an independent line of approach to the east bank of the river at the English Turn, sixteen miles from New Orleans. It was only navigable by small boats.

4. *The Bayou St. John* — This waterway begins at Lake Pontchartrain and extends straight west till, at a distance of four miles from the origin, it is within two miles of what were then the city limits. The bayou was navigable only for small boats, it could be made impassable in a few hours by felling trees, and the swamps on either side were considered quite impenetrable.

5. *The Bayou La Fourche* — This was situated west of the Mississippi. Beginning at the gulf shore eighty miles from the mouth of that river it extends north to a point where it "forks from the Mississippi." It was reported to be easily navigable

---

[1]Claiborne to Jackson, November 4; Jackson to Claiborne, December 10, 1814, Jackson Mss.

but narrow and readily obstructed. It was estimated that 1,000 men stationed midway between the fork and the city could march to the bayou on the appearance of an enemy and hold him off.

6. *Barataria Bay* — Seventy miles west of the mouth of the Mississippi, with a channel ten feet deep and capable of easy defense, this bay offered through a number of connected bayous and the canals on the west bank a communication with the river immediately opposite the city. This line was difficult and a block house with a few cannon at a point called "The Temple" would, it was thought, make it secure.[1]

When Jackson assumed command of the seventh district, the defenses of New Orleans were much neglected. At Fort St. Philip were twenty-eight heavy guns, twenty four-pounders; and there was a battery at English Turn, designed for nine pieces, but its platforms, magazines, and barracks were unfinished. Fort St. John, at the mouth of the bayou of the same name, was also designed for nine pieces, but only four of them were mounted and the place was in charge of a subaltern with twenty men. Another small fort on Lake Pontchartrain was at Petites Coquilles, in such a state of decay that it would take 60 men two months to make it defensible.[2]

The forces in the city and its dependencies in July included 120 men in the city barracks, 95 in Fort St. Charles — an old and useless fort well surrounded by the houses of the citizens — the 44th regiment numbering 337, and 128 men in garrison at St. Philip. In all, there were 680 men, of whom at least 208 were not present for duty.[3] Beside these the 7th

---

[1] This description and enumeration of approaches to the city are taken from the letter which the committee of citizens of New Orleans appointed September 14, 1814, sent to Jackson and which is preserved in the Jackson Mss.

[2] McRea to Jackson, September 9 and 19, and October 20, 1814; Schamburg and Morgan to Jackson, October 31, and Wollenstonecraft to Jackson, September 27, 1814, Jackson Mss. But the report of the last mentioned does not quite agree with McRea's or with itself.

[3] See *Monthly Report* for July, Jackson Mss.

regiment, was at Tchifonte with 465 men and at the request of McRea it was added to the force in the city.[1] New Orleans was a naval station under the command of Commodore Daniel T. Patterson. His effective force was six gunboats and one schooner and these were short of sailors.[1] The fleet had long been blockaded by the British ships at the mouth of the Mississippi, which also kept in the river a large number of trading vessels. Vast quantities of supplies and of cotton and sugar, the accumulation of two years of blockade, were also in the city. It was not so easy for the enemy to close the entrance to Lake Borgne and out of it small ships were accustomed to escape with cargoes for Pensacola.

In the beginning of the campaign serious fears were felt for the loyalty of the French and Spanish population in Louisiana. Governor Claiborne, of that state, himself said as much to Jackson in the middle of August.[3] But a month later he was able to report that sentiment was changing and that the people seemed to be rallying to the call for troops.[4] This change of sentiment was probably due to the early successes of the Americans, their active appeals to the natives, and the allegation, always repeated and by many believed, that the British intended to arm the slaves against their masters.[5] So fast did the revival of interest proceed that, by November 20th, 1,000 of the state's militia and some hundreds of volunteers were in the field from Louisiana.[6] From La Fourche southward each

[1]McRea to Jackson, September 19 and October 12; also *Monthly Report* of the 7th regiment, December 23, 1814, Jackson Mss.

[2]Claiborne to Jackson, November 4, 1814, Jackson Mss.

[3]Colonel François Colliel, a prominent Creole, was discovered sending a Spanish officer at Pensacola a description of the defenses of New Orleans and expelled from Louisiana. But Colliel gave it as his opinion that if Jackson appeared with enough forces to command public confidence the people would support him. See Colliel to Morales, October 10; Claiborne to Jackson, October 28, and November 4, 1814, Jackson Mss.

[4]Claiborne to Jackson, August 16, September 20, 1814, Jackson Mss.

[5]Claiborne to Jackson, August 16 and 20, September 20, October 24, 1814; also J. Smith to Jackson, August 30, 1814, Jackson Mss. See also Gayarre, *History of Louisiana*, IV., 341-348.

[6]Claiborne to Jackson, November 20, 1814, Jackson Mss.

bank of the river was settled by rich sugar planters. In this region there were said to be twenty-five slaves for each white person,[1] and the proportions in other parts of the state were not much smaller. In view of the fears in regard to the slaves it was not to be expected that a more general response should be made by the population.[2] Nevertheless, the sensitiveness of the legislature in their relations with Jackson indicates that there was ever a little hesitation in the minds of the people.

It was August 27th, when Jackson at Mobile learned that Nicholls was at Pensacola announcing himself the herald of a great expedition which should take Louisiana. The information was soon in New Orleans, and urgent letters were sent to the commander of the district requesting him to go to the city. He steadily refused: he would go to the Mississippi, he said, in good time, when the defenses of Mobile were satisfactory and not sooner. "My whole force," he said impatiently, "would not satisfy the demands they [the people of New Orleans] make."[3]

Meantime, he placed Lieutenant-Colonel McRea in command of the city and ordered him to put the forts in the best possible condition of defense. McRea was soon in conflict with the commandant of Fort St. Philip, who refused either to obey him or to coöperate. Jackson promptly placed all the troops in Louisiana under the command of the lieutenant-colonel and there was harmony in the place. But he needed for New Orleans an officer of higher rank and reputation, and he asked the secretary of war to send him one. In compliance with the request Brigadier-General Edmund Pendleton Gaines was ordered to New Orleans,[4] but he proceeded so slowly that he did not arrive there until February 4, 1815. Jackson also sent his inspector-general to examine the works around the

[1] New Orleans committee to Jackson, September 15, 1814, Jackson Mss.
[2] In 1811, there was a negro insurrection in Louisiana and the memory of its terror was fresh in the minds of the people. Gayarre, *Louisiana*, IV., 266.
[3] Jackson to secretary of war, October 10, 1814, Jackson Mss.
[4] Jackson to secretary of war, August 25; Monroe to Jackson, December 7, 1814, Jackson Mss.

city. The reports of that officer showed that strengthening the fortifications was going forward as rapidly as possible with the slender resources of the district and the confused state of the local authority. Had Jackson himself been there he could hardly have done more than was done.

While these orders were being executed, a part of the force at New Orleans was used to suppress the lawless Baratarians, with whose immunity from arrest the governor of Florida so caustically reproached Jackson. These men had the technical status of privateers. They collected from various sources at the island of Guadaloupe and sailed as privateers under French licenses; but the capture of that island by the British in 1810, and the subsequent expiration of their licenses made it necessary for them to get other governmental authority. They turned to the newly proclaimed revolutionary republic of Cartagena, which gladly received such an accession of maritime strength and gave them new licenses. They had, however, to find a new rendezvous and place for the disposal of their prizes They seized Barataria Bay, which was excellently situated for their purposes. On the island of Grande Terre, in this bay, they sold their captured ships and cargoes as freely as if the trade was unquestioned. Latour confesses with shame that planters and merchants of the best standing bought supplies and other goods there, sending them into the city or parishes without paying import duties. "The frequent seizures made of those goods," says he, "were but an ineffectual remedy of the evil, as the great profit yielded by such parcels as escaped the vigilance of the custom-house officers, indemnified the traders for the loss of what they had paid for the goods seized. . . . This traffic was at length carried on with such scandalous notoriety that the agents of government incurred very general and open reprehension, many persons contending that they had interested motives for conniving at such abuses, as smuggling was a source of confiscation from which they derived considerable benefit."[1] The Baratarians received protection from a group of interested men in New Orleans, among whom was Edward Livingston, a brilliant but not too scrupulous lawyer who acted as their retained counsel. It was frequently charged that most of the ships had no commissions and were really pirates; but Latour, who has the advantage of contemporary knowledge at first hand, says this was never proved. He thinks all had licenses of some kind, though he is willing to admit that some papers may have been forged. Granting that all had commissions from Cartagena they were, under the interpretation of international law then in vogue,[2] technically pirates until the United States recognized the belligerency of that republic.[3] Moreover, their presence in Barataria Bay was an offense against the neutrality obligations of the United States. Thus, there were three grounds on which they ought to have been suppressed. Governor Claiborne endeavored to drive them away. Several expeditions accomplished nothing but to force them into temporary flight with all their goods, and they returned when danger ceased.[4] Neither Wilkinson nor Flournoy showed a disposition to apprehend them, but in Jackson they found a quick and determined foe, although it was to the navy that their final dispersion was due.

The head of the Baratarians in 1814 was Jean Lafitte, French born and formerly a New Orleans blacksmith, a man of courage, energy, and acknowledged leadership. Colonel Nicholls knew his capacity and sought to draw him into the British service. September 3, 1814, the sloop *Sophia*, Captain Lockyer in command, appeared before Grande Terre with letters from

---

[1]Latour, *Historical Memoir*, 15.

[2]Lawrence, *Principles of International Law*, section 122.

[3]Rumor said they disposed of the crews of their prizes in genuine pirate fashion. Ross to Jackson, October 31, 1814, Jackson Mss.

[4]Gayarre, *Louisiana*, IV., 289, 301, 312, 370.

Nicholls. Jean Lafitte and his followers were invited to join the British in the campaign against the Americans. To the former was offered a commission and to the latter assignments of land; but the freebooters must agree to distress the Spanish commerce no longer, to sell their ships to the British, and to obey the orders of the British admirals. It was demanded that Lafitte should restore the goods he had taken from the English, but, to save his pride, it is said, he received a verbal offer of $30,000 as a gratuity. This was not a bad bargain for Jean Lafitte, against whom the Americans were about to take action of quite another kind; but he thought he could make a better bargain elsewhere, and to gain time, refused to give a positive answer. He asked Lockyer to come again at the end of a fortnight, when he would accept the proposition — *"Je serais tout à vous."*[1]

Lafitte was willing to give up his roving career, but he preferred to trust himself in American hands. Much of his booty was of English origin, and he was not sure that an Englishman would keep a promise so liberally made. On the other hand, he had friends among the Louisianians, many of his followers were of American birth and sympathy, he knew that the Southwest had no real scruples about the kind of warfare he was waging on Spanish subjects, and, more important still, he had a brother in a New Orleans prison on a serious charge and hoped by a reconciliation to get him released. He saw in Lockyer's offer a means of rendering himself serviceable to the Americans. He sent copies of the Briton's letters to New Orleans and offered to surrender himself to Governor Claiborne if past offenses were forgiven. He offered to defend Barataria Bay against the enemy and asserted that he was so true to the government that, if his offer was not accepted, he would sail away with his establishment rather than fight against the United

---

[1] The original of Lafitte's letter, September 4, 1814, as it seems, is in the Jackson Mss.

States. At this juncture, as he must have known, a body of regulars were about to be sent to disperse or capture his force, and it would be a shrewd turn if he could place himself and his accumulated booty under the protection of the American flag in time to avert the blow.

The authorities in New Orleans, state and national, considered his proposition a trick to gain time and its only effect was to hasten the departure of the regulars. Edward Livingston, however, had good reason to know the truth in the communication and succeeded in convincing the officials and the people that the offer of Nicholls to Lafitte was evidence that the city was in danger. But it does not appear that he any more than Jackson suspected the overwhelming nature of the force which was about to be thrown against the city.

September 16th, the American expedition was before Grande Terre. Lafitte did not stay to oppose it. With his best ships and most of his followers he escaped out of the bay, and the victors burned all the spoil which they could not take away. They captured eight small vessels, a number of prisoners whom they held for trial, a large amount of merchandise, 7,500 gun flints, and many of Lafitte's papers. Among the last was the reply to Lockyer, which the writer was careful not to send to New Orleans when he revealed the overtures made to him. Its apparent acceptance of the Englishman's offer now made an impression very unfavorable to the Baratarians.[1] A short time later news came that Lafitte was again on the coast and had headquarters at Cat Island, near the mouth of La Fourche, and that he was still engaged in smuggling. This did not tend to modify the wrath of the authorities; but he genuinely desired peace and continued to make overtures through Livings-

---

[1] Colonel Ross to Jackson, October 3, 1814, report of the capture of Lafitte's stronghold; Wollenstonecraft to Jackson, September 13; Lafitte to Lockyer, original French copy, September 4, 1814; Jackson Mss. Lafitte's correspondence, translated, and other matter of a similar nature is in Latour, *Historical Memoir*, Appendix, numbers 4, 5, and 6. Also Jackson to Claiborne, September 30, and Jackson's comment on back of Monroe to Jackson, December 10, 1814, Jackson Mss.

ton. He seems to have had no trouble with the state officials, but the cases against him were for smuggling, and the national officers were not so much inclined to leniency, probably because they were not so much affected by local influence. His friends were able to get the legislature to pass resolutions requesting the district attorney to abandon the cases if the pirates would agree to serve in the army.[1] The request was not granted by that officer; but later, after Jackson's arrival in the city, Lafitte sought an interview, coming to the place under a guarantee of safety from Judge Hall, of the federal court. Up to this time, Jackson would make no concessions to the lawbreakers, but he saw in the chief of the sea rovers a man of remarkable personality, brave, and filled with the war spirit. He was impressed, also, by his evident honesty and after the arrival of the British agreed to receive the Baratarians into the military service of the government.[2] Some of them formed a corps and in the defense of Jackson's lines below New Orleans served with great success batteries three and four. Others joined one of the three companies of marines and acquitted themselves well. The indictments against them were subsequently dropped. The Baratarians made a good impression on contemporaries. Latour, writing in 1816, speaks well of their loyalty.[3] They add a touch of romance to the history of the day, and their story has been told with effect — probably with too much warmth — by many writers.

The communication from Lafitte and other information from various sources convinced the people of New Orleans that their city was in danger. The place was filled with produce from the interior, accumulated through a two-years' blockade,

---

[1] Copy of the resolutions in Jackson Mss.

[2] The Baratarians were on an island in the swamps, below Baton Rouge, when Coffee arrived on the Mississippi, and he was anxious to take steps looking to their suppression. See Coffee to Jackson, December 15, 1814, Jackson Mss.

[3] Claiborne to Jackson, September 20 and October 17, 1814; also resolutions of Louisiana legislature, without date; all in Jackson Mss. See also Gayarre, *Louisiana*, IV., 356, 369, and 411.; Latour, *Historical Memoir*, 71.

credits were swollen and continued to increase in expectation of the final day of liquidation, and specie, even for fractional currency, was extremely scarce. If the city should be seized many a fortune would collapse. Thus self-interest as well as patriotism prompted the leading inhabitants to strive to beat off the danger.

September 16th, a public meeting was called to promote the cause of defense. It was especially desired to arouse the support of the native French population, about whose loyalty there was much doubt. Edward Livingston was, of all the prominent American residents, most influential with this class. He came forward prominently in the movements now about to be made and it proved to be an important step in his career. He introduced resolutions in the meeting of September 16th, pledging the state and city to their best exertions, and when a committee was appointed to carry out the will of the meeting he was made its chairman. In this capacity he came into correspondence with Jackson in Mobile, later became his aide,[1] and laid the foundation of a friendship which was destined to make him a member of the cabinet and foreign minister.

Livingston's committee strove to arouse enthusiasm. It was appointed the day after Lawrence drove back the British ships at Fort Bowyer, and the news of that event gave support to its efforts. The old French population was divided in its sympathy between the Bourbons and Napoleon. Of the latter party were a number of persons who left France after the collapse of their leader earlier in the same year. One of them was General Humbert, who offered his services to Jackson. Enlistments were stimulated and arguments were employed to convince the Creole planters that their interests demanded

---

[1]Livingston improved his opportunity as chairman of the committee to ask Jackson to give him the rank of aide. The latter declined because he did not approve of appointing an aide detached from headquarters and because he had two already, the number allowed him by the government. Jackson to Livingston, September 30, October 23, 1814.

American success. Much was made of the rumors that the British would stimulate a slave rising. Seconding these efforts came Jackson's proclamation of September 21st, written in exultation over the defeat of the British at Fort Bowyer. "Louisianians!" he exclaimed, "The proud Briton, the natural and sworn enemy of all Frenchmen, has called upon you by proclamation to aid him in his tyranny, and to prostrate the whole temple of our liberty. Can Louisianians, can Frenchmen, can Americans ever stoop to be the slaves or allies of Britain!" Referring to the Baratarians he said: "Have they not made offers to the pirates of Barataria to join them, and their holy cause? And have they not dared to insult you by calling on you to associate, as brethren, with them and this hellish banditti!"[1] Neither of these utterances was tactful. The Creoles resented the reference to slaves of the British, for it implied a reflection on the French government, to which they were attached; and there were many who did not like the uncouth words in which the Baratarians were denounced.[2]

Another class to whom Jackson appealed were the free Negroes, of whom the city held more than six hundred, and some of whom were wealthy. Under Spanish rule these people were called upon in times of trouble and served well. The Americans did not look favorably on such service, but allowed a small battalion of them to continue its organization under Colonel Fortier and Major Lacoste, with colored men for company officers. August 11, 1814, Governor Claiborne had an interview with these officers and found them faithful to the government. They suggested that all the free men of color in New Orleans be enlisted. The governor acquiesced and transmitted the suggestion to Jackson, who accepted the idea with enthusiasm. "Our country," he said, "has been invaded and

---

[1] Latour, *Historical Memoir*, Appendix, number 16.
[2] The French newspaper criticized it, and Gayarre supports the criticism, *Louisiana*, IV., 354.

threatened with destruction. She wants soldiers to fight her battles. The free men of color in your city are inured to the Southern climate and would make excellent soldiers. They will not remain quiet spectators of the interesting contest. They must be either for, or against, us. Distrust them and you make them your enemies, place confidence in them, and you engage them by every dear and honorable tie to the interest of the country, who extends to them equal rights and privileges with white men. I enclose you a copy of my address to them for publication and wish an experiment made for raising a regiment of them."[1]

The proclamation was expressed in the warmest terms. "Through a mistaken policy," it ran, "you have heretofore been deprived of a participation in the glorious struggle for national rights in which your country is engaged. This no longer shall exist. As sons of freedom you are now called upon to defend your most inestimable blessing. As Americans, your country looks with confidence to her adopted children, for a valorous support, as a faithful return for the advantages enjoyed under her mild and equitable government. As fathers, husbands, and brothers, you are summoned to rally round the standard of the eagle, to defend all which is dear in existence." To such as should volunteer were offered the regular bounties — 160 acres of land and $124 in cash — and the regular pay, rations, and clothing of a soldier. They were to be commanded by white commissioned, and colored non-commissioned, officers.[2]

This liberal attitude toward the Negroes brought out the opposition of those inhabitants of Louisiana who believed that repression rather than confidence was the best policy to be pursued with regard to these people. They protested against putting arms into their hands, saying that it would render them

---

[1] See Jackson to Claiborne, September 21, 1814, Jackson Mss. Also Gayarre, *Louisiana*, IV., 335.
[2] Latour, *Historical Memoir*, Appendix, number 17.

insubordinate in times of peace and give them an undesirable acquaintance with the art of war, and they declared that the free Negroes were especially disloyal. All these objections were laid before Jackson, but he did not relent.[1] The battalion under Lacoste was enlarged and drilled, and when Jackson arrived on December 1st, it paraded before him by the side of the uniformed companies of the city and won his special commendation.[2] Later it served with credit in the operations against the British. Another battalion was organized from the Santo Domingo Negroes, of whom a large number were in the city as refugees from the British. It numbered 210 men and was mustered into service a few days before the landing of the enemy.[3] Under Major Daquin it did excellent service in the night battle of December 23d, and on Jackson's lines.

The assistant district paymaster was one of those who did not approve of enlisting Negro and Indian troops, and he questioned Jackson's authority to have them in the service. What else he said does not appear; but he received a letter from Jackson which reduced him to submission in short order. It ran:

Be pleased to keep to yourself your Opinions upon the policy of making payments to particular Corps. It is enough for you to receive my order for the payment of the troops with the necessary muster rolls without inquiring whether the troops are white, Black, or Tea. You are not to know whether I have received authority from the War Department to employ any particular description of men, and will, upon the receipt of this make payment of the Choctaws upon the muster rolls of Major Blue.[4]

Another source of friction between Jackson and the Louisi-

[1]Claiborne to Jackson, October 17 and 24; Jackson to Claiborne, October 21 1814, Jackson Mss.
[2]Latour, *Historical Memoir*, Appendix, number 20.
[3]Jackson to Claiborne, December 18, 1814, Jackson Mss.
[4]Jackson to W. Allen, December 23, 1814, Jackson Mss

anians came from attempts to export provisions from the city to Pensacola, where prices rose with the approach of the British. As soon as Jackson knew that the enemy was bound for that place he gave strict orders that no vessels laden with food be allowed to pass through the lakes. Nevertheless, there were merchants in New Orleans who, it was reported, evaded the law daily, and Jackson, hearing of it, directed that the ship-owners and captains concerned be arrested and tried by military law. He spoke with a feeling of chagrin, and his orders were executed with precision. The only relaxation he would make was that vessels bound for Mobile might sail if they gave bond in approved security that their cargoes should be landed in that place. So effective was the embargo that Pensacola in December, appealed to him in the name of humanity to let enough rice, flour, and other food be sent thither to keep the inhabitants from starvation.[1] The incident served to increase Jackson's distrust of the people of New Orleans and contributed to the friction which later arose between civil and military authorities.

Another source of anxiety came from the chaotic political conditions. Claiborne, the governor, was honest, patriotic, and industrious, but he lacked tact and the power to make himself obeyed. He had, also, many enemies who opposed him in the press and defeated his recommendations when they could, in the legislature. Late in 1813, the United States government withdrew one regiment of the scant force at New Orleans, and Flournoy asked the governor to call out 1,000 militia for six months to fill their places, chiefly in the garrisons around New Orleans. Claiborne complied, sending out his call on December 25th. Four hundred men from the counties adjacent to Baton Rouge and in the eastern part of the state, mostly of

---

[1]Jackson to Claiborne, August 30; to McRea, October 14; to Patterson, October 14, McRea to Jackson September 3, 9, 22, October 12, 17, 1814, Jackson Mss.

Anglo-American stock, came down to the city for duty. But the inhabitants of New Orleans and of the river banks south of Baton Rouge refused to respond. They alleged that there was no need of their services; and it was, in fact, not usual to call the militia out for garrison duty unless there was grave imminent danger. Claiborne referred the matter to the legislature, but his opponents there were able to defeat resolutions in support of his position. The up-country militia offered their services to force their brethren of the city to perform their duty, but the governor was too wise to precipitate a civil war and declined the offer. The spring and summer of 1814 were passed in apathy, and the governor was deeply discouraged. But his chagrin was not entirely justified. When it became evident that there was real danger from an enemy, it was no longer possible for his opponents to convince the people that they need not take up arms. They did not now oppose a call for the militia, but were satisfied to tie the hands of the executive in other ways. They supported a spirit of dissatisfaction which left room to doubt the loyalty of the state, although it is not likely that the suspicion was well founded. One result was the appointment of a legislative committee on the war which, with the citizen committee, was a source of confusion. Another was to prolong the session of the censorious assembly which was called to secure funds for defense and not to sit in judgment on the conduct of the war.

Thus Louisiana, against which more than 10,000 troops were about to be hurled, passed through the months of August, September, and November, slowly calling out its militia, repairing its fortifications, and putting its house in order for the shock of battle. The well-intentioned Claiborne could not bring unity to its discordant population; but riding during these last days of the dull autumn along the road from Mobile to New Orleans was a horseman who had both the will and the power to silence opposition and to concentrate the resources of the place in the single process of saving it from the hands of the invader.

CHAPTER XI

A CHRISTMAS "FANDANGO"

IN 1814, Admiral Cochrane commanded the British fleet in American waters, and his chief duty was to supervise the blockade. In the spring, he was ordered to make observations along the coast of the Gulf of Mexico with a view to operations in Louisiana. In the summer he reported that 3,000 men with the co-operation of the Indians and discontented natives, could take Mobile and New Orleans. His language indicates that he had in mind an expedition through Mobile, which was also Jackson's conception of the military problem from the invader's standpoint. The English ministry were not so sanguine as Cochrane. In the expedition which they were about to send forth they engaged three times the troops suggested by the admiral and adequate naval protection. The army was drawn from several quarters. Ross's force which was operating against Washington and Baltimore made a part, and as a reward for his success in that service Ross was given command of the whole movement. Other troops were sent from Ireland and France, and some black regiments from the West Indies because they were believed to be adapted to the climate and to other conditions in Louisiana. The death of Ross before Baltimore made no change in the plans, except that the chief command was assigned to Lieut.-Gen. Sir Edward Pakenham, a man of recognized ability and brother-in-law of the Duke of Wellington. He was sent out in haste to overtake the expedition before it came to its destination, but in that he was not successful. He arrived on the shores of Louisiana, December 25th, after the advanced

stages of the attack were passed. Under him served Major-
Generals Gibbs, Keane, and Lambert, all men of tried courage
and experience, Keane being in command till the coming of
Pakenham.[1]

The leader was instructed to proceed from Jamaica, the
point of rendezvous, on November 20th, directly to New Orleans or indirectly through Mobile, as he saw fit. He was
informed that the object of the expedition was to command the
mouth of the Mississippi and by holding it to be in a position
"to exact its cession as a price of peace." He was instructed
to conciliate the native Louisianians, to assist them with arms
and provisions, to organize them into military bodies, and to
encourage them to commit themselves by an overt act against
the United States. He was not to allow them to think that they
would become permanent subjects of England, or an independent
state; but to lead them to believe that they would return to
the Spanish allegiance. He was also "by no means to excite
the black population to rise against their masters"; since the
whole Creole element, who were slaveholding in interests, would
be repelled if they believed that an insurrection of slaves was
planned.[2]

Jackson's earliest intimation of this danger was received
on August 27th, in Mobile, and was contained in letters from
Pensacola announcing the arrival of Colonel Nicholls at that
place. The boasts, proclamations, and other proceedings of
this faithful courier showed that something serious was planned
by his superiors, but all evidence pointed to Mobile as the point
of initial attack. This coincided with Jackson's view. "A real
military man," he said, "with a full knowledge of the geography
of that and this country [the surroundings of Mobile and New
Orleans] would first possess himself of that point, draw to

---

[1]Gibbs arrived with Pakenham.
[2]Adams, *History of United States*, VIII., 315.

his standard the Indians, advance by way of Fort Stephens, and march direct to the Walnut Hills, and by a strong establishment there and being able to forage on the country, he could support himself, cut off all supplies from above, and make this country [Louisiana] an easy conquest."[1] This opinion, given February 18, 1815, before controversy arose on the point, expresses Jackson's conception of the military situation from the British standpoint. It was also his opinion on December 10, 1814, when the British were concentrating off Cat Island, and he avowed it in a letter to the secretary of war.[2] Fort Stephens was on the lower Tombigbee, the Walnut Hills were the site of the present city of Vicksburg, and the intervening country was sparsely settled. The difficulty of supporting a force of several thousand men through this region was much underrated by Jackson.

The rumors from Pensacola reached Washington in due time and Monroe, secretary of war, forwarded them to Mobile with confirmatory information from other sources. Ten years later Jackson's political opponents charged that he loitered too long in Mobile, and that it was only Monroe's insistency that finally drove him out, just in time to save New Orleans. The truth is, Jackson took his own time at Mobile and left it entirely of his own volition. Moreover, all his advice from the secretary up to October 30th, was to the effect that the enemy would attack through that place. The remoteness of his situation and the confusion then existing in the war department left him largely to his own resources, and his is the credit or blame for the results.

It was late in September when the government became convinced that Louisiana was in danger. At once Monroe sent out calls for militia to the governors of Kentucky, Georgia, and

[1] Jackson to Monroe, February 18, 1815, Jackson Mss.
[2] Jackson to secretary of war, December 10, 1814, Jackson Mss.

Tennessee. From the first and second he required 2,500 men respectively, and from the third 5,000 in addition to the 2,500 which were called out in the preceding July for garrisons in the Creek country. Jackson was informed of these requisitions and wrote letters seconding them.[1]

The response was generous. Kentucky, although she had contributed liberally to the war in the Northwest, sent 2,228 men under General Adair.[2] Georgia sent an equal number under General McIntosh. Tennessee sent 2,800 mounted men under General Coffee, something less than two thousand infantry from the eastern counties under General Taylor, and as many more from the west — by way of the Mississippi — under General Carroll. Mississippi Territory furnished a battalion under Major Hinds 150 strong, and the Louisiana militia, including the volunteer organizations in New Orleans, furnished nearly three thousand.[3] Jackson's total force was a little more than fourteen thousand militia and 2,378 regulars. Of these he left all the Georgia and East Tennessee militia with nearly two thousand regulars and riflemen to protect Mobile and its surroundings. The remainder, about eleven thousand five hundred, he ordered to concentrate at New Orleans; and on November 22d, with a small escort, he started for that city. He rode deliberately, in order to inspect the approaches to the city. His judgment was that it was impossible for a hostile army to move from Mobile to New Orleans by the direct land route.

[1]Monroe to Jackson, September 27, and October 10, 1814; Monroe to Governor Blount, September 25, 1814; Jackson Mss.

[2]Smith, *Battle of New Orleans* (Filson Club Publishers), 179-202, where the muster rolls are given.

[3]In the summer of 1814, the secretary of war called for one thousand detached Louisiana militia to serve six months. November 20, Claiborne reported that they were raised and with others brought the total number of Louisianians in the field up to twelve hundred: Claiborne to Jackson, November 5 and 20, 1814, Jackson Mss. The San Domingo Negroes, Baratarians, and others mustered in before December 23, brought the number to at least sixteen hundred. When the British arrived the whole body of the state's militia was called out and by the end of December they were arriving in force. From the thirtieth until the fourth of the next month, the total accessions were twelve hundred, and many others came after the battle of the eighth. See Col. Robert Young to Jackson, January 1, 1815; Claiborne to Jackson, January 7, 1815, Jackson Mss. Gayarre, *Louisiana*, IV., 450, 458; Latour, *Historical Memoir*, 204. Most of the Louisiana militia were without arms.

When he left Mobile he still entertained the impression that it would be attacked. Three of his five regiments of regulars were ordered to garrison it, and the horse, under Coffee and Hinds, were stationed in such positions that they could easily be called back if needed. The first of these officers was sent to the neighborhood of Baton Rouge, forage being scarce in New Orleans; the second, commanding the Mississippi dragoons, except the company which was with Blue, was placed midway between the two cities so that he might be called to either at a moment's notice.

Coöperating with the army was a small naval force under Master-Commander Daniel Todd Patterson, a man of energy and good judgment.[1] It consisted of six of the gunboats which marked President Jefferson's policy of naval defense, and a number of smaller vessels. One of the gunboats was sent to Fort St. Philip, on the Mississippi,[2] and the others, five in number, were on Lake Borgne, to protect the city from an approach from that quarter and to keep open the inland water communications with Mobile. The gunboats were small. The five on Lake Borgne carried a total of twenty-three guns and 182 men. Besides these there were two vessels— a schooner, the *Carolina*, and a ship, the *Louisiana*—in the river before New Orleans. At Tchifonte, on Lake Pontchartrain, was an uncompleted flat-bottom frigate built to carry forty-two guns.[3] Work on it was stopped some months earlier, probably by the advice of Flournoy; and although both Jackson and Patterson urged that it be resumed, nothing was done in that direction. The vessel was now worse than useless; for it was necessary to send the *Ætna*, a brig much needed elsewhere, to

[1] The historians generally, even Latour, who was a military man and wrote in 1816, speak of Patterson as "commodore"; but his rank was master-commander, one grade lower than a naval captain. The rank of commodore was not created in America until 1862 and is a grade higher than that of captain. Jackson and other contemporaries call him "commodore."

[2] Latour, *Historical Memoir*, 74.

[3] Latour says forty-two; Reid and Eaton forty-four. Latour seems more reliable under the circumstances.

Tchifonte to protect the frigate, which was nearly ready for its armament.

It was in the morning of December 1st, that Jackson entered New Orleans, passing down the streets to the residence of a rich merchant where the governor, Master-Commander Patterson, and others waited to welcome him. The people of the city had heard much of his military achievements. To most of them a great general was distinguished in appearance, after the fashion of the recent French and Spanish officials. They were surprised and somewhat disappointed when there appeared a tall and emaciated figure, showing signs of recent severe illness, with a clean shaven and sallow face, and sandy hair just beginning to gray under his forty-seven years. He was clothed in a well-worn leather cap, a short Spanish cloak of old blue cloth, and great unpolished boots whose vast tops swayed uneasily around his bony knees. But his eyes were cool and penetrating, his mouth was always firm and in repose gentle, and his carriage was grave, dignified, and suggestive of mastery of self and of others. When they first saw him the people were disappointed. He seemed only another of the frontier flat-boatmen, of whose uncouthness they knew rather too much. But when they saw him and heard him speak their disappointment became enthusiasm. All accounts agree that he won the sympathy of the people of New Orleans on that first day of his visit. After the well-intentioned governor made his prolix speech of welcome, and after the general delivered his reply and heard it translated by Edward Livingston into French for the benefit of the Creoles he turned to business. First he reviewed the city militia composed of the uniformed companies under Major Plauché and the battalions of free men of color under Majors Lacoste and Daquin, complimenting both on their soldierly appearance. Then he went to dinner with Livingston, where he met a company of fashionable ladies and charmed them by his grave deference and natural courtesy. Rising from the table, he hurried off to meet his chief engineers and with them went carefully and exhaustively over the plans of the defenses. Two days later he began a tour of inspection, going first down the river as far as Fort St. Philip, where it was planned to give the enemy the initial check on this line of approach. He ordered two auxiliary batteries to be constructed to strengthen it and rode back to the city six days after he set out examining every mile of the way carefully. At once he departed for a similar inspection of the lake shore. At Chef Menteur, at the head of Lake Borgne, he ordered a new battery to be placed as additional protection to the Gentilly road. His quick and spirited manner of taking up the business before him made an excellent impression on the city, which for months had suffered from the confusion and the supineness of the authorities. It was not that he brought more technical skill to the situation—his orders were given by the advice of engineers, who were on the spot before his arrival. It was his mastery of the situation, through a forceful speech and a compelling will, which gave the people confidence and made them willing to obey his commands.

From this inspection, he concluded that the enemy would come by the river, and he believed that when the defenses there were strengthened as he ordered they would be unassailable. A few days after his arrival on the Mississippi the British fleet began to come into Pensacola Bay, and information was promptly sent to New Orleans. When he returned to the city from his first trip of inspection he learned that their ships were beginning to anchor off Cat and Ship Islands, at the entrance of Lake Borgne. He considered this but a ruse to turn his attention from the river, and went on with his inspection of works: nor had he yet given up his opinion that the enemy aimed at Mobile and by a movement into the interior would seize the Mississippi and isolate New Orleans.[1]

Writing to Coffee at his ease on December 11th, he said: "Your position is a favorable one to cover Amite, and prevent the enemy from advancing through Lake Maurapa, and up the Manshock [the Manchac pass]. The vessels of the enemy has made their appearance on the coast near Ship and Cat Islands, and the Contractors Vessels on their voyage to Mobile has returned. I expect this is a faint, to draw my attention to that point when they mean to strike at another. However I will look at them there and provide for their reception elsewhere." And then forgetting for a moment the scenes around him and turning in his mind back to Tennessee, he says: No news from home "since I saw you except I see in the Nashville *Gazette* that '*Packolett has beat the noted horse Doublehead with great ease.*'" Then again to military matters: "Keep your brigade ready for service at a moment's notice; We may, or we may not, have a fandango with Lord Hill, in the Christmas holidays. If so you and your Brave followers must participate in the frolic."[2]

On the afternoon of the thirteenth,[3] while he was still inspecting on the lakes, news came to the city that the enemy's vessels at Cat Island were greatly augmented, that they were supplied with gun barges suitable for operations on the lakes, and that it was no longer to be doubted that they were about to land from their present anchorage. On the thirteenth, Jackson was within easy communication with the city and must have received Patterson's news by the morning of the fourteenth; yet he took no steps that day to call down his forces from the

[1] Jackson to secretary of war, December 10, 1814, Jackson Mss.

[2] Jackson to Coffee, December 11, 1814, Jackson Mss. "Pacolet" belonged to Jackson, who had ordered that he should not be raced during the war. See James Jackson to Jackson, Nashville, November 27, 1814, Jackson Mss. The British ministry first intended to give the command of the expedition to General Lord Hill.

[3] Latour, *Historical Memoir*, 55.

upper country. He seemingly remained convinced that the assemblage off Cat Island was a ruse, and if this surmise be true he was utterly at sea in regard to the situation, which was, in fact, very grave. Within the city were no more than 1,500 armed men to be thrown against a landing party from the fleet, and the only means of checking a landing was the five gunboats on Lake Borgne.

The situation hardly assumed this form when even the hope from the gunboats was destroyed. These vessels were ordered to avoid a struggle on the lake and meet the enemy at the southern extremity of the Rigolets; but on the thirteenth, while retreating from too venturesome an approach to his fleet, they found themselves pursued by a large number of his barges. They sought to reach the designated spot, but becoming becalmed on the morning of the fourteenth were forced to anchor in line of battle and receive the attack of the enemy. Against them were brought forty-three barges each carrying a cannon, and three smaller boats without such armament, all manned by 1,200 men. Unable to maneuver and feeling themselves doomed to capture, the Americans fought as well as they could until their commander was badly wounded and struck his flag. They lost forty-five, killed and wounded; and the British, ninety-five.[1] The victors now had all the lake at their disposal. They seized the Isle aux Pois, east of the Rigolets, landed an advanced division on it, and explored the western shore of the lake for the best place to reach the environs of New Orleans.

The gunboats were taken at noon on the fourteenth, and it was the afternoon of the next day when the news reached New Orleans, forty miles away. Jackson hastened from Chef Menteur to the city. He was at last fully conscious of his danger, and from that moment he was all activity. A letter was hur-

---

[1] The report of the American commander is in Latour, *Historical Memoir*, Appendix, number 19; that of the British commander is in James, *Military Occurrences*, II. 523.

riedly sent to Coffee, twenty miles north of Baton Rouge, ordering him to march day and night till he reached headquarters and charging him to send messengers with like orders to Carroll and Thomas higher up the river and to Hinds at Woodville, Mississippi. Coffee heard the news gladly. On the seventeenth at four o'clock in the morning he wrote that he would march at sunrise and would be in New Orleans in four days if all went well. He took 1,250 of his men with him, all who were fit for duty, and in the early morning of the twentieth he arrived in New Orleans with 800 of them, leaving the others to follow as fast as they could, having covered 135 miles in a few hours more than three days.[1] Carroll arrived on December 21st, and about the same time came Hinds with 100 dragoons.

Jackson's problem was now to determine by which of the approaches from the lake the British would attempt to land. He concluded they would not try to pass Petites Coquilles with small boats, and this eliminated the idea of an approach by Lake Pontchartrain. He made another inspection of the shores of Lake Borgne and determined that they must come by Bayou Sauvage and Chef Menteur. This line of communication begins at the northern shore of the lake about fifteen miles from the Isle aux Pois and nine from the Rigolets. It leads through a marsh for ten miles, when the surrounding land becomes firm and opens into a plain around the village of Gentilly, five miles west of which was the city. It was on this elevated ground that Jackson expected to fight the battle. He sent thither all

---

[1] Of the two letters ordering Coffee down, one was from Robert Butler, adjutant-general, and was probably written on the fourteenth, although dated the fifteenth, since it says the British fleet appeared off Cat Island in force on the preceding evening. It is improbable, also, that a letter dispatched on the fifteenth reached Coffee, one hundred and twenty miles away, by the morning of the sixteenth when, as we know, Coffee knew of Jackson's summons. (Cf. John Hynes to Coffee, December 16, 1814, Jackson Mss.) The other letter was written by T. L. Butler, Jackson's aide, after the gunboats were known to be taken. Coffee called in his troopers and marched at dawn on the seventeenth. His command was much depleted by sickness and fatigue. His own letters to Jackson show that the story repeated by Reid and Eaton and by Jackson himself, that he marched to New Orleans in two days is erroneous. Cf. Coffee to Jackson, December 13, 17; Coffee to his contractors, December 16, 1814; and Jackson to Monroe, February 17, 1815; Jackson Mss, and Reid and Eaton, *Life of Jackson*, 29.

the troops he could spare, ordered additional redoubts and other works, and placed at the extremity of the line the battalion of free Negroes under Major Lacoste. Even after the foe landed elsewhere, he believed that they were attempting a ruse in order to divert his strength from Chef Menteur. He was as persistent in this notion as formerly in the belief that the assembling at Cat Island was a trick to deceive him; and he did not relinquish it till he saw three quarters of the British army actually before him on the Villeré and adjacent plantations.

One must approve every feature of the campaign of the British except their rash frontal attack on Jackson's lines on January 8th. Particularly skilful was their landing. Chef Menteur was too obvious: ten miles west of it was the mouth of Bayou Bienvenue, which the British writers call Catalin. Through somebody's neglect it was not obstructed by fallen timber, although Jackson early gave strict orders to that end for all bayous opening on the lakes. In this region the country between the river and the lake is of three kinds, high ground which borders the river and is a mile or less in width, cypress swamp lying cast of that about three miles wide, and still eastward a belt of trembling marsh called locally "prairies." The first of these belts is cultivated, and through it pass drainage canals which empty into the sinuous water courses in the swamps, which collecting into larger main channels make into the bayous. From the mouth of Bayou Bienvenue one may pass by a large tributary to the entrance of a canal which drains the Villeré plantation, lying on the river about nine miles from the city. The Bayou Bienvenue, therefore, offered a safe communication with the high ground adjoining the river at a point near New Orleans. Villeré's with the adjacent plantations offered a wider space of solid ground than that which bordered the Chef Menteur road. This space was to be the field of the battle.

Near the mouth of Bayou Bienvenue was a village of twelve

huts occupied by Spanish and Portuguese fishermen. These people proved traitors and came to an understanding with the British soon after the arrival of the fleet off Ship Island. On December 20th, they brought two English officers to their village, carried them up the bayou and canal till they were able to take a drink of water from the Mississippi. Their report pleased their superiors and no time was lost in hurrying on the advance.

On the twenty-first the Americans sent a picket of twelve men in one boat to the Spanish village. They found most of the inhabitants absent, spent that day and the next in watching the waters of the lake for signs of the enemy, and on the night of the twenty-second slept in fancied security with only one sentinel posted. Some time after midnight he heard a noise and awakened his comrades. In the dim moonlight they could make out five barges full of armed men, coming up the bayou. Not daring to fire on so many men they hid behind a house till the barges passed. Then they tried to get away in their boat by way of the lake in order to give information to the city. In their haste they attracted the attention of the intruders and all except one were seized. He after three days' wandering through the swamps found his way to Chef Menteur. The prisoners, on being questioned, assured their captors that there were 18,000 men in New Orleans and at the English Turn. The effect was to hasten the movement of the attacking party, and by four o'clock on the morning of the twenty-third the whole advanced division consisting of 1,688 rank and file were at the point where Villeré's canal emptied into the bayou, three and a half miles from the Mississippi. Landing in the canebrakes they rested for six hours and then resumed their journey. After an hour's marching through the soft soil on the banks of the canal they came to firmer ground. Stunted cypresses met their eyes, then orange trees appeared, and pushing through these they found open fields of cane stubble beyond which at a distance of from eight hundred to a thousand yards were the waters of the Mississippi. On the tilled plain were the houses of General Villeré's plantation, and in them was a company commanded by his son, a major of militia. With a sudden dash these were surrounded and the militia captured, although Major Villeré escaped by leaping out of a window and rushing to the river, where he found a boat in which he reached the opposite bank. When this was done it was about noon.

Villeré's plantation was on the public road leading to New Orleans and many other estates were near it, but all this movement, from midnight till noon, was without the opposition, or even the knowledge, of the Americans. The responsibility was primarily Major Villeré's, who failed to guard the bayou properly; but it was shared by Jackson, who ought not to have left so important a place in the hands of militia without adequate supervision by a trained officer. Up to this moment Jackson was hardly master of the situation. His military genius was of the kind that does one thing splendidly, hurling into it with superhuman energy both himself and all who were under him. It was not of the kind that organizes well and manages the most complex situation through mastery of details. It is interesting to think what would have happened had the British met Jackson in some open country where there was opportunity for maneuvering.

While the enemy made this advance to the Mississippi there was confusion and hurry in the city. Not knowing just where the blow would fall, it was, nevertheless, understood that it would be a severe one and that the most extraordinary efforts were necessary to sustain it. Both the governor and the general were apprehensive of the legislature. The city was believed to be full of British agents, and it was feared that they might persuade the assembly to take some ill-advised steps toward submission. Claiborne, in order to meet the emergency, took the unusual step of asking the legislature to adjourn itself for two or three weeks. The reply was not surprising: the assembly saw many reasons why it should continue to sit and it would not disperse. Then Jackson declared martial law in the following words:[1]

Major-General Andrew Jackson, commanding the Seventh United States military district, declares the city and environs of New Orleans under strict martial law, and orders that in future the following rules be rigidly enforced, viz. Every individual entering the city will report at the adjutant-general's office, and on failure to be arrested and held for examination.

No person shall be permitted to leave the city without a permission in writing signed by the general or one of his staff.

No vessels, boats or other crafts, will be permitted to leave New Orleans or Bayou St. John, without a passport in writing from the general or one of his staff, or the commander of the naval forces of the United States on this station.

The street lamps shall be extinguished at the hour of nine at night, after which time persons of every description found in the streets, or not at their respective homes, without permission in writing, as aforesaid, and not having the countersign, shall be apprehended as spies and held for examination.

ROBERT BUTLER,
Adjutant-General.

December 16, 1814.

This step was supported by a ringing proclamation, in which Jackson warned the citizens that there were spies in their midst and called for aid in arresting them.

In the meantime, the summoned troops were hastening to the danger point, Carroll making the best time. All the way down the river in flat-bottomed boats he drilled his men as well as he could, so that when they arrived on the twenty-first,

---

[1] Niles, *Register*, VII., 317.

they were not quite so raw as they would have been but for this foresight. They brought reinforcements to the number of 2,500. The Baratarians were sent out to their posts, the Louisiana militia, the uniformed companies of the city, and the free men of color in their two battalions — all were distributed at points believed to be threatened; many of them to the east of the city along the road to Chef Menteur, some others in the city itself where they could be used for emergency, and some others in the outlying posts. None of them were on the road which led from New Orleans to Villeré's plantation.

We have fortunately a letter from Jackson to one of his most intimate friends, Col. Robert Hays, of Nashville, which shows what grasp the writer had on the military situation at the moment when Keane's troops were pushing through the cane brakes along Villeré's canal. The letter runs:

SIR: Before this reaches you, you will have heard of the capture of our gunboats on the lakes, since which the British has made no movement of importance. The Fort at Petit Cocquil, they have not yet attacked. That is the only Barier between them and the entire peaceful possession of the lakes. They are said to be in great force. The citizens of this place, since my arrival, has displayed a great show of ardor, and una nimity. Genl. Coffee and Genl. Carroll have both arrived their Troops in good health for the climate and in high spirits, and have a hope should the British effect a landing at any point, I will be able to check them. The Kentuckians has not reached me, neither have I heard from them. I have not received a letter or paper from Tennessee since the last of October. I am anxious to know whether Mrs. Jackson has sailed from Nashville[1] under the expectation that she has, has been the reason why I have not wrote her. If she is still at home say to her the reason I have not wrote her, and say to her and my little son god bless them. I am more than anxious to see them.

[1]Mrs. Jackson was preparing to join her husband at headquarters when she learned that the British had landed, and on that account, she deferred her visit.

I send you for your perusal the orders and address to the citizens of this place. I hope under every circumstance, and let what will happen, you will hear that I have done my duty. *All well.*"[1]

The ink of this letter was hardly dry before travel-stained fugitives began to arrive at headquarters with the news that the foe was going into camp eight miles away. It was then 1:30 in the afternoon of December 23d. Immediately orders were issued to send as many troops as possible down the river road to face the enemy's position. If Jackson was at sea when expecting the British landing, now that they were before him and his problem was reduced to the simple task of meeting them on the field, he became the incarnation of energy. His decision was taken instantly. When the messenger finished telling of the arrival at Villeré's the general turned to some officers and said, "Gentlemen, the British are below: we must fight them to-night." Coffee, Plauché commanding the uniformed companies, Daquin with the battalion of St. Domingo Negroes, the 7th and 44th regulars, and Hinds's dragoons with two field-pieces, were assembled on the river road south of the city and hurried forward, Coffee's troops in the van. Commander Patterson was asked to send any available vessels down the river to coöperate in the proposed attack. Complying he embarked on the schooner *Carolina* and dropped down to a position opposite the British camp, the ship *Louisiana* following. They numbered, by the American reports, besides the men on the *Carolina*, 2,131. General Morgan, commanding a body of Louisiana militia, at English Turn — south of Villeré's — was directed to create a diversion during the night from that side.

About sunset the British advanced post noticed a body of

---

[1] Jackson to Colonel Robert Hays, December 23, 1814, Jackson Mss.

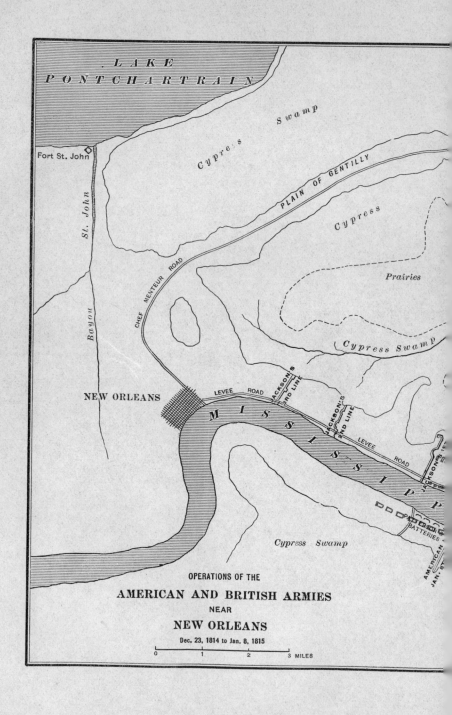

OPERATIONS OF THE

AMERICAN AND BRITISH ARMIES

NEAR

NEW ORLEANS

Dec. 23, 1814 to Jan. 8, 1815

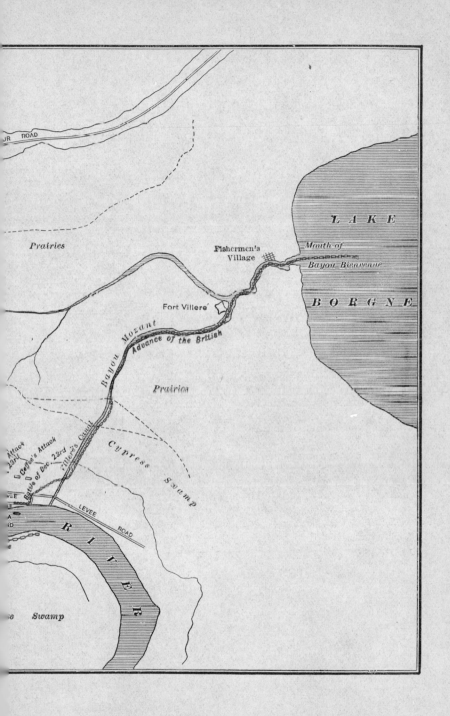

two hundred horse approaching on the road from the north. A part of them came within a hundred yards and wheeling in excellent form rode away; but one squadron charged with great boldness up to the picket and did not retire till it had received a volley with fatal effect. An English officer who was present gives us the following interesting statement of the impression it made on his comrades:

This was the first occasion, during the course of our Trans-Atlantic warfare, that the Americans had in any way ventured seriously to molest or threaten our posts, or shown the smallest disposition to act vigorously on the offensive. I cannot deny that it produced a curious effect upon us. Not that we experienced the smallest sensation of alarm. We held them in too much contempt to fear their attack; I question whether we did not wish that they would hazard one; yet we spoke of the present boldness, and thought of it too, as a meeting on which we had no ways calculated, and for which we could not possibly account. It had not, however, the effect of exciting an expectation, that the attempt would be renewed, at least in force; and though we unquestionably looked upon our position, from that moment, with a more cautious eye, we neither felt nor acted upon the supposition, that any serious danger would be incurred, till we ourselves should seek it.[1]

This frank avowal of the contempt in which they held their opponents goes far to explain the defeat which awaited Pakenham's soldiers. The force before them was unlike any other the British had met in America; but the difference was not so much due to the men as to the spirit infused into it by its leader. Jackson, by his personality, could have made in a short time a fighting machine out of any body of average American militia.

The British troops went into camp on the river bank near the centre of Villeré's plantation, at a point at which the levee

[1] *A Subaltern in America* (1833 ed.), 219.

and public road make an angle.   Half a mile north they
stationed a strong advanced guard on the road from New Orleans, which in all this region paralleled the river bank.   Still
farther in front they placed a picket guard on the river, and
from this point a series of such guards was extended at an acute
angle from the river till it reached the border of Villeré's plantation two thirds of a mile away.   Pickets were also placed on
the batture, or exposed bed of the river between the water and
the levee, which was from two hundred to three hundred
and fifty yards wide.   Their artillery consisted of only two
unused three-pounders.[1]   These arrangements made, the British
felt safe from attack, and as the weather was cold great camp
fires were lighted, which revealed their position plainly.

Jackson was before the enemy by sunset on this short winter
day.   Giving Coffee command of 732 men, including his own
dismounted riflemen, the Mississippi dragoons, and the Orleans
Rifle Company, he ordered him to move to the left and fall on
the enemy's front at a point midway between the advanced
guard and the main body.   The rest of the Americans were
held in readiness in front of the advanced guard, who were in
a position to be cut off from Keane's chief force and captured
or cut to pieces.   The *Carolina* and *Louisiana* were ordered
to coöperate from the river, and the former did good service.[2]
The fire from these vessels was to be the signal for the general
attack.

At seven o'clock the *Carolina* came up to the brink of the batture in front of the British camp at a distance of three hundred
yards.   The invaders took her for a trading ship and crowded over
the levee down to the water's edge to see what her business could
be.   Their brilliant camp fires behind them made them excellent targets for the gunners, who suddenly opened fire.   So

---

[1]Gayarre *History of Louisiana*, IV., 431.
[2]The *Louisiana* could not be brought up in time to take part in the battle.

great was the confusion that it was ten minutes before the British recovered themselves, seized their guns, and extinguished the fires. The schooner remained in her place and did so much damage during the engagement that the British were forced to keep well under the protection of the levee.

Soon after the schooner opened fire, the main body of the Americans under Jackson began to move against the advance guard of the enemy. At a distance of one hundred yards the fighting became general and was well sustained on both sides. Plauché's battalion of uniformed companies and Daquin's battalion of St. Domingo Negroes were assigned to a position on Jackson's left, but they were not able to come into it at the very beginning of the engagement. This left the American line shorter than that of the enemy, who tried to envelop it on his right flank. While the movement was progressing, he ran into Daquin first, and then Plauché, deploying in the dark, received a shock from their cool and persistent attack, and falling back, carried the whole line till it re-formed and stood again about three hundred yards in the rear of its first position.

In the meantime, Coffee, his men dismounted and deploying to the left, came into the position assigned, and closed in behind the portion of the enemy who were engaged with Jackson. In doing so, he met and drove back to their camp some of the British who were thrown out in front of their main body. Keeping ever to the right, he approached the rear of the advanced guard, who were prudently falling back. Coffee concluded that in the darkness it would not be safe to get between them and the main body, especially as to do so would draw him pretty close to the line of fire from the *Carolina*. He contented himself with moving so far to his right as to pass this body on their right, and take position in front of them where he was content to await developments.

It was now half-past nine, the fighting had continued for

two hours, the enemy were heavily reinforced and on the alert for other attacks, and Jackson concluded that the affair had yielded all the advantage possible. He drew off his men to a position six hundred yards north of the enemy and across the road to New Orleans to await daylight. The British spent the rest of the night in anxiety, posting double guards, and responding to the slightest alarm. The Americans lost, by their own report, 24 killed, 115 wounded, and 74 missing. Among the slain was Colonel Lauderdale, of Coffee's Tennessee riflemen, a brave officer and a loyal supporter of his leader. The British reported a loss of 46 killed, 167 wounded, and 64 missing.[1]

The British writers speak of this action as an American defeat. It is true that Jackson did not accomplish his announced purpose of driving the enemy from American soil; but he, nevertheless, achieved important results. The army acquired confidence in themselves and in their leader, they learned how to act together, and they lost some of their dread of British regulars. The British themselves found that they had before them another kind of opposition than they had met in America, with the result that they continued the advance slowly and cautiously and gave Jackson time to construct the fortifications without which Louisiana must have been lost. As a test of the superior fighting ability of the two sides the engagement proved nothing. Until the arrival of reinforcements near the close of the fighting, Jackson was in superior strength, both from actual numbers and from the presence of the *Carolina* and two guns which were served down the road during the entire action. The British seem not to have brought into use the small guns which were landed with their advance division.

The battle of the twenty-third proved what Jackson an-

---

[1]Jackson's report of this action is in Latour, *Historical Memoir*, Appendix, number 25. For losses see *Ibid*, No. 29. For the British report, see James, *Military Occurrences*, II., 529 and 532.

nounced to Coffee, a Christmas "fandango." It was an answer to a boast of the English admiral that he would eat his Christmas dinner in New Orleans. After it each side realized that there was serious fighting ahead, and each began to make the best preparations for a contest which would bring out its utmost strength.

CHAPTER XII

JANUARY THE EIGHTH, 1815

WHEN Jackson was fighting the battle of December 23d, he was still uncertain about the plans of the enemy. He feared that Keane was attempting a ruse in order to draw the Americans to Villeré's while the main body of the British landed at Chef Menteur and seized the city. Not daring, under these circumstances, to take all his troops with him, he ordered Carroll's 2,000 with three regiments of city militia to hold the road to Chef Menteur, at the eastern extremity of which Lacoste was stationed with his battalion of city Negroes. In fact, Jackson suspected that Lacoste was already taken; but soon after the battle he had definite news from that officer, who reported that the main body of the enemy were passing his position and entering Bayou Bienvenue. Convinced that no ruse was intended, Jackson at once ordered half of Carroll's force to his aid. His first impulse was to renew the fight at dawn, but on reflection he "determined not to play so deep a game of hazard as to attack them in their strong position,"[1] but to select a protected situation and await battle. There was a midnight conference with the engineers and it was decided to establish defenses at McCartey's old mill race, otherwise called Rodriguez's canal, two miles north of the scene of the night battle. It was no more than a dry ditch ten feet wide,

---

[1]From a fragmentary *Journal* of the battle of New Orleans in Jackson's own hand, covering the period from December 23, 1814, to January 19, 1815. It seems to have been prepared some time after the battle but it was certainly before the death of Major Reid, in the winter of 1815-16. The sheets are missing which deal with events between December 28 and January 25 and from January 7 and to the battle on the west bank on January 8. It is among the Jackson Mss. in the Library of Congress.

running three quarters of a mile from river to swamp, but it was the best natural protection in the neighborhood, and it was thought that with batteries placed at intervals it could be held against the enemy.

The withdrawal of the troops began at four o'clock in the morning of the twenty-fourth. They broke away from the left, Coffee first, then Carroll, who was already on hand, and last the regulars. At sunrise they held the mill race, the regulars next the river and Coffee next the swamp, in the same order as they were formed before the British a few hours earlier. Hinds's dragoons and a small company of horse from Feliciana Parish were left to observe the enemy.

The British knew nothing of this movement but remained huddled on the field during the night and offered battle early in the morning. When no attack was made on them they withdrew, at eight o'clock, to their camp. All day reinforcements were hurried forward from the fleet, and by the morning of the twenty-fifth all the army which had arrived at the anchorage was landed. An old levee paralleled the new one at a distance of 300 yards and between the two the soldiers found some protection from the fire of the *Carolina* and *Louisiana* on the river and from the threatened attacks of Coffee's horsemen whom Jackson sent to annoy them by land. Here Pakenham found them when he arrived on the morning of the twenty-fifth. The first thing he did after taking command was to move them to the plain, placing a large body near the cypress swamp and extending his outposts across the intervening space to the river. By this time the two armies faced each other at an interval of two miles, one preparing to march straight on the city, the other utilizing every hour given it in erecting the works which would defeat such an advance.

Pakenham was an able general but a methodical one. With 5,500 troops in his camp he might have seized the American line, now barely more than a skeleton. But the *Carolina* and *Louisiana* annoyed his right flank, and he determined to silence or drive them away before he moved. By great exertion he got batteries in place during the night of the twenty-sixth and opened on them on the following morning with shell and hot shot. The second discharge of the latter fired the *Carolina*, which could not be taken away on account of contrary winds and a strong current. The batteries played on her for an hour, when she blew up. Meantime, the *Louisiana* with difficulty was towed out of range and saved. These operations delayed the British advance four days and gave the Americans a valuable opportunity to construct works of defense.

When Jackson fell back on the twenty-fourth his first care was to order heavy guns and entrenching tools from New Orleans. At 1 P. M., fifty spades and mattocks arrived and ground was immediately broken for the first battery. The general watched it with feverish anxiety, expecting at any moment to receive the advance of the British. At four o'clock he learned that they were being heavily reinforced and that they kept in close line formation. He concluded that they would not come at once and redoubled his effort on the works, sending to the neighboring plantations for all available implements. Three times each day he rode down the lines and kept a part of his staff on them constantly. Although suffering from serious illness he did not sleep for three days and nights while the entrenchments were going through their first stages. He was "determined there to halt the enemy," as he himself said, "or bury himself on the ruins of that defense."[1]

Among Jackson's manuscripts is a fragmentary journal in which he gives us a view of the events of these trying days. In it we have a glimpse of the anxious haste with which were utilized the four days of grace which Pakenham fortunately

---

[1] Jackson's fragmentary *Journal*, Jackson Mss.

allowed. During the night of the twenty-fourth the two six-pounders which served in the night battle were put in position six hundred yards from the river, being battery five on Latour's plan.[1] The next morning, the twenty-fifth, Hinds reported the British still in camp and fortifying on their flank. This seemed a good omen, and every effort was made to complete the three batteries then being constructed. The twenty-sixth, Hinds reported that the enemy during the night were busy bringing up heavy artillery, which indicated that they were not yet pre-pared to move forward. During the day three American batteries were completed, being numbers two, three, and four, commanded respectively by Lieutenant Norris, Captain Domi-nique, and Lieutenant Crawley. The morning of the twenty-seventh, Hinds reported that the British were still in camp but showed signs of activity. Early on the twenty-eighth he gave notice that they were forming in columns as if to advance. His messenger was hardly gone when the dragoons were attacked in force and compelled to withdraw behind the American lines. Following closely on their heels came the whole British army in two compact columns, one near the river and the other march-ing parallel to it near the swamp. The sight of the American works surprised them, but they approached within cannon shot. The river column was immediately exposed to a heavy fire from the batteries on the line and from the *Louisiana* and floating batteries on the river: it was glad to seek any cover which offered and remained till evening in an uncomfortable position next to the levee from which it was brought with some loss and the appearance of a retreat. The other column deployed through the swamp where it encountered Coffee's riflemen and fell back when he prepared to outflank it. Pakenham was unwilling to try to carry the works and encamping at nightfall out of range of Jackson's cannon, sent for his great guns and

---

[1] Latour, *Historical Memoir*, map number 7.

prepared to erect batteries with which he could beat down his opponent's defenses. At that time the American earthworks, if we may believe a British eyewitness, were no more than "a few abattis with a low mound of earth thrown up in the rear."[1] Near the swamp they were weakly protected by the batteries, and it seems probable that a strong column massed here under the protection of the woods could have brushed away any defense Coffee and Carroll could have offered. It was the last opportunity the British had to break through: when their batteries were established, Jackson had strengthened his own works until they were impregnable.

For three days after the demonstration of the twenty-eighth, the cautious and methodical Pakenham gave himself to the task of erecting batteries in front of Jackson's lines. They began at the river, 700 yards from the Americans, and the first battery, containing seven light, long-ranged guns,was brought to bear on the river and the opposite shore where Commander Patterson had erected a battery. The Americans learned from deserters that hot shot were continually ready in these batteries for the *Louisiana*, if she should come within range. Facing Jackson's lines were four batteries with seventeen guns, eight eighteens, four twenty-fours, and five howitzers and field-pieces probably of twelve- and nine-pound capacity. It is estimated from the best sources that they threw a broadside of as much as 350 pounds of metal.

The British delay gave Jackson an opportunity to increase his artillery strength. On the twenty-eighth he had five guns in position, on the first of January fifteen. Three of these, one twenty-four and two long twelves, were on the west bank of the river, opposite the British batteries at a distance of three quarters of a mile. They were taken from the *Louisiana* and under Patterson's command did important service on January 1st.

[1] *Subaltern in America* (edition 1833), 235.

On the east bank the twelve guns were placed in eight batteries, thirty-twos, twenty-fours and smaller pieces. Together
they threw a broadside of 226 pounds.[1]

At 8 o'clock on New Year's morning these two lines of cannon
began the best sustained artillery engagement of the war. The
British were the attacking party, their object being to dismount
the batteries so that the waiting infantry might go through the
line. They had the opportunity to dismount, if they could,
the opposite batteries one at a time by concentrating their
fire. If they did not do so within a reasonable time their attack
was a failure. The task of the Americans was to sustain the
fire of their opponents, and in this respect they had the advantage
of better earthworks, because they had longer time to construct
them. They sought also to disable the opposing batteries and
drive them from the attack. The infantry of the two sides remained, for the most part, inactive during the battle.

The British had great confidence in their artillerists, who now
opened vigorously and incautiously, sending their shot for a
time too high and thus wasting much of the ammunition which
was brought from the fleet with great difficulty. The Americans
began slowly, observing the effect of their fire and seeking the
proper range. As they found it their fire grew stronger till
in the course of an hour it became so accurate and penetrating
that the British were surprised and forced to admit its superi-
ority. Some of their cannon were dismounted, and five were
reported as abandoned on the field. By noon most of their
batteries were silent, but their guns nearest the river were able
to keep up a response at intervals till three in the afternoon.
The British used hogsheads of sugar in their works, which proved
to have slight power of resistance. To this they attributed the
failure. In the night they withdrew their artillery, having lost

[1]This statement of artillery strength is taken from map five in Latour, *Historical Memoir;* his statement in
the text (page 147), is slightly different, where he omits the two four-pounders and includes a howitzer in
battery number one, making a total weight of metal of 224 pounds.

something less then seventy-five men. "Such a failure in this boasted arm," said Admiral Codrington with a tinge of professional jealousy, "was not to be expected, and I think it a blot in the artillery escutcheon."[1] But we must not demand the impossible. The failure was due to the resistance of Jackson's earthworks and the excellence of his gunnery.

The Americans suffered little. In the cheeks of the embrasures of their batteries bales of cotton were placed, which were knocked out of position by the enemy's shot to the confusion of the gunners.[2] Three guns were somewhat damaged, two caissons were exploded, and thirty men were killed or wounded — a small price to pay for the knowledge that American gunners could meet their English brethren on equal terms. Jackson was satisfied with his success. Till nightfall the British guns lay in the empty batteries, but he made no attempt to bring them off. He realized that it behooved him to be cautious. His trenches and his army were the only defenses against conquest. It was for his antagonist to decide what the next move should be.

Pakenham's decision was duly made. He planned to throw to the west of the river a body of troops large enough to seize Patterson's guns which he would turn on Jackson's army on the east side, while with his main force he stormed the formidable works which sheltered the Americans. The movement was well designed, and if carried into effect with precision would be a dangerous one for Jackson. But the event showed that it was not easy to make the attack on the west bank at the right moment for coöperation with the assault on the east.

The experiences of the past fortnight had given the British

---

[1] *Life of Codrington* I., 334.
[2] Much has been said by later writers of this incident, which contemporaries barely mention, Reid and Eaton seem to say that Jackson continued to use cotton bales in his earth-works till after January 8, *Life of Jackson*, 357. Jackson, on the other hand, said in his old age, when his memory was entirely reliable, that no cotton bales were in his works. See Parton, *Jackson*, III., 633.

greater respect for the resistance of the Americans, and their general was disposed to move cautiously. Major-General Lambert was daily expected with the 7th and 43d regiments numbering together 1,570 men, and it was decided to await their arrival. Colonel Thornton, who led brilliantly the advance at Bladensburg, was appointed to command the movement on the west bank. To put him across the river, orders were given to dig Villeré's canal deep enough to carry the ships' barges, and on the night of the sixth the whole army by shifts labored silently to accomplish this vast undertaking. The boats might have been transported on rollers with less labor; for they were lighter than the artillery which the men had dragged up, but Pakenham preferred the canal since it would make it easier to conceal the movement of the boats, and, in order to make the deception surer, he commanded troops to maneuver in front of the canal while the boats were being moved. All this precaution was unnecessary; for, on the seventh, Patterson from the opposite side observed all that was done and understood its significance. It was not until January 6th, that Lambert arrived in camp and gave the occasion for the final advance. On the seventh, fifty boats were ordered to be placed on the Mississippi for the embarkation of Thornton's command at nightfall.

These activities gave Jackson an opportunity to make further preparations for meeting his foe. The cannonade on the first showed that his works were not thick enough and they were ordered strengthened. To his men it seemed a hardship, this eternal digging, which might as well be left to the Negro slaves: the men came to fight, not to build fortifications. One of the battalions refused point-blank. Jackson, alarmed at this symptom of mutiny, sent for the officers of the discontented organization and told them plainly that he was prepared to take the most energetic measures if the men persisted in disobedience. The officers were impressed by his manner and assured him there would be no more trouble, and the promise was kept.[1]

On January 5th, Major Peire suggested that a bastion be placed on the levee at the right and in front of the line to rake the flank of a charging column. Jackson objected on the ground that it would obstruct his fire, but yielded when Colonel Hayne, whose opinion he valued highly, seconded Peire's opinion. It was against his judgment that he gave in and it was, as he says, "for the first time in my life."[2] The event tended to justify his opinion. The bastion was easily seized by the British on the eighth; for its two six-pounders and small company of defenders were not able to resist the force concentrated against it; and retaking it was expensive.

January 2d, General John Adair rode into Jackson's camp with the cheering news that the expected Kentuckians were near at hand. Two days later they arrived, 2,268 in all, commanded by Maj.-Gen. John Thomas. They were badly armed, two thirds having no guns of any kind. Seven hundred and fifty, only 500 of whom had muskets, were stationed in the rear of Carroll's men as a support. They were under the command of Brig.-Gen. John Adair. The rest of the Kentuckians were placed on Jackson's second line at Dupree's plantation. Although strenuous efforts were made to get arms they were only slightly successful, and these good troops were nearly useless in the battle which was about to begin. But on January 7th, Adair armed 400 more of his men with guns he got in New Orleans and sent them to the advanced line. On the eighth, therefore, 1,100 Kentuckians fought by the side of Carroll's Tennesseeans.

Jackson's lines of defense were three and consisted of three parapets, each extending from the river to the swamp. The

[1] Jackson's fragmentary *Journal*, Jackson Mss.
[2] From Jackson's fragmentary *Journal*, Jackson Mss.

first was five miles from the city along Rodriguez's canal, the second two miles north of this at Dupree's plantation, and the third at Montreuil's, a mile and a quarter nearer New Orleans. The second and third lines were designed for rallying points in case it should be necessary to abandon the first. As no such necessity arose, this description is concerned with the details of the first line only.

When Jackson took possession of Rodriguez's canal it was a dry ditch, twenty-five feet wide and four or five feet deep. By cutting the levee a quantity of water was let into it, but the quick subsidence of the river left it very shallow. Thirty yards behind the canal a palisade of fence pales and other boards was made and the soil was banked against it in the rear. The supervision of the engineers was not strict, and the citizen soldiers of the various corps followed their own ideas, with the result that the parapet when completed was very irregular in height and width. In some parts it was twenty feet wide at the top, and in others it was hardly strong enough to stop a cannon-ball. Everywhere it was as much as five feet high and in some places higher. The batteries were placed in three groups, one bearing on the approach along the river road, one covering the centre of the plain, and the other covering the approach along the edge of the swamp. Number one was seventy feet from the river with the bastion a short distance in front and to the right, number two was ninety yards farther east, number three was fifty yards beyond that, and number four twenty yards farther. These made the first group. Number five was 190 yards beyond number four, and number six about thirty-six yards farther, and these made the second group. Number seven was 190 yards beyond number six, and number eight — the crippled brass howitzer — was sixty yards still farther, and these made the third group. Fifty yards beyond number eight the line plunged into the woods, here not impassable, for 750 yards and then bent backward at right angles to its former direction until at the distance of 200 yards it ended in an impracticable swamp. The part within the woods had no batteries and was only thick enough to withstand rifle shots. Whenever necessary, the parapet was provided with a banquette.[1]

Besides the artillerymen, the troops behind the line consisted of the 7th regiment next the river and from that point in order Plauché's battalion, Lacoste's and Daquin's battalions of Negroes, the 44th regiment, General Carroll's command supported by Adair 400 yards in the rear, and Coffee's command which guarded the lines from the point at which it entered the woods, to the end. The total strength of these various bodies was 3,989 men.[2] Behind the line were 230 cavalry, in four small groups; and along the edge of the woods were posted 250 Louisiana militia to prevent surprise in that quarter. Four hundred yards behind the line was placed a strong row of sentinels to prevent any soldier leaving the line without permission. In front of the line at a distance of 500 yards were the outposts. In this excellent position Jackson awaited the attack which various signs and bits of information led him to expect on the eighth of January.

The point at which Pakenham proposed to break this defense was at battery number seven, which could be approached within two hundred yards with some protection from the woods. In front of this position he formed a column of 2,150 men under the command of Major-General Gibbs, supporting it on the right by a regiment of West Indian Negroes, 520 strong, with direction to advance through the woods and occupy Coffee's attention, breaking his lines if possible. While Gibbs led this column in the charge on the right, a second column consisting of 1,200 men under Major-General Keane was formed to advance

---

[1] Latour, *Historical Memoir*, 145.

[2] This estimate is based on Latour, *Historical Memoir*, 150, and is not far from the estimate made by Jackson two years after the battle, when he was in his controversy with Adair.

along the road by the edge of the river, making a demonstration in force against Jackson's right and drawing his fire, while Gibbs did the real work of carrying the line. A third column of 1,400 men under Major-General Lambert was held in reserve near the centre of the field. During the night of the seventh, six eighteen-pounders were thrown forward to one of the redoubts erected for the artillery battle of the first and played on the American line during the attempted assault. Gibbs's and Keane's columns were ordered to form two hours before dawn on the eighth, and it was planned to hurl them against the Americans while it was still dark enough to conceal their movements. Pakenham hoped that the attack might take his opponent by surprise, but in that he was to be disappointed. Had no external agency informed Jackson of what was coming, his sleepless activity would have prevented a surprise.

In accurate coöperation with this assault were to be Thornton's operations on the west bank. With 1,400 men, 200 of whom were seamen and 520 of whom were blacks from the West Indies, he was directed to embark by nightfall on the seventh, cross the river to a point three miles below the American defenses, thence march in the night up the river, seize Patterson's batteries, and await the signal for the attack on the east bank. On getting it he was to turn Patterson's captured guns on Jackson's flank with all possible energy. It was a well arranged plan; for if at the moment of crisis in his front Jackson should find himself galled by his own guns from the west, the effect could be little less than demoralizing.[1]

Thornton's success, however, depended on accurate coöperation and this proved to be impossible. The capricious Mississippi suddenly fell leaving only two feet of water in the precious canal and the boats had to be dragged along slowly by the men. The caving of the banks stopped some of the largest ones and

---

[1] *Subaltern* (edition 1833,) page 257, James, *Military Occurrences*, II., 374-380.

that created further delay. It was three o'clock before Thornton pushed off with a third of his force, and when he landed unopposed on the opposite side he heard the reports of the British batteries which opened the battle. It was nearly three hours before he could come within striking distance of Patterson's guns.

But not all of the delay was with Thornton. Pakenham had the misfortune to appoint the 44th regiment to lead Gibbs's column. The selection is unaccountable; for it was notorious in the army that Lieutenant-Colonel Mullins, then in command, was incapable, and if Pakenham did not know it, the fault was his own. Fascines made of bundles of sugar cane with ladders were collected behind the place designated for the formation of the charging column, and the 44th was ordered to take them up as they proceeded to the head of the division. When they arrived they had neither fascines nor ladders, and it was time for the assault to be made. Three hundred men were hurried back to get them, leaving the 44th at the head of the column with 127 men. As the moments elapsed, the dawn began to appear and all the advantage of a concealed attack was lost. Through this the troops became impatient and uneasy under the American cannonade which then began and the signal was given for the attack before the formation of the 44th could be restored. With this element of confusion at the head of the column Gibbs's advance lost the precision which was necessary in the severe ordeal to which Jackson's deadly fire subjected it. The men forgetting their duty to rush the works with the bayonets began to fire, the detail of the luckless 44th, rushing up with fascines and ladders, threw down their burdens and began to fire likewise, and the advance became a wavering, confused mass.

Gibbs was now in despair. All his commands were wasted, his column recoiled, and he rushed up to Pakenham a short distance in the rear exclaiming, "The troops will not obey me; they will not follow me!" Gibbs turned and dashed to the head of the column and Pakenham, his hat in his hand and shouting encouragement to his men, followed on horseback. Two hundred yards from the parapet the latter's horse was killed and the rider was wounded. He hardly mounted another when a grapeshot brought him to the ground and he was borne to the rear in a dying condition. Gibbs reached the head of the column which was now rallying and carried it forward up to the very lines of his opponents, but in the deadly fire from their rampart he fell mortally wounded within twenty yards of the canal. At the same moment Keane was severely injured and when the soldiers saw their three leaders carried off the field, they lost courage and fell back. Lambert coming up with reserves had not the hardihood to repeat the costly attempt.

Meantime, Keane on the left flank had been in action. With the signal for battle his brigade advanced along the river road, driving the sentinels so rapidly that his advanced companies rushed the bastion before its defenders could fire more than two rounds at them. Had the whole column now followed with vigor, the result might have been disastrous for the Americans; but mindful that his duty was merely to make a demonstration, Keane held his men back, while the Americans rallied and drove, out the captors of the bastion. His main column was halting at a respectful distance from the American fire. Seeing the plight of Gibbs's division near the woods, he obliqued across the interval to their assistance. It was rashly considered but bravely done in the face of the American fire. It accomplished nothing: Keane himself was severely wounded at the brink of the canal and his troops fell back with the others. The charge began at six: at half past eight, the fire of the musketry ceased and at two the cannonade ended.[1]

[1] For the details of the British charge see Lambert's report, James, *Military Occurrences*, II., Appendix, number 96; also the testimony of Majors Tylden and McDougal quoted in the same, pages 375 to 379; *Subaltern*, chapter 21; Gleig, *Campaigns in America*, 323-7; Latour, *Historical Memoir*, 154-164; and Reid and Eaton, *Jackson*, 365-70. *Subaltern* alone, mentions Keane's oblique movement, but he does it so explicitly that it is impossible to ignore him.

But for the confusion in Gibbs's column the British charge was made splendidly. It was received by the Americans with equal courage and without confusion. All night they lay on their arms in two equal shifts which relieved one another at the ramparts. The first clearing of the horizon at dawn revealed the enemy drawn up in line more than four hundred yards in front of the ditch. The American batteries opened at once, while the British gave the signal for the charge. With grim determination and some admiration the backwoods riflemen saw the red line narrow itself into a compact column sixty men broad and start at double quick for that part of the works which was defended by Carroll and Adair. They had ample time for preparations and concentrated their forces at the danger point in several ranks which fired and loaded alternately. At easy musket range the American infantry delivered a murderous fire, shaking the column, while the batteries, loading with grape and canister, ploughed wide lanes through the compact mass. The roll of musketry was like continuous peals of thunder. The first onslaught lasted twenty-five minutes, when the column recoiled to its original position, where it was reformed and brought back. Again the Tennesseeans and Kentuckians received it with a hail of musket-balls and grape-shot. A few of the attackers crossed the canal, probably two hundred, and endeavored to climb the slippery sides of the parapet. Some succeeded, only to be killed or captured on the top, and others remained in comparative safety at the bottom till they rejoined their retreating colleagues. When the smoke of battle cleared away, a broad space before the seventh battery was red with the prostrate forms of British soldiers. "The ground," says *Subaltern*, "was literally covered with dead; they were so numerous that to count them seemed impossible." They were[1] counted, however, the dead and wounded

---

[1]Edition 1833, page 262.

on the east bank, and the number was 1,971. Jackson's loss on this side was six killed and seven wounded. Among the British casualties were one lieutenant-general, two major-generals, eight colonels and lieutenant-colonels, six majors, eighteen captains, and fifty-four subalterns. This excessive proportion of the officers engaged shows the excellence of the frontier marksmanship.

On the west bank the battle went otherwise. Jackson was accustomed to concentrate his energies on one thing at a time. While he gave himself to driving the British from Pensacola, he neglected New Orleans, although he might have done much good by riding thither at least once while he waited for Coffee. In the same manner he gave his attention to the east bank and left the west side to others. It does not appear that he was once on that side during the sixteen days that the British were pushing their way toward the city. He left the defense there to Maj.-Gen. David Morgan, of the Louisiana militia, a man of little military experience or ability, and gave him a body of militia who had never seen service of any kind. And although the river was only three quarters of a mile wide at this place no boats were provided for crossing so as to allow means of quick reinforcements. On January 7th, Morgan had 550 militia, when it was known that he would be attacked during the night. To reinforce him Jackson in the afternoon ordered 500 of the unarmed Kentuckians to proceed to the west bank by way of the city, where they were expected to get some arms which the mayor was retaining for an emergency. In the city they learned that Adair got these arms earlier in the day, but after some delay they got seventy muskets at the naval station which, with some inefficient arms they had before, made 170 who had guns. The rest did not feel called upon to hurry into danger without arms and went into camp a little south of the city. The armed ones, under command of Colonel Davis, proceeded and came to Morgan's lines at 4 o'clock in the morning of the eighth. They had marched in twelve hours from Dupree's line to Morgan's line, a distance of eight miles, not enough to exhaust them, but under such conditions that they were tired and discouraged. Morgan received them gladly, and keeping the larger part of his Louisiana troops in his line sent the Kentuckians at once farther down the river to meet the enemy. It was not a cheerful detail to men who were expecting an opportunity to rest, but they departed without protest.

Earlier in the night Morgan sent Major Arnaud, with 100 militia down the river road to prevent the landing of the British. Finding no enemy on the bank he bivouacked his command at midnight three miles from Morgan and placed a single sentinel on the road southward from it. At dawn Thornton with 600 men and three gun-barges on the river manned by about a hundred sailors moved northward as rapidly as possible. They soon came upon Arnaud's faithful sentinel, who gave his comrades fair warning of their danger and enabled them to escape in safety. A mile from Morgan they joined the Kentuckians under Colonel Davis, who took command of both bodies, formed them on a canal, and awaited Thornton's attack. It came promptly with an attempt to turn the right, where Arnaud was placed. The Louisianians were thrown into confusion and fled incontinently, so demoralized that very few of them saw further service during the day. Davis was forced to fall back, and he joined Morgan who assigned him to a place on his right flank. Thornton followed aggressively, annoying the Americans both on land and from his three gun-barges, which continually raked the bank with grape-shot.

Morgan's line, on the opposite side of the river and a mile southward of Jackson's line, was badly located. It began at the southern end of Patterson's batteries, which covered nearly a mile of the bank, and ran with a canal from the river to the swamp, a distance of 2,000 yards. To hold such a line properly would require 2,000 men. It was selected against the advice of Jackson's engineer, who pointed out a position half a mile northward where the plain was only half as wide. But that position would leave half of Patterson's batteries south of the line; and since Morgan decided after conferring with Patterson, it is not unfair to assume that the desire to protect the batteries had something to do with Morgan's decision. Entrenchments were thrown up on the line for 200 yards from the river, and in this part were placed one twelve-pounder and two six-pounders with that part of the militia which remained after Arnaud's flight. This left 1,800 yards undefended, and when Davis arrived about eight o'clock, hard pressed by Thornton, he was ordered to take position upon it. Between him and the militia was an interval of 200 yards, his own command of less than 200 men was stretched out to cover 300 yards, and the rest of the line to the swamp was without defense except for a picket guard of eighteen men. The whole force was a little over 600, some of whom were badly armed.

Thornton was as quick as he was energetic. Seeing Morgan's exposed right he determined to turn it. He sent a part of the 85th regiment to make this flank movement by way of the woods and out of range of any guns which Patterson or Morgan could bring to bear on them. With another part of his force he made a feint along the road, and with still another sought to enter the gap between Davis and the militia. The Kentuckians stood well for a time, but realizing that they were about to be surrounded, withdrew from their position, leaving the militia exposed on their right with the result that these also retreated. Both Morgan and Patterson expected that the batteries of the latter would protect the line, but in the actual conflict it was seen that the defenders of the line so obstructed the fire that they could not be used on an enemy approaching from the south. Thornton's success on the line forced Patterson to withdraw. He had time merely to spike his long-range guns, which had served so well in annoying the enemy on the east bank, and to withdraw his gunners. Thus it happened that about the time the attack on the east side was a failure that on the west was completely successful. Thornton pursued the retreating Americans for two miles. Holding the west bank for a mile above Jackson's line the British were now in a position to force him out of his position, had they been disposed to follow Thornton's success.

Fortunately for the Americans, the British were satisfied with the situation. They had suffered too much on the east bank to utilize their success on the west, and Major-General Lambert, who was now in command, after finding that it would take 2,000 troops to hold what Thornton had won — which Jackson tried to hold with 600 — ordered the left column to recross the river during the night. Thus ended an engagement in which Jackson lost six killed and wounded, sixteen pieces of artillery, and the key to his first line of defense. It cost the enemy seventy-three killed and wounded, and Thornton was among the latter. The entire losses for the day were for the British 2,137 and for the Americans seventy-one, fifty of which were sustained in a sortie from Jackson's line.[1]

Responsibility for the disaster on the west bank rests on Morgan and Patterson, who adopted an impossible line of defense, and on Jackson, who was ignorant of the conditions there and who failed to send enough troops to hold it. For two weeks 1,000 of Carroll's men had lain on the Chef Menteur road in the unwarranted expectation that the enemy would divide his force and carry that approach before it could be strengthened from the American lines on the river. Had these Tennesseeans

[1]For the battle of the west bank see Latour, *Historical Memoir*, 164-176, Reid and Eaton, *Jackson*, 373-378, Gayarre, *Louisiana*, IV., 478-496, Smith, *The Battle of New Orleans*, (Filson Club Publications, number 19), 89-121, Jackson's and Patterson's reports in Latour, *Historical Memoir*, Appendix, number 29, Thornton's and Lambert's reports, *Ibid*, number 66, and in James, *Military Occurrences*, Appendix, numbers 96 and 97.

been ordered to join Morgan on the afternoon of the seventh, the story of the battle would probably have been different.[1]

Jackson did not recognize this responsibility and, with both Morgan and Patterson, placed it on the detachment of Kentuckians. In the moment when Gibbs and Keane were repulsed, the commander-in-chief, standing on the levee by his line, saw through the mists the maneuvers of Thornton a mile and a half away. Events immediately in front of him gave him confidence and he waited to see a like success on the west bank. To his disappointment the flashes of the guns through the fog revealed the retreat of the Kentuckians and Louisianians. "At the very moment," runs his report, "when the entire discomfiture of the enemy was looked for, with a confidence amounting to certainty, the Kentucky reinforcements, in whom so much reliance had been placed, ingloriously fled, drawing after them, by their example, the remainder of the forces." This was his official indignation. His unofficial wrath burst out in violent abuse that morning on the levee, as he saw the men falling back. He ordered General Humbert, distinguished in the French army of Napoleon but now serving as a volunteer private in the American ranks, to take 400 men, cross the river, and recover the lost position at any cost. Humbert obeyed with pleasure, but on the other side found that some of Morgan's officers objected to serving under a man who was not a citizen, and as Jackson had neglected to give him written authority for assuming command he returned in disgust. The withdrawal of Thornton made it possible for the Americans to reoccupy their former position, where a better line was established and Patterson's batteries were remounted in a better location.

At noon of the eighth there was a Bengal from the enemy

[1] Gayarre, *Louisiana*, IV., 422, and Jackson's fragmentary *Journal*, December 23. Jackson's assertion that only sixteen hundred of Carroll's men had arms seems doubtful, but even if it is correct, he still had six hundred of Carroll's men, whom he could have spared to Morgan. See Jackson to Monroe, December 24, 1814 and February 17, 1815, Jackson Mss.

on the east bank and a flag of truce approached with a letter asking for an armistice to bury the dead. Desiring to conceal the loss of the three senior officers, Lambert signed the request without naming his rank. Jackson desired to gain time and replied with explicit terms, which he hardly expected Lambert to accept. The latter took it under consideration, promising an answer by ten o'clock on the ninth. Lambert hesitated, because Jackson insisted that operations should not cease on the west bank and that neither party should reinforce his troops there.[1] By next morning Thornton's command was safe on the east bank, and Lambert accepted the armistice. The dead and the severely wounded, left on the field during the night, were now removed. Gleig, a British officer who rode out to the scene, tells us what he saw. "Of all the sights," he says, "I ever witnessed, that which met me there was beyond comparison the most shocking and the most humiliating. Within the small compass of a few hundred yards were gathered together nearly a thousand bodies, all of them arrayed in British uniforms. Not a single American was among them; all were English; and they were thrown by dozens into shallow holes, scarcely deep enough to furnish them with a slight covering of earth. Nor was this all. An American officer stood by smoking a segar, and apparently counting the slain with a look of savage exultation; and repeating over and over to each individual that approached him, that their loss came only to eight men killed, and fourteen wounded."[2]

From the eighth till the eighteenth the armies were inactive except for a desultory cannonade from the American line and a spiritless British bombardment of Fort St. Philip, on the Missis-

---

[1] See Jackson's report, January 9, 1815, Latour, *Historical Memoir*, Appendix number 29, and Reid and Eaton, *Jackson*, 383. But Jackson's fragmentary *Journal* and a letter from Lambert to Jackson, January 8, both in the Jackson Mss, seem to show that the armistice was accepted on the eighth. Jackson thought that Lambert was frightened by the demand that neither side should reinforce the west bank, and delayed till he could bring Thornton over.

[2] Gleig, *Campaign at Washington and New Orleans*, 332.

sippi. Major Hinds, whose conduct in this campaign marks him for a man of singular ability, asked permission to attack with the cavalry. Jackson refused, lest Hinds should do something which would bring on an engagement in the open field. He advised with Adair and Coffee, both of whom urged him not to attack in the open. The former said: "My troops will fight when behind breastworks or in the woods, but do not hazard an attack with raw militia in the open plain: they cannot be relied on. The officers are inexperienced, the soldiers without subordination or discipline. You would hazard too much by making an attack with them in the open plain against well disciplined troops."[1]

On the fifteenth, signs of activity in the camp showed that the British were about to depart: on the morning of the nineteenth their lines were deserted. They had constructed fortifications at the mouth of Bayou Bienvenue and withdrawn behind them till the army could be carried slowly to the fleet riding in deep water sixty miles away. Hinds with 1,000 men was sent to cut up their rear, but found them so well defended in the narrow passes of the swamps that he considered it unwise to attack.[2] On the twenty-seventh, the difficult work of embarking was completed; but bad weather detained the fleet at its anchorage until February 5th, when it was at last able to stand away to the east. Two days later it came to a halt off Dauphine Island, where the army was disembarked for a period of rest after a most exhausting and demoralizing experience. Its total loss, by the British account, since December 23d, was 2,492, while its opponents lost only 333.[3]

On the morning of the nineteenth, Jackson and his staff rode to the abandoned camp. They were met on the way by a British surgeon with a letter from Lambert announcing his departure

---

[1] Jackson's fragmentary *Journal*, Jackson Mss.
[2] *Ibid.*
[3] Latour, *Historical Memoir*, Appendix, number 29; James, *Military Occurrences*, II., 388.

from Louisiana and asking considerate treatment for eighty wounded who could not be moved. Jackson received the messenger with courtesy and sent his chief medical man to aid in caring for the wounded men, and later he visited them himself. On the ground the enemy left fourteen pieces of artillery so disabled as to be useless. On the twenty-first, the major part of the American army was withdrawn from the lines and entered the city amid demonstrations of joy by the inhabitants. On the twenty-third a *Te Deum* was sung in the cathedral with great pomp. As the general proceeded across the square to the edifice he passed under a triumphal arch under which two maidens presented him with laurel wreaths; farther on other maidens strewed flowers in his path; at the door the Abbé Dubourg delivered a laudatory address to which Jackson replied in studied moderation; and a guard of honor escorted him to his lodgings.

In his address the abbé referring to the recent victory said: "The first impulse of your religious heart was to acknowledge the signal interposition of Providence." A "religious heart" has rarely been considered one of Jackson's possessions, yet in this case the priest's words were appropriate. Several of the grim warrior's letters witness his conviction that his success, marvellous to himself, was partly due to Divine intervention. To his friend, Col. Robert Hays, he wrote: "It appears that the unerring hand of providence shielded my men from the shower of Balls, bombs, and Rockets, when every Ball and Bomb from our guns carried with them a mission of death. Tell your good lady and family god bless them."[1] Nor did he hesitate to give the same opinion in his official dispatches. To Monroe he wrote: "Heaven, to be sure, has interposed most wonderfully in our behalf, and I am filled with gratitude when I look back to what we have escaped; but I grieve the more

---

[1] Jackson to Hays, January 26, 1815, Jackson Mss.

that we did not, with more and more industry use the means with which she had blessed us. Again and again I must repeat, we have been always too backward with our preparations. When the enemy comes we begin to think of driving him away; and scarcely before." [1]

It is true that Jackson realized the military situation slowly. It was not till the British were actually at hand that he realized the importance of guarding New Orleans: it was not till the gunboats were taken that he realized that he ought to concentrate his forces: it was not till December 29th, that he ordered New Orleans to be searched for entrenching tools;[2] it was not till the British held Bayou Bienvenue that he realized its importance: it was not till the militia were about to arrive without arms that he realized how few muskets he had: it was not till Jean Lafitte suggested that the extreme left of his line ought to be bent backward so as to rest on an impassable swamp that this position was made secure;[3] and it was not till Thornton held the left bank that he realized fully its importance in the general scheme of defense.

A serious embarrassment in this campaign was the lack of arms. Jackson tried to throw the responsibility on others. His apologists say[4] he asked for a supply in the summer of 1814, but no reference to this is made in his extensive preserved correspondence in the summer and early autumn. He even drew 500 stands from New Orleans to Mobile in September.[5] The first specific reference to the subject in the correspondence is in a letter to Governor Blount, October 27th.[6] Coffee had just arrived without a full equipment and that seems to have roused his interest for the first time. Up to that time he seems to have

[1] Jackson to Monroe, February 17, 1815, Jackson Mss.
[2] Livingston to Mayor Girod, December 29, 1814, Jackson Mss.
[3] Livingston to Jackson, December 25, 1814, Jackson Mss.
[4] Latour, *Historical Memoir*, 66.
[5] Captain Humphrey to Jackson, September 6, 1814, Jackson Mss.
[6] Jackson Mss.

overlooked the fact that his division was without arms, which was quite in keeping with his failure to give attention to detail. He was now, however, urgent enough. Monroe, at last aroused to the necessity, ordered the commandant at Fort LaFayette, near Pittsburg, to send a supply immediately. November 8th 5,000 stands were sent by sail boats from that place with the expectation that they would arrive in twenty days. The time was ample, but the captains loitered to trade and the delay was fatal. One of the boats was fast enough to fall in with Carroll on his way to the place of danger, and he took the responsibility of taking 1,100 stands to make up the deficiency in his command: the rest arrived at their destination after the battle of the eighth.[1]

Nor was Jackson quite correct in saying that he had only 3,200 stands at the time of the battle. The regulars, Carroll's men, Coffee's men, the Louisiana militia, and 1,000 of the Kentuckians, over 6,000 in all, must have had arms. Besides, the returns of his ordnance department show that 2,404 stands were issued from December 18th till January 8th.[2]

Deficient as he sometimes was in the science of warfare, he was nevertheless an excellent fighter. Wherever he fought, fighting was good. Mutiny frequently appeared in his camp because of the great exertion he demanded of his men, but neither in the Creek nor in the New Orleans campaign did the soldiers directly under his authority ever flinch on the field of battle. Had he been present on the west bank on the morning of January 8th, the result, doubtless, would have been less humiliating. Good officers, as he wrote down in his journal, will make good soldiers:[3] his own influence showed the truth of the statement.

General Jackson's qualities made a good impression on his opponents. James, the British historian of the war, says: "He

---

[1]Jackson to Carroll, October 31; Jackson to Monroe, October 31, 1814; Wollesley to Jackson, November 8, 1814; Monroe to Blount, November 3, 1814; Jackson Mss.
[2]Jackson Mss.
[3]Jackson's fragmentary Journal, January 18, 1815, Jackson Mss.

proved himself at New Orleans, not only an able general for the description of country in which he had to operate, but, in all his transactions with the British officers, both an honorable, and a courteous enemy. In his official despatches, too, he has left an example of modesty, worthy of imitation by the generality of American commanders, naval as well as military."[1] The characterization is correct. Jackson had a strong sense of dignity. When his antipathy was aroused, he was most perverse, stickling over punctilios, blustering, and absolutely wrongheaded, but under normal conditions he treated his antagonist with the consideration of a brave man, who is not afraid to be generous. An illustration of this quality is the cordial manner in which in the following note he restored the sword of General Keane who requested to be allowed to redeem it:

"The general commanding the American forces, having learned that Major-General Kean of the British army had expressed a wish for the restoration of his sword, lost in the action of the eighth of January in consequence of a wound, feels great satisfaction in ordering it to be returned to him. Mr. Livingston, one of his volunteer aids, is charged with the delivery of it. The undersigned, feeling for the misfortune of the brave, begs that General Kean will be assured of his wishes for his speedy restoration."[2]

Unfortunately, many things happened in connection with the New Orleans campaign which illustrate a less attractive side of Jackson's character. The bountiful crop of strife which he reaped must be reserved for the next chapter.

---

[1] James, *Military Occurrences*, II., 390.
[2] Jackson to General Keane, February 4; G. M. Ogden to Jackson, February 3, 1815; Jackson Mss.

CHAPTER XIII

NEW ORLEANS UNDER MARTIAL LAW

THE two months following the departure of the British on January 18th brought Jackson almost as much anxiety as the two months preceding it, with the difference that it was due to petty rather than to important public matters. Although a treaty of peace between England and the United States was signed by the commissioners on December 24, 1814, news of the event did not reach New York until February 11, 1815, and it was not known in New Orleans until it arrived by way of the British fleet on February 19th. American newspapers soon confirmed the intelligence, but the official despatches which ought to have brought the news to Jackson were delayed in the post-office so long that it was not until March 13th that he had advices from his government. The interval between the receipt of unofficial and official information was a period of uncertainty. Jackson properly refused to reduce his strength or relax his vigilance until he knew that peace was made. The legislature and many of the people of Louisiana, naturally censorious, clamored for the repeal of the edict proclaiming martial law and for the dismissal of the militia; Governor Claiborne and United States Judge Hall were drawn into the affair; and an unhappy state of confusion followed which the tactless efforts of Jackson only made worse. Along with the consideration of these facts one must observe certain final stages of the actual campaign, as the attack on Fort Bowyer, and the punishment of a notable mutiny. All these events bring Jackson's personality into prominence and give additional basis for an opinion on his ability as a public man.

After the first attack on Fort Bowyer, September 15, 1814, Jackson ordered its defenses to be strengthened, taking for that purpose a number of heavy cannon from New Orleans. Major Lawrence was left in command, and with his twenty-two guns and his garrison of 366 men[1] he felt sure of defending the place against any number of hostiles. From the water the fort was, indeed, impregnable; but on the land side its walls were no more than three feet thick and composed of an earth wall held up by boards, while the interior was without cover for the gunners or any other means of protection against explosives thrown into the enclosure. Moreover, certain sand-mounds within easy range offered an enemy the opportunity of securing, if he fortified them, absolute command of the position. To defend the place, therefore, from a land attack there must be enough force to hold an enemy at a safe distance from this danger point. A thousand troops were not too many for such a task.

Lambert arrived with the British army at Dauphine Island on February 6th, determined to carry his arms against Mobile, and his first concern was Fort Bowyer. He saw that the place could not be taken from the water and decided to invest it. For this duty he selected the second brigade, then about twelve hundred men strong,[2] which early on the eighth landed on the peninsula two and a half miles east of the fort. It was supported by artillerists, sappers and miners, and marines, making probably as many as 450 in this auxiliary force. Its first step was to establish a line across the peninsula in order to cut off possible reinforcements from the mainland. The garrison withdrew into their defenses and the British approached within three hundred yards of the walls. They began parallels, seized the sand-mounds, constructed batteries which the American gunners

[1]The British returns of captured made the garrison 375, but the American authorities speak of them as 366. See James, *Military Occurrences*, II., 573; Latour, *Historical Memoir*, Appendix, number 38.

[2]Composed of the 4th, 21st, and 44th regiments, which had 1974 men before January 8. On that day, they lost 1089; if half of their wounded were recovered, they now had 1170. James, *Military Occurrences*, II., 373, 555.

could not destroy by using their severest fire, and on the morning of the eleventh had four eighteen-pounders and two eight-inch howitzers trained on the fort at a distance of 100 yards, besides ten smaller pieces at a distance of 300 yards or less. At ten o'clock Lambert sent forward a flag of truce with a demand that the fort surrender. Lawrence conferred with his officers, asked for time to consider, and in the afternoon agreed to surrender on the following day. With the fort and garrison went twenty-eight pieces of artillery, 351 stands of arms, and an ample supply of ammunition. The loss of the British in killed and wounded was twenty-one; that of the Americans was eleven.[1]

The easy capture of Fort Bowyer was largely due to the negligence of Winchester, who at this time had been for two and a half months in command at Mobile with ample forces to guard it. It was his duty to protect it or abandon it, and he did neither. It was not until the tenth that he ordered Major Blue, with 1,200 whites and Indians, to go to the aid of the garrison. Contrary winds kept them back so that they did not arrive until the twelfth.[2] Some one was to blame, also, for the short supply of provisions in the fort, and the unprepared state of the defenses on the land side.

As to Jackson's responsibility, it is certain that he did not realize the danger in which Mobile stood. In spite of his former predilection for the place, he gave it little attention after he arrived in New Orleans. One thing at a time was his way. When the enemy left Cat Island he assumed they were bound for Bermuda to await orders and hastily forwarded his reassuring opinion to Winchester. January 30th, he wrote again to his subordinate, "I have no idea that the enemy will attempt Fort Bowyer on your quarter, still you cannot be too well prepared and too vigilant."[3]

---

[1] Latour, *Historical Memoir*, 207, Appendices, 39, 40, 49, 46; Reid and Eaton, *Jackson*, 400; James, *Military Occurrences*, II., 391, 570-575; Gleig, *Campaigns in America*, 351; Niles, *Register*, VII., 32, 58.

[2] Niles, *Register*, VII., 32, 58.

[3] Jackson to Winchester, January 19 and 30, 1815, Jackson Mss.

The loss of Fort Bowyer was particularly disappointing after the brilliant affair at New Orleans, and Jackson felt it very keenly. With the same kind of excited judgment which precipitated the quarrel with the Kentuckians he criticized Lawrence in his report for surrendering before the enemy fired a round from the commanding batteries. Lawrence felt the injustice of the charge and demanded an inquiry, which was granted: the result was complete vindication.[1]

Jackson began to plan to retake the fort as soon as he knew of its fall. February 21st, he received from Admiral Cochrane a note enclosing a copy of a bulletin received from Jamaica containing an account of the peace signed at Ghent on December 24th, and with it the admiral's congratulations. Nothing was said about suspension of hostilities pending the receipt of official intelligence, and Jackson in his reply inquired on what footing the admiral was pleased to consider the two armies since the receipt of the information. While thus appearing to give full credence to the information, he privately professed to see in it the possibility of a ruse and wrote to McIntosh, who was about to supersede Winchester, to suggest that they unite their forces and expel the British from Mobile Bay and thus wipe out the stain of the surrender of Fort Bowyer. He believed it could be done since the combined forces would be double what he had at New Orleans when he repelled the attack of this same British army.[2] It was a piece of thoughtless bravery, and a moment's reflection must have convinced him that if the peace rumor were true the position would be given up without loss of life. If it proved untrue it would still be very difficult for the 6,000 Americans now in Mobile to protect the town and recover the fort into which the enemy could place 2,000 men and still have left for operations against the town more men than the

---

[1]Latour, *Historical Memoir*, Appendix, number 40.
[2]Jackson to McIntosh, February 22, 1815, Jackson Mss.; also his proclamation, February 19, 1815; Latour, *Historical Memoir*, Appendix 41.

whole American army contained, and this over and above their advantage from the control of the bay. Jackson was no doubt in a tortured frame of mind. To Governor Holmes, of Mississippi, he wrote on February 21st: "I am prepared for anything war or peace. If an honorable peace I hail it with heartfelt satisfaction: if dishonorable it will meet my hearty imprecations. But the Lord's will be done. The fall of Fort Bowyer is truly grating to my feelings."[1] He was accustomed to demand of his subordinates the most implicit obedience, but he rarely showed the same spirit toward his own superiors.

On the very day he received Cochrane's announcement of peace the six mutinous militiamen met their fate at Mobile. This event, which was in itself only a matter of army discipline and created no criticism at the time, was later utilized by Jackson's political enemies to oppose his election. The incident is related as follows:

In the spring of 1814, the governor of Tennessee, under the authority of the secretary of war, called out 1,000 drafted militia for garrison duty in the Creek country, specifying in the call that they should serve six months from June 20th, the date of mustering in. When the commander of the division arrived at Fort Jackson in July, 1814, he found the place in a neglected condition: he rather abruptly ordered the garrison on fatigue duty, to cut down trees, remove undergrowth, open ditches, and do the other similar things necessary to make a new site habitable and defensible. Along with this came the dog days with much of the dreaded "Coosa fever," and the result was a great deal of dissatisfaction among the men at Forts Jackson, Strother, and Williams.

As in the preceding autumn, the discontent crystallized into a claim that the tour of duty of the militia was three, instead of six, months. By clever arguments a doubt was thrown on

---

[1] Jackson to Governor Holmes, February 21, 1815, Jackson Mss.

the governor's right to call them out for six months, but the matter was never anything but a case for judicial determination, and the governor's action from the standpoint of the objectors was not void but voidable. The remedy of the militia, if a wrong was done them, was in the courts and not in mutiny.

The garrison at Fort Jackson belonged to the 1st regiment of West Tennessee militia, commanded by Colonel Pipkin, and as September 20th approached, they became particularly demonstrative. All the experiences of Fort Strother in the distressful days of November and December, 1813, were repeated. Some of the officers supported the demands of the men. On the night of September 2d, the following lines were attached to the gate-post of the fort:

> Look below we are the Boys,
> That fear no Noise,
> Nor Orders that we hear.
> Eighteen days more,
> And then we go,
> Or be found in gore,
> And never come here no more,
> To suffer as we and many others have Before.
> Liberty Street.[1]

September 14th, there was an open demonstration of the discontented ones. A few of them got a fife and drum and beat up and down the lines till they drew to them nearly two hundred others. Then they seized a quantity of bread and set the bread house on fire, while threatening to take stores and cattle and march back to Tennessee.[2]

A leader of this group was John Harris, a Baptist preacher who was nearly as illiterate as the others. His influence as a minister ought to have been more worthily exerted than in promoting disobedience; but having convinced himself that

---

[1] Enclosed in Colonel Pipkin to Jackson, September 4, 1814, Jackson Mss.
[2] Thomas Hoagland to Jackson, September 15, 1814, Jackson Mss.

a tour of duty ought to be three months, he took the law into his own hands and went about with a list of men who were pledged to go home. On September 20th, he and 200 others set out for Tennessee, where some of them arrived in due time. But the majority were met and arrested by the reinforcements on their way to the front and carried back to Fort Jackson. Harris and a few others of those who reached their homes learned the fate of their comrades and went back of their own accord to stand trial, so convinced were they of their innocence.

This reappearance of the spirit of mutiny at a time when invasion was threatened exasperated the higher officers of the army. Col. Robert Butler, adjutant-general, in sending the arrested ones to Fort Jackson expressed the hope that they would be ordered to Mobile and said to Jackson: "The rascals should be taught what it is to disgrace the state and the American character. You can manage them when there in perfection."[1]

Jackson did, in fact, order the regiment to Mobile, and as he was departing for New Orleans appointed a court-martial composed of officers of the Tennessee militia to try the mutineers. The hearing began on December 5th. From the beginning there was no doubt of the guilt of the accused. The only question was, should their honest opinion that they were bound for a three months' tour of duty be taken as an extenuating circumstance? The court, whose members were serving under the same law as the accused, took a negative view of the matter. All the prisoners to the number of 205 were convicted: six of them were condemned to death, and the others to penalties less severe. Jackson kept the verdict in his hands during the trying days of the British stay below New Orleans and finally approved it on January 28th, a week after the evacuation of the British camp. On February 21st, just as the rumor

---

[1]Butler to Jackson, September 22, 1814, Jackson Mss.

of peace began to circulate on the coast, the six unhappy militia-men were shot, dying firmly and protesting their innocence of wrong intention.[1]

Jackson approved of the finding of the court-martial, but he was not responsible for it. It is not charged that he tried to influence it. The weight of the allegation against him is that he did not modify the sentence. He ought to have done this if he believed the good of the service demanded it. But he might well believe that the good of the service demanded that the spirit of mutiny be suppressed and that the militia be taught that it was not for them to interpret their rights under the law at the risk of demoralizing the defense of the nation. But for the later political agitation the matter would have been forgotten. The case of Harris appealed to the agitators especially: they believed that it would arouse the indignation of the Baptists, who were numerous in some of the doubtful states. The whole affair is only interesting as a manikin which has been made to play a part in a past political struggle.

While the career of the six militiaman was drawing to a close at Mobile, Jackson became involved in a blazing quarrel with several persons and groups of persons in New Orleans. In this affair one event followed another with increasing effect until the situation was acute; but probably the most important cause was Jackson's sensitive temper which would glow at the slightest blowing. When he arrived in the city, conditions, it is true, were abnormal, but they were not so bad but that a wise administrator could get along without a quarrel with legislature, governor, and United States courts.

When Jackson appeared, the legislature was generally loyal. Its quarrel with Claiborne was suppressed, but probably not forgotten. The Creoles, in the assembly and out, while not enthusiastic for a war to perpetuate American control, were

---

[1]Parton, *Jackson*, II., chapter 22, deals fully with the execution of the militiamen.

supporting it without difficulty. The state's quota of drafted militia was 1,000 and these were in the field by the time Jackson arrived in New Orleans, to say nothing of more than five hundred volunteers. After the British landed, the reserve militia was called out and responded to the number of several hundred.[1] The legislature voted liberal sums to clothe the Tennessee militia[2] and they promised to furnish Negroes to work on the fortifications, although it seems that the United States paid wages to the masters.[3] This attitude on the face indicates complaisance, although it was Jackson's opinion after the controversy was acute that they were not genuinely cordial. "On my arrival," he said, "I was flattered by the greetings of all; and while I returned to all the salute of entire confidence, I must own that I manifested somewhat more than I felt. . . . Notwithstanding the great unanimity which appears, very generally to have prevailed among the inhabitants since my arrival, I am fearful that if reverses had overtaken us, or if disaffection could have hoped for favor I should have been compelled to witness a very different scene — I am fearful I should have witnessed it, where it ought least to have been looked for."[4]

The refusal of the legislature to adjourn after the capture of the gunboats led Jackson to declare martial law, and in doing so he expressed his intention to remain master of the situation. A week later the British surprised him by landing at Villeré's. Taking this fact in connection with his inexperience many of the natives concluded that he had little military capacity. At this time a rumor began to run through the city that he intended, if forced to fall back, to burn the town and its large store of produce rather than have them fall into the hands of the enemy. The citizens were alarmed and began to think of

[1]Claiborne to Jackson, November 20. 1814, Jackson Mss.
[2]Latour, *Historical Memoir*, 141, note.
[3]Jackson to Monroe, December 10, 1814, Jackson Mss.
[4]Jackson to Monroe, February 17, 1815, Jackson Mss.

their property. Some of them asked Capt. Thomas L. Butler, then in command in the place, what were his orders if compelled to evacuate the city. Butler refused to divulge his commands, and the ill-feeling increased. The citizens thought that the refusal confirmed their suspicions: Jackson believed that the demand was made in connection with some concerted plan of action to save their property, by making terms with the enemy. The successful check of the British in the night battle alleviated the popular alarm, but it did not destroy it.

It was, in fact, destined to have an early resurgence. December 27th, Colonel Declouet, a prominent and loyal Creole citizen, and commander of a militia regiment then in service, had an interview with Speaker Guichard, of the house of representatives. The testimony of the two in a later investigation differs as to what was said in this conversation; but it is evident that Declouet carried away the opinion that, if Jackson were defeated, the legislature would try to make terms with the British rather than have their city destroyed. He seems to have thought, also, that some steps would be taken by the leaders on the morning of the twenty-eighth. That was the morning when the enemy made their first demonstration against the American lines. It passed with great anxiety in New Orleans, for it was not believed that Jackson could hold his lines, then not more than half complete. Declouet, full of the common terror and weighed down by the secret he had gained from the speaker, rode to the camp to confide his opinion secretly to the commander-in-chief. When near there he met Abner Duncan, one of Jackson's several volunteer aides, a New Orleans lawyer of prominence, and through him sent his message to Jackson. Duncan had the misfortune to twist the words of his informant. Jackson declared that as he was riding across the field of battle, just before the advance of the enemy, he noticed Duncan much agitated, and asking the cause of agitation the aide replied that the governor had sent a message to the effect that the legislature was about to make terms with the enemy. The general expressed doubt as to the correctness of the statement, but sent word to Claiborne, quoting from his statement to the legislature, "to make strict inquiry into the subject; and if true to blow them up."[1] Riding away on this mission Duncan soon met Colonel Fortier, aide to Governor Claiborne, and by him forwarded the message. But he softened the words somewhat. Fortier returned toward the city, but met Claiborne on his way to the camp and said to him: "Major-General Jackson has received the information that the legislature is on the point of assembling to give up the country. His orders are that the governor should immediately close the doors of the state house, surround it with guards, and fire on the members should they persist in assembling." Claiborne was surprised at the information, but executed the instructions without delay. Here we have an important matter transferred from Guichard to Declouet, then to Duncan, then to Jackson with his orders back to Duncan, then to Fortier, and finally to Claiborne; and at no stage in the process is it reduced to writing. All of these men gave evidence of what was said to them, and no two statements agree. It is easy to see that they were all in an agitated frame of mind that December morning. It is evident, also, that Jackson spoke truly when he said that his orders were "to blow them up," and Duncan, more level-headed at the moment, was justified in modifying the command to simple exclusion from the legislative hall.

December 29th, the exclusion was revoked and the legislature, humiliated and angry, resumed its sittings. Its first action was to appoint a committee to investigate recent events. February 6th, a report was adopted exonerating the body from

---

[1] Jackson's testimony is quoted in Gayarre, *History of Louisiana*, IV., 540: it is confirmed by Plauché to Phillips, January 17, 1843, Jackson Mss.

treasonable designs. At the bottom of its lengthy testimony and diffuse summing up one finds no reason to think that the assembly were willing to surrender to the British without a battle. It is also evident that there was great anxiety among the people and legislators in regard to the general conviction that Jackson was prepared to destroy much property to prevent its falling into the hands of the enemy, and the legislature was disposed to prevent this. But it is difficult to see where they could draw the line between loyalty and treason. A capitulation when Jackson was in full flight would modify little the conduct of either the British or American General. A capitulation made before that time would not be accepted by Jackson; it would disorganize the American resistance, and it would, in fact, be disloyalty.[1]

It is likely that Jackson would have destroyed the large amount of stores in the city, if forced to evacuate it, so as to make the place as useless as possible to the enemy in a military sense. The burning of Moscow was then fresh in the minds of men, and strenuous patriots like Jackson regarded it as a most praiseworthy deed. In 1824, he gave an account of an interview at this time with a delegation who came from the legislature to his camp to learn his intention in regard to burning the city. He says: "To them I replied: 'If I thought the hair of my head knew my thoughts, I would cut it off and burn it' — to return to their honorable body, and say to them from me, that if I was to be so unfortunate as to be driven from the lines I then occupied, and compelled to retreat through New Orleans, they would have a warm session of it."[2]

At this stage the quarrel with the legislature merges into a controversy with the governor. At first Jackson and Clai-

---

[1]For a discussion of this incident see Martin, *History of Louisiana*, passim, and Gayarre, IV., 539-577, who is more judicious.

[2]Jackson to the postmaster general, March 22, 1824; Affidavit of T. L. Butler, May 23, 1815; Jackson Mss. Gayarre, *Louisiana*, IV., 563.

borne coöperated cordially; but after martial law was proclaimed on December 16th, they became less harmonious.
Claiborne, commander-in-chief of the militia, now found himself subordinate to a man whose nature it was to demand implicit obedience. Probably without realizing it, the governor
reacted against his own occultation, while conscious that he
gave himself unreservedly to the defense of the state. A sense
of wounded dignity, a rather morbid disposition to make a virtue
of self-effacement, and various intermittent fits of self-assertion
all united to put him into an agitated state of mind.
Jackson, in the meantime, always self-satisfied, bending
himself and all others whom he could reach to the one task
before him, caring little for the feelings or foibles of others,
moved forward imperiously and even contemptuously — when
he might have well shown some forbearance — and thus at last
the governor forgot his old political enemies and came to support the legislature in the struggle against military domination.

Claiborne attributed his loss of favor to the influence of
the volunteer aides, whom Jackson appointed on December 17th,
all former enemies of the governor. "These men," he said at
the time, "will do me much harm if the General suffers himself
to be imposed upon." Claiborne soon found confirmation of
his suspicions. December 23d, while troops were hurrying
to meet the British at Villeré's plantation, the governor, of his
own initiative, set out for the front at the head of three Louisiana
regiments. He was met by an order from the general to take
position on the Gentilly Road. He complied, but considered
the order part of a plan to keep him in the background.[1]

The first evidence of a strained relation is in a letter from
Claiborne to Jackson, December 22, 1814. "*The times require
our union,*" says the governor, "nor is there anything I more
desire than to maintain with you, the most friendly under-

---

[1]Gayarre, *Louisiana*, IV., 596.

standing, and a coöperation zealous and cordial. With this object in view I request of you a *private interview* on this day, at such hour as may suit your convenience."[1]

Jackson's reply, if he made one, is not preserved in his papers; but the governor continued to coöperate as cordially as possible. With the general, Claiborne pledged his joint credit to buy blankets for the soldiers.[2] Until January 17th, he remained in command of the Louisiana militia encamped on the Gentilly Road; and after that date he assumed command of the state militia on the west bank and maintained a semblance of order in that quarter until the disappearance of danger.[3] Jackson's attitude toward him was unbending, and when during the battle of January 8th, the governor was found in safety at the hospital he took pleasure in attributing it to cowardice.[4]

As military affairs lost some of their prominence the civil government began to think of resuming its functions. But Jackson continued to exercise martial law with its absolute authority, always strengthening the defenses of the city, and embodying the reserved militia till at the end of January he had twice as many armed men as on the eighth of the month. The prolongation of martial law was borne without open protest by the civil authorities until the receipt of unofficial information of the treaty of peace; but there was suppressed friction and in regard to the recovery of the slaves an explosion seemed for some time to be imminent.

While the British were before New Orleans, 199 slaves took refuge on the fleet expecting to be carried away on it.[5] This must have been done with the consent of some higher officers, although General Lambert, whose generally honorable conduct

[1] Jackson Mss.
[2] Claiborne to Jackson, December 22, 1814, Jackson Mss.
[3] Claiborne to Jackson, January 16 and 17, 1815, Jackson Mss.
[4] T. L. Butler to Claiborne, December 31, 1814; certificates of Dr. Ker and Major Davezac, April 6, 1815, Jackson Mss.
[5] Gayarre, *Louisiana*, IV., 511.

entitles him to full credence, said that he knew nothing of it until he returned to the fleet after he evacuated his camp at Villeré's plantation. He immediately wrote to Jackson saying he had taken pains to persuade the Negroes to return to their homes and offering to deliver them to their masters if the fugitives could be got to return voluntarily. He said that as the British law did not recognize slavery he did not feel authorized to force them to leave against their wills.[1] Jackson replied immediately and appointed Captain Henly to receive the slaves, but nothing was done and unofficial information led him to believe that their surrender was hardly to be hoped for. Early in February, he sent Edward Livingston and Manuel White to receive the fugitives, but Lambert would not force the slaves to depart and all the messengers could say would not lead them to give up the near prospect of freedom. From that time there was much correspondence between the two commanders on the subject, but nothing was gained. The Americans claimed that the clause in the treaty for the restoration of property would apply to the slaves, and the British asserted that they could not recognize the slaves as property but as individuals who came voluntarily into the British lines.[2] The matter was afterward referred to arbitration by Russia, who on the interpretation of the treaty gave judgment for the United States.[3]

Negotiations with the British army properly fell within the scope of the military authority, but the civil government was not able to keep hands off when the recovery of the slaves was at stake. January 31st, a week after Jackson first wrote to Lambert on the subject, he received a letter from Claiborne

---

[1]Lambert to Jackson, January 20, 1815, Jackson Mss.

[2]The following letters on this subject are in the appendix of Latour, *Historical Memoir*, at the pages indicated, and those noted with a J are in the Jackson Mss.: Jackson to Lambert, March 7, page 99; March 13, page 100; Lambert to Jackson, February 8, page 82 and J; February 27, page 93 and J; March 18, page 120 and J: Jackson to Cochrane, February 20, page 85 and J: Woodruff to Jackson, March 23, page 119 and J. See also Jackson to Lambert, February 4, Jackson Mss. All these letters are dated 1815. See also Gayarre *History of Louisiana*, IV., 511.

[3]Moore, *International Arbitration*, I., chapter XI., pages 350-390.

ANDREW JACKSON IN 1815.   AGE 48

From a miniature on ivory by Jean François Vallée.   It was painted in New Orleans just after the victory over the British.   The artist, a Frenchman, has managed to give his subject a Napoleonic countenance

asking what was accomplished in the matter and saying that he himself would make application by three distinguished citizens. Jackson resented this interference and caused his adjutant-general to write a stiff reply announcing Henly's appointment and adding that it seemed that nothing would be done by the British. Claiborne laid the correspondence before the legislature, which approved of his course and appointed a commission of four members to make personal application to Lambert.[1] Aroused by this prospect of two negotiations Jackson hurried off Livingston and White, as has been said, and we hear nothing more of the plans of the civil authorities. But he let it be known that he would have no meddling. "Be assured," he said to Claiborne, "if either the assembly or yourself attempt to interfere with subjects not belonging to you, it will be immediately arrested. I am pledged for the protection of this District, having the responsibility I trust I know my duty and will perform it."[2]

Just at this time the legislature was completing its investigation of its suspension on December 28th. Jackson probably thought that they were about to deal severely with him, for, on February 6th, in a sharp note to the governor, he demanded a copy of the report they were about to make, repeating his demand two days later and threatening, if it were not complied with, to hold an investigation himself.[3] The menace was probably intended to induce the legislature to make a mild report; and if that was the purpose it succeeded. When the report was handed to him on the fifteenth[4] it completely exonerated Jackson and threw the blame on other shoulders. Not even the benign Gayarre is able to reconcile it with the known attitude of the assembly at that time toward the commander of

[1]Claiborne to Jackson, February 4, 1815, Jackson Mss.
[2]Jackson to Claiborne, February 3, 1815, Jackson Mss.
[3]Jackson to Claiborne, February 8, 1815, Jackson Mss. Gayarre, *Louisiana*, IV., 555.
[4]Secretary Louisiana senate to Jackson, February 15, 1815, Jackson Mss.

the seventh military district.[1] The situation seems more singular
when we remember that on February 2d, the assembly voted
its thanks to every prominent contributor to the recent success
but the chief one. When Carroll, Adair, Coffee, and Thomas
received this token of public appreciation and Jackson received
no notice, the omission was too pointed to be misunderstood.

The assembly adjourned early in February, and its quarrel,
soon forgotten, was followed by trouble of another kind. Jackson would not disband the army while the enemy were in force
on the coast. The Tennesseeans and Kentuckians did not
complain of this lengthened service, but the volatile Louisianians bore it with impatience. The reserved militia were
first dissatisfied, and the governor appealed to Jackson to discharge them.[2] The detached militia manifested their feeling
by leaving their commands with or without leave until companies
were reduced to mere skeletons. A sharp reprimand from Jackson checked the practice, but did not remove its cause. Soon the
Creoles thought of another expedient. Repairing to the French
consul, Toussard, they registered themselves as French citizens
and applied to Jackson for discharges from military service.
The demands were granted until they became so numerous
that the trick was evident. Then the general dealt with them
in a characteristic manner. February 28th, he ordered all
French citizens to retire to a distance of 120 miles from the
city. The command produced consternation: Toussard protested to Governor Claiborne, who replied that he could do
nothing and referred him to the federal courts. When Jackson
learned of this he ordered the consul out of the city. There
was much excitement among the Creoles, and on March 3d,
there appeared in the city paper an anonymous letter protesting
in severe terms against the order concerning the French. It

---

[1]Gayarre, *Louisiana*, IV., 556-558.
[2]Claiborne to Jackson, February 24, 1815, Jackson Mss.

amounted to defiance of the military power which it denounced, and the writer could only have expected to have a bout with that authority. Jackson left him in little suspense. Learning that the objectionable letter was written by Louaillier, a member of the assembly — who had been a loyal supporter of the campaign — he directed his arrest by a file of soldiers. Counsel for Louaillier at once applied to the state courts for his release on a writ of *habeas corpus*. The request was refused on the ground of no jurisdiction. Louaillier then made his demand of Dominick A. Hall, the federal district judge, an unbending defender of his official dignity and authority. He was not submissive to the proclamation of martial law in the first instance and accepted the opportunity to try his strength with the commander-in-chief. He granted Louaillier's request, stipulating that Jackson should have notice before the writ was served on him. When the general received this notice he wrote the following order to one of his subordinates:

Having received proof that Dominick A. Hall has been aiding and abetting and exciting mutiny within my camp, you will forthwith order a detachment to arrest and confine him, and report to me as soon as arrested. You will be vigilant; the agents of our enemy are more numerous than was expected. You will guard against escapes.

This order was to be expected, but the insinuation that Hall was an agent of the enemy was discreditable to Jackson's intelligence.[1]

Just at this time came a messenger from Washington with an important letter for the general and an open order to postmasters to facilitate the progress of the bearer of news of peace. Jackson eagerly broke the seal and found that by some error the wrong letter was enclosed. The instructions to the postmasters

---

[1] Louaillier's communication and the orders for arrest are given by Parton, *Jackson*, II., 309-316, but Parton gives no suggestion of Jackson's wrongheaded attitude in the week which followed.

and the word of the messenger made it evident that the war was over, but Jackson would not relax martial law. His only concessions were to dismiss the Louisiana reserved militia and to repeal his order for the exclusion of the French residents, an order which had not been obeyed. Hall was kept in prison and when the district-attorney applied to a state judge for his release on *habeas corpus* proceedings, both attorney and judge were ordered under arrest.

The situation was grave. The people of New Orleans were generally for the civil government, and the officers who filled the streets and coffee-houses were for the military authority. Public meetings were held by the citizens, and officers and citizens came to the point of blows when a group of the latter tore down an illuminated picture of Jackson in a house of public entertainment. Claiborne, at last at the head of a popular movement, contended for the integrity of the civil power and instructed the Louisiana attorney-general to resume his functions and protect the citizens from military arrests.

At this point came Louaillier's trial by a court-martial, presided over by General Gaines, who had recently arrived. The letter published on the third was made the basis of seven charges, one of which was that Louaillier was a spy. The accused urged that as he was not in the army or militia he was without the jurisdiction of a court-martial. The court allowed the plea with reference to every charge except that of being a spy, and acquitted him on that because he was not found lurking about the camp or fortifications. No court with a sense of humor would seriously consider the charge that a spy would publish a letter like the defendant's in the columns of a newspaper which appeared in the very camp of the commander against which it was hurled.

The sentence of the court displeased Jackson. March 10th he reviewed it in general orders and gave his view of the nature and scope of martial law. This is a subject about which military men are apt to differ from the jurists, and the war of 1812 was the first under the constitution in which it came up for adjustment. Commanders were inclined to follow the English precedents which gave wide interpretation to martial law, making it nearly identical with the will of the general. In every case which arose in this war and went to the courts for revision, the judges overthrew this view and announced limitations which sought to make martial law as little arbitrary as possible. It was not until the Civil War era that the subject received definite statement in the case *ex parte* Milligan.[1] In his general orders Jackson took the older and broader view. Making no distinction between a military commission and a court-martial he held that the latter could take cognizance of violations of martial as well as military law and that it had jurisdiction over cases of mutiny. He, therefore, set aside the sentence of Gaines's court-martial and retained Louaillier in prison. Realizing that it was useless to try Hall before the court-martial which had acquitted Louaillier he sent him, March 12th, out of the city with orders not to return until peace was regularly announced or the enemy had departed from the coast. The next day came official news that the treaty was ratified. Jackson revoked martial law immediately and released his prisoners. Toussard and Judge Hall came back to town amid the acclamations of the populace and Jackson prepared to send home the detached militia from Louisiana, Tennessee, and Kentucky.[2]

Hall, whom his friends described as "a magistrate of pure heart, clean hands, and a mind susceptible of no fear but that of God,"[3] was determined to vindicate the majesty of the civil government. Waiting until the rejoicings over peace were

[1]United States Supreme Court's Reports, 4, Wallace, 2.
[2]These incidents are described by Gayarre, *Louisiana*, IV., chapter 12, with evident fairness. See also Martin, *History of Louisiana*.
[3]Martin, *History of Louisiana*, II., 416.

expended, he issued on March 21st, an order summoning Jackson into court to show why he should not be held in contempt for his recent refusal to recognize the court's writ of *habeas corpus*. March 27th, Jackson appeared in company with Major Reid, one of his aides. He submitted a written statement of reasons why he was not in contempt and withdrew, leaving Reid to read the paper. The reading of it was hardly begun when the court interrupted to ask the nature of what followed. Reid replied that it came within the scope of rules the court had laid down. Upon this the judge announced that he would take advice and suspended the sitting until the next day. On re-assembling Reid was not allowed to proceed and argument was heard. Jackson's counsel would offer none since he protested the jurisdiction of the court. After argument by the prosecution court adjourned until the next day, when Jackson came in person with a written protest against the sentence which was about to be given.

Among Jackson's papers is a draft of this protest in the hand-writing of Abner L. Duncan, one of the volunteer aides and a lawyer of ability: It runs: "I will not answer interrogatories. I may have erred, but my motives cannot be misinterpreted. . . . The law can be satisfied without wounding my feelings whose dictates under such circumstances, I most candidly acknowledge, it would be difficult, if not impossible to restrain." This apologetic statement was not used. The protest which was offered survives in the handwriting of Reid and runs: "I will not answer interrogatories. When called upon to show cause why an attachment for contempt of this court ought not to run against me, I offered to do so. You have, nevertheless, thought proper to refuse me this constitutional right. You would not hear my defense although you were advised that it contained sufficient causes to show that no attachment ought to run. Under these circumstances I appear before your Honor to receive the sentence of the court, and with nothing further to add. Your Honor will not understand me as meaning any disrespect to the court by the remarks I make; but as no opportunity has been furnished me to explain the reasons and motives which influenced my conduct, so it is expected that censure will form no part of that punishment which your Honor may imagine it your duty to perform."[1]

Before this dignified protest Judge Hall bore himself with equal credit. In imposing a fine of $1,000, he remarked that the duty was unpleasant, that he could not forget the important services of the defendant to the country, and that in consideration thereof he would not make imprisonment a part of punishment. "The only question," he added, "was whether the Law should bend to the General or the General to the Law," and under such conditions the court could not hesitate an instant. Jackson paid the fine, and when his admirers raised the amount for him by popular subscription he waived it aside with characteristic generosity asking that the sum be used to relieve the families of those who fell in defense of the city. At the final hearing Jackson's friends offered in court an account of the trial from his standpoint and requested that it might go into the record. Hall refused the request, remarking that he did not wish to encumber the record and saying, as they reported, "that he knew what we would be at."

Jackson's bearing at the trial was as excellent as his protest, which has been quoted. When he appeared, he was followed by an excited crowd of supporters, soldiers, and civilians, among them a number of Baratarians who had cause to remember the frown of Judge Hall. When these persons faced the court they raised a great shout of defiance. Jackson quickly rose to his feet, faced the rabble, and, with a splendid look and gesture, awed it into respectful silence. Then bowing to the bench he

[1] See Jackson Mss.

resumed his seat. After the sentence was announced he was drawn in a carriage by his admirers to the Exchange Coffee-House, where he spoke in the following excellent manner: "I have during the invasion exerted every one of my faculties for the defense and preservation of the constitution and the laws. On this day I have been called on to submit to their operation under circumstances which many persons might have thought sufficient to justify resistance. Considering obedience to the laws, even when we think them unjustly applied, as the first duty of the citizen, I did not hesitate to comply with the sentence you have heard, and I entreat you to remember the example I have given you of respectful submission to the administration of justice.[1]

This was Jackson at his best, and, even if it was due to the suggestions of his advisers, it did him credit. Unfortunately, it was marred by an early return to what an opponent termed "an obstinate and morbidly irascible temperament." A few days later he published the statement which the judge refused to admit to the record with a preface in which he attacked Hall in a severe personal manner. He charged and offered to prove, if the judge denied it, certain objectionable things: the challenge was accepted, in a prompt newspaper utterance, but Jackson failed to pursue it further.[2]

Amid the rejoicing that followed the end of the campaign the quarrel with Hall was discounted and soon forgotten. The American people cared little for the ruffled feelings of a judge whom they believed too punctilious, and they were ready to forgive much to him who defeated Pakenham. The incident, therefore, left Jackson's glory undiminished, except in the pages of history, where it is a warning that a general must use martial

---

[1] Gayarre, *Louisiana*, IV., 625, Martin, *History of Louisiana*, passim, and Reid and Eaton, *Jackson*, 419. The account in the last differs in some respects from that which Martin, a contemporary, gives, and which Gayarre follows.
[2] Gayarre, *Louisiana*, IV., 626.

law moderately and an example to encourage a just judge to maintain the supremacy of the laws.

While this affair transpired, Jackson was preparing to return to Nashville. During the last weeks of his stay Mrs. Jackson was his visitor. She was a striking figure in the social life of the gay French city. As her husband was the soul of honesty and primitive honor, she was the essence of kind-heartedness and religious devotion. Accustomed to the best position in the less polished society of Tennessee, they took with ease, if not with grace, a similar position in New Orleans, where they were long remembered with kindness. April 6th, they set out for Nashville, received at every stopping place with demonstrations of joy. Cities gave dinners and legislatures voted swords and addresses. From that time Jackson was the "Hero of New Orleans."

Reports of Jackson's clash with Judge Hall reached Washington and some persons demanded that he be court-martialed. As soon as he received intimations of this from Madison and Dallas, secretary of war, he set out for Washington to impeach Hall, first sending his informant severe letters in denunciation of his opponents. In the capital both President and secretary were complaisant, and the latter in a letter justified all that the general had done. But there was an interview in which the superior officer offered, as Jackson says, "a chart blank, approving my whole preceedings." He then abandoned his plan to impeach the judge.[1]

In the spring of 1815, the army was reorganized on a peace footing. Two divisions were created with a major-general over each. Jackson was given the command in the South and Gen. Jacob Brown in the North. From his headquarters at Nashville he directed the distribution and operations of the

---

[1] Jackson to Kendall, June 18, 1842, *Cincinnati Commercial*, February 5, 1879.

forces south of the Ohio. Brigadier-General Gaines commanded on the Florida frontier, where there was most danger; and his superior might remain for long periods at the "Hermitage," enjoying the honor and comfort to which his high services entitled him.[1]

[1]*United States Statutes at Large*, III., 224.

XIV

CRUSHING THE SEMINOLES IN FLORIDA

GENERAL GAINES was well pleased to command on the south-eastern frontier. Both Indian affairs and our relations with Spain made active service in this region seem probable. The fugitive Creeks, held in check during the winter of 1814-15, were still hostile and waiting for an opportunity to renew the struggle. It was evident to most men that the United States must soon have Florida; and the Southwest viewed skeptically President Monroe's long drawn out diplomacy to that end, believing that force would eventually be employed. Jackson shared these opinions and enjoyed the prospect of becoming the agent who would make Florida American territory.

Of these two probable events the most imminent was war with the Creeks. During the recent struggle the British took the Creeks under their protection, leading them to think that the lands would be restored which were lost by the treaty of Fort Jackson. Had the British campaign in Louisiana been successful, some attempts to execute this promise would doubtless have been made. But the treaty of Ghent was silent on the subject, and the savages were forced to assume the appearance of peace.

A clause of this treaty provided that the United States should surrender all lands taken during the struggle from any Indians with whom they should be at war when the treaty was signed. The British may have had the Creeks in mind when the clause was written, but it could make no impression on the United States, since they held that the treaty of Fort Jackson, August, 1814, ended the war with these Indians. The fugitive Creeks repudiated the agreement made at Fort Jackson, but England was not disposed to insist on an interpretation friendly to their position. The savages hardly concealed their disappointment, and certain representatives of Great Britain, who remained with them, worked to keep it alive, through either good or bad intentions, until it should at last lead to open war. They assured the ignorant red men that England would see justice done them and the treaty be put into operation.

When Colonel Nicholls arrived in Florida in the summer of 1814, he was accompanied by Capt. George Woodbine,[1] to whom was assigned the work of organizing, training, and leading the corps of red men whom it was intended to employ. Arms and uniforms were distributed liberally, and soon seven hundred warriors were enlisted. This produced consternation on the border, where the inhabitants thought that a white man who would lead Indians against white men was nearly as bad as one who would organize Negroes against white men. Captain Woodbine — "the notorious Woodbine" he was called — became exceedingly unpopular and much regret was expressed that he did not fall into American hands during Jackson's second dash into Florida. A great deal of the wrath which sprang up on his account found vicarious outlet in the death of Arbuthnot and Ambrister.

Colonel Nicholls accompanied the British to New Orleans but took no part in the battle. After their departure from the coast he returned to Florida and resumed his course as friend to the Indians. He hoped to perpetuate British influence and in the spring of 1815 made an offensive and defensive alliance with them in behalf of his sovereign. So far as this related to Indians resident within the borders of the United States it could

---

[1]December 30, 1814, he signed himself "Captain 1st Battalion Royal Marines, and British Agent at the Talapues," *American State Papers, Foreign*, IV., 491.

have no force, and if ratified by the English government it must have produced trouble. He repaired the fort built the preceding year on the Apalachicola, stored it abundantly with arms and ammunition, and presented it to his allies as a base of future operations. He sought to give them, also, a better form of organization. At a great assembly of chiefs he spoke effectively of the duty of punishing Indians who wronged white men and succeeded in getting the Creeks to appoint administrative officers to restrain such offenders; and he encouraged Indians who had grievances against white men to bring their cases to him. After investigating such complaints he would appeal for justice to Colonel Hawkins, the United States agent among the Creeks. It is conceivable that a benevolent man in this position might under ideal conditions have exerted a fortunate influence on the relations between the two races; but Nicholls's spirit was not benevolent, his reputation was sinister, the situation was unpropitious, and his letters to Hawkins were so positive that the Americans considered them arrogant. To the people of the frontier he was an irritating intermeddler.

An illustration is the case of Bowlegs, a Seminole chief, who complained that the Americans had killed some of his men and driven off some of their cattle. Nicholls heard the case and May 12th, wrote to Hawkins. He recounted the wrongs of Bowlegs[1] and added:

Now, sir, if these enormities are suffered to be carried on in a Christian country, what are you to expect by showing such an example to the uncultivated native of the woods? (For savage I will not call them — their conduct entitles them to a better epithet.) I have, however, ordered them to stand on the defensive, and have sent them a large supply of arms and ammunition, and told them to put to death, without mercy, any one

---

[1]This chief signed himself "Bolick, chief of the Seminole Nation at Sahwahna," *American State Papers, Foreign*, IV., 493, but he was generally called "Bowlegs" by the whites.

molesting them; but at all times to be careful and not put a foot over the American line. In the mean time that I should complain to you; that I was convinced you would do your best to curb such infamous conduct. Also that those people who have done such deeds would, I was convinced, be disowned by the government of the United States and severely punished. They have given their consent to await your answer before they take revenge; but, sir, they are impatient for it, and well armed as the whole nation now is, and stored with ammunition and provisions, having a stronghold to retire upon in case of a superior force appearing, picture to yourself, sir, miseries that may be suffered by good and innocent citizens on your frontiers, and I am sure you will lend me your best aid in keeping the bad spirits in subjection. . . . I am also desired to say to you, by the chiefs, that they do not find that your citizens are evacuating their lands, according to the ninth article of the treaty of peace, but that they were fresh provisioning the forts. This point, sir, I beg of you to look into. They also request me to inform you that they have signed a treaty of offensive and defensive alliance with Great Britain, as well as one of commerce and navigation, which, as soon as it is ratified at home, you shall be made more fully acquainted with.[1]

When this letter was written, the Americans were preparing to run the line which, by the treaty of Fort Jackson, would separate the lands retained by the Creeks from those ceded to the United States, General Coffee being one of the commissioners. The Indians were greatly excited, and Big Warrior was reported to be urging the Choctaws to join his people in a war against the whites. General Gaines, with 1,000 men under him, felt none too strong to handle the situation. While he called for 5,000 men to reduce the Indians to a condition in which they would be either "friendly or harmless" he proposed to gain time by holding a council. He met the chiefs on June 7, 1815, and by much persuasion and the distribution of pro-

---

[1] *American State Papers, Foreign*, IV., 549.

visions softened their temper slightly; but his own confidence in the situation was not restored. Nicholls, also, was actively brewing discord. What he said to the Indians is not reported, but it may be inferred from a letter of June 12th, repudiating the treaty of Fort Jackson and warning the whites that they would occupy the ceded district at their peril.[1]

Gaines called on the governor of Georgia for troops and when the commissioners to run the line met in the autumn at the confluence of the Flint and Chattahoochee rivers he had 800 men on the spot. This show of force cowed the Creeks, and the surveyors proceeded without opposition; but the sullen savages muttered that there would be trouble when settlers appeared on the lands.[2] This state of irritation bore the usual fruits. Indians raided the white settlements, taking life and property, and as soon as claims were staked out in the disputed region reports of outrages began to go northward.

In the summer of 1815, Nicholls returned to England about the same time that the American government forwarded thither a protest against his ambitious schemes with the Indians. Lord Bathurst lost no time in repudiating the plans of the intermeddler, although the chiefs who accompanied him were received with prudent flattery in both official and unofficial circles. One of them, the prophet Francis, was made a brigadier-general in the royal service and received at court in a brave red uniform. He was given money and other presents and returned to Florida in the following year confident that he was in high favor with his new friends and protectors. These occurrences were calculated to create as much misapprehension among the Americans as among the too credulous Indians.

Meanwhile Colonel Nicholls's red friends showed how little

[1]Gaines to Jackson, June 8 and October 8, 1815, Jackson Mss. Nicholls to Hawkins, June 12, 1815, Jackson Mss.

[2]Benjamin Hawkins to Jackson, December 1 and 8, 1815; Gaines to Jackson, November 4, 1815; Gaines to Governor Early, October 13, 1815; Jackson Mss.

they were able to profit from his help by losing control of the fort he had given them. In northern Florida a band of fugitive American Negro slaves were organized for their own protection. They hated the Seminoles, who were accustomed to hunt them down and deliver them to their former masters. They had a good leader named Garçon and at an auspicious moment seized the fort on the Apalachicola with its 3,000 muskets, carbines, and pistols, its 763 barrels of gunpowder, its 300 kegs of rifle-powder, and its ample supply of ball and other necessaries;[1] and they held it against all the efforts of the Indians to retake it. They encouraged other fugitives to join them, raided across the border, and made the "Negro Fort" a menace to the slave property of southern Georgia. Even the Spanish authorities looked upon it with apprehension.

Gaines was alarmed at the situation and offered the Seminoles fifty dollars for each Negro captive if they took the fort. Jackson, also, took up the matter and was pleased when the government ordered him to destroy the place if the Spaniards would not do it.[2] He wrote to the governor of Pensacola expressing such a determination and asking if the "Negro Fort" was under the protection of the King of Spain. The reply convinced him that Spain would make no serious objection if the Americans suppressed the banditti.[3] The prospect of energetic action pleased him, but before he could make a move a terrific accident removed the object of solicitude.

The Americans were building Fort Scott on the Apalachicola just north of the Florida line. In July, 1816, four vessels, two of them gunboats, came up the river with supplies for this work. Gaines took the precaution to send Colonel Clinch with 116 men to act as escort, but with orders not to attack the Negroes, unless they should first open fire. Near the fort he met a body

[1] *American State Papers, Foreign*, IV., 560.
[2] Gaines to Jackson, May 14, 1816; Crawford to Jackson, March 15, 1816, Jackson Mss.
[3] Governor Mauricio de Funigia to Jackson, May 26, 1816, Jackson Mss.

of Seminoles hunting for Negro captives and the two bands
joined forces. From a captured bandit Clinch learned that
several days earlier Garçon seized and slew a boat's crew from
the four American vessels, which now lay at the mouth of the
river. Considering this an attack within the meaning of his
instructions he invested the hated fort and ordered the gunboats to come up the river. The Negroes gathered their women
and children in the place and showed their contempt for their
opponents by wildly firing their thirty-two pounders into the
forest. After several days of this pantomime the gunboats
were warped up the river against adverse winds and on July
27th, opened fire. Their small solid shot made no impression
on the strong English built walls, and hot shot were secured.
The first one of these had the fortune to penetrate a large magazine within the fort and there was a terrific explosion, which
cost the lives of 270 of the inmates and wounded sixty-one more.
Of the 334 occupants only three escaped unhurt. One of these
was Garçon, who was hanged in retaliation for turring and
burning one of the crew of the captured boat of the whites. One
unfavorable complication clouded this overwhelming success.
Clinch had promised the coöperating Seminoles the arms
taken from the fort, and he could hardly do otherwise since
they were originally Seminole property. Many were found in
the ruins and handed over to the red men. These guns were
later used by the Indians against the Americans.[1]

The Negro menace was now gone but the Indian discontent
remained. The unhappy Creeks realized their helplessness.
When Gaines appeared on the border to lay out the walls of
Fort Scott he called the neighborhood chiefs to a council. They
took the pipe of peace with listlessness saying, as he reported,
"that they were too poor to oppose us and therefore had deter-

---

[1]See report of Sailing-master Loomis commanding the gunboats that destroyed the fort, *American State
Papers, Foreign*, IV., 559.

mined to sit still and hold down their heads."[1] But some unbending spirits among them took up the tomahawk, slew white
men, and escaped to Florida.   Then the indignation of the settlers
was aroused and thoughout Georgia and Alabama ran a demand
for war.   Desperate white men made reprisals and one of the
slain was "a beloved woman."   When her murderers were
arrested they were released on a writ of *habeas corpus*.   Gaines
ordered their re-imprisonment and placed them in the same
jail with some Indians held for killing white persons.[2] But
this was unusual justice, and the Creeks were dismayed at the
inequity of their ordinary treatment.   "If the Indian murderers,"
said Big Warrior,writing to Jackson in reference to another case,
"were as completely in my power as this murderer was in yours,
you should see what I should have done for him."[3]

By March, 1817, several thousand white people were settled on
the rich lands taken from the Creeks. They came with the
heedless haste characteristic of the first comers in a new region
and soon suffered for lack of supplies.[4] This hardship made
the increasing Indian depredations seem heavier. When the
Indians demanded punishment for the slayers of their brethren
they were told that no white man would be killed for slaying
an outlaw. Then the savages renewed their depredations.
The whites demanded that the responsible parties be given up.
Then ten Indian towns united and sent their defiance. Ten
red men, they said, had been killed, and only seven whites: let
the Americans know that three more white men must die before
scores would be even. The message, as Gaines reported to Washington, was really a declaration of hostilities.[5]

About this stage in the story Alexander Arbuthnot becomes
prominent. This intelligent and benevolent Scotch trader

[1]Gaines to Jackson, April 18, 1816, Jackson Mss.
[2]Gaines to Jackson, June 3, 1817, Jackson Mss.
[3]April 16, 1817, Jackson Mss.
[4]Gaines to Jackson, March 6, 1817, Jackson Mss.
[5]Gaines to Jackson, October 1, 1817, Jackson Mss.

appeared in Florida early in 1817. Interested in the welfare of the Creeks he became both trader and political adviser, assuming in the latter relation almost exactly the position formerly occupied by Nicholls. They trusted him and gave him a power of attorney to treat for them. When the Americans in July proposed a conference he replied in behalf of one of the chiefs partly as follows:

I have received your letter requiring me to attend you to hear a talk authorized by the President of America. It is not convenient for me to attend personally, but I will pay every attention to your talk if you will send it to me in writing, and I assure you by this, that it is my wish to be good friends with the Americans, as well as all other people. I beg you to attend to no foolish talk or reports, that me or any of my people wish to disturb the Americans who do not encroach on us. We are peaceable and wish to let others be so; but there are people with the Nation who make trouble. Listen not to them.[1]

In taking up the work of Nicholls, Arbuthnot assumed the former's unpopularity with the whites, and the day was to come when he would rue it. Gaines pronounced him "one of those *self-styled philanthropists* who have long infested our neighboring Indian villages in the character of British agents."[2] The people of the frontier identified him with "the notorious Woodbine," and there were some who considered him the same individual under an assumed name. Among the latter was Niles, editor of the famous Baltimore weekly, *The Register.* He published a letter from Arbuthnot to the commandant of Fort Gaines in which the writer said: "The head chiefs request I will enquire of you why American settlers are descending the Chattahoochee, driving the poor Indian from his habitations, and taking possession of his home and cultivated fields." He

---

[1] See Gaines to Jackson, July 10, 1817, Jackson Mss.
[2] Gaines to Jackson, April 2, 1817, Jackson Mss.

appealed, he said, in the name of humanity and not by authority, but he gave warning that the British government would send to see "that the boundary lines, as marked out by the treaty, were not infringed." Niles, reprinting this letter, pronounced it "about as impudent a thing as we ever saw," adding that if Arbuthnot were captured he should be punished "with far less pity than is due to a sheep-killing dog."[1] In November, 1817, Gaines said that the hostile Indians numbered 2,000 with 400 Negroes.[2]

While relations with the Indians were thus becoming warlike, the old irritation against Spain, overshadowed for a time by the campaign in Louisiana, sprang again into vigorous life. Jackson's army was hardly disbanded before restless adventurers in New Orleans were planning an expedition against Mexico. Aurey's expedition to hold Galveston Bay had in it many who served under Jackson. General Humbert and Major Peire were among them, and they were quickly followed by the Lafittes, who had doffed the cloak of patriotism to assume again the more profitable garb of privateer. Edward Livingston himself remained in New Orleans lay adviser of the movement, even as he was formerly paid friend and mediator for the Baratarians. He and others kept Jackson informed of the movement and wished that the latter might lead it.[3] Jackson gave no open encouragement to it, neither did he try to suppress it; and the affair served to keep alive the popular feeling against Spain.

Another incident, trivial in itself, further irritated the borderers and aroused the feelings of Jackson and his military subordinates. The Americans were building Fort Crawford on the Spanish frontier and were sending supplies to it by way of the Escambia, which empties into Pensacola Bay. The supplies

---

[1] Niles, XII., 211, 287, XIV., page 168, n.
[2] Gaines to Jackson, November 21, 1817, Jackson Mss.
[3] Livingston to Jackson, November 7, 1816; Colonel Gibson to Jackson, January 12, 1817; Gaines to Jackson, February 14, 1817; Jackson Mss.

were under the charge of Colonel Brearly. In anticipation of his arrival at Pensacola, Gaines sent a messenger thither to ask the Spanish governor to allow the boats to pass without hindrance, giving the messenger a guard of seven soldiers for protection against the Seminoles. At first the governor objected to the request because he could not allow goods to be imported free of duty. If the Americans wanted to buy provisions in Pensacola, he said, they might do so as freely as he could buy them in the United States, and if they desired they might refer the case to the governor-general in Havana. The messenger remained in the town, persisting in his demands, keeping his guard posted — a source of irritation — and awaiting the arrival of Brearly. After much delay and the renewal of the demands by Brearly when he had arrived, the Spaniard relented on the ground that the provisions were needed for the sake of humanity. This happened in April and May, 1817. Twice later he made the same concession under the same pretext; and finally in April, 1818, he refused to pass other supplies unless a Spanish merchant were made agent to forward them, paying the regular duties.[1] In this position the governor was within his rights, since the Escambia was not by treaty or accepted international law open to American navigation. But his denial of the privilege was taken as a wrong by Gaines, who wrote to the governor a letter, May 12, 1817, which for raw and undignified manner ought to make any courteous American blush to this day.[2]

Meanwhile President Monroe was negotiating for the purchase of Florida. In some doubt of his final success he was pleased to have Jackson in a position to seize that province, if it should be necessary. In fact, the President, feeling that war was imminent, was making preparations for such an event. June 2, 1817, he wrote that England was preparing to help Spain

---

[1] Gaines to Jackson, April 2 and May 8, 1817; Governor Jose Mascot to Gaines, April 12, 21, 1817 ; Governor Jose Mascot to Jackson, April 15, 1818; Jackson Mss.
[2] Jackson Mss.

subdue her revolting colonies in return for commercial privileges in South America.[1]

Nothing could please Jackson better then the prospect of getting his hands again on the rich prize, which he joyfully held for a brief moment in 1814. Between him and the President there was complete understanding. Referring to the invasion of 1814, Monroe wrote: "It is true I was not very severe on you for giving the blow, nor ought I to have been for a thousand considerations, which I need not mention."[2] There could not be much real anger beneath the official frowns of such a superior.

The first step into Florida came in connection with the Amelia Island incident. This place, on the Atlantic coast just south of the American line, was seized in 1817, by McGregor, an Irish adventurer who had been concerned before that in a filibustering expedition against Mexico. It became the resort of smugglers and a scene of discord, which was as intolerable to Spain as to the United States. Early in November Gaines was directed to occupy it till further orders. The adventurers made no resistance and time was granted them to withdraw.

When Gaines was sent to Amelia Island hostilities with the Seminoles were already begun. Fowltown, a particularly independent Indian town, lay on the American side of the new line. Its chief gave prompt notice to the commandant of Fort Scott that the land taken by the Americans was his and that he should resist all attempts to deprive him of it. Gaines waited not a moment to conciliate him; he treated the defiance as a declaration of war and ordered Major Twiggs with 250 men to seize the defiant chief. Twiggs reached the place on November 21st, was fired on by the savages, returned their fire, and drove them into the forest, with four warriors slain and many more wounded. Gaines reported this action to his

[1]Jackson Mss.
[2]Monroe to Jackson, July 3, 1816, Jackson Mss.

superiors and awaited instructions to carry the struggle against all the hostile Indians.[1] The operations against McGregor called him away from these scenes, which promised such active campaigning. The secretary of war — it was now Calhoun — did in fact on December 18th, and again on December 26th, order him to attack the Seminoles, through East Florida if it seemed advisable, pursuing them into Florida if necessary,[2] but when these instructions reached him the conduct of the principal attack was entrusted to other hands.

December 26th, the day he ordered Gaines for the second time to advance, Calhoun also ordered Jackson to Fort Scott to assume the chief direction of the war. He was authorized to concentrate at that point all the troops in his department, including 1,000 Georgia militia recently called into service, and to call out other militia if needed.[3] The order found him at the "Hermitage" alive to the situation. He believed the time was come to seize Florida, and January 6, 1818, before he left Nashville, he suggested as much to Monroe in the following letter:

SIR: A few days since I received a letter from the Secretary of War, of the 17th ult., with enclosures. Your order of the 19th ult. through him to Brevet Major-General Gaines to enter the territory of Spain, and chastise the ruthless savages who have been depredating on the lives and property of our citizens, will meet not only the approbation of your country, but the approbation of Heaven. Will you, however, permit me to suggest the catastrophe that might arise by General Gaines's compliance with the last clause of your order? Suppose the case that the Indians are beaten: they take refuge either in Pensacola or St. Augustine, which open their gates to them; to profit by his victory, General Gaines pursues the fugitives, and has to

---

[1] *American State Papers, Military*, I., 566.
[2] Jackson Mss.; also *American State Papers, Military*, I., 689, where the date of the former letter is given December 16, 1817.
[3] *American State Papers, Military*, I., 690.

halt before the garrison until he can communicate with his government. In the mean time the militia grow restless, and he is left to defend himself by the regulars. The enemy, with the aid of their Spanish friends and Woodbine's British partisans, or, if you please, with Aurey's force, attacks him. What may not be the result? Defeat and massacre. Permit me to remark that the arms of the United States must be carried to any point, within the limits of East Florida, where an enemy is permitted and protected, or disgrace attends.

The Executive Government have ordered, and, as I conceive, very properly, Amelia Island to be taken possession of. This order ought to be carried into execution at all hazards, and simultaneously the whole of East Florida seized, and held as an indemnity for the outrages of Spain upon the property of our citizens. This done, it puts all opposition down, secures our citizens a complete indemnity, and saves us from a war with Great Britain, or some of the continental powers combined with Spain. This can be done without implicating the government. *Let it be signified to me through any channel (say Mr. J. Rhea) that the possession of the Floridas would be desirable to the United States, and in sixty days it will be accomplished.*

The order being given for the possession of Amelia Island, it ought to be executed, or our enemies, internal and external, will use it to the disadvantage of the government. If our troops enter the territory of Spain in pursuit of our Indian enemy, all opposition that they meet with must be put down, or we will be involved in danger and disgrace.[1]

This letter was sound in its military ideas and unsound in its notion of foreign policy. It was certain that the Indians, if attacked, would flee to Florida, and if pursued thither they would seek refuge in Spanish towns; so that if hands might not be laid violently on such place of refuge, it would be well to make no appeal to arms in the first instance. But the suggestion that Florida be held as indemnity was impracticable.

Later, Jackson asserted that while on his way to Fort Scott,

---

[1] Benton, *Thirty Years' View*, I., 169.

in February, 1818, he received from Rhea the expected assurance and that it was in consequence of that information that he carried his army boldly into Florida. He also asserts that he preserved Rhea's letter till the Seminole controversy of the succeeding winter became warm and that he then, April 12, 1819, burned the letter at Rhea's request, who said that he urged it at Monroe's solicitation. He also said that he wrote a note to this effect on the margin of his letter-book the day the communication from Rhea was destroyed, and that his friend, Judge Overton, saw the letter while it was extant.

Monroe's story differs totally from Jackson's. He says that he was ill when the letter of January 6th was received, that he read only two lines of it and seeing that it pertained to the Seminole situation laid it aside for Calhoun, that when the secretary of war read it he returned it with the remark that it required the President's own perusal, that it was shown to Crawford, a Georgian and secretary of the treasury, and that he, Monroe, then laid it aside and did not read it until his attention was called to it by Calhoun after congress met in December, 1818, when he looked it up and saw for the first time the suggestion as to seizing Florida.

The historian must choose between the statements of the two men. Both are persons of conceded honesty, and we cannot impugn the intentions of either. But Monroe, as an educated man and a trained official, probably had a more reliable memory. Jackson's defense, which he prepared at the time but did not publish, shows that he was not judicially minded. There is more probability that his memory was poorer than Monroe's. Moreover, certain other facts weaken Jackson's story: (1) He gave only a most general account of the contents of the letter. Even if it were written we cannot be sure that his memory did not play a trick in regard to its meaning.[1] (2) Although he says he made in the margin of his letter-book a note opposite the copy of the letter of January 6th, no letter-book for this date is found in the large collection of papers which he has left, and neither Benton, nor Parton, nor Kendall, nor any other of the earlier historians who saw the collection in its undiminished state, except the unreliable Henry Lee, has mentioned it. It would seem that Jackson would have been careful to preserve this bit of corroborating evidence after the loss of its main piece, if he had it. (3) What real harm could Rhea's letter have done commensurate with the commotion caused by its assumed destruction? It is said its publication would have made Spain unwilling to sign the Florida cession treaty, but the treaty was signed at Washington seven weeks before the letter was said to have been destroyed. It was then expected that Spain would ratify at once; and as the letter was safe in Jackson's hand and only destroyed to prevent its coming, by his death or some accident, into the hands of persons who might not conceal it — a contingency which was not imminent — its destruction could hardly have been necessary to make ratification sure. (4) When Rhea was called on later to corroborate Jackson he was so old that his faculties were weak. He wrote at least three letters to Jackson before he was able to recall all that Jackson desired and he did not succeed till he received some important promptings. In one letter, January 4, 1831, he said:

I observe by my papers that you was in Washington in January, 1819. As yet nothing more. At that time I was continually occupied with business before the committee of pensions and revolutionary claims, and therefore I desire to

---

[1] A copy of Overton's statement is in the Jackson Mss. He says that in 1818, while preparing Jackson's defense in the Seminole Controversy, he saw Rhea's letter in the original, which "in substance conveyed the idea that he had conversed with the President, who showed him your confidential letter; that he approved of your suggestion, etc." Which suggestion?

have something to bring the matter to my recollection. You did not write it to me but I see by the newspapers what is going on. I request you to send me to Blountsville a copy of the letter (in which you mention my name) to Mr. Monroe. I am desirous to have it and trust all will come to light. As you are on the defensive I will help you all I can. I desire nothing to be known of me in the business, until I speak out as fully myself as I can and therefore this letter so far *confidential, confidential.*

Jackson complied with his friend's request, forwarded copies of his letters to Monroe and related the whole matter as he remembered it. March 30th, Rhea was still calling for information and saying, "You think you will have to come out if so, be not in haste."[1]

December 18, 1818, Rhea seems to have known nothing of such a letter as Jackson later described. Writing to the latter he said: "I will, for one, support your conduct, believing as far as I have read that you have acted for public good. There

[1] The letters from Rhea to Jackson, January 4, March 30, April 2, 1831, are in Jackson Mss. I venture a possible explanation of the discrepancy between the statements of Monroe and Jackson, mostly a conjecture for it cannot be proved. Early in 1817, Jackson learned that the acting secretary of war had withdrawn from his division Major Long, a subordinate, and assigned him to duty elsewhere without informing the commanding general of the fact. He sent a vigorous remonstrance to President Monroe, and getting no reply within a reasonable time, published an order warning his officers to obey no instructions in the future which did not come through his hands. A dispute was thus brought to the public attention between General Jackson and the acting secretary, which the pacific Monroe was not able to settle. But when Calhoun took the war office, December 10, 1817, he wrote a conciliatory letter to Jackson and restored his good temper. Late in November, while the affair was still unsettled, Rhea, who was a member of congress from Tennessee, had a conversation about it with Monroe, in which the latter said many complimentary things about Jackson. November 27th and again December 24th, Rhea wrote Jackson in regard to the matter, expressing the President's high regard for the general. All of this shows that Rhea considered himself a mediator between his two friends in this matter. Now the bearing of this situation on the letter of January 6th is this: It is possible that some approving expression of Monroe in a later conversation with Rhea was reported by the latter to Jackson in such a way that the general would take it for the hint to invade Florida. Neither Monroe nor Rhea, then knew about the suggestion of January 6th, and an approving expression of the former may have been innocently reported by the latter in such a way as to convey a world of meaning to the expectant Jackson. We can hardly doubt that Jackson burned, as he alleged, a letter from Rhea containing some statement, which he took for permission; the statement so interpreted must, therefore, have referred to something else. This explanation seems more probable, since neither Jackson nor Overton gives any definite notion of how the permission in the burned letter was worded. The alternative to this theory, so far as I can see, is to hold that either Jackson or Monroe made false assertions, with the probability in favor of Jackson's guilt. It is difficult to believe this of either man. (For the letters from Rhea to Jackson mentioned in this note see Jackson Mss; also see Monroe to Jackson, December 2, 1817. in the same collection.) — J. S. B.

has been (as you no doubt will have observed, in the public papers,) an attempt made to investigate, but failed — the resolution was postponed — indefinitely. I confess I had rather that everything that could have been alleged had come out, but it was otherwise ordered."[1] The tone of this letter and the lack of others from Rhea at this time seem to indicate that he knew little about the beginning of the Seminole War.

Senator Williams, of Tennessee, claimed that he suggested to Monroe to order that the Indians be followed into Florida, that he believed Jackson would seize the opportunity if warranted in doing so by his orders, and that when the controversy arose in 1819 he knew from Crawford, and said to many friends, that Calhoun in Monroe's Cabinet desired to reprimand Jackson. Williams added that Jackson was told this but was so infuriated against Crawford that he would not believe it.[2]

Whatever the truth about the suggestion of January 6th, the secretary's orders of December 26th, to take command of the campaign put General Jackson into quick motion. It was January 11th that the order reached the "Hermitage." It reminded the commander that there were 800 regulars and 1,000 Georgia militia under arms in the southern division, and it authorized him to call on the governors of neighboring states for other troops if they were needed. Eighteen hundred men were enough to beat the Indians but they were not enough to seize and hold Florida, and it was the latter object that Jackson had in mind. One thousand mounted men from Tennessee and Kentucky were believed to be necessary for this movement; but they could not be called out at once by the governor, who was on a visit to the Cherokees. With characteristic initiative Jackson called together some of his old officers, authorized them to raise the required number of men on his own responsibility,

---

[1] Jackson Mss.
[2] John Williams to Van Buren, March, 22, 1831. Van Buren Mss.

and join him at Fort Scott as soon as possible. He assumed rightly that the governor would later approve of the action. January 22nd, with 200 men from the vicinity of Nashville, he set out by the shortest roads for the scene of danger. At Hartford, in northern Georgia, he was joined by Gaines, who had hastened back from Amelia Island before he knew he was superseded in the campaign, and March 9th the commander reached Fort Scott.[1]

In the meantime, the Indians were in much confusion. The best estimates make them not more than twelve hundred, although the warlike Gaines was disposed to have the number twice as large. They had no concerted plans for resistance. All their hopes lay in aid from the British and even Gaines said that they would submit as soon as they realized that this hope was vain.[2] Arbuthnot could give them no comfort and exerted himself to save his red friends from the ruin which threatened them. They were too much infuriated to submit to the Americans, but their resistance was never formidable, and it seems probable that they would have made peace after a few vigorous raids against their towns, if the Americans had not coveted Florida.

The Indians took the attack on Fowltown, November 21st, as the beginning of war. They remained armed in the vicinity and a few days later attacked a body of troops which were sent to reconnoitre. November 30th, they ambushed a boat in the Apalachicola and killed or captured all but six of its forty-seven occupants, including soldiers and seven women.[3] This could only provoke the utmost vengeance of the United States. The hostiles realized it and heard with awe that their punishment was committed to the terrible Jackson. They dared not with-

[1] *American State Papers, Military*, I., 687, 690, 696, 698.
[2] *Ibid*, 691, 686.
[3] *Ibid*, 686, 687.

stand him and fled before his face into the bounds of the Spanish province.

At Fort Scott, Jackson commanded less than 2,000 men, 800 regulars, 900 Georgia militia and a small body of friendly Creeks. These were threatened with starvation and he marched immediately for the mouth of the river, where he knew ships with provisions from Mobile were detained by adverse winds. March 16th he arrived at the site of the Negro Fort and began to repair it for a fortified base. At the same time he received ample provisions from the river. He was now fifteen miles from the gulf at the dividing line between East and West Florida, 200 miles east of Pensacola and 250 from St. Augustine. The intervening country, with the exception of a few posts, was as virgin forest as in the days of De Soto. So far as Spanish resistance was concerned the whole province was at his mercy.

He took little time to make up his mind what to do. Reports came that the hostile Indians were assembled at the post of St. Marks, seventy-five miles eastward on a small river and ten miles from the coast. He decided to take it, and writing to the secretary of war, March 25th,[1] justified himself as follows:

The Governor of Pensacola informed Captain Call, of the 1st infantry, (now here,) that the Indians had demanded arms, ammunition, and provisions, or the possession of the garrison of St. Marks of the commandant, and that he presumed possession would be given from inability to defend it. The Spanish government is bound by treaty[2] to keep her Indians at peace with us. They have acknowledged their incompetency to do this, and are consequently bound, by the law of nations, to yield us all facilities to reduce them. Under this consideration, should I be able, I shall take possession of the garrison as a depot for my supplies, should it be found in the hands of the Spaniards,

---

[1]*American State Papers, Military*, I., 698.
[2]By the treaty of 1795, the Spaniards agreed to restrain the Indians within their borders from attacks on the United States.

they having supplied the Indians; but if in the hands of the enemy I will possess it for the benefit of the United States, as a necessary position for me to hold, to give peace and security to the frontier, and put a final end to Indian warfare in the South.

March 26th, he set out straight overland for the fort, sending to the same place a fleet of small gunboats which had joined him from Mobile and New Orleans with orders to scour the coast and intercept any fugitives, "white, red, or black," who sought to escape his vengeance. On the march he was joined by a body of friendly Indians under the chief McIntosh and by a part of the delayed West Tennessee troops. The Indian towns which lay in his way fared badly. At one place the occupants dared to oppose him, but a vigorous attack sent them hurrying to St. Marks, where many of their friends were already assembled. The victor paused long enough to burn the houses of the hostiles and seize their supplies of cattle and provisions. Among the spoils were found more than fifty fresh scalps, some of which were recognized as those of the party recently slain on the Apalachicola. Following the fugitives rapidly the army came to St. Marks, which was not in Indian hands. The weak garrison could make no resistance, the place was handed over to the Americans, who gave receipts for the movable property and established their own garrison within it.

Learning then that another body of hostiles were assembled at Bowlegs' town of Suwanee, Jackson marched on April 9th for that place, hoping to take it by surprise. On the sixteenth he came to the outskirts of the place but not until the inhabitants had information of his approach. His attempt to surround the warriors proved futile, and they succeeded, much to his disappointment, in escaping across the river with the loss of nine Negroes and two Indians killed and nine Indians and seven Negroes captured. At this time the whole power of re-

sistance of the Seminoles was broken, and their villages were
burned and provisions seized or destroyed with impunity.
Results had shown that they were not prepared for war, however
hostile may have been their feelings. Before Jackson's force
of nearly three thousand white troops and two thousand Indian
allies their scattered towns made, and could make, the faintest
opposition. As a military feat the war came to little. It does
General Jackson credit only as showing his remarkable power
of quick and unrelenting pursuit in the face of many difficulties
from bad roads and scant supplies of provisions.[1]

Reporting his movement Jackson said, while at St. Marks,
"Foreign agents, who have long been practising their intrigues
and villanies in this country, had free access to the fort." He
referred chiefly to Woodbine, who was fortunate enough to
escape before the arrival of Jackson, and Arbuthnot, who trusted
unhappily to the sanctity of Spanish neutrality and was promptly
made prisoner. At Suwanee was found an adventurer of kindred
character, Robert C. Ambrister, an English officer who was
certainly where he had no business to be. Both were held
prisoners for trial by court-martial.[2]

Two other captives were the Indian chiefs Francis and Himollimico. Awaiting in despair the arrival of Jackson, they
were cheered to learn that a boat was in the harbor flying the
British flag. Francis was recently returned from England and
believed it was help from that quarter, with arms and supplies.
Taking his trusted assistant, Himollimico, he rowed ten miles
to the anchorage and went aboard in all confidence. He was
received with tokens of friendship and laying aside his arms
went below to drink with the commander. At a signal he was
seized and bound, and when he protested was informed that he
was a prisoner on an American gunboat. It was, in fact, one

[1]*American State Papers, Military*, I., 699, 700.
[2]*American State Papers, Military*, I., 700.

of the fleet which Jackson despatched to the coast to intercept fugitives. The commander displayed the British flag to attract the flying Indians. The next day the two prisoners were sent to the fort where they were summarily hanged by the orders of the commanding general.[1] The manner of taking them, though no worse than the ruses ordinarily practised by the Indians, has usually shocked the Americans' sense of fair play. The relentlessness of the execution and the courageous bearing of Francis, who had the charm of manner of the best specimens of his race, have served to contrast the characters of the two warriors, American and Indian, without disadvantage to the latter.

The fate of the two white prisoners was equally severe, although pronounced with more formality. The court-martial before which they were sent was taken from a population accustomed to hate Woodbine and who had till very recently believed that "Arbuthnot" was an *alias* for "Woodbine." The escape of this leader of Negro and Indian troops before the arrival of the army was a disappointment, and put them into a frame of mind to have a vicarious victim, and this boded ill for the veritable Arbuthnot. He was charged with inciting the Indians to war against the United States, he being a citizen of Great Britain, and with acting as a spy for the Indians and furnishing them with arms and other assistance. A third charge alleged that he had incited the Indians to kill Hambly and Doyle, two American traders, but the court decided that it had no jurisdiction over that matter.[2]

In support of the first charge it was specified that Arbuthnot advised the Creek chief, Little Prince, not to execute the treaty of Fort Jackson and that the United States were infringing the treaty of Ghent: also, that he volunteered to transmit complaints

---

[1]Parton, *Jackson* II, 454, gives a spirited account of the execution of the two chiefs. See also statement of commanding officer, *American State Papers, Military*, I., 763.

[2]The minutes of this court-martial are in *American State Papers, Military*, I., 721.

to the British government to induce it to interfere to see that the Indians received their rights. The prosecution offered as witness the interpreter who translated the letter for the Little Prince, but the letter itself was not in evidence. Letters were also produced from Arbuthnot to the governor of the Bahamas and to the British minister in Washington, showing that the writer was accepted by the Indians and acted as an agent for them. Another piece of evidence was a power of attorney signed by twelve chiefs, three of whom were old red sticks, some of whom lived in Florida and some in the United States, giving him full authority to represent them in any business whatever and to write letters for them.

The second charge, aiding the enemy, was supported by a letter from Arbuthnot at St. Marks, written four days before Jackson's arrival there, to his son at Suwanee warning him to convey the father's property to a place of safety and transmitting to Bowlegs the advice that it was useless to oppose the Americans. This information, it was believed, enabled the savages to escape to the forest and thus to disappoint Jackson's desire for vengeance. The prosecution showed also that the accused had ten kegs of powder for the Indians and Negroes.

The prisoner introduced little evidence and spoke in his own defense, although he was offered counsel. He objected to the evidence of the interpreter, since by criminal procedure the contents of a letter might not be introduced by parol, if the letter itself was obtainable; the letter to his son was written merely to save his property and to warn the Indians to submit to the Americans; and finally, he said ten kegs of powder were no more than enough for hunting by the Indians and Negroes with whom he traded. It was not a strong defense considering the temper of his judges. The story of the interpreter has marks of genuineness and other documents supported the contention that the accused was intermeddling with the interpretation of the treaty. The court also could see that, whatever the object of the writer the letter to his son enabled the foe to escape the conqueror: they knew, also, that ten kegs of powder sold at just this time to the enemy of the American arms would make a difference in the warlike attitude of that enemy. After secret deliberation the prisoner was found guilty on each charge by a two-thirds vote of the court. The verdict was in no sense Jackson's. The court was presided over by Gaines, then brevet major-general, as well trained in military law as any officer in the army. Of the twelve other members six were of the regular army and six of the militia, all but one of a higher rank than captain. It was a representative court-martial, and it sentenced the prisoner to death by hanging.

Had the Seminoles been civilized Arbuthnot's intermeddling would have been less objectionable; but his course when taken with savages could not fail to produce dissatisfaction and lead to border massacres and pillaging. He was too wise a man to fail to understand this. He imprudently placed himself in a position as dangerous to his person as profitable to his commerce. The fate which overtook him, though not deserved, would have been avoided by a man of ordinary prudence.

The court-martial next took up the case of Ambrister. He was a British citizen, formerly a lieutenant of marines, nephew of the governor of New Providence, and now about to return to England where he expected to be married. But the love of adventure was so strong that he turned aside to become involved in the Indian troubles brewing in Florida, having in mind the achievement of Woodbine. To many he said that he came on the latter's business. He was charged with aiding the Indians and Negroes and inciting them to resistance, and with leading and commanding them in their war against the United States. Evidence shows that he bore himself arrogantly from the time of his arrival, seizing property for the use of himself and his rabble of Negro followers, giving out ammunition and paint to the Indians, and, when he knew of Jackson's approach, sending his followers to oppose him with arms. Several compromising letters of the prisoner were introduced, and one of them contained these words: "There is now a very large body of Americans and Indians, who I expect will attack us every day, and God only knows how it will be decided; but I must only say this will be the last effort with us. There has been a body of Indians gone to meet them, and I have sent another party. I hope Your Excellency will be pleased to grant the favor they request."

Ambrister's defense was weaker than Arbuthnot's. The letter just quoted showed that he both incited the Indians and led them. He pleaded not guilty of the former charge and guilty with justification of the latter; but at the last threw himself on the mercy of the court. The verdict was guilty and the sentence was death by shooting. After sentence was announced a member of the court asked for a reconsideration, which was granted, and the sentence was changed to fifty lashes on the bare back and a year's imprisonment at hard labor. This leniency seems to have been due to the fact that Ambrister had been led on solely by love of adventure: the court probably felt that Arbuthnot, who was an old man, acted from design and was more culpable. But Jackson had no leniency for either prisoner. He approved of the verdicts as orginally given, setting aside the second sentence of Ambrister on the ground that the court had no right to reconsider. His position has this in its favor, that if a court can revoke its sentences it assumes the pardoning power, which it was never meant to exercise. The court ended its labors on April 28th, during the night Jackson gave his approval to the verdict, and at daylight on the twenty-ninth he set out for Fort Gadsden. A few hours later Ambrister was shot and Arbuthnot hanged from the yard of his own vessel. The spectacle of their two British friends, whom they had thought all powerful, thus summarily disposed of by the relentless Jackson produced a deep and lasting impression on the hostile Indians.

In his order confirming sentence Jackson said: "It is an established principle of the laws of nations that any individual of a nation making war against the citizens of another nation, they being at peace, forfeits his allegiance, and becomes an outlaw and pirate." This doctrine has no basis in international law. Citizens of neutral nations may, and do, take part in the wars of belligerents without becoming outlaws; they become prisoners of war and if captured are dealt with by the rules of civilized warfare. But the case is usually regarded otherwise in savage warfare, which is considered a species of organized assassination. A man who assumes the responsibility of bringing on such a calamity is in a sense a party before the act to its horrors and is not dealt with in the same way as a soldier in recognized warfare.[1] This was the position of Adams, American secretary of state, when the matter was taken up by the British government. He asserted that Arbuthnot with others was responsible for the war and that they deserved the punishment of death.[2] The British government was thus given no opportunity to dispute Jackson's definition of neutral rights but had to decide whether or not they would ask retribution for the punishment given their citizens, if it seemed excessive. They held after discussion that the penalty was not too great, on the ground, as Rush, our minister to London, reported, that Arbuthnot and Ambrister "had identified themselves, in part at least, with the Indians, by going amongst them with other purposes than those of innocent trade, by sharing in their sympathies too actively when they were upon the eve of hostilities with the United States;

---

[1] Wharton, *International Law Digest*, III., 328, 348.
[2] Adams to Erving, Minister to Spain, November 28, 1818 *American State Papers, Foreign*, IV, 539, 544.

by feeding their complaints; by imparting to them counsel; by heightening their resentments, and thus at all events increasing the predisposition which they found existing to war, if they did not originally provoke it."[1] The fate of the two men serves as a warning that irregular agents, whose interests or enthusiasm lead them into rash actions, may not with impunity imperil the peaceful relations of their respective nations by their unauthorized interference.[2]

The incident made temporarily a powerful impression on both the American and British public. Jackson's compatriots approved his course heartily. They believed he had done justice upon two bad characters, and they admired the boldness of a man who could break so successfully the red tape of the foreign office. Englishmen were indignant that two of their fellow-citizens were so summarily killed by an angry frontier general. They demanded an explanation; but it is probable that there was some exaggeration in Castelreagh's subsequent remark to Rush that war might have then occurred "if the Ministry had but held up a finger."[3]

Having crushed and intimidated the Indians there was now no reason why Jackson should not retire to American territory if his sole object was to deal with the savages. He left St. Marks garrisoned by 200 American troops, saying they were necessary to keep the Indians quiet. But they were too few if there was a real danger from that source and too many if the savages were crushed, as he alleged. His true reason must have been, as he said in the secret letter of January 6th, to hold Florida as indemnity. This supposition finds confirmation in his further movement in Florida. West of the Apalachicola

[1]Rush to Adams, January 25, 1819, Mss. reports in state department.

[2]The case is discussed in Moore, *International Law Digest*, VII., 207. See also *British and Foreign State Papers*, 1818-1819, page 326, where the correspondence between the two governments is given.

[3]Rush, *Memoranda of a Residence at the Court of London*, (Edition 1833) page 488. For Rush on the negotiations see *Ibid*, 464, 473.

was a broad territory, in which the Indians were not trouble-
some, but which was significant because it contained the town
of Pensacola, without which American control of Florida would
be impossible. Into this region he penetrated, on May 10th,
with 1,200 men to scour the country, as he put it. He met
no opposition from the Seminoles but on the twenty-third
received from the governor of Pensacola a written protest against
this-invasion of Spanish territory. Jackson was then within
a day's march of the town and on the same day sent peremp-
torily an announcement of his purpose to occupy the town
and its defenses. He supported his position by recounting the
violations of neutrality at St. Marks, which, if they justified
interference at that place, had nothing to do with Pensacola. He
also alleged that Indians received succor at the latter place.
The affidavits by which he tried to support the second charge
are extremely flimsy and hardly weaken the governor's straightforward declaration that he helped only a small number of
non-combatants and a party of eighty-seven men, women, and
children who were collected and sent northward with the sanction
of an American officer.

When he left Fort Gadsden, Jackson was told that 500 warriors
were assembling at Pensacola. He said he would occupy the
place if the report were true. No kind of evidence which he
has preserved shows that any Indians were now there, yet he
proceeded to take the town and hold it subject to the orders
of his government. His own reports and accompanying documents make it probable that his real reason here, as at St. Marks,
was the determination to hold West Florida, of which Pensacola
was the controlling point.[1] His attitude is further shown by
the fact that he ordered Gaines to seize St. Augustine. There
was now no other reason for such an order than the purpose

---

[1]For documents respecting the movement against Pensacola see *American State Papers, Military*, I.,
701-721.

to hold Florida, and the department of war revoked the command.[1]

His plans were accomplished with his usual promptness. May 24th he entered Pensacola and sent the governor, who took refuge in the Barrancas, a formal justification of his conduct, announcing that he would "assume the government until the transaction can be amicably adjusted by the two governments." The Spaniard replied politely, defending his conduct, requiring the invaders to leave Spanish territory as soon as they obtained necessary supplies, and closing by saying: "If contrary to my hopes, Your Excellency should persist in your intention to occupy this fortress, which I am resolved to defend to the last extremity, I shall repel force by force; and he who resists aggression can never be considered an aggressor. God preserve Your Excellency many years." To this Jackson replied as follows:

SIR: The accusations against you are founded on the most unquestionable evidence. I have the certificates of individuals who, on the 23rd inst., at or near the little bayou, counted seventeen Indians in company with several Spanish officers.[2] I have only to repeat that the Barrancas must be occupied by an American garrison, and again to tender you the terms offered, if amicably surrendered. Resistance would be a wanton sacrifice of blood, for which you and your garrison would have to atone. You cannot expect to defend yourself successfully, and the first shot from your fort must draw upon you the vengeance of an irritated soldiery. I am well advised of your

---

[1]Parton, *Jackson*, II., 555.

[2]Jackson seems to have referred to the following certificates: By Richard Brickham; "I certify that on the 23d of May, being in the bayou, which enters Pensacola Bay, one and a half miles from the town, I saw at the ferry, on the road to the Barrancas, a number of Indians, I think about seventeen, in company with four Spanish officers. The officers were carried over, and the boat returned to ferry over the Indians. I saw one boat-load landed on the side next the Barrancas. The Indians concealed themselves in the bushes on discovering us."

By John Bonners:"I certify that I was in a boat with Brickham at'the place and time mentioned in the above certificate; that I saw several Indians in company with four Spanish officers. The officers were ferried over with one Indian. I did not see the Indians ferried over; they concealed themselves on discovering us."

It is not alleged that these Indians were warriors, or even warlike; the number is not definite; and nothing in the statements contradicts the governor's admission that he aided peaceful Indians who lived around Pensacola in small numbers, as he had a right to do.

strength, and cannot but remark on the inconsistency of presuming yourself capable of resisting an army which has conquered the Indian tribes, too strong, agreeably to your own acknowledgement, to be controlled by you. If the force which you are now disposed wantonly to sacrifice had been wielded against the Seminoles, the American troops had never entered the Floridas. I applaud your feeling as a soldier in wishing to defend your post; but when resistance is ineffectual, and the opposing forces overwhelming, the sacrifice of a few brave men is an act of wantonness, for which the commanding officer must be accountable to his God.

Approaching the Barrancas the Americans were received with a brisk fire, and prepared to carry the place by storm; but the besieged governor would not allow matters to go to that stage. Feeling that his resistance was enough to show his loyalty to duty, he surrendered the fortifications, marching out with the honors of war. Jackson agreed to transmit him, the soldiers, and the civil officials to Havana, to receipt for military and other public property, and to hold the town and province subject to the determination of the American and Spanish governments. "The terms," reported Jackson to his government, "are more favorable than a conquered enemy would have merited, but, under the peculiar circumstances of the case, my object obtained, there was no motive for wounding the feelings of those whose military pride or honor had prompted to the resistance made." To his friend Campbell he wrote more confidentially: "All that I regret is that I had not stormed the works, captured the governor, put him on trial for the murder of Stokes and his family and hung him for the deed."[1]

The Barrancas surrendered May 28th, and the next day its captor was on his way to Tennessee. He left the Spanish civil administration intact, except as to the customs. The

---

[1] Cited by Parton, *Jackson*, II., 500. Stokes was an American recently murdered in an Indian raid.

United States revenue laws were ordered in force, a revenue collector with necessary subordinates was appointed to execute them, and a garrison gave the proper support. At a banquet in Nashville in honor of the returning hero one of the toasts was: "Pensacola — Spanish perfidy and Indian barbarity rendered its capture necessary. May our government never surrender it from the fear of war." This toast voiced the popular feeling that Florida must be retained. Many persons believed that it would never return to Spain, among them land speculators who bought extensively in real estate at Pensacola. One of them was the colonel commanding the garrison left there. Subsequent developments punctured the boom and the venturesome colonel confessed that he had "burnt his fingers."[1] But before this episode was accomplished the invasion of Florida was made to play a prominent part in the nation's diplomacy and politics.

---

[1]Col. William King to Col. R. Butler, December 9, 1818, Jackson Mss.

CHAPTER XV

THE SEMINOLE WAR IN RELATION TO DIPLOMACY AND POLITICS

JACKSON'S invasion of Florida produced important historical results in both diplomatic and political affairs. It thrust itself into the midst of a long and delicate negotiation for the purchase of Florida, threatening at the time to defeat it, and probably helping to bring it at last to a favorable conclusion by showing Spain how precarious was her hold on the province. It became a rallying point for antagonistic groups of politicians, placing Clay in life-long opposition to the Tennessee hero, whom it drew to the ranks of his opponents; and in this sense it may be regarded as the starting point of a thirty-years' conflict between the two men.

Our negotiations for Florida began as early as Jefferson's administration. They were complicated by many matters and made no progress for ten years; but in 1817, there was a change of ministry in Madrid which favored our hopes. George W. Erving, our minister at that court, was surprised to receive, on August 17th, from Pizarro, the Spanish minister, a proposition to cede Florida in exchange for all of Louisiana west of the Mississippi, from its source to its mouth.[1] The offer, of course, was impossible; but President Monroe took it as sign of yielding, and redoubled his efforts. The negotiations were transferred to Washington and went forward under the immediate supervision of Secretary Adams. In an interview on December 19th, Onis, the Spanish minister in Washington, began these fresh

---

[1] *American State Papers, Foreign*, IV, 445.

negotiations; the date was three days after Calhoun first gave Gaines permission to pursue the Indians into Florida but with orders not to attack a fortified post.

For three months the discussion proceeded tediously but hopefully, much argument being held on the questions of boundaries and claims. While the business was in this stage, Monroe asserted, in a message of March 25, 1818, that most of the hostile Seminoles lived in Florida; that Spain failed to restrain them from attacking the Americans, as by treaty she was bound to do; and that the United States would be justified in entering Florida to punish the savages, but without insult to the Spanish authorities there, withdrawing as soon as their object was accomplished. Onis resented this criticism and protested to Adams with many arguments to show that Spain had kept faith.[1]

Soon after this the newspapers began to speak of Jackson's expedition into Florida and to hint at further designs than punishing the Indians. Onis discounted such rumors and made no protest until at the middle of June he received official information from the governor of West Florida. His indignation burst forth immediately and treaty negotiations were suspended. "How was it possible," he exclaimed, "to believe that at the very moment of a negotiation for settling and terminating amicably all the pending differences between the two nations, and while Spain was exhibiting the most generous proofs of a good understanding, and the most faithful observance of all the duties of good neighborhood, the troops of the United States should invade the Spanish provinces, insult the commanders and officers of their garrisons, and forcibly seize on the military posts and places in those provinces?" He closed a catalogue of wrongs by saying: "In fine, General Jackson has omitted nothing that characterizes a haughty conqueror but the cir-

---

[1] *American State Papers, Foreign*, IV., 486.

cumstances of adding to these monstrous acts of hostility the contradictory expressions of peace and friendship with Spain."[1]

The wrath of Onis was not greater than that of Pizarro. During the summer he conducted with Erving a most amiable negotiation, and several of the disputed points were already removed when news came in August of the course of Jackson in Florida. At first, he contented himself with a protest, assuming, as it seems, that Jackson would be disavowed; but when Onis reported that no such action was taken in Washington the resentment of the minister burst forth. Renewing his protest he declared:

In consideration of the nature of the said injuries and acts essentially hostile, the course of the pending negotiations between the two governments shall be, and accordingly is, suspended and interrupted, until the Government of the United States shall mark the conduct of General Jackson in a manner correspondent with its good faith, which appears to be no other than by disapproving the aforementioned excesses, giving orders to reinstate everything as it was previous to the invasion, and inflicting a suitable punishment on the author of such flagrant disorders.[2]

Monroe was, indeed, slow to act in the matter, for there were many difficulties. He was anxious to complete the negotiations for Florida, and individually he disapproved of its occupation, but Jackson's popularity was so great that the administration dared not comply with all of Pizarro's demands. The matter first came up in the cabinet on July 15, 1818, in reply to Onis's protest. Monroe and all his advisers but the secretary of state believed that Jackson had violated his instruction. Calhoun was especially strong and gave the impression that he was touched in his pride because his orders were not

[1] *Ibid*, 495.
[2] *Ibid*, 522.

followed. Adams held that all Jackson did in Florida was defensive and incident to his main duty to crush the Seminoles, and he added that Pensacola ought to be held until Spain gave guarantee to restrain her Indians from attacks on the United States; but he changed the latter position when convinced by argument that territory cannot be acquired under the constitution without an act of congress. A long debate resulted in three documents: (1) A letter to Onis announcing that Pensacola and St. Marks would be given up; (2) a letter to Jackson calculated to soften the blow and preserve his good-will by explaining the constitutional objections to the acquisition of Florida by invasion; (3) a letter by Wirt, attorney-general, for publication in the *National Intelligencer* by which it was sought to secure popular support.[1]

In these discussions Adams, whose diplomacy was apt to be aggressive, was disappointed because Monroe did not take a more positive position. But when, in November, despatches came from Erving, inclosing Pizarro's notes of the preceding summer, he welcomed the opportunity to go to the bottom of the matter. His reply was excellent.[2] It began with the assertion that Jackson occupied Florida not by orders, but as an incident "which occurred in the prosecution of the war against the Indians"; and since Pizarro intimated that the situation might result in war, it would be well to review the Seminole troubles from their origin. They began with the arrival of Nicholls and Woodbine, who made Pensacola their base of operations, and, when driven out by Jackson, planted themselves on the Apalachicola to send forth the Indians and Negroes to distress the defenseless American settlers. But all this might be buried in oblivion with other transactions of war but for the conduct

1Adams, *Memoirs*, IV., 107-120.   For the documents see: 1. *American State Papers, Foreign*, IV., 508; 2. Monroe, *Writings*, VI., 54; 3. *National Intelligencer*, July 27, 1818.
2*American State Papers, Foreign*, IV., 539. With Adams's despatch are published many documents on the invasion of Florida, *Ibid*, 545-612.

of Nicholls and Woodbine after the return of peace. They fired the resentment of the Creeks by the assurance that the treaty of Ghent protected them, by holding out the hope of aid from Britain, by making a pretended treaty with them, by sending threatening letters to the American officials, by constructing the fort on the Apalachicola, by furnishing arms and ammunition, and by many other actions which tended to incite them to war on the United States, until at last the maddened savages sallied across the frontier and killed American citizens. All this was done in plain view of the Spanish officials who did not try to check it. Nor did it cease with the departure of Nicholls. Arbuthnot and Ambrister took up his work fanning the flame of discontentment, the Indian outrages continued and became more severe, until at last it was necessary for the United States to begin war. But how should the enemy be humbled without crossing the Spanish line, since they made it a safe refuge between their raids? General Jackson believed it was necessary to follow the foe into Florida, not as an enemy of Spain, but solely to reach an insolent foe. As he approached St. Marks he learned that it was likely to fall into the hands of the Indians, who were collected there in large numbers — and the information was from the governor of Pensacola himself. For this reason he occupied the fort, as he announced, till Spain was able to garrison it strongly enough to hold it against the Indians. Also, he learned that the governor of Pensacola, ruling over West Florida, had given various acts of assistance to the enemy, and he marched into that province. When he received from the governor a warning that he would be expelled by force if he did not leave at once, he took it as a challenge and to prevent his own ejectment seized the town of Pensacola and its defenses. He continued to hold the two places because he believed they would be used to protect the Indians if he left them in the hands of Spain. Regardless of this very justifiable precaution the United States had shown its good intentions by ordering the posts to be given up unconditionally; "but the President," continued the secretary, "will neither inflict punishment, nor pass a censure upon General Jackson, for that conduct, the motives of which were founded in the purest patriotism; of the necessity for which he had the most immediate and effectual means of forming a judgment; and the vindication of which is written in every page of the law of nations, as well as in the first law of nature — self-defense." On the contrary, the President thought that Spain ought to order an inquiry of the conduct of the governors of Pensacola and St. Marks. Adams came more closely to the point in the following candid and strong statement:

If, as the commanders both at Pensacola and St. Marks have alleged, this has been the result of their weakness rather than of their will; if they have assisted the Indians against the United States to avert their hostilities from the province which they had not sufficient force to defend against them, it may serve in some measure to exculpate, individually, those officers; but it must carry demonstration irresistible to the Spanish Government, that the right of the United States can as little compound with impotence as with perfidy, and that Spain must immediately make her election, either to place a force in Florida adequate at once to the protection of her territory, and to the fulfilment of her engagements, or cede to the United States a province, of which she retains nothing but the nominal possession, but which is, in fact, a derelict, open to the occupancy of every enemy, civilized or savage, of the United States, and serving no other earthly purpose than as a post of annoyance to them.

The force of this argument was not lost on Pizarro. Nothing further appears in regard to the demand that Jackson be punished, and the Florida negotiations, which were already resumed, proceeded so fast that on February 22, 1819, Monroe was able to send to the senate a treaty which gave us the long-sought territory.

Adams's defense of Jackson was the strongest that could be made, but it smacked of the advocate and it had certain weak points. Spain's responsibility for Nicholls, Arbuthnot, Ambrister, and Woodbine, her complicity with England, who was allowed to use Pensacola as a base in the war of 1812, her harboring fugitive Creeks, who sallied forth to attack the American frontier during that war, and, later, her failure even to try to restrain her own savages from similar attacks, and her weakness in guarding her territory are all points well taken; but they lose some of their force because American territory was for a long time safe refuge for filibusters against Spain. Weaker still is Adams's contention that it was necessary to take St. Marks to keep it from falling into Indian hands, since such a catastrophe was in nowise imminent; nor can one pay considerable attention to Jackson's reason for seizing Pensacola. Weakest of all was the defense of Jackson's holding West Florida and the district adjoining the Apalachicola on the east under the pretext that such a course was necessary to keep down an enemy who, according to Jackson's own statement, was utterly crushed. The American government recognized this, and announced at once that it would restore the province to its rightful owners, not, as Adams blandly said, as an act of grace, but because it had no justifiable ground for doing otherwise. Adams's pugnacious arguments were useful to make Spain realize her insecure hold on Florida. With Central and South America gone from her grasp, Jackson's easy conquest warned her that it was good policy to sell for cash what otherwise she would eventually lose at the expense of war and national disgrace.

The acquisition of Florida involved the sacrifice of Texas; for Spain secured by the treaty the recognition of the Sabine as the Louisiana boundary on the southwest. Several things combined to induce Monroe to make this concession. One was the influence of Crawford, who sought to give safety to the borders of Georgia, his own state; another was the desire to avoid aggravating the slavery controversy, then already sufficiently annoying in the Missouri question; and still another was the conviction that Florida at that time was worth more to the nation than Texas. Secretary Adams resisted the abandonment of our claim to the Southwest, but his opposition was not public. Clay, on the other hand, denounced the proceedings in congress. Although not openly concerned in the discussion, Jackson agreed with Monroe, partly through his general support of the administration, partly because he disliked Clay, and partly from his long-cherished desire to acquire Florida. Monroe, who at this time had a nervous respect for his opinion, wrote him his reasons for approving the Florida treaty. Jackson's reply contained the following expression:

I am clearly of your opinion that, for the present, we ought to be content with the Floridas — fortify them, concentrate our population, confine our frontier to proper limits, until our country, to those limits, is filled with a dense population. It is the denseness of our population that gives strength and security to our frontier. With the Floridas in our possession, our fortifications completed, Orleans, the great emporium of the West, is secure. The Floridas in the possession of a foreign power, you can be invaded, your fortifications turned, the Mississippi reached and the lower country reduced. From Texas an invading enemy will never attempt such an enterprise; if he does, notwithstanding all that has been said and asserted on the floor of Congress on this subject, I will vouch that the invader will pay for his temerity."[1]

In 1836 the advocates of Texan annexation were denouncing the treaty of 1819. Their opponents replied that Jackson

[1] Jackson to Monroe, June 20, 1820, Parton, *Jackson* II., 584; Monroe to Jackson, May 23, 1820, *Writings,* VI., 126, Niles, *Register,* LXII., 138; Adams, *Memoirs,* IV., 275.

supported that treaty, and John Quincy Adams in the house described an interview in which General Jackson, in 1819, freely expressed himself to that effect for the benefit of President Monroe. Jackson pointedly denied the interview. Adams supported himself from his diary, and the two men were left before the public with an unsettled point of veracity between them. Each was doubtless honest, but in view of the evidence of Adams's diary we are led to suppose that the irritable and convinced mind of Jackson had played him a trick.[1]

When the cabinet adopted its Florida policy, it left to Monroe the task of pacifying Jackson, whose strong temper was well known. Calhoun might have had the duty, but it was wiser to leave it to the President, who was an old friend and whose disposition was smooth and pliant. His letter of July 19, 1818, met all expectations. With the greatest show of candor he promised in the outset to conceal nothing that his correspondent ought to know and proceeded as follows:

In calling you into active service against the Seminoles, and communicating to you the orders which had been given just before to General Gaines, the views and intentions of the Government were fully disclosed in respect to the operations in Florida. In transcending the limits prescribed by those orders you acted on your own responsibility, on facts and circumstances which were unknown to the Government when the orders were given, many of which, indeed, occurred afterwards, and which you thought imposed on you the measure, as an act of patriotism, essential to the honor and interests of your country.

It was proper to follow the Indians into Florida, but an order by the Government to attack a Spanish post would assume another character. It would authorize war, to which, by the principles of our Constitution, the Executive is incompetent. Congress alone possesses the power. I am

---

[1]Seward, *Adams*, 277.

aware that cases may occur where the commanding general, acting on his own responsibility, may with safety pass the limit, and with essential advantage to his country. The officers and troops of the neutral power forget the obligations incident to their neutral character; they stimulate the enemy to make war; they furnish them with arms and munitions of war to carry it on; they take an active part in their favor; they afford them an asylum in their retreat. The general obtaining victory pursues them to their post, the gates of which are shut against him; he attacks and carries it, and rests on those acts for his justification.

Was evidence ever more ingeniously distorted in the mouth of a special pleader? It was not charged that Spanish officers stimulated the Seminoles to war, or that they furnished arms, or took part in the struggle; nor is it quite true that Jackson pursued his enemy to St. Marks and Pensacola. But this clever array of assumptions was calculated to please Jackson, and it was made to introduce a still more subtle appeal to his vanity.

The affair is then brought before his government by the power whose post has thus been attacked and carried. If the government whose officer made the attack had given an order for it, the officer would have no merit in it. He exercised no discretion, nor did he act on his own responsibility. The merit of the service, if there be any in it, would not be his. This is the ground on which the occurrence rests as to his part.

But as to the government: it was now face to face with the question of war.

If the Executive refused to evacuate the posts, especially Pensacola, it would amount to a declaration of war, to which it is incompetent. It would be accused of usurping the authority of Congress, and giving a deep and fatal wound to the Constitution. By charging the offense on the officers of Spain, we take the ground which you have presented, and we look to you to support it. You must aid in procuring the documents necessary for this purpose. Those you sent by Mr. Hamby were prepared in too much haste, and do not, I am satisfied, do justice to the cause. This must be attended to without delay. Should we hold the posts, it is impossible to calculate all the consequences likely to result from it. It is not improbable that war would immediately follow. Spain would be stimulated to declare it; and once declared, the adventurers of Britain and other countries, would under the Spanish flag, privateer on our commerce. The immense revenue which we now receive would be much diminished, as would be the profits of our valuable productions. The war would doubtless soon become general: and we do not foresee that we should have a single power in Europe on our side. Why risk these consequences? The events which have occurred in both the Floridas show the incompetency of Spain to maintain her authority; and the progress of the revolutions in South America will require all her forces there. There is much reason to presume that this act will furnish a strong inducement to Spain to cede the territory, provided we do not too deeply wound her pride by holding it. If we hold the posts, her government cannot treat with honor, which, by withdrawing the troops, we afford her an opportunity to do. The manner in which we propose to act will exculpate you from censure, and promises to obtain all the advantages which you contemplated from the measure, and possibly very soon. From a different course no advantage would be likely to result, and there would be great danger of extensive and serious injuries.

These were excellent arguments and were calculated to impress Jackson, after he was properly prepared for them by the preceding deft phrases of flattery. They were followed by as barefaced a connivance at trickery as a President of the United States could well commit. Said Monroe:

Your letters to the Department were written in haste, under the pressure of fatigue and infirmity, in a spirit of conscious rectitude, and, in consequence, with less attention to some parts of their contents than would otherwise have been bestowed on them. The passage to which I particularly allude, from memory, for I have not the letter before me, is that in which you speak of the incompetency of an imaginary boundary to protect us against the enemy — the ground on which you bottom all your measures. This is liable to the imputation that you took the Spanish posts for that reason, as a measure of expediency, and not on account of the misconduct of the Spanish officers. The effect of this and such passages, besides other objections to them, would be to invalidate the ground on which you stand and furnish weapons to adversaries who would be glad to seize them. If you think proper to authorize the secretary or myself to correct those passages, it will be done with care, though, should you have copies, as I presume you have, you had better do it yourself.

Jackson was little impressed by Monroe's subtleties. Brushing aside all suggestions of Spanish responsibility, danger of war, and amendment of despatches, he confined his reply to Monroe's two assertions, "That I transcended the limits of my orders and that I acted on my own responsibility." In the first place, he desired to say that he did not shirk responsibility: "I have passed through difficulties and exposures for the honor and benefit of my country; and whenever still, for this purpose, it shall become necessary to assume a further liability, no scruple will be urged or felt." In spite of a suggestion of brag this statement was absolutely true. With no allusion to a Rhea letter he justified himself by the order of December 26, 1817, which authorized him to "adopt the necessary measures to terminate a conflict which it has ever been the desire of the President, from motives of humanity, to avoid." This order was sweeping, and he considered it broad enough to allow him to do what he thought fit in the emergency. "The fullest discretion," he said, "was left with me in the selection and application of means to effect the specifical legitimate objects of the campaign; and for the exercise of a sound discretion on principles of policy am I alone responsible."

October 20th, Monroe replied more complaisantly than ever.

Finding that you had a different view of your power, it remains only to do justice to you on that ground. Nothing can be further from my intention than to expose you to a responsibility, in any sense, which you did not contemplate. The best course to be pursued seems to me to be for you to write a letter to the Department, in which you will state that, having reason to think that a difference of opinion existed between you and the Executive, relative to the extent of your powers, you thought it due to yourself to state your view of them, and on which you acted. This will be answered, so as to explain ours, in a friendly manner by Mr. Calhoun, who has very just and liberal sentiments on the subject.

It was not candid in Monroe to allow Jackson to believe that Calhoun was his friend in the Seminole matter. It created a false opinion in the mind of the general which the secretary was weak enough to approve by his silence, and that made greater the explosion when the truth at last came out. Throughout their dealing with the incident the President and most of the cabinet showed that they were afraid of their subordinate whom the people considered a hero. But Monroe's doubtful suggestions were met with Jackson's accustomed directness. He repeated the assertion that he had not transcended instructions and refused to be put in a position to open a discussion, but he would not avoid one if it was forced upon him, and he said in dismissing the affair:

There are no data at present upon which such a letter as you wish written to the Secretary of War can be bottomed. I have no ground that a difference of opinion exists between the government and myself, relative to the powers given me in my orders, unless I advert either to your private and confidential letters or the public prints, neither of which can be made the basis of an official communication to the Secretary of War. Had I ever, or were I now to receive an official letter from the Secretary of War, explanatory of the light in which it was intended by the government that my orders should be viewed, I would with pleasure give my understanding of them.'

Calhoun did not send the requested letter and this phase of the Seminole affair closed. Already another phase was opening, a political investigation supported primarily by those who wished to discredit the administration and connived at by some others who feared Jackson as a political factor. Now, as at other times, it proved that his opponents underestimated his power with the people. Their fulminations returned to their own heads, the administration was not injured, and Jackson's position as a party man became stronger and more definite.

When Jackson, the military hero, appeared on the stage of national politics he was not an inexperienced politician. For many years he was an eminent character in Tennessee. He belonged to the faction in which acted James Robertson and the Donelsons, in the West, and the Blounts, in the East, all prominent socially as well as politically. Probably this faction was a little more aristocratic than that led by Sevier, the people's hero. Strength of will, self-assertion, physical and intellectual boldness, ability to make himself obeyed and feared, were all qualities of success in Tennessee. Although his quarrels weakened his leadership for a time, he had many friends who wanted to bring him back into office. The opposition to him

---

¹For Monroe's part of the correspondence see Monroe, *Writings*, VI, 54, 74, 85: for Jackson's part see Parton, *Jackson* II., 518-528, where Monroe's part is also given. Jackson's letters in this affair show traces of another mind than his. The assistant was probably Overton, who was at this time engaged in preparing the general's defense in the Seminole affair (Jackson to Eaton, November 19, 1819, Jackson Mss.) Eaton and Butler were in Washington and could not have helped in the writing, and it could not have been by Lewis.

was chiefly personal, and yielded quickly before the successes in the Creek country and at New Orleans. The year 1815 was not gone before shrewd men in the West began to say that with proper management he could be made President.[1] There were many suggestions to this effect at this time, all with reference to the election of 1816.[2] But it soon became evident that the prize was now Monroe's.   Jackson acquiesced willingly both because he disliked Crawford, Monroe's chief competitor, and because of his long friendship for the Virginian.   It was, in fact, in association with the Macon-Randolph-Monroe group of republicans that he began to take interest in national politics. Like the others of the group he disliked Jefferson and opposed the election of Madison in 1808.[3] In 1815, he was in a position to have influence with the coming administration and the long future seemed hopeful.   After a trip to Washington in the autumn he gave himself up for several years to the duties of his department, receiving reports, making infrequent trips of inspection as far south as New Orleans, and visiting the Indians to make treaties or establish more friendly relations.   He was often in communication with Tennessee leaders: Eaton, who was then completing the biography which the death of Reid early in 1816 left incomplete; White, Overton, Felix Grundy, and Major W. B. Lewis.   It was a busy group of friends, bent on his elevation in due time.   The first and second were United States senators, the third was a state judge of character and ability, a loyal adviser through many years, the fourth was a rising young politician of great shrewdness, and the last an industrious lieutenant who, although of ordinary mind, had much influence with the chief and was destined to render various important services in the years to come.   They all had their

---

[1] Andrew Hynes to Jackson, October 24, 1815; Anthony Butler to Jackson, November 7, 1815, Jackson Mss.
[2] One came from Aaron Burr, but it seems to have had no influence on later events.   Burr to Alston, November 20, 1815; Parton, *Jackson*, II., 351.
[3] S. Williams to Jackson, April 25, 1808, Jackson Mss.

eyes on the election of 1824, when Monroe should have had his full allotment of service and honor.

In the meantime, four other men hoped for the succession. Crawford, of Georgia, excellent politician and administrator, was Monroe's chief republican contestant in 1816 and withdrew from the canvass before the election because, as it is assumed, he was promised the Virginia support in 1824. He became secretary of the treasury under the new President, and throughout the eight years of his incumbency had the support of the New York-Virginia alliance, then very powerful in the election of Presidents. Another candidate was Adams, secretary of state from 1817 until 1825, selected because of his ability and because it was believed wise to have a New Englander in the cabinet. Still another was Calhoun, whom Monroe made secretary of war with some hesitation, and after the place was declined by Jackson. He was young, ambitious, and a defender of national interests, and not yet enslaved by the states' rights ideas of South Carolina. These three, being in the cabinet, gave support to the administration, although Crawford proceeded with a certain air of independence, as became a man whose ambitions were countenanced by the old régime.

The fourth candidate was Clay. He had wished to be Monroe's secretary of state, because the office was supposed to carry the succession; but when it went to Adams he refused to be consoled with the war office, which he might have had, and in the house of representatives he became the leader of those who could be brought to oppose the administration, seizing eagerly on everything which could serve his purpose and fighting so hotly that some of his opponents thought him more selfish than patriotic. In the spring of 1818, Monroe asked congress to pay the expenses of a commission to report on the condition of affairs in the new South American republics. Clay opposed it and moved that a minister be sent to the "United

Provinces of Rio de la Plata." He supported his motion in his loftiest style, but it was lost by a vote of 115 to 45. Stung by his defeat, he was in a mood to undertake much to retrieve his position when news of the invasion of Florida came northward. Monroe's second message, November 16, 1818, gave him the opportunity to take up the matter. It approved of Jackson's action in Florida on the grounds of necessity, throwing the responsibility upon the Spanish officials in the province. The message was referred to the house committee on military affairs. As early as this Jackson's friends in Washington reported that some "back stairs influence" was being exerted to secure a report unfavorable to him. Georgia's representatives were hostile and New York's were supposed to be willing to support them. The former were probably under the influence of Crawford, between whom and Jackson unfriendly relations had sprung up in a manner much like the origin of most of Jackson's quarrels. It was as follows:

By the treaty of Fort Jackson, 1814, the Creeks ceded a wide strip of land from the Tennessee to the old West Florida boundary, giving a broad, open path to Mobile. Early in 1816, a Cherokee delegation appeared in Washington with a claim to that part of this strip which extended south of the Tennessee River for nearly one hundred miles, and Crawford, then secretary of war, allowed the claim under a construction of an old treaty. Jackson heard of the impending negotiations and wrote a protest which arrived too late to prevent the convention with the Cherokees. When he learned that all his plans for an open path southward were thus blocked, he sent a vigorous objection to the secretary, his superior. It is the only paper in connection with the Cherokee treaty of this year which seems to have been written by himself. Full of his characteristic logic and bluster, it concludes by saying: "I have now done: political discussion is not the province of a military officer. As a man

I am entitled to my opinion and have given it freely."[1]   In the following September he met the Cherokees for a treaty and was forced to buy back the land which the recent convention confirmed to them.   He relieved his feelings in a private letter in which he said: "My whole time and thoughts are occupied in finding out the wilds of the deceitful, and to obtain if possible the object in view, and finally disappoint the would-be President."[2]   Crawford's letters to Jackson were direct and without that tone of timorous compliment which even his superiors were accustomed to use toward him.[3]   Neither man was likely to yield to the other, the quarrel became bitter, and for more than eight years, Jackson lost no opportunity to defeat the plans of "the would-be President."   Crawford, less passionate and outspoken, was willing in 1818 to use any proper political opportunity to discredit his enemy, who was likely to be a rival, and the Seminole matter seemed to afford just such an occasion.   Thus Clay openly and Crawford secretly were prepared, for political reasons, to inquire into Jackson's invasion of Florida.

Jackson in Nashville knew well that trouble was brewing in Washington and through his friends kept informed of the situation.   Eaton, fearing that the general's temper would not be controlled, urged him not to come to the capital.   But Robert Butler, an old companion in arms and a faithful defender, thought differently, writing on December 15th, that his chief's presence was needed, and the master of the "Hermitage" hesitated no longer.[4]   After a hard trip over wretched roads, he arrived in the city on January 27, 1819.

[1]*American State Papers, Indian Affairs*, II., 110.   Parton says that Jackson made his protest to Crawford while in Washington in the winter of 1815-1816, but the correspondence indicates that his protest from New Orleans on April 11 was his first interference in the matter.   Cf. Parton, *Jackson*, II., 355.

[2]Jackson to R. Butler, September 5, 1816, Jackson Mss.

[3]See *American Stage Papers, Indian Affairs*, II., 88-91, 100-113.

[4]Eaton to Jackson, December 14, 1818; Poindexter to Jackson, December 12, 1818; Butler to Jackson, December 15, 1818, Jackson Mss.

The situation was already acute. A fortnight earlier the house military committee reported against the execution of Ambrister and Arbuthnot. The report went to the committee of the whole, where Cobb, of Georgia, Crawford's leading supporter in the house, moved to amend by declaring (1) that a bill be introduced to forbid the execution, without the approval of the President, of any captive taken in time of peace or in an Indian war; (2) a disapproval of the seizure of St. Marks and Pensacola, "contrary to orders, and in violation of the constitution"; (3) that a bill ought to pass to prohibit the invasion of foreign territory without authority of congress, except in fresh pursuit of a defeated enemy. Cobb's speech introduced a three-weeks' debate, called forth some able speeches in the house, and produced a deep impression on the public. At the end the report of the military committee was lost by a vote of 63 to 107 and Cobb's amendments by 70 to 100.[1]

The most notable speech for the minority was from Clay, who now first appeared in open opposition to Jackson. Disclaiming personal animosity either to him or to the administration, he asserted that important principles were involved and that he should examine them candidly. First of all, he attacked the treaty of Fort Jackson, which he rightly saw was the beginning of the Seminole war, and which he read for the first time in order to get material for this debate. "This treaty," he said, "aroused his 'deepest mortification and regret. A more dictatorial spirit he had never seen displayed in any instrument,' not even in the treaties which Rome forced from the Barbarians. It spared to the poor Indians neither their homes, their property, nor their prophets. 'When,' he would ask, 'even did conquering and desolating Rome fail to respect the altars and the gods of those whom she subjugated!' Let me not be told that these prophets were impostors, who deceived

---

[1] *Annals of Congress*, 15th congress, 2nd session, volume I., 138, 588, 1136.

the Indians. They were *their* prophets — the Indians believed and venerated them, and it is not for us to dictate a religious belief to them. It does not belong to the holy character of the religion which we profess, to carry its precepts, by force of the bayonet, into the bosoms of other people. Mild and gentle persuasion was the great instrument employed by the meek founder of our religion. We leave to the humane and benevolent efforts of the reverend professors of Christianity to convert from barbarism those unhappy nations yet immersed in its gloom. But sir, spare them their prophets! Spare their delusions! Spare their prejudices and superstitions! Spare them even their religion, such as it is, from open and cruel violence." Clay went on to say that the treaty of Fort Jackson was void because it was signed by a minority of the Creek chiefs, and consequently the treaty of Ghent would operate to restore the Creek lands.

The suggestion that Jackson aimed to convert the Creeks was laughable, the plea for their religion was whimsical, and the assertion that the Creek lands should be re-ceded was ill advised. They must have been made through a reckless desire to construct arguments. They were seized on by the opposition to show how little Clay knew of the subject about which he was speaking.

But from this point the Kentuckian proceeded with more caution. The capture of the Indian chiefs at St. Marks was condemned because it was done by placing a British flag where only the American colors should be; their execution, because it was our first use of retaliation, only to be allowed when it acts as a deterrent, which could not here be alleged. The argument was specious: false colors are allowed as ruses of war, and the Indians were expert in devising similar decoys; moreover, the execution of Francis was calculated to have a deterrent force with the savages who had believed him all powerful through his relation with England.

I do not find in Clay's speech that moderation which his best biographer attributes to it.[1] He was ever a brilliant advocate, rarely a man of balanced judgment. He made many telling hits, but they were usually obscured by exaggeration or weakened by omissions. For example, he demolished Jackson's definition of international law as applied to Arbuthnot and Ambrister, but he would not see the point made by Holmes, of Massachusetts, that white men who instigate savage war ought not to be allowed to plead the laws of civilized warfare. Nor was it fair to compare the execution of Ambrister to that of the Duc d'Enghein; for though there were similar outward circumstances, and these Clay stressed, the purposes of the two acts were entirely different. But the speech was nevertheless a good one and not so turgid as most of the others in the debate.

The weakest point in Clay's speech is in the following:

Recall to your recollections the free nations which have gone before us. Where are they now and how have they lost their liberties? If we could transport ourselves back to the ages when Greece and Rome flourished in their greatest prosperity, and, mingling in the throng, ask a Grecian if he did not fear some daring military chieftain, covered with glory, some Philip or Alexander, would one day overthrow his liberties? No! no! the confident and indignant Grecian would exclaim, we have nothing to fear from our heroes; our liberties will be eternal. If a Roman citizen had been asked if he did not fear the conqueror of Gaul might establish a throne upon the ruins of the public liberty, he would have instantly repelled the unjust insinuation. Yet Greece had fallen, Cæsar had passed the Rubicon, and the patriotic arm even of Brutus could not preserve the liberties of his country! The celebrated Madame de Staël, in her last and perhaps best work, has said, that in the very year, almost the very month, when the President of the Directory,

---

[1]Schurz, *Life of Clay*, I., 154.

declared that monarchy would never more show its frightful head in France, Bonaparte, with his grenadiers, entered the palace of St. Cloud, and, dispersing with the bayonet the deputies of the people, deliberating on the affairs of the state, laid the foundations of that vast fabric of despotism which overshadowed all Europe. He hoped not to be misunderstood; he was far from intimating that General Jackson cherished any designs inimical to the liberties of the country. He believed his intentions pure and patriotic. He thanked God that he would not, but he thanked him still more that he could not, if he would, overturn the liberties of the Republic. But precedents, if bad, were fraught with the most dangerous consequences. Man has been described by some of those who have treated of his nature as a bundle of habits. The definition was much truer when applied to governments. Precedents were their habits. There was one important difference between the formation of habits by an individual and by governments. He contracts it only after frequent repetition. A single instance fixes the habit and determines the direction of governments.[1]

This utterance was pointless if it did not imply that Jackson as a military hero was a menace to the country, not so much for what he had done as for what he might do. The public so understood it, and it proved the beginning of many repetitions of the same charge. It was a foolish imputation, because, as Clay admitted in making it, Jackson neither would nor could overthrow the popular attachment to the constitution. It could hardly injure Jackson, because the populace, to whom it would ordinarily appeal, were safely won by his military achievement. Moreover, it was the kind of speech which would wound most severely Jackson's self-esteem. The cry of military hero was raised many times after this in derogation of his ambition, but it did not lessen his popularity.

Jackson arrived in Washington on January 27th, when the

[1] *Annals of Congress*, 15th congress, 2nd session, volume I., 653.

tide ran in his favor, so far as the house debate was concerned. He remained at his hotel, refusing to accept invitations to dine until the vote of the representatives on February 8th acquitted him of wrong-doing. But he had not the same feeling in regard to the senate, where another investigation was pending. February 11th, he set out for New York, allowing himself to be fêted on the way like a conqueror. In Philadelphia the festivities lasted four days. In New York the freedom of the city was presented in a gold box, and Tammany gave a great dinner at which the leading guest, much to the dismay of the young Van Buren and other supporters of Crawford, toasted DeWitt Clinton, the leader of the opposing republican faction. In Baltimore, on the return trip, there was more rejoicing. Admirers gave a dinner and the city council asked him to sit for a picture by Peale for their council room. Everywhere there were overwhelming popular demonstrations which gratified Jackson and strengthened him in the conviction that his course was right. Keen-eyed politicians, friends of the administration and opponents, watched the ovations closely, and many wondered what effect they would have on the deliberations of the senate, whose report was not made when Jackson left the capitol.

But the senate, little impressed by outdoor clamor, proceeded with accustomed dignity. The Seminole matter was in the hands of a select committee of which Abner Lacock, of Pennsylvania, a friend of Crawford, was chairman. He was a quiet gentleman, indefatigable in collecting evidence and unterrified when rumor said that Jackson, blustering at his hotel, was swearing he would cut off the ears of any member of the committee who opposed him. February 24th, Lacock submitted a long report which was printed the next day in *The Intelligencer*. Its tone was calm and argumentative and its conclusions altogether against the invasion of Florida. Jackson said that he first saw it on March 1st, in Baltimore, and that leaving that city at nine at night he rode back to Washington before dawn of the second in order to meet the new crisis. It is rather singular that it took the report four days to arrive in Baltimore and only eight hours for Jackson to cover the same distance southward. He came in a great rage and the streets were full of his threats. A story generally believed at the time and not positively denied by Jackson[1] was that he was only prevented by Commodore Decatur from personally attacking Eppes, a member of the senate committee, for strictures made on him.

But all this excitement was unwarranted. The committee, with or without design, had waited so long to submit the report that it was impossible to debate it. It was ordered to be printed and lie on the table, from which it was not taken before the session expired by constitutional limitation on March 4th. Its publication in *The Intelligencer* brought forth in the same paper some "Strictures on Mr. Lacock's Report,"[2] and this was followed by a reply from Lacock.[3] Before it was published Jackson was off for Tennessee, where he was received with éclat from Knoxville to Nashville. The latter place provided a dinner and an address of welcome in which the country was assured that he was still the hero of his own people.

Jackson's friends attributed the investigation to the desire of the Clay and Crawford groups to discredit a rival. Direct evidence here is hardly to be expected, but it is difficult to believe that all the zeal against Jackson was disinterested. When the matter came up the administration had already settled it in a manner which has the sanction of posterity. The posts would be relinquished, and thus Jackson's design for permanent occupation was repudiated. Why disturb all that had been done in order to censure our foremost commander whose error, if there were one, was excessive zeal in defeating the enemy

[1] See Parton, II., *Jackson*, 569-571.
[2] *Intelligencer*, March 8, 1819.
[3] *Ibid*, March 20, 1819.

and adding to the national patrimony? As to Arbuthnot and Ambrister, why should his own government punish Jackson on their account when not even the British government resented their fate? Jackson's candidacy disturbed two of his antagonists in the presidential race: it lessened Clay's hold on the West and Crawford's on the South. Calhoun, Southern though he was, was not so much affected. He had, it is true, some strength in North Carolina, where Jackson might expect to compete with him. But his only other Southern strength lay in South Carolina, which was safe enough. Calhoun's greatest hope was in those middle states which were attached to the tariff and to internal improvements, and in the chance that he might get New England if Adams could not be elected.[1]

Before the investigation ended its promoters realized that it was likely to make more friends than opponents for Jackson. The country tired of the house debates long before they were concluded: it would not tolerate a repetition in the senate, and it was wise to drop the matter. Moreover, publishing the committee's report accomplished all that could be expected from a fuller investigation. It submitted Jackson's conduct to the consideration of thoughtful people, so that they might determine whether or not he was the kind of a man who ought to aspire to the presidency.

An incident which occurred in connection with Lacock's report gives us, also, a view of Jackson's mind and may help us to answer the question which his opponents in 1819 desired to submit to the public. As the story goes Capt. James Gadsden wrote Jackson that Crawford was said on good authority to have written a letter to Clay proposing a combination to defeat the reëlection of Monroe. The general must have repeated the gossip; for when he arrived in Washington he had

---

[1] In 1831, Jackson with weak arguments charged Calhoun with promoting the investigation of 1819. Lacock and Calhoun denied it. See Benton, *View*, I., 180, and Parton, *Jackson*, II., 553.

a call from General Swift, Gadsden's informant, in which the visitor asked who was authority for the statement. Jackson, not knowing that Swift had spoken to Gadsden, gave the name of the latter, when Swift said: "He has not treated me generously; but it is true: I am the man: I saw the letter and read it," adding that he and Crawford were now friends and that he hoped the matter would be dropped. Later Jackson called on Monroe, who said that Crawford denied writing such a letter to Clay. The President added that Crawford would be a villain if he, a member of his cabinet, should attempt such an intrigue. Then Jackson said to him: "Say to Mr. William H. Crawford from me that he is a villain, and that he dare not put his pen to paper and sign his name to the declaration that he never wrote such a letter to Mr. Clay: if he does, say to him from me, if I do not prove it upon him, I will apologize to him in every gazette in the United States." Monroe replied by cautioning Jackson against relying too much on Swift, who in a pinch might "trip." But the general replied that "tripping was out of the question with me: no man should do it."

Swift did indeed prove a broken reed. Hearing that his name was used he called on Jackson and said that Crawford's letter was merely a letter of introduction. The Tennesseean was thunderstruck and assuming his sternest tone said that he could not be mistaken. The caller remained silent a moment and asked if there was no way of reconciling Jackson and Crawford. "I told him," said the former, "that there was none, I knew him [Crawford] to be a villain, that I had made it a rule through life never to take a rascal by the hand knowing him to be such, that I never gave hand where my heart could not go also; believing as I did of Mr. Crawford I never would take him by the hand." Here the immediate quarrel rested. Before that Jackson had been told that Lacock's report would not be submitted to the senate, but when it at last came forth he concluded that Crawford, having failed to secure a truce with his enemy, had decided to carry the matter as far as possible.[1] Gadsden was from South Carolina, as was A. P. Hayne, brother of the famous antagonist of Webster. Both were military men with good records of service under Jackson, and both seemed at this time to have hopes of political careers under his protection. Both were drawn into association with Calhoun and went into eclipse with that unfortunate leader. A letter of this period from the second shows to what degree of flattery one of his intimates was willing to go in propitiating the favor of the chief. "What does the President of the United States not owe you," exclaimed Hayne, "for the prompt support you have always given his administration? In 1814 and 1815, you snatched the republican party and Mr. Monroe from almost inevitable destruction, and in the present instance you have most effectually saved the latter. Your personal presence has silenced all opposition to his administration; and has ensured his second election."[2]

General Jackson regarded the Lacock report as a manifesto of his enemies and insisted that it should be answered. Overton tried to dissuade him, but he replied that this issue ought to be met whenever raised. Overton yielded and during the autumn completed, under Jackson's supervision, the defense of the Seminole war. "The answer," said the general in sending it to Eaton for submission to his friends, "is drew with Christian mildness, brings before the reader the facts, and a reference to the documents proves them . . . In this as in every other thing pertaining to this unpleasant business I leave [all] to your and my friends Judgment, after having expressed my opinion on the subject; let all your deliberations be founded on this: that I fear not investigation, but court it, wherever it

[1]Jackson to Gadsden, August 1, 1819; Gadsden to Jackson, February 6, 1820, Jackson Mss.
[2]Hayne to Jackson, March 6, 1819, Jackson Mss.

is necessary for the understanding of the nation."[1] This letter probably expressed the writer's true relation to the friends who brought him into the political arena; he had his way in essentials but yielded much to their guidance in matters of detail,

Eaton, receiving the memorial, conferred with Rufus King, of New York, and William Pinckney, of Maryland, both supporters of the administration; and it was decided to soften some of the parts and to omit those which imputed malice to the Lacock committee. A reference to Crawford as "the *gentleman* who was the chief juggler behind the scenes" was dropped and Eaton explained it to Jackson by saying that nobody would believe anyway that Lacock could write the report. February 23, 1820, King presented the memorial in the senate and Pinckney made a speech in its support.[2] Many people were annoyed at the prospect of opening again the Seminole matter, but their fears subsided when King agreed to be satisfied if the memorial were printed and made a matter of record. His desire was granted and here the Seminole affair ended. It pleased Jackson that his cause in the senate was defended by such prominent men as King and Pinckney; and the rosy accounts Eaton sent of the effects put him in good humor.[3]

One of the charges against Jackson in connection with the Seminole war involved his personal integrity. It was alleged that he was concerned in a land speculation in Pensacola and that he seized the town in order to enhance his property there. This damaging story had no other basis than this: In the autumn of 1817, eight of his Nashville friends formed an association to buy real estate in Pensacola, believing that Florida would soon be acquired and that lands there would increase in value. Jackson gave their agent a letter of introduction to the Spanish

---

[1] Jackson to Eaton, November 19, 1819, Jackson Mss.
[2] *Annals of Congress*, 15th congress, 2nd session, volume 2, 2308.
[3] Eaton to Jackson, March 11 and 15, April 2 and 16, 1820, Jackson Mss.

governor, in order to vouch for the respectability of the promoters. The agent left Nashville in November and bought some land in and near Pensacola. The whole transaction was completed before the news that Jackson was ordered to conduct the Indian campaign reached Nashville. Eaton, who was one of the speculators, asserted that it was undertaken solely because it was believed that Florida was about to be acquired. He may have had some inkling of the progress of the negotiations, then just re-opened by Pizarro; but there is no reason to doubt his assertion that Jackson was in no sense a beneficiary of the scheme.[1] The interest of the latter in the acquisition of the province was wholly patriotic: he did not at that time suspect he was destined to have the honor of becoming its first governor under American rule.

---

[1] *Annals of Congress*, 15th congress, 2nd session, volume 2, 2300.

CHAPTER XVI

GOVERNOR OF FLORIDA

BEFORE following Jackson into the field of national politics it is necessary to consider his governorship of Florida, the last phase of his public career before he became a presidential candidate. To receive the province from Spain, to wave adieu gracefully to the former masters, and to inaugurate American rule with the least friction possible was a delicate task. It required more tact and consideration for others than Jackson possessed. For this reason this episode is the least credible of his national career.

Soon after the Seminole war Jackson expressed a desire to leave the army, but did not withdraw, probably because of the congressional investigation. After that was past there was some probability that Spain's unwillingness to ratify the Florida treaty would lead to war, and in such a situation he would not resign. But on February 22, 1821, the treaty was at last proclaimed by Monroe, and Jackson prepared to fulfil his purpose. Before he could do so the Florida governorship was offered.

To many people it seemed but proper that he who had twice raised the American flag in Pensacola should first unfurl it there in token of permanent American possession. Monroe thought as much and opened the matter when Jackson was in Washington in 1819, but the offer was then declined. It was renewed January 24, 1821, and at first the general was inclined to accept; "but," as he said, "on more mature reflection added to the repugnance of Mrs. Jackson to go to that country I have declined and so I have wrote to the President and secretary of war." But later than this he yielded, his chief purpose being, as he admitted, to place some of his friends in the subordinate offices which he thought would be filled through his suggestion.[1] His commission was dated March 10th, and modified on March 20th, but he did not assume the government until June 1st, when he relinquished his military office.[2]

His powers as governor were ample. Until the end of the next session of congress he was to exercise all the authority which belonged under the old régime to the captain-general of Cuba and to his subordinate governors of East and West Florida. He might suspend officials not appointed by the President, but he might not lay new taxes or grant public lands, and his salary was $5,000, the same as when a major-general. He was also made commissioner to receive the territory with authority to appoint a deputy and with additional allowances for expenses.[3]

Before Jackson arrived in Pensacola to receive the province, Colonel Forbes was sent to Havana with orders from the Spanish government to the captain-general to deliver Florida to the American commissioner, together with the public archives and all papers relating to the titles of private property, which by treaty were to be surrendered. When he received from Havana the necessary orders to the officials at Pensacola and St. Augustine, he was to repair to the former place. At the same time the Spanish minister in Washington asked that American troops should not enter Pensacola until the Spanish troops were withdrawn, and the request was allowed. Thus Jackson's prompt entrance into his government depended on the early completion of the negotiations in Havana.[4]

[1]Monroe to Jackson, January 24, 1821; Jackson to Bronaugh, February 11, June 9, 1821; Jackson to Monroe, August 4, 1821, Jackson Mss.
[2]See Jackson Mss. March 10 and 20, 1821.
[3]Adams to Jackson, March 12, 1821, Jackson Mss.
[4]Adams to Jackson, March 12, 1821; Adams to de Anduciga, November 2, 1821; Adams to Forbes, March 10, 1821; Jackson Mss.

But Forbes had all kinds of difficulties in Cuba, due, it seems, to the lack of good will in the officials there. He wasted six weeks in fruitless endeavors to get the archives and at last departed without them, arriving in Florida about June 1, 1821.' Meantime, Jackson, accompanied by his wife and a group of friends, was proceeding to his post. In New Orleans they were received with marked respect, and April 30th, they halted at Montpelier, in southern Alabama, to await the movements of Forbes. Here they remained five vexatious weeks, Jackson's mind filled with suspicion of Spanish treachery. At length he proceeded into Florida and halted fifteen miles from Pensacola at the home of a Spanish gentleman. Mrs. Jackson and most of the companions found quarters in the town, but he declared that he would not see it until he could go under his own banner to plant his flag for the third time on its walls. There were various other delays, and it was not until July 15th that, all difficulties removed, he prepared to enter Pensacola. He was now in the best of spirits and wrote to a friend in town as follows:

General Jackson with his compliments to Dr. Brunough informs him that the General will be in Pensacola to break-fast on Tuesday at half after six A. M. and a number of the officers of the army as well as officers of the navy from the *Hornet*. Will the Doctor have the goodness to aid Lt. Donaldson in making the necessary preparations for Brakfass, and also Dinner. The Scripture says return good for evil, in this feeling I intend asking the govr and his secretaires to dine with me. He is as I suppose, very sore, and if he was devoid of urbanity I mean to show him I at least possess magnanimity by which I will heap coals of fire upon his head. Had I agreed with the ceremony this day proposed by him we would have had no time for dinner; but as useless ceremony is a great tax upon me I have

---

¹In 1832, Jackson, when President, demanded from Spain, the archives taken from Florida to Havana and got what he asked, Richardson, *Messages and Papers, of the Presidents.* II., 593.

waved all that could be dispensed with and I suppose we will get through about eleven o'clock and have the star spangled banner waving over our dinner. I have been compelled to-day to respond to three long letters. My answers were short.

The designated Tuesday was July 17th, and promptly at 7 A. M., the American troops approached the place, their band playing joyously. Natives and eager American speculators and office-seekers lined the streets, all anxious to see the beginning of a new era in the sleepy town. The procession moved down Main Street, passed the great house from the balcony of which Mrs. Jackson looked fondly at the straight horseman who led it, and halted at the government house, where Governor Callava with garrison in ranks awaited the final ceremonies. These were soon over. The keys were handed to the new owners, the Spanish flag flapped down the flag-staff, the American emblem took its place, and the garrison at word of command turned from the scene to embark on vessels which were waiting in the harbor. The next morning the hot gulf breeze wafted them away, the last vestige of Spanish authority in West Florida, the American ship *Hornet* gallantly acting as escort. They carried 367 soldiers and ninety-seven civilians. Thirty-six officers and 137 others were allowed to stay on condition that they should go at their own expense within six months.[2]

To Mrs. Jackson these scenes appealed strongly. The departure of the Spaniards excited the sympathy of her gentle soul, but the amusements of a Spanish Sunday shocked her stern Presbyterianism till she must interfere. "I sent," she wrote, "Major Stanton to say to them that the approaching Sunday would be differently kept. . . . Yesterday I had the happiness of witnessing the truth of what I said. Great order was observed; the doors kept shut; the gambling houses

1Jackson to Bronaugh, July 15, 1821, Jackson Mss.
2Callava's agreement August, 1821, Jackson Mss.

demolished; fiddling and dancing not heard any more on the Lord's Day; cursing not to be heard."[1] Another incident illustrates the sharp break in ideas for the province. As the American flag rose to the top of its staff a Methodist missionary, passing through the crowd, began to distribute tracts to the natives. He soon encountered an indignant Catholic priest who began to remonstrate against his action. For reply the missionary merely pointed to the new flag: his disappointed interlocutor silently turned away.[2]

Governor Jackson's first dinner was hardly over before he was deep in a quarrel with his predecessor, Governor Callava. By the treaty Spain must surrender the forts intact and the United States furnish transportation for the garrisons. Nothing specific was said about cannon and provisions for the transported garrisons. Secretary Adams, foreseeing trouble on this point, instructed Jackson that the guns ought to go with the forts and that he ought to furnish supplies, but that if Callava proposed to take away the cannon the provisions ought to be withheld as an offset. The contingency which Adams foresaw occurred. After much negotiation it was agreed to leave the guns and furnish provisions, and that the matter be referred to the two governments for adjustment, receipts being given for both cannon and provisions. When the cession was about to be made and Callava was sought to receipt for the supplies, he reported that he was sick and could not be seen. His secretary gave his word that the receipt would be sent and the Americans delivered the provisions. But when the document arrived and was translated it was seen to be no receipt but a certificate that supplies had been delivered in accordance with the treaty. This duplicity put Jackson in a rage: he wrote some plain letters to the Spaniard, from whom he received no satisfaction, and

---

[1]Parton, *Jackson*, II., 604. Parton has undoubtedly improved Mrs. Jackson's language.
[2]*Ibid*, II., 608.

he closed the correspondence abruptly on August 3d, with the assurance that he had no further confidence in the statements of his correspondent and would have no further dealings with him. To Adams he expressed "a hope that my government will stamp his perfidy with such marks of displeasure, as will convince Spanish officers hereafter to comply with their engagements of honor."[1] Yet in spite of his declaration he was to have much more to do with Callava.

His governorship was hardly begun before office-seekers began to beset him. Some were former political friends, others were his old soldiers, for whom he was ever sympathetic, and to all he gave patient hearing. One of the applicants, David Cowan, more importunate than the others, enlisted the sympathies of Mrs. Jackson by picturing the distressed condition of his family. She, who understood not the wiles of the office hunter, replied that if there was an office in her husband's gift that would relieve Cowan's condition she would use her influence to have it go to the petitioner. The condition was not hard to meet, since he was willing to be inspector of provisions, or he could, to quote his own words, "with equal capacity and dignity fill the office of notary public, city magistrate, or sheriff, by the advice of an attorney who has promised his assistance." He became port-warden and within a month was in a squabble with the merchants of the town because of his large fees.[2] In this incident appears Jackson's conception of his duty as dispenser of patronage; later and in a higher office he showed it was not improved.

Launching the new government was made more difficult by the lack of the important subordinate officers. Of those whom Monroe had appointed, not one was in Florida on July 17th. Jackson found a remedy in assigning their duties to his staff

[1] Adams to Jackson, March 12, 1821; Jackson to Callava, August 3, 1821, Ibid to Monroe, August 4, 1821, Jackson Mss.
[2] Cowan to Jackson, July 13, 1821, Jackson Mss.

chiefly to Dr. Bronaugh, R. K. Call, and H. M. Brackenridge, the last of whom spoke Spanish. A deputy commissioner was sent off to St. Augustine to receive the surrender of East Florida. July 27th, came Eligius Fromentin, one of the two newly appointed federal judges. He was already known in Pensacola where he was United States agent pending the completion of the treaty; and on his departure he left numerous debts for which judgments were obtained in his absence. When Jackson arrived he was shocked to see notices of these judgments posted on the street corners, according to custom in such cases. It was not the first unfavorable impression he had of the judge. "I have no unfriendly feeling towards Mr. Fromentin," he wrote at this time to Monroe. "He is a polite, gentlemanly man, but from the character given him both here and in Orleans, both as to his capacity as a judge and his moral character, I cannot confide in him."[1] When Jackson could not "confide" in a man he was in a fair way to quarrel with him.[2]

In the meantime, Callava remained in Pensacola, undoubtedly losing his character as governor. The treaty provided that cession should be complete within six months after ratification, or by August 22d, and if any authority inhered in him by reason of his former governorship it might be considered to have ceased at the end of this period. But he was also commissioner to make the transfer. International comity would allow him reasonable time to complete his business as commissioner, and his continuation in the place was with Jackson's consent. He was a Spanish officer for a particular purpose and had personally the status of an accredited agent. As such he was exempt from arrest and trial by the ordinary courts of the

---

[1]Jackson to Monroe, August 4, 1821, Jackson Mss.

[2]Fromentin, a French Jesuit, was expelled from France during the Revolution, came to Maryland, where he married into an influential family, read law and settled in New Orleans to practise that profession. His character and talents were poor; but by suavity and boldness he secured a short term in the United States senate, and through the efforts of his wife's relatives, President Monroe, not knowing his qualifications, appointed him federal judge in Florida. He was thoroughly incompetent for the duties of the office.

country, and his property, domicile, and the public papers in his charge were inviolate as long as he kept within the limits of his official duty.

Callava and Fromentin were soon closely associated, and with them was John Innerarity, Pensacola representative of the rich Mobile traders, Forbes & Company. This great house, long enjoying under Spanish protection special advantages in the Indian trade, was unpopular with the Americans, who thought it stimulated Indian outrages, and Jackson shared their prejudice. He was chagrined, also, to learn that some of his own officers fell, soon after their arrival, under the influence of Callava's circle. Thus, an explosion was imminent, and the lawsuit of the Vidal heirs furnished the necessary occasion.

Nicholas Maria Vidal, a Spanish military auditor, died in 1806, leaving large landed property near Baton Rouge and other effects in Pensacola. By will he left his estate, after his debts were paid, to his mulatto children in Pensacola. The property went into the hands of Forbes & Company for settlement. It was not quite clear what they did about it; but after some years the heirs had received no returns and applied to the courts to force a settlement. Several orders to Innerarity to deliver the papers to the court were avoided in one way or another till 1820, when he at last was compelled to deliver the papers, ten years after he assumed the task of executing the Vidal will. The auditor, Saures, who received them, declared that proceedings under the will had been wholly irregular and confused and he recommended that suit be brought to annul all that had been done and to force the executors to account to the heirs. The recommendations were not acted upon, but on July 10, 1820, Callava signed a decree ordering Innerarity within ten days to make report of his accounts as executor, and to deposit in the royal treasury certain sums within five days. This decree, also, was evaded. By this statement of the facts, taken from the report of Alcalde Brackenridge,[1] there was appearance of fraud and an investigation was justified.

About the end of July, 1821, the new *alcalde* was visited by Mercedes Vidal, quadroon and natural daughter of the deceased Vidal. She demanded justice against Innerarity, exhibited a record of proceedings in the case until 1820, admitted that she secured it clandestinely in the fear that it would be taken away by Callava with other records, and declared that she knew not the whereabouts of the will and other testamentary papers. A few days later she reported that they were in the hands of Sousa, a clerk of Callava, and that she was allowed to make copies by taking them out piecemeal. Brackenridge scented illegality and got her to bring him an instalment as evidence. He then spoke to Jackson, who said that if proof were sufficient he would make a formal demand for the papers. Accordingly, on August 21st, formal demand was made to Sousa, who refused to deliver the documents, pleading that he was but an agent; and he seized the first opportunity to send his papers to the house of his superior. He was promptly arrested and taken, much terrified, before Governor Jackson, who, himself much excited, ordered that the prisoner be carried under guard to the house of Callava, there to surrender the required papers, in default of which he was to be thrown into the town prison.

By this time it was the afternoon of the twenty-second, and Callava was at dinner with Innerarity, Fromentin, Captain Kearney, of the navy, and others, ladies and gentlemen, at the house of Colonel Brooke, of the 4th infantry; and Brooke's residence was in the immediate neighborhood of Callava's. It was half past four o'clock when Colonel Butler, Brackenridge, and Dr. Bronaugh stopped at the house of the Spaniard and learned that he was still at the house of Colonel Brooke at dinner. Not

[1] *American State Papers, Miscellaneous*, II., 811.

desiring to disturb him they returned half an hour later to be told that he was still absent. They then went to the house of the host and sent word that they would like to see Callava at his own home. It is inconceivable that he did not know well enough all that was passing in this interval. In fact, by his story, Sousa appeared at the dinner table to tell him what was wanted and an aide was sent to Jackson to say that if a list of the desired papers was furnished they would be given up if they were such as ought not to be taken away. The messenger soon returned saying that he found Jackson in a towering rage walking about and shouting, "Colonel Callava to the dungeon!" This announcement, says Callava at the table where company was assembled, "could not but raise a blush in my face, and disorder in my stomach, in the very act of eating, and in the convalescent state in which I was I felt myself attacked by a deadly pain (which I almost habitually suffered and which had frequently attacked me in the preceding days)." But he bravely concealed his inconvenience and left the table to reflect on what course he ought to pursue.

In the street he encountered the American officers who told him with as much kindness as the situation warranted that they must have the papers or arrest him. They assured him that Governor Jackson could consider him in no other light than as a private person. There was further conversation to this effect, and feeling the pain returning he told them he was ill and that they must tell "Don Andrew Jackson" that he was ill and could not leave his house, whereupon they went away. Now "Don Andrew Jackson" well remembered that in the preceding month Callava evaded his promise in regard to the receipt for provisions on the ground of sickness, and he was in no mood to allow such a pretext to serve again for purposes of deceit. Moreover, the American officials were reasonably gentle with him. "An hour, at least," says Brackenridge, who acted as interpreter, "was taken up in the conversation; everything was fully explained: the written order from the Governor, containing a specification of the papers, the declaration of Sousa that they had been delivered to his steward; and repeated demands were made for them. He insisted on his alleged rights as commissioner; he said, if the papers were demanded of him in that capacity, or as late governor, and by writing, he would reply" — all of which shows that Colonel Callava had his own share of stubbornness.

As they were withdrawing to report his refusal he said that if a list of the documents was delivered to him he would send them, neglecting to say that he spoke as a commissioner of his government. Half an hour later Brackenridge returned with such a list. He found Callava packing up papers, preparing a protest, and acting generally as if he thought everything he owned was to be taken from him. He was assured that only certain documents were wanted, a list of which was delivered, and he was informed that the papers desired would be called for in two hours. He said he would reply to the demand if it was directed to him as commissioner, and this part of the interview closed. Callava, feeling rather depressed, now went to bed.

In the meantime, a report of the whole transaction was made to Jackson. He was very angry and wrote the following order to Colonel Brooke, Callava's late host:

SIR: — You will furnish an officer, sergeant, corporal, and twenty men, and direct the officer to call on me by half past eight o'clock for orders. They will have their arms and accoutrements complete, with twelve rounds of ammunition.

No news coming from the Spanish commissioner, the guard marched to his house at nine o'clock. They found the place dark.

"Leaving the guard at the gate and in the street," says Brack-enridge, who was present, "we entered the garden in front of the house, after removing the bar by which the gate was fastened. The house was shut up; the door locked. On our entering the porch, we heard a bustle inside resembling the rattling of arms. Admittance was three times demanded by me in Spanish, but no answer was returned. I then went round, and discovered several persons in the porch on the side fronting the bay. The guard was ordered round, and formed in front of high steps which lead up to the porch; they had a short time before been ordered into the garden, and had been drawn up before the front door. On ascending the steps, inquiries were made for Colonel Callava; they all remained silent: on the question being repeated, it was observed by some one that he did not know. The only light was a candle burning in one of the rooms. Colonel Butler ordered a candle to be brought from some of the neighbouring houses. After waiting fifteen minutes, it was resolved to enter the hall, and some one brought out the candle. Two or three of the soldiers were then ordered up; we then entered the room where the candle had been burning, and Colonel Callava rose from the bed, with his coat off, and expressed great surprise at our entering his house at that time of night. The papers were then demanded of him, as is stated in the report of Colonel Butler and Dr. Bronaugh. He persisted in the same reason which he had before repeatedly alleged. Every possible means was used to induce him to surrender the papers; the boxes containing them were in view, and he was told that if he would not break them open we would take them. He was at length told, that, having refused to deliver the papers, he must go before the Governor, who was then sitting in his office and waiting our return. He at first said that he might be assassinated or murdered, but that he would not leave his house alive. Colonel Butler told him repeatedly that he might consider himself as taken forcibly from his house, and hoped he would not render it necessary to use actual force. It was impossible to have used greater delicacy to any one under similar circumstances. When the guard was at length ordered up, and the officer ordered to take him into custody, he consented to go;

more than half an hour having passed from the time of our entering the house."[1]

Unfortunately, Callava's account does not agree in details with that of Brackenridge. "They surrounded my bed," he said, "with soldiers having drawn bayonets in their hands, they removed the mosquito net, they made me sit up, and demanded the papers or they would use arms against me." He told them that as they had used force the boxes and papers were in their hands and he would appeal to the United States government. He had a written protest by him which one of his friends tried to translate to the officers, but they forbade him. After a while an officer told him he was under arrest. "I answered," he says, "that I was so, but he would have the goodness to observe that I was so sick as that I ought not to be taken out of my house at that hour. He made no answer to the interpreter, and remained silent, but one of the three boldly ordered me to dress; I dressed in my uniform, was going to put on my sword, but on reflection thought it better to deliver it to the officers. I did so and one of the three took it from his hands, and threw it upon the chimney, and in this manner I was conducted through the streets among the troops."

It was now ten o'clock, but the governor was waiting in his office in the capacity of judge. The prisoner was given a seat and Brackenridge was directed to act as interpreter. Being informed why he was brought to court, Callava rose to protest, saying that he was commissioner of Spain and not answerable in a private capacity. Then Jackson declared he would receive no protest against his jurisdiction. After some argument it was agreed that Callava might answer in writing. "I sat down," he says, "to write a regular protest, that I might go on to answer afterwards, but I had hardly begun, when Don Andrew Jackson took the paper from before me, and with much

[1] *American State Papers. Miscellaneous.* II.. 830.

violence, and furious gestures, spoke for some time looking at the bystanders, and when he had concluded the interpreter told me that he ordered me to give no other answer to all that he had asked me but yes or no."

The scene was now most exciting. In the centre sat the principals both very angry; around them in the lamplight were the crowd of onlookers. Callava persisting in his contention was quivering with emotion. Jackson was raging violently, now threatening his opponent and now his own supporters. "Why do you not tell him, sir, that I will not permit him to protest?" he exclaimed to Brackenridge. The latter in the confusion called on Cruzat, Callava's secretary, to assist in interpreting, but Cruzat refused. The turmoil continued for some time, when the Spanish commissioner finally remained silent, declaring that he would answer in writing and as a commissioner of Spain or not at all. Then was called Fullarat, the steward into whose hands Sousa delivered the boxes of papers. He testified that the boxes were in the house of his master: this was the necessary proof that the papers were in Callava's possession, and they were formally demanded. Callava and Jackson then began a heated dialogue. "The governor," says Brackenridge, "in the same manner, enforced his demand of the papers by a variety of reasons; he observed, they were such papers as were contemplated by the second article of the treaty, which was read to him; that it was his duty to see, for the safety of the inhabitants, and the protection of their rights, that all papers relating to the property of individuals should be left. The conversation, as is natural, was warm on both sides and some expressions were softened by me in the interpretation, and others, tending only to irritate and provoke, omitted altogether. These were principally the appeals of Colonel Callava to the bystanders, which were frequent, loud, and inflammatory; and, on the part of the governor, strong expressions against what he considered a combination between him and others to withdraw the evidences of the right of property required by individuals; which combination I understood, and so expressed it, to be between Colonel Callava, Sousa, and the steward Fullarat, but which seemed to excite some indignation, as he said, 'Sousa is my domestic, my servant; he is nothing in this business.'" This scene lasted till midnight, Jackson being much fatigued from irritation and from having sat as judge from forenoon with slight intermission. At length he "rose from his seat, and called on me distinctly to state that Colonel Callava must deliver the papers, or abide by the consequences; he, at the same time, called upon the friends of Colonel Callava who understood English to explain to him the situation. It was fully explained to him. This was several times repeated, and, at length, a blank commitment, which had been prepared in case of necessity, was signed, and Colonel Callava committed to prison. The next day I presented petition to open the boxes and seize the papers, which was accordingly done."[1] To prison went, also, Fullarat and Sousa.

Callava wrote an account of this painful interview which he handed to the Spanish minister in Washington with his protest against the whole incident.[2] His account of the close of the trial is interesting. "When the commitment was read," says he, "I got upon my feet. I begged the interpreter to ask him if he did not shudder and was not struck with horror at insulting me, and I pronounced a solemn protest against his proceedings. The interpreter informed him, and he replied that for what he had done he had no account to give but to his government, and he told me I might protest before God himself." Callava was taken to prison at midnight, his house open and in the possession of United States officers, his money-chests and

---

[1] Brackenridge's account is in *American State Papers, Miscellaneous*, II., 828.
[2] Callava's protest, October 3, 1821, *American State Papers, Foreign*, IV., 768.

other property at their mercy. He received in the prison the
treatment of a common criminal, "and lastly," as he says,
"by a respectable citizen of the United States and by my officers,
at two in the morning a couch was spread for me and my other
assistants, to throw ourselves down upon: for by Don Andrew
Jackson I was permitted to throw myself, sick as I was, upon
the bricks of the prison."

When "Don Andrew Jackson" sought his own couch that
night he probably consoled himself with the thought that he
at last had a Spanish governor where he wanted him. Behind
his violent action lay a long series of official delays and subter-
fuges which made the faith of a Spanish official an offense in
the eyes of most Americans who had aught to do with it. It was
not improved by the conduct of Callava and his friends in the
prison on this same night. To him came a number of his officers
and friends with food, wine, and cigars: a feast was improvised,
jests and laughter filled the apartment, the recent trial was
mockingly reënacted, and the rest of the night was turned into
day. All traces of the commissioner's oft-pleaded illness had
vanished.

Early next morning American officers seized the papers in
Callava's possession, took out of the boxes those which had
been demanded, and sealed up the cases without disturbing
other property. The Vidal suit was then brought to trial before
the supreme court of the province, Jackson presiding with a
local justice. Forbes & Company's plea of no jurisdiction was
overruled, and three auditors were ordered to examine the
accounts of the firm with the Vidal estate. October 6th, they
reported, approving the settlement of the estate by the Spanish authorities in 1810, but stating that the expenses of the affair,
$1,315.62 for property valued at $10,101.50, were excessive.
They attacked the account at another point, disallowing a
payment of $200 to Edward Livingston for suing out an attach-

ment in New Orleans, not because it was exorbitant — as they might well have held — but because it was not properly chargeable to the estate. On this and other grounds they held that Forbes & Company had $496 belonging to the estate: and they suggested that the court determine whether or not the firm be held for two other claims which it was said they had paid but for which no receipts were produced. On consideration the court decided to demand the payment of the latter claims. Thus it was held that Forbes & Company, after allowing some deductions, owed to the estate $683.06 as an undivided asset, which with interest since 1810 was ordered to be paid within sixty days. In December, when Jackson was gone, the defendant petitioned for a new trial, giving such clear and satisfactory reason for it that the decision just cited seems overthrown at every point.[1] Unfortunately the means of determining the exact merits of the controversy are not now at hand.

In the meantime, let us return to Callava. On the morning after his arrest his friends invoked the aid of Federal Judge Fromentin, who as a former resident of New Orleans should have remembered the experiences of Dominick Hall. On verbal request and without asking to see the warrant of commitment, he issued a writ of *habeas corpus* and in the absence of the marshal served it by a private citizen on the officer of the day who had Callava in custody. Then the judge, awaiting the arrival of the prisoner, busied himself in writing a bail bond for the liberation of a man, the legality of whose detention he was yet to determine. While thus engaged he received a citation to appear before Governor Jackson "to show cause why he has attempted to interfere with my authority as governor of the Floridas, exercising the powers of the captain-general and intendant of the island of Cuba over the said provinces,

---

[1] *American State Papers, Miscellaneous*, II., 848-863, 873.

respectively, in my judicial capacity as supreme judge over the same, and as chancellor thereof."

Jackson's commission gave him authority:

To exercise, within the said ceded territories, under such circumstances as have been, or may hereafter be, prescribed to him by my instructions, and by law, all the powers and authorities heretofore exercised by the Governor and Captain General and Intendant of Cuba, and by the Governors of East and West Florida, within the said provinces, respectively.

Under this grant of power Jackson believed himself possessed of the function of high judge, which was once exercised by the governor of West Florida; but the belief was not absolutely justifiable. It is true the governor was once a judge, but in 1820 the Spanish *cortes* adopted a new constitution by which the colonial governors were restricted to military, political, and financial functions, distinct judges being created for the trial of cases. This constitution was promulgated in Havana in January, 1821, and it seems not to have been promulgated in Florida, probably on account of the coming transfer of authority. Jackson held, and with much plausibility, that the mantle of the old governor fell to him unshorn of the judicial power. Moreover, congress and the President evidently intended the governor of Florida to have temporarily the same wide powers as the first American governor of Louisiana. On the other hand, Callava declared to Brackenridge before the events of August 22d strained their relations that in the last months of Spanish possession there was in the province no official who could legally decide a lawsuit.[1] Jackson, ignoring this opinion, created a city government for Pensacola, county courts for the outlying settlements, and reserved the highest judicial function for himself.

---

[1] *American State Papers, Miscellaneous*, II., 902-907.

His judicial authority was assailed on still another side. Fromentin was commissioned United States district judge and arrived in Pensacola thinking he would exercise the usual powers of such a judge. To his surprise Jackson showed him instructions from Washington by which only two United States statutes, those dealing with the revenue and the importation of slaves, were to be enforced in the province for the present: for other affairs the old law was to be administered. Fromentin's duties, as Jackson argued — and the judge agreed with him — were limited to these two subjects. But contact with Callava and Innerarity gave the judge other views as well as the courage to enforce them; and August 23d, he was bold enough to issue the writ of *habeas corpus* for the release of his friend.[1]

Jackson's position as judge was undoubtedly irregular, but the situation was unusual. A governor in this transition period ought not to be hampered by the formalities of English law, nor could an American official be expected to be proficient in Spanish practices. Much must be left to his judgment, and tact was essential. Now Jackson's judgment was good for main points; but it vanished before passion, and he lacked tact. When his authority was crossed he was apt to forget forms of legality and even of propriety in order to carry his point. He was not a proper man to have the wide discretionary powers with which Monroe's commissions invested him.

When Fromentin, on August 23d, received the citation to appear and show cause why he interfered with the governor's authority he replied that he had rheumatism and could not comply. The next day he was better and called on his excellency. The interview was exciting. At its close the judge signed a memorandum to the effect that the writ of *habeas corpus* was granted in an unusual manner. He admitted, but not in writing, that the writ was issued hastily and on insuffi-

---

[1] *American State Papers, Miscellaneous*, II., 801, 822.

cient information and promised not to interfere again with the governor's authority.[1] "The lecture I gave the judge when he came before me," wrote Jackson to the secretary of state, "will, I trust, for the future, cause him to obey the spirit of his commission, aid in the execution of the laws and administration of the government, instead of attempting to oppose me, under Spanish influence."[2]

A week later Fromentin learned that this signed memorandum was described by Jackson as an apology and opened a correspondence whose personalities did no credit to either of the two highest officials in the province. Each side appealed to Adams, secretary of state, filling his ears with charges and counter-charges. After investigation he supported Jackson. Fromentin's letters show how completely he was unfit for the position of judge, and he was soon removed from the position. The controversy was brought before congress by inconsiderate opponents of Jackson; but wiser heads, unwilling to give him another opportunity to appear as a martyr, let the matter drop.[3]

August 27th, Callava, though still weak from illness and mortification, set out for Washington to lay his case before the Spanish minister. The protest which came duly from that official brought from Secretary Adams one of his usual clear and aggressive despatches. The occurrence at Pensacola, he said, was wholly due to the delay of the captain-general in Havana, to whom royal orders were delivered by the American agent, Colonel Forbes, on April 23d, directing the delivery of Florida with certain archives. There was no reason why this should not be done within a week: there were twenty boxes of documents in Havana relating to Florida, most of which ought to have gone to Forbes, but not one was delivered; after vainly

---

[1] *American State Papers, Miscellaneous*, II., 821.
[2] *Ibid*, 801.
[3] Bronaugh to Jackson, February 8, 23, 1822; Adams to Fromentin, August 26, 1821, Jackson Mss.

demanding them six weeks he was forced to depart without them but with the captain-general's promise to send them to Pensacola, a promise still unperformed. These documents were all from Florida originally, they related chiefly to land transfers, and were safeguards against fraudulent sales. Adams also reminded his correspondent that Callava refused to show Jackson his credentials as commissioner of transfer, saying that he would surrender the province as governor and not by special authority. Thus by his own act he was debarred from claiming immunity as a commissioner and he became after the transfer a private citizen. And his willingness to be liberated on bail shows that he acquiesced in this status; for the plan was to release him on bail, he agreeing to appear for trial when required and not to carry away the boxes of papers. The secretary discreetly said little about the trial of Callava, contenting himself with the approval of its results. He summed up the case in declaring:

On a review of the whole transaction, I am instructed by the President of the United States to say, that he considers the documents in question as among those which, by the stipulations of the treaty, ought to have been delivered up, with the province, to the authorities of the United States; that they were on the 22nd of August, when in the possession of Domingo Sousa, within the jurisdiction of the United States, and subject to the control of the governor, acting in his judicial capacity and liable to be compulsively produced by his order; that the removal of them from the possession of Sousa, after the governor's orders to deliver them had been served upon him, could not withdraw them from the jurisdiction of Governor Jackson, and was a high and aggravated outrage upon his lawful authority; that the imprisonment of Col. Callava was a necessary, though by the President deeply regretted, consequence of his obstinate perseverance in refusing to deliver the papers, and of his unfounded claim of diplomatic immunities and irregular exercise even of the authorities of governor of Florida, after the authority of Spain in the province had been publicly and solemnly surrendered to the United States."[1]

To this communication the Spanish minister returned a peppery reply, announcing that he would await instructions from his government. But there was no prospect of gain to either side from a prolonged discussion of such a trivial incident, and the affair of "Don Andrew Jackson" and "Colonel Don Callava" ceased to disturb the diplomats. The country soon forgot it. Nobody wanted war, and the popular disapproval of Spain's general conduct overshadowed whatever technical wrong she may have suffered: Jackson remained the people's hero.

Thus closed the Jackson-Callava incident. Although the papers were demanded in a tactless manner, they were such as ought not to have been taken away. They were not properly military papers but were documents relative to a lawsuit still pending. In contending that Callava was merely a private individual Jackson was not so clearly right. The Spaniard had his status from his commission, and although a notification that no further business would be held with him might render him useless as a commissioner, it did not destroy that status. As long as he was allowed to remain in the province he was entitled to the ordinary immunity in person and property of a diplomatic agent.

Jackson's administrative achievements were less striking than his quarrels. The Florida treaty was proclaimed February 22, 1821; and in the remaining ten days of the existing congress there was only time to create a temporary government for the new province. The President was authorized to continue the older system, with the exception of the revenue laws and the

---

[1] Documents relating to the diplomatic side of the incident are in *American State Papers, Foreign*, IV., 765-808. Adams to de Anduaga, April 15, 1822, is on pages 802-807.

laws relating to the importation of slaves. The act was practically like that of 1803, in which a transition government was established in newly acquired Louisiana. The powers of the first American governor in New Orleans were, therefore, very large; and Jackson expected to have equal authority in Pensacola. His commission, as construed by himself and allowed by the President, granted him most of the functions of government. He was local lawmaker, judge, and executive; and immediately after the transfer of the province he embodied what he thought the most needed reforms in a series of ordinances. The first provided a municipal government for Pensacola with Brackenridge for *alcalde*, or mayor; another made regulations for preserving the public health; another created counties; and still another established county courts. Altogether they were wisely planned.[1] The kind of government which Florida needed, he said, was one which was "simple and energetic." He advised that the region should not be joined to Georgia and Alabama, but that it be made one territory with the hope of ultimate statehood. Whatever we may say of the system of government he established in West Florida, it was more definite and practicable than that which it displaced.

Jackson has been pronounced "guilty of high crimes and misdemeanors"[2] for not enforcing the Spanish constitution, particularly where it required a popular election of the *alcalde*. His instructions were to continue the government and laws he found in existence, and although Callava promulgated the constitution on May 26, 1820, and swore to obey it, it was not put into force. The system which he found on his arrival was arbitrary and chaotic, and he decided to reform it. Must his reforms follow the unenforced Spanish constitution? If Callava, in view of the coming transfer, would not enforce the instrument,

---

[1] *American State Papers, Miscellaneous*, II., 904-908.

[2] Thomas, *Military Government in Newly Acquired Territory of the United States*, (Columbia University Studies, **XX**.) 75.

should Jackson observe it, now that Spanish authority was destroyed? If Callava's government was temporary, so was Jackson's, since by law it was to give place to a permanent government by the end of the next session of congress. It was not in keeping with Spanish laws to put a liberal government on its feet in such a time of confusion. As to the municipality of Pensacola, which was needed to preserve order, existing conditions did not favor its election by the unorganized citizenry; and Jackson thought himself justified in appointing both mayor and council. The practical wisdom of his action is confirmed by the approval of the President of the United States. Nor was it clearly illegal. Callava, without criticism from his government, suspended the enforcement of the constitution after its promulgation: Jackson, who stood precisely in his shoes, had, under the circumstances, equal if not greater reason to hold it in abeyance. At any rate, the situation was doubtful enough to warrant the exercise of discretion without committing "a high crime and misdemeanor."[1] Moreover, the incident illustrates his character as an administrator of laws. He was practical and bold and did not hesitate to override the letter in order to enforce the spirit of a law. The practice, of course, may endanger the existence of the laws, but the people who made them trusted Jackson's honesty and common sense, and they never rebuked his assumption of responsibility.

Long before Callava and Fromentin ceased to annoy him Jackson determined to resign his governorship. He was not suited to administrative routine and did not like it: he was disgusted because the Washington politicians distributed the Florida patronage to the exclusion of his own friends, his health was wretched, Mrs. Jackson did not like the country and longed for the familiar faces at her home, and his friends, who had other

---

[1] Professor Thomas is hardly warranted in including Jackson's governorship in his generally excellent treatment of *Military Government in Newly Acquired Territory of the United States*. It was not military government: Jackson was not then an officer in the army, and his government was purely civil.

plans for his future, realized that nothing was to be gained by keeping their candidate in Pensacola. He left Florida early in October on the plea of his wife's health, promising to return on short notice if his presence became necessary, and November 4th, he arrived at the "Hermitage." Soon afterward he placed his resignation in the hands of the President, who accepted it, to take effect December 1st.[1]

The retirement of private life was welcome. For the past four years his health was extremely bad: chronic diarrhœa and indigestion several times brought to the verge of life a body which was never strong. Residence in the Southern wilderness both in 1818 and again in 1821 aggravated the trouble, and many friends now felt that his chances of recovery were small. But rest and an iron will brought recuperation; the care of his farm and blooded horses gave added stimulus; and in a few months the loss of strength was repaired. A new residence gave additional interest to life. It was the commodious brick structure which, though later burned and rebuilt, still survives as one of the historic homes of America. The hero of two wars, the idol of a large portion of the people, and prospective candidate for the presidency, he made it the centre of hospitality for a wide circle of notable men. A fine carriage drawn by four handsome gray horses, with servants in livery, added to his state. To the ordinary observer he appeared as a man of reserved and dignified manners: to his intimates he was cordial and rarely either yielded himself to anger or relapsed into the swaggering braggadocio of earlier days. He satisfied the Tennesseeans of his time, who pronounced him as great as the greatest who came to their prosperous young capital.

One of his last official acts in Florida was to expel the few Spanish officers whom for one reason or another he had allowed to remain in Pensacola after July 17th. They were active

---

[1] *American State Papers, Miscellaneous*, II., 911; Bronaugh to Jackson, December 26, 1821, Jackson Mss.

sympathizers with Callava and published a protest against his arrest. Their action was ill advised and could have no other effect than to arouse the antagonism of the native population. Jackson construed it as interference with his government, and he sent them away on four days' notice. They were forced to submit, but sent a parting shot against their antagonist in the shape of a protest which no Florida paper would print, but which found a better reception at the hands of *The Intelligencer*, of Washington, already leaning strongly toward Crawford.

Ever suspecting his opponents he soon came to think the Florida governorship was offered to him through their influence, in order that when off his guard he might discredit himself and thus be sacrificed to the interest of Crawford. In some curious notes which survive in his own hand he asserted as much and said this was why his recommendations for appointments in Florida were ignored, and why Fromentin was preferred to John Haywood, of Tennessee, for judge. Noting the opinion of the Richmond *Enquirer*, a Crawford journal, that Callava ought to have been confined in his own house but his subordinate might have been sent to the common jail, he answered by citing the Mosaic law, "upon which," he said, "our republican constitution is founded; Deutronomy, chapter 1, vers. 17 — 'Ye shall not respect persons in judget.; but ye shall hear the small as well as the great; ye shall not be afraid of the face of man; for the judget. is Gods, etc.'"[1] This sentiment is characteristic of Jackson, who in early life was irreligious but never skeptical. Moreover, the heroic in his own nature responded fully to the stern justice of the Hebrew lawgiver.

The Florida governorship brought about a coolness between Jackson and Monroe. When Fromentin submitted his case

---

[1] These notes seem to have been intended as outline of a reply to his opponents in the proposed congressional investigation of 1822. They are in the Jackson Mss. and are without date.

to the authorities in Washington he received a letter from Adams in which the secretary said that the President "is persuaded that your motives and intentions were entirely pure, though he deeply regrets the collision of authority and misunderstanding which has arisen between the governor of the Territory and you." Another feature of the letter was the secretary's assurance that Fromentin's authority was limited to two laws: "in the execution of those laws, in your judicial capacity, the governor has been informed that you are considered amenable only to the government of the United States."[1] This was bad, in Jackson's eyes, but worse still was Monroe's annual message, December 3, 1821, because it was directed to congress, where Crawford and Clay had many supporters. It repeated the President's expression of confidence in Fromentin with provoking impartiality, and although it sought to balance this by warm praise of the patriotism and gallantry "of the officer holding the principal command," the sting was deep.[2] Jackson's friends in Washington soon knew how he felt. He attributed Monroe's lukewarmness to the influence of Crawford; and Dr. Bronaugh, then his most confidential representative in the capital, told Monroe's son-in-law as much one night at a ball. Next morning Bronaugh was summoned to the White House and received a long explanation which he was requested to transmit to the "Hermitage." Even this made little impression on the general, and three months later, May 30th, the President wrote a letter himself, filling it with assurances of friendship. It brought a mild reply from Jackson, who professed satisfaction and assured his correspondent that nothing could interrupt their friendship. But by this time he was fairly launched on his presidential canvass, and Monroe was too closely identified with the Virginia influence which was working for Crawford

[1] *American State Papers, Miscellaneous*, II, 848.
[2] Richardson, *Messages and Papers of the Presidents*, II., 192.

to permit the restoration of the most cordial relations with the Tennesseean.[1] The political situation was shifting rapidly, and for Jackson destiny was closing one portal and opening another. Before the summer was gone he was definitely before the country as a candidate for the presidency. *fopulrely*

[1] Jackson to Gadsen, May 2; to Bronaugh, July 18; to Monroe, July 26: Bronaugh to Jackson, February 23, 1822. Jackson Mss.; Monroe, *Writings*, VI., 291.

CHAPTER XVII

THE PRESIDENTIAL CAMPAIGN OF 1824

THE time at which Jackson became a presidential candidate was auspicious for forming new political parties. The chief problems of Jefferson's day, economy, peace, and the payment of the debt, passed away as soon as war ceased in Europe and America. Eighteen hundred and fifteen brought new issues, and the republicans were practical enough to accept them. The tariff, the bank, and internal improvements seemed necessary to the national development. They were matters of social improvement at national expense and violated Jefferson's theory of states' rights. But the party had new leaders, young men who placed expediency above the doctrines of 1798; and they convinced congress that experience during the recent war proved the new policies necessary. As the years passed social development at national expense became less popular and the republican party began to divide into two groups, one supporting the new, and the other the older, view. The former group had its most aggressive leaders in Clay and Calhoun, two positive men who could not themselves agree to act together. With them went for a while Crawford, but his ardor cooled when he found on the other side the old Virginia influence, led by Monroe and countenanced by Madison and Jefferson, who were still oracles for a great many republicans. Van Buren, his chief lieutenant in the North, had pronounced views in favor of the principles of 1798.[1] Adams was a nationalist, also,

---

[1] Van Buren's unpublished Mss. *Autobiography*, Library of Congress, passim.

but gave himself to the duties of his office of secretary of state and in consequence his views were not prominently before the public.

General Jackson's attitude on these matters at this time is not clear. He was probably indifferent both on the bank question and in regard to internal improvements. He supported the tariff on the ground that domestic manufactures would make us independent of foreign markets in time of war, but he was not an extreme protectionist. A man of action, he had few theories, but these were of the school of 1798. In his early political career he followed Macon, Randolph and Monroe and opposed Jefferson and Madison. When the theories of that school were revived after 1820, he came back to them. He wrote Monroe a letter in congratulation of the veto of the Cumberland Road bill[1]— the first striking evidence of the revival—and later he steadily held that internal improvements and the bank were unconstitutional. But he never changed his opinion on the tariff, either because of a sense of consistency, or because some of his strongest support in the North was protectionist, or because the low tariff movement was led by Calhoun and the nullifiers, whom he disliked greatly.

The campaign of 1824 was fairly opened in 1822, and the territorial support of the several candidates became a subject of general importance. Now the old Virginia-New York alliance was strong, because Virginia could speak for a group of Southern states, and New York had influence in the North. Kentucky was an obedient daughter of the Old Dominion; North Carolina, always weak in initiative, surrendered herself to the leadership of her northern sister and with her carried her own daughter, Tennessee. Georgia acted with these four states, and the five, during the time of the Virginia hegemony, had an average number of fifty-nine electoral votes. New York during the

[1]Jackson to Monroe, July 26, 1822, Jackson Mss.

same period had an average of twenty-three votes, to say nothing of those of New Jersey which she usually controlled. Together the alliance cast eighty-two votes, while for the period under consideration the average total number of votes was one hundred and ninety. The basis of the coöperation was the assignment of the presidency to Virginia and the vice-presidency to New York; and the arrangement was observed throughout the Virginia hegemony, except during the Clinton defection. The figures[1] here given will show how easy it was for this powerful group, bound together by self-interest, to dominate the fortunes of the republican party.

In 1822 the ancient alliance was greatly shorn of its strength. The two principals did indeed hold together, giving their influence for Crawford; but Kentucky had her own son in the race and was not to be counted on by the old combination. Tennessee was in the same situation. South Carolina, also, had a candidate; and North Carolina was more inclined to divide her votes between Jackson and Calhoun than to give them to Virginia's favorite, himself a Georgian. Crawford, therefore, could count on nothing more than his own state and Virginia, with whatever he could wring out of the legislature of New York, where, in spite of the influence of the republican organization, old federalism was rearing its head again.

None of the other candidates seemed to have better chances than Crawford. Calhoun was known as a leading champion of internal improvements, and his feeling was broadly national. Pennsylvania liked him for both reasons, and the politicians there were united on him, probably through the influence of the capitalistic element of the party. New England also liked him next to Adams, its own son. Clay had his own state and most of the votes from the region north of the Ohio, and he had

---

[1] These figures would be more significant if they were based on votes in caucus, but, unfortunately such votes are not preserved by states.

hopes in New York and the lower Southwest. Adams could count on New England, and that part of the republican party which was most allied to federalism was his instinctively. Such was the general situation when General Jackson, the last of the candidates to arrive on the field, made his appearance.

The jealousy of other states of Virginia tended to unite them against Crawford, Virginia's candidate. The Jackson managers shrewdly utilized it in cutting North Carolina, in spite of the influence of Nathaniel Macon, out of the old alliance. The situation there as early as 1822 was the field against Crawford. A "People's Ticket" was planned on which were some Calhoun, some Jackson, and some Adams electors, the agreement being that they should all combine at last for the man most likely to beat the Georgian. When Calhoun ceased to aspire to first place, and Adams ceased to be seriously considered in the state, this became a regular Jackson ticket. Just before the election, Eaton, confident of victory, wrote the North Carolina managers as follows:

What will Virginia do? What can she do? Her old allies Pennsylvania and North Carolina have thrown off their leading-strings, and arrogated to themselves the right of thinking for themselves. On them the dictatorial voice of Virginia is lost. Will Virginia separate now from those two states and thus jeopardize her future political consequence? Those leaders in the state, who have managed heretofore the people, as a village school master his little boys, will think well of this 'ere the hour of trial arrives. Strange that she should act upon the principle of pressing, long as possible, one of her own citizens; and when the race is extinct then to look for a *collateral* residing in another state. None but a native Virginian is qualified and fit to rule the affairs of this country, as her politicians and leading men would maintain.[1]

---

[1] Eaton to Colonel William Polk, September 12, 1824, Mss. in possession of William H. Hoyt, of New York City.

Before 1822 many people had Jackson's possible candidacy in mind, and he must have been conscious of the fact; but his intimate correspondence fails to show any plan on his own part, or knowledge of the plans of others, which would promote his election. On the contrary, he was interested in the chances of the other candidates opposing Crawford and Clay and favoring either Adams or Calhoun. Adams's defense of the Seminole war and of the arrest of Callava aroused his admiration, and Calhoun's support in the congressional investigation of 1819 brought the general and the secretary into cordial relations. The South Carolinian carefully cultivated this friendship, and it seems rather singular to hear this cool master of logic say to the passionate and usually biased Tennesseean; "Your country's fame and yours is one. I would rather have your good opinion with the approbation of my own mind than all the popularity which a pretended love of the people, and a course of popularity hunting can excite."[1] The date of this utterance was March 7, 1821, a year before Jackson definitely decided to run for the presidency.

Throughout this year he remained undecided, thinking more about the others than himself. December 6th he wrote in apparent frankness to a Calhoun supporter repudiating the notion that Crawford might carry Tennessee, and saying: "Nor need they expect any other than Mr. Adams to be supported in this state unless some Southern candidate should arise — and I am certain no man in the South could concentrate the votes of the South and West, but Mr. Calhoun — and you are at liberty to say in my name both to my friends and enemies — that I will as far as my influence extends support Mr. Adams unless Mr. Calhoun should be brought forward, and that I have no doubt but Mr. Adams will outpole Mr. Crawford in the

---

[1]Jackson Mss. See also in the same, Calhoun to Jackson, April 1, 1821, and Jackson to Calhoun, May 22, 1821.

South and West. . . . P. S. As to Wm. H. Crawford you know my opinion. I would support the Devil first."[1] This letter was shown to Calhoun and gave him much satisfaction. At this time Jackson's friends were probably still in doubt about bringing him forward.[2] They watched carefully the situation, which changed continuously. December 3d, Eaton in Washington summed it up as follows:

While *he* who now fills the halls of the White House is slowly closing his eyes upon the rich trifles of the world, like an old father he stands surrounded by three full grown sons, each seeking the inheritance on his departure. John Q., from the favors bestowed by the old man in his life time has been deemed a favorite always: J. C., however, from being possessed of a sanguine temper, sets up also pretensions to the inheritance. William and the old gentleman, you know, it has been reported are constantly disagreeing in opinion and are hence not quite so friendly, as father and son should be; be this as it may, it seems pretty well settled that the Virginia estate if not already done, will be apportioned to the Latter.[3]

The conviction that Adams was losing ground ought, by Jackson's declaration of December 6th, to have given the Tennessee influence to Calhoun; but other plans were made, and the information from Washington that Calhoun was gaining rapidly[4] made prompt action necessary. Accordingly, in January, 1822, the first open steps were taken in behalf of the new candidate. The newspapers of Nashville began to urge him for President, and party leaders watched the journals of the country to see what impression was made. The suggestion was well received, especially in Pennsylvania, and the Jackson group decided to go further. One of them, Felix Grundy, on

[1]Jackson to Gadsden, December 6, 1821, Jackson, Mss.
[2]Calhoun to Maxey, December 31, 1821, Marcou Mss., Library of Congress.
[3]Eaton to Jackson, December 3, 1822, Jackson Mss.
[4]Dr. Bronaugh to Jackson, January 7, 1822, Jackson Mss.

June 27th, wrote to Jackson to ask if any reason unknown to
the public existed why Jackson should not be nominated for
the office of President at the approaching session of the legislature.[1] The reply was characteristic: he would, he said,
neither seek nor shun the presidency. This was all that his
supporters desired. July 20th, the Tennessee legislature adjourned for a few minutes and, the speaker and members keeping their seats, the following resolutions were passed:

The members of the general assembly of the state of Tennessee, taking into view the great importance of the selection
of a suitable person to fill the presidential chair at the approaching election for the chief magistracy of the United States, and
seeing that those who achieved our independence, and laid the
foundations of the American republic, have nearly passed away;
and believing that moral worth, political requirements and
decision of character, should unite in the individual who may
be called to preside over the people of the United States, have
turned their eyes to *Andrew Jackson*, late major-general in the
armies of the United States. In him they behold the soldier,
the statesman, and the honest man; he deliberates, he decides,
and he acts; he is calm in deliberation, cautious in decision,
efficient in action. Such a man we are willing to aid in electing
to the highest office in the gift of a free people. The welfare
of a country may be safely entrusted to the hands of him who
has experienced every privation, and encountered every danger,
to promote its safety, its honor, and its glory. Therefore,
Resolved, As the opinion of the members composing the general
assembly of the state of Tennessee, that the name of major-
general Andrew Jackson be submitted to the consideration of
the people of the United States, at the approaching election for
the chief magistracy.[2]

A week later he wrote to an intimate friend in apparent
sincerity: "I have no desire, nor do I expect ever to be called

[1]Grundy to Jackson, June 27, 1822, Jackson to Grundy, Bronaugh, July 18, 1822, Jackson Mss.
[2]Niles, *Register*, XXII., 402.

to fill the Presidential chair, but should this be the case, contrary to my wishes or expectations, I am determined it shall be without any exertion on my part."[1]

The address of the Tennessee legislature contained both truth and error. Jackson was undoubtedly honest, patriotic, efficient, and ready to make great sacrifices for the interest of country; but it was sheer adulation to say that he was "calm in deliberation, cautious in decision." His nomination violated all precedents and his opponents pronounced it ridiculous. Webster thought the nominee entirely unfit and told of an interview with Jefferson in 1824, in which the latter is alleged to have said:

I feel much alarmed at the prospect of seeing General Jackson President. He is one of the most unfit men I know of for such a place. He has very little respect for law or constitutions, and is, in fact, an able military chief. His passions are terrible. When I was president of the senate, he was a senator, and he could never speak on account of the rashness of his feelings. I have seen him attempt it repeatedly, and as often choke with rage. His passions are, no doubt, cooler now; he has been much tried since I knew him, but he is a dangerous man.[2]

Webster's report has been widely quoted; but it is hardly to be reconciled with the following expression in a letter from Jefferson to Jackson, December 18, 1823:

"I recall with pleasure the remembrance of our joint labors while in senate together in times of great trial and of hard battling. Battles indeed of words, not of blood, as those you have since fought so much for your own glory and that of your country. With the assurance that my attamts. [attachments] continue undiminished, accept that of my great respect and considn."[3]

[1] Jackson to Bronaugh, August 1, 1822, Jackson Mss.
[2] Webster, *Private Correspondence*, I., 371.
[3] See Jefferson Mss. Library of Congress.

Jackson's strength lay with the people, that of most of his opponents lay with the members of congress and other politicians, whose influence was accustomed to carry the elections. Most of these leaders were committed to one of the other candidates when Jackson was nominated. They did not think him qualified for the presidency, they were not drawn by his masterful personality, and they did not think he would win. His managers felt that newspapers and an organization of their own were necessary in order to make active his strength with the people. They succeeded in creating such an organization and it finally attracted the majority of the voters out of the camp of the older leaders into that of the new. The process was crude for two reasons: (1) the people were reached by illiberal arguments; and (2) the new politicians were apt to be uncouth, some of them being repudiated leaders in the older groups, others new men of little experience, others mere adventurers, and still others men of great natural ability who were destined to achieve eminence. As Jackson's fortunes improved many of the older politicians joined him. Leadership now became more conventional and appeals to voters less passionate; but it was a long time before Jacksonian democracy lost its distinctively popular quality.

The first field in which Jackson's managers tried their strength was Louisiana, where, in the spring of 1823, they sought to get the legislature to nominate their candidate. The attempt was not successful. Clay's friends were numerous, the enemies whom Jackson made by his quarrels at New Orleans were united against him, and the French speaking members of the legislature were drawn the same way, so that thirty-four of the sixty members were induced to sign resolutions in behalf of the Kentucky candidate. The attempt to make Jackson President had not at that time the approval of some of his best friends in the state: Livingston, Duncan, and Grymes, all his defenders in ordinary matters, refused to support the movement in the legislature. But Clay could not maintain the advantage he had gained: in the election in the following year, Louisiana gave two of her electoral votes to Adams, three to Jackson, and none to Clay.[1]

The next state to attract attention was Pennsylvania, where Thomas J. Rogers, a member of congress and a manufacturer, and S. D. Ingham, a popular lawyer, organized the politicians for Calhoun as early as 1821.[2] But the Pennsylvania farmers felt little interest in him, particularly those who lived in the western half of the state, where the Scotch-Irish predominated. Jackson was the son of a Scotch-Irish immigrant, and his most prominent qualities were characteristic of that stock. As soon, therefore, as he was urged for the presidency, the Calhoun leaders of this region began to have trouble. Henry Baldwin, of Pittsburg, was chief of them and had much difficulty in deciding which way he should go. He first leaned to Jackson till laughed out of it by the supporters of Crawford and then turned away just as the Jackson wave overwhelmed the community. A letter from Edward Patchell, an ignorant preacher of the neighborhood, tells how the crisis came to Pittsburg.

Patchell was the leader of a group of Jackson men from an earlier stage of the contest and became so prominent in it that he was nicknamed "Old Hickory." In 1824, he was elected brigadier-general of militia because of his sobriquet, as he said. He had long had political ambitions, but being uneducated he "stood in the rear ranks," as he himself said, "and never ventured in the front until Andrew Jackson, the son of my dear countryman, was announced a candidate for the first office in the people's gift." He established *The Alleghany*

---

[1] Isaac L. Baker to Jackson, February 26, May 3, 1823: David C. Ker to Jackson, November 23, 1824; Jackson Mss.

[2] Hunt, *Calhoun*, 48.

Democrat with one of his "meer boys" for editor and asserted, with apparent sincerity, that he did not desire office. His account of his conduct in regard to the nomination, spite of some errors of facts, illustrates well the Western upheaval. He continues:

Altho I well knew that my talents were unadequate to the task, yet I depended not only in my personal courage alone, but I trusted in my God, and your God, whome hath raised you up for to be a Saviour and a deliverour for his people. I considered you were justly entitled to the nation's gratitude, and altho I well knew that I was not a poletetion, yet nevertheless ware I to try I could do something. And if Henery Baldwin had, as he promised assisted me, I would not have had the half of the trouble or difficulty in turning the people on the straight course that I had. Mr. Baldwin wrote the advertisement for the call of the first meeting which was held in the Courthouse in favour of your Election, and sent it to me to get it published. The meeting was very numerous, much larger than ever had been known here. After the chairman and the secretaries ware appointed Mr. Baldwin states the object of the meeting, and your name ware placed at the foot of the list. Wm. H. Crawford got one vote, H. Clay five, J. Q. Adams two, J. C. Calhoun four, and Gen. Andrew Jackson upward of 1000. A resolution was then offered that "Henry Baldwin be appointed to write an address" to the democratic republicans throughout the United States. But the very next day, as I have understood, Mr. Baldwin met with Judge Riddle, your old boot-maker, and he hooted him and fully persuaded him that Mr. Wm. H. Crawford would be taken up in caucus, and would be elected President beyond any manner of doubt. From that day until this, Mr. Baldwin was never known to write the scrape of a pen either for or against you — But I believe has ever since been praying good God, good Devil not knowing whose hands he might fall into. I was then drove to the alternative of inlisting a young lawyer under my banner, meer boys, as Judge Riddle used to call them. But with the assistance of the boys I have accomplished wonders. I have reduced the

Lousie party here from ten thousand to something less than fifty, and they are chiefly the antient and notorious wire workers, they are the office holders and office hunters, and all they can do now is grin and shew their teeth. . . . Had I been in possession of the learning, talents and political knowledge of Henry Baldwain, I have the vanity to think that long ere now, I would have reduced the people into a sense of their duty. But Jackson, I must repeat it, I have done no more than my duty, and I even forbid you to return me thanks: And should we fail this Election, I will pray my God to spare life until I see Andrew Jackson President of the United States, and then let me close my eyes in peace.[1]

Patchell spoke for Pittsburg; a meeting at Carlisle, in the central part of the state, showed the same temper. It was called by Calhoun supporters to get him endorsed for the presidency. When resolutions to that effect were about to be voted on, it was moved to substitute Jackson's name for Calhoun's and the motion was carried with enthusiasm. The politicians could not misread such signs as these. George M Dallas, at first for the South Carolinian, showed them what must be done to preserve their leadership when he threw a Philadelphia meeting into the Jackson camp, remarking as he did so that he acted merely in obedience to the will of the people. Calhoun's hope in Pennsylvania was, indeed, gone; and March 4, 1824, a state convention at Harrisburg declared for Jackson by what was practically a unanimous majority. The same meeting nominated Calhoun for vice-president, thus announcing to the world a compromise which had been quietly arranged between the supporters of the Tennesseean and South Carolinian.[2]

The sudden swing of the state from his column, as shown in the Philadelphia meeting and the Harrisburg convention of February, 1824, brought dismay to Calhoun. He had built

[1] Edward Patchell to Jackson, August 7, 1824, Jackson Mss. Henry Baldwin was for Jackson in a timorous way in the preceding year. See his letter to Jackson, January 2, 1823, Jackson Mss.
[2] Parton, *Jackson*, III., 28.

his hopes on the politicians: Jackson's rested with the people. To one of his confidential lieutenants Calhoun unburdened himself as follows:

The movement at Philadelphia was as unexpected to me as it could have been to any of my friends. It has produced the deepest excitement. Mr. Dallas had informed me about a week before that he thought the cause was lost in Pena. and that we should have to yield there, at the Harrisburg convention. Tho' prepared for defeat [at] Harrisburg, no movement in advance was anticipated. What took place was unprecedented and under a sudden impulse received from the caucus nomination here, and the loss of Berks which decided the contest in favor of Genl. Jackson in Pena. I have no doubt the motives were pure; and tho' ill timed as it regards Dallas and our cause, yet not unfavorable to the great point of defeating the radicals. Our friends have come to the conclusion that we ought to hold to our position, and wait events. It is thought to be the best in every point of view, whether it regards the country, or ourselves. Nor will there be much difficulty. South Carolina and Jersey can easily be restored as they are. In North Carolina, the friends of Jackson will not start another ticket, with the understanding that the one formed will support him, should I have no prospects in Pena. a ticket will be formed favourable to me as a second choice, and the same course will be pursued in Louisiana, Alabama, Mississippi, Missouri, and Tennessee. In Maryland it is highly desirable that my friends should run in as many districts as possible, taking Jackson if necessary as a second choice, or taking position simply against the caucus with the determination to support the strongest.

Jackson's friends indicate a disposition to add my name to his ticket in Pena. as V. P. We have determined in relation to it to leave events to take their own course, that is to leave the determination to his friends. Standing as I do before the American people, I can look to no other position, than that which I occupy. Had Pena. decided favourably the prospect would have been most fair. Taking the

U. S. together I never had a fairer prospect than on the day we lost the state.[1]

Calhoun's interests, it was thought, would be advanced by the combination now made. He was still a young man and could afford to wait for honors. He and Jackson were united by their opposition to Crawford, then considered the most formidable candidate for the common goal. Moreover, it was not difficult to effect the coöperation. Jackson and Calhoun were friends before the former was nominated by Tennessee in 1822, and although their friendship cooled after that event it did not disappear entirely. It was possible for the latter to say in 1823: "I find few with whom I accord so fully in relation to political affairs as yourself. I have a thorough conviction that the noble maxim of yours, to do right and fear not is the basis, not only of Republicanism, according to its true acceptance, but of all political virtue; and that he who acts on it, must in the end prevail. The political quibblers will fail. The cause of the Georgian is, if I mistake not, rapidly declining. It has no foundation in truth, and can only be propped by false pretenses. Should he fail in New York, as I think he must, he will not have the least prospect of success."[2] That the towering mind of Calhoun could speak such platitudes with apparent unction indicates that he was exceedingly anxious to preserve the good will of Jackson.

A similar combination was attempted between Clay and Crawford, but without success. Rumors of it reached Jackson in the summer of 1823, and Calhoun said that he believed such a purpose existed among the friends of those candidates. "I hope," he said, "we shall never present the example of coalition, intrigue or management advancing any citizen to the highest

[1]Calhoun to V. Maxey, February 27, 1824, *Marcou Papers*, Library of Congress.
[2]Calhoun to Jackson, March 30, 1823, Jackson Mss. See also Gadsden to Jackson, July 30, 1823, in the same collection.

honor of the country. The influence of such an example would be pernicious in the extreme. If the people can be cheated, they will not be served. Virtuous servants would be discouraged and the unprincipled only would thrive."[1] Thus spoke the bargaining Calhoun in condemnation of the bargain of Clay.

Crawford's lieutenants seem to have been responsible for the approaches to the supporters of Clay, and Van Buren was active in the business. He dwelt upon the shattered state of Crawford's health, which, he said, would surely cause Clay, in 1828, to come into first place in the combination. Crawford's Virginia friends were pleased at the prospects of securing Clay's support, but thought the initiative in announcing him should not come from their state, since Crawford, also, was a son of the Old Dominion. Clay discouraged the movement and it was not consummated. He thus lost an opportunity to acquire most of the Crawford following[2]. It was especially significant that he allowed Van Buren and the chief group of New York republicans to go to Jackson after fulfilling its duty to the Georgian. But this did not operate in the election of 1824. Crawford was still in the field; and the union of Jackson and Calhoun brought into coöperation Tennessee, Pennsylvania, and South Carolina, with fifty votes, and gave them a hope of carrying North Carolina, Alabama, and Mississippi, with twenty-three votes.

Early in 1824, efforts were made to combine the other candidates against Crawford, whom all feared and disliked. R. M. Johnson, of Kentucky, approached Adams and asked if he would coöperate to defeat the Georgian. "I told him," says Adams, "that I would cordially contribute to this object to the utmost of my power; that to this end I had authorized my friends

[1]Calhoun to Jackson, July 31, 1823, Jackson Mss.

[2]Van Buren to B. Ruggles, Aug. 26; P. N. Nicholas to Van Buren, October 19 and 31; J. A. Hamilton to *Ibid*, December 12; Van Buren to Crawford, November 12, to Butler, December 27, 1824: also Van Buren *Autobiography*, 113: all in Van Buren Mss.

in the pursuit of it, if they should think it expedient, to set me altogether aside, and to concur in any arrangement necessary for the union of the republican party and the public interests." Two days later a plan was submitted to him by which he was to have the presidency, Jackson the vice-presidency, Clay the state department, and Calhoun the treasury. To this proposition, which was said to have originated with Calhoun, Adams made no reply. Two weeks later the republican caucus was held, and Crawford developed so little strength in it that all thought of a combination against him was dropped.' Echoes of these plans reached Jackson, but he put them aside. He would make no bargain, he said: let his friends do what was best for the country, and he would be satisfied.

The incident has further interest because it shows the relative importance in which the four candidates were regarded by one who had good ground for an intelligent opinion. Jackson now stood in second rank. Even Adams conceded this. He declared that Jackson was fit for the vice-presidency, that the place suited Jackson, and that it would be well to have a President from the East and a vice-president from the West. "His name and character," he added complacently, "would serve to restore the forgotten dignity of the place, and it would afford an easy and dignified retirement to his old age."'

Before these attempted combinations ceased Tennessee itself was to be fought for. One of the enemies whom Jackson's temper made was Col. John Williams, of Knoxville, recently commanding the 10th regiment, in which Thomas H. Benton was lieutenant-colonel. In 1815 Williams became United States senator and in 1823 was up for reëlection. He was openly against Jackson, supporting in 1819 the resolutions to

'Adams, *Memoirs*, VI., 241; Talmadge to Jackson, March 6; Jackson to Talmadge, March 12, 1824; Jackson Mss.

'Adams, *Memoirs*, VI., 253, 333.

censure the general for the invasion of Florida, and, it was alleged, ridiculing the nomination by the Tennessee legislature and saying it would not be seriously supported by the people of the state. Mutual friends tried to make peace between the two, but Jackson steadily refused to receive any advances unless Williams acknowledged his error and apologized, and this the senator would not do.[1] His reëlection in 1823, it was felt by Jackson's supporters, would be a blow to their interests; and they sought to bring out a man who could defeat him. They first thought of John Rhea, but on that basis they lacked a majority by several votes. They then decided that only Jackson could defeat Williams. He was very unwilling to have the office and H. L. White, one of his wisest supporters, feared its effects, lest it should be considered an electioneering scheme; but the necessity was great and the election was carried by a safe majority. Of the twenty-five members of the legislature who stood by Williams and voted against the people's favorite only three were reëlected at the next election.[2]

This danger past, the Jackson managers had time to consider the party caucus, then a most serious obstacle. It was in the control of Virginians, and in the days before nominating conventions it was very influential with the party. The Virginians were likely to carry it for Crawford, and every other candidate was, therefore, against it. They all pronounced it a futile means of suggesting a presidential candidate; but Jackson, the popular favorite, was peculiarly interested in breaking down this centre of the politician's power.[3] His supporters in the Tennessee legislature in 1823 passed resolutions denouncing the caucus, instructing the state's congressmen to vote against it, and calling on other legislatures to take similar action. Many

---

[1]McNairy to Jackson, September 3; Jackson to McNairy, September 6, 1823. See also, Jackson to Gen. John Brown, October 8, 1819; Jackson Mss.
[2]Jackson to Polk, October 25, 1835.
[3]Parton, *Jackson*, III., 23.

states acquiesced, and so strong was the sentiment against the caucus that in Virginia itself a resolution to instruct the Virginia delegation to support it was lost by one vote. The agitation succeeded in its purpose: it made the caucus so unpopular that but sixty-eight out of a total of two hundred and sixty-one congressmen would attend it, when it met on February 14, 1824, and of these sixty-four voted for Crawford, who was declared the republican nominee.[1]

Another source to which the Jackson managers looked for votes was the remnant of federalists in the Southern and Middle states. These persons were too much against the regular republicans to accept Crawford, and old animosities ranged them against Adams. Calhoun had been a favorite with them, and his alliance with Jackson made it seem that they could be won for the Tennesseean. To influence their opinions the managers brought out an old correspondence which was supposed to be agreeable to them. The story, which Parton under the influence of the garrulous Major Lewis seems to have distorted, is as follows:

October 23, 1816, Jackson wrote to Monroe, about to be elected President, recommending the appointment of Col. W. H. Drayton, of South Carolina, a war federalist, as secretary of war, basing his advice on military grounds.[2] Before a reply could be made he wrote again, November 12th, urging Drayton on political grounds. "Pardon me," he said, "for the following remark for the next presidential term. Everything depends upon the selection of your ministry, both as to yourself and country. In every situation party, and party feeling ought to be laid out of view (for now is the time to put them down) by selecting those the most honest, possessing capacity, virtue, and firmness; by this course you'll steer the national ship to

---

[1] McMaster, *United States*, V., 60-64.

[2] The letter is in draft in Jackson's hand, Jackson Mss. See also Parton, *Jackson*, II., 357, where the text has been improved.

honor and preferment, and yourself to the united plaudits of a happy country. Consult no party or party feelings in your choice, pursue that unerring Judgment you possess, that for so many years has added so much to the benefit of our common country."[1]

The suggestion suited Monroe's theories. As an old protester against the regular republicans of Jefferson's time, he was disposed to be liberal in his appointments, and for the same reason he had opposition from the regulars. This obstacle prevented the nomination of Drayton; but Monroe was not displeased and became continually more liberal. In his second administration he openly announced an "amalgamation policy" in appointments. His acceptance of Jackson's theory brought a third letter from the latter, in which he said, in expressing his horror of the Pickering federalists: "Had I commanded the military department where the Hartford Convention met, if it had been the last act of my life, I should have hung up the three principal leaders of the party."

These letters were written with Jackson's usual directness, but Major Lewis revised and embellished them before they were sent to the President-elect. It is to Lewis that we owe the oft-repeated phrase, "the monster called party spirit." Later he told Parton that he considered them important when they were written, and kept them in mind. From this information the biographer constructed a theory that they were written with an eye to the future. The theory is unsupported; for Jackson himself said they were not written for publication,[2] and the reference to the Hartford Convention would hardly have appeared if such an event had been foreseen. So far as their author was concerned, they were probably only a candid

---

[1]Jackson to Monroe, October 23, November 12, 1816, and January 6, 1817; Jackson Mss. See, also, Parton *Jackson*, II., 357-368.

[2]Jackson to Lewis, December 28, 1826, Jackson Mss. See also *Bulletin New York Public Library* IV. 312.

expression of his opinion in regard to the attitude the government ought to take toward the moderate federalists.

The first use of these letters in the campaign of 1824 was made privately. Lewis in 1822 read copies of them to Col. William Polk, of Raleigh, the leading federalist in North Carolina. The latter, says Lewis, was convinced by them and thenceforth worked successfully for the Tennesseean in North Carolina.[1] So far as we may judge from the facts which appear on the surface, the Jackson managers were satisfied to use the correspondence in this discreet manner. To publish it was likely to displease both the strict party republicans and the extreme federalists of New England. It was not, therefore, through their efforts or consent that it was at last given to the public. The story of the publication shows how large a part intrigue played in the political history of the day.

In his second term Monroe, following his "amalgamation policy," nominated Irish, a federalist, as a marshal in Pennsylvania. The two senators from that state were republicans and protested to Monroe against the appointment. He, in justifying himself, read them Jackson's letters of 1816–1817 and within a short time repeated the argument with other republicans. But the Pennsylvanians were not convinced and induced the senate to reject Irish by a vote of twenty-six to fourteen, the majority being all republicans.

From this affair the public first knew of the correspondence. Crawford's supporters dwelt on the information, pleased to have an argument to show that Jackson was not a good republican. For a time the attack produced consternation in western Pennsylvania, where republicanism was a tradition with the Scotch-Irish. The Jackson newspapers, however, nervously denied the existence of the correspondence, and George Kremer, whose fame rests chiefly on his participation in a more noted squabble,

---

[1] Parton, *Jackson*, III., 15.

wrote to ask Jackson if the alleged letters were really written. Now the published reports had distorted the contents of the correspondence, and the general was literally correct when he said in reply that he did not write what was attributed to him. Kremer published this reply and said that he had talked, also, with Monroe, who confirmed Jackson's denial. This left the Pennsylvania senators in a bad position. One of them was a supporter of Jackson and kept quiet; but the other, Walter Lowrie, a Crawford man, resented the imputation against his integrity and called on the President to publish the correspondence which was read to him and his colleague. Monroe's relations with Jackson were already strained on account of the Fromentin affair and he refused to take a step which would make them worse. Lowrie was thus left in an awkward position, but relief was at hand. One morning he received an anonymous letter postmarked "Richmond," which contained a copy of the President's reply to Jackson's second letter. Part of it was in the handwriting of Jackson, who declared that it was stolen from his papers, and part in that of Hay, Monroe's son-in-law. By threatening to publish the letter which fortune sent him, Lowrie was able to force action by his opponents. After some squirming on their part, Eaton, acting for his leader, published the whole correspondence in May, 1824. The effect was considerable, though not as decisive as was anticipated. Some republicans were alienated and many federalists were won. But these results were not permanent. The disappearance of Crawford after 1825 gave most of his followers to Jackson; and issues were such in 1828 that most of the federalist accessions of 1824 were lost. Some of the Crawford republicans in process of transition found the Monroe correspondence a stumbling-block; but Van Buren, their principal leader, reassured them saying that Jackson was once a good republican and "we must trust to good fortune, and to the effects of favora-

ble associations for the removal of the rust they [his principles]
have contracted in his case, by a protracted non-user, and the
prejudicial effects in that regard of his military life."[1]

Jackson's allusion to the Hartford Convention was bitterly
resented in New England, but he did not retract. In a private
letter he justified himself by saying: "It is true that I wrote
hastily these letters to Mr. Monroe to which you refer, and
that I never calculated that they would be published," but
they had not done as much harm as his enemies expected.
As to the Hartford Convention, his utterances were, he declared,
well founded. The papers charged the leaders with treason and
a military commander has power to deal with treason; where-
fore, "if there is no mistake about the powers referred to, and
if there had been none in the public prints, when they charged
the Hartford Convention with carrying on illicit correspondence
with the enemy by its agents, with a combination to disobey
the calls of the President, for the just *quotas* of militia, thereby
paralyzing the arm of government, and aiding and assisting
the enemy by withdrawing themselves illegally from the ranks
of their country, I ask if the conduct as charged against the
members of the Hartford Convention and its correspondence
with the British agents (if true) did not bring them within the
purview and meaning of the fifty-sixth and fifty-seventh articles
of war — if not then they are a dead letter and ought to be
expunged . . . I have no hesitation in saying that if I had
been placed in command in that country by the orders of the
President, I should have at once tried the strength of the powers
of the government in a state of war, whether it was competent
to wield its physical force in defence of our country by punishing all concerned in combinations to aid the enemy and para-
lyze our own efforts. In this case if my judgment had been

[1]Van Buren, *Autobiography*, III., 20-27, Van Buren Mss. *Bulletin New York Public Library*, 1900, 194; Lowrie to Monroe, March 15, 1824; Jackson to Donelson, January 16, 18 and 21, 1824, to Monroe, April 9, Monroe to Jackson, April 10, 1824, Jackson Mss. See also Jefferson, *Writings* (Ford edition), X., 304.

condemned, all good men would have at least commended the motive." [1]

Jackson took his seat in the senate December 5, 1823. He was made chairman of the committee on military affairs and member of the committee on foreign relations. He resigned his seat two years later after the legislature nominated him for the second time to the presidency. His duties were performed conscientiously, and for a new member who had no talent for speaking he was fairly prominent. He presented the business which pertained to his committee with brief but effective speeches; and on the whole his career was satisfactory to those who made him their representative. [2]

Internal improvements and the tariff were then prominent political questions, and each was before the senate in the first session he attended. Both measures were popular with his friends in the North, particularly in Pennsylvania, and unpopular with most of his Southern supporters. His managers feared that his outspoken nature would be unequal to so delicate a situation, but for once he was discreet. He voted for all the road bills which came up except one — and in that case did not vote at all — but he justified himself on the ground of military necessity. On Calhoun's project for a general survey of roads and canals he voted steadily with the majority which, rejecting all amendments, passed the bill in the form in which it came from the house. [3]

In regard to the tariff of 1824 he displayed the same kind of courage and decision. The bill came from the house, stamped with the insignia of protection. Amendment after amendment was introduced to lower the schedules, most of them without success. Of the attempts to reduce the duties by amendment in the committee of the whole, Jackson's vote was for the pro-

1Jackson to Lewis, December 28, 1826, Jackson Mss.
2Annals of 18th Congress, 1st session, Volume I., *passim*.
3*Ibid*, 137, 296, 253-256, 570.

tectionists twenty-two times, for lower rates four times, for compromise once, and in three cases it is not possible to determine how it should be classified.[1] His one vote for the free list had reference to frying pans. In far the majority of cases he voted with Lowrie and Findlay, senators from the staunch protectionist state of Pennsylvania.

At this time it was generally reported that Jackson favored the "protecting duty policy"; and Dr. L. H. Colman, a Virginia supporter who professed opposite views, wrote to ask his tariff opinions. The reply, which became famous, was as follows:[2]

SIR: I have had the honor this day to receive your letter of the 21st instant, and with candor shall reply to it. My name has been brought before the nation by the people themselves without any agency of mine: for I wish it not to be forgotten that I have never solicited office, nor when called upon by the constituted authorities have ever declined — where I conceived my services would be beneficial to my country. As my name has been brought before the nation for the first office in the gift of the people, it is incumbent on me, when asked, frankly to declare my opinion upon any political or national question pending before and about which the country feels an interest.

You ask me my opinion on the Tariff. I answer, that I am in favor of a judicious examination and revision of it; and so far as the Tariff before us embraces the design of fostering, protecting, and preserving within ourselves the means of national defense and independence, particularly in a state of war, I would advocate it and support it. The experience of the late war ought to teach us a lesson; and one never to be forgotten. If our liberty and republican form of government, procured for us by our Revolutionary fathers, are worth the blood and treasure at which they were obtained, it surely is

[1] Annals of 18th Congress, 1st session, Volume, I., 583-738, passim.
[2] Jackson to Dr. Colman, April 26, 1824, Parton, Jackson, III., 35.

our duty to protect and defend them. Can there be an American patriot, who saw the privations, dangers, and difficulties experienced for the want of a proper means of defense during the last war, who would be willing again to hazard the safety of our country if embroiled; or rest it for defense on the precarious means of national resources to be derived from commerce, in a state of war with a maritime power which might destroy that commerce to prevent our obtaining the means of defense, and thereby subdue us? I hope there is not; and if there is, I am sure he does not deserve to enjoy the blessings of freedom.

Heaven smiled upon, and gave us liberty and independence. That same Providence has blessed us with the means of national independence and national defense. If we omit or refuse to use the gifts which He has extended to us, we deserve not the continuation of His blessings. He has filled our mountains and our plains with minerals — with lead, iron, and copper, and given us a climate and a soil for the growing of hemp and wool. These being the grand materials of our national defense, they ought to have extended to them adequate and fair protection, that our own manufactories and laborers may be placed on a fair competition with those of Europe; and that we may have within our own country a supply of those leading and important articles so essential to war. Beyond this, I look at the Tariff with an eye to the proper distribution of labor and revenue; and with a view to discharge our national debt. I am one of those who do not believe that a national debt is a national blessing, but rather a curse to a republic; inasmuch as it is calculated to raise around the administration a moneyed aristocracy dangerous to the liberties of the country.

This Tariff — I mean a judicious one — possesses more fanciful than real dangers. I will ask what is the real situation of the agriculturalist? Where has the American farmer a market for his surplus products? Except for cotton he has neither a foreign nor a home market. Does not this clearly prove, when there is no market either at home or abroad, that there is too much labor employed in agriculture? and that the channels of labor should be multiplied? Common sense points out at once the remedy. Draw from agriculture the superabundant labor, employ it in mechanism and manufactures, thereby creating a home market for your breadstuffs, and distributing labor to a most profitable account, and benefits to the country will result. Take from agriculture in the United States six hundred thousand men, women, and children, and you at once give a home market for more breadstuffs than all Europe now furnishes us. In short, sir, we have been too long subject to the policy of the British merchants. It is time we should become a little more *Americanized*, and instead of feeding the paupers and laborers of Europe, feed our own, or else in a short time, by continuing our present policy, we shall all be paupers ourselves.

It is, therefore, my opinion that a careful Tariff is much wanted to pay our national debt, and afford us a means of that defense within ourselves on which the safety and liberty of our country depend; and last, though not least, to our labor, which must prove beneficial to the happiness, independence, and wealth of the community.

This is a short outline of my opinions, generally, on the subject of your inquiry, and believing them correct and calculated to further the prosperity and happiness of my country, I declare to you I would not barter them for any office or situation of temporal character that could be given me. I have presented you my opinions freely, because I am without concealment, and should indeed despise myself if I could believe myself capable of acquiring the confidence of any by means so ignoble.

This letter, so characteristic of Jackson's mind, was well adapted to his object. The military argument appealed to all voters, and the home market theory pleased the buoyant West. It did not convince the planters of the South and the theoretical free traders elsewhere, but these were either hopelessly attached to Crawford or safely led into the fold through their devotion to Calhoun. Moreover, Jackson believed in what he wrote; his entire honesty will relieve from the imputation of self-conceit the flamboyant sentiment with which he closed the letter.

The reference to the moneyed aristocracy was at once an echo of 1798 and a prophecy of 1832.

When the letter was published the expression, "judicious tariff" caught the eye of the public. It strengthened the impression, already created by the letters to Monroe, that the author was not a man of extreme views. Clay perceived the force of the utterance and when he heard of it shrugged his shoulders and exclaimed, "Well, by —, I am in favor of an injudicious tariff!"[1]

Jackson's dilemma during the discussion of the tariff bill is illustrated by the following story in Van Buren's unpublished autobiography. A proposition to impose a duty of four and a half cents a yard on cotton bagging, the chief factory of which was in Lexington, Ky., was opposed strongly by the supporters of Crawford and Calhoun. Jackson's Southern friends frequently called him into the side aisles to urge him to vote for a motion by Macon to strike out the proposed duty. Although opposed to the particular duty, he favored the bill and feared that to amend it in one clause would lead to general revision. Van Buren's seat was on the side aisle, and he necessarily heard these repeated consultations. When Macon's amendment was put, both Tennessee senators voted "nay," and it was defeated by a vote of twenty-two to twenty-three. Suddenly realizing that his vote, if cast in the affirmative, would secure an opposite result, Jackson turned to Van Buren and exclaimed, "You give way, sir!" The New Yorker refused, and in a few minutes his interlocutor, realizing the impropriety of his demand, returned with an apology. But some of his supporters declared that Van Buren's vote was a trick to make Southerners think that Jackson had defeated the amendment, an imputation which was stoutly denied by the crafty little Northerner, whose own friends were disposed to boast of it as a mark of their leader's

[1] Van Buren, *Autobiography*, I., 29, Van Buren Mss.

sagacity. All this happened when the tariff bill of 1824 was before the committee of the whole; when it came before the senate, Jackson and Holmes, of Maine, changed their votes on the same amendment and the duty on cotton bagging was stricken out.[1]

In September, 1823, Crawford was stricken with paralysis and for a year his condition was precarious. If he should die who would get his "old republican" support? Would it be Clay, the opponent of the administration and champion of a protective tariff? or Adams, whose New England reserve aroused no enthusiasm in the South? or Jackson, supporter of the administration, milder than Clay on the tariff question, and long a friend of Monroe, but a relentless enemy of Crawford? The situation was interesting, and perplexing. Crawford's friends asserted,—as it turned out, truthfully—that their leader would not die, they minimized the seriousness of his illness, and when, two months before Election Day, he began to mend, their spirits and their confidence returned.

But his improvement did not make his election more probable. It only made it more certain that neither of the four candidates would have a majority of the electoral college, and that the ultimate choice would fall in the house of representatives, where the state delegations voting each as a unit select for President one of the three highest in the electoral college. Who would be the three fortunate ones? The slow-coming election returns at last answered the question. Jackson had ninety-nine electoral votes, Adams eighty-four, Crawford forty-one, and Clay thirty-seven. Calhoun was safely elected vice-president, but the contest for the presidency entered a second and more exciting stage.

---

[1]Van Buren, *Autobiography*, I.,29, Van Buren Mss.; Annals of 18th Congress, 1st session, Volume I., 708, 733

CHAPTER XVIII

ELECTION BY THE HOUSE OF REPRESENTATIVES

OF THE three candidates whose names now went before the house of representatives Crawford was eliminated by the state of his health. He barely held the states committed to him by undeviating loyalty and could not expect to draw from either of the other candidates. Of the other two, Adams, patriotic and fearless, was an educated man, long experienced in political affairs, and in sympathy with the best traditions of statesmanship. Jackson, equally patriotic and honest, was uneducated, inexperienced in national politics, and lacking in judgment and self-control. An intelligent man actuated solely by love of country might well prefer the former.

But the choice was not to be made under such happy conditions. Each candidate had a group of managers who worked in his behalf, and who, at the same time, had eyes on their own proper advancement. They were practical politicians and planned to get votes for their leaders by any reasonable means. Flattery, promises of future support, and threats of future opposition were their ordinary arguments. The candidates themselves cannot be charged with participation in this process of manipulation. They must have known the game too well to take open part in it; but it is inconceivable that they were ignorant of what transpired.

There were then twenty-four states in the union, and in the house, the winning candidate must control the delegations of thirteen of them. Clay, long speaker and leader of a devoted group of representatives, could influence enough delegations to determine the result. He and his followers at once became objects of solicitude to all the other parties. His own letter cleverly describes the situation:

I am sometimes touched gently on the shoulder by a friend, for example, of General Jackson, who will thus address me: "My dear sir, all my dependence is upon you; don't disappoint us, you know our partiality was for you next to the hero, and how much we want a Western President." Immediately after, a friend of Mr. Crawford will accost me: "The hopes of the Republican party are concentrated on you; for God's sake preserve it. If you had been returned instead of Mr. Crawford, every man of us would have supported you to the last hour. We consider him and you as the only genuinely Republican candidates." Next a friend of Mr. Adams comes with tears in his eyes:[1] "Sir, Mr. Adams has always had the greatest respect for you, and admiration of your talents. There is no station to which you are not equal. Most undoubtedly, you are the second choice of New England, and I pray you to consider seriously whether the public good and your own future interests do not point most distinctly to the choice which ought to be made?" How can one withstand all this disinterested homage and kindness?[2]

Politics, indeed, make strange bed-fellows, and the strenuous Jackson was not exempt from the application of the rule. The preceding year, he made friends with Thomas Hart Benton, whose views and temperament made him a Jackson follower, and who was as much interested in the reconciliation as the Tennesseean. Benton, formerly for Clay, was now won over and labored hard to carry the Missouri representative for Jackson. Another scheme was to bring Jackson and Crawford together. The health of the latter prevented an open meeting, but the men were induced to say pleasant things about each

[1]There is an allusion here to Adams's watering eyes.
[2]Colton, *Private Correspondence of Clay*, 109.

other and Mrs. Crawford called on Mrs. Jackson, from which political lieutenants deduced the most reassuring conclusions.[1]

In the winter of 1824-5, friends undertook the greater task of establishing cordial relations between the general and the President-maker. Clay and Jackson were brought together at a dinner, from which the former drove home in the carriage of the latter; then each gave a dinner to the other, and afterward they met with appearances of good will. The advances came from Jackson's side, but it is not known how much he and how much his managers were responsible for them. He seems to have believed in the genuine good will of his rival, and was no doubt in a position to offer him a place in the cabinet if the election resulted favorably. While Clay had opposed Adams's policies during Monroe's administration, he had declared that Jackson was personally unfit for the presidency. He must, therefore, have found it more difficult to come around to the latter than to the former.

But Clay's mind was made up early in the contest, certainly before the middle of December. January 8th, he announced to his intimates that he would go for Adams. He might have justified himself on the ground of the superior fitness of Adams; but he chose the less defensible position that he would save the country from the "dangerous precedent of elevating, in this early stage of the Republic, a military chieftain, merely because he has won a great victory." "As a friend of liberty," he writes to Brooke with an eye to publication, "and to the permanence of our institutions, I cannot consent in this early stage of their existence, by contributing to the election of a military chieftain, to give the strongest guaranty that the Republic will march in the fatal road, which has conducted every republic to ruin."

---

[1]John Branch to Colonel William Polk, January 25, 1825; Mss. in possession of William H. Hoyt, New York City.

"My friends," he says in another letter, "entertain the belief that their kind wishes toward me will in the end be more likely to be accomplished by so bestowing their votes [i. e., on Adams]. I have, however, most earnestly entreated them to throw me out of their consideration in bringing their judgments to a final conclusion, and to look and be guided solely by the public good."[1]

Clay's fine self-denial need not detain us long. He was a practical politician and as keen in his own interests as his lieutenants. He knew his advantages from the election of Adams. The New Englander was not likely to become a permanent party leader. He had little strength outside of New England, and the more popular Clay might fairly hope that a union with him would lead to the succession. The growing popularity of the tariff, Clay's pet measure, in the region normally for Adams, gave additional reason for such an alliance, and to it may be added the Kentuckian's feeling for the capable classes as against the revived doctrines of popular government for which Jackson stood. On the other hand, coöperation with Jackson was difficult; for both were Western men and neither was willing to take a subordinate position in a combination. Moreover, Calhoun was already in coalition with Jackson and it was generally admitted that he was to be heir apparent to that leader. These and other practical considerations, which were well known to his supporters and which seem clear to the historian, must have been thoroughly understood by Clay when he made up his mind that the interests of the country demanded the election of Adams.

Clay did not avow his intentions until shortly before February 9th, the date set for the vote in the house of representatives. In the meantime there was much discussion, each side thinking it had a chance,[2] and in it, Jackson's followers advanced

---

[1] Colton, *Private Correspondence of Clay*, 110, 111, 112.

[2] January 7, Macon thought Jackson's prospect the best and Cobb, of Georgia, was uncertain on January 15. See Shipp, *Life of Crawford*, 179.

the claim that he was entitled to be considered the people's favorite, because he had the largest number of electoral votes and because he probably received the largest popular vote; but there is little certainty about the latter statement, since six states chose electors by legislatures, and in those states it was impossible to estimate the popular vote. Jackson's advocates made much of the argument. They went so far as to say that the will of the people would be defeated if their candidate was set aside, and this, they said, was in spirit, if not in fact, a violation of the constitution, which intended that the people should choose the President. The argument was weak; the constitution did not provide for elections by the people, and it was clear that if the majority of the people had wanted Jackson above the other candidates, they would have expressed themselves accordingly in the choice of electors. But the contention was popularly plausible. It had no influence on the politicians in Washington, and its advocates probably expected as much, but it impressed the people at large, with whom the hero of New Orleans was increasingly influential. It served to support the feeling, skilfully stimulated by the supporters of the friend of the masses, that the corrupt manipulators of affairs at the centre of government no longer cared for the will or the interests of the people. The votes finally given by the states of Illinois and Missouri give some color of truth to the charge.

Jackson watched these affairs from his seat in the senate with silent interest. Easily suspicious of his opponents and confiding in his friends, he saw no other intrigues than those directed against him. What he observed filled him with horror. "I would rather," he exclaimed, "remain a plain cultivator of the soil as I am, than to occupy that which is truly the first office in the world, if the voice of the nation was against it." [1] He was

---

[1] Jackson to S. Swartwout, December 14, 1824, Jackson Mss.

then living with Mrs. Jackson at the same hotel at which Lafayette, on his famous visit to America, was living, and he found much to interest him in the company of the revolutionary hero. There is evidence, too, that his strength of character made a strong impression on the Frenchman. His position made him a man of note, but, through natural qualities, he was distinguished. His bearing was good, he avoided complicity in the intrigues of the day, he asserted with an earnestness which carried conviction the loftiest political ideals, and he practised with all sincerity the simpler duties of private life. His shortcomings of inexperience and bad temper did not appear to the casual observer, and his outspoken frankness gave him apparent advantage over the busy politicians around him.

Much has been said about Mrs. Jackson's social capacity, and her appearance in Washington aroused great interest. The following naïve extract from the letter of a Jackson man shows what impression she made:

The visit of Mrs. Jackson to this place has given a damper to those who have used her as an argument against him (Jackson). She has proven the falsity of the thousand slanders, which have been industriously circulated of her awkwardness, ignorance and indecorum. I have been made acquainted with her and find her striking characteristics to be, an unaffected simplicity of manners, with great goodness of heart. So far from being denied the attentions usually extended to strangers, as was predicted, she has been overpowered by the civilities of all parties. Policy makes it necessary that they should thus demean themselves toward her for *they* will not be forgotten by her husband, who deny her the rights of a stranger. The old General's health is very delicate, owing to which, he seldom goes into company of an evening. At General Brown's he was on the night of the "8th January" and received more court than all the company beside. Several buildings were illuminated in the neighborhood of his lodgings and an artillery company

at night turned out and fired him a salute over a con-
flagration of tar barrels.[1]

Among those men who actively tried to elect General Jackson,
was George Kremer, of Pennsylvania, destined to play a conspicuous part in the intrigues of the day. He was a man of the
people, who had won the confidence of his constituents by his
outspoken denunciations of his opponents, an extreme product
of the new movement. He was a man of originality and
boldness, and in spite of poor educational advantages and
peculiarities of manner, he won influence in his party. But
circumstances were about to thrust him into an adventure for
which neither his physical nor moral courage was adequate.

Kremer was an enthusiastic admirer of Jackson and suspicious
and credulous enough to take seriously the charges of corruption
which were uttered by his party against their opponents. Early
in January, James Buchanan, also of Pennsylvania, told Kremer
in apparent alarm, if we may accept Kremer's story, that as a
friend of Clay, he knew a great intrigue was in progress about
which he thought Jackson ought to be informed, and that if he
was as good a friend of Jackson as Kremer, he would inform him.
The plot, he said, was that Adams's friends were proposing to
Clay's supporters to get the secretaryship of state for Clay if he
would use his influence for the Eastern candidate. Buchanan
said Jackson was in great danger unless he would make the same
offer to Clay, since the Adams men proclaimed that Jackson,
if successful, would surely keep Adams secretary of state.
Buchanan, therefore, suggested that the Tennesseean at least
authorize the assurance that he, as President, would not continue
the present incumbent. To this proposition, Kremer says he
returned the answer that his candidate would make no promises
and if elected, it must be by principle. His statement was

[1]John S. Ellis, January 11, 1825, Mss. in possession of William H. Hoyt, of New York City.

embodied in a letter to Jackson, and to it he appended the following postscript: "Mr. Buchanan stated that him and Mr. Clay have become great friends this winter, this he said as I thought to inform on my mind the authority from whence he had derived his information."[1]

So far Mr. Kremer. When the matter became public controversy, Buchanan was appealed to, and made the following statement:

On the 30th of December, 1824 (I am able to fix the time, not only from my own recollection, but from letters which I wrote on that day, on the day following, and on the 2nd of January, 1825), I called upon General Jackson. After the company had left him, by which I found him surrounded, he asked me to take a walk with him; and, while we were walking together upon the street, I introduced the subject. I told him I wished to ask him a question in relation to the Presidential election; that I knew he was unwilling to converse upon the subject; that, therefore, if he deemed the question improper, he might refuse to give it an answer: that my only motive in asking it, was friendship for him, and I trusted he would excuse me for thus introducing a subject about which I knew he wished to be silent. His reply was complimentary to myself, and accompanied with a request that I would proceed. I then stated to him there was a report in circulation, that he had determined he would appoint Mr. Adams Secretary of State, in case he were elected President, and that I wished to ascertain from him whether he had ever intimated such an intention; that he must at once perceive how injurious to his election such a report might be; that no doubt there were several able and ambitious men in the country, among whom, I thought Mr. Clay might be included, who were aspiring to that office; and, if it were believed he had already determined to appoint his chief competitor, it might have a most unhappy effect upon their exertions, and those of their friends; that, unless he had so determined, I thought this report should be promptly contradicted under his own authority. . . . After I had

---
[1] Kremer to Jackson, March 6, 1825, Jackson Mss.

finished the General declared he had not the least objection to answer my question; that he thought well of Mr. Adams, but he never said or intimated that he would, or would not, appoint him Secretary of State; that these were secrets he would keep to himself—he would conceal them from the very hairs of his head.[1]

Years later, Jackson declared that Buchanan did not do him full justice and repeated the charge, which is clear in Kremer's letter, that Buchanan said it was necessary to fight Adams's supporters with their own weapons, that is, to make an offer to Clay. On the face of the matter, it seems that Buchanan did seek to get from Jackson a statement which he could use with the Clay men, and that having failed in his purpose, he sought a few days later to induce Kremer to move Jackson to the same purpose. How much he had in heart a bargain with Clay is seen by a statement of the latter in his old age. Buchanan, he said, called at his lodgings where the two were together in the presence of Letcher, of Kentucky. Clay, speaking of himself in the third person, tells us what happened:

Shortly after Mr. Buchanan's entry into the room, he introduced the subject of the approaching Presidential election, and spoke of the certainty of the election of his favorite (Jackson), adding that "he would form the most splendid cabinet that the country had ever had." Mr. Letcher asked, "How could he have one more distinguished than that of Mr. Jefferson, in which were both Madison and Gallatin? Where would he be able to find equally eminent men?" Mr. Buchanan replied that he "would not go out of this room for a Secretary of State," looking at Mr. Clay. This gentleman playfully remarked that "he thought there was no timber there fit for a cabinet officer, unless it was Mr. Buchanan himself." Mr. Clay, while he was so hotly assailed with the charge of bargain, intrigue, and corruption,

---

[1] Buchanan to the Editor of the Lancaster (Pennsylvania) *Journal*. See Buchanan's *Writings* (Moore, Editor), I., 263-7; also Parton, *Jackson*, III., 114.

during the administration of Mr. Adams, notified Mr. Buchanan of his intention to publish the above occurrence; but, by the earnest entreaties of that gentleman, he was induced to forbear doing so.[1]

None of this evidence shows that either Jackson, Clay, or Adams was bargaining for the presidency. But it made it pretty certain that Mr. Buchanan had his dreams, and that his attempt to realize them was clumsily made.

Clay's intention to support Adams was known to intimate friends by the middle of December,[2] and a rumor to that effect was abroad. The Jackson party discounted it at first, but as February 9th, the day of the final choice, approached, they began to realize its truth. They now became very bitter toward Clay, partly desiring, as it seems, to shake some of his support out of his hands and partly to take vengeance on him for his opposition. For some days the air was full of charges, and on January 28, 1825, appeared in the *Columbian Observer*, of Philadelphia, an unsigned letter, in which was the following indictment:

For some time past, the friends of Clay have hinted that they, like the Swiss, would fight for those who pay best. Overtures were said to have been made by the friends of Adams to the friends of Clay, offering him the appointment of Secretary of State, for his aid to elect Adams. And the friends of Clay gave the information to the friends of Jackson, and hinted that if the friends of Jackson would offer the same price, they would close with them. But none of the friends of Jackson would descend to such mean barter and sale. It was not believed by any of the friends of Jackson that this contract would be ratified by the members from the States which had voted for Clay. I was of opinion, when I first heard of this transaction, that men, professing any honorable principles, could not, or would not be

---

[1]Colton, *Life of Clay*, I., 418.
[2]Benton, *Thirty Years' View*, I., 48.

transferred, like the planter does his negroes, or the farmer does his team of horses. No alarm was excited. We believed the republic was safe. The nation having delivered Jackson into the hands of Congress, backed by a large majority of their votes, there was on my mind no doubt that Congress would respond to the will of the nation by electing the individual they had declared to be their choice. Contrary to this expectation, it is now ascertained to a certainty that Henry Clay has transferred his interest to John Quincy Adams. As a consideration for this abandonment of duty to his constituents, it is said and believed, should this unholy coalition prevail, Clay is to be appointed Secretary of State.

This charge ought not to have surprised an experienced politician, but the language in which it was made, was calculated to annoy. It is easy to explain it as the vaporing of an uncouth popular leader; but how can we excuse the violence of Clay's reply, February 1st, in the *National Intelligencer*? He wrote:

The editor of one of those prints, ushered forth in Philadelphia, called the *Columbian Observer*, for which I do not subscribe, and which I have never ordered, has had the impudence to transmit to me his vile paper of the 28th instant. In this number is inserted a letter purporting to have been written from this city, on the 25th instant, by a member of the house of representatives, belonging to the Pennsylvania delegation. I believe it to be a forgery; but if it be genuine, I pronounce the member, whoever he may be, a base and infamous calumniator, a dastard and liar; and if he dare unveil himself, and avow his name, I will hold him responsible, as I here admit myself to be, to all the laws which govern and regulate men of honor.[1]

Two days later Kremer in the same newspaper tendered his respects to the Honorable Henry Clay, acknowledged the authorship of the letter in the *Columbian Observer*, offered to prove its truth, and, saying nothing about the laws of honor, planted

[1]Colton, *Life of Clay*, I., 297.

himself behind the bulwark of public duty, proclaiming that as a representative of the people he would "not fear to 'cry aloud and spare not,' when their rights and privileges are at stake." Clay could hardly insist on a duel with the eccentric Kremer, whose card made no reference to the speaker's challenge. He contented himself with demanding in the house a full investigation of the charges against him and added with some show of contempt that "emanating from such a source as they did, this was the only notice which he could take of them." When he sat down, Forsyth, of Georgia, a Crawford man, moved that a select committee of investigation be appointed, and after two days' debate, the motion was carried and a committee was chosen from the followers of Adams, who was charged with complicity in the bargaining, and from the supporters of Crawford, Jackson's most bitter enemy. Had they been taken from other factions they must have been partisans of either Clay or Jackson, which shows that the situation was difficult.

When Clay demanded an investigation, Kremer rose at once to promise that every portion of his charges should be proved to the satisfaction of the house. But when summoned before the committee to give evidence, he refused to attend. He attempted to justify himself in a long letter, which he evidently did not write and which with some probability has been attributed to S. D. Ingham.[1] The committee could not proceed without the chief witness, and the investigation collapsed.

Kremer lacked courage for a fight, and he had no case; but had he been a better fighter, he might have been appalled by the situation which presented itself. His charge was made against some of the friends of Clay, but the Kentuckian with characteristic magnanimity shouldered the responsibility by asking that he be investigated. But in the debate on the motion to appoint a

---

[1] Kremer's reply is in Colton, *Life of Clay*, I., 307.

committee, it became evident that in the minds of many Kremer himself was on trial, and that if he failed to satisfy the committee, he might expect punishment for maliciously attacking a high officer of the house. Moreover, it would be difficult to prove his charge, since his witnesses, congressmen friendly to Clay, would hardly care to repeat to the committee the rumors out of which Kremer had formed his opinion. If the charges failed, Jackson's cause would be discredited with those necessary followers of Clay without whom he could not be elected. This last phase of the question must have appealed strongly to Jackson's managers; and it is not improbable that at this stage they took the whole case out of Kremer's hands. The affair, which he probably opened himself with the cognizance of friends, was become so large that he might well retreat while he could.

Kremer justified his refusal on the ground that it was proposed to hold him responsible for communicating proper information to his constituents. Such a proposal, said he, was neither constitutional nor expedient, and he denied the jurisdiction of the house in the matter. He asserted that the contention that a member might not criticize the political action of a high officer of the house was worse than the sedition law of 1798. "It may be proper to remark," he added, "in explanation of the admission which I may seem to have made of its jurisdiction: Whatever assent I may have given, was done hastily, relying on the conscious rectitude of my conduct, and regarding my own case, without having reflected duly, on the dangerous principles involved in the proceedings, and cannot therefore be considered as a waiver of my rights." He closed by asking that the case be left to the American people or to the courts. As applied to Kremer's responsibility, this argument has a certain plausibility, although it falls before the undoubted right of the house to discipline its own members. But he was not the defendant, and his reply has no bearing on the question of Clay's responsibility.

In the meantime, the work of the politicians was being brought to a close. When congress convened, Adams was sure of Maryland and New England, seven votes. Jackson felt certain of New Jersey, Pennsylvania, Tennessee, South Carolina, Indiana, Alabama, and Mississippi. Crawford counted on Georgia, Virginia, and Delaware, and he controlled the North Carolina delegation, although the electoral vote of that state was for Jackson. His supporters hoped that in case of a deadlock, he might have a chance at the prize or cast the deciding vote in favor of one of the other candidates. Of the six other states Clay could carry the delegations of Ohio, whose electoral vote he also had; Kentucky, in spite of instructions for Jackson by the legislature; and Louisiana, which cast its electoral vote for Jackson. In New York, whose electoral vote was for Adams, the representatives were divided, seventeen for Adams, two for Jackson, and fifteen for Crawford, so that there was likely to be a deadlock in the delegation. Illinois cast its electoral vote for Jackson and its one representative, D. P. Cook, announced soon after his arrival in Washington that he should consider this as instructions. But he was known to favor Adams on personal grounds, and the friends of that gentleman were able to induce him to change his mind. Missouri, the other state, cast its electoral vote for Clay, but when he was out of the race, the sentiment of the state turned to Jackson. It was represented in the house by a single delegate, John Scott, who for a time was undecided. Benton, in the senate, was strongly for Jackson and labored hard with Scott but failed at last, because, as is alleged, the delegate was promised certain favors in regard to the public printing with the assurance that his brother should not be removed from a federal judgeship for taking part in a recent duel.[1]

---

[1] Adams, *Memoirs*, VI., 472, 473.

By this means, Adams acquired five states, four of which came through Clay's influence, and had altogether twelve, just half of the total number.

Such was the situation when the house on February 9th took its first vote. It was generally expected that the result would be Adams twelve, Jackson seven, Crawford four, with New York divided; and politicians were actively planning for future ballots. Rumor said that eventually Crawford would join Jackson, making eleven votes, with New York evenly divided between Jackson and Adams, a most interesting situation. But all these prospects vanished on the first ballot, when by the change of one Crawford representative, New York went for Adams, who thus received thirteen votes and was declared elected. Clay is called the president-maker of 1825, and either Cook or Scott might have changed the result, but the last necessary touch to complete the election was actually given by this member of the New York delegation. Martin Van Buren in his unpublished autobiography gives a singular explanation of the incident.

One of the New York representatives was Stephen van Rensselaer, very wealthy and very pious. He was a brother-in-law of Alexander Hamilton and therefore much opposed to the Adams family. Van Buren, a Crawford leader, was anxious to prevent an election on the first ballot, probably in order to have the credit of throwing necessary votes to Adams on a later ballot.[1] He relied on Van Rensselaer, who declared more than once that he would not vote for Adams. But on the morning of the ninth as Van Rensselaer went up to the capitol he fell into the hands of Clay and Webster, who beset him strongly with such arguments as would appeal to a man of wealth and religious conviction. His purpose was shaken and he began to ask himself if he had a right to settle so important a matter on personal grounds. He formed the resolve that he would not vote for Adams on the

[1] Van Buren does not admit this purpose, but Hammond, *Political History of New York*, II., 190, says he had it on the best authority. See also Alexander, *Political History of New York*, I., 341-343.

first ballot, whatever he might do later on. "He took his seat," says Van Buren, who had the story from Van Rensselaer himself, "fully resolved to vote for Mr. Crawford, but before the box reached him, he dropped his head upon the edge of his desk and made a brief appeal to his Maker for guidance in the matter — a practice he frequently observed on great emergencies — and when he removed his hand from his eyes, he saw on the floor directly before him a ticket bearing the name of John Quincy Adams. This occurrence at the moment of great excitement and anxiety, he was led to regard as an answer to his appeal, and taking up the ticket, he put it in the box. In this way, it was that Mr. Adams was made President."[1]

The election of 1825 was an unusual opportunity for intrigue. Never before and but once since has so great a prize been at the disposal of political manipulators. Considering the situation in all its possibilities, the issue was as good as could have been expected. Adams, the man chosen, was the best candidate, and the country was satisfied with the choice.

Jackson himself showed no resentment until he knew Clay would go into the cabinet. His old friendship for Adams lasted throughout the campaign, and as late as July 4, 1824, he expressed his confidence in him, adding, "There is no conduct of Hypocritical friends that can alter these feelings."[2] When his friends first spoke of offers of bargains, he believed that Adams had no part in them. On the evening of February 9th, the two men came face to face at a presidential levee, Jackson with a lady on his right arm. Bystanders were curious to see what would happen. Each man hesitated a moment, and then the tall general stepping forward said heartily: "How do you do Mr. Adams? I give you my left hand, for the right, as you see, is devoted to the fair: I hope you are very well, sir." To which

---

[3] Van Buren's *Autobiography*, I, 17, Van Buren Mss.
[4] Jackson to Judge Fulton, July 4, 1824, Jackson Mss.

the other replied coolly, "Very well, sir: I hope General Jackson is well"; and with that they resumed their progress. Observers concluded that the Westerner took the better part in the encounter.

February 14th, he learned that Clay would be secretary of state and turned bitterly against Adams. "I have, as you know," he wrote to Lewis, "always thought Mr. Adams an honest, virtuous man, and had he spurned from him those men who have abandoned those principles they have always advocated, that the people have a right to govern, and that their will should be always obeyed by their constituents, I should still have viewed him as an honest man; and that the rumors of bargain and sale was unknown to him."[1]

In this letter Jackson rests his opposition to Adams chiefly on other grounds than the bargain with Clay; and the same is true of a letter he wrote to Swartwout two days later.[2] On inauguration day he was the first to congratulate the new President, which elicited marked approval from the press of the country. But Clay's nomination for secretary of state seemed to him to confirm all his suspicions, and he began openly and bitterly to denounce what he called a corrupt bargain. Six months later, when the country rang with the controversy, he recounted his progress in the matter as follows:

I had esteemed him (Adams), as a virtuous, able and honest man; and when rumor was stamping the sudden union of his and the friends of Mr. Clay with intrigue, barter and bargain I did not, nay, I could not believe that Mr. Adams participated in a management deserving such epithets. Accordingly when the election was terminated, I manifested publicly a continuation of the same high opinion of his virtue, and of course my disbelief of his having had knowledge of the pledges which many

---

[1] Jackson to W. B. Lewis, February 14 and 20, 1825, in Parton, *Life of Jackson*, III., 73, and Mss. collection of New York Public Library.

[2] Jackson to Swartwout, February 22, 1825, in Parton, *Jackson*, III., 75, and in Jackson Mss.

men of high standing boldly asserted to be the price of his election. But when these strange rumors became facts, when the predicted stipulation was promptly fulfilled, and Mr. Clay was *secretary of state*, the inferrence was irresistible. . . . From that moment I withdrew all intercourse with him, not however, to oppose his administration when I think it useful to the country.[1]

Here Jackson speaks of his public attitude toward Adams: a private letter written at the time of the inauguration shows a less dignified state of mind. He says:

Yesterday Mr. Adams was inaugurated amidst a vast assemblage of citizens, having been escorted to the capitol with the pomp and ceremony of guns and drums not very consistent in my humble opinion with the character of the occasion Twenty-four years ago, when Mr. Jefferson was inducted into office, no such machinery was called in to give solemnity to the scene. He rode his own horse and hitched himself [*sic*][2] to the inclosure. But it seems that times are changing. I hope it is not so with the principles that are to characterise the administration of justice and constitutional law. These, in my fervent prayers for the prosperity and good of our country, will remain unaltered, based upon the sovereignty of the People, and adorned with no forms or ceremonies, save those which their happiness and freedom shall command.[3]

Adams's diary contains interesting evidence about his relations with Clay during this famous winter, and it must be summed up here, even at the risk of making the subject appear tedious. For example, Adams visited James Barbour, senator from Virginia, to know how that important state would vote. He was assured that it would support Crawford at first and in no event

---

[1] Jackson to H. Lee, October 7, 1825, Jackson Mss.
[2] Of course the word "hitched" is used intransitively. The story that Jefferson tied his horse to the fence is discredited by the best evidence.
[3] Jackson to Swartwout, March 5, 1825, a copy, Jackson Mss.

would go for a military chieftain.[1] The reply illustrates the feeling of utter hostility which the old-line republicans, Virginia at their head, had for the new democratic-republican movement which centered around Jackson and Calhoun. Clay was willing enough to be president-maker and was anxious to secure an election on the first ballot, before Crawford's supporters, who must support their candidate at first, could have a chance to cast the deciding votes.

December 17, Letcher, of Kentucky, Clay's "mess-mate," called on Adams. Speaking as a friend of Clay, but on his own authority, he inquired as to Adams's sentiments toward that gentleman. The reply was reassuring: He once felt Clay had treated him badly and was partly responsible for Jonathan Russell's attack in regard to the treaty of Ghent; "but having completely repelled that attack, I feel no animosity toward any person concerned in it." He was assured that Clay felt no hostility toward him, and the conversation ran on for some time, the drift being, says the diary, "that Clay would willingly support me if he could thereby serve himself, and the substance of his *meaning* was, that if Clay's friends could *know* that he could have a prominent share in the administration, that might induce them to vote for me, even in the face of instructions." It is one of the provoking features of this persistent diary that it rarely tells what Adams said to the man who interviewed him. In this case, we are only told, "In my answers to him, I spoke in more general terms."[2]

December 23d, came Letcher again, saying he was anxious that Adams should have the votes of Kentucky, Ohio, Illinois, Indiana, Missouri, and Louisiana, that is, all the states which the Clay men pretended to control. Here the diary is most tantalizing; for it only says that Adams observed that he supposed

[1] Adams, *Memoirs*, VI., 466.
[2] *Ibid*, VI., 416.

he could not even get the vote of Kentucky, and that Letcher replied that this state was "uncommitted."[1] This offer would mean the presidency on the first ballot! Can we think it only evoked a shrug from one man and a reassuring nod from the other?

Clay must have formed a favorable opinion from these overtures; for on January 9th, he asked for an interview, and, although it was Sunday, Adams gave him the whole evening. He announced that he preferred Adams for President, but that, without any reference to himself personally, he would like to know his host's views on certain public affairs. Many questions must have been discussed between the two men, but the diary says nothing about them. It does not even tell us what were the matters about which Clay desired Adams's opinion. January 29th, Clay called again, "and sat with me a couple of hours discussing all the prospects and probabilities of the Presidential election. He spoke to me with the utmost freedom of men and things." Evidently the two men were now equal political partners.[2]

In these four interviews, the most interesting things were communicated. They probably convinced Adams that he would be President if Clay were made secretary of state. He believed that this would be a fit appointment. What did he say in reply? We are not told specifically. It could not have been discouraging to Clay, or he would not have sought his first interviews. Can it be doubted that there was about this matter a reasonable understanding between the three men, Letcher, Clay, and Adams, all of them experienced players of the political game?

The day after the election, Adams avowed to persons concerned that he would ask Clay to become secretary of state. Next day he received a defiance from Calhoun: If the Kentuckian went into the cabinet, a determined opposition to the new

[1] Adams, *Memoirs* VI., 452.
[2] *Ibid*, VI., 464, 483.

administration would be formed with Jackson's name at its head, and with New York doubtful, Virginia in opposition (through the antagonism of the Crawford following to Clay), the West generally leaning to Jackson; and, the rest of the South turning away from the North, it would make a formidable combination and Adams would be left with no reliance except New England. Calhoun went so far as to name the cabinet, which would suit him: Poinsett, Cheves, John McLean, and Southard, all Calhoun supporters, and not one from the Jackson wing of the combination. Adams ever disliked Calhoun, whom he believed to be unscrupulous in accomplishing an inordinate ambition. He took this challenge as but an attempt to frighten him out of his design to appoint Clay; and he proceeded as he had determined.[1]

Clay was as little to be frightened as the new President. His letters show that he summed up the advantages and disadvantages of an acceptance with much penetration.[2] As he himself states them, his reasons for declining seem now to be overwhelming. Why did not Clay understand this? Why did he take the weaker side? Probably because on that side was his bold love of battle, which overcast his judgment on more than one occasion.

Clay knew of the threats to form an opposition and affected to disbelieve them. He was soon to know that they were real. The air became full of plans to defeat his nomination in the senate. It seemed that there would be a long wrangle, but at last his opponents contented themselves with merely voting against him. The result was twenty-seven for, and fifteen against confirmation of the nomination, with seven senators absent. Jackson was one of the fifteen, and the rest were from his, or

---

[1] Adams, *Memoirs*, VI., 506. It is characteristic of Adams that in spite of these threats, he appointe Poinsett minister to Mexico on March 7. See Calhoun *Correspondence* (Jameson, Ed.), 224.

[2] Clay to Brooke, February 18, 1825, Colton, *Correspondence of Clay*, 114.

Calhoun's, or Crawford's following. It was a strong vote in a weak cause; and it evidently rested on a deeper foundation than the belief that Clay had made a corrupt bargain with Adams. It was the initial skirmish of a long conflict.

THE LIFE OF
ANDREW JACKSON

ANDREW JACKSON IN 1845.   AGE 78

From a portrait by G. P. A. Healy, commissioned by Louis Philippe to paint it with the portraits of
other Americans for the palace at Versailles.   It was executed a few weeks before
Jackson died and was considered a good likeness

THE LIFE

OF

ANDREW JACKSON

By

JOHN SPENCER BASSETT, Ph.D.

*Professor of American History in Smith College on the
Sydenham Clark Parsons Foundation*

VOLUME TWO

Illustrated

NEW EDITION

" *If you would preserve your reputation, or that of
the state over which you preside, you must take a
straightforward determined course; regardless of the
applause or censure of the populace, and of the forebodings of that dastardly and designing crew who,
at a time like this, may be expected to clamor
continually in your ears.*" — *Jackson to Governor
Blount, 1813.*

New York

THE MACMILLAN COMPANY

1916

CONTENTS

ILLUSTRATIONS

VOLUME II

VOLUME II.

CHAPTER XIX

THE CAMPAIGN AGAINST JOHN QUINCY ADAMS

ADAMS'S administration is interesting because in it were organized two new political parties and because it saw the progress of the long and unhappy war on Adams and Clay. The political situation was rather chaotic, and methods of opposition were uncouth and violent; but it was the seed-time of democracy, and it opened a new phase of American history.

National politics in 1824 were personal. After 1815, the republican party began to ignore the principles on which Jefferson founded it and to follow expediency. It established a national bank five years after it declared such an institution unconstitutional, it adopted Hamilton's theory of a protective tariff, and it favored roads and canals at national expense and passed two bills to that effect, which were vetoed by Madison and Monroe, two statesmen who still clung to the politics of Jefferson. Men who believed in, and others who opposed, these divergent policies were all accepted as republicans. A party which embraces such dissimilar groups can hardly have any other principle than the desire for success.

Another peculiarity of the situation was that neither of the five leading candidates for the presidency, all recognized republicans, stood distinctly for any one policy. It is true that Crawford, special heir of Virginia influence, was considered a champion of state rights, but there were so many republicans of avowed national tendency that he dared not speak loudly for his doctrines. In the same way was the freedom of the others limited, of Calhoun, who stood for internal improvements, of Clay, who advocated the tariff, and of Adams, who leaned to strong government generally. Jackson alone was not associated in the public mind with any particular policy — neither his length of service nor his political aptitude gave him the opportunity — but, his supporters, who favored him on personal grounds, were of such varied views that he dared not speak emphatically on any important subject. Personality was the principal basis of the canvass, and in such a canvass, it was natural that there should be much overpraising and much abuse.

The new parties were personal. They were a Jackson party and an anti-Jackson party. After a time, Jackson's bold measures, which he justified by principles, aroused protests from persons who believed in opposite principles. Thus personality was merged with theory, and parties again became groups of persons who desired the same measures.

The anti-Jackson men were composed chiefly of the supporters of Adams and Clay. While the first of the two was not popular in New England, he was trusted as a representative of Eastern interests, and Jackson, the frontiersman, was distrusted as a representative of ideas foreign to the older states. Clay's logical support was in the West, but he had just taken a dangerous liberty with it. No one could doubt that this section would prefer Jackson to Adams in a clear contest between the two men. Yet Clay defied the sentiment, in some respects in the face of positive expressions of it, and by entering the cabinet made plausible the charges that he acted for his own gain and that he cared not for the will of the people. These charges, it is true, counted for little with men who admired Adams and his secretary of state; but they were accepted by the great mass of people, very numerous in the West, who thought originally that Jackson would make a better President than Adams. How little he added to the combination with which he threw in his fortunes is shown by the fact that in the election of 1828 Adams received not one Western electoral vote.

The Jackson party, when fully developed, embraced its own followers and most of those of Calhoun, Crawford, and Clinton, the last not very numerous, but important in New York. Early in 1825, the Crawford forces had not joined it, although in certain matters — as in the opposition to Clay's nomination — some of them acted with it.

"The Jackson men being in the field," wrote Van Buren from Washington, on December 25th, "are of course looking out for the weak points in the enemies' lines and are ready for the assault where opportunity offers. We of the Crawford school lay upon our oars and will not lightly commit ourselves except in defense of old principles."[1] The shrewd New Yorker was only hesitating through a sense of dignity. He could have no objection to an alliance with a promising Jackson faction. A year earlier, August 26, 1824, he was proposing a union between Clay and Crawford, the former to be vice-president. This, he then said, would lay the foundation of a grand republican party with which he would be happy to coöperate permanently, and it would be easy to see that the condition of Crawford's health would give the vice-presidency under him a peculiar value.[2] The scheme failed and the grand republican party was left to be formed by other means. In the spring of 1826, Crawford was entirely eliminated from national politics and Van Buren was acting with the Jackson leaders in the plans which were laid against Adams. He admits he had then determined to cast his lot with a man from Tennessee.[3] He carried most of his faction with him, but it was a bitter pill for the Virginians, long the political arbiters of the country, to follow the leadership of the Western statesmen. From 1789, until the triumph of Jackson,

[1] Van Buren to Butler, December 25, 1825, Van Buren Mss.
[2] Van Buren to Benjamin Ruggles, August 26, 1824, Van Buren Mss.
[3] Van Buren, *Autobiography*, I., 90, Van Buren Mss.

with the exception of two years under Madison, there was always a Virginian in the cabinet: from that triumph until the administration of Tyler, there was not another in that body.

In 1825 the Jackson and Calhoun wings of the party were quite distinct. With the latter were most of the experienced politicians of the party. Calhoun, college bred, socially prominent, and long experienced in high office, was looked upon by many as the redeeming force in the crude group. He was supported by the capable Pennsylvania leaders in the party and the Jackson men themselves realized his strong position within the organization. But they did not relish the confidence with which some of his lieutenants viewed his prospects. It was through his efforts that General Duff Green was made editor of the party organ, *The Daily Telegraph*, published at Washington. Green was more careful of the interests of his patron than of the party, and as time passed his policy irritated the leaders of the other wing. In that group the Tennessee senators, White and Eaton, were most prominent. They were not able to cope with the men of the Calhoun wing, either through intellect or political capacity. It seemed to them unequal that the particular followers of Jackson, whose popularity was the basis of the party's hopes, should be overtopped by the Calhounites, who for their ambition were grafted on the organization. All this they felt, but in the presence of party perils they considered it wise to subordinate their feelings. Outwardly, therefore, all was serene, but when success should remove the pressure of a common danger, serious dissensions were likely to appear.

Crawford hated Calhoun cordially and charged him, for nationalistic views, with treason to republicanism. Van Buren inherited this dislike, and that was enough to induce him to side with the Tennessee faction in the new party. But his interests also drew him in the same direction. There had been an heir presumptive since 1800, Madison to Jefferson, Monroe to Madison, and Crawford to Monroe; it had become a normal phase of American politics, a position to be fought for; and the sagacious Van Buren saw an opportunity to win it through the support of Jackson and those members of his party who were most closely associated with him. Nor was his accession unwelcome to the Tennessee faction. They found him a valuable ally in resisting the threatened predominance of Calhoun, and his social position was a blessing to a party which was sensitive under the criticisms of the rather supercillious society of the capital. In these unannounced dissensions was the foundation of a bitter future conflict.

The position of Jackson in the coming campaign was a quiet one. Returning from Washington in March, he was received with ovations by his supporters in Pennsylvania and along the Ohio. He spoke freely about recent events and openly charged Clay with purchasing a cabinet position by making a President. In Nashville, he was given a great dinner at which many toasts were made in his praise. He then retired to the "Hermitage" and passed the days in dignified ease, as became one who believed in the theory, then generally esteemed, that a good patriot should never seek and never decline office. The managers in Washington charged themselves with the burden of consolidating the various interests which could be brought to his support. He was made to see that he could not aid them by remaining in the public view, and the faithful Lewis was placed at his side to act at once as a restraining force on his impulsive temper, and as a convenient intermediary between him and the Washington manipulators.

But Jackson was not a tool of his subordinates. They knew how strong was his will and were most cautious in trying to influence it. Ordinarily he was a cool and shrewd politician, and his course was not as much shaped by impulse as we are apt to think from the occasional outbursts, which the picturesque school of historians have often described. He was a man of the people, sharing their opinions of government, their suspicions and their credulity; and on most questions he knew how the people would feel. His absolute courage made him willing to appeal to the voters over the heads of the politicians on some of the most important matters of his time. He left much to his managers, but he usually understood their plans, and never interfered capriciously. In the most serious affairs, he took charge of the situation with the confidence of an autocrat, and in every case with success. Such a man could not be a mere figure-head, however much of the ordinary direction of affairs he may have surrendered to others.

When he was defeated in 1825, it was generally understood that Jackson would be a candidate in the next campaign. It was no surprise, therefore, when in the following October the Tennessee legislature again recommended him to the people as a candidate for the presidency. A few days later, he appeared before that body to resign his seat in the senate. Inclination, he said, prompted him to retire to private life and the recent action of the assembly seemed to make such a step proper. To this simple announcement he added a political appeal. He endorsed a constitutional amendment then being discussed before the public to limit the President to one term of four or six years, and he suggested another amendment by which a member of congress should not be appointed to an administrative office during the term for which he was elected and for three years thereafter. The language in which he supported the suggestion is strong and apparently sincere. In view of his later appointments, it is worth quoting:

The effect of such a constitutional provision is obvious. By it Congress, in a considerable degree, would be free from that connection with the executive department which, at present, gives strong ground of apprehension and jealousy on the part of the people. Members, instead of being liable to be withdrawn from legislating on the great interests of the nation, through prospects of the executive patronage, would be more liberally confided in by their constituents; while their vigilance would be less interrupted by party feelings and party excitements. Calculations, from intrigue or management, would fail; nor would their deliberations or their investigations of subjects consume so much time. The morals of the country would be improved, and virtue, uniting with the labors of the Representatives, and with the official ministers of the law, would tend to perpetuate the honor and glory of the government. But if this change in the constitution should not be obtained, and important appointments continue to devolve on the Representatives in Congress, it requires no depth of thought to be convinced, that corruption will become the order of the day, and that under the garb of conscientious sacrifices to establish precedents for the public good, evils of serious importance to freedom and prosperity of the republic may arise.[1]

Here was evidently an allusion to Adams's appointment of Clay to a cabinet position; but in Jackson's first cabinet five of the six members were taken from congress.

When congress met in December, it was known that Adams would be opposed at every possible point. The Jackson-Calhoun men were alert and not very scrupulous. They had their first opportunity in the President's annual message, which was, indeed, an unfortunate utterance. Jefferson advocated the smallest sphere of governmental activity compatible with the public welfare. Adams desired a generous policy of governmental supervision, the spirit of which was certainly non-Jeffersonian. Just at this time public men were disputing over the power of congress to construct roads, canals, light-houses, and harbors; but here was an academic argument for a general system of public improvements. "The great object," the message said, "of the institution of civil government is the improve-

[1] Niles, *Register*, XXIX, 157.

ment of the condition of those who are parties to the social compact." This could be partly obtained through roads and canals, "but moral, political, and intellectual improvement are duties assigned by the Author of our Existence to social, no less than to individual man." To be more specific, the government should maintain a national university, geographical and astronomical observatories, and explorations of coasts, rivers, and interior plains. In his enthusiasm he declared: "It is with no feeling of pride as an American that the remark may be made that on the comparatively small terrestrial surface of Europe, there are existing upward of one hundred and thirty of these light-houses of the skies, while throughout the whole American hemisphere there is not one." The closing sentence was most unwise: "While foreign nations, less blessed with that freedom which is power than ourselves, are advancing with gigantic strides in the career of public improvement, are we to slumber in indolence or fold up our arms and proclaim to the world that we are palsied by the will of our constituents? Would it not be to cast away the bounties of Providence and doom ourselves to perpetual inferiority?"[1]

This message must have emanated solely from the author's faculty of theorizing, since it is impossible to see how he could have justified it on any ground of policy then plausible. Those who favored internal improvements were committed to Calhoun, and in the Jackson combination, the Crawford faction, which still held out, was sure to take fright at doctrines so like the old federalist arguments of 1800, and the repudiation of strict accountability to constituents was entirely opposite to the trend of the times. All these points were quickly seized by the opposition, and the country rang with jeers and denunciation. The expression, "light-houses in the skies," was particularly unfortunate: it was too much like "castles in the air." As might

[1]Richardson, *Messages and Papers of the Presidents*, II., 311-317.

have been expected, Virginia, the home of old republicanism, was particularly offended. Ritchie, editor of the Richmond *Enquirer*, long the exponent of that school, opened fiercely on the administration, publishing its indignation in a series of articles by W. B. Giles, a bold defender of radical state rights theories.[1] In congress another Virginian, no less a personage than John Randolph of Roanoke, opened the vials of his wrath, denouncing the union of Adams and Clay in the well-known words, "the coalition of Blifil and Black George — the combination, unheard of till then, of the Puritan and Blackleg." Thus the Crawfordites were led to coöperate with the Jackson-Calhoun combination; and this threatened a general Southern and Western movement against the occupant of the President's mansion.

Along with this statement of Adams's loose construction view came notice of the proposed Panama Congress. This was a meeting of delegates from South and Central American states at the Isthmus, to which the United States in the preceding spring was invited to send delegates. Clay favored the scheme from the first; but the President, more cautious in diplomacy, deferred action until he was informed more definitely of the subjects to be considered. It was not until November that they were submitted by the South Americans. There was not entire unanimity in the propositions of the various states, but it was evident that the republics of the South desired to have a league with our government, by which the attempt of any European power to interfere in American affairs should be resisted. The league was to have a biennial congress, to be governed by a majority of its members in time of war, and have authority to apportion the contribution of each state in troops and money. Adams justly realized that we should suffer in such a partnership, and, while he appointed commissioners, he instructed them to assent to nothing, till it was submitted to our congress.

[1] Adams, *Memoirs*, VII., 104.

The cause of South America was ever popular in the United States. Clay's championship of it in Monroe's administration. was one of his most popular actions. The Monroe Doctrine, with which Adams was largely concerned, was received with satisfaction by the people. This last step in the same direction, for which it was thought Clay was chiefly responsible, created alarm among his opponents. They feared that it would be popular because it stood for liberty and because it was aimed at the Holy Alliance, which American opinion held in special horror. They also saw in it, says Van Buren, something that would draw attention from the bargain and corruption cry, and by uniting Clay and Adams in a popular undertaking serve to justify their association in the government.[1] They resolved to attack the mission as vigorously as possible. In doing so it served their purpose to describe the project, not as Adams had limited it in his instructions to the commissioners, but as it was designed by the South Americans, as a plan to found a permanent league. The construction was unfair, but it was not designed for a very discriminating audience. For some time the man- agers debated whether the mission should be opposed in the senate, on the confirmation of the commissioners whom Adams had nominated, or in the house on the necessary vote of money for expenses. It was finally decided to make the fight in the senate, since there the Jackson forces had their best speakers.[2] The discussion was prolonged as much as possible to enable public opinion to form itself; but in the end the senate sustained the President by a vote of twenty-four to nineteen. The fight was renewed in the house on the appropriation of money, but it was there lost by a majority of one hundred and thirty-four to sixty. The most important result for the young Jackson party was that it gave an opportunity to perfect its new organi-

[1]Van Buren, *Autobiography*, I. 93.
[2]*Ibid*, 94.

zation; and it was significant that in the senate Van Buren took prominent part against confirmation.

The opposition also brought slavery into the discussion, with eyes shrewdly cast toward the effect on the South. It was then feared that France or England might get possession of Cuba and Porto Rico, and the proposed congress would likely desire to fit out an expedition to make them free of Spain. This would involve the liberation of the slaves there, as in the other revolutionized Spanish colonies. The congress would also discuss the suppression of the slave-trade, and the recognition of the independence of Hayti, both measures distasteful to the South. Should the government lend its influence to a movement which had it in so great a menace for the South? It was ever easy to arouse Southern voters on this question, and Hayne's fiery rhetoric was sagaciously expended in a speech, a characteristic part of which was as follows:

With nothing connected with slavery can we consent to treat with other nations, and, least of all, ought we to touch the question of the independence of Hayti in conjunction with revolutionary governments, whose own history affords an example scarcely less fatal to our repose. These governments have proclaimed the principles of liberty and equality; and have marched to victory under the banner of universal emancipation. You find men of color at the head of their armies, in their legislative halls, and in their executive departments. . . . Our policy, with regard to Hayti, is plain. Other states will do as they please—but let us take the high ground that these questions belong to a class which the peace and safety of a large portion of our union forbids us even to discuss. Let our government direct all our ministers in South America and Mexico to protest against the independence of Hayti. But let us not go into council on the slave-trade and Hayti.[1]

On this phase of the opposition, South Carolina, Georgia, and Tennessee stood side by side with all the rest of the South.

---

[1] *Congressional Debates*, 1825-6, Vol.II., Part I, 166.

This debate drew Calhoun, presiding over the senate, into its vortex. When the abuse of the President began, he was asked to rule out of order such attacks on a high officer of the government. He declined to do so on the ground that the senate had no rule on the subject and that he, as servant of that house, had not the authority to make one. He was probably technically correct, but it was believed that partisanship and an unwillingness to offend the Jackson party by seeming to repudiate them, helped him to realize the nature of the technicality. The incident led to a heated correspondence in the newspapers. He was attacked by a writer signing himself "Patrick Henry," who was reported to be Adams himself, and defended by one calling himself "Onslow," who was Calhoun.[1] It was not agreeable to see the two highest officers of the government wrangling thus in the press; and it shows how far the vice-president had become actively enlisted in the attack on the administration.

The debate on the Panama Mission was drawn out until late in April, 1826; and although the delegates were despatched, it was too late for the congress, which adjourned after a short session without accomplishing anything. During the winter and spring the "Friends of Jackson," as the party called itself, made several minor moves against the President and his secretary of state. Amendments to the constitution were demanded prohibiting the appointment of congressmen to office, forbidding the reëlection of a President, and defining the powers of congress in regard to internal improvements so that state rights should not be imperiled. Resolutions were offered asking the President to report how many members of congress had been appointed to office by the Presidents since the adoption of the constitution. These attempts to involve Adams in the error of abusing the patronage seem absurd, coming from the party which was destined to go to the greatest extremes in the same direction. In

---

[1]Hunt, *Life of Calhoun*, 58. The "Onslow" numbers are in Calhoun, *Works*, VI., 322-348.

fact, Adams was trying, much to his political damage, to resist the current, which then ran strongly for political appointments. "Patronage," as then used, meant the expenditure of public money which brought benefits to a certain part of the voters. Benton uses the term to indicate all the national expenses except the public debt.[1] He speaks of "executive patronage," meaning political emoluments, as appointments and the public printing. He probably would have called appropriations for canals and roads some other kind of patronage. With the growth of the revenue came an enlargement of executive patronage, and in a system of appointments, which had no other test of merit than the judgment of the appointer, inefficient men came into office and political appointments were numerous. As long as there was no opposition party this made little difference, but with the organization of the Jackson group to embarrass Adams it was natural that the evils of the system should be saddled on him. Old republicans, country gentlemen, and many others believed that the tendency was dangerous; and the Jackson managers deemed it politically worth while to attack it. The appointment of Clay seemed in a striking manner to give opportunity to connect the administrations with the evil.

Macon was selected to bring the matter up in congress. At his suggestion a committee was appointed to bring in a report on the reform of executive patronage. May, 1826, Benton for the committee reported six bills and a long argument for reform. The bills dealt with the public printing, officers who handled the revenue, postmasters, cadets, and midshipmen, and provided that military and naval officers should not be dismissed from the service at the will of the President. The argument of the report was so sound that it has in later days been cited by civil service reformers as a landmark in the progress of their cause; but to

[1]Benton, *Thirty Years' View*, I., 81.

apply it to Adams was absurd. How skilfully they attacked him is shown in the following extract:

The King of England is the "fountain of honor": the President of the United States is the source of patronage. He presides over the entire system of Federal appointments, jobs, and contracts. He has "power" over the "support" of the individuals who administer the system. He makes and unmakes them. He chooses from the circles of his friends and supporters, and *may* dismiss them, and upon all the principles of human action, *will* dismiss them, as often as they disappoint his expectations. His spirit will animate their actions in all the elections to State and Federal offices. There may be exceptions, but the truth of a general rule is proved by the exception.[1]

The condition here described was a possibility, it was even a tendency of the day, but it is certain that Adams did all he could to resist it. The imputation that he did otherwise was a political *ruse de guerre*, unworthy of those who used it, but liable to be used by their opponents if opportunity offered. It also described exactly the condition the patronage was going to assume under Jackson triumphant.

A week later, Benton called up the bills and asked that Macon, who had long interested himself in the subject, be heard in their defense. But that gentleman announced that he was too ill at that time to assume the task and moved that the matter be laid on the table. It was not again taken up, which was probably as far as it was meant to carry it from the beginning. Ten days later congress adjourned, and the "Friends of Jackson" returned to their constituents. Another election was on hand, the issue of which justified all their hopes: both houses of congress passed into their control, and the result in 1828 seemed assured. They took courage and prepared for battle.

---

[1] *Congressional Debates*, 1825-6, Vol. II., Part I., 672, 707; Part II., Appendix, 133, 136.

These charges against the administration seem rasping enough from the turbulent Benton, but they are especially unpleasant from the experienced and cultivated Calhoun. "It must be determined in the next three years," he wrote to Jackson, "whether the real governing principle in our system is to be the power and patronage of the Executive, or the voice of the people. For it is scarcely to be doubted that a scheme has been formed to perpetuate power in the present hands, in spite of the free and unbiased sentiment of the country; and, to express it more correctly, those now in power act on a scheme resting on the supposition, that such is the force of the Executive influence, that they, who wield it, can mould the public voice at pleasure, by an artful management of patronage."[1] Could Calhoun have believed his words, or did his desire to flatter the impulsive Jackson run away with his discretion?

The question of patronage being thus presented to the public, the managers turned to the bargain between Adams and Clay, chiefly with the purpose of breaking down Clay. All Jackson's utterances in this affair indicate his sincere belief in the charge. He was convinced that Buchanan in approaching him came with authority from Clay. But his managers were not so ingenuous. In October, 1826, Duff Green knew from Buchanan himself that the charge could not be substantiated, and yet he used it with the greatest assurance. "I had no authority," said the man from Pennsylvania, "from Mr. Clay or his friends to propose any terms to General Jackson, in relation to their votes, nor did I make any such proposition. . . . I am clearly of opinion that whoever shall attempt to prove by direct evidence any corrupt bargain between Mr. C—— and Mr. A—— will fail."[2] For all this, Duff Green and his colleagues made the cry do their service.

---

[1] Calhoun to Jackson, June 4, 1826, Jackson Mss.
[2] Buchanan, *Writings* (Moore, Editor), I., 218.

In the spring of 1825, Jackson, in his correspondence and his private conversation, spoke freely his belief in Clay's complicity in the affair. He said he would have been elected had the will of the people not been thwarted by this "Judas of the West." There is no reason to believe he did not speak as freely during the following two years to persons with whom he was thrown, but no such conversation was reported in the press, possibly because nothing was to be gained by it. But in March, 1827, an unsigned letter appeared in the Fayetteville, N. C., *Observer*, reporting a conversation at the "Hermitage," in which Jackson repeated explicitly the story that Clay's friends proposed to his friends to make him, Jackson, President if they were assured that Adams should not continue secretary of state. The letter was widely reprinted and called forth a card in which Clay denied all knowledge of such a bargain and said he doubted if Jackson made the statement attributed to him. Then the anonymous correspondent, Carter Beverly, of Virginia, uncovered himself, and called on Jackson to verify what was printed in the *Observer*. Jackson complied with becoming reluctance. It was true, he said, that in the privacy of his own fireside, he declared his belief, but since the matter was repeated abroad he did not hesitate to avow his opinion. He then repeated the substance of the proposition which he alleged the friends of Clay made to him in the beginning of January, 1825, which was that if assurances were given that Adams should not remain secretary of state, Jackson would have the support of Clay's friends.

When Clay saw this letter in print, he felt he could afford to reply. He published a denial and called for the name of the man who made the proposition to Jackson. He was duly informed that the proposition came from James Buchanan, of Pennsylvania, whose participation in the affair has already been discussed. Buchanan now published a statement which supported

Jackson's up to the critical point, and failed there because it did not allege that an actual bargain was offered. But it was strong enough for the Jackson papers, who heralded it as complete vindication of their hero. The hero himself, as we have seen, inwardly chafed because it was not more emphatic.[1] But the public were satisfied. If there were certain things lacking in the proof, did not Clay's acceptance of the secretaryship more than make up for them? The argument was effective with the least thoughtful part of the voters.

While this matter proceeded successfully for Jackson, the tariff question came up again and brought serious danger to his cause. The champions of protection were active in the North. They had passed beyond the infant-industry argument and were proclaiming the advantages of a home market through the growth manufacturing towns. The appeals were attractive to the farmers of Pennsylvania and New York, and found response even in the trans-Alleghany region, where all classes were enthusiastic for the development of their splendid resources. But the South was equally unanimous against the tariff. Virginia, strong in the old republican school, opposed it on constitutional grounds; South Carolina, more practical and less wedded to old theories, rested her opposition on sectional interests, and by strenuous fighting was becoming the leader of a new school of Southern politics. It seemed impossible to reconcile the two views, and herein lay Jackson's peril: for he depended as much on South Carolina and the far South as on Pennsylvania, New York,[2] and the West. It would take careful management to steer his cause safely between the groups. How cleverly it was done we shall see.

In the first place, his own record favored his plans. He voted in congress for a tariff which would develop the military resources of the country. This moderate position need alarm

---

[1] See above, II., 361.
[2] W. L. Marcy to Van Buren, June 25, 1827; January 29, 1828; Van Buren Mss.

neither side. Such a man, said his friends in the North, could be relied on to see that the blessings of protection were not sacrificed to the Southern demands. Such a man, said his advocates in the South, could be relied on to oppose the selfish plans of that section which would build up their own interests at the expense of those of another. Adams and Clay stood openly for protection and were not embarrassed by defection in their camps.

In the second place, the Jackson congressmen and party workers generally were more anxious for the success of their presidential candidate than for the passage of a tariff. But they were afraid of their constituents North and South. The task, then, resolved itself into preparing a line of conduct which would satisfy the voters, and all the movers of the pawns were in secret accord as to the ethics of their conduct.

The plan followed is supposed to have been devised by Van Buren. Whether it was his or not, he gave his best efforts to carry it through. The speaker of the new house was Andrew Stevenson, of Virginia, an old republican who followed Van Buren into the Jackson camp. For some time committees had been non-partisan, which was not unnatural under Monroe's and Adams's policy of "amalgamation." But Stevenson signalized the advent of a new party system by giving their control to his own friends. He placed two Adams, and five Jackson men on the committee on manufactures, to which was allotted the task of bringing in the new tariff bill.

After much delay the committee introduced its bill. It happened then, as later, that states which wanted higher duties on most articles wanted lower rates on others. Thus, New England, demanding protection on her manufactures, asked for free raw materials. The bill now reported placed duties generally high on all articles, including the raw materials used in New England. The bill would please the Middle states and the West, but it would be unpopular in the South and New England. It was the purpose of the framers to resist all attempts to amend the bill, in the belief that on the final vote it would be defeated through the decisive action of New England members. The South was induced to vote down all the New England amendments in the belief that the bill would thus finally be defeated, and the measure came to its last vote in nearly the same shape as it came from the committee. But here the unexpected happened: the South, as was anticipated, voted against the bill it had vigorously refused to amend, but enough New Englanders voted for it, with all its faults, to make it a law. Nobody but the Jackson managers was pleased with the result; but the political effects were good. The Southern members could report to their constituents that they voted against it, although they had not the satisfaction to say they defeated it. The Northern Jackson members could report that they voted for it. It was a lucky deliverance for the party.[1]

The tariff of 1828 was only one incident in a campaign of excitement. Each party was bitter and personal in its abuse of the other. All the squabbles of Jackson's early life were brought up to show he was not fit to be President. The hanging of Arbuthnot and Ambrister, the unauthorized invasion of Florida, and the quarrel with Callava were cited to show his lack of respect for law. The execution of mutinous militiamen in the campaigns of 1813 and 1814 was recalled to show his ferocious temper; and when a Philadelphia editor published a hand-bill showing a coffin with the victims standing by its side, the idea was caught up eagerly and repeated in all parts of the country. Jesse Benton, the cause of the quarrel of 1813, also contributed his mite, a hand-bill in which his version of the dispute was given to show that Jackson was truculent and treacherous to an opponent. Van Buren thought that this abuse served to keep

[1]Taussig, *Tariff History of the United States*, 5th edition, 86-108. In 1837, Calhoun in a speech in congress, explained this bargain, in which he thought the Southerners had been deceived. See his *Works*, III., 47.

the candidate's name before the people, who otherwise might have forgotten his pretensions.

The worst and least justifiable of these personal charges was reviving the story of his marriage. The irregularity of this ceremony was brought up to his disadvantage in his early career in Tennessee politics, and it was not to be expected that it should be omitted in this campaign; but we are hardly prepared to find that it was a main argument in the leading opposition newspapers. It appeared in the *National Journal*, a paper published in Washington, apparently under close supervision of the President. Jackson thought, and correctly, it seems, that if Adams had used his influence the matter would have been kept out of its columns. He held, therefore, that his antagonist was constructively responsible for the attack and felt justified in withholding from him the ordinary social courtesies of gentlemen.

Some of Jackson's supporters were willing to reply to these charges in kind, and the story was started that Adams, while minister to Russia, was concerned in delivering a beautiful American girl to a life of shame in order to gratify the lust of an aristocrat. The tale as told was entirely untrue. Duff Green, editor of the *Telegraph*, went even further. "I saw the necessity," he wrote, referring to the attack on Mrs. Jackson, "of bringing home the matter to Mr. Adams's own family and by threats of retaliation drove the *Journal* to condemn itself. This you have no doubt seen and understood. The effect here was like electricity. The whole Adams corps was thrown into consternation. They did not doubt that I would execute my threat, and I was denounced in the most bitter terms for assailing female character by those very men, who had rolled the slanders on Mrs. Jackson under their tongues as the sweetest morsel that had been dressed up by Peter Force and Co., during the whole campaign.'"[1] To this shameless avowal Jackson re-

[1] Green to Jackson, July 8, 1827, Jackson Mss.

plied that it would be well now and then to throw into the enemy's camp a few firebrands in the shape of facts, "but that female character should never be introduced by my friends unless a continuation of attack should continue to be made against Mrs. Jackson, and that by way of *just retaliation* upon the *known* GUILTY. My great wish is that it may be altogether *evaded*, if possible, by my friends. *I never war against females*, and it is only the base and cowardly that do."[1]

It was fortunate for Jackson that while these charges were being made, he was at the "Hermitage" under the soothing influence of Major Lewis and Judge Overton. Inwardly he raged, as is shown by an allusion to Clay in one of his letters. "I have lately got an intimation of some of his secret movements, which, if I can reach with positive and responsible proof, I will wield to his political and, perhaps, to his actual destruction. He is certainly the basest, meanest, scoundrel that ever disgraced the image of his god — nothing too mean or low for him to condescend to, *secretely* to carry his cowardly and base purposes of slander into effect: even the aged and virtuous female is not free from his secrete combinations of base slander — *but enough, you know* me, I will curb my feelings until *it becomes proper* to act, when retributive *justice* will visit him and *his panders heads*."[2]

In another case he was not so well controlled. In 1826, Southard, secretary of war, in a private conversation at Fredericksburg, Va., criticized the defense of New Orleans and praised Monroe's activity as secretary of war at the time, attributing to him much of the merit of saving the city. An exaggerated account was carried to Jackson, who wrote a severe letter to Southard and sent it unsealed by Samuel Houston. This messenger showed the communication to some of the party managers in Washington, who agreed that it ought not to be

[1]Jackson to Green, August 13, 1827, Jackson Mss.
[2]Jackson to Houston, December 15, 1826, Jackson Mss.

delivered. It was, in fact, withheld and an appeal was made to the writer, with the result that some weeks later Southard received a written demand for an explanation. It contained no other denunciation than a cool statement that Jackson considered the criticism of his campaign as a blow from the administration. Southard in reply denied that he intended to reflect on the military conduct of his correspondent, and here the matter rested so far as the campaign was concerned;[1] but it was destined to play an important part in another interesting phase of our story.[2]

This incident illustrates Jackson's relation to his party managers. They were alarmed because they realized that his fiery temper was liable to burst forth at any time, and they took steps to restrain it. Several of them wrote him in the most cautious manner, urging such arguments as they believed must convince him that he ought to keep quiet. Eaton spoke earnestly: "Many friends," he wrote, "begged him to urge Jackson not to notice things Clay was saying." My reply to these anxious friends was, "*Fear not*, General Jackson will not so far insult his friends as to take his own cause into his own hands and from his friends.' . . . They only ask of you under any and all circumstances, to be still and let them manage whatever is to be done.'"[3] Caleb Atwater also wrote, from Ohio: "For Heaven's sake, for your country's sake, do remember that but one man can write you down — his name is Andrew Jackson."[4]

At first Jackson was not docile under these attempts at control. To Polk, who begged him to make no reply to an expected request for his views on internal improvements, he wrote with some spirit: "I have no disguise with my friends, but am not

---

[1]Adams, *Memoirs*, VII., 218, 220, 221, 222, 223, 225; also Jackson to Houston, November 22, 1826, Jackson Mss. Jackson published in a pamphlet his two letters to Southard and the latter's reply.
[2]See below, II., 500.
[3]Eaton to Jackson, January 21, 1828, Jackson Mss.
[4]Atwater to Jackson, September 4, 1828, *Ibid*.

in the habit of gratifying enemies. I have nothing in my political creed to keep secrete, it was formed in the old Republican school, and is without change. I have no secretes, nor have I, nor do I wish to conceal my opinions on the powers of the general government, and those reserved to the states respectfully [*sic.*] as it respects internal improvements, I never have withheld them when I spoke upon this subject, and I am sure I never will, and I am sure the general government has no right to make internal improvements within a state, without its consent first had and obtained."[1]

So spoke the leader in December, 1826: a year later he was in a more cautious frame of mind and when he was appealed to for his opinion on the tariff, referred the inquirers to his votes in congress and his letter to Dr. Coleman.[2]

In this connection the following letter has much interest. It is written to Major Lewis from Washington, is signed "B——," and seems to come from Benton.

The present administration is the most effective enemy of internal improvements that has ever appeared among us. They are ruining the cause by prostituting it to electioneering, and will be attacked upon that ground. I think it probable that Jackson will be catechized upon this subject, either by some overzealous friend or insidious enemy. I have talked with V. B. and others about it. They think as I do, that things are well enough now and ought not to be disturbed. If, therefore, a friend should put interrogatories, we think he ought to be made to comprehend that there is no necessity for any public answer. If an enemy should do so, and at the same time be so respectable as to make an answer indispensable, we think that it ought to be given rather by a *general* reference to the votes given by J—— in the Senate than by a *particular* confession of faith. The right of the people to know the political sentiments of a public man, might be admitted; the declining of declaring these sentiments,

---

[1] Jackson to Polk, December 27, 1826, Polk Calendar.
[2] Jackson to Polk, March 23, 1828, Polk Calendar.

on the eve of an election, might be stated; and then the necessity of a declaration in this case might be obviated by a general statement that his votes in the Senate would show his opinions. These votes will be satisfactory to most of the advocates of the doctrine, and at the same time, they do not go the whole length, as is well known in Virginia and elsewhere. If nothing but newspaper calls should be made, I think they should be left to newspaper answers. Adams's votes in the Senate upon this subject will be fully exposed. He voted against every measure of the kind ever proposed in that body while he was a member. These, with his old federal votes against the West and Louisiana will appear in bolder relief than they have ever yet been seen in. We are all divided here according to our politics, just as they were in '98. Our friends mean to fight it out; if they are conquered they want no quarter, and if they are victorious, they will owe no favors.[1]

A long letter to Jackson from Robert Y. Hayne has much of the same tenor, and throws some light on the character of the writer.

"We know Mr. Clay well enough to understand," he says, "the course that will be pursued in matters where his will is law. Altogether unprincipled, ambitious, daring, bold, and without the smallest regard either to the courtesies or decencies of life, he inspires his political followers with a spirit not unlike that which distinguishes a savage warfare, sparing no age, sex, or condition. There is still another motive that lurks beneath the unmanly and ungenerous course of the administration, it is the desire to betray you into some indiscretion. They have taken pains to impress the public mind with the belief that your *temper* unfits you for civil government. They know that a noble nature is always liable to excitement, and they have put, and will continue to put, into operation, a hundred schemes to betray you into some act or expression, which may be turned

---

[1] "B" [Benton], to Jackson, February 22, 1827, Jackson Mss.

to their own advantage." Adams, he added, refused to answer political questions because he was President; and was not Jackson the saviour of his country and the representative of the people, equal to Adams in dignity?

Then Hayne came to affairs near his own heart, the tariff and Calhoun's position in the party. It is true, he said, that the Southern people "deny the power of Congress to legislate on these points,[1] yet we feel that our interests are safe in your hands." As for the party itself, its greatest danger was from dissensions between its parts, which before uniting with it had their own mutual differences.[2] It was a mild hint at the rivalry of Calhoun and Van Buren, then well established.

Thus labored the little group in Washington, Van Buren, hand in hand with the Tennesseeans, and Calhoun's friends co-operating, all nervously anxious about their relations with the chieftain whose name was their best card. John Quincy Adams called them the "privy council," and they foreshadowed the "Kitchen Cabinet" not yet in existence. In Nashville a similar group was preparing pamphlets and newspaper articles in the common cause, its most appreciated work being a long defense of the marriage of the leader. In it were Judge Overton, a companion of Jackson's earliest days in the West and a true friend through life, and Major Lewis, whose personal influence with the candidate was strong for many years. Twenty-five years later, Parton, then writing his *Life of Jackson,* came strongly under the influence of Major Lewis, who made him believe that much of the political history of the period came out of the latter's activity. Later historians have been apt to speak of him as an astute and far-sighted party manager. From the many traces we have of him in the Jackson correspondence, the impression seems to be erroneous. Lewis had much to do

---

[1] Hayne was referring to the tariff and internal improvements.
[2] Hayne to Jackson, June 5, 1827, Jackson Mss.

with appointments to office and with Jackson's conduct toward men, but others seem to have devised party moves. His letters show us a garrulous man, with no noticeable power of initiative, but industriously active in flattering his leader and ministering to his prejudices. It is probable that Jackson's advice to Polk in 1844, indicates Lewis's true ability: "Keep Blair's *Globe* the administration paper," he writes, "and William B. Lewis to ferret out and make known to you all the plots and intrigues hatching against your administration and you are safe."

Van Buren says that it was predicted in 1825, that Jackson's popularity would pass before 1828. The energy of his managers, and abuse from his opponents, gave the lie to the prophecy. By the end of 1827, Adams seemed sure of nothing but New England: to his enemy were conceded Pennsylvania, Virginia, the Carolinas, Georgia, Alabama, and Mississippi, with good prospects in the Northwest. The debatable states were New York, Missouri, Kentucky, and Louisiana. In all these states the greatest activity existed on each side.

The situation in New York was exceedingly important. Here the republicans were in two factions, Van Buren's, which supported Crawford in 1824, and De Witt Clinton's, which first supported him for the presidency in that campaign and later toyed with both Jackson and Adams. Clinton had long desired the presidency, but his lukewarmness toward the War of 1812, won him the opposition of the Virginians, who gave Tompkins the vice-presidency in 1816 and thus satisfied New York while they ignored Clinton.

After the election of 1825 Clinton coquetted with both parties. Adams refused to encourage him because it was unwise "to make one scale preponderate by weights taken from another."[1] He feared to offend Van Buren, of whose coöperation he had some hopes; but he only angered Clinton, and soon both republi-

---

[1] Adams, *Memoirs*, VII., 185, 202. See also, Alexander, *Political History of New York*, I., 335-7.

can factions were supporting Jackson. Clinton desired the vice-presidency, and Van Buren seconded the pretension as a means of uniting the New York republicans and of embarrassing Calhoun. The Tennesseeans were also favorable to Clinton. It shows how much the organic nature of the party was developed that Jackson remained apparently neutral to the matter. But Calhoun was deeply concerned,[1] and a lively dissension was imminent in the party when in February, 1828, Clinton died. Van Buren realized the importance of this event and moved quickly to capture the dead man's followers. With all solemnity the New York delegation arranged a memorial meeting for the deceased at which Van Buren presided and made a speech in honor of the man whom he had long opposed. Much other labor was expended on the subordinates in the faction, with the result that they came under the command of their old rival, but not in a very docile frame of mind. They retained much of their old feeling and made trouble in the distribution of federal offices, but they voted with the party and made Van Buren the topmost figure in New York politics.[2]

In the West the Clay support fought with great spirit and in Louisiana they were particularly vigorous. If we may believe Edward Livingston and other correspondents, federal office-holders in New Orleans were most partisan and worked continually for the administration. The same, it may be said, was alleged of the officials in parts of Ohio, while Adams complained that in the New York election of 1827, the federal officers in the state were against the administration.[3] To overcome the opposition in Louisiana, and to make a good impression everywhere, it was planned to have on January 8, 1828, a great celebration of the battle of New Orleans. Jackson, who had

---

[1] D. Green to Jackson, October 22; Branch to *Ibid*, December 11, 1827; Jackson Mss.

[2] Adams, *Memoirs*, VII., 370. P. N. Nicholas to Van Buren, October 13; Marcy to *Ibid*, December 10 J. A. Hamilton to *Ibid*, December 21, 1826; Van Ness to *Ibid*, February 22, 1827; Van Buren Mss.

[3] I. L. Baker to Jackson, September 1, 1827; E. Livingston to Jackson, August 12; *Ibid* to Jackson, November 15, 1828, Jackson Mss; Adams, *Memoirs*, VII., 349.

refused to visit a Kentucky watering-place for fear it might be pronounced electioneering, gave himself to the scheme and arrangements were made to make the occasion as conspicuous as possible. Politicians from as far as New York came to join the company of friends who escorted the leader. The occasion was made a fruitful scene of intrigue for the favor of the hero until some of his old and non-political friends became disgusted and were only induced to remain with the party by the argument that a withdrawal would be interpreted unfavorably by his enemies.[1] Jackson newspapers heralded the events of the journey far and near. A committee of citizens of New Orleans met him at Natchez, and the party arrived at the battle field on the anniversary of the victory. Four days were spent in festivities during which the city of New Orleans gave itself up to extravagant demonstrations of joy. Never was a historical celebration made to contribute to political ends with better success.

Jackson's utterances on this occasion were praised by his friends as illustrations of his eloquence and good sense. The public did not realize how well he was coached beforehand. Andrew P. Hayne, brother of the South Carolina senator and old companion in arms, took care that they should say just the right things. There were to be three speeches, he said to Jackson beforehand, but he hoped only one would be published; and there were two ideas he wanted to see in them: (1) that Jackson, like Cincinnatus, left his home at his country's call, performed the task required of him, and returned to his home again; (2) a mild but manly reference to the wicked attacks on Mrs. Jackson. Beside this he hoped that the speech would be entirely military and that the speaker, like Washington, would read it.[2] That Jackson carefully filed this communication among the papers

[1] Dunlap to Jackson, August 10, 1831, Copy in Library of Congress. See also *American Historical Magazine* (Nashville), IX., 93.

[2] Hayne to Jackson, December 27, 1827, Jackson Mss.

he kept for the future historian shows that he valued highly the advice in it. John Quincy Adams tells us the speech delivered was written by Major Henry Lee, a ready hack writer of the time, then intimately associated with the general.[1]

Already it was evident that the popular enthusiasm for Jackson was overwhelming. The frigid honesty of the existing President could not withstand its power, and he early foresaw the end. He was a bad loser, as his father was before him, and expressed his contempt for his detractors in language which might rather be expected from them. He confided to his diary that Ingham, Randolph, Hamilton, and some others were "skunks of party slander who had been squirting round the House of Representatives thence to issue and perfume the atmosphere of the Union."[2] For Calhoun he expressed an equally vigorous, if less picturesque, opinion. "Calhoun," he wrote, "is a man of considerable talent and burning ambition; stimulated to frenzy by success, flattery, and premature advancement; governed by no steady principle, but sagacious to seize upon every prevailing popular breeze to swell his own sails; showering favors with lavish hands to make partisans, without discernment in the choice of his instruments, and the dupe and tool of every knave cunning enough to drop the oil of fools in his ear."[3]

For Clay, also, the situation had little comfort, and he talked gloomily with his chief. When the latter remarked that after the people had four years of Jackson, they would be disgusted and turn to the Kentuckian, Clay said that the reaction would, indeed, come, but not till he was too old to profit by it. He was deeply dejected and offered to retire from the cabinet, but Adams, knowing this would be taken as a sign of defeat, urged him to take a rest instead.[4] Thus, with discouragement for the ad-

[1] Adams, *Memoirs*, VII., 477.
[2] *Ibid*, VII., 431.
[3] *Ibid*, VII., 447.
[4] *Ibid*, VII., 382, 518, 520, 521.

ministration and with uproarious enthusiasm for its opponents the country came to the election day.

There could be no doubt of the result. The autumn was hardly at hand before congratulations began to arrive at the "Hermitage." They came from old friends and new ones, from those who offered sincere admiration and those who expected favors. Among the well-wishers was Gen. Thomas Cadwalader, of Philadelphia, social leader in the city and valuable salaried lobbyist for the United States Bank, who paid compliments to the fine climate, soil, and people of Nashville, invited Jackson to visit him in Philadelphia, and added: "Mrs. Cadwalader desires me to say that no endeavor will be spared to supply to Mrs. Jackson the places of those warm friends whom she will leave behind her."[1] The Cadwaladers were as prominent in Philadelphia as the Livingstons were in New York and New Orleans. Did the doughty General Thomas dream of an influence over the incoming President like that which Edward Livingston established over him at New Orleans? If so, he was to be rudely disappointed. Jackson could see the difference between the efficient organizer of the resources of defense and the pompous agent of the bank, as our story will unfold later. Nor was Hayne, the nullifier, less courteous. He wrote that Mrs. Hayne would like to make any necessary arrangement for Mrs. Jackson's comfort before the arrival in Washington.[2]

The election results justified the expectations of both friends and flatterers. Every electoral vote south of the Potomac and west of the Alleghanies went for Jackson, together with those of Pennsylvania. All of New England except one vote in Maine, and all of Delaware and New Jersey were for Adams. New York gave twenty and Maryland five for Jackson and they gave respectively sixteen and six for Adams. In all, Jackson

---

[1]Cadwalader to Jackson, June 21 and October 15, 1828, Jackson Mss
[2]Hayne to Jackson, December 18, 1828, Jackson Mss.

had one hundred and seventy-eight electoral votes and Adams had eighty-three. Calhoun had all the Jackson votes except seven of Georgia's nine, which Crawford's hatred took from him for the benefit of William Smith, of South Carolina.

The country now rang with shouts for the victor, and all eyes turned toward Nashville. There were political servitors who sought their reward, "old republicans" who rejoiced that the nationalizing tendencies of Adams were checked, believers in democracy, who thought that the reviving aristocracy was crushed, and low tariff men who considered the defeat of Clay a public blessing. All turned expectantly to the one who had saved them. Bustle invaded the quiet of the "Hermitage," and rejoicings mingled with preparations for a new phase of life for its occupants. In Nashville men of both parties united to give their first citizen a public dinner, which should be worthy of his success. Suddenly all these expressions of joy withered before the brief illness and death of Mrs. Jackson.

Spite of its irregularity Jackson's marriage was a very happy one. His wife had little education, but she was naturally intelligent; and she had that intense feeling for goodness and innate beauty which sanctifies love. She had the esteem of most of the people who knew her, and some of her friends loved her deeply. She was fond of young people and assumed a motherly attitude toward them which they appreciated highly. To a large circle of such admirers she was known as "Aunt Rachael." Her affection was deep enough to win her husband's strong nature and make him her lover as long as he lived. Her devotion to religion broke down his indifference on that subject — he was, it seems, never antagonistic to it — and he became in the latter part of his life a loyal, if not a devout, Presbyterian.

His care of his wife was constant, and he never forgave those who injured her. Much as he was enraged by the attacks on her in the campaign of 1828, he kept from her all knowledge that her name was used until she accidentally discovered the fact after the election. An account of her death which has survived among those who were most intimately associated with him presents the following story: About a month after the election, she drove into Nashville to purchase clothes for use in her new station. She was quite happy in the occasion and went from shop to shop with interest till her strength was gone. Then she retired to the private office of a newspaper editor, one of her relatives, to rest until her carriage was ready for the return. Here she came upon a copy of the pamphlet issued by her husband's friends in her defense. It came as a surprise and she was overwhelmed. When her companions came an hour later, they found her crouching in a corner, weeping and hysterical. On her way home she made every effort to resume her composure, so as to avoid giving pain to her husband, but she was not successful. The forced gaiety which she assumed attracted his attention at once and he had the story of the day's happening. From that time, says the narrative, she grew worse, at last taking to her bed and dying on December 23d.[1] For some years her health had been poor, and the final collapse was attributed to heart disease, but Jackson believed that her grief was a cause. The blow left him dazed, and he sat by the body for a whole night in the belief that life was not entirely extinct. He buried her in the garden at the "Hermitage," near the little Presbyterian church which, chiefly from his own funds, he built in 1823 for her gratification.[2] One of the last acts before his departure for Washington was to order a suitable monument for the grave.

Mrs. Jackson's memory was after this the gentlest spot in his life. When accusations were brought against the good name

---

[1] The author had this account from Mrs. Elizabeth Blair Lee, daughter of F. P. Blair, Sr., who remembered it from her youth, when she had it from Major Lewis. She considered it probable; but Parton, who had a marked faculty for using a good story, and who used Lewis freely, says nothing of it.

[2] A receipt among his papers, 1823, shows that he gave $150 to its erection and furnished materials; but for the latter he rendered a bill.

of Mrs. Eaton, it was sufficient for him that she had been received by his departed wife. His wife's natural goodness and strength of character won the respect of many of his friends. She was in Washington with him during the winter of 1824-5, and one of the acquaintances she made was Lafayette, who stopped at the same hotel with her. When she was dead he expressed his sympathy to Jackson in a letter in which he said: "You know how very kind and affectionate your excellent lady has been to me; the opportunities I had to appreciate her worth had more particularly attached me to her. I was daily anticipating the general approbation she could not have failed to obtain in her situation."[3]

Many years afterward, the "Hermitage" became the object of pilgrimage for patriotic and curious travelers, and an old servant of its former owner was employed to show it to such visitors. He had a reverent respect for Jackson and would show, with great pride, the objects associated with the general's political and military life. In Jackson's bedroom was a picture of Mrs. Jackson, which the old Negro would describe as follows: "This is de picture of Miss Rachael. Every morning de general would kneel before it and tell his God that he thank him to spare his life one more night to look on de face of his love."

But however crushing the personal affliction, political affairs did not wait. The funeral was hardly over before the preparations for Washington demanded his attention. He hurriedly gathered up his thoughts and turned his face toward a new field of duty.

---

[3]Lafayette to Jackson, February 26, 1829, Jackson Mss.

CHAPTER XX

CABINET-MAKING AND THE INAUGURATION

IT WAS the middle of January, 1829, when Jackson set out for Washington amid the plaudits of his countrymen. Reform of abuses was the cry of the campaign just ended, and he was gratefully hailed as the giver of better things. One admirer thanked God that he had seen the overthrow of John I and John II, and he hoped he would not live to see another of that race and the same country on the throne.[1] John Brown, of Virginia, who described himself as "an old revolutionist and one of your warmest friends, and an individual of the near two hundred thousand freemen, which I hope have taught congress a lesson not soon to be forgotten," also gave his opinion of the situation. He was especially anxious that the "court etiquette and pompous perade" in Washington be reformed. Such display was not in keeping with republicanism. It is true it was practised by "General La Fiatte," but he could be forgiven because he had the "voletile fancy of a Frenchman." The writer did not think such flattery could please any really wise man, and he hoped Jackson would discourage it. It was the simple letter of a countryman, a man who held the views of the people around him, but Jackson did not disdain the advice; and he filed the letter after endorsing it thus, "a friendly letter — worth reading — private."[2] Jackson was an average man; and his power to appreciate the views of average men was one of his best traits.

---

[1] D. C. Ker to Jackson, November 11, 1828, Jackson Mss.
[2] John Brown to Jackson, March 10, 1829, Jackson Mss.

The President-elect proceeded on his journey by easy stages. From Nashville he reached the Ohio at Louisville, thence up the river to Pittsburg, and at last over the mountains to the capital. Duff Green, desiring that he should appear under the prestige of the Calhoun faction, planned a great cavalcade to meet him at Pittsburg and escort him by relays to the end of the journey. But Van Buren opposed the scheme on the ground that it would be unacceptable to Jackson, and it was abandoned.[1] The people along the route made up by their enthusiasm all the éclat that was lost in the absence of an escort. At last the party came to Washington on February 11th, the day the electoral votes were counted in the senate.[2]

The city was full of anxious faces. So much had been said about electioneering by office-holders that it was generally believed that wholesale removals would be made. Later, when dismissals for cause did not yield enough vacancies to satisfy the many applicants they insisted that removals without cause should be made, and the demand was frequently granted.

Office-seekers and others flocked to Jackson's hotel, urging their claims on him and on whatever friend they thought had influence with him. For Adams, whose gifts were all exhausted, they had no thought. Even Jackson ignored him. On the ground that Adams was responsible for the continuance of the attacks on Mrs. Jackson, he refused to make the usual call of the incoming upon the outgoing President. A few confidential friends consoled the correct and unbending New Englander; he remained in the White House until the day before the inauguration, when he removed to a place on Meridian Hill, near the western boundary of the city, and left his rival to take informal possession of the official residence.

When Jackson arrived, February 11th, cabinet-making was already the chief object of interest. A small group of confidants

[1] J. A. Hamilton to Jackson, November 24, 1828, Jackson Mss.
[2] Niles, *Register*, XXXV, 401, 409.

gathered to advise with him, and the remainder of the political world looked on as rumors came from the centre regarding the fate of one or another aspirant for office. Senators White and Eaton and Major Lewis were continually with him. Van Buren was absent, detained in Albany by his duties as governor; but he was represented at Washington by J. A. Hamilton, who wrote frequently about the progress of events.

The onlooking politicians were divided, according to their interests, into several groups. Most noticeable were the supporters of Van Buren. They had a certain theoretical alliance with the constitutional views of the Crawford party, but their chief concern at this time was the future of their leader and the distribution of state offices. For some time it was known that the New Yorker would have choice of the cabinet positions. He was, next to Calhoun, the ablest man in his party, and his party services were preëminent. In 1828, he resigned his seat in the senate and ran for governor of his state, because it would unite the party for the benefit of Jackson. The appointment was, therefore, eminently proper from a party standpoint, and it was filled with credit, as later events showed. Some of his friends desired him to become secretary of the treasury because of the large number of offices to be disposed of in that department,[1] but the secretaryship of state was offered, and accepted, because its incumbent, by the prevailing opinion, was heir-apparent. Jackson offered the state department on February 15th, after consultation with Hamilton; and it was accepted on the 20th, with the stipulation that it should not be necessary for the duties to be taken up until the legislature of New York should adjourn, probably at the end of March.[2]

To fill the office temporarily, became the object of one of the

---

[1]Silas Wright, Jr., to Van Buren, December 9, Verplanck to *Ibid*, December 6; Thomas Ritchie to *Ibid*, March 11, 1828; Van Buren Mss.

[2]Jackson to Van Buren, February 15; Van Buren to Jackson, February 20; J. A. Hamilton to Van Buren, Febuary 12, 1829; Van Buren Mss.

minor moves on the board. Hamilton desired the position and Van Buren approved of his ambition; but an obstacle appeared in Henry Lee, a scheming hack writer, who had attached himself to the Nashville group and who by flattery of Lewis and by a plan to write a life of Jackson had worked himself into favor. The gravest charges were alleged against his private life, but this seems not to have been known to Jackson. Lee now desired to be chief clerk in the state department, an office held long and efficiently by Daniel Brent; and if Lee were chief clerk it ought to devolve on him to preside over the department during the absence of the secretary. Hamilton, therefore, set his face to defeat the hope of Lee, who was strongly fortified because he had a letter of endorsement from Lewis. He attacked his opponent on the ground of moral character. White, to whom he took his complaint, was shocked at the state of the case, declared that Lee must be shaken off and said that he would be considered an offense, if the truth were known, to the honor of the general. He also condemned "in unmeasured terms" Lewis, whose error of judgment is very evident. The upshot was that Van Buren interfered and wrote to Jackson asking that Hamilton might be secretary *pro tempore*, and the request was granted.[1] Lee was shunted off into a small foreign consulship, for which the senate rejected him. He was deeply disappointed and turned against the administration.

Calhoun's influence hung over all cabinet appointments, although it is impossible to connect him directly with any one selection. Van Buren's friends feared him greatly, but they dared not oppose him openly. They were disposed to credit him with more ability in intrigue than he possessed, and some of them even thought that bringing Van Buren into the cabinet was a scheme by which the latter could be discredited before the country. When it was seen how weak was the cabinet,

---

[1] J. A. Hamilton to Van Buren, January 1, February 12, 18 and 25, 1829; Van Buren Mss.

Van Buren himself had doubts, as we shall see, about the wisdom of his acceptance.[1]

Pennsylvania offered two candidates for position, S. D. Ingham and Henry Baldwin. Jackson favored the latter on personal grounds, but the Calhoun interest in the state centered so strongly on the former that he yielded, and it was decided that Ingham should have an offer of a cabinet position. Calhoun's strong supporters pressed him for secretary of the treasury, finding, it seems, some fitness in giving the second place in the cabinet to a Calhoun man, if Van Buren was to have the first.[2]

In this affair Calhoun himself was in a rather delicate situation because his own state was opposed to Ingham, and supported for second choice a man who had the backing of Van Buren himself. They were committed to nullification in its first stages and did not want to see the treasury controlled by a man with the tariff views of the Pennsylvanian school. They urged Langdon Cheves, of their own state, and if he could not be appointed, Lewis McLane, of Delaware. Cheves was soon seen to be out of the question, and they clung to McLane the more fiercely; but he had no chance, although Van Buren himself wrote a letter in his behalf to Eaton. Another aspirant was Albert Gallatin, whom Van Buren, through Hamilton, suggested for treasurer. The approach was made through Lewis, who rejected it at once saying: "The old man, if he comes here, *will have the whole credit of the administration. There is no use in having him. He wanted to be Secretary of the Treasury.*"[3]

Another object of concern was John McLean, of Ohio. He was in Calhoun's interest and was looked upon with disfavor by the Van Buren men.[4] He was postmaster-general under Adams and

[1]E. K. Kane to Van Buren, February 19, 1829, Van Buren Mss.

[2]L. McLane to Van Buren, February 19; J. Hamilton, Jr., to Van Buren, February 19, 1829; Van Buren Mss.

[3]J. A. Hamilton to Van Buren, March 6, 1829, Van Buren Mss.

[4]*Ibid* to *Ibid*, February 13, 1829, Van Buren Mss.

used his office against the election of his superior. He could not be ignored, because of his recognized ability, and he caused some embarrassment by aspiring to a higher rank than he then held. Moreover, he was popular in the West and with the Methodists in the country at large. It was good policy to keep him in the cabinet, and after much hesitation he consented to remain where he was, his office being raised to full cabinet rank, which before this it did not have.

In the meantime, the Virginians stood pathetically aside. It was the first cabinet-making in our history in which they had no share. Mr. Speaker Stevenson, Editor Ritchie, and others waited in vain to be called into council. Van Buren, old Crawford leader and friend of the new régime, received their confidences, as we may see in his correspondence, but did nothing.

Jackson was not favorable to Virginia, but Calhoun urged that some attention be shown and L. W. Tazewell was offered the war department. He refused it, probably because he wanted nothing less than first place. He was then assigned to the British mission and accepted it; but March 11th, when popular opinion ran strongly against the new administration, he declined it on the ground of business interests.[1] When Tazewell was passed over for cabinet rank, Virginians turned to P. P. Barbour, whom they desired to make attorney-general.

The war department was given to Senator Eaton. Jackson said he thought he ought to be allowed to have a personal friend in the cabinet, on whose confidential advice he might lean,[2] and no one objected. The choice was between Senators White and Eaton. The following extract from a letter from Eaton to his colleague seems to indicate that it was left to the two men to decide which should be chosen.

---

[1] Hamilton, J. A., *Reminiscences*, 91.
[2] L. McLane to Van Buren, February 19, 1829, Van Buren Mss.

A letter, received some time ago, from General Jackson, stated he desired *you* or *me* to be near him. In a recent conversation with him, he remarked that he had had a full and free conversation with you; and at the close remarked that he desired to have me with him. I presumed, without inquiring, that he had probably talked with you on the subject, and that you had declined accepting any situation, as you before had told me would be your feelings. Nothing definite has taken place on this matter between General Jackson and myself, and I hope you know me well enough, and my regard and friendship for you, to know this, that I should never permit myself to stand in competition with any desire you may entertain. If you have any desire, say so to me *in confidence*, and it shall so be received. If you have none, then in reference to any and all considerations I should consent to any such appointment. Think of this and give me your opinion frankly.[1]

White was a man of honor and has preserved the respect of the historian. He could do nothing but decline to stand in the way of his friend, which is undoubtedly what Eaton expected of him.

The navy department went to John Branch, senator from North Carolina and former governor. He was noted for nothing but his good dinners and correct manners; and the impression got abroad that he was brought forward because it was felt that something must be done to promote the social prestige of the new party. Eaton stood strongly for Branch,[2] however, and it is reasonable to assume that he did so because he wanted to withstand Virginia's claims, which were pressed in favor of Tazewell and probably because he felt that the weak-willed Branch would at least be manageable. The appointment displeased many people, and McLane probably voiced a general opinion when he wrote: "By what interest that miserable old woman, Branch, was ever dreamed of no one can tell."[3]

---

[1] Eaton to White, February 23, 1829, *Memoirs of H. L. White*, 266.
[2] C. P. Van Ness to Van Buren, March 9, 1832, Van Buren Mss.
[3] McLane to Van Buren, February 19, 1829, Van Buren Mss.

The attorney-generalship only remained unprovided for. The Virginian leaders were especially anxious about this office; and Ritchie, sending suggestions on the subject, made it plain that there ought to be "a strong constitutional Attorney-General."[1] P. P. Barbour proved to be the Virginia candidate; and he and Berrien, of Georgia, finally were the two leading candidates. The Tennessee managers were for the latter, and he was selected, Eaton's influence being the determining factor.[2]

Ten days after the arrival of Jackson all these arrangements were made. Intimations of what was going on reached the outer group of politicians from time to time. They did not know what was happening, but realized that they were ignored. The South Carolina school with Hayne and James Hamilton, Jr., at their head, and the Virginians, led by Stevenson, Archer, and Tazewell, were much chagrined. One morning the *Telegraph* announced that the President-elect would be glad to see persons who desired to offer advice about the cabinet; but not one of them budged toward Jackson's lodgings, by this time popularly dubbed "the Wigwam."[3] February 17th, by one account, he told Calhoun that he had the highest confidence in these gentlemen, calling several Virginians and South Carolinians by name, and would like to confer with them. They called immediately. Hamilton, of South Carolina, was spokesman and began by praising the selection of Van Buren. Then he came to the chief point of his anxiety. There was, he said, great concern about the treasury. Here Jackson interposed, saying Ingham was to have that place to meet the united demand of the Pennsylvania delegation. Then Hamilton suggested that Cheves would be suitable for secretary of the treasury, but

---

[1]From a memorandum in Jackson's handwriting headed "Mr. R——e, R——, Va." It contains suggestions for cabinet members and seems to be based on a conversation, either directly or indirectly. It is without date; Jackson Mss.

[2]C. P. Van Ness to Van Buren, March 9, 1832, Van Buren Mss; J. A. Hamilton's assertion (*Reminiscences*, page 91), that Berrien was a Calhounite was probably an afterthought.

[3]Mrs. M. B. Smith, *First Forty Years of Washington Society* (G. Hunt, Editor), 283.

Jackson replied that this was impossible. He also set aside the suggestion that it be McLane and closed the interview by saying that he should take a middle course on the tariff, striving to pay the debt and taking steps to reform the public service. With this the conference ended. The invited gentlemen went home dazed and indignant. They went to the meeting to give advice; and not to learn that all was arranged. "I assure you," said James Hamilton, jr., in closing his account of the interview, "in the words of Sir Anthony Absolute, 'I am perfectly cool — damn cool — never half so cool in my life'." McLane spoke more plainly. "How lamentably," he exclaimed, "stands the old man on his two prominent grounds of commitment — a reasonable disregard of old party distinctions, and an unnecessary resort to congress for cabinet appointments." All the circle were drawn from one party and four of them were from congress, three of the four being "of the least capacity."[1]

The announcement of the cabinet could now no longer be delayed. The first impression was unfavorable. J. A. Hamilton later said it was "the most unintellectual cabinet we ever had."[2] Besides those who were disappointed, there were many who were grieved to see inexperienced men selected. But most singularly the first opposition was from Tennessee, where Eaton was well known. The state's delegation protested against his appointment. They did not like his ambition and his evident purpose to manage the President. The protest was futile. Jackson declared that it made him feel well again to get such opposition and sent the delegation a severe reproof.[3] It was not like him to give up a friend because objection was made to him.

The cabinet was a surprise to Van Buren himself. No one, he says, was more disappointed than he, and, he added, Ingham

---

[1] Hayne to Van Buren, February 14; J. Hamilton, Jr., to *Ibid*, February 19; L. McLane to *Ibid*, February 14; and J. A. Hamilton to *Ibid*, February 14; 1829—;Van Buren Mss.

[2] Hamilton, *Reminiscences*, 215.

[3] J. A. Hamilton to Van Buren, February 23, 1829; Van Buren Mss.

was the only appointee whom he had heard mentioned beforehand for the cabinet.[1] McLane advised him directly to have nothing to do with the administration, and in Washington, other friends spoke to the same effect. Lewis was uneasy lest Van Buren's assent be withdrawn, and assured J. A. Hamilton that Van Buren was not out of favor. Jackson was somewhat concerned till assured that the New Yorker would accept. Lewis summed up the situation in saying: "It is a Cabinet which is decidedly favorable to Van Buren. He has not a more devoted friend than Eaton, and Branch is the same." "Be assured Calhoun is disappointed," adds Hamilton, "and he now hopes that Jackson may be thrown into his arms by your refusal."[2]

This ebullition served to draw the line between the specific Jackson faction, and the old controlling force in the republican party. It also aroused Jackson's resentment against the Virginians and anti-tariff South Carolinians. It was not a serious affair; and Cambreleng estimated it rightly when he wrote to Van Buren, March 1st:

The short and long of the matter is this — The democrats are all not only satisfied but gratified with the cabinet, while the whole federal phalanx is shocked at the idea that the plebeian race should have the ascendency in the councils of the President. The cabinet is infinitely better for harmony, for all practical purposes, for the interest of *New York*, and for the country than it would have been if the treasury had been occupied by a gentleman of the immoveable pertinacity of Mr. Cheves and the navy by the vanity and eccentricity of Mr. Tazewell. You would have had all leaders and no wheel-horses, and the first hill you reached would have upset you all. Murmurings are now pretty secret. But when Mrs. L——, Mrs. H——, Mrs. S——, and Mrs. McL—— hold one of their caucuses, ye gods what a storm![3]

[1]Van Buren, *Autobiography*, I., 15, Van Buren Mss.
[2]J. A. Hamilton to Van Buren, February 21, 1829, Van Buren Mss.
[3]Cambreleng to Van Buren, March 1, 1829; Van Buren Mss. Probably Mrs. Livingston, Mrs. Hayne, Mrs. Sargeant and Mrs. McLane.

The prediction of Cambreleng proved correct. James Hamilton, jr., before a month passed, wrote that he was satisfied with the cabinet. He added with characteristic bluntness that he learned "that old venal Swiss Gallatin is fishing for France. I hope to God that the General will not disgrace himself by countenancing the rapacity of this old vulture. . . . Thank God I want nothing for myself, as I would not give a damn 'to call the king my Brother.'"[1]

Another echo of public opinion in South Carolina came from Dr. Thomas Cooper, long an extreme republican and then president of the state university. Van Buren he wrote confidingly, was now the "master mover" at Washington, adding "take care to be so. You aspire to the succession: do not count on New England but look to the South and West: your great competitor will be Calhoun, but support of internal improvements will sink him unless he repudiates it." Cooper closed by urging that South Carolina would secede if the tariff policy of the past was continued. The letter shows how close Van Buren up to this time was to the nullifiers, and how little they were associated as yet with Calhoun.[2]

Before Jackson's administration fairly began, his cabinet lost one of its strongest men in the resignation of John McLean. It was with reluctance that he consented to remain postmaster-general, and his unwillingness increased as the days went by. There was vacancy on the supreme court bench, and the day after the inauguration McLean expressed his willingness to take that instead of a cabinet position. The suggestion pleased Lewis and the Van Buren men, for it gave them a chance to remove a Calhoun supporter from the President's council; but they had to overcome one obstacle. W. T. Barry, the recently defeated Jackson candidate for governor of Kentucky, was slated for the

1J. Hamilton, Jr., to Van Buren, March 25, 1829; Van Buren Mss.
2Thomas Cooper to Van Buren, March 24, 1829, Van Buren Mss.

court vacancy and it was proposed that he should exchange places with McLean. The Jackson supporters from that state opposed Barry's elevation to the bench because he was of the relief party in Kentucky politics,[1] but with some difficulty they were brought to consent to his nomination. They must now be induced to consent to place him in a still higher position, and the appointing council realized that it was difficult. J. A. Hamilton undertook to convince one of them, T. P. Moore, of Kentucky, taking him before breakfast, because, as he said, a man is not so proud when his stomach is empty. The result justified the tactics, but it is not certain whether it was the hour of approach or some intimation of the appointment as minister to Columbia, which Moore later received, that worked his conversion. "Calhoun," says Hamilton in reporting the affair to his leader, Van Buren, "is cut up by this measure, as is very manifest. He begins to feel that there is an influence beyond that he can hope to exercise." Branch, Eaton, and Berrien were opposed to the change because they thought it would weaken the cabinet.[2] They were right: Barry was in no sense fitted for the position, and through his inefficiency the post-office came into great confusion.

In actual operation, the cabinet proved better than was expected, partly on account of the superior administrative ability of the secretary of state and partly because it existed during quiet times. Ingham succeeded in the treasury at a time when there were no financial difficulties. Eaton made a good secretary of war when the only business of his department related to Indians, and Branch made no mistakes in managing a navy which could hardly be said to exist. McLane hesitated to become attorney-general because, as was said, he feared to encounter

---

[1]The relief party favored the relief of debtors, opposed the United States Bank, and advocated the overthrow of the old courts which declared their measures unconstitutional. See Sumner, *Life of Jackson*, Chap. VI.

[2]J. A. Hamilton to Van Buren, February 27, and March 6 (2), 1829, Van Buren Mss.

at the bar Webster and Wirt,' but Berrien, a weaker man took the office without fear, and was lucky enough to survive. Barry alone fell into positive disgrace through mismanagement. The reorganization of the cabinet two years after it was appointed may, however, have saved other departments from misfortune.

These events mark the last stage in the disintegration of the Virginia hegemony. A new combination was formed in which the West and Southwest were the controlling force, and that region took two places in the cabinet. The two extremes of the old combination, New York and Georgia, were bound to the new by the gift of two cabinet positions, and another symbolized the loyalty of Pennsylvania. The old slave states could not be ignored, but here the representation went to North Carolina. This large but unaggressive state had generally followed Virginia's leadership, and it was good policy to cut it away from the old alliance, which was thus shorn of influence at every point. The proud old state accepted the situation with as good grace as possible. The announcement of her humiliation produced astonishment in Richmond, and "it required," said Stevenson, "all our skill and prudence to quiet" the people.²

But the task of reburnishing the state's prestige was better assigned to Ritchie, whom the picturesque Randolph called with some exaggeration "the Janus-faced editor of the Richmond *Enquirer*, who has contrived to keep in with every administration, save the short reign of John Adams, the second, and then he kept an anchor out to windward for Henry Clay."³ Ritchie wrote to Editor Noah, of New York, co-worker in the cause of democracy:

I am deeply sensible of the compliment you pay to the principles of Virginia. But I have no idea that the sceptre will come

¹Verplanck to Van Buren, December 6, 1828, Van Buren Mss.
²A. Stevenson to Van Buren, April 19, 1829, Van Buren Mss.
³Colton, *Private Correspondence of Henry Clay*, 363.

round to her, for several years to come. We are content to be without it; and even without any hand in the administration. If General Jackson can do better elsewhere be it so; but we shall not, on this account, be less anxious to support the administration of the man we have supported, if he guides his course by liberal and enlightened principles. I pledge you my honor that all the little hints you may have seen in the coalition prints about the discontent and disaffection of Virginia are utterly false and unfounded.

As for the future, said Ritchie, all his hopes were in Van Buren, in whose "tact, sagacity, and knowledge of mankind, temper and admirable talents" he had confidence. "But all these will be of little avail unless he has the courage to tell General Jackson the truth. Some of his friends have doubts on this respect. I confess I have none . . . If you should see Mr. Van Buren, be so good as to present this subject in the most striking way you see best."[1]

The only glimpses we get of the inner working of the circle which considered the cabinet appointments indicates that Jackson was the final appeal in the selections. Thus, Hamilton in one letter says that Jackson and White are going to ride and he thinks much will be settled on the ride. He was a man difficult to move when his mind was made up; but he was approachable to influence before he decided. Like most men of passion, his choice could be determined by some trifle of temper or accidental mood, and for this reason those who sought to direct his will were ever cautious about their manner of approach.

Cabinet-making was soon forgotten in the delights of the inauguration. Ten thousand visitors crowded Washington to see their favorite take the oath-of office. "I never saw such a crowd before," said Webster. "Persons have come five hun-

---

[1] Ritchie to Noah, March 15, 1829; Van Buren Mss.

dred miles to see General Jackson, and they really seem to think that the country is rescued from dreadful danger."

March 4th was a sunny day with a suggestion of spring. "By ten o'clock," says an eye-witness who was not a Jacksonian, "the Avenue was crowded with carriages of every description, from the splendid Baronet and coach, down to wagons and carts, filled with women and children, some in finery and some in rags, for it was the people's President; the men all walked."

Before noon the steps, porticos, the surrounding terraces, and the large enclosed yard to the east of the capitol were alive with humanity. Francis Scott Key, long used to great spectacles, looked on from the gate of the yard and exclaimed, "It is beautiful, it is sublime!" At length persons on the west front, looking down Pennsylvania Avenue, the view of which was then not obstructed by the trees in the grounds, saw a small company, approaching on foot. All wore their hats but a tall gentleman in the middle, whose erect figure and white head were recognized as Jackson's. The procession followed the avenue up the hill on the south side of the capitol, and crowds rushed thither to get a view of the hero. "There, there, that is he," exclaimed some, "he with the white head." "Ah," murmured others, "there is the old man and his gray hair, there is the old veteran, there is Jackson!" Through such eager, pressing crowds he passed slowly into the capitol.

On the east front the crowd awaited the taking of the oath and after that the address. On the portico was a table covered with a red cloth, behind it, the closed door from the rotunda. The portico and the steps were filled with ladies in gay colors, the ground was covered with the expectant multitude, "not a ragged mob, but well dressed and well behaved, respectable and worthy citizens." At length the door behind the table opened. Out came the marshals, the judges of the supreme court, and behind them, the white-haired Jackson. He bowed gravely to the people, who responded with a great shout in unison. Then came the inaugural address, read in a low voice, which many strained their ears in vain to hear. Then the oath was administered by the chief justice, the aged Marshall, whose life was a protest against the political views of the Jackson party, and an attendant presented the Bible. Taking it in his hands, the President kissed it, laid it down reverently, and bowed again to the people. At this his admirers, no longer restrained, rushed past the officials up the steps and seized his hand to congratulate him. With difficulty, he pushed through the throng to a gate, at which his horse awaited him. Here he managed to mount and set off for the White House followed by a promiscuous multitude in carriages, in carts, on horseback, and afoot. "Countrymen, farmers, gentlemen, mounted and dismounted, boys, women and children, black and white" were in the train.

At the Mansion, refreshments had been provided for a large number of ladies and gentlemen; but there were no police arrangements to preserve order and the rabble rushed in with the better class of people. They crowded around the President until he was only saved from bodily harm by some gentlemen, who made a circle in front of him and kept back the intruders by main force. He shook hands with the curious until at last he was glad to escape by a side entrance to his lodgings at Gadsby's hotel. The rabble fell on the refreshments, jostling the waiters as they appeared at the doors, breaking the china and glassware, standing in muddy boots on damask covered chairs, spoiling the carpets, and creating such a press that it was no longer possible for those on the inside to escape by the doors. The windows were used for exits for the suffocating masses. Mrs. Smith, who visited the place after three in the afternoon, found the President gone and the parlors in possession of "a rabble, a mob of boys, Negroes, women, children, scrambling, fighting, romping." Several thousand dollars' worth of broken china and cut glass and many bleeding noses attested the fierceness of the struggle. Where the chaos would have ended is not to be determined had not some sagacious ones thought of the expedient of sending tubs of punch out to the lawn and thus turned aside a part of the incoming stream.[1] Among the guests was James Hamilton, Jr., the nullifier, whose description of the scene is as follows:

'It was a glorious day yesterday for the *sovereigns*, who assembled here to the amount of 15 or 20,000, who hailed the chief with the most enthusiastic applause, and greetings. The ceremony went off well, and the principal person acquitted himself with a grace and a 'composed dignity' which I never saw surpassed. The address itself is excellent, chaste, patriotic, sententious, and dignified. It says all that is necessary to say on such an occasion and exposes no weak flanks that it may be necessary [to] defend hereafter. As far as I have heard (although I confess I have not conversed with the ultra-tariff men), it has given universal satisfaction. It has a commendable brevity, the limits of which I hope in none of his state papers he will ever transcend.

After the ceremony the old chief retired to the Palace where we had a regular Saturnalia. The mob broke in, in thousands. Spirits black, yellow, and grey, poured in in one uninterrupted stream of mud and filth, among the throngs many subjects for the penitentiary and not the fewest among them where [*sic*] Mr. Mercer's tyros for Liberia. It would have done Mr. Wilberforce's heart good to have seen a stout black wench eating in this free country a jelly with a gold spoon at the President's House. However, notwithstanding the row Demus kicked up the whole matter went off very well through the *wise neglect* of that great apostle of the "fierce democracy," the chairman of the central committee, which body corporate, so far from being defunct by the election of Old Hickory, seems now to have

[1]This account is based on the narrative of Mrs. M. B. Smith, *First Forty Years of Washington Society* (Hunt, Editor), 290-298. The quotations in the text are from this work.

gathered fresh vitality and has, I believe, even taken the old man under their parental guardianship.[1]

The inaugural address which pleased Hamilton was not the one which Jackson brought with him to the capital. In the large collection of papers which the general left to posterity is a copy of the inaugural address in his own hand, and indorsed by him, "Rough Draft of the Inaugural Address." As an expression of ideas, language, and political principles, it is the best outcome of the thinking of this remarkable self-made statesman and, in spite of its length, it deserves publication. It reads:

Fellow Citizens:—About to enter upon the duties to which as president of the United States, I have been called by the voluntary suffrages of my country, I avail myself of this occasion to express the deep and heartfelt gratitude with which a testimonial of such distinguished favor has been received. To be elected under the circumstances which have marked the recent contest of opinion, to administer the affairs of a government deriving all its powers from the will of the people — a government whose vital principle is the right of the people to control its measures, and whose only object and glory are the equal happinesss and freedom of all the members of the confederacy, cannot but penetrate me with the most powerful and mingled emotions of thanks, on the one hand, for the honor conferred on me, and on the other, of solemn apprehensions for the safety of the great and important interests committed to my charge.

Under the weight of these emotions, unaided by any confidence inspired by past experience, or by any strength derived from the conscious possession of powers equal to the station,—I confess, fellow citizens, that I approach it with trembling reluctance. But my country has willed it, and I obey, gathering hope from the reflection that the other branches of the Government with whom the constitutional will associates me, will yield those resources of Patriotism and intelligence by which the administration may be rendered useful, and the honor and

[1] J. Hamilton, Jr., to Van Buren, March 5, 1829, Van Buren Mss.

independence of our widely extended republic guarded from encroachment; but above all, trusting to the smiles of that overruling providence, "in the hollow of whose hand," is the destiny of nations, for that animation of common council and harmonising effort, which shall enable us to steer the Bark of liberty through every difficulty.

In the present stage of our history, it will not be expected of me on this occasion to enter into any detail of the first principles of our government. The atchievements of our fathers, our subsequent intercourse with each other, the various relations we have sustained with the other powers of the world, and our present attitude at home, exhibits the practical operations of these principles, all of which are comprised in the sovereignty of the people. This is the basis of our system, and to its security from violation and innovation must our practice and experience as a government be dedicated. To the administration of my illustrious predecessors, I will be permitted to refer as mirors, not so much for the measures which may be demanded by the present state of the country, but as applications of the same principles to the various exigencies which have occurred in our history, and as shedding light upon those which may hereafter arise. It is thus the great moral race we are running, connects us with the past, and is tributary to the events which are to come: thus, that every period of our government is useful to that which follows, not as a source of principle, but as guides on that sacred fountain to which we must often go for the refreshment of our laws, and the invigoration of the public morals. It is from this source that we derive the means of congratulating ourselves upon the present free condition of our country, and build our hopes for its future safety. In fine, Fellow Citizens, this is the bulwark of our liberties.

. Among the various and important duties that are confided to the President, there are none of more interest than that which requires the selection of his officers. The application of the laws, and the management of our relations with foreign powers, form the chief object of an Executive, and are as essential to the welfare of the union as the laws themselves. In the discharge of this trust it shall be my care to fill the various offices at the disposal of the Executive with individuals uniting as far as possible the qualifications of the head and heart, always recollecting that in a free government the demand for moral qualities should be made superior to that of talents. In other forms of government where the people are not regarded as composing the sovereign power, it is easy to perceive that the safeguard of the empire consists chiefly in the skill by which the monarch can wield the bigoted acquiescence of his Subjects. But it is different with us. Here the will of the people, prescribed in a constitution of their own choice controuls the service of the public functionaries, and is interested more deeply in the preservation of those qualities which ensures fidelity and honest devotion to their interests.

Provisions for the national defense form another class of duties for the Representatives of the people, and as they stand in delicate connection with the powers of the general and State Governments when understood to embrace the protection of our own labour, merit the most serious consideration. Legislation for this object encouraging the production of those articles which are essential in the emergencies of war, and to the independence of the nation, seems to me to be sanctioned by the constitution as lawful and Just. The general safety was the great motive for the confederation of the States, and never would have been effected without conferring on the Federal Government the power to provide those internal supplies which constitute the means of war, and which if left to the ordinary operations of commerce, might be witheld at a time when we most needed them. A Judicious Tariff imposing duties high enough to insure us against this calamity will always meet with my hearty coöperation. But beyond this point, legislation effecting the natural relation of the labour of the States are irreconcilable to the objects of the union, and threatening to its peace and tranquility.

Recollecting that all the States are equal in sovereignty, and in claims to the benefits accruing from the confederation, upon the federal principle of providing by taxation for the wants of the Government, it seems Just that the expenditures should be distributed regard being first paid to the national debt, and the appropriations for the support of the Government, and safety of the union. The necessity of conforming more closely to this principle is illustrated by the dissatisfaction which the expenditures for the purposes of improvement has already created in several of the States. The operation of the principles, as fixed on this equitable basis, will give to the States the fiscal prosperity of the nation, and secure harmony by removing the grounds of jealousy.

Between the powers granted to the general government, and those reserved to the States and the people, it is to be regretted that no line can be so obviously drawn as that all shall understand its boundaries. There will be a teritory between them, which must be governed by the good sense of a nation always ready to resist oppression, and too high minded to forget the rights of the minority. It is the inheritance of that sentiment of conciliation, and spirit of compromise which gave us the constitution, and which is to enable us in the progress of time to amend such defects in the system as experience may detect. Fully sensible of the necessity which I shall have for the exercise of this spirit on the part of my fellow citizens, I shall notice with pleasure an unreserved examination of the measures of my administration, and shall be the last to cry out treason against those who interpret differently from myself the policy, or powers of the government.

Some of the Topics which shall engage my earliest attention as intimately connected with the prosperity of our beloved country, are, the liquidation of the national debt, the introduction and observance of the strictest economy in the disbursements of the Government, a Judicious tariff, combined with a fostering care of commerce and agriculture, and regulated by the principles before adverted to, a Just respect for State rights and the maintainence of State sovereignty as the best check of the tendencies to consolidation; and the distribution of the surplus revenue amongst the States according to the apportionment of representation, for the purposes of education and internal improvement, except where the subjects are entirely national. With the accomplishment of these objects I trust the memorials of our national blessings may be multiplied, and the scenes of domestic labour be made more animating and happy.

Among Jackson's papers there is also a manuscript endorsed in his own hands, "Inaugural Address as 'Delivered." It is in the hand of a copyist and on a peculiar large sheet of foolscap like that of the "Rough Draft." A third copy also is found in the same collection, tied together with ribbon, written on one side of an ordinary sheet, and evidently that from which Jackson read. Now the interest of this is that the three copies are all different. They seem to represent three stages in the preparation of the document. The "rough draft" was Jackson's own, the second copy, or the "address as delivered," was the result of consultation with his friends at the "Hermitage," and the third copy, or the copy with the ribbon, was that which survived after it was inspected by his friends in Washington, and from which he actually read. It is like the copy in *The Messages and Papers of the President.*

The second copy, much unlike the first, differed from the third in several respects, the most important being that where the seventh paragraph of the printed address, the third copy, deals with internal improvements it merely says that they and the diffusion of knowledge are important and should be encouraged. The second copy, evidently the one brought from Tennessee with the intention of delivering it, gives this paragraph and adds the following:

After liquidating the national debt, the national income will probably exceed the ordinary expenses of government, in which event, the apportionment of the surplus revenue among the states according to the ratio of their representation for these purposes, will be a fair, federal, and a useful disposition of it. Every member of the Union, in peace and in war, will be benefitted by the improvement of our inland navigation, and the construction of highways in the several states. And the Representative principle, upon the virtue of which our state and federal governments are founded, can reach its *maximum* value, only by a wide and efficacious diffusion of instruction — knowledge and power being in this respect coexistent qualities.

It is not too much to suppose that this paragraph was cut out after his arrival in Washington. The tenth paragraph of the third draft must have been added in the capital, since it does not appear in the second copy. It relates to the reform of the patronage. There is in none of the copies an allusion to the United States Bank, which is remarkable, since Jackson five years later made a contradictory statement in reply to a question from Polk. He said:

The President with his respects replies to Colonel Polk, that he understood him correctly, that the original draft of his inaugural address was made at the Hermitage, that his views of the *United States Bank* were incorporated in it, and also his views of the surplus funds that might casually arise in the treasury. These two paragraphs were by the advice of his friends here, both left out of the inaugural address, and were both introduced into his next annual message. It was thought that both these topics were better suited to an annual message, than an inaugural address, and thus you, if necessary, may use it. Every one that knows me, does know, that I have been always opposed to the U. States Bank, nay all Banks.[1]

Unless there was a copy of the address which is not preserved, we must conclude that Jackson's memory played him a trick in regard to the bank matter. Washington gossip in 1831 said his memory was bad.[2]

The address delivered is easily accessible to the reader. It contained the usual expression of respect for the presidency, and promised to protect the rights of the states, to practise economy, and to try to pay the national debt. It gave a cautious approval to a tariff which would "equally favor" agriculture, commerce, and manufactures, except that special encouragement should be given to the production of articles "essential to our

---

[1] See Polk to Jackson, December 23, 1833, Polk Papers, Library of Congress. On the back of this letter Jackson writes the above.
[2] Mrs. M. B. Smith, *First Forty Years of Washington Society* (Hunt, Editor), 320.

national independence." It pronounced internal improvements and the diffusion of knowledge "of high importance"; it promised not to increase the army, but to keep it and the navy at their existing state of efficiency; and it praised a patriotic and well organized militia as an "impenetrable ægis" which in spite of imperfections would protect us from foreign foes. It announced a just and liberal policy toward the Indians, undertook to reform abuses of the patronage, and closed by invoking Divine assistance for all his efforts. It was, as Hamilton, of South Carolina, said, a satisfactory address, dignified enough and not likely to arouse the opposition of any important section of public opinion.[1]

The impression was general at the time that Jackson did not write the address. Adams thought it was by Henry Lee, and Col. J. A. Hamilton says he had much to do with it in Washington. This impression was connected with the feeling that Jackson could not write such a paper as appeared in print. But his opponents were apt to underestimate his ability. The rough draft, or first copy, which has survived and was undoubtedly his own work, indicates that he could write a very good paper. The changes subsequently made by the advice of his friends were made for reasons of political expediency.

The first weeks of the administration were full of doubts. The persistence and crude manners of the office-seekers filling the hotels and public buildings seemed to show a deterioration in public life. Persons who did not get a cabinet position did not conceal their disappointment; and less interested observers began to shake their heads, while the Adams-Clay opposition gleefully declared that the victors were discredited in the very beginning. No man then in the administration could check this tendency to confusion, Jackson least of all, whose daily companions were Eaton and Lewis, themselves leaders of the forces

---

[1] Richardson, *Messages and Papers of the Presidents*, II., 436.

of devastation. So great was the danger that even R. M. Johnson, of Kentucky, on his way home, wrote to urge the President to dismiss his unofficial advisers, adding that people said Jackson needed no organized committee to sustain him or enlighten his councils.[1] From this situation, Van Buren's quiet dexterity probably saved the government. He alone of the cabinet had the confidence of the older politicians, he alone could remove from administration circles the appearance of social crudeness, and he alone had the address to bind up the wounds of disappointed leaders, satisfying them with some of the higher diplomatic positions not yet assigned.

Van Buren left Albany for Washington late in March. In New York he met Levi Woodbury, of New Hampshire, who had been urged in vain for cabinet position as the representative of New England. He was disappointed and talked freely about affairs at the capital. At Philadelphia, the traveler encountered Edward Livingston, who had no cause for dissatisfaction; for he was first offered a seat in the cabinet and refusing that was offered the ministry to France, of all places the one he most wanted. Yet Livingston and his wife were full of forebodings, complaining especially of the lack of social dignity in the White House. They could not foresee, said Van Buren, that Jackson's receptions would eventually become as elaborate, brilliant, and popular as those of any of his predecessors. Continuing his journey the secretary met at New Castle, Del., the disappointed McLane, from whom came the same doleful tale. From Washington came the same story in a large number of letters from personal admirers who did not like the looks of things, and some of whom advised him not to become secretary of state.

Van Buren reached Washington in the evening. His carriage was hardly at the hotel before he was surrounded by candidates for office. They followed him to his room, where he lay on a sofa

[1] Johnson to Jackson, March 9, 1829, Jackson Mss.

and said he would call on the President in an hour but would hear their claims in the interim. At last he set out for the White House, and his own account of his reception gives us an excellent picture of the lonely occupant of the mansion. He says:

A solitary lamp in the vestibule and a single candle in the President's office gave no promise of the cordiality with which I was, notwithstanding, greeted by Genl. Jackson on my visit to the White House. I found no one with him except his intimate friend, Major Lewis. His health was poor, and his spirits depressed as well by his recent bereavement of his wife, as by the trials of personal and political friendship which he had been obliged to encounter in the organization of his cabinet. This was our first meeting as political friends, and it was certainly a peculiar feature of that interview and no insignificant illustration of his nature that he received with most affectionate eagerness at the very threshold of his administration the individual destined to occupy the first place in his confidence, of whose character his only opportunities to learn anything by personal observation had been presented during periods of active political hostility. He soon noticed my exhaustion from sickness and travel and, considerately postponing all business to an appointed hour next day, recommended me to my bed. From that night to the day of his death, relations, sometimes official, always political and personal, were inviolably maintained between that noble old man and myself, the cordial and confidential character of which can never have been surpassed among public men.[1]

Van Buren does not overstate the matter. The two men first met, but in a purely formal manner, in the winter of 1815-1816. They next saw one another when the elder became senator from Tennessee in 1823. They discovered then that they agreed in principles but were opposed in personal feelings. In 1819 Jackson visited New York and gave a toast at a Tammany dinner in honor of Clinton. He was largely prompted to this by his dis-

---

[1]Van Buren, *Autobiography*, I., 11-15, Van Buren Mss.

like of Crawford, whom Clinton opposed; but the affair offended Van Buren, Crawford leader in the state. After Jackson retired from the senate in 1825, no communication passed between him and the New Yorker, except one letter introducing a friend and one or two others of a formal nature.[1] The interview at Washington was, therefore, literally the beginning of the intimacy of the two men. Van Buren intimates that the relation developed rapidly, that it sprang out of Jackson's spontaneous feeling and was returned at once by its object. The statement may well be true. Affliction left him isolated; he was too strong by nature to be satisfied with the political wisdom of men like Lewis and Eaton and turned to the ready sense of the secretary of state. He found in him a certainty of purpose and judgment which relieved his own inexperience while it satisfied the friends of the administration.

The first business between the two men referred to diplomatic appointments. Jackson admitted that he had made a mistake in offering Tazewell the mission to England and Livingston that to France. Van Buren as frankly replied that if he had been consulted, he would not have made the offers. Each position involved much work on incomplete diplomatic business and young men, he thought, ought to be sent to fill them. Since the offers were made it was believed that nothing could be done to withdraw them, but it was decided to urge each to hasten his departure, a course which solved the difficulty; for when Tazewell and Livingston found they were expected to set out at once they both declined. At this interview Jackson asked the secretary to suggest a minister to Spain. The latter mentioned the name of Woodbury, and the President, willing to conciliate New England, adopted the suggestion. But Woodbury, after much hesitation, also declined.

When Tazewell declined, Berrien, the new attorney-general,

[1] Van Buren, *Autobiography*, I., 16-71

was suggested for the English mission; and Jackson, pleased with the idea, made the offer.[1] It was considered certain that the tender would be accepted; and Van Buren seized the opportunity to satisfy the federalists and the disappointed South Carolinians by offering the attorney-generalship to McLane, who gladly assented. But here, much to the surprise of all, Berrien announced that he would remain in the cabinet, and McLane, his pride somewhat hurt, consented to go to England. It was arranged, however, that if there should be a vacancy on the supreme court bench McLane should be recalled to take it. He was a man of ability, but possessed of an unsteady ambition which was destined to limit his ultimate success.[2] His wife was a brilliant social leader in the capital, and it was supposed that his eagerness to enter the cabinet was partly due to her influence.

When Livingston refused the mission to France on account of the condition of his private affairs, Van Buren saw in it an opportunity to soothe Virginia. He selected for the place, W. C. Rives, who accepted. He was of the younger school of his state's leaders and filled Van Buren's ideal, that to endure the rebuffs of the French ministry and persistently follow until they would settle our claims, it was necessary to have an agent in Paris who had a career to make, not one who would feel disposed to rest on his laurels rather than subject his dignity to the slights of an indifferent government. The appointment justified this expectation. Rives took up the task required of him with assiduity and by his insistence forced the French ministry to come to an agreement as to our claims, although it took the threats of Jackson at a later day to make them actually pay over the money.[3]

Having thus smoothed out the political situation, Van Buren turned to the condition of official society, which was much

[1]Lyttleton Tazewell to Jackson, March 20, 1829; Jackson Mss.
[2]Van Buren, *Autobiography*, I., 47-56. Van Buren Mss.
[3]See below, Chapter XXX.

disturbed by the lack of prestige on the part of the Tennessee group. He says that when a senator he came, "as a brother Dutchman" into close friendship with Baron Huygens, minister from Holland, and with Sir Charles Vaughn, the English minister. Relying on these to help him, he invited all the diplomatic corps to meet him at the White House to be presented to the President. He then told Jackson that in an informal interview these two diplomats had expressed the opinion that if, in the coming presentation, the assurances of the inaugural address were repeated it would enable the ministers to make such reports as would have good effect at home. The secretary, therefore, advised the President not to make a formal address but to say that he stood by the inaugural, that he desired peace with all the world, that he had no prejudices nor predilections among foreign nations, and that he should try to advance his own nation through unselfish and frank negotiations. The reader will observe that these suggestions went further than the inaugural; but Jackson followed them, delivering himself, as Van Buren says, in his "invariably happy and expressive manner." The diplomats were well pleased. A short time afterward, they were invited to a dinner which was served in a creditable manner and at which "the simple yet kindly, old fashioned manners of the host" surprised and captivated the guests. And thus, says our informant, the anxiety of these foreign gentlemen was relieved and their prejudices softened "by the most approved diplomatic machinery."[1] Moreover, when it was known in Washington that the diplomats were pleased, popular apprehensions were lessened. Thus the first weeks of the administration passed without calamity and with some degree of success.

---

[1]Van Buren, *Autobiography*, I., 68-70, Van Buren Mss.

CHAPTER XXI

JACKSON'S APPOINTMENTS TO OFFICE

THE power the President gets from appointing the administrative officials puts a severe test on his judgment. Neither the constitution nor the laws provided any other means of determining the capacity of the appointee than the will of the appointer; but as party developed the choice became less a spontaneous act of the President and more an expression of partisan feeling.

Under Jackson the political party achieved a new stage in its development. It took a more popular basis and evolved the nominating convention as a means of expressing its will in one important phase of its activity. The party thus gained in self-expression. It took greater control over its leaders and forced them to follow in some degree its wishes in making appointments. This process is seen in Monroe's administration; it was resisted by Adams with results unfavorable to his popularity; it found its full opportunity under Jackson. The last-mentioned President did not create the spoils system: it came with new conditions. His responsibility was that he did not oppose but approved it through his sympathy with the new party ideals.

It is difficult to determine on what principle the early Presidents arrived at their estimate of an applicant's fitness for office. The recommendation of friends probably had much weight and party lines were usually followed. Thus, Washington in the beginning of his administration selected most of his subordinates from persons who had favored the adoption of the constitution. In Rhode Island and North Carolina, the two states which entered the union after it was formed, the customs officers were anti-federalists in accord with prevailing state politics. Washington appointed the large majority of their successors from the federalists.[1] If it should be said in extenuation that he believed the union would be safe only in the hands of officers loyal to its establishment, it would be pertinent to say in reply that this is the ordinary justification of party appointments.

When Jefferson became President he found the offices full of federalists. He proposed to appoint republicans until they equaled their opponents, but with the disappearance of the federalist party all the civil service was filled with republicans. With a design of building up his own support, Monroe announced what he called an "amalgamation policy," selecting officers from both sides. This displeased those who believed themselves the genuine representatives of republicanism. Later these were mostly Crawfordites and carried their feeling for party appointments into the larger Jackson party which was formed after the election of 1824. Partisanship, therefore, was never quite absent from the choice of officials before 1829.

On the other hand, personal favor and various other reasons than fitness for the office decided the selection within party lines. Sometimes women in Washington sought office for their friends: for some applicants poverty, or a large family, or kinship with a man of prominence, or the favor of an ex-President were made grounds for appointment. A letter from Monroe to Jackson, 1821, in regard to the new officials selected for Florida has this interesting statement:

Mr. Alexander Scott, of Maryland, is appointed to the Collector of the Customs, Mr. Steuben Smith, of New York, Naval officer, Mr. Hackley, of Virginia, Surveyor, and Mr. Baker, of this place, Inspector of Pensacola. The first mentioned is a man of considerable literary acquirements and strict integrity, well connected in his State. The second is the son of Col. Wm.

[1]Fish, *The Civil Service and Patronage*, 11-13.

Smith, who was Aide-de-camp to General Washington in the revolutionary war, and afterwards Secretary of Legation at London, where he married the daughter of Mr. Adams, former President. He is the nephew of the present Secretary of State, and his wife is the sister of Mr. Adams. Of Mr. Hackley you may have heard in Spain, his wife is the sister of Governor Randolph of Virginia, and Mr. Madison and others, our friends, have strongly recommended him to me. As these persons are, I believe, literally poor, as is indeed, Mr. Baker, who was formerly consul in Spain and Italy, and in whose favor Mr. Jefferson takes an interest, I wish you to place them, if possible, in some of the public buildings, of which I presume there are some not necessary for your own accommodation. It is I believe customary for the revenue officers to be thus provided, wherever it is practicable, and in no instances can such provision be more important, or indispensable to the parties than the present.[1]

Monroe does not avow personal reasons for the choice of all the officials in Florida, but the frank reference to them here seems to indicate that such reasons were not unusual in his mind. The idea is supported in the following extract from a letter by Mrs. Margaret Bayard Smith:

I have tried and other friends have tried, to procure a clerkship for him.[2] Mrs. Porter did her best and I used all manner of persuasion and argument with the kind, good natured secty. of War.—"My dear Madam, what am I to do? When we ask Congress for more Clerks in the Dept and tell them the present number is insufficient for the duties of the offices, the reply is, If you continue to fill the offices with *old men*, no number will be sufficient. Get young men and fewer will answer and the work be better done. This is too true, the public benefit is sacrificed to private interest and charity. The Departments are literally overstocked with old, inefficient clerks. I cannot serve your friend, consistently with duty."[3]

[1] Monroe, *Writings*, VI., 183.
[2] The reference is to a relative of her husband. Rush was secretary of war.
[3] *First Forty Years of Washington Society* (Hunt, Editor), 276.

In another connection Rush spoke of the war department as the "octogenarian department." [1]

The old method of appointment made possible, and by this evidence it actually created, inefficiency in office. Jefferson made many removals which were really political, but he usually managed to find some other reason to justify his action.' The party once established in power, removals were infrequent; political reasons ceased to act; and it was so hard to prove a charge of inefficiency that it was rarely attempted. Moreover, there was a prevalent notion that office was properly a safe refuge for deserving old men who had served the public. These difficulties gave a strong reason for passing the Four Years' Law of 1820. Crawford probably wrote the bill, and he undoubtedly supported it. For tenure during good behavior of a large number of officers who handled the revenues, chiefly in the treasury department, was now substituted a four years' term. By leaving incumbents subject to reappointment the secretary was able to control their action, if he chose to do so.' It is possible that Crawford favored the law for its bearing on his coming canvass for the presidency, but it is not clear that he did so; for the chief support of the theory is the diary of John Quincy Adams, not always reliable when dealing with one of the diarists' political rivals. Apart from any such purpose, the bill made removals of inefficients easy, but it applied to only a portion of the officials.

The overthrow of the caucus, like everything else that gave the political party a more popular basis, tended to the spoils system. Under the caucus the member of congress had a feeling of proprietorship in the offices. He freely asked for them for himself and for his friends. Under the later system he lost his controlling influence with the appointing power and with the growth of democracy looked more carefully to the will of his

[1]Colton, *Private Correspondence of Clay*, 188.
[2]Fish, *The Civil Service and Patronage*, 42.
[3]*Ibid*, 66-70.

constituents. That will was now embodied in the demands of political lieutenants and supporting editors, the persons who are ever at the bottom of demands for party rewards. They were the class that supplied the office-seekers: they felt that reward for loyal service was theirs by right.

The conviction that the public service suffered from favoritism and inefficiency and the growth of democratic party organization were two reasons for the development of the spoils system. A third was the belief in rotation in office. Long terms seemed to favor the creation of an official aristocracy and to produce an official class who were indifferent to popular approval. More than all else, party lieutenants believed that the rewards of party fidelity ought to be distributed among the workers with approximate equality. When the system was logically developed, rotation in office would apply within party lines as well as without.

Partisan appointments have long existed in English-speaking countries. They were used in the colonies to support the crown influence, and after the revolution many states saw them adopted to support party power. But they took their earliest and most complete development in New York, where the people from an early period were used to little local self-government. A large number of militia and civil offices were appointive — in 1821 there were over 8000 of the former and 6,663 of the latter — and the first state constitution created a council of appointment, consisting of four members and the governor, who were to fill this large number of places. From 1777 to 1795 and from 1801 to 1804 George Clinton was governor, and his own rule was merged so completely and quietly into that of his nephew, De Witt Clinton, that it may be said to have persisted till the death of the latter in 1828. These two men built up by skilful management of the appointments a devoted party, in most respects like the modern political "machine." Their example was imitated by others; and although in 1821 the number of appointive offices was greatly reduced and the council of appointment abolished, the spoils system remained a firm characteristic of party life. To control the many political subordinates and to direct them efficiently in the elections there now came into existence a small central group of party leaders called the "Albany Regency," at the head of which, in the period of which we are speaking, was Martin Van Buren.[1]

New York was not alone in the development of partisan appointments. Pennsylvania has been pronounced as bad, and the evil was not unknown in New Hampshire, Rhode Island, and Massachusetts. The aristocratic caste of Southern society was not favorable to rotation in office, but in the West, which was dedicated to social equality, rotation was demanded as necessary to democracy, and politicians there were alive to the opportunity of turning it toward an effective system of party appointments.[2]

Thus we see that by 1824 the spoils system was established in many of the states and was in fair way to be adopted in the national government, had not President Adams intervened. He would lend himself in no manner to the introduction of the system. His appointments took no partisan nature, nor would he remove an official because he took part in politics. He was so rigid that he won the disapproval of not only his more selfish followers but his most intelligent and liberal supporters. Edward Everett, a fair representative of the latter class, declared in 1828:

We both probably know cases — I certainly do — of incumbents, who have actually become hostile, on the calculation that they are safe now, and can make themselves so, in the contingency of a change. For an Administration then to bestow its patronage, without distinction of party, is to court its own de-

Fish, *The Civil Service and Patronage*, 86-91.
Ibid, 92-103.

struction. I think, therefore, that Fidelity to itself requires, that every Administration should have the benefit of the cordial coöperation of all its members. It cannot be supposed, considering how nearly equal the parties are in numbers, that there are not good men, for any and every service, on the side of the Administration. And tho' I would apply the general rule, with the greatest possible lenity, in the individual case, yet the rule ought to be, that, other things being equal, the friends of the Administration sh'd have the preference. Our present chief magistrate made the experiment of the higher principle, of exclusive regard to merit; and what has been his reward? A most furious opposition, rallied on the charge of the corrupt distribution of office, and the open or secret hostility of three-fourths of the office-holders in the Union.[1]

Everett's sense of the drift of political opinion was correct. The country was turning toward a new doctrine, and Adams's attempt to hold it back was futile.

It was well known during the campaign that Jackson would favor partisan appointments. His strong and oft repeated charge that the offices were filled with inefficient and corrupt men was but laying a basis for removals. Leading Jackson papers said he would, if elected, remove all who deserved it. General Harrison was heard to say he would not support him if he did not believe Jackson would, the day he arrived at Washington and without the formality of a trial, hand up every rascal of them.[2] So strong was the expectation among the followers of the general that Everett thought Jackson could not be elected if he were now to avow the sentiments in the Monroe letter of 1816.[3]

It is too much to expect absolute consistency of a statesman. In 1798 Jackson characterized a proposition to fill the offices

---

[1] Everett to John McLean, August 1, 1828, *Proceedings of the Massachusetts Historical Society*, February 1908, 361.
[2] *Ibid to Ibid*, August 18, 1828, *Ibid*, 372.
[3] *Ibid*, 376.

with federalists as an "insolent attack" on liberty.[1] He probably merely expressed a temporary feeling of resentment against his opponents; for when later in the same year he resigned his seat in the senate to become judge, his new appointment and that of his successor were made strictly on party lines, and without objection on his part.[2] The apparent liberality in the Monroe letter, 1816, may be explained on the ground of his strong military feeling. He was chiefly concerned that federalists who fought in the war should be considered in the appointments, and we must not forget that to Lewis's embellishing hand we owe some of the strongest expressions in the letter.

As a soldier he would be pleased to lessen party spirit which would prevent a national coöperation in resenting the foreign wrongs. It was a worthy ideal, but it did not deny the feeling that offices should be given to gentlemen who deserved to be taken care of for past services. He was disappointed when, as governor of Florida, he was not allowed to fill the subordinate offices there with friends and old military associates. In 1818 he recommended to Monroe the wishes of an old revolutionary soldier in words which explain his view at that time better than any words of the historian. He wrote:

Colonel Sherburne, Chickasaw agent, requested me to name to you that he was wearied with his situation, of which I have no doubt; his age and former habits of life but little calculated him for happiness amidst a savage nation. But being dependent for the support of himself and sister on the perquisites of his office, he can not resign; but it would be a great accommodation to him to be transferred to Newport, should a vacancy in any office occur that he was competent to fill. I have no doubt but he is an aimable old man; and from his revolutionary services, I sincerely feel for him. He is unacquainted with Indians,

---

[1] Jackson to Overton, January 22, 1798, a copy in the Library of Congress, original in Nashville, Tennessee.
[2] Willie Blount to Sevier, July 6 and August 12, 1798, *American Historical Magazine* (Nashville), V., 121-123.

and all business which relates to them; but at the treaty, as soon as he did understand our wishes and that of the government, he aided us with all his might.   The colonel never can be happy amidst the Indians.   It would afford me great pleasure to hear that the colonel was comfortably seated in an office in Newport, where he could spend his declining years in peace and happiness with his own countrymen and friends.[1]

One who could write thus in 1818 could not, consistently, criticise the administration ten years later for having the service full of old and inefficient men.

So much was said about the abuse of the patronage during the campaign of 1828 that Jackson himself came to believe it and heard of election results with a grim determination to make changes.   "I know the General is resolved," wrote Major Lewis, "on making a pretty general sweep of the departments. It is expected he will cleanse the Augean stables, and I feel pretty confident he will not disappoint the popular expectation in this particular.   He is determined on making a radical change in the offices — on giving them a complete overhauling; and to do this effectually an almost entire new set must be put in."   Lewis was then at Jackson's elbow and must have known his superior's private feeling in the matter.   His opinion, also, is corroborated by J. A. Hamilton, who wrote Van Buren to the same purport on February 27.[2]   And yet a clean sweep was not made.   Some hand, it may have been Van Buren's,[3] intervened to secure moderation.   A great many more removals, however, were made than at the beginning of any preceding administration, and this, with the prevalent apprehensive terror made the period remembered as a debauch of partisanship, a characterization it hardly deserves.

[1]See Parton, *Life of Jackson*, II., 526.
[2]Lewis to J. A. Hamilton, December 12, 1828; Hamilton to Van Buren, February 27, 1829; Van Buren Mss.   Also Jackson to Van Buren, March 31, 1829, Jackson Mss.
[3]Van Buren to Jackson, enclosing letter from Ritchie, March 31, 1829; Jackson Mss.

For the distress of the ejected Jackson had warmest sympathy. "My feelings have been severely crowded by the various applications for relief," he wrote ten weeks after the inauguration, ". . . Would you believe it, that a lady who had once rolled in wealth, but whose husband was overtaken by misfortune and reduced to want, and is, and has been an applicant for office, and well recommended, applied to me with tears in her eyes, soliciting relief, assuring me that her children were starving, and to buy them a morsel of bread she had to sell her thimble the day before. An office I had not to give her, and my cash was nearly out, but I could not withold from her half of the pittance I had with me."[1]

Much was said by the Jackson men before election about the corruption of the office-holders. They entered office themselves with the desire and expectation of finding much fraud. But search as they might, they could find only one wrong-doer, Tobias Watkins, fourth auditor. He was short in his accounts, and was indicted and sentenced to imprisonment. Jackson ordered a label to be displayed over the door of the unhappy man's prison cell announcing that it led to the "Criminal Apartment."[2]

During the first weeks of the administration Washington was filled with gloomy tales of suffering among office-holders and office-seekers. Those who were in office trembled for their futures: those who sought positions displayed the most distressed conditions as a means of recommending themselves to the sympathy of the appointing power. Wherever one went were signs of woe. "We have not had leisure yet," said Jackson on May 26th, "to make the necessary arrangements of reform. We are progressing, and such is the press for office, and the distress here, that there are for the place of messengers (for the Departments)

---

[1]Jackson to Cryer, May 26, 1829, *American Historical Magazine* (Nashville), IV., 231.
[2]Sumner, *Life of Jackson,*(revised edition), 189.

at least twenty applicants for each station, and many applicants who have been men of wealth and respectability. Still if our friend Gwinn wishes to come on here, when we finally organize the Departments, and turn out the spies from our camp, I will preserve an office for him. But we are now having a thorough investigation into the situation of all Departments, and the inquiry will be made how many, if any, clerks can be dispensed with."

The clamor of the public did not deter Jackson, who wrote in his private journal some time between May 18 and June 23, 1829:

There has been a great noise made about removals. This to be brought before Congress with the causes, with the propriety of passing a law vacating all offices periodically — then the good can be re-appointed, and the bad, defaulters, left out without murmurs. Now, every man who has been in office a few years, believes he has a life estate in it, a vested right, and if it has been held twenty years or upwards, not only a vested right, but that it ought to descend to his children, and if no children then the next of kin. This is not the principles of our government. It is rotation in office that will perpetuate our liberty.

There can be no doubt that he acted from what be believed to be the best interests of the public, and our condemnation must fall on his capacity of forming a correct decision, rather than on his intention. A letter to Mrs. Pope, wife of a prominent Frankfort, Kentucky, supporter, who intervened to secure the retention of a postmaster, shows how rigorously he appreciated his duty. It also may help to show that the situation was less severe than has been supposed. He wrote:

Your letter of the 30th ultimo has been received, and I embrace the first leisure moment since, to explain to you the reasons which produced the removal of Mr. H —— Acting upon the information contained in your first letter on the subject,

I felt a pleasure in the supposition that he could be retained without violating a proper regard for the duties of my office, or for the opinion of the great body of the people interested in that which he filled. This pleasure I assure you, Madam, was heightened by the respect which I entertained for your wishes; and it was not without much pain that I felt constrained to act upon the belief that you had mistaken his true character. Unquestioned authority has been lodged in the department of the Postmaster General for the assertion that Mr. H—— intemperate[1] habits disqualify him, in a great degree, for the personal discharge of the duties of the office, and that he had been in the custom from this cause, of entrusting its keys to individuals obnoxious to the community in many points of view. An extract of the memorial on this subject I enclose for your satisfaction. . . . It is a painful duty to be the instrument of lessening the resources of a family so amiable as that of Mr. H—— but when the public good calls for it, it must be performed. As a private individual, it would give me the greatest happiness to alleviate their distress, but as a public officer, I cannot devote to this object the interests of the country.[2]

When he came into office Jackson found that many officials were insolvent and deeply in debt. It revolted his honest soul, and he directed all such persons to be dismissed. He would not have the government service a refuge for such defrauders. He ordered a search of the jail records, which showed that eighty-eight persons were thus delinquent. Some of them had taken the bankrupts' oath twelve times in a few months.[3]

A story preserved among his friends tell show his love of honesty once brought to pay debts long ignored, a man over whom he had no official authority. The keeper of a boarding-house in the capital had for lodger a congressman who evaded his obligations to her. At length she saw no other hope than to

---

[1] The word "intemperate" is erased in the text.
[2] Jackson to Mrs. F. Pope, June 8, 1829, Jackson Mss.
[3] From an undated memorandum in Jackson's hand. It undoubtedly refers to the beginning of his administration. Jackson Mss.

take the matter to Jackson, who heard her story and said, "Have him give you a note for the amount due and bring the paper to me." The delinquent readily gave his note, for it was worth nothing. When Jackson received it he endorsed it and gave it to the woman with the remark, "I think he will pay it now." The expectation was a just one: no member of congress was willing to lose his hold on presidential favor by forcing the chief executive to pay his board bill, or to have his constituents know that he threw his money obligations on the shoulders of the hero of New Orleans.

The prospect of wholesale removals brought protests from some of the prominent men in the party. They feared the influence on public opinion, and one of them used the sagacious argument that it would be better to keep the applicants unsatisfied, saying, "The hope of office will secure you more support than the enjoyment of it."[1] Jackson endorsed the letter to be kept carefully and filed it among his special papers. The appointment of editors brought the loudest protest. A partisan editor of the day was apt to be a hired hack-writer for whom his own employers had little respect. He was rewarded with contracts to print the laws and with other government publishing, but he was not expected to have office. In the democratic upheaval which brought Jackson to power this specious distinction tended to disappear. Editors worked as hard in the canvass as political speakers and asked for the same rewards. Jackson complied with their requests, showing his favor for the profession by appointing Amos Kendall, a Kentucky editor, an auditor in the treasury department and taking him for one of his confidential advisers. The objection to such appointments was strongest with the Virginians, long attached to the traditions of official propriety. Their disappointment reached the President through several sources, most notably in a letter from Ritchie to Van

[1] John Pope to Jackson, February 19, 1829, Jackson Mss.

Buren.[1] But the protests did not change his attitude. He believed he was right, and he justified himself in a long letter from which the following is an extract:

You will recollect that in the recent political contest it was said, and truly said, to be a struggle between the virtue of the American people and the corrupting influence of executive patronage. By no act, by no solicitation of mine, and apart from any interference of myself, did the people in their kindness, present me as their candidate. The different presses of the country acting upon their own impulses, espoused one side or the other, as judgment or other cause operated. Those who stept forward and advocated the question termed the side of the people, were a part of the people, and differing only in this that they were the proprietors and conductors of the press — in many cases purchased by themselves expressly for the purpose of aiding in the "grand cause." And to what motive other than the love of country and the exercise of a sound judgment could their course be ascribed? I was not abroad seeking popularity, nor did I trammel or commit myself by pledges to remove partisans in the event of success. No one has ever accused me of doing so, and hence we are bound to believe that they were disinterested in their support of me. Many maintained and believed, and especially the politicians of the country, that no efforts of the people, would be found sufficient to counteract the subsidizing influence of government. Upon this ground then, whatever motive could arise founded on self, was of a character to invite chiming in with the powers that were then in existence. Yet many editors did not, and hence can we resist the impression that they were actuated by the same generous and patriotic impulse that the people were?

If these suggestions be founded in truth, why should this class of citizens be excluded from offices to which others, not more patriotic, nor presenting stronger claims as to qualification may aspire?

[1]Van Buren to Jackson, March 31; Jackson to Van Buren, March 31, 1829; Jackson Mss. Ritchie to Van Buren, March 27; W. S. Archer to Van Buren, May 6, 1829; Van Buren Mss. Jackson to J. Randolph, November 11, and J. Randolph to Jackson, November 22, 1829; Jackson Mss.

To establish such a precedent would I apprehend, have a powerful tendency to place the control and management of the press into the hands of those who might be destitute of principle; and who prosecuting their profession only as means of livlihood and lucre, would become mercenary, and to earn their penny would abandon principle, which ought to be their rule of action.

The road to office and preferment, being accessible alike to the rich and the poor, the farmer and the printer, honesty, probity and capacity constituting the sole and exclusive test, will I am persuaded, have the happiest tendency to preserve unimpaired freedom of political action; change it and let it be known that any class or portion of citizens are and ought to be proscribed, and discontent, and dissatisfaction will be engendered. Extend it to editors of papers, and I re-iterate, that men of uncompromising and sterling integrity will no longer be found in the ranks of those who edit our public journals. I submit it then, to your good sense and calm reflection, what must be the inevitable result of things in this country, when the press and its freedom shall become so depressed and degraded as to be found altogether under the control of men wanting in principle and the proper feelings of men?[1]

This letter, the draft of which exists in Jackson's own hand, well illustrates his grasp on political matters. The naïveté with which he passes judgment on the motives of the editors measures his manner of estimating his supporters. His indifference to the influence of the dignified classes appears in his readiness to accept the editors as equal advisers and supporters. His belief in the people as the source of political authority and his confidence in his own cause appear in all the phases of the letter. It marks him as an honest, credulous, determined, uninformed, and uncompromising leader of a democratic upheaval, a man who does not hesitate to put into force a new idea through fear of violating established procedure.

Later in his administration he was surrounded by skilled

---

[1] Jackson to Z. L. Miller, May 13, 1829, Jackson Mss.

observers of human nature and they were able to protect him from too ready confidence in impostors; but in his first days this defense was not established, and the effect was sometimes bad. It was notably so in the case of Samuel Swartwout, an adventurer who came seeking any office which might offer. He had facility and assurance, beneath which the credulous President was not able to penetrate. He carried off one of the best prizes in the government, collector of the port of New York. The position controlled the appointment of many subordinates, it involved the handling of much money; and it had an important relation to the merchants of the greatest importing city in the country. Through the custom of taking the bonds of the merchants to secure deferred payments of duties, large discretion was left to the collector; and he ought to be a man of sound business judgment. Measured by any of these needs Swartwout was not a success. He had no experience, he had not the confidence of the business men of the city, he was an inveterate speculator, and he considered office an opportunity to make money. He was well known in New York, and Van Buren opposed his appointment. But Swartwout had won Jackson's confidence and had petitions numerously signed. As some of the New York congressmen were for him and the senators did not work against him, he carried all before him.

In making this appointment Jackson's personal feeling went against the recommendation of every friend who ought to have had influence in the matter. Ingham, in whose department the New York collectorship lay, was against it. Cambreleng, a congressman from the state, wrote: "If our collector is not a defaulter in four years, I'll swallow the treasury, if it was all coined in coppers."[1] The assurance which enabled Swartwout to win Jackson made him a popular official and for a while he

[1]Van Buren, *Autobiography*, 70-82; Cambreleng to Jackson, April 15, Van Buren to Dudley, April 20; *Ibid* to Cambreleng, April 23, 25, and another letter of the same month, but without date to Cambreleng and Bowne—1829; Charles E. Dudley to Van Buren, April 29, 1829; Van Buren Mss.

got on without difficulty. The President was pleased with this and sometimes rallied Van Buren and the New Yorkers at the failure of their forebodings. But beneath this suave exterior the collector was nevertheless a defaulter. His peculations began in nine months after he entered office and continued until when they were discovered in 1838 they amounted to a million and a quarter.[1]

Jackson's rage when he heard the news was characteristic. The delinquent, who had fled the country, ought, he wrote, to be captured and thrown into prison. Many times the writer advised him not to speculate while a government official and he always promised to follow the advice. "Can he live after this? or will he cut his own throat?" It must be evident to all that Swartwout could not have defrauded the government without the assistance of the United States Bank, and the event, said Jackson, ought to show the country that there should be a complete divorce between banks and the government.[2] His allusions to the matter are innocent of self-condemnation.

Swartwout established in New York the Seventh Ward Bank to help in his personal schemes. It was a political institution and relied on government deposits. In 1834 he desired to get a government deposit and appealed directly to Jackson. Postmaster-General Barry, he wrote, desired a loan from the bank on account of the post-office department and he was willing to accommodate him if fifty thousand dollars of the funds for building the new custom house were placed in the bank. All this he related in a letter to the President,[3] in which was enclosed the following to the secretary of the treasury:

My dear sir: It is so recent that the commission for building the Custom House have received 50,000 Dollars, for that object,

---

[1] Felix Grundy to Jackson, November 13, 1828, Jackson Mss.
[2] Jackson to Blair, January 5, 1839, Jackson Mss.
[3] Swartwout to Jackson, March 8 (1834 or 1835), Jackson Mss.

that they do not wish to press the Department for a further loan. Yet I can assure your excellency, that a draft for another sun of 50,000 Dls. would be of great importance to many of our friends who wd. be infinitely benefited by its use in the shape of Loans, who can not get it out of the Depsts. Banks. This I know. While Millions lay in the vaults of these Institutions, many of which are opposed to us in politicks, this little patriotic Institution is working its way among our friends, loaning all it can to our friends and sustaining the administration by all the means in its power. If, therefore, a further sum of 50,000 Dls. could be placed to the credit of the commission we would place it in that institution, and it would be used, I can assure you, for the benefit of the administration and its friends. Your kind interference might do this for us and we should be infinitely obliged thereby.

The application seems to have been successful; but apart from that, it is discreditable to a President of the United States that he was approachable in such a matter; and that he should have preserved the letter without evidence of displeasure at its contents is at least surprising.

Removals under Jackson are believed to have been very numerous; but the available evidence shows that while they were more than under former Presidents, they were not so many as in later administrations. The newness of the system and the vehemence of party feeling have unduly impressed the imagination of the historian. There were then 612 presidential officers, and only 252 were removed. Of more than 8,000 post-masters and their deputies only 600 met a like fate. Deputy post-masters were not presidential officers until 1836, and they had small salaries; so that changes here may be attributed to resignations or the caprice of the immediate superior quite as readily as to the spirit of the administration.'

Nine months after his inauguration Jackson summed up his view of appointments in his first annual message, saying:

¹Fish, *The Civil Service and Patronage*, 124-128.

There are, perhaps, few men who can for any length of time enjoy office and power without being more or less under the influence of feelings unfavorable to the faithful discharge of their political duties. Their integrity may be proof against improper considerations immediately addressed to themselves but they are apt to acquire a habit of looking with indifference upon the public interests and of tolerating conduct from which an unpracticed man would revolt. Office is considered as a species of property, and government rather as a means of promoting individual interests than as an instrument created solely for the service of the people. Corruption in some and in others a perversion of correct feelings and principles divert government from its legitimate ends and make it an engine for the support of the few at the expense of the many. The duties of all public offices are, or at least admit of being made, so plain and simple that men of intelligence may readily qualify themselves for their performance; and I can not but believe that more is lost by the long continuance of men in office than is generally to be gained by their experience. I submit, therefore, to your consideration whether the efficiency of the Government would not be promoted and official industry and integrity better secured by an extension of the law which limits appointments to four years.

In a country where offices are created solely for the benefit of the people no one man has any more intrinsic right to official station than another. Offices were not established to give support to particular men at the public expense. No individual wrong is, therefore, done by removal, since neither appointment to nor continuance in office is matter of right. The incumbent became an officer with a view to public benefits, and when these require his removal they are not to be sacrificed to private interests. It is the people, and they alone, who have a right to complain when a bad officer is substituted for a good one. He who is removed has the same means of obtaining a living that are enjoyed by the millions who never held office.[1]

Jackson's extreme democracy made him oblivious to the dangers from partisan appointments. He saw the evils of

---

[1] Richardson, *Messages and Papers of the Presidents*, II., 448.

long terms when incumbents were selected on personal grounds; but he was incapable of understanding how his own system would bring greater inefficiency. His assertion that all men could easily learn to perform the duties of the public offices was palpably false, and experience quickly proved it. There was as much dishonesty among his own appointees as among their predecessors and as much inefficiency. George Bancroft, himself a democrat, who had business to transact with the treasury department in 1831, said: "Talk of reform! The departments are full of the laziest clerks, and men are paid large salaries for neglecting the public business."[1]

The permanent effect of this change has often been pointed out. Although it was, as just stated, an out-growth of forces beyond Jackson's control, it received from the capricious nature of many of his selections an exaggerated viciousness which was apparent to his best supporters. Even Marcy, supposed to have had no conscience about bad appointments, declared privately that Jackson made many "mis-appointments"; and Gideon Welles said the President allowed himself "to be importuned" into "very improper" selections. Welles added: "Office seeking and office getting has become a regular business where impudence triumphs over worth."[2]

From what has been said it is evident that while the spoils system was a development in connection with the general evolution of democracy, Jackson did not try to check its progress but facilitated it. His removals were not as numerous as those under many later Presidents. President Cleveland, elected as a reformer, and acting under the pressure of party organization, removed many more.[3] It was in the nature of the case that the system should appear in connection with the forces which ruled public life at the time. Any man who could have been an

---

[1]Howe, *Life of George Bancroft*, I., 197.
[2]Marcy to Van Buren, February 12, 1838; Welles to *Ibid*, April 27, 1838; Van Buren Mss.
[3]Dewey, *National Problems*, 35-39.

exponent of the democratic movement would probably have believed as Jackson believed in regard to appointments.

The group who advised with Jackson in making the cabinet continued to surround him after the inauguration and furnished the beginning of what came to be known as the "Kitchen Cabinet." Its membership varied from time to time; but W. B. Lewis, Amos Kendall, and A. J. Donelson, the President's private secretary, were generally in it. But Donelson was independent and was usually opposed to the Eaton-Lewis interest.[1] Van Buren was included also, but he was a member of the regular cabinet part of the time and his advice was probably on large matters rather than on the general affairs which are supposed chiefly to have engaged the attention of the "Kitchen Cabinet." Eaton was a member until he left Washington in 1831. Duff Green may have been admitted to council in the earliest months of the administration, but he could not have had a full membership. After the *Globe* was established in 1830, F. P. Blair, its editor, was a regular member.

The influence of this group was believed to be great. Jackson might well be sensitive on the point, since it tended to belittle him. "In regard now to these complaints," he said to John Randolph, "and others of a similar character founded on a pretended distrust of *influences* near or around me, I can only say that they spring from the same false view of my character. I should loath myself did any act of mine afford the slightest color for the insinuation that I followed blindly the judgment of any friend in the discharge of my proper duties as a public or private individual."[2]

---

[1]Van Buren, *Autobiography*, III., 189; Van Buren Mss.
[2]Jackson to Randolph, November 11, 1831, Jackson Mss.

CHAPTER XXII

"THE EATON MALARIA"

THERE were better phases of Jackson's presidency than adopting the spoils system. We may have varying degrees of commendation for his attitude toward internal improvements, his destruction of the United States Bank, his introduction of vigor into our foreign relations, his prompt disposal of the Indian question in Georgia, and his opposition to nullification in South Carolina; but his course in regard to each has a defense which satisfies many fair minded men. This more attractive side of Jackson now lies before us; but before it can be considered another chapter must be given to party intrigue. An unpleasant episode here intervened and was utilized by the masters of the two factions in the party in such a way that it become an important historical event.

"The Eaton embroglio," says Van Buren, was "a private and personal matter which only acquired political consequences by its adaptation to the gratification of resentments springing out of the formation of the cabinet, and, as was supposed, to the elevation or depression of individuals of high position."[1] As Van Buren himself was one of the individuals referred to, his statement has peculiar interest. Abundant evidence has been given to show how much the Calhoun-Van Buren rivalry was present in making the cabinet.[2] It persisted after that event, and as Eaton was active in the interest of the secretary of state and the ladies who refused most strongly to receive Mrs. Eaton

[1]Van Buren, *Autobiography*, 47; Van Buren Mss.
[2]See above, II., 410-418.

were associated with the friends of Calhoun, the matter was presented to Jackson as a conspiracy against Eaton by the Calhounites, and the presidential wrath which resulted was used to break down the vice-president's position in the party. Similar intrigues are found in the history of other nations; and they usually exist there, as in the case before us, in a circle which surrounds some ruler whose powerful will is not restrained by calm judgment.

When Eaton arrived in Washington in 1818 to become a senator he became a boarder at the tavern of William O'Neil, an Irishman whose ready wit made him popular among members of both houses of congress. "Peg O'Neil," daughter of the host, was growing up into a dashing young woman whose rather free manner won her the disapprobation of the best society. Disagreeable stories were told about her, and they did not cease when she married Timberlake, a dissipated purser in the navy. He was frequently absent from home for long periods, during which she remained with her father and saw much of the boarders. It seems to have been during this period that her name and Eaton's began to be associated. History can have no object in proving that these persons did wrong: it is only essential to remember that many people of the day believed it. In 1828 Timberlake committed suicide at sea. Some said it was because of his own dissipation, others that it was from humiliation at the conduct of his wife. The following New Year's Day, Senator Eaton, intimate friend and party manager of the now triumphant Jackson, married the widow in Washington. His best friends felt that it was an unfortunate step.[1] Official society was already shocked at the crudeness of the manners of the new party: they were not willing

---

[1]"Poor Eaton is to be married tonight to Mrs. T——! There is a vulgar saying of some vulgar man, I believe Swift, on such unions — about using a certain household...[sic] and then putting it on one's head."— Cambreleng to Van Buren, January 1, 1829, Van Buren Mss. Cf. the following; "This is as they say, to beray the panier, and then put it on your head."—Montaigne, *Essays*, (Temple Classics), V., 109.

to tolerate in addition a person whose reputation was assailed by common rumor.

Eaton's promotion to the cabinet was unpopular on the political side. Many Tennesseeans disliked him, and the delegation in congress protested to Jackson himself. Judge White, the other senator, would have been more readily received as the man most worthy of recognition from the state. Eaton and Lewis were brothers-in-law, and both were committed to the cause of Van Buren. "No man," said Lewis long afterward when speaking of the New Yorker, "exerted himself more in his behalf than I did, or stood by him with more unshrinking firmness in the darkest hour of his political existence."[1] In the controversy over the treatment of Mrs. Eaton he was Jackson's personal adviser. Many of the letters in the affair are copied in his own hand. He was living in the President's mansion in close personal relations with Jackson. There can be little doubt that he stimulated the old man's suspicion and resentment and gave them a turn against the Calhoun faction. His manner of making himself feared by the office-seekers is seen from a protest of Gen. R. G. Dunlap, an outspoken Tennesseean who long had acquaintance with the most prominent men in the state. "His only importance," wrote Dunlap to Jackson with the freedom of an old friend, "is that by his hinting impudence when out of your presence, of being in the Prest [President's] confidence he assumes the mark of an adviser. This holds you responsible for his silly conduct."[2] But the protest was futile, and Lewis kept his position of confidential adviser in small matters.

The announcement that Eaton would be in the cabinet brought protests from many people in Washington. Jackson heeded them not: he said he welcomed the opposition, that he felt happier

---

[1]Lewis to Jackson, August 30, 1839, Mss in possession of W. C. Ford.
[2]Dunlap to Jackson, June 30, 1831, copy in Library of Congress.

in a storm, and that he would not abandon his friend.' But his determination did not improve Eaton's position in the city. "To-night," says a writer who could speak for society, "the bosom friend and almost adopted son of General Jackson, is to be married to a lady whose reputation, her previous connection with him both before and after her husband's death, has totally destroyed. She is the daughter of O'Neal who kept a large tavern and boarding house. . . . She has never been admitted into good society, is very handsome and of not an inspiring character and violent temper. She is, it is said, irresistible and carries whatever point she sets her mind on. The General's personal and political friends are very much disturbed about it; his enemies laugh and divert themselves with the idea of what a suitable lady in waiting Mrs. Eaton will make to Mrs. Jackson. . . . We spent the evening at Dr. Simm's last night. All present were Jacksonians — Dr. Simm the most ardent and devoted. He had lately received a letter from Gen'l. J. which he promised to show me. I wanted to see it immediately, suspecting, as I told him, if he deferred showing it, it would be with the intention of correcting the orthography. He laughed and joked on the subject very good naturedly and about Mrs. Jackson and her pipe in the bargain."[2]

At the time this letter was written Mrs. Jackson was in her grave and Mrs. Andrew J. Donelson, wife of the private secretary of the President, was designated for mistress of the official household. She was a woman of strong and placid character, competent to sustain the dignity of the station, and by no means disposed to tolerate the kind of woman Mrs. Eaton was reputed to be. Her husband was not strong for the Eaton-Lewis influence. He resented their methods and re-

[1]J. A. Hamilton to Van Buren, February 23, 1829, Van Buren Mss.
[2]Mrs. Smith, *First Forty Years of Washington Society* (Hunt, Editor), 252. Like many women of the frontier, Mrs. Jackson smoked a pipe.

belled when he felt that political faction was to be made to cover social impropriety. He was more emphatic than his wife in regard to the Eatons.[1]

At the first official functions Mrs. Eaton was received with studied indifference by the wives of other cabinet officials. If they were in the same receiving party with her, they ignored her presence; if they were at dinner with her they spoke not; and all that Jackson could do to show his favor brought her no more consideration than at first. "With the exception of two or three timid and rather insignificant personages, who trembled for their husbands' offices," says our informant, "not a lady has visited her, and so far from being inducted into the President's house, she is, I am told, scarcely noticed by the females of his family."[2] The supporters of Adams and Clay observed this situation with pleasure and were willing to make it as unpleasant as possible. Observing their actions Jackson came to believe that all the trouble which fell on Eaton was designed by Clay. A few weeks later he thought the trouble began with Eaton's enemies who, despairing of office as long as the secretary of war had influence, wished in this manner to overthrow him. It was some months later when Jackson attributed the "conspiracy" to Calhoun.[3]

The storm burst on Jackson soon after the inauguration. Rev. J. M. Campbell, pastor of the New York Avenue Presbyterian Church at which the General and Mrs. Jackson formerly worshiped, felt impelled to remonstrate with him. He was a young man and did not dare approach Jackson himself, but got Rev. Ezra Stiles Ely, of Philadelphia, an old friend and correspondent of the President then in attendance on the inauguration, to promise to make the protest. Doctor Ely did not find an opportunity to do this in the capital, but on his return to his

---

[1]Van Buren, *Autobiography*, 189, Van Buren Mss.
[2]Mrs. Smith, *First Forty Years of Washington Society* (Hunt, Editor), 288.
[3]Jackson to ——, April 26, 1829, Jackson Mss.

home wrote at length, reciting the stories reported against Mrs. Eaton. Jackson's reply was characteristic. His correspondent did not know, he said, that the stories alluded to sprang out of Clay's contrivance and were circulated to blacken the writer through his friend. As for Mrs. Eaton he believed her a chaste and maligned woman, and his departed wife had believed her above reproach, and nothing short of absolute proof would convince him to the contrary. There is no record that Jackson ever changed an opinion once formed, whatever the proof offered to him. Now committed in this quarrel he remained till the end of the unhappy struggle firm on the side of what he thought injured honesty. "This," he said, "was a righteous course founded upon the principles of that gospel, which I not only profess to believe, but do religiously believe."[1] "I told them," he wrote to another, "I did not come here to make a Cabinet for the ladies of this place but for the nation, and that I believed, and so I do, that Mrs. Eaton [is] as chaste as those who attempt to slander her."[2]

The inner circle of the administration party desired to keep the affair out of politics, but their opponents forced it forward. Jackson's wrath could be counted on, and it was fair game to stimulate it to his own ruin. The Van Buren group also realized the opportunity it gave them to injure Calhoun; and so both forces coöperated to deepen the scandal.

During the spring and summer of 1829, Jackson, thoroughly bent on restoring the reputation of Mrs. Eaton, sent to various parts of the country to get evidence which would support his views. Finally on September 10th, when the affair had stewed for six months, he summoned the cabinet for the consideration of the matter. All the evidence he had collected was submitted to it and two of the chief accusers of Mrs. Eaton were brought

[1]Jackson to Mr. S.—New York, September 27, 1829, Jackson Mss.
[2]Jackson to————, April 26, 1829, Jackson Mss.

forward to testify in person. One of them remarked that he believed Eaton innocent, when the President exclaimed, "And Mrs. Eaton also!" The other replied, "On that point I would rather not give an opinion"; at which Jackson exclaimed, "She is as chaste as a virgin!" The second accuser desired to be heard, explaining that he had not meant to arraign the administration but to save it from discredit. He began to argue against the sufficiency of the evidence produced in support of the wife of the secretary of war, when Jackson sharply reminded him that he was summoned to give evidence and not to pass upon it. With this the meeting dissolved, the cabinet-members going away in a rather disgusted mood, and Jackson remaining satisfied with the investigation in which he played the parts of advocate and judge.[1]

But poor Mrs. Eaton's postition was no better than formerly. Mrs. Calhoun was against her; the ladies of the cabinet — even Mrs. Branch and Mrs. Berrien, whose husbands were brought into office through Eaton's influence, in order to weaken Calhoun — were all against her; the White House ladies were firmly of the same opinion; and some of the women of the diplomatic corps were as defiant as the American ladies. Society was rent in twain, and some prominent men left their families at home rather than encounter the perils of entertaining socially.

Van Buren was a widower, and thus had a rare opportunity to increase Jackson's friendship for him. He gave a dinner at which the slighted lady received from him every mark of respect. He called on her and in other ways showed his confidence in her. Through his influence Sir Charles Vaughan, the British minister, who was also unmarried, came to treat her with consideration. The two men with the President formed the centre of the Eaton party. At this time Van Buren was thrown into intimate relations with his superior in office. They

[1]Parton, *Life of Jackson*, III., Chapter 18.

rode together daily, breakfasted together frequently, and exchanged views on most matters of governmental policy. But the secretary was too shrewd to refer to the bearing of the affair on his own case. Jackson later absolved him from any attempt to promote it as a means of defeating his rival.

By autumn, 1829, the situation in official society was acute. During the spring the government was newly organized and during the summer society was chiefly out of the city, so that there was no obligation to entertain officially. Until November no cabinet dinners were given, Jackson fearing that the ever present discord might embarrass them. But private entertainment was waiting, according to custom, on official hospitality, and people were remarking the condition into which society was drifting. The President and his secretary conferred and invitations were sent forthwith for a cabinet fête. All the members attended with their wives at the appointed time, which pleased the chief. He assumed his most courteous air and took out to dinner Mrs. Ingham, who was entirely committed to the insurgents. Van Buren took Mrs. A. J. Donelson. Both men tried to make the dinner table a scene of mirth; but they failed signally. They could make no impression on the stolid faces of the company, where rebellion was written on every feature. At length the company departed, leaving a sore and disappointed host. The occasion, as the secretary put it, was "a formal and hollow ceremony."

Next came, by regular usage, the dinner of the secretary of state. Whether in politics or society Van Buren was a good diplomatist, and he used all his ability to make his dinner a success. He expected, and he said as much to Jackson, that the opposition, unwilling to oppose the President openly, would take this as the occasion to show their hand, and that the cabinet ladies would decline to attend. With this in view he invited to the dinner Mrs. Randolph, a daughter of Thomas Jefferson, and caused it to be known that the event was in a sense given in her honor. Her presence would repair the loss of prestige if all the cabinet wives were absent. His anticipations were correct: Branch and Ingham came to dinner, but their wives declined. Eaton and Barry also came, but their wives acting together remained at home. Berrien, the remaining member, had an engagement out of town. But Mrs. Randolph was present and charmed the company by her distinguished manners, and the dinner passed off very successfully.

Soon afterward the Russian minister, Baron Krudener, also a bachelor, gave a ball to the cabinet. As Mrs. Ingham was absent he took in Mrs. Eaton, next in rank in the cabinet precedence, and to Secretary Eaton fell Madame Huygens, wife of the Dutch minister. At this the Dutch lady was greatly offended and expressed her chagrin openly, and refused to remain in the dining-room when she saw she was to sit by Mrs. Eaton. She declared, so it was reported, that she would give a ball to which the upstart would not be invited, and Mrs. Branch, Mrs. Berrien, and Mrs. Ingham were said to have promised to do the same.[1] The report, whether true or not, made a great impression in the city. The inner White House circle pronounced it conspiracy to crush Mrs. Eaton, and since it could not be attributed to Clay it was laid at the doors of the vice-president, or his friends. When, a few days later, an anonymous letter appeared in a city paper attacking Van Buren for trying to force an objectionable woman on good society it was taken as confirmation of the charge. It was about this time that the intrigue was made to operate against Calhoun.

In the meantime, Mrs. Eaton made no progress. Entertainments in private houses were generally denied to her, but she continued to attend public affairs throughout the early winter. At last she was the object of such contempt at a ball

---

[1] These events are described in Van Buren's *Autobiography*, III., 186-213, Van Buren Mss.

on January 8, 1830, that she could no longer expose herself
to the chance of further indignity, and she began to remain
at home.¹

Jackson was now deeply angry. He felt that his will was defied, and this touched him in the most sensitive spot. One
morning before breakfast he summoned Van Buren, who found
him in a state of excitement. His eyes were bloodshot and he
admitted that he slept none the preceding night. He announced that he had come to a fixed determination as to his
course in the much discussed affair, that he would investigate
and if the reports of Madame Huygens's threat were true he
would send her husband back to Holland and dismiss the cabinet
for conspiring to bring him into contempt. Van Buren sought
to quiet him. If there was a conspiracy, he said, the proposed manner of dealing with it was entirely proper, but he
doubted if the Dutch lady made the threat attributed to her,
and he offered to find out if she was guilty. He called on Huygens, with whom "as a brother Dutchman" he was on terms
of friendship, and from both him and Madame Huygens secured such a plain denial of the alleged conspiracy that the
President was satisfied.

But Jackson was not reassured. It was not his nature to
submit to defiance, and Washington was plainly in arms against
him. The rebels were women, safe from his vengeance, but
he undertook to reach them through their husbands. Late
in January he again summoned the secretary of state and showed
him a paper he proposed to read to the cabinet. The visitor
objected that the paper did not say clearly enough that Jackson
had no intention of interfering with the domestic affairs of his
advisers, and he suggested that it be read to the cabinet and not
sent to them in writing.² The suggestion was followed, and

¹Mrs. Smith, *First Forty Years of Washington Society*, (Hunt, Editor) 311.
²Van Buren, *Autobiography*, III., 209-212, Van Buren Mss.

Ingham, Branch, and Berrien were summoned to an interview which Jackson described as follows:

Several members [of congress] came to me and after reporting these facts [in relation to the alleged conspiracy], asked if I intended to permit such an indignity to be offered to me unnoticed: I assured them I would not, and that I would call for explanations from them. I therefore sent and had an interview with these Gentlemen. I informed them of the information I had recd of the combination from the members of congress, and the plan having been carried into execution and that I had sent for them for explanation and enquiry whether the information I had recd was correct. When we met I read them the following statement:—

The personal difficulties between some of the members of my cabinet have assumed an aspect and received a bearing in regard to myself which requires an expression of my personal feelings. To prevent future misunderstandings I have deemed it expedient to have this interview with Mr. Ingham, Mr. Branch, and Mr. Berrien. When we met I said to them (Mr. Ingham, Mr. Branch, and Mr. Berrien)[1] that the course pursued by them to Major Eaton and his family as reported to me, was in my opinion, under the circumstances not only unjust in itself but disrespectful to myself. The grounds upon which this opinion is founded are substantially these:

I do not claim the right to interfere in any manner in the domestic relations or personal intercourse of any member of my cabinet nor have I ever in any manner attempted it. But from information, and my own observation on the general course of events I am fully impressed with a belief that you and your families, have in addition to the exercise of their own undoubted rights in this respect taken measures to induce others to avoid intercourse with Mrs. Eaton and thereby sought to exclude her from society and degrade him. It is impossible for me on the fullest and most dispassionate view and consideration of the subject to regard this course in any other light than a wanton disregard of my feelings and a reproach of my official

---

[1]The text has been followed literally. It is not always in direct quotation.

conduct. It is I, that have without solicitation or design on his part called Major Eaton into my cabinet, and it is I, that with the fullest conviction of the injustice of the imputations which as I firmly believe malice and envy have cast upon his wife continue him there. If her character is such as to justify active measures on the part of the members of my cabinet to exclude her from virtuous society it is I who am responsible to the community for this alledged indignity to the public morals. I will not part with Major Eaton from my cabinet and those of my cabinet who cannot harmonize with it had better withdraw, for harmony I must and will have. It is in vain to attempt to disguise the true aspect of the question, and it is not in my nature to do so if I could; nor can I consent to harbor any feelings toward those with whom I am in the habit of daily association without distinctly expressing and apprising them of these opinions. My whole life has been at variance with such a course, and I am too old to practice it now. I must cease to respect myself when I find I am capable of it. Therefore have I sought this interview, to assure you that if there be any truth in the report that you have entered into the combination charged, to drive Major Eaton from my cabinet that I feel it an indignity and insult offered to myself, and is of a character that will remain hereafter to be condemned.[1]

On this paper Jackson endorsed:

This was read to them, and being informed by the gentlemen that as far as their influence went, it was exercised differently, and their wish was to harmonize the cabinet, I determined not to dismiss them.

But he sent them away with the suggestion that they "arrange their parties in the future so that the world should not get this impression"; i. e., the impression that they were determined not to recognize the Eatons.

"The Eaton Malaria," as Van Buren aptly called it, was

[1]The memorandum quoted exists in Jackson's own hand. Several copies of it are in the Jackson Mss. See also Jackson to Eaton, July 19, 1830, Jackson Mss. For Berrien's account of the affair, see Niles, *Register*, XL., 381-384 and *ante*.

now come to its most noxious stage. Washington gossip talked of nothing else, public business halted, and there was general expectation that the cabinet would be reorganized. But some calm head, it could hardly have been Jackson's, worked for restraint. The paper read to the cabinet members suggests two explanations, in each of which there is probably some truth. In one sense it was an expression of an egotistical man's sense of indignity at being thwarted in his will; in another it may well have been presented to the three gentlemen in the hope that through a sense of resentment or propriety they would resign their positions. When the wrath of the President abated somewhat and the rebuked officials did not resign, the situation became slightly less strenuous. The administration would have welcomed their withdrawal, but it was not willing to assume the responsibility of disrupting the cabinet on such grounds. It was extremely doubtful if even Jackson's popularity could at this time stand the odium of dividing his party to serve an intriguing favorite.

The culmination of this quarrel marks also a change in the President's relation to the city in which he was now the leading citizen. At his arrival he was much talked about. In spite of what his enemies said of his policy and capacity, his character remained unimpeached. People had a feeling of sympathy for the frank and brave old man, now burdened by domestic afflic- tion, whose shortcomings sprang chiefly from neglected oppor- tunities. Mrs. Smith, an intimate friend of Clay's family and wife of the president of the branch of the United States Bank, wrote: "I think I shall like him vastly when I know him — I have heard a number of things about him which indicate a kind, warm, feeling and affectionate heart.— I hope sincerely he may get safely over the *breakers* which beset his entrance into port, and when in — God grant the good old man a safe anchorage in still waters." A year later the same writer was entirely in sympathy with the opposition. "Altho' I sincerely believe him to be a warm, kind-hearted old man," she wrote "yet so passionate and obstinate, that such a subserviency must be very galling and hard to bear. In truth, the only excuse his best friends can make for his violence and imbecilities, is, that he is in his dotage."[1]

Mrs. Eaton's withdrawal from social functions relieved somewhat the acuteness of the situation. The cabinet went on without open friction, but still without cordial coöperation until in the following year it was reorganized by the resignation of a part and the dismissal of all the rest of the members but one.

Major Eaton's friends speak of him as good-natured and able. In Washington he was undoubtedly popular, and but for his wife's controversy he might have maintained himself in the party he did so much to organize. Spite of the loyal support of his chief, success was now impossible. Moreover, the controversy embittered his temper and made him a host of enemies and was, through the plans of his wife, shifted to Tennessee, where he had opponents also. In the summer of 1830 the couple were in that state. Jackson was there, also, to spend a vacation. The preceding hot season he passed at the Rip Raps, a pleasant islet which the government owned in Hampton Roads; but now he returned to the "Hermitage," doubly dear by reason of its association with his departed wife. The old scenes brought a revival of his sorrow and increased his feeling of loneliness; for the all pervading controversy had divided his own household.

In the "Hermitage," scowling and bemoaning the ingratitude of those for whom he had done so much, he heard that the Eatons were coming to the state capital and that the leading society there were determined not to receive them. He aroused himself instantly; the travelers were invited to make a visit to his home, and preparations were made to give the affair all

---

[1]Mrs. Smith, *First Forty Years of Washington Society*, (Hunt, Editor), 285, 321.

possible éclat. His own connections, that is to say, Mrs. Jackson's relatives, were divided by the controversy, but steps were taken to bring them together so that the family should not appear to be inharmonious.

All eyes turned to the "Hermitage," and Jackson's friends in the Tennessee towns through which Eaton must pass arranged dinners which must satisfy the utmost vanity of the visitors. The Nashville banquet was to be especially distinguished, but many people, some of them leading democrats, refused to attend. To Jackson this was conspiracy — a part of the Washington conspiracy, he said. It seemed essential to have a more successful reception at his home, and this could not be done unless the Donelsons were united. To secure such union he appealed to General Coffee, next to himself the most prominent member of the connection. That gentleman labored hard and patched up a truce, by which all parties agreed to come to the "Hermitage" and show formal respect to its visitors. "My dear Major," now wrote the host to Eaton with satisfaction, "I send my son to meet you at Judge Overton's, and to conduct you and your lady with our other friends to the Hermitage where you will receive the heartfelt welcome that you were ever wont to do, when my Dr. departed wife was living. Her absence makes everything here wear to me a gloomy and melancholy aspect, but the presence of her old and sincere friend will cheer me amidst the melancholy gloom with which I am surrounded. My neighbours and connections will receive you and your Lady with that good feeling which is due to you, and I request you and your Lady will meet them with your usual courtesy."[1] Thus outward peace was restored, while beneath the surface were still bitterness and war.

With the coming of autumn the storm shifted its centre to Washington, but there was no yielding on the part of "the

---

[1] Jackson to Eaton, August 3, 1830, Jackson Mss.

conspiracy." In fact, it laid a firmer hold on its object by depriving him of A. J. Donelson, on whose services he was much dependent. Mrs. Donelson, presiding over her uncle's establishment, received Mrs. Eaton as her uncle's guest, but she would not call on her. This finally irritated Jackson so much that he gave his niece the option between yielding or leaving the White House. She chose the latter, and nephew and niece went back to Tennessee. The lonely old man was deeply hurt and voiced his despair as follows:

If my family and professed friends had remained faithful to me, and the great interests of their country, instead of falling into the trap of the great intriguer Mr. Calhoun, how much better for them, and gratifying to me. They have decided and withdrawn from me. I rest upon providence and the good sense of the people for my support, and I am sure it is the best. The only thing to be regretted is, I am thrown upon strangers, who I have to rely [sic], instead of those I took great pains in educating that they might be a comfort and aid to me, in my declining years. I have hitherto had sufficient energy to pass thro' any and every difficulty that presented, and I still trust that a kind providence will not forsake me in the severest trouble.[1]

In September, 1831, Donelson and his family returned and peace again ruled in the mansion,[2] but at this time the Cabinet was renewed, and the source of discord was happily removed from the city. Jackson said he hoped they came "with all those feelings which ought at first to have accompanied them hither. They know my *course and my* wishes, and I hope they come to comply with them."[3]

In these later stages the "Eaton Malaria" runs into the Calhoun quarrel and the general party upheaval which accompanied

[1]Jackson to Rev. H. M. Cryer, May 20, 1830, *American Historical Magazine* (Nashville), IV., 234.
[2]W. B. Lewis to Van Buren, September 17, 1831, Van Buren Mss.
[3]Jackson to Van Buren, September 5, 1831, Van Buren Mss.

the steady advance of Van Buren into the position as heir apparent.

Before we consider these things we must know about Jackson's relation to the general political progress in the early part of his administrations.

CHAPTER XXIII

CHECKING THE DESIRE FOR INTERNAL IMPROVEMENTS

THE first congress under President Jackson met December 7, 1829. Andrew Stevenson, a Virginia republican, was chosen speaker of the house by the votes of 159 of the 194 members present. His following represented all who opposed Adams and Clay, and most of it would probably have gone for the new President had he favored the old Monroe policies. But Andrew Jackson had his peculiar support and he was going to have his peculiar policies. Out of them sprang the historic democratic party, whose birth may well be placed at this period. It was Jackson's vigorous personality and the advancement of Martin Van Buren which drove this dividing wedge into the older organization. Clay gathered up as far as he could all the riven fragments and united them with what was left of the Adams-Clay following, with an eye to the election of 1832. The group which grew out of his efforts became the whig party.

The new cabinet was approximately representative of the combined interests which voted for the victor, but the new policies were chiefly dictated by one section of the cabinet. Monroe and Adams and their predecessors treated the cabinet as a council of state, which adopted policies on the initiative of the President. Many of Jackson's wisest supporters desired him to follow the same practice, since that would give the more experienced men in the party an opportunity to modify the course

475

to be pursued. But he decided otherwise.[1] A short
time after the inauguration he ceased to call cabinet meetings.
Heads of departments he treated as high administrative officers,
and the consideration of policies was left to informal consultations with those intimate friends in whom he had confidence.
He tended to reduce the cabinet to the rank of administrative
subordinates.[2] After the reorganization of 1831 he showed
less of this purpose. He consulted freely in reference to the
removal of the deposits. But when his mind was made up on
an important affair he was apt to override cabinet opinion.

The first annual message contained both old and new ideas.
Of the former were its recommendations that internal improvements ought to be undertaken but by some means which would
be constitutional and which would not create discord among
the lawmakers, that the public debt ought to be paid, and that
the Indians should not be allowed to set up a state within the
jurisdiction of Georgia. Two other principles must have disappointed the strict republicans, although they were calculated
to please members of the party who supported the national
program which Calhoun had favored. They were: (1) That
free trade is desirable, but since "we must ever expect selfish

---

[1]Among the Jackson Mss., without date, but classified as of October, 1828, is a "memorandum of points
to be considered in the administration of the government." It is in Jackson's hand and reads: "Mr. R——
R——, Virginia: 1st A strong constitutional attorney-general.

"2nd   A genuine old-fashioned cabinet to act together and form a councel consultative.

"3rd   No editors to be appointed.

"4th   No members of Congress, except heads of Departments or Foreign Ministers, to be appointed.

"5th   No foreign missions to be originated without the Senate &c &c.

"6th   The Public Debt paid off, the Tariff modified and no power usurped over internal improvements.

"7th   A high minded enlightened principle on the administration of the govt. as to appointments
and removals. These things will give a brilliant career to the administration."

  I cannot think this paper contains Jackson's own views.   It seems to have been a memorandum he made
for his guidance in summing up the views of another man.   The line at the top, "Mr. R — e R — Va," suggests Ritchie, editor of the Richmond *Enquirer*, whom Van Buren in writing to Jackson the following spring
called the most influential editor in the country. He spoke for the Virginia faction and was heard far and wide.
There is no evidence that he visited the "Hermitage" before the inauguration, but the summary of his views
could have been made by Jackson after an interview with some intermediary, or as a deduction from Ritchie's
editorials. The second and third points of the memorandum are clearly contrary to Jackson's opinions, which
would make it improbable that the paper was intended to record his ideas.— J. S. B.

[2]For a good discussion of Jackson's relation to the cabinet, see MacDonald, *Jacksonian Democracy*, 226.

legislation in other nations" we must continue "to adapt our own to their regulations," that the existing tariff had brought neither the ills nor the benefits predicted for it and should be modified, and that all sections "should unite in diminishing any burthen of which either may justly complain";[1] and (2) That the surplus revenue after the debt was paid should be distributed among the states. Calhoun, in common with all who opposed a high tariff, objected to distribution because by diminishing the surplus it lessened the need of tariff reduction, but many of his older followers in the Middle States and the West gave it hearty support. Another recommendation, although it rested logically on old republican principles, was in its practical import essentially new and was destined to become the most characteristic measure of the democratic party in its early phase. It referred to the United States Bank and said that in the opinion of the President it was not too soon to consider the recharter of the institution and that it was certain that some of the objects for which the bank was founded were not accomplished.

Jackson took his immense popularity for approval of his policy, and he was right in doing so; for although his military reputation brought him before the people, the feeling that he represented them and could be trusted to act for them served to sustain him in his long period of public life. He considered his own ideas the people's ideas. No President kept a more watchful eye on congress to see that they did not violate the will of the people. Excluded from congressional halls by custom, through friends he kept well informed of all that transpired there. Either A. J. Donelson or Major Lewis was usually there and made quick report to the chief. Thus the leader added to the ordinary feeling of party loyalty the force of a mild terror, increasing the coherence of his own party and embittering the attitude of his opponents.

---

[1]Richardson, *Messages and Papers of the Presidents*, II., 442.

The house was tractable but the senate was otherwise. The removal of officials particularly displeased it. It debated for some time a resolution questioning the President's power of removal; but the practice was too long established to be overthrown. The senate showed displeasure by rejecting some of the nominations and by making others appear so dubious that they were withdrawn by the President. One of the unfortunates was Isaac Hill, of New Hampshire, a relentless champion of democracy in whose newspaper the most cruel things were said about the enemies of Jackson. The senate refused to confirm his nomination and he went back to New Hampshire in a rage. He soon had his revenge. Levi Woodbury, a senator with higher ambitions, was induced to resign his seat and, in 1831, Hill came back to Washington as senator-elect in his stead. When the cabinet was reorganized in the same year Woodbury's self-denial had its reward. It pleased Jackson and the whole administration party to see him whom the dignified upper chamber thought unfit for second comptroller of the treasury taking at the behest of the people a seat in the very body which rejected him. But the senate had too much respect for the President's popularity to embarrass him with many rejections. Later, when feeling ran higher, they were not so considerate of his wishes. Daniel Webster correctly described the situation in saying: "Were it not for the fear of the outdoor popularity of General Jackson, the senate would have negatived more than half his nominations. There is a burning fire of discontent that must, I think, some day break out. When men go so far as to speak warmly against things which they yet feel bound to vote for, we may hope they will soon go a little further."[1]

There was undoubtedly discontent in the party, but Jackson's courage and strength were to prove sufficient for its control.

---

[1] Webster, *Private Correspondence*, I., 501.

It was excellent strategy to force Hill on the senate as a vindication of his nomination and as a way of letting the world see how General Jackson could make himself obeyed. The world was going to see in a few years many similar illustrations of his capacity for political command.

Some of the signs of discontent came from followers of Calhoun. They did not relish Van Buren's steady march into presidential confidence, and Duff Green's columns revealed their cooling ardor. Jackson urged Green to write more incisively, saying with his usual plainness that congress was giving itself chiefly to president-making. The editor showed his pique in his reply. How could he defend the administration's policies unless he knew what they were, he said. Since the cabinet met no longer to consider policies of government, no one felt authorized to defend a measure as an expression of party purpose.[1] Green's reply had much truth in it, but it made no impression on Jackson. The influence of Van Buren steadily increased and through it an issue was made in this very session of congress which, while it struck openly at Clay, dealt Calhoun a severe blow in a less obvious way. It was the veto of the Maysville Road Bill, which checked the impulse for roads and canals at national expense, a measure on which rested much of the South Carolinian's strength.

Calhoun was most prominently identified with internal improvements, one of the movements for domestic development which became popular after the war of 1812. He was responsible in 1817 for the bill to use for this purpose the bonus of the Second United States Bank, which Madison vetoed on constitutional grounds. Accompanying the veto was a suggestion that the constitution be amended to allow the expenditure of money for public improvements, but nothing came of it. The people of the Northwest were especially anxious for roads and

---

[1]Cited by Parton, *Life of Jackson*, III., 277.

canals; they were not able to construct them by private enterprise, the new state governments were not rich enough for
the task, and they turned to the national government. Pennsylvania, through whose territory lay the route to the West
most talked about, also supported the movement. Besides
these, a few people everywhere believed that the government
should undertake such works. Federalists supported the movement as it suited their interests rather than from principle, it
seems, since New England, the centre of federalism, but already
supplied with roads and somewhat equipped with canals, went
strongly against the measure.

Madison's veto did not end the agitation. Military roads
were from the first favored by a larger number of people than
non-military roads; and there was now disposition to place the
whole movement on that basis. Resolutions were passed asking
the secretary of war, Calhoun, to report a system of such internal improvements as were necessary to the public defense.
He complied willingly and in 1819 submitted a comprehensive
plan which he said would be "among the most efficient means
for the more complete defense of the United States." But he
was careful to add that the work should not be authorized
unless it was considered constitutional and that he did not enter
into that phase of the question.[1] The report served for propaganda, as was doubtless intended, and three years later the
feeling for roads and canals was still stronger. Both principle
and local interest combined to make a majority for it in congress.
The strict republicans, with the Virginia leaders at their head,
viewed this growth of opinion with alarm, and Monroe was
not sorry for an opportunity to give it a check. He made a
bill to collect tolls on the Cumberland road serve as an occasion.
In vetoing it on May 4, 1822, he submitted his "Views on the
Subject of Internal Improvements," a historical discussion of

---

[1] *American State Papers, Miscellaneous*, 534.

the question from the constitutional standpoint; and he added that there should be an amendment to permit the construction of roads and canals.[1] This document was well received by the strict republicans, and Jackson wrote its author in terms of warm commendation for its principles.

Nevertheless, the subject would not down. In 1824 a bill was passed to authorize a survey of such transportation routes as were necessary to the commercial, military, and postal needs of the country Monroe approved the bill on the ground that it was in the province of congress to ascertain what was needed in this nature. The execution of the task fell to Calhoun, still secretary of war. The series of roads and canals which he now recommended was large enough to offer something to every important section of the union. It embraced: (1) A canal from Washington to the Ohio to be extended later to Lake Erie; (2) An inland waterway along the Atlantic coast from the Potomac to Boston harbor; and (3) A road from Washington to New Orleans. Calhoun added that there were other improvements which, while not essential, were "deemed of great importance in a commercial and military view." They were canals connecting the Savannah, Alabama, and Tennessee Rivers, the James and the Kanawha, the Susquehanna and the Allegheny, the St. Johns in Florida with the Gulf of Mexico, and the St. Lawrence with Lake Champlain. Nor was this all: in due time other routes were recommended, as a road from Baltimore to Philadelphia, another from Washington to Buffalo, the extension of the Cumberland Road to the capital of Missouri, and a canal from Lake Pontchartrain to the Mississippi. This survey was defended on the ground that it would be an intelligent suggestion for the expenditure of private and state funds. The strict republicans opposed it on the ground that it sought to combine the interests of all parts of the union in

[1]Richardson, *Messages and Papers of the Presidents*, II., 142, 183.

a congressional majority large enough to override a presidential veto. It was undoubtedly calculated to whet the popular desire for internal improvements. Jefferson and his Virginia followers declared with dismay that this tendency was irresistible.[1]

Of the candidates for the presidency then before the country, Clay, Adams, and Calhoun were openly for internal improvements and they were willing to avoid constitutional objections by trusting to a favorable interpretation of the right of congress to establish post roads, or to regulate interstate commerce, or to provide for the public defense. Calhoun's constitutional position was not quite so clear as Clay's and Adams's, probably because of South Carolina's trend to strict construction. Jackson also favored internal improvements when they could be shown to contribute to the military safety of the nation. But he held some decided opinions about state rights, and it could be foretold how he would act if the matter were robbed of its military significance.

Only Crawford, of the five candidates, was clear in his opposition to the policy, and when he was eliminated by illness there was much discouragement among those who thought that the government should not play into the hands of politicians who stimulated the demands of interested voters. The election of Adams and his combination with Clay made it seem probable that this policy would gain rapidly in the country. On the other hand drawing Crawford, Calhoun, and Jackson into the opposition gave strength to those who objected to internal improvements. Van Buren was strongest in the combination and sought to carry it over to the strict republican view. December 20, 1825, he introduced a resolution denying the power of congress to construct roads and canals, but the senate left it unnoticed.

[1]*Writing of Jefferson* (Memorial Edition), XVI., 140.

While no great work of internal improvement was authorized under Adams, smaller works, roads and harbors, were ordered to the extent of more than two millions, which was two and a third times as much as was spent for the same purposes under all the preceding Presidents. Each appropriation stimulated the demand for others, and the success of the Erie Canal, completed in 1825, seemed to add confirmation to all favorable prophecies. There was undoubtedly a strong tide running for public improvements at the close of this administration, held back only by the factious quality of the opposition to Adams. But with the advent of a new President other results seemed likely.[1]

Jackson's views of the constitution were formed through feeling rather than intellect. They were formed in the early school of Monroe and Randolph, and although he voted for military roads and for the systems of surveys of 1824, he was likely to come over to the opposition when shown that it took the same position as the party to which he gave his first allegiance. The veto of 1822 served such a purpose. "My opinion has always been," he wrote to Monroe, "that the Federal Government did not possess the constitutional right; that it is retained to the states," and that in time of war the national authority may repair roads and control them but must surrender them when peace returns.[2] In the first draft of the inaugural address, however, he showed that he was carried away by the Western sentiment, saying that internal improvements, when not of an entirely local character, should be built by the national government. When the address had gone through the hands of prudent advisers in Washington it merely declared that "internal improvements and the diffusion of knowledge, so far as they can be promoted by the constitutional acts of

[1] Turner, *Rise of the New West*, 224-235, 286-288.
[2] Jackson to Monroe, July 26, 1822, Jackson Mss

the Federal Government, are of high importance." In his first annual message he came again to the subject and said that the surplus revenue after the debt was paid should be divided among the states in proportion to population for internal improvements. The old method of distribution by congress directly he said was bad, meaning, as it seems, on account of the jobbery in applications. He did not appear to realize that distribution to the states would largely transfer this jobbery from congress to state legislatures. But even here Jackson guarded himself by saying that if the constitution would not allow the suggested course an amendment should be submitted to the people to secure the desired permission.[1]

Van Buren, apparently, was sincerely opposed to the policy of internal improvements. He voted for some of the earlier bills, but Monroe's veto put him to thinking, and he concluded that the policy was both dangerous and unconstitutional.[2] Afterward he opposed it as opportunity offered but noticed that it gained continually in public opinion. He at length decided that nothing could stand against it but Jackson's popularity; and he determined to try to bring that to bear. As early as possible after he entered the cabinet he discussed the matter with the President.

The two men proved to be at one in the matter. A careful consideration showed that they felt it necessary to check the course of public opinion, and it was agreed that the secretary should keep his eye on congress and report to the President when a bill was being debated which seemed proper for veto. The design was kept quite secret by the two men, which was ever Van Buren's inclination in regard to contemplated actions. In politics he liked to move quickly and unexpectedly on an adversary.

---

[1]Richardson, *Messages and Papers of the Presidents*, II., 451.
[2]Van Buren, *Autobiography*, III., 149, 152-158; Van Buren Mss.

Affairs in Pennsylvania at that time made it a delicate thing to oppose internal improvements. The state was largely committed to that policy both because any direct approach to the upper Ohio must pass through its bounds, and because a number of wealthy contractors in Philadelphia were actively agitating at the national capital and among the people at large in behalf of appropriations, from which they expected to reap large profits. They had strong influence with the state politicians and controlled a number of newspapers. Beside this, the Quakers, a numerous body of voters, were already displeased at Jackson because he favored the removal of the Cherokees in Georgia; and if he had any definite plans against the United States Bank he must have realized that he would need, in order to carry them through in Pennsylvania, the home of the parent bank, all possible popularity in that state. These various things were duly considered by Van Buren, but he concluded that the President's popularity was enough to overcome even these difficulties and Jackson, agreeing to take the responsibility, it was determined to go ahead with the program.

April 26, 1830, McDuffie, of South Carolina, was in the midst of a stately speech on the inequalities of the tariff. At the end of two hours he paused and said that he had now submitted the dry and less interesting part of his argument, that the remainder would be more pleasing, and that with the permission of the house he should like to discontinue at that time and conclude the next day. He was indulged, and Fletcher, of Kentucky, suggested that the rest of the sitting be given to some minor bill that could be passed in a short time and moved a consideration of the bill to subscribe to the stock of a road from Maysville, Ky., to Lexington, in the same state. Then in the most confident tone he explained that the Kentucky legislature had incorporated the company to build and operate the road, that while it was within the state entirely, it was part of what would be a great national road when completed, and that by taking stock in so promising an enterprise the government could not lose its investment. He spoke briefly and was followed by a Georgian who was surprised that Fletcher should fancy the bill would have no opposition. It was essentially a local bill, and it precipitated a debate which ran through three days before the house passed it by a vote of 102 to 86. The senate debate on the measure is lost but it passed that body safely and went to the President about May 20th.

The Maysville Road was as local as any important road within a state could be. It was in the state in which Clay lived and the bill was supposed to be a kind of challenge from that gentleman, both of which facts, it seemed to Van Buren, would appeal to the President. As soon as the house approved the measure he mentioned it to Jackson in one of their daily rides on the Tenallytown road. He offered to submit reasons — which he had already prepared — why the bill should not become a law. The offer was accepted, and the paper which was handed over was kept for five days without intimation of the President's opinion on it. Jackson then announced his entire acquiescence and asked the secretary to prepare a statement of the constitutional grounds on which a veto might rest. This kind of a document had also been previously prepared in anticipation of such a request, and it was duly handed to the head of the government. Van Buren also suggested that if a statement of the national finances were made it would show that there was not enough money in the treasury to pay the due proportion of the national debt, provide for the expenses of government, and support internal improvements. This suggestion was followed also.

The bill represented a popular opinion, and a veto needed all possible support. Not one in twenty, says Van Buren, believed that Jackson would venture to reject it, and it was the intention of the secretary of state that they should not know it until the bill was passed. He feared that Clay, if he thought a veto imminent, would drop the bill and bring in another less local and one in which a larger group of people were interested. Jackson at first was for opening the way for the veto by proper editorials in the newspapers and as soon as the plan was settled said, "Give it to Blair," which he habitually pronounced "Bla-ar." But the arch-schemer induced him to conceal his intentions.

In spite of these precautions an inkling of what was coming got abroad, and the Kentuckians were much disturbed. They sent R. M. Johnson, at that time a close friend of Jackson's, to ascertain what he would do. The visitor was given to grandiloquent language, even in private conversation. When he entered the President's office the secretary of state was prudently present. As the visitor proceeded with his argument his language became warm. He said that the state of Kentucky demanded the Maysville Road, and that to veto the bill would defeat the democratic party in the state. "If this hand were an anvil," he exclaimed, extending the left arm with the palm upward, "and a fly were sitting on it, and a sledge-hammer should come down on it like this" — bringing down his right hand with a blow — "that fly would not be more surely crushed than the democratic party in Kentucky would be crushed by this veto."

At this point Jackson, whose interest grew with Johnson's, rose to his feet with an air which meant danger. Had the speaker considered the state of the treasury balance? "No," was the reply. "Well, I have," said the general hotly; and he went on to say that he was elected to pay off the national debt, how could this be done and the proposed internal improvements constructed without borrowing? — and borrow he would not.

The President's fervor disconcerted his interlocutor, who

hesitated and prepared to leave the room. Van Buren watched the scene with deep interest. He feared, he tells us, that Jackson's temper had revealed too much of his purpose and observed to Johnson that he must not think the President's mind was made up, and, in fact, that he and Jackson were just going over the Maysville bill when the visitor arrived. At this Jackson took his cue, changed his tone, and succeeded in restoring the Kentuckian to what Van Buren calls "his accustomed urbanity." Johnson faithfully reported to his colleagues all these occurrences. Then they asked him what he thought Jackson would do with the bill. He replied that in his opinion nothing short of a voice from heaven could prevent "Old Hickory" from vetoing the bill, and he doubted if that could prevent it.

Interest in the outcome was now stronger than ever, but no one cared to risk a second interview with Jackson. They went to Van Buren instead, both friends and opponents of the bill. He had much trouble to keep them from finding out what was to be done; but mysterious silence was one of his peculiar qualifications, and he employed it here so well that he not only deceived the interrogators but even created the opinion that he was opposed to the veto. One of the reasons said to have been given for rejecting him as minister to England in 1832 was that he favored the Maysville Road.

The senate was debating the bill while this was going on, and in due time they gave their assent. The Western states and Pennsylvania now looked anxiously to Jackson. Van Buren was also deeply concerned, and he kept close to the President's side. On the morning the veto was sent to congress, he breakfasted at the White House, Barry, Eaton, Lewis, and Felix Grundy being present also. The others had long faces, knowing what was coming and believing it would damage the party. Jackson was extremely weak from illness, and the secretary of state while assisting him up the stairs remarked that the others seemed alarmed. "Yes," was the reply, "but don't mind that. The thing is here [touching his breast-pocket] and shall be sent up as soon as congress convenes."

The veto was addressed to the house of representatives, in which the bill originated. Its reading was received with severe silence. It not only defeated the Maysville Road, but it challenged the principle of internal improvements. Some of the democrats were alarmed, some were angry, some predicted that the result would be fatal in Pennsylvania and the West, and others saw in it a shrewd electioneering move, worthy of the astute secretary of state. Care had been taken to write the veto so that it would appeal to the largest number of people. Those whose interests would be injured by it were ignored — their opposition was taken for granted; but every possible phase of constitutionality and expediency was exploited to convince the people at large that to appropriate the [national funds for roads and canals was illegal and unwise.

The defeat of the measure pleased the old republicans. They attributed it largely to Van Buren and on it founded a hope that the Western influence would not entirely direct the party. In Virginia a number of them assembled to give John Randolph a parting dinner before his departure for Russia. One of the toasts was, *The rejection of the Maysville Road Bill — It falls upon the ear like the music of other days.* This was drunk standing with three times three cheers. In Pennsylvania the impression was not at first so favorable. A congressman from that state remonstrated with Jackson in person. He was patiently heard and told to say no more until he consulted his constituency. He promised to do this and a short time after he reached his district he wrote to say that the voters endorsed the President.

"The veto,"[1] says Van Buren, "was the wedge which split the party of internal improvements, a party which was 'wielded by a triumvirate of active and able young statesmen as a means through which to achieve for themselves the glittering prize of the Presidency, operating in conjunction with minor classes of politicians, looking in the same general direction, and backed by a little army of cunning contractors." Calhoun, Clay, and Adams had each leaned hard on internal improvements, from them each drew much of his popularity; and the removal of the issue from the field of active politics was a sad blow to each. Clay and Adams could have expected little else, but to Calhoun it gave notice that he was losing position in the democratic party and that his rival was in the lead. The fact that the defeat of internal improvements would weaken Calhoun probably added to the secretary of state's zeal in the matter; although it must be remembered that the advisers from Tennessee, generally opposed to the vice-president, were not now against him, but held back on account of what they considered party expediency.

The Maysville veto was skilfully written. Its purpose was to overthrow a well-rooted popular feeling. An embarrassing feature was that Jackson himself had voted for the survey bill of 1824 and for some other minor bills to construct roads. The document, therefore, must not make him appear inconsistent or seem to despise the popular fancy. Little regard was paid to the opinion of the politicians, for it was believed that they would acquiesce if public opinion could be reached. As to the contractors, they were equally ignored; for their opposition was certain whatever was done against them, and their rage would only serve to show they were speculators disappointed of their profits, and that all Jackson had said about them was true.

[1]Van Buren tells the story of the Maysville veto with full details and with apparent frankness. See *Autobiography*, III., 152-169, Van Buren Mss.

In his argument Jackson emphasized the local character of the proposed road; and while he did not openly dispute the principle of appropriations of this kind, he depicted incidentally many of the evils he thought would come from it. We had gone too far, he said, from the principles of 1798 to take a stand now on the strictest construction of the constitution in regard to appropriations. Jefferson, Madison, and Monroe signed bills to construct roads, and as for Adams, it was well known that he was committed fully to internal improvements. The apparent reluctance with which this was admitted would please the strict republicans, and the willingness to accept things accomplished would please many who held a different view.

What was the principle on which Jefferson, Madison, and Monroe acted? From Madison's and Monroe's vetoes it was seen to be that the government had power to appropriate money for public works which were not local, but whose benefit was to the nation. The Maysville Road was local, and therefore he opposed it. He thus reconciled his argument with his votes in congress all of which he could defend on the ground that they looked to national benefits.

Two principal arguments were added to reconcile the people to a reversal of a policy which evidently was agreeable to them:

1. Certain revenues were pledged to pay the national debt, while congress was then in the very act of reducing duties on certain articles. Yet the demand for expenditures was great: if to the necessary expenses of government were added the appropriations for internal improvements then proposed there would be for the current year a deficit of ten millions. Thus we should have either to give up such appropriations, or abandon the payment of the debt, or increase taxes. But if the money may not be raised now, the people need not be discouraged. The intelligent American people could be trusted to carry this policy through at a time more auspicious than the present.

Let us, however, give all present efforts to extinguish the debt. How much would it not strengthen the national character in the eyes of the world to see a republic founded as an experiment, come successfully through two great wars, prosperous, free from debt, and united in its spirit! How much better was this than "a scramble for appropriations that have no relation to any general system of improvement!"

2. Assuming that congress could by the constitution construct improvements, it was certain that it could not "prosecute" them. But there was so much uncertainty as between the two rights that it was unwise to proceed further until the constitution was amended so as to make its meaning perfectly clear. If the people really desire improvements they will not fail to make such an amendment, which was particularly desirable in order to enable congress to regulate and conduct such improvements without infringing the jurisdiction of the states in which they lay. The Cumberland Road was an example of the evils under present conditions; for years the right of congress to conduct it was questioned, and sometimes funds were voted for that purpose, and sometimes they were refused. All such confusion would be avoided if the people were asked to pass on the subject by a proposed amendment.[1]

Public appropriations for internal improvements have several times been considered by the American people, either in congress or in state legislatures, or in municipalities. There has usually been a well-defined consciousness of the need of such appropriations to secure desired utilities; but practical wisdom has generally halted before the evident danger of jobbery in selecting the works to be constructed or in awarding the contracts. Jackson's allusion to this danger was wise; for the people are slow to trust themselves with the supervision of so

---

[1]Richardson, *Messages and Papers of the Presidents*, II., 483-493.

large a system of expenditures for a purpose in which selfish motives can operate so easily.

From Madison's veto to Jackson's was a period of thirteen years. Holding back internal improvements during that time was fatal to those who hoped to have them through national aid. The movement was already transferring itself to the states. Pennsylvania and the states west of it were particularly extravagant, and the results were repudiation of debt or heavy embarrassments. The Maysville veto undoubtedly turned a large part of this financial waste away from the national treasury.

The congressional elections of 1830 supported the administration, and this was taken as endorsement of the veto. The vehemence with which the opposition denounced that policy during the campaign warrants the assertion that the public had ample opportunity to repudiate it if they had so desired. Van Buren, watching the situation, feared, as he tells us, that the antipathy to improvements would go so far as to include among forbidden things such necessary works as light-houses, fortifications, and harbor improvements. He wanted to get before the public some statement of sound principles which should show what might and what might not be provided.

In order to bring up the question again in a proper way, and to make friends for his policy, he wrote to Madison, living in Virginia at the age of seventy-nine. The Maysville message assumed that Madison's veto of 1817 conceded "that the right of appropriation is not limited by the power to carry into effect the measure for which the money is asked, as was formerly contended."[1] This, as Van Buren reveals in confidence, was a doubtful construction of the early veto, but it was used in the hope of bolstering up the argument of 1830. It was a good point on which to hang a restatement, and probably a modifi-

---

[1] Richardson, *Messages and Papers of the Presidents*, II, 486.

cation of Jackson's position, and he desired to open a correspondence which should give him such an opportunity.

He proceeded cautiously, sending Madison, in the first place, a copy of the veto message with a simple note of personal compliment. As he expected, the eye of his correspondent fell on the questionable allusion to the message of 1817, and a protest followed. The intention of Madison's veto, said the writer of it, was "to deny to Congress as well the appropriating power, as the executing and jurisdictional branches of it," which was the general understanding at the time the veto was delivered.

The situation was now to the liking of the clever secretary. Replying at once he said that the question of internal improvements was not settled, that it would come up again in the future, and the President would be pleased to have his predecessor's opinion on four points: (1) A precise view of the government's power to appropriate money to improvements of a general nature. (2) A rule to govern appropriations for light-houses and harbor improvements. (3) The expediency of refusing internal improvements until the national debt was paid. (4) The strong objection to subscriptions by the United States for stock in private companies.

Madison's reply to the first question was less definite than his interrogator desired. It enumerated certain works on which the government might expend money, declared that discretion ought to be left to the legislature, that funds should be apportioned among the states according to population, but that there were certain objections to this. As for light-houses and harbors, that depended on whether they were local or general, and on how much a given work was local and how much it was general, and each case was to be decided on its merits. The replies to the other two points were equally indefinite: the national debt ought to be paid with all possible expediency, but some conceivable expenditures would take precedence, each to be considered on its own merits; and the government ought sometimes to aid, and sometimes to refuse to aid private corporations. To these categorical statements he appended a general opinion that internal improvements are unconstitutional but that they are highly important when properly selected, which was but reasserting the veto of 1817.[1] Such a response could have given little comfort to Van Buren. It neither supported his contention nor contradicted it so directly as to furnish the basis for an opposing argument. By July, when the reply was written, it was evident that public opinion was so far with the veto that it was needless to say more than had been said. It was good policy to let well enough alone.

But Jackson was too practical to go to extremes. Appropriations for light-houses and harbors were continued, and funds were granted to keep in proper condition certain works already undertaken. For example, the Cumberland Road, which received before the Maysville veto total grants for $1,668,000, received after that event during Jackson's administrations $3,728,000.[2]

A year later Jackson wrote to Kendall: "I wish you to look at the Harbor Bill, and compare it with my veto message on the Maysville Road Bill, and my message to Congress in 1830. I have left in the hands of Major Donelson, Genl. Gratiot's report on the items in the bill, from which you will find that many are local and useless; few that are national. I am determined in my message, if I live to make one to Congress, to put an end to this waste of public money, and to appropriations for internal improvements, until a system be adopted by Congress and an amendment of the Constitution; in short to stop this corrupt, log-rolling system of Legislation." But harbor appropriations continued to be made after the old manner.

---

[1] Madison, *Letters* (Edition 1884), IV., 87-93.
[2] Report of Colonel Albert: See Wheeler, *History of Congress*, II., 124.

The history of the Maysville message illustrates Jackson's relation to his advisers. He could not have written this message; but its significant ideas were his. He could not have planned actions so well calculated to manipulate the situation for his advantage, yet he gave intelligent approval to the plans when made by another and had the courage to carry them through. Moreover, the veto is not far beyond the clause in the draft of the first inaugural where he declared against internal improvements of a local nature. Most of his important policies are found in an undeveloped form in his earlier doctrines.

The Maysville message has an importance in the history of American politics not at first observed. It was the first distinctive measure of the Jacksonian democracy. It marked the complete union of the old Crawford group with the original Jackson men. Finally, it robbed Calhoun of a popular policy and weakened him so much that his enemies dared to proceed to destroy him utterly. How they realized their final plans in this process and the part Jackson took in it is the subject of the next chapter.

CHAPTER XXIV

By 1830 the two factions among those who voted for Jackson in 1828 were well developed. Their rivalry entered into the selection of the cabinet, the Eaton embroglio, the Maysville veto, and the ever-present hopes of the succession in 1832. It was the chief phase of public life in the early years of the administration. If an office-seeker failed to get Van Buren's support he was likely to attach himself to Calhoun, and *vice versa*. Each faction was too strong to yield to the other, and war to the end was necessary. Each was composed of politicians; for the dissension did not reach the mass of voters, who thought of Jackson only. He became the arbiter of the dispute. The last move of the Van Burenites was to excite his terrible anger against their enemy. Before its force no appeal to justice and no revelation of political intrigue was able to stand.

Jackson's friendship for Calhoun was as early as the Seminole affair, which began late in 1817, just as the latter of the two men became secretary of war. It was doubtless stimulated by his hatred of Crawford and Clay. He thought that the secretary of war supported him when the other two would censure him for invading Florida, and while on his way to Washington to defend himself in that matter he gave for toast at a dinner, "John C. Calhoun — an honest man the noblest work of God." Calhoun did not entirely deserve this confidence; for in the earliest cabinet councils on the matter he said that the leader of the Florida invasion ought to be disciplined for violating orders. Jackson knew nothing of this, and Calhoun allowed him to remain uninformed. He seems to have been a little in awe of the fiery Tennesseean.

In the campaign of 1824 Jackson favored either Calhoun or Adams before he himself was announced as a candidate. The alliance between his and Calhoun's groups was probably arranged by their respective lieutenants without much aid from the principals. Letters exchanged by the two men at infrequent intervals do not mention any such bargain. Jackson wrote with his usual directness, but Calhoun was apt to show a nervous attempt to please, as though his position was unpleasant and involuntarily taken. "I would rather have your good opinion," he wrote in 1821, "with the approbation of my own mind, than all the popularity which a pretended [?] love of the people, and a course of popularity hunting can excite." "I find few with whom I accord so fully in relation to political affairs as yourself," he wrote in 1823.[1] Calhoun was not naturally uncandid, and he must have found it hard to flatter. He was very ambitious and bowed before the Jackson wave through the hope that he might at last ride on its top. The health of the Tennesseean was exceedingly bad, and he openly declared for only one term: it was a fair prospect for him who could hope for the succession. Very few letters between the two men are preserved for the period from 1824 to 1829, but all obtainable evidence shows that personal relations between them were friendly. Jackson knew of the opposition of his particular supporters to the South Carolinian, but he did not give himself to it. Party harmony was essential in the campaign and in the first months of the new administration.

Calhoun seen from a distance was a man after Jackson's own heart. He had courage, vigor, and candor; and these qualities won the Tennesseean. But closer contact showed a man who was cold, correct, and intellectual, a public man of

---

[1]Calhoun to Jackson, March 7, 1821, and March 30, 1823, Jackson Mss.

the old Virginia manners, and one who could not bend to the will of a leader. If he had won the friendship of the Tennessee group in 1825, before they gave themselves to another, his future would have been different.

The course of Duff Green was another disturbing factor. Brought from Missouri to Washington in 1826 to establish the *Daily Telegraph*, he attached himself to Calhoun's interests. He was rash, arrogant, and turbulent. He made it clear that Calhoun was to have the succession, as though he would frighten off other aspirants; and in many ways irritated the opponents of the South Carolinian. January 17, 1828, he announced Jackson and Calhoun as the republican ticket, seeking to commit the party and to defeat those members of it who at that moment were scheming to bring forward De Witt Clinton. This was borne patiently throughout the long fight against Adams and in the early years of the first administration, and he received his reward in the lion's share of the public printing; but the stronger grew the opposite faction the less willingly they gave him the position of editorial oracle. His paper reflected the change of temper: when Jackson in the winter of 1829–30 chided him for not defending the policies of the government, he replied that he was no longer informed of those policies.[1] A more facile man than Green would have been better suited to his chieftain's purposes. On the other hand, one must remember that the Jacksonian democracy was organized in Jackson's own spirit of absolute leadership. From an editor who served it military obedience was demanded. If Green would not give himself to the cause body and soul he must give place to some one who was more obedient.

It does not appear when the anti-Calhoun faction began to urge Van Buren for the succession. They concentrated on De Witt Clinton for vice-president in the winter of 1827–28 and

---

[1] Silas Wright to Van Buren, December 9, 1828, Van Buren Mss.

had he lived he might have become a formidable antagonist of the South Carolinian. But his death in February, 1828, left the opposition headless. Many of them were for Van Buren before this, but he was not taken at once for the vacant position. He was little known in national politics, he was closely associated with Crawford whom many Jackson men hated, and he was unpopular through having the reputation of a shrewd manipulator. As a member of cabinet he commanded great respect, but he was not in 1828 the man to defeat Calhoun for second place in the administration.

You are now the "master mover" in Washington: "take care to be so." Thus wrote in substance Dr. Thomas Cooper, March 24, 1829, in recognition of Van Buren's preëminence in the cabinet. We have seen the prediction fulfilled. He not only managed his department with credit; but he saved the administration's prestige in social matters, he steered himself safely through the dangers from the "Eaton malaria," he brought the President to support the old republican view of internal improvements, and he made himself the most trusted friend of Jackson and the glorified hero of the "Kitchen Cabinet." While he thus advanced, his rival, Calhoun, was steadily falling into disfavor with the President.

The first noticeable rift in the relation between Jackson and Calhoun occurred in 1826. In that year some of Jackson's enemies criticized his defense of New Orleans, and a friendly paper in Tennessee replied with the countercharge that Monroe, then secretary of war, did not support him fairly in that military expedition. It was at this time that Jackson became involved in the controversy with secretary of the navy, Southard, over the latter's assertion that Monroe saved the New Orleans campaign from failure.[1] This touched the feelings of Monroe who undertook to refute the editor of the Tennessee newspapers.

---

[1] See above, II., 396.

He wrote to Senator White, of that state, offering to submit documents in substantiation of his assertion that he gave all possible aid to the operations in Louisiana. White was reassured in a measure and showed the letter to Jackson, who passionately pronounced Monroe guilty of deception.

While this affair transpired some unknown hand brought Calhoun into it. Sam Houston, then a Tennessee member of congress and in full sympathy with the anti-Calhoun faction, got possession of a letter from Monroe to Calhoun, written September 9, 1818, in which the President told his secretary of war what should be done with the invader of Florida. It showed that neither of the two men approved that invasion, which was contrary to Jackson's understanding of their attitude at the time. Houston sent the letter to the "Hermitage," where the effect was decided. "It smelled so much of deception," said Jackson, "that my hair stood on end for one hour."[1] He was then warm against Monroe, which was some protection to Calhoun. He thought that the latter caused the matter to be revealed to him to show how false was the former.

It has never been explained how this letter was taken from Calhoun's possession. He was conscious that a letter had been purloined, but had no description of it until nearly a year later, when he learned that it was in Jackson's hands. The mischief-maker, who sprung the trap in February, 1827, evidently wished to leave the men most concerned without a chance to explain. Calhoun now approached White and Eaton, saying that if the letter in question was Monroe's of September 9, 1818, it was written, as he knew, with friendly intent to the general. The latter was forced to acknowledge the date of the letter, and Calhoun placed in the hands of the intermediaries a long correspondence between himself and Monroe, and those gentlemen

[1] Monroe, *Writings* (Hamilton, Editor), VII., 93, 104. Jackson to H. L. White, February 7, 1827, March 30, 1828, Jackson Mss.

professed themselves satisfied.[1] They could have no object
in discrediting Monroe, no longer a factor in politics, and the
vice-president's reputation with Jackson had suffered the
first taint, which was all that the plotters could expect at that
time.

Toward Monroe the attitude of Jackson was frigidly dignified,
but to the South Carolina statesman he was formal and courteous. He was, as Calhoun himself said, a man of "good sense
and correct feelings, when not under excitement." He had
been unwisely left in ignorance of the ancient division in the
cabinet and he was naturally shocked when undeceived. While
he froze toward the ex-President, he was excessively polite
toward Calhoun. If the latter, so he wrote to White, claimed
that the letter was stolen from him, it should be returned.
Two months later he wrote directly to the vice-president in
full explanation of his position in 1818, expressing himself in a
restrained manner, entirely worthy of a public man.[2]

In the meantime, Crawford, ill enough to be put out of politics
and well enough to try to mar the hopes of his old enemies,
took a hand in the attack on Calhoun, whom he pronounced a
burden on the ticket. White and Felix Grundy, to whom he
revealed his plans, gave little heed, but he proceeded to scheme.
He made up his mind that Macon, of North Carolina, ought
to be vice-president and to that end wrote letters to prominent
men in all the states outside of New England. He tried to get
Van Buren to carry New York for Macon, but that wily leader
would not range himself openly against his antagonist. Crawford was very bitter and worked unrelentingly. He asserted
that if Calhoun could be defeated for second place on the ticket
he could be kept out of the cabinet of the new President. "I
will myself," he said, "cause representations to be made to

---

[1] Calhoun, *Letters* (Jameson, Editor), 254. See also Calhoun to Jackson, July 10, 1828, Jackson Mss
[2] Jackson to White, March 30, 1828; *ibid* to Calhoun, May 25, 1828, Jackson Mss.

General Jackson that will prevent his being taken into the cabinet of General Jackson."[1] It seems evident also that Lacock, an opponent of Jackson, knew in 1819 of Jackson's much-discussed letter to Monroe, asking for permission to invade Florida, and it is not likely that Crawford left him in the dark in regard to other features of the situation.[2]

Both Crawford and Van Buren were in correspondence with Alfred Balch, who lived near Nashville and worked against the Calhoun supporters in Tennessee. The election of 1828 was hardly over when he wrote to the New Yorker that the two factions in the state were already organizing with an eye to the succession. Two years earlier, he said, he began to recruit for Van Buren there, and his success was remarkable. He added, " J^n appears to be well but (entre nous) he is wearing away rapidly. It is strange, but it is as true as holy writ, that already J$^{n's}$ successor is as much spoken of as J$^{n's}$ late success."[3]

After the inauguration both sides held themselves in restraint, not wishing to embarrass the common cause; but when congress convened in December there were many opportunities for misunderstandings, and the Eaton affair as well as the rise of Van Buren in presidential confidence heightened the tendency. Calhoun was clearly losing ground and his opponents were more sure of themselves. It began to be reported that his friends would like to see the general discredited so that they would seem the most capable element of the party. Calhoun denied the charge, saying: "So far from opposing, we may appeal with confidence to the proceedings of both Houses to prove, that our support has been more uniform and effective that any other portion of congress. It is an object of ambition with

---

[1]Crawford to Van Buren, December 21, 1827, and October 21, 1828; Van Buren to Crawford, November 14, 1828; Van Buren Mss. Crawford to White, May 27, 1827; and Grundy to Jackson, November 20, 1828; Jackson Mss.

[2]Parton, *Life of Jackson*, II., 553.

[3]Van Buren to Jackson, September 14, 1827; Balch to Van Buren, November 27, 1828; Van Buren Mss.

us to carrry the General through with glory; and while we see with pain every false move, we have never permitted our feelings to be alienated for a moment. Ours is the position of honest and sincere friendship, and for us a perfect contrast to that pursued, in the quarter to which I allude."[1]

Another important fact in this connection was the rise of nullification. This movement sprang up in South Carolina without the aid of Calhoun, but in 1829 it had full possession of the state and he gave it his powerful support. From its inception it had Jackson's opposition, as will be shown in the proper place; and it, therefore, furnished another means utilized by the surrounding circle, to turn him against the vice-president.

The spring of 1830 brought the first preparations for the coming congressional elections. With it came revived talk about the next presidential contest, and one of the matters of speculation was the possibility of Jackson's accepting a second term. All the anti-Calhoun element desired such an event, well knowing that Van Buren could not take first place from the South Carolinian in an open field. They probably had little difficulty to induce the leader to agree with them on this point, although there is no positive evidence on the matter; and they turned themselves to the business of disposing of Calhoun. Their reliance was on the secrets of Monroe's cabinet when it met to consider Jackson's invasion of Florida in 1818. They proposed to create rupture between the two men and the month of May was the time when it seemed best to bring it about.

On the twelfth of that month, the very day they put the final proofs into Jackson's hands, Calhoun wrote as follows:

My true position is to do my duty without committing myself, or assuming unnecessary responsibility, where I have no control. The times are perilous beyond any that I have ever witnessed. All of the great interests of the country are coming

---

[1]Calhoun, *Letters* (Jameson edition), 272.

into conflict, and I must say, and with deep regret I speak it, that those to whom the vessel of state is entrusted seem either ignorant, or indifferent about the danger.   My great ambition is to see our country free, united and happy, and placed where I am, I owe it as a duty to myself and country to preserve unimpaired the public confidence.   Thus acting, the first step is to postpone all questions as to myself, till it becomes necessary to decide, and the one to which you refer among the others:[1] when the time comes it will present a grave question, to be decided wisely only by weighing fully considerations for and against.

I consider it perfectly uncertain, whether General Jackson will offer again or not.   Some who regard their own interest more than his just fame are urging him to offer, but it will be difficult to reconcile the course to his previous declarations, unless there should be the strongest considerations of the public good to justify him.[2]

On the following day the writer of this letter received formal notice from the President that hostilities were begun.

What was Jackson's attitude toward Calhoun before this time? It is difficult to say, but there is strong circumstantial evidence that he was already determined to repudiate him.   Lewis's position goes far to show as much.   "You cannot but recollect, General," he wrote in 1839, "that before your installation into office even, I had several conversations with you upon the subject, and importance of looking to Mr. Van Buren as your successor for the same office.   From that time to the day of his election I spared no pains, but exerted every honorable effort in my power to accomplish that object."[3]   Van Buren himself says that Jackson was against Calhoun before May, 1830, but that it was late in the same year when he first told the New Yorker that he was to be successor.   Moreover, knowledge of Calhoun's position in 1818 came to Jackson gradually, and was so clearly

---

[1] I. e., the succession.
[2] Calhoun, *Letters* (Jameson edition), 272.
[3] Lewis to Jackson, August 30, 1839, Mss. of W. C. Ford, Boston.

delayed for the critical moment that we wonder if the President could have been entirely ignorant of the earlier stages of the matter.

The story of the breach of relations, so far as can be gathered from available evidence, is as follows: Col. James A. Hamilton, of New York, old supporter of Crawford and friend of Van Buren, attended the celebration of the anniversary of the Battle of New Orleans, January 8, 1828. He joined General Jackson's personal party at Nashville and went down the river with them, winning the general by his ready tongue and political standing until he was taken into the bosom of the family. He became very intimate with Major Lewis, with whom he had much in common. The two men played their game so openly and persistently that they disgusted some of the general's older and more disinterested friends.[1]

Hamilton offered to use his influence to bring Crawford to support Jackson and proposed to return north by way of Georgia, in order to talk with the old chieftain. He and Lewis discussed the differences between the two men, and the latter said that Jackson thought Crawford wanted to court-martial him in 1818. Jackson was approached and gave such preliminary overtures as were necessary to effect a reconciliation.

At Milledgeville, Ga., Hamilton found that Crawford was absent from home for a fortnight. Deciding not to wait, he unburdened himself to Forsyth, then governor, who undertook to see the absentee and write the result of the effort. In due time a letter came from the governor saying that Crawford was friendly and that he avowed that it was Calhoun who favored the punishment of Jackson in 1818. Hamilton kept the letter and says he told Lewis nothing about it, but it is hardly to be thought that so important a piece of in-

[1] R. G. Dunlap to Jackson, August 10, 1831, Copy in Library of Congress. Also in *American Historical Magazine* (Nashville), IX., 93. Also Van Buren, *Autobiography*, IV., 27, (Library of Congress, Transcript)

formation was allowed to lie dormant in the hands of Calhoun's enemies.

April 3, 1828, Lewis, in Nashville, heard that his daughter was ill in Philadelphia, and set out the next day to visit her. He went through Washington, which, if he traveled the usual route by Pittsburg, must have been out of his way, and learned there that his daughter was better. Incidentally he met Van Buren for the first time. In Philadelphia he was completely reassured as to his daughter, "and," he adds, "as I was anxious to get back home I hurried on to New York, which, never having visited, I desired to see." There he was shown Forsyth's letter to Hamilton. He was surprised at the contents but did not mention the matter to Jackson when he returned to Tennessee. He feared that the general, whose feelings were then highly wrought up over the attacks on Mrs. Jackson, might break into some explosion which would injure his chances of election. The letter was concealed more than a year.

So far the plausible Lewis; but there is reason to suppose that the affair did not proceed quite so properly. On the boat which carried Jackson to New Orleans for the celebration of 1828 was Gen. R. G. Dunlap, old friend and a comrade in the Seminole war; and he was not a politician. He told what he saw and heard on the boat, not for publication but to Jackson himself for his information. He said that Hamilton spoke to him of his proposed visit to Georgia and continued: "He then stated that it was believed that General Jackson was to be assailed either by Mr. Adams or Mr. Monroe in relation to the affair of the Seminole War in Florida, and that some of the General's friends (stating that he and Major Lewis had talked about the matter) believed that Mr. Crawford could give evidence growing out of Mr. Monroe's Cabinet councils which would vindicate the General against such an attack." After saying this Hamilton went on to express doubt of Calhoun's loyalty to Jackson. Dunlap gave him little comfort, saying he cared not what Calhoun felt in 1818 if he would only act fairly now. "I felt a contempt," he said to Jackson, "which I had tried to suppress for several days for the conduct of some of your suite, whom, I believed, were feeding your fears and passions with a view exclusively to fasten themselves on your kindness." He was so much chagrined that with General Smith and Colonel Martin he agreed to leave the party in New Orleans and stop at another hotel; but they were dissuaded by Houston, lest Jackson's friends should seem to be divided.[1] From this it is evident that Hamilton knew while still on the Mississippi what Crawford would say to him; and if that be true it goes far to show that the visit to Milledgeville, which plays so central a part in Lewis's general story, was a cut and dried affair to give Crawford a suitable opportunity to launch his secret on its fatal course.

But let us return to Lewis. Through most of the year 1829 Jackson was ignorant of Forsyth's letter, but in the autumn it was thought fit to bring it to his attention, and the means used were worthy of the genius of a man like Lewis. In November Monroe dined with Jackson. Lewis, Eaton, and Tench Ringgold were also present. At the table Ringgold remarked that in 1818 Monroe was the only member of the government who favored Jackson in the Seminole affair. Lewis innocently asserted that Calhoun was said to have been on that side, but the other held to his original statement. When the guests were gone Lewis and Eaton remained. Jackson called for his pipe and fell into a reverie, the two others talking between themselves as he smoked. Was Eaton not surprised, said the ingenuous Lewis, at what Ringgold said? Then the general, catching the drift of things, started up asking what Ringgold had said. Lewis told him, but Jackson said there was some mistake.

"I replied," says Lewis, "I am not sure of that."

---

[1] Dunlap to Jackson, August 10, 1831, copy in Library of Congress.

"Why are you not?" inquired the general.

"Because I have seen a letter written eighteen months ago, in which Mr. Crawford is represented as saying that you charged him with having taken strong grounds against you in Mr. Monroe's cabinet, but in that you had done him injustice, for it was not he, but Mr. Calhoun, who was in favor of your being arrested, or punished in some other way."

Jackson now demanded to see the letter from Forsyth, and Lewis hurried to New York to get it; but Hamilton objected that it ought not to be surrendered without the consent of the writer. It was then agreed that as Hamilton and Forsyth would both be in Washington at the approaching session of congress, the matter might be left in suspense until then.   But the Georgian, on his arrival, insisted that Crawford's original statement be secured, to which Jackson agreed.   So says Lewis; but there is an unexplained lapse of time in the affair: congress convened on December 7th, Forsyth, who was a senator, took his scat on December 9th, the letter to Crawford was not written until April 16th following,[1] and that was the day after the celebrated Jefferson anniversary dinner.[2]   Crawford's reply, written April 30th, reached Jackson May 12th, and it confirmed everything.

The next day, May 13th, the President enclosed the Crawford letter with a note to the vice-president inquiring frigidly if the statement was true.   Calhoun acknowledged receipt instantly and promised to reply more fully in a short time.   He expressed satisfaction "that the secret and mysterious attempts which have been making by false insinuations for years for political purposes, to injure my character, are at length brought to light." Calhoun had his faults: he was ambitious, unsympathetic, chary of friendship, and willing to follow the tide of popular favor where it counted in his career.   He had tried to ride the

---

[1] Calhoun *Works*, VI., 360.
[2] See below page 555.

Jackson wave, and was about to be submerged by it. In this respect we can have little sympathy for him; but as the victim of the cheap and heartless strategy by which he was now cast out of the political household he awakens our interest. Van Buren, the beneficiary of the plot, is said to have known nothing of it. It is entirely probable. It was a part of the game that he should be ignorant, and at the time he doubtless knew that he was ignorant of it; but he received the cloak of the despoiled victim and wore it in public without shame.

May 29th Calhoun's promise was fulfilled. In a letter, covering twenty-two pages of his *Works* he took up one by one the accusations of Crawford and rebutted them completely, so far as they implied treachery to Jackson. He also made it clear to any impartial man that the charges proceeded from the hatred of him who made them. "I should be blind," he continued, "not to see that this whole affair is a political maneuver, in which the design is that you should be the instrument, and myself the victim, but in which the real actors are carefully concealed by an artful movement. . . . I have too much respect for your character to suppose you capable of participating in the slightest degree in a political intrigue. Your character is of too high and generous a cast to resort to such means, either for your own advantage or that of others. This the contrivers of the plot well knew; but they hoped through your generous attributes, through your lofty and jealous regard for your character, to excite feelings through which they expected to consummate their designs. Several indications forewarned me, long since, that a blow was meditated against me."[1]

The writer could not have expected to convince Jackson at this stage of the affair. Foreseeing that things tended to an exposure he was putting the case as well as possible for that purpose. It was to this end that his letter abounded in fine-

---

[1]Calhoun, *Works*, VI., 362.

spun arguments from which, in fact, he never could escape. They convinced nobody, and the severe terms in which he arraigned the plotters, though well deserved, were futile, both as to Jackson and as to the public. He would have done better to admit his original position in 1818, and to have shown that what he did was in accordance with his sense of duty and without intention of injuring the general. That he had allowed Jackson to remain undeceived through these years was the weak side of his position, and his failure to deal with it gave the latter an opportunity to reply with good effect.

I had been told, said the President in substance, that it was you and not Crawford who in 1818 tried to destroy my reputation. I repelled the charge with indignation "upon the ground that you, in all your letters to me, professed to be my personal friend, and approved *entirely* my conduct in relation to the Seminole campaign. . . . I had a right to believe that you were my friend, and, until now, never expected to have occasion to say of you, in the language of Cæsar, *Et tu, Brute!*"[1] The communication closed with an intimation that the affair would be laid before the public at the proper time.

Now followed a warm correspondence between Jackson, Calhoun, and Forsyth, extending through the summer. The President at last closed it, leaving "you and Mr. Crawford and all concerned to settle this affair in your own way." Calhoun, irritated by this summary dismissal, threw aside all semblance of deference and wrote a scathing denunciation of the whole intrigue. Why should Jackson, he asked, who boasted of his fairness have turned to Crawford, the writer's bitterest enemy, to know what transpired in Monroe's cabinet? The letter was not answered, but endorsed on it in the great slanting handwriting of the President one reads: "This is full evidence of

---

[1] C. Crocker to Scott, March 16, 1826, as follows, "But it was in the spirit of *Et tu, Brute*,"—Lockhart, *Life of Scott* (Riverside edition), VIII., 48.

the duplicity and insincerity of the man and displays a littleness and entire want of those high, dignified, and honorable feelings which I once thought he possessed."[1]

While this correspondence progressed Calhoun received a biting letter from Crawford, with the information that a copy was sent to Jackson also. Its character is indicated by some extracts. "I make no doubt," said the writer of it, "that you would have been very glad to be spared the trouble of making so elaborate a comment upon a letter of three pages. I make no doubt that you dislike the idea of being exposed and stripped of the covert you have been enjoying under the President's wings by means of falsehood and misrepresentation." And again: "A man who knows, as I well do, the small weight which any assertion of yours is entitled to in a matter where your interests lead you to disregard the truth, must have other evidence than your assertion to remove even a suspicion." And finally this: "From the time you established the *Washington Republican* for the purpose of slandering and vilifying my reputation, I considered you a degraded and disgraced man, for whom no man of honor and character could feel any other than the most sovereign contempt. Under this impression I was anxious that you should be no longer vice-president of the United States."[2] The venom of this letter ought to have discredited Crawford as a witness with any fair minded man.

This controversy showed Jackson and his immediate supporters that it was necessary to have another organ than Green's *Telegraph*. Of the latter he said: "The truth is, he has professed to me to be heart and soul against the Bank, but his idol controls him as much as the shewman does his puppits, and we must get another organ to announce the policy, and defend the

---

[1]Calhoun to Jackson, August 25, 1830, Jackson Mss. See also Calhoun, *Works*, VI., 400.

[2]Crawford to Calhoun, October 2, 1830, Jackson Mss. See also Shipp, *Giant Days, or the Life and Times of W. H. Crawford*, 238.

administration, in his hands it is more injured than by all the opposition."[1] Looking around for an editor he hit upon F. B. Blair, formerly a Clay supporter in Kentucky, who had become an advocate of "relief" and "new court" policies, and as such defended Jackson in 1828. Blair was deeply hostile to the Bank of the United States. He was a friend of Kendall, who now urged that he be brought to Washington. He accepted the proposition made to him and on December 7, 1830, brought out the first number of the *Globe*, destined to be the most influential American newspaper of this time. He began without capital, but the administration used its influence and soon got him two thousand subscribers to which was added a share of the public printing. He made an admirable partisan editor. His style was forceful, biting, and uncompromising. Jackson found in him a kindred Western spirit entirely at his service. When Jackson desired to lay a matter before the public he would exclaim, "Send it to Bla-ar," pronouncing the word in the old North-of-Ireland way. Blair, for his part, admired Jackson greatly and with sincerity. From his letters we have interesting glimpses of the President, one of which is as follows:

It is a great mistake to suppose that Old Hickory is in leading-strings, as the coalition say. I can tell you that he is as much superior here as he was with our generals during the war. He is a man of admirable judgment. I have seen proof of it in the direction which he has given to affairs this winter, in which I know he has differed from his advisers. . . . He is fighting a great political battle, and you will find that he will vanquish those who contend with him now as he has always done his private or the public enemies.[2]

Van Buren has long been supposed to have brought on the attack on his rival. Lewis says that neither the secretary of state nor himself played such a part, but that it came about as

[1] Jackson to Lewis, June 26, 1830, Mss. New York Public Library.
[2] *Atlantic Monthly*, LX., 187.

an accident. But it must have been taken with full knowledge of the supporters of the man from New York. When Calhoun's first long statement was received, the letter of May 29th, Jackson was in a violent temper and sent the communication to Van Buren for his opinion of it. The latter read the first page and handed it back to the messenger remarking that it would probably produce a rupture with the President and that it would be better if he, the secretary, could say that he knew nothing of it. When it was returned Jackson asked what his favorite thought of it.

"Mr. Van Buren," said Lewis, "thinks it best for him that he should not read it," and he gave reasons for the opinion. The general smiled and said: "I reckon Van is right. I dare say they will attempt to throw the whole blame upon him."[1]

Long afterward, when the heat of the controversy was past, and Calhoun and Van Buren had gone through the formality of reconciliation, Jackson sent the latter the following statement:

Hermitage, July 31, 1840

DEAR SIR:

It was my intention as soon as I heard that Mr. Calhoun had expressed his approbation of the leading measures of your administration and had paid a visit to you, to place in your possession the statement which I shall now make, but bad health and the pressure of other business have constantly led me to postpone it. What I have reference to is the imputation which has some times been thrown upon you, that you had an agency in producing a controversy which took place between Mr. Calhoun and myself in consequence of Mr. Crawford's disclosure of what occurred in the cabinet of Mr. Monroe relative to my military operations in Florida during his administration. Mr. Calhoun is doubtless already satisfied that he did you injustice in holding you in the slightest degree responsible for the course I pursued on that occasion; but as there may be others who may

[1]For Lewis' narrative, see Parton, *Jackson*, III., 310-330.

be still disposed to do you injustice; and who may hereafter use the circumstance for the purpose of impugning both your character and his, I think it my duty to place in your possession the following sympathetic declaration, viz., *That I am not aware of your ever saying a word to me relative to Mr. Calhoun which had a tendency to create an interruption of my friendly relations with him — that you were not consulted by me in any stage of the correspondence on the subject of his conduct in the cabinet of Mr. Monroe, and that after this correspondence became public the only sentiment you ever expressed to me about it was that of deep regret that it should have occurred.*

You are at liberty to show this letter to Mr. Calhoun, and make any other use of it you may think proper for the purpose of correcting the erroneous impressions which have prevailed on the subject.[1]

This statement was in keeping with Jackson's generosity toward a friend. It was supported by Van Buren's own assertion in his unpublished autobiography. He was too wise a political manager to become involved in a quarrel which related so closely to himself, and which must inevitably be made public.

With the end of this correspondence late in the summer of 1830, there was a lull in the controversy. Calhoun busied himself in getting letters from other members of Monroe's cabinet of 1818, all of whom, except Crawford, gave evidence to support him. Monroe himself made a statement to the same purport. Even R. M. Johnson, a friend of Jackson, gave assurance that in 1819 Calhoun in reference to the invasion of Florida "always spoke of you (Jackson) with respect and kindness."[2] All this was in anticipation of publication, but each side hesitated to commit itself to the public. Each desired the advantage of being able to pronounce the other the aggressor, and, therefore, the disturber of party harmony.

The administration felt that it was not a time for dissension

---

[1] Van Buren Mss.

[2] R. M. Johnson to Jackson, February 13, 1831, Jackson Mss.

in the household. Clay was rallying his friends and joining to them the friends of the bank and internal improvements. Nothing must be done before the November elections, and their results were not so overwhelming that opposition could be ignored. Calhoun undoubtedly underestimated his difficulties. He did not realize how much he was hampered by nullification. It turned from him the great body of Northern sentiment at a time when he needed all his strength. He took the hesitation of the administration for weakness and believed that he could blast Van Buren by showing what a nefarious scheme had been concocted: January 13, 1831, he wrote:

The correspondence between the President and myself begins to excite much attention and speculation. I arrived here [Washington] before New Year's day some three, or four days, and as I did not attend on that occasion, it confirmed the rumours already in circulation of a seperation between us. Mr. Crawford's correspondence with Mr. Adams and Mr. Crowinshield placed the opponents of the administration in possession of the knowledge of the correspondence between us, and their policy has been to force it out. As far as I am concerned, it would be desirable, but as I have acted on the defensive thus far and intend to do so throughout, I will not publish unless it should become absolutely necessary. In the meantime, I permit whatever friend desires to read the correspondence, which has given a pretty general knowledge of its contents here. The result has been, in the opinion of all my friends, to strengthen me, and to weaken those who have got up the conspiracy for my destruction. Every opening was made for me to renew my intercourse with the President, which I have declined, and will continue so to do, till he retracts what he has done. His friends are much alarmed.

To another he wrote: "Those who commenced the affair are heartily sick of it."[1]

Van Buren corroborates to a certain extent this view of the situation. He admits that about the beginning of the year

[1] Calhoun, *Letters* (Jameson edition), 279, 283.

overtures for reconcilation between Jackson and the vice-president were made and nearly succeeded, and that if they had not failed the South Carolinian would have reached the goal of his ambition.[1] Failure came because Calhoun was too eager to strike Van Buren behind the President's cloak. His friends, and probably some others, flattered him that by exposing the intrigue he could destroy the chances of the secretary of state. They believed the latter a shrewd upstart, who had no weapon but trickery, and that this would be ineffective if the people could see how it worked. They forgot, if they ever knew, Jackson's power of friendship.

Calhoun even fancied that the publication could be directed so pointedly toward his rival that Jackson would be indifferent about it. With that object in mind he submitted to Eaton the long pamphlet he had prepared and asked this confidential friend of the President to remove before publication all points which would be personally disagreeable to the chief. Eaton promised to submit the manuscript to Jackson, but he failed to do so and returned it without saying the President did not see it. No corrections had been made in the text, and Calhoun, believing that there was plain sailing ahead, with the aid of Duff Green, proceeded with the plans for publication. February 15th, by way of preparing the public, Green published in the *Telegraph* a number of extracts from Van Buren papers, the purport of which was to bring out their candidate for the presidency in case Jackson declined to run. This was to show that the Van Buren faction had introduced discord into the party. Two days later the complete pamphlet was given to the world.[2]

Jackson prepared a reply but on consideration decided not to publish it. He felt, says Benton, that it was not becoming for a President of the United States to become a party to a

---

[1] Van Buren, *Autobiography*, IV., 33-37 (Transcripts).
[2] *Telegraph*, February 15 and 17, 1831: See also Niles, *Register*, XL., 11, and Calhoun, *Works*, VI., 349-445.

newspaper controversy. The defense remained unpublished for over twenty years and was at last incorporated with certain omissions in Benton's *View*.[1]

Calhoun's disillusionment was rapid. The administration party showed eager hostility and ranged itself on the side of Van Buren. Blair's newly established *Globe* gave the pace for a hundred other newspapers. "Mr. Calhoun's publication," it said after reviewing the events which preceded its publication, "therefore, was wholly uncalled for. It is a firebrand wantonly thrown into the Republican party. Mr. Calhoun will be held responsible for all the mischief which may follow."[2] In a short time the whole country rang with the conflict, and all hope of peaceful relations between President and vice-president was destroyed.

Fighting for life, Calhoun set about to organize his group to break the power of Van Buren, safely ensconced under the wing of the popular idol. "He came in like a mercenary," said Duff Green of the secretary of state, "and having divided the spoils among his followers he seems resolved to expel the native troops from the camp. I will expose him."[3] A movement was launched to unite all opponents of the secretary of state. The old Clinton faction of New York was approached and gave assurances of support; the dissatisfied Virginians offered another body of recruits and arrangements were made to establish a newspaper to sustain them under the editorship of R. H. Crallé; in Pennsylvania Calhoun counted on Ingham, already alienated from Jackson and about to resume through the dissolution of the cabinet his former position as state leader;[4] and in the South he had a strong following among those who resented the high

---

[1] Benton, *View*, I., 167.
[2] *Globe*, February 21, 1831.
[3] Duff Green to Cabell and Co., April 16, 1831, Green's letters, Library of Congress.
[4] Duff Green to "Cabell Esquire," June 21, 1831. Duff Green's letters to Crallé and others in the Library of Congress throw much light on the Calhoun movement from 1831 to 1836.

tariff.   His efforts were expended within the party with the object of defeating the nomination of Van Buren in 1832, for either first or second place on the ticket.

All this aroused Jackson.   He came out openly for his favorite, consenting to take reëlection as a means of carrying through his policy.   Leading his well-organized party, he attacked every show of opposition with the ardor of a military man, and the people followed him tumultuously.   In the face of such a force the insurgents could do nothing.   Calhoun was isolated.   Broken and desperate he became a sectional leader, but it was not until Jackson's hand relaxed its grasp on the democratic party that he again became an important factor in national politics.

XXV

THE CABINET DISSOLVED

THE reorganization of the cabinet followed hard on the rupture with Calhoun. It was a shrewd move in the interest of Van Buren, and the evidence seems to show that it did not originate with Jackson. It removed Calhoun men from the cabinet, eliminated the disturbing Eaton affair, weakened the criticism of the new favorite for the succession, assured a united cabinet, and placed the anti-Calhoun faction at the head of the party. It completed the evolution of the Jacksonian organization which was about to establish a rigid control of public affairs.

Calhoun's pamphlet produced a powerful effect. Intelligent men who were not biased by party feeling could not but see the intrigue which had been used, and politicians feared the results. In Richmond, Va., his friends were very active and proposed to give him a dinner on his return from Washington, but by the greatest effort, the opposing faction was able to prevent it on the ground that party harmony ought to be preserved. The action of Virginia in this crisis would have exerted much influence in other states, and each faction was anxious to control it.

Friends in Richmond kept Van Buren informed of the situation there. "In my opinion," wrote Archer on March 12th, "nothing can restore the administration to popularity but a thorough reorganization of the cabinet. This cannot in my judgment be done till after the next election. The government is too much weakened to give any more local disgusts. This hazard can't be run now. At another time it must be accomplished, and what will be the greatest obstruction, I fear, Mr. Eaton (toward whom as you know, I have personally a kind feeling), must be induced to accept some honorary form of retirement." It was a fortnight after he received this letter before Van Buren, by his own account, decided to resign. Three weeks after it was written Andrew Stevenson wrote: "We shall probably have *war to the knife*, and shall lose some of our forces."[1]

By this time, many party leaders realized the burden of carrying Eaton. They also knew how hopeless it was to expect Jackson to repudiate him. One day on Pennsylvania Avenue, General Overton, a close friend of Jackson, met Major Bradford, another friend of the President. Both were Tennesseeans. "Bradford," said he, "there must be a change in the cabinet or we cannot get along."

"Change! What change, sir, do you mean?"

"I mean, sir, that Major Eaton must be removed."

Overton added that over one hundred congressmen would go home dissatisfied, unless something was done. Bradford replied, "If the whole country were in a body to press Andrew Jackson to this act they would not succeed without showing better cause than, as yet, is known."

"Well, sir," replied Overton, "it will be tried, for there is to be a meeting for that very purpose very soon."

Bradford consulted Barry who was much concerned at the news and by his advice Jackson was approached.

"After I had made my communication," says Bradford, "he [Jackson], instantly raised himself to the height of his noble stature and with eyes lighted up with feeling and determination, he uttered these words: 'Let them come — let the whole hundred come on — I would resign the Presidency or lose my life sooner than I would desert my friend Eaton or be forced to

[1] W. S. Archer to Van Buren, March 12 and 27, 1831; A. Stevenson to Van Buren, April 4, 1831; Van Buren Mss.

do an act that my conscience may disapprove. I shall send for General Overton to-morrow and sift this affair to the bottom.'"[1] Thus there was small hope for Eaton's dismissal: we shall see that by skilful maneuvering he was brought to resign.

Van Buren's interests coincided with the desire for a new cabinet. By getting out he would relieve himself from the charge of directing the government in his own behalf, he would suffer no loss but rather gain strength with Jackson, who would now regard him as a generous and self-denying man, and he would remove himself from what might be an unpleasant storm centre. He considered the matter carefully and decided to withdraw. He resolved, as he says, to broach the matter to Jackson on one of their daily rides, but time after time as he thought to speak his courage failed and he deferred the matter. His son, who knew his father's resolve chaffed him privately for these postponements. Finally, one day, as President and secretary rode through Georgetown into the Tenallytown road, the latter found opportunity to declare his purpose.

In their general conversation, Jackson referred to the discord in his councils and said that he had hopes of peace. "No, General," said the other, "there is but one thing can give you peace." "What is that, sir?" said Jackson quickly. "My resignation." "Never, sir," exclaimed the general: "even you know little of Andrew Jackson if you suppose him capable of consenting to such a humiliation of his friends by his enemies!"

It took four days, says Van Buren in his circumstantial account of the affair, to convince the old man of the wisdom of the proposed action. What arguments were used we are not told, but in a long ride that took them beyond their usual turning point at the Tenallytown gate, he was at last brought over. It was then that the President suggested the English mission for his companion.

---

[1] Major Samuel Bradford to Jackson, February 28, 1832, Jackson Mss.

Next morning Van Buren was early at the White House. Jackson was much agitated and said with his usual directness that it was his custom to release from association with him any man who felt that he ought to go, and that he would accordingly let his secretary follow his desires. This, says the latter, was precisely the turn he had most feared: his request, after a night's reflection, was construed as indicating a wish to leave an unpopular association. With much warmth and unfeigned concern the secretary withdrew all he had said and declared he would keep his place until dismissed. This earnestness and evident candor touched the old man's heart and complete harmony was restored.

During the afternoon of the same day, they again rode horseback. It was now agreed that the matter might be discussed with Barry, Eaton and Lewis; and the next night, the five men dined together at Van Buren's house. Up to this point Van Buren's resignation only was under discussion. Nothing had been said about Eaton's, but the whole drift of the argument must have pointed to that as a logical outcome of the situation. Eaton was thus forced to take a position, and in the night's conversation he said that inasmuch as he was the original cause of the entanglement, he also would withdraw in the interest of harmony. Van Buren then asked what Mrs. Eaton would say of this and her husband replied that she would gladly consent. The matter was definitely determined at this meeting, and next evening the party assembled again, Eaton reporting that his wife approved of the proposed arrangement. Her compliance could hardly have been hearty, however; for when a few days later Jackson and Van Buren on one of their strolls, made her a visit, their "reception was to the last degree formal and cold." When the secretary alluded to this, Jackson only shrugged his shoulder and said it was strange. After Eaton's announcement at the meeting referred to, it was agreed that both men should resign in writing and that the letter from the secretary of war should be dated earlier than the other.[1]

Eaton's letter had date of April 7th, and Van Buren's, April 11th, but they were not announced in the *Globe* until April 20th, when Van Buren's note and Jackson's reply were given in full. Eaton's gave a desire to retire to private life as the ground on which it rested, but his friend's was more delicately drawn. Alluding in guarded terms to the charge that he was aiming at the presidency, the writer declared that he sought only to relieve the President from such false imputations, and that he would have done this sooner had not public business which was just completed, made it necessary to remain in office. The matter referred to was negotiations with England and France, two complicated affairs, which were just completed with credit and success. Jackson accepted these resignations in two courteous notes, which left no doubt that he parted with the men in the most friendly spirit.[2]

It was not a great sacrifice on the part of either of the two men. In reorganizing the cabinet, McLane, by the arrangement made, would return from London and Van Buren would have the vacant place. Eaton, it was expected, could be made a senator from Tennessee, and he would thus be able to continue his struggle against his Washington foes without seeming to retreat before them.

The public knew little of what was going on behind the scenes and the first intimations of resignations caused friends of the two secretaries, to think them out of favor with the President. Van Buren's supporters in New York were in consternation until he sent a letter to Butler, his old law partner, with specific reassurances. His retirement, it said, was of his own initiative and would not have been allowed by the President, "if he had

---

[1] Van Buren, *Autobiography*, IV., 82-92.
[2] Parton, *Life of Jackson*, III., 347-352.

not been satisfied by me that it was called for by the public interest and could not be ultimately prejudicial to me." It closed by suggesting that his friends be given an intimation of the true state of affairs and by hinting that other resignations would follow.[1]

Virginia also gave the outgoing secretary of state much anxiety. He wrote a precautionary letter to Ritchie, editor of the Richmond *Enquirer*, and completely won that variable personage. A reassuring reply came quickly, one feature of which was an injunction not to take an office by way of substitute for the surrendered secretaryship. This was in order that the very suspicion of collusion should be avoided. Two weeks later, when it was known that Van Buren was to be minister to London, the Richmond editor took the opposite point of view, writing a long argument to show that it was Van Buren's duty to take the proffered appointment. The squirming of poor Ritchie is one of the pathetic things in the process by which Virginia was shorn of her political prestige, and it was likewise a partial cause of that disaster.[2]

These efforts were seconded by Jackson, who made one of his visits to the Rip Raps, in Hampton Roads, in the early summer of 1831. He received calls from many Virginians and talked freely of the situation. To the visitors he affirmed his undiminished confidence in the New Yorker. In fact, from now on he made no secret of his wishes in regard to his favorite.[3]

The withdrawal of two cabinet members gave opportunity to dismiss the others. They came in as a unit, said Jackson, and they should go out as a unit. The assertion was not true, but it served the purpose of him who made it; and there was undoubtedly truth in the notion that the President ought to have a harmonious council. Accordingly, April 19th he informed

[1]Van Buren to B. F. Butler, April 16, and B. F. Butler to Van Buren, April 22, 1831; Van Buren Mss.
[2]Ritchie to Van Buren (no date, about April 22), and April 30, 1831; Van Buren Mss.
[3]Jackson to Van Buren, July 11, 1831; Van Buren Mss.

Ingham and Branch of the retirement of their colleagues and intimated that he would be pleased to reorganize the cabinet. They resigned promptly and with as much good temper as could be expected under the circumstances. Berrien was absent on public business. On his return Jackson expressed his wishes in a conversation and a letter of resignation was immediately sent, June 19, 1831. Barry, postmaster-general, was allowed to remain in office. He was a weak man and neither side considered his presence important.

The formal dignity with which the secretaries retired was not to last long. Early in May, Duff Green in the *Telegraph* began to refer pointedly to Mrs. Eaton, going so far as to say that Ingham, Branch, and Berrien refused to receive her. As neither of these gentlemen denied the assertion Eaton took it for acquiescence in the charge. If no cloud had been cast on the lady's fame, his conduct would have been natural, but in view of the Washington gossip for nearly two years past, the husband expected too much. He was wildly angry and in a note asked Ingham if he approved Green's assertion. His former colleague replied contemptuously: "You must be a little deranged, to imagine that any bluster of yours could induce me to disavow what all the inhabitants of this city know, and perhaps half the people of the United States believe to be true." This reply doubtless relieved its author's pent-up feelings, but it was rude and unnecessary. Eaton followed it by a demand for "satisfaction," but the other only belittled the demand. Then the Tennesseean sent a note in a tone of lofty bluster in which his feelings found their highest expression in the assertion that his adversary was a coward.[1]

Ingham was now handing over the keys of office, which he had retained in order to complete some unfinished work in establishing a system of standard measurements, and he was on

---

[1] Parton, *Life of Jackson*, III., 365.

the point of leaving Washington. It was Saturday, June 18th, that the report was concluded, and on that day he sent his reply to Eaton's first note. Hurrying his preparations for departure while he ignored the second note seemed, therefore, to give color to the opinion that he was running away from the quarrel. Eaton was bent on having an encounter and on the same Saturday vacated the war office, which he had retained temporarily. Dr. P. G. Randolph, husband of Mrs. Eaton's sister, was placed temporarily in charge. Next morning he intruded himself into Ingham's private apartments and inquired if the latter intended to answer the challenge which had been sent. Ingham replied that he would answer when he saw fit, and Randolph announced that if an acceptance were not received, Eaton would take prompt measures to redress his wrongs. For this the visitor was shown the door.[1]

Next day, Monday, Ingham gave up his office, sent Eaton a contemptuous reply to the challenge, and prepared to leave the city. During the morning he made some calls on friends, and when he returned home at one o'clock learned that Eaton had inquired for him at the treasury department and had subsequently spent much of the forenoon at a grocery store from which Ingham's residence could be watched. He was also told that Eaton, Randolph, Major Lewis, J. W. Campbell and others had been seen together as though they were united to carry out some design. He concluded that his life was in danger and armed himself, but when he later went out with friends to the treasury department, he was not molested. In the afternoon Eaton was seen to walk several times past the house, as though he were looking for Ingham.

All this the retiring secretary of the treasury construed as a conspiracy. He remained at home on Tuesday and at four o'clock Wednesday morning set out for Baltimore. Before he

---

[1] Niles, *Register*, XL., 317, 331, 367.

went he sent Jackson a silly letter charging a conspiracy to assassinate him, the writer.   If he believed what he wrote, his duty was to have made his charge before the police authorites and to have remained in town as a witness.   The complaint was referred by Jackson to the parties implicated.   They all denied concerted action, but Eaton admitted that acting for himself alone he had sought an encounter with Ingham in order to redress his wrongs.   Thus passed the "assassination" of Ingham, except as it was used by the newspapers for political effect.[1]   It created a great deal of talk, and ten days later it was the chief object of conversation at Quincy, Mass., where Adams remarked to a caller from the South that he thought Eaton did right and was much persecuted in his relations with the cabinet members, but that he ought to have retired without making an issue of his wife's character before the American people.[2]

General Coffee's opinion of the affair is also interesting.   This old companion in arms of Jackson was in retirement but kept a close eye on all that touched his old friend and commander. The Washington troubles gave him much concern and he relieved his mind in a confidential letter to Jackson.   Eaton's position, he said, was proper but the time was badly chosen.   It might add serious embarrassment to the administration.   "At suitable seasons," he continued, "I expect he will go the whole hog round." Let him be patient; a favorable opportunity would undoubtedly occur when a meeting could be made to "come on by accident."[3]

Dissolving the cabinet gave joy to the opposition.   What could these wholesale resignations mean? said their press with affected simplicity.   They were, replied the *Globe*, purely political and not mysterious, a necessary step to preserve the equilibrium of factions within the party.   The discreet silence which

---

[1]Niles, *Register* XL., 302, 331.
[2]Massachusetts Historical Society *Proceedings*, XLIII., 73.
[3]Coffee to Jackson, July 9, 1831; Jackson Mss.

the outgoing cabinet members preserved supported this view; but men who knew the situation best believed that something was behind the scene. The *Telegraph*, whose editor, said General Coffee ought to be challenged for a duel, also knew the secret, and his remarks concerning the administration were very bitter. Ingham's friends in Pennsylvania followed the lead of the *Telegraph*. The opposition seized on every intimation of a rupture in the councils of their enemies and sought to widen the breach. The blustering of Eaton against Ingham was particularly interesting to them, and Niles, in full sympathy with their side, continually reminded his readers that it was all very significant. At this time Branch and Berrien began to talk, and it was about the interview in January, 1830, in which Jackson tried to induce the cabinet members to drop the discriminations against Mrs. Eaton.[1]

To Duff Green belongs the credit of prying open this phase of the controversy. He charged Jackson with saying that the cabinet should receive Mrs. Eaton or lose their places. Blair, coming to the aid of the President, demanded proof. Green gave none, but it became known that Berrien would substantiate the charge. Blair then turned on Berrien, who at length published a statement in which he asserted that the President in the interview referred to, made the recognition of Mrs. Eaton the condition on which he, Branch, and Ingham should remain in the cabinet, and he denied that Jackson in that interview read from a written statement or other paper.[2] Ingham and Branch corroborated the statement in formal notes,[3] evidence not to be reconciled with a memorandum, several copies of which exist in Jackson's handwriting, but which was then unpublished.

The President observed the controversy with great interest, and although Ingham and Berrien made more than one effort to draw some explosion of temper from him in regard to it, he

[1]See above, II., page 467.
[2]Niles, *Register*, XL., 381-384.
[3]Jackson to Van Buren, July 11, 1831, Van Buren Mss.

remained discreetly silent. So far as he was concerned, the dissolution of the cabinet was accomplished peacefully. He ignored the outbreak of temper between Eaton and Ingham, and when the latter referred the alleged conspiracy to him he acted with becoming fairness. To the published statement of Berrien, he also offered a dignified appearance. But inwardly he was deeply agitated.

At first Calhoun was the object of his temper. Berrien, he said, July 11th, was going out like a gentleman, but the vice-president was continuing "his old course of secrete writing and slandering me. I have a few extracts from his letters sent to me, which in due time, will aid *in finishing a picture I mean to draw of him!*" If this intention refers to his formal reply, we know that its publication was wisely deferred.[1] A fortnight later, when the *Globe's* caustic attacks brought Berrien into the controversy, Jackson changed his mind about that gentleman. But his greatest scorn was reserved for Ingham; and when that person published a letter to him before it had time to arrive, he caused a secretary to write a frigid reply refusing to receive further communications. The secretary's letter was promptly published in the *Globe*.[2]

The autumn after Eaton left office, he visited Tennessee. The Jackson party there exerted themselves with great success to make his reception brilliant. Every lady in Nashville except Mrs. Dr. McNairy, so wrote Judge Overton, called on Mrs. Eaton; and fifty-four out of the sixty-nine members of the legislature attended a dinner to Eaton. Branch was then traveling in Tennessee and arrived at Nashville at just this unlucky moment. "He reached Nashville the evening of the dinner," writes Jackson to Van Buren, "and, on the next day went to the Assembly room, where Mr. Bell and Major Eaton were by invitation, and after remaining in the *lobby* for some time with-

---

[1] See above, II., 517.
[2] N. P. Trist to Ingham, see the *Globe*, July 11, 1831.

out any attention being paid to him, he retired. He doubtless exclaimed in his anguish 'Farewell, a long farewell to all my greatness,' as he now discovers his sad mistake in supposing that he, Ingham, Berrien, Calhoun, Duff Green & Co., could raise up and crush whom they pleased at pleasure, and destroy me by prostrating Eaton and yourself. Those men have fallen unwept, unhonored and unsung. . . I fear them not, nor need you. You are gaining strength daily in the nation and will continue to do so, and rise in public estimation in opposition to all their intrigues to prevent it. Your enemies might as well attempt to change the running of the water in the Mississippi, as to prevent you from obtaining the increased confidence of the people.'"[1]

His personal affection for the favorite came out in many little touches. July 23rd, when the controversy was warmest, he hung a picture of his friend in his own apartment. "It appears to look and smile upon me as I write," he said.[2] And two days later he wrote; "Let me hear from you, and any idea that may occur to you worthy to be presented to Congress, suggest it to me."[3] To Dunlap he wrote: "I never acted with a more frank and candid man than Mr. Van Buren.—It is said that he is a great magician —I believe it, but his only wand is good common sense which he uses for the benefit of his country."[4] To Judge White, he wrote: "I say to you frankly, that Van Buren is one of the most frank men I ever knew, with talents combined with common sense, but rarely to be met with — *a true man* with no guile."

In the meantime, the guileless Van Buren succeeded in keeping himself untouched by the prevailing controversies. He left the country late in the summer. He wrote frequent letters to Jackson, but he has kept the historian as much at sea as his

[1] Jackson to Van Buren, November 14, 1831, Van Buren Mss.
[2] Jackson to Van Buren, July 23, 1831, Van Buren Mss.
[3] *Ibid* to *Ibid*, July 25, 1831; Van Buren Mss.
[4] Jackson to Dunlap, July 18, 1831, copy in Library of Congress. Jackson to White, April 9, 1831, Jackson Mss.

contemporaries. Later in life he asked Jackson to return his letters, and the old man with accustomed sincerity complied without retaining copies. Van Buren gave as the ground for his request the desire to use them in his autobiography; but the completed manuscript of that work contains few references to the letters to Jackson.

But Jackson's confidence in his friend was not misplaced. Van Buren was by far the wisest and coolest head among those who conducted the administration. He was always restrained, always master of his tongue and pen, suggesting more than he said, and careful to leave no positive impressions on others which might embarrass him in the future. In success and defeat he remained true to the old chieftain. Beneath the cool exterior of the one was the capacity to understand the genuine qualities which lay beneath the crude and turbulent nature of the others.

Many of Van Buren's friends were opposed to the appointment to England. They feared he would lose control of the situation through absence. His judgment was to the contrary: he believed his influence at the White House was strong enough to withstand absence. In fact he had the assurance of Jackson himself that all his power would be exerted to make the New Yorker the next President. Moreover, it was evident that by going abroad, he would lessen the strength of his opponent's argument that he was the shrewd manipulator of the President and those who controlled the party machinery. When in the following winter his short-sighted foes defeated his nomination in the senate, he became a martyr in the eyes of his party and it was now a point of honor to carry him through the democratic nominating convention. Up to that time, his nomination in 1832 seems not to have been a part of the plan arranged by the inner circle in Washington.

The work of filling the cabinet vacancies was taken up in connection with the task of getting rid of the former incumbents, Van

Buren remaining in Washington to assist. At Jackson's suggestion, he wrote on April 9th to Edward Livingston. "The President," he said, "wants you to come here at once and to manage
so that your destination is unknown; and he will judge of your
fitness for the duty he has in view by the secrecy and promptness with which you execute this request."[1] The communication
was essentially a military order, and the recipient obeyed with
alacrity. He was now out of debt and willing to exchange his
seat in the senate for the first position in the cabinet. He was
a nationalist in his views and his appointment was unpopular
with the strict constructionists of New York and Virginia; but,
as Ritchie said, they did not complain since Jackson asserted
that he would "give the rule" and that it would be the part of
the secretaries to execute his views.[2]

Filling Eaton's place was more difficult. The plan had been
that H. L. White should resign his seat in the senate to take the
war department and that Eaton should have the vacant senatorship. Although Van Buren suggested White for a place,[3] Jackson himself assumed the task of inducing the Tennessee senator
to comply with the first phase of the plan. April 9th, the day Van
Buren summoned Livingston, he himself wrote White in a far
less commanding tone. The letter gives such an intimate view
of Jackson's mind at this time that it is well worth publishing in
its entirety. It runs:

Strictly confidential.

Washington, April 9th, 1831[3]

My Dr. Sir

When first elected President of the United States, my first
concern was to select a cabinet of honest talented men, and good
republicans, amonghst whom, I might have one, from personal
acquaintance, I could with safety confide You and Major

[1] Van Buren Mss.
[2] Niles, Register, XL., 169.
[3] Van Buren, Autobiography, III., 4; Van Buren Mss.

Eaton were the only men with whom, I had such acquaintance and intimacy that ensured me my entire confidence were well placed (and who could be tho't of to fill such a place), one of whom I tho't it necessary for the success of my administration, should be in my Cabinet.   Both of you had taken a prominent share in my election, which drew me from my chosen retirement, I therefore thought I had claims upon you to aid me in the administration of the government.   With these feelings, on the close of the election in 1828, I addressed you, asking you to come into my Cabinet, and requesting if anything of an imperious nature should deprive me of your services, make your determination known to Maj. Eaton, as I calculated that one or the other of you would.

When I reached Washington, for reasons which you assigned as imperious, you declined, and it was with great reluctance and much difficulty, and persuasion, Maj. Eaton consented.   He has made known to me his intention to withdraw, and has tendered his resignation.   It is with the greatest reluctance I part with him, but *his decision is final*.   You know the confidence I have in him, but knowing how much he has unjustly suffered I cannot longer detain him contrary to his wishes and to his happiness.   He has been cruelly persecuted, and from a combination of sources, that until lately, some of them I did not suspect.

I have in my reply to Major Eaton's letter of resignation, closed mine thus, "I will avail myself of the earliest opportunity to obtain some qualified friend to succeed you, and until then I must solicit that the acceptance of your resignation may be deferred."   I have therefore a right to claim your aid as my faithful friend, Eaton has determined to retire.   The reasons that influenced your determination in 1829, does not now exist. It is true you have drank the cup of bitterness to the dregs, your bereavements have been great — with me you can live (I have a large room for you) who can sympathize with your sufferings, and you can keep your little son and daughter with you and attend to his education, and the duties of your office will give employ to your mind.   This must be employed to preserve life, and in this employment you will not only render important services to your country, but an act of great friendship to me. I cannot hesitate to believe, but that you will yield your consent. I shall await your answer with much anxiety.

I pray you to look about and you will see the great difficulty, not to say impractibility [sic] of supplying your place in case of refusal, and I therefore feel the more justified in adding the claims of private friendship, to considerations of public character.

You must not my dear friend refuse my request. If at any time you should find the duties of the office too much for your health or other opportunity should offer to place you in a situation more congenial with your past pursuits, we will have time and opportunity to prepare for the gratification of your wishes, which shall continue as they have heretofore been the rule of my conduct in whatever relates to yourself always, satisfied that they will be none other than such as are reasonable.

Mr. Van Buren has also intimated to me his intention to withdraw, of course, a reorganization of my cabinet (proper) will be made. The Postmaster-genl. will only remain. When Eaton and Van Buren goes, justice to them, and to myself, and that electioneering scenes in congress may cease, or the intriguers exposed, will induce me to re-organize my Cabinet. This I regret, but have a long time foresaw, admonished but could not controle; my Cabinet must be a unit. I sincerely regret to loose Eaton and Van Buren two more independent republicans does not exist, who have laboured with me, with an eye single to the prosperity of the union. Still Mr. Van Buren, was singled out as a plotter. The cry plot, plot in Mr. Calhoun's book bro't me in mind of the old story — rogue cries rogue rogue first to draw the attention from himself, that he might escape. I say to you frankly, that Van Buren is one of the most frank men I ever knew, with talents combined with common sense, but rarely to be met with — *a true man* with no guile. With my kind solicitations to you and your little family and your connections believe me,

Your friend,
ANDREW JACKSON.[1]

The Honorable
   H. L. White.

---

[1] Jackson Mss.

White's afflictions, to which allusion was here made, were the loss of most of his family, the latest being the death of his wife on March 25, 1831. It is usually asserted that these misfortunes caused him to refuse the proffered secretaryship; but his reply to the letter quoted does not mention them. The reasons there assigned are that he was unfit for the position and too old to learn, that he could not afford to leave his property in Tennessee, and that it was against his principles to take office from a personal friend.[1]

The receipt of this letter was followed by a conference to which Van Buren, Eaton, and Livingston were summoned. "It will now be proper," said Jackson to them, "to make a selection and the task is one of some difficulty."[2] It was, in fact, as hard to get a man for the place, not tainted with Calhoun influence who would command the respect of the country, as to find another way of providing for Eaton. The result of the conference was a still more urgent letter from Jackson to White trying to shake his decision. All White's arguments were disposed of —they were not formidable—the duties of the department could be easily learned and his property interest at home could be taken care of. Surrounded as he was, said Jackson, by bank men, nullifiers, and advocates of internal improvements, it was hard to find a man in whom he could confide. He must have one to whom he could unbosom himself, and who should it be but his old friend? "I could get," he added, "Col. Drayton, perhaps, who might be in favor of rechartering the Bank, acquainted with military matters, but unacquainted with Indian matters and whose appointment would arouse half of South Carolina and let it be remembered that he has been a strong Federalist. I like the man but I fear his politics — and having taken Mc-Lane (a Federalist), into the Treasury, I do not like to be compelled to take another."[3]

[1] White to Jackson, April 20, 1831, Jackson Mss.
[2] Jackson to Van Buren, May 20, 1831, Van Buren Mss.
[3] Jackson to White, April 29, 1831, Jackson Mss.

This entreaty was seconded by the personal intercession of Major F. W. Armstrong, a mutual friend, who pled so well that White gave a reluctant consent; but a month later this was withdrawn on the ground that another daughter had developed consumption and he felt it his duty to remain near her in Tennessee. But we may look behind his excuses; his desire for retirement did not prevent his retention of his senatorship, and his grief did not keep him from a second marriage in the following year.[1] It seems that he had deeper reasons for his refusal than those assigned. He well remembered, if we accept the gossip of the day, the manner in which Eaton elevated himself into the cabinet, he was not in sympathy with the Eaton-Lewis influence in administration circles, he was not enthusiastic for Van Buren, and he was not now disposed to play the part which the combination arranged for him. He thus won the opposition of the inner circle in Washington, we eventually find him cooling toward the administration, and in 1836, he ran against Van Buren for the presidency.

The war department was now offered to Drayton, who declined, and it was then accepted by Lewis Cass, who had a good record as governor of Michigan. Lewis McLane, returning from London, became secretary of the treasury, realizing an old ambition for cabinet honors. The navy department was given to Levi Woodbury, of New Hampshire, a man of excellent capacity, whose one fault, in the eyes of Isaac Hill, was that in Portsmouth he and his family associated with the aristocracy and not with the Jackson party there.[2] Roger B. Taney, a promising lawyer of Baltimore, became attorney-general, and his ability justified the selection. Barry remained postmaster-general. It was a respectable cabinet, devoted to Jackson, submissive to his leadership, favorable to Van Buren, and for the most part com-

---

[1] Armstrong to Jackson, May 22; Jackson to White, June 1; and White to Jackson, June 15; 1831; Jackson Mss. See also, *Memoir of White*, 419, 447-450.
[2] Massachusetts Historical Society *Proceedings*, XLIII., 72.

mitted to those aggressive measures into which the administration was about to throw itself. Establishing it was a gain in the working strength of the party.

The new cabinet indicated a new party control and new ideals. It announced that power was gone from Virginia and South Carolina and centered in a combination of the newer states of the West and Southwest with the large democratic states of the middle sea coast.

Eaton's future was a source of anxiety to Jackson, who clung stubbornly to a friend in distress. Since it was impossible to thrust him into White's seat, Eaton turned to that of Grundy, the other Tennessee senator, whose term expired in 1833. Grundy supported Jackson, who was thus forced to assume a neutral position. Each side claimed sympathy, but the President persisted in outward impartiality, although there are indications that secretly he leaned to Eaton.[1] But Grundy's appeal to the people was successful, and Eaton, who had little strength in the state when deprived of Jackson's open support, was forced at last to give up the fight. He was then willing to accept the governorship of Florida. The place did not please him, and he gave broad but vain hints that he wanted the governorship of Michigan, then vacant through the death of Governor Porter. In 1832, he was a delegate to the Baltimore convention. It was reported that he would vote against Van Buren, probably because the New Yorker's disfavor in Tennessee lessened Eaton's chances for the senatorship. But his rebellion disappeared with an intimation that Jackson expected him to do his duty.[2] In 1836, he was made minister to Spain. Richard Rush, Adams's candidate for vice-president in 1828, but now a

---

[1] McLemore to Jackson, September 25; Jackson to D. Buford, September 10, 1832; William Carroll to Jackson, August 9 and December 3, 1833; Grundy to Jackson, May 6 and August 7, 1833; Jackson Mss. In the Jackson Mss. is a letter in Eaton's behalf, September,—1832. It is addressed "Gentlemen", and is in Jackson's handwriting. If sent at all, it was probably intended for discreet use.

[2] Parton, *Life of Jackson*, III., 421.

fervid Jackson man, made the journey across the Atlantic in the
same ship with Eaton and wrote enthusiastically of him.   Mrs.
Eaton and her daughters, he said, were the life of the party
aboard.[1]   In 1840, Eaton turned openly against Van Buren and
supported the enemics of Jackson.   It completed a series of
disappointments, which his capacity and character did not deserve.   His unfortunate marriage wrecked a career of much
promise.   When Jackson heard of his course in 1840, he pronounced Eaton "the most degraded of all the apostates fed,
clothed, and cherished by the administration."

The events of 1831 brought into high light the position of
the "Kitchen Cabinet."   Many men, some of whom were
friends of the administration, thought that the trouble grew
out of the course pursued by this group of irresponsible persons.
Eaton's association with the group strengthened the idea in the
popular mind.   The candid Dunlap expressed his opinion of this
phase of the situation in the following words to Jackson: "While
the nation may admire the firm friendship by you manifested for
Mr. Eaton, they cannot but rejoice at the hope of his retirement.
Mr. W. B. Lewis, almost too small to write about, occupies a
position before the nation alone from his presumed and assumed
intimacy with you, which merits little attention.   Send him
home and no longer hold yourself accountable to the free and
enlightened people for the arrogant follies of such a small
but busy man. . . .   To speak plain, the opinion prevails
at large that W. B. Lewis is one of your most confidential
councillors.   This fact does, whether it be true or false, seriously
affect the public.   It raises a suspicion of your fitness to rule;
paralyzes every noble feeling of your friends when it is said
Billy Lewis is your Prest councillor."[3]   Alfred Balch, another
Tennessee supporter and a friend of Van Buren, spoke quite as

---

[1] Rush to Jackson, September 26, 1836, Jackson Mss.
[2] Jackson to Kendall, September 23, 1840; *Cincinnati Commercial*, February 5, 1879.
[3] R. G. Dunlap to Jackson, June 30, 1831, copy in Library of Congress.

plainly. The feeling is general, he said, that in Washington there is "a power behind the throne greater than the throne itself. . . . It is my most decided opinion that Major Lewis should set up an establishment for himself — should till the close of the next session of congress disconnect himself from you and see you only in a ceremonious manner. It is also my opinion that Mr. Kendall should attend only to the duties of his office and let you wholly alone."[1] These things did not destroy Jackson's hold on the Tennesseeans: he was their one hero and his grasp on the state organization was absolute; but the popular impatience expressed itself in defeating Eaton's attempt to be a senator and in the alienation of White.

The "Kitchen Cabinet" was not abolished, but it underwent two important changes. In the first place its *personnel* changed. The removal of Van Buren and Eaton took away two of the strongest members. Lewis opposed Jackson on the bank question, and weakened his influence. After 1831, the most influential friends of the President were Kendall, Blair, A. J. Donelson, and Taney. Thus we see the "Kitchen Cabinet" went through a reorganization of its own. In the second place, the party machinery was growing and the "Kitchen Cabinet" became less of a personal affair and more of an expression of party will. The increasing tendency to leave the patronage to members of congress, the removal of faction which caused the group to spend much energy in intrigue, and the crystallization of well defined party principles operated to the same end. This renewed group was less repugnant to the people than its predecessor.

But one act remained to complete the readjustment of the party, the nomination of Jackson and Van Buren in 1832. National nominating conventions had suddenly sprung into existence: the anti-masons held one in 1830 and another in 1831, the

---

[1] Alfred Balch to Jackson, July 21, 1831; Jackson Mss.

national republicans held one in 1831, and the democrats followed the example in May, 1832. Jackson was induced to stand for a second term by the assurance that it was necessary to preserve the union and by his innate repugnance to allowing himself to be driven by his opponents.[1]   Delegates to the convention were chosen for loyalty to him, and his power was enough to carry them for his favorite.   Major Lewis was the chief instrument through which this will was made manifest to the members of the convention.   By correspondence and by personal solicitation he caused them to see that they would have the opposition of the leader if they did not vote for Van Buren.   On the first ballot the New York received two hundred and eight votes while his two opponents had together only seventy-five.

When Van Buren sailed for London, it was not determined that he should be the candidate for vice-president.   Jackson, in fact, had a plan by which his friend should stay in Europe for two or three years, then come back to the cabinet and be in a position to be urged for first place on the ticket in 1836.   "The opposition," he said —he was writing to Van Buren and the date was December 17th — "would be glad to reject your nomination as minister if they dared, but they know it would make you too popular."   Referring to Livingston's desire to go abroad he said:

I am anxious again to have you near me, and it would afford me pleasure to gratify both.   I find on many occasions I want your aid and Eatons.   I have to labour hard, and be constantly watchfull.   Had I you in the state department and Eaton in the war, with the others filled as they are, it would be one of the strongest and happiest administrations that could be formed. We could controle the little federalist leaven, in that high-minded, honorable, and talented friend of ours, Mr. McLane.   Cass is an amiable talented man, a fine writer, but unfortunately it is hard for him to say no, and he thinks all men honest.   This is a virtue

---

[1] Jackson to Van Buren, September 18, 1831; Van Buren Mss.

in private, but unsafe in public life. . . . You are aware of the friendship I have for Livingston, and the respect I have for his talents; that he is a polished scholar, an able writer, and a most excellent man, but he knows nothing of mankind. He lacks in this respect that judgment that you possess, in so eminent a degree, his memory is somewhat failing him. . . . I would not be surprised if contrary to your declared wishes, you should be run for vice-presidency. As sure as the senate makes the attempt to reject your nomination, I am told it will be done.[1]

January 25th the threatened rejection was carried in the senate, the opposition resting on Van Buren's instructions to McLane in 1829 and Calhoun with four faithful followers coöperating with them on the ground that the New Yorker had seduced the mind of the President and formed plots within the party. The rejection was carried by the deciding vote of the vice-president.[2] Instantly the country was in a state of excitement. Meetings to endorse the rejected man were held in New York and throughout the country. The Jackson party declared that the insult was really against Jackson and the President agreed with the assertion. "This is your flood-tide," wrote the faithful Marcy to the absent one in London, "and if you wish to make your voyage, you should not neglect it. If there is hazard in the game, I think you still should play it."[3] He added that if Van Buren did not come forward others would do so, that P. P. Barbour, of Virginia, was being pressed by the anti-tariff men and if not chosen for second place would be a strong candidate for first honor in 1836.

Jackson also wrote. "The insult to the executive would be avenged," he said, "by putting you into the very chair which is now occupied by him who cast the deciding vote against you. Hayne voted against you and his reasons for it shows that he

[1]Jackson to Van Buren, December 17, 1831, Van Buren Mss.

[2]See Benton, *View*, I., 214-220, for an interesting account of Van Buren's rejection. See also Isaac Hill to Van Buren, January 29, 1832, Van Buren Mss.

[3]W. L. Marcy to Van Buren, January 26, 1831, and February 12, 1832, Van Buren Mss.

has fallen from the magnanimous position that we always assigned him."[1] While this letter was crossing the ocean, it passed another coming westward to the writer of the first. "My dear friend," it began, "I looked over the papers by the last Packet with no small degree of impatience for a letter from you — not that you owed me one, for I am ashamed to say that on that point, I am greatly your debtor, but from my anxiety to learn the precise effect which the extraction of a ball from your arm has had upon your health and comfort. The several grave suggestions in your long and interesting letter will not be lost sight of, but will be deferred without prejudice until things become a little more settled with you and we see things in a clearer light than at present. The opposition are feeding fat their old opposition against me I see, and what I confess surprises me a little, is to find that Mr. Clay is so blind as not to see the advantage which in the eyes of all honorable and liberal men he gives me over him by his course in the senate in respect to my nomination." I have never seen the old aristocratic and federal spirit, he continued in substance, support a man of whom they did not feel sure that he was untrue to the democracy. They supported you at first on account of your letter to Monroe, but when you announced democratic views in later letters they turned against you. "They ruined Burr beyond redemption, they crippled Clinton, gave Calhoun his first mortal wound, and to form a correct estimate of the havoc which they have made with poor Clay, it is only necessary to contrast his present situation with what it was when he was the leader of the Republican Party in the House of Representatives."

At this point the letter was interrupted till the next day, and in the interval came news of his rejection in the senate. His mail was full of advice as to coming home. Most of his correspondents advised him to return at once to look after his

[1]Jackson to Van Buren, February 12, 1832, Van Buren Mss.

affairs, but Lewis and Cambreleng thought it would be wise to wait until the nominating convention had met, and he decided to take their suggestion, thus, as he said, giving the lie to those who accused him of intrigue and "leaving my fate to the unbiased disposal of our political friends."[1]

Late in March, he left London for a short visit on the continent and arrived in America early in July. In England he was diplomatically successful, and the king, in telling him farewell said: "Well Mr. Van Buren, I cannot, of course, take part in the decision of your government, nor any branch of it, but I may be permitted, without any impropriety, to express my regret that it has been thought necessary to remove you from us." And as a token of esteem, the departing minister was invited to visit Windsor Castle from Saturday until Monday, where the king and queen, Lord Palmerston, and Mr. Vaughan, former minister to Washington, did all they could to make his stay pleasant. He confided it all to Jackson with the intimation that it would be unwise to tell it abroad, lest it be thought that he was not a democrat; but he felt these attentions would counteract the attempts of his enemies "to mortify me in the presence of the assembled representatives of Europe, and the aristocracy of this country, and through that means to reach you."[2]

Andrew Jackson could not have suspected how skilfully his favorite was identifying his cause with that of the leader. To him it was all a piece of downright wickedness on one side and suffering virtue on the other. He showed his appreciation of the latter and his power to put down the former in the work of the Baltimore convention. When the repudiated minister arrived, the die was cast. He was accepted candidate for yoke-fellow in the canvass; and from all sides came demands for his counsel in meeting the crisis which the party now faced.

---

[1] Van Buren to Jackson, February 20; and Van Buren to John Van Buren, February 23, 1832, Van Buren Mss.
[2] Van Buren to Jackson, March 28, 1832, Van Buren Mss.

XXVI

JACKSON AND NULLIFICATION

IN THE process by which Jacksonian democracy separated itself from the older republican factions in Virginia and South Carolina, the destruction of the movement for nullification was an important and instructive incident. It preserved the national basis of the party, saved the union from attempted separation, and gave the world an illustration of the strong personality of the man who directed the affairs of the central government. A further result was that it crystalized a certain powerful influence in the extreme South, which under Calhoun's leadership was to give direction to later history.

In the beginning of the national government, the federalists were supreme in South Carolina, following a group of which C. C. Pinckney was the chief ornament. The republicans carried the state for Jefferson, but their leaders were personally not able to cope with those of the opposite party. The state resented the inferior position to which the Virginia leadership assigned it and was one of the first to range itself with those who threatened to overthrow that leadership before the beginning of the War of 1812. Three leaders now appeared, Lowndes, Cheves, and Calhoun, either of whom was the equal of any Virginian then in active politics. In their reaction against the old school and partly because of the continuance of the old federalist leaven in the state, they became more national than the strict republicans. A protective tariff, a national bank, and internal improvements all found place in their philosophy. They became leading advocates of each of these policies and had their followers in many parts of the country. In the breakdown of the Virginia influence during Monroe's second term, Lowndes and Calhoun had ambitions for the presidency. The former was nominated by the state legislature for that high station in 1821, and he was endorsed as a nationalist. His death a year later, removed him from the arena, and Calhoun received a similar nomination, although it is doubtful if he was as popular with the mass of South Carolinians as Lowndes. In the same year, 1822, Robert Y. Hayne was elected United States senator as a nationalist, defeating William Smith, against whom a strong argument was that he favored secession rather than accept the Missouri Compromise.[1] All these incidents show that at this time the state was safely national, in spite of a strong and rather radical state rights party, and that Calhoun, while not very popular with the masses, had the support of the dominant group of politicians and was everywhere honored as a man of great ability and as a son who was likely to bring honor to the state.

Ten years later, this condition was reversed. The state rights party was in control of the government, the voters were warmly committed to nullification, and leaders who formerly spoke of the blessings and glories of the union had hurriedly given in their allegiance to a group who looked upon separation as possible and under certain conditions as desirable.

The cause of this change of political sentiment was the tariff. It seemed as if the manufacturers of the North would never be satisfied with moderate protection and that they were determined to have their desires regardless of the interests of the agricultural South. Whatever they asked, they managed to find a way to carry through congress, and when at last they carried the tariff of 1828, Southern feeling was bitter. South Carolina was particularly violent, and its violence looked to action.

[1] Jervey, *Robert Y. Hayne and his Times*, 125, 143, 144.

While Virginia talked about strict construction and constitutional theory, this more aggressive community began to devise some practical means of counteracting the so-called wiles of the North. Nullification was invented as an instrument of war: its legitimacy was accepted by the state at large. The people of South Carolina were ever sensitive in resenting what they considered discrimination. They were accustomed to fervid electioneering from early days; and when the supporters of nullification suggested this extreme measure as a fundamental right they made it the occasion for a crusade of liberty. This extremity of fervor was not calculated to lead to wise action or correct thinking. It caused the state to exaggerate its wrongs and to accept a constitutional theory which its well wishers in other Southern states would not adopt for their own.

But behind the tariff was slavery. Calhoun, in 1830, expressed a recognized truth when he said, speaking for his people:

I consider the Tariff, but as the occasion, rather than the real cause of the present unhappy state of things. The truth can no longer be disguised, that the peculiar domestic institution of the Southern States, and the consequent direction, which that and her soil and climate have given to her industry, has placed them in regard to taxation and appropriations in opposite relation to the majority of the union; against the danger of which, if there be no protective power in the reserved rights of the states, they must in the end be forced to rebel, or submit to have their permanent interests sacrificed, their domestic institutions subverted by colonization and other schemes and themselves and children reduced to wretchedness. Thus situated, the denial of the right of the state to interfere constitutionally in the last resort, more alarms the thinking, than all other causes; and however strange it may appear, the more universally the state is condemned and her right denied, the more resolute she is to assert her constitutional powers, lest the neglect to assert should be considered a practical abandonment of them, under such circumstances.[1]

---

[1]Calhoun to Maxey, September 11, 1830, Marcou Mss.

The leading opponents of the tariff in South Carolina were Crawford men, who disliked Calhoun intensely, among them Dr. Thomas Cooper, William Smith, and James Hamilton, Jr. They began serious agitation after the passage of the tariff bill of 1824 and were well received by the people of the state. Each advance of the tariff in national politics increased their hold in South Carolina. Fighting for power as well as for principles, they turned the popular resentment against everything Northern. They attacked Adams for his centralizing policies and arraigned internal improvements in terms that made Calhoun wince. Few state politicians dared withstand them, and many followers of the vice-president, among them Hayne and McDuffie, gave in their support.

The wincing Calhoun did not long hesitate. Much as he valued his national influence, he realized that it was worth little if he had not the support of his own state. He gradually shifted his position on the tariff and in 1827 defeated the woollens bill by his casting vote in the senate. He thus lost an important part of his support in the North, while he made himself secure in the South. As to his presidential ambition, he hoped that the shifting of the political current might soon leave the tariff high and dry and that his connection with the Jacksonian democracy might bear him forward in its successful sweep. But the tariff would not down. The law passed in 1828 was more objectionable than any of its predecessors, and in spite of the fact that its worst features were introduced by Southerners to make it so objectionable that New England would vote against the bill, the South was deeply resentful. The wrath of the South Carolinians was, therefore, proportionally increased and Calhoun's complication with their cause was further augmented. Both he and they were now irrevocably launched in the course of nullification.

Calhoun did not originate the nullification theory. In 1827, there appeared a series of essays under the title of *The Crisis*, dealing with the situation in the state and announcing nullification as a remedy. They were written by Robert J. Turnbull, a prominent leader of the state rights party. At that time, the majority of the anti-tariff men in South Carolina favored pacific measures to carry their purpose. They talked about the ballot-box, the influence of public opinion, and the results of coöperation among all the states which were opposed to protection. Turnbull threw all this aside. "Let South Carolina be bold and resist oppression," he said. The union was not yet enough consolidated to make it possible to coerce a state: the conduct of of Georgia in regard to the Indians showed this. It was never intended that the supreme court, a part of the general government, should be arbiter in a dispute between that government and a state: its decisions ought not to extend to political matters. Let the legislature of a sovereign state protest, there was no tribunal of last resort, and the state might do as it saw fit. In its assertion of the compact theory and the denial of the arbitrament of the supreme court, this doctrine undoubtedly bore resemblance to the Virginia-Kentucky resolutions, and it was the unshaped form from which Calhoun evolved his perfected theory.[1] It did not contain the word "nullification," the proposed plan of meeting the situation being described merely as "resistance."

Turnbull's appeal met with little response at once, but in the following year, the "tariff of abominations" brought an actual crisis. Some of the state's delegation in congress were for resigning as a protest, but after consultation, it was agreed to try to temper the popular resentment until after the election, and then to let the people's wrath have its own course.

This hesitancy was due to anticipations in regard to Jackson. The South Carolinians had much hope that he would oppose the

---

[1] See *The Crisis* (1827); also Houston, *Nullification*, 71-73.

tariff. It is true he was mildly for protection in 1824, and his utterances in the campaign were exceedingly cautious; but this was only politics. Was he not a Southern man, a cotton planter, and if Calhoun, one of the partners in the great national game could be shaken from his position why not the other? So they reasoned, and they would do nothing rash in the crucial year of 1828, nothing that would throw the election into the hands of Adams and Clay, from whom they could expect no help at all.

The election was hardly over before they threw themselves on the administration. Cooper, an old Crawford leader, opened correspondence with the New York Crawfordites. If the tariff was not repealed, he said, there would be no union at the end of the new administration, and New York especially might take warning lest the South goaded to anger should transfer the "Southern agency" to London. By "Southern agency" he meant the function of handling Southern products and purchases.[1]

These protests were made to Van Buren as controling member of the cabinet, and they kept up until well into 1830. His own letters in reply, so far as they are preserved, were most non-committal. But the confident tone in which his correspondents continued to write indicate that they were not repulsed. Cambreleng and J. A. Hamilton, who also received letters, were more alarmed and felt that a compromise ought to be made.

But Cooper and his associates did not wait to see what Jackson would do. Before the election of 1828 was decided, they made arrangements for a vigorous campaign as soon as that event was out of the way. In the summer of 1828, several of them visited Calhoun at his South Carolina home. He talked to them freely, and at their suggestion stated his views in his famous *Exposition*. This, with little change, was presented to the legislature the following autumn, as the report of a committee. It was not adopted, but five thousand copies were

---

[1]Cooper to Van Buren, March 24, 1829, Van Buren Mss.

ordered printed for distribution. It was a formal and complete statement of the theory of nullification, furnishing a constitutional argument for doing what Turnbull declared could and ought to be done. It was known at the time by a few of those most concerned that it came from the pen of the vice-president.[1] When in 1831, after his definite break with Jackson, Calhoun threw himself openly into the cause of nullification, he re-stated his position in *An Address to the People of South Carolina.* The argument in these two papers was so subtle that few of those who tried to explain it, gave evidence of understanding it. So many interpretations were given that in 1832, Calhoun, at the request of James Hamilton, Jr., wrote an amplification of his doctrine known as the *Fort Hill Letter.* From these three papers posterity has derived its knowledge of the theory of nullification. To quote the words of the author, "The great and leading principle is, that the general government emanated from the people of the several states, forming distinct political communities, and acting in their separate and sovereign capacity, and not from all the people forming one aggregate political community; that the constitution of the United States is, in fact, a compact, to which each state is a party, in the character already described; and that the several states, or parties, have a right to judge of its infractions; and in case of a deliberate, palpable, and dangerous exercise of power not delegated, they have the right, in the last resort, to use the language of the Virginia Resolutions, *'to interpose for arresting the progress of the evil, and for maintaining, within their respective limits, the authorities, rights, and liberties appertaining to them.'* "[2]

Out of this was constructed the principle that a state might annul a law of congress which it pronounced unconstitutional, and that the general government was an agent of the states, in fact,

[1]Hunt, *Life of Calhoun*, 108, 109.
[2]Calhoun, *Works*, VI., 60.

an agent of any particular state, so far as the will of that state was concerned. It was a doctrine of more devastating effect than secession. Secession would have split the union in twain; nullification was calculated to dissolve it state by state.

Developments in South Carolina attracted attention in other states and in Washington. Anti-tariff men generally, and particularly the Southerners, felt sympathy for the movement, but hesitated to commit themselves to so unexpected a doctrine. Nullifiers were exceedingly anxious to get the support of Virginia, which might carry that of other states, and that probably is why they stressed the connection between their movement and the resolutions of 1798-1799.

One natural result was to stimulate the feeling for union, and the two sides thus formed soon came to a clash in the debates in congress, Webster and Hayne being the opposing champions. The latter rejoiced in the opportunity to set before the world the doctrine of the new school, and his great speech did all for the cause that could have been expected of him. It won more respect from Southerners of the day than posterity has given it. Benton praised it highly, and in South Carolina it was hailed as a "complete answer" to the aggressive North. Later it was asserted, but without specific supporting evidence, that the President at that time held the same view. He considered himself a state rights man, and probably approved Hayne's defense of the cause. But we must not take very seriously his estimate of a constitutional argument. His opinions were chiefly formed through feeling, and they were apt to change with the occasions.

Through all this period, Jackson's attitude toward the nullifiers was candid but discreet. To James Hamilton, Jr's., assurance, May, 1828, that the state would "take no strong measure until your election is put beyond a doubt," he replied in words which would have been understood by a man less devoted to his enthusiasm. It was much to be regretted, he said, that the tariff came up for discussion at this time: "There is nothing I shudder at more than the idea of a separate Union. . . . The State governments hold in check the federal and must ever hold it in check, and the virtue of the people supported by the sovereign states, must prevent consolidation, and will put down that corruption engendered by the executive, wielded, as it has been lately, by executive organs, to perpetuate their own power. The result of the present struggle between the virtue of the people and executive patronage will test the stability of our government."[1]

September 3d Hayne wrote. He denied that his people desired disunion, as charged from some quarters, and declared they were loyal to Jackson and believed in his fairness. "Should Mr. Adams be reëlected," he said, "and should his administration continue to act on the policy of wholly disregarding the feelings and interests of the Southern States; should they push the manufacturing system to the point of annihilating our foreign commerce, and above all, should they meddle with our slave institutions, I would not be answerable for the consequences. I think our Legislature will probably take strong grounds on these subjects, but I have no apprehension of their going at this time beyond a formal manifesto setting forth the injuries of the South, and giving a solemn warning against the consequences of a *continuous disregard* of our rights and interests. Should you be elected, as there is every reason to believe, we shall look to you as a *Pacificator*."[2] The manifesto, to which he referred, was undoubtedly Calhoun's *Exposition*.

Hayne's letter was a warning and a suggestion. There is no evidence of Jackson's real feeling about the matter. Outwardly, at that time, he gave no token of opposition, but he yielded noth-

[1] J. Hamilton, Jr., to Jackson, May 25, 1828; Jackson to J. Hamilton, Jr., June 29, 1828, Jackson Mss.
[2] Hayne to Jackson, September 3, 1828, Jackson Mss.

ing to the nullifiers in their desire to have a secretary of the treasury favorable to a lower tariff. Calhoun's connection with the movement was soon known in Washington, at least as early as inauguration day, but this could hardly have affected Jackson. Nullification was as yet entirely theoretical, it was in touch with the Southern party, he was still well disposed toward the vice-president, and party harmony was essential. But the controling faction was opposed to Calhoun, and in that was the possibility of much hostility.

The bold challenge of 1828 was followed by a year and a half of singular calm. Did they wait for the expected triumph of Calhoun in 1832, or were they endeavoring to learn what Jackson would do if the program should proceed at once? Neither question can be answered, but Calhoun's expectations in the former respect must have been deeply bound up with those of the South Carolina party, and a realization of this gave courage to his enemies. The Webster-Hayne debate in January, 1830, placed the two theories of the union definitely before the nation. People everywhere were taking sides, and it began to be asked on which the President would be found. Within three months of the famous debate the question was answered at the Jefferson dinner.

In the autumn of 1829, the President learned of Calhoun's position in regard to the invasion of Florida, during the winter and early spring the Eaton affair was in its most annoying stage, and that also bore on his feeling toward Calhoun. It was, therefore, natural that he should have made the occasion of denouncing nullification that for striking Calhoun a severe and unexpected blow. April 15th, was Jefferson's birthday, long observed by democrats for renewing their devotion to party principles. As the day approached in 1830, the South Carolina group prepared to take prominent part in its celebration. Their object, says Van Buren very plausibly, was two-fold; (1) to get the sympathy of Virginia by exalting Jefferson and by stressing the relation of their own doctrine to the resolutions of 1798, and (2) to please Georgia, long opposed to South Carolina, by praising her position in the affair of the Cherokees, itself a kind of nullification.

Invitations were sent as a matter of course to Jackson and Van Buren. The two took counsel and agreed that Jackson at the dinner should give a toast which should announce the hostility of the administration to nullification. The sentiment was written down and placed in his pocket before he went to the dinner. When called on he arose and proposed: "Our Union, it must be preserved!" Consternation seized the state rights group. Hayne, quick witted and resourceful, hastily suggested to the speaker that the word "federal" be placed before the word "union." He thought this would make the toast lean somewhat to a state rights interpretation. Now this, says Van Buren, was the way the sentiment was first written, but Jackson, scrawling it off on his toast-card just before he arose, omitted "federal." No objection was made to its restoration.

Calhoun, who followed, gave a toast more expressive of South Carolina principles — "The Union, next to our liberty most dear! May we all remember that it can only be preserved by respecting the rights of the States and distributing equally the benefit and the burthen of the Union!"[1] It lacked the laconic force of Jackson's utterance, nor did it come with the same sense of authority. It is noteworthy that the next day Forsyth wrote to Crawford the letter which brought forth the avowal of Calhoun's attitude in the Seminole affair.[2]

The South Carolinians did not take offense at the toast but tried to lessen its effect by asserting that it must be understood in a "Pickwickian sense." Some of them took comfort out of

---

[1]Van Buren, *Autobiography*, IV, 99-107, Van Buren Mss.
[2]See above, II., 509.

the Maysville veto, which came a month later, but among them were few of those who followed Calhoun closely. In the state, they tried to create the feeling that they had the President's support. About this time — in May, 1830 — Joel R. Poinsett, returning from Mexico, arrived in Washington and had a frank talk with Jackson about South Carolina affairs. The latter showed that he was committed against nullification which he pronounced madness. Poinsett proceeded to South Carolina, where an active union party was being organized. In it were former Governor Taylor, D. R. Williams, D. E. Huger, James L. Petigru and Hugh S. Legare. Between these two parties there was much scowling with some stronger action during the second half of 1830. Early in the next year, Calhoun published his attack on Van Buren and Jackson, and in the following summer he uncovered his position as champion of nullification and gave a vigor to the protesting party in his state which up to that time it did not have.

These events seem to indicate that throughout the quiescent period in 1830, the movement waited on Jackson. The vice-president arrived in Washington a few days before New Year's determined to keep aloof from the President. He refused to attend the New Year's reception at the White House and showed to whomever asked to see it the hostile correspondence of the preceding summer. To his friends, he wrote in deprecation of their confidence in the President: "The position which General Jackson has taken of halting between the parties," he said, "as if it were possible to reconcile two hostile systems, must keep us distracted and weakened during his time. To expect to be able to support him, taking the position he has, and to unite the South in zealous opposition to the system, which he more than half supports, is among the greatest absurdities. Had he placed himself on principle, and surrounded himself with the talents, virtue and experience of the party, his personal popularity would, beyond all doubt, have enabled us to restore the Constitution, arrest the progress of corruption, harmonize the Union, and thereby avert the calamity which seems to impend over us; as it is, that very popularity is the real source of our weakness and distraction. . . . Believing that an united effort of the South is hopeless during his time, we must next look to the action of our own state, as she is the only one, that can possibly put herself on her sovereignty. Nothing must be omitted to unite and strengthen her, for on her union and firmness, at this time, the liberty of the whole country in no small degree depends."[1] In the *Exposition* Calhoun established himself as covert leader of nullification; in this letter he came out as open leader of the cause.

An incident of midsummer, 1830, shows how the game was played in the plan to win Jackson for one side or the other. When Poinsett arrived in Charleston, the union faction gave him a dinner which was intended to rally their own followers. The nullifiers decided to have a dinner of their own and made the arrival of Senator Hayne the occasion. The event was a great success and attracted notice throughout the country. James Hamilton, Jr., sent an account of it to Van Buren, with whom he was in frequent correspondence.[2] He added a warning against Poinsett, charging him with a declaration against devolution, that is, against handing the presidency down to a successor. And then Hamilton shrewdly observed that he himself was for the reëlection of Jackson and that the influence of the United States Bank in the state was against the nullifiers. He evidently hoped this would draw the sympathy of the man at Washington, of whom, Calhoun declared a half year later, as we have seen, that he only could unite the whole South in the cause of nullification.

---

[1] Calhoun, *Correspondence* (Jameson, Editor), 280.

[2] J. Hamilton, Jr., to Van Buren, September 20, 1830; Van Buren to Jackson, July 25, 1830; Van Buren Mss.

It is impossible to say how near Jackson came during this period of waiting to fulfil the hopes of the nullifiers. With most of their leaders he was on friendly terms, but whether his motives were political or otherwise does not appear. In his ordinary moods he was a good politician and quite as capable of a deep game of delay as some who were not so violent in their moments of excitement.

Van Buren's attitude at this time is more easily seen. Hamilton's letters impressed him, and on the one just mentioned, he endorsed the opinion that the letter showed that in the Charleston dinner, the nullifiers went further than they intended. A few days after he heard of that affair, he wrote to Jackson that nullification was declining and the more reliable element among its supporters would soon return to a better state of mind. This shrewd politician was very timid and dependent on his colleagues for his views. Both failings here tended to bring him into acquiescence with the part of the scheme it was desired to make him play.

Having brought Van Buren to a yielding state of mind, the nullifiers sought through him to affect the will of Jackson himself. Hayne cautiously made the approach. October 28th— it was still 1830 — he wrote to Van Buren in anticipation of approaching events. The situation in South Carolina, he said, was exaggerated by enemies out of the state. No measures had been adopted or contemplated looking "in the remotest degree" to a dissolution of the union: the announcement of an abstract right on the part of a state to judge of an infraction of the constitution and to provide means of redress, he asserted, "no more implies the immediate and rash exercise of that power than the assertion of the right of a state to secede from the Union (which all seem to admit), implies that the Union ought to be immediately dissolved. . . . 'The extreme medicine of the State is not likely to become our daily bread.' If our friends in Washington have the smallest uneasiness at the state of affairs in South Carolina, bid them dismiss their fears. No rash measures will be adopted — but tranquility will never be restored to the South until the American System is abandoned, and if the federal government shall go on in the assumption of unconstitutional power, *collision with the States* will sooner or later become inevitable."[1]

As to practical affairs, Hayne admitted that the legislature was about to vote on a convention, but since a two-thirds vote was necessary to call such a body, he thought it would not carry. But if it should be called, it would undoubtedly be more conservative than the legislature. Its effect would be to draw the attention of the country to the burden of the South on account of the tariff, and that would give Jackson an opportunity to intervene as a "pacificator." The letter reveals the part the nullifiers hoped to get the President to play, and this probably accounts for their quiet attitude in 1830. They were willing to award to Jackson the glory of making a compromise, if he could only be relied upon to play the right part at the proper time.

But Jackson was not suited for the part he was desired to assume. The only pacification he was apt in making was such as he gave to the Creeks in 1814 and to the army of Pakenham a few months later—the peace of submission. He was already determined that the plans of the nullifiers were "mad projects," and he caused his friends to know his position.[2] In the autumn the attempt to call a convention was defeated in the legislature by the efforts of the active union party, who were already beginning to assert in the state that the President was on their side. They could cite his Jefferson birthday speech as well as his declarations to friends to show that he was against the nullifiers.

[1] Van Buren Mss.
[2] Jackson to Robert Oliver, October 26, 1830, Poinsett to Jackson, October 23, 1830; Jackson Mss.

Calhoun's special friends knew of the quarrel of the preceding summer, and they must have known how hopeless it was to expect help from Jackson. The vice-president, fresh from consultations with these friends, arrived in Washington late in December and began at once to prepare the pamphlet he soon hurled at Van Buren. He would have been pleased, as we have seen,[1] to keep the President out of the quarrel entirely, but that was impossible. From that time, Calhoun became the chief reliance of the nullifiers, and his powerful aid, with the surrender of thoughts of compromise, gave the party the dominance in the state.

In the summer of 1831, two Charleston merchants, both nullifiers, undertook to test the constitutionality of the tariff laws. They refused to pay the bonds they had given to guarantee the payment of duties on certain commodities, alleging the illegality of a protective tariff. The district-attorney was instructed to prosecute them, but he, a nullifier, refused and resigned his office. Jackson's first impulse was to impeach him for violating his oath, but that was too impracticable, and he contented himself with sending a secret agent to Charleston to report on the progress of events while proceedings to collect the bonds were halted. At the same time, he was in constant correspondence with the union leaders in the city, particularly Poinsett, from whom he received full information. Letters to and from these leaders constitute a valuable source of information for this phase of the movement.[2]

While things hung in the balance, almost at the last moment before the appearance of the Calhoun pamphlet, Hayne and his friends undertook to get one of their supporters appointed district-attorney in South Carolina. Jackson refused to make the

---

[1] See above, II., 517.

[2] They are found in the Jackson Mss., in the Library of Congress, and in the Poinsett papers in the possession of the Pennsylvania Historical Society. The latter collection has been freely used by Stillé in a sketch of *The Life and Services of Joel R. Poinsett* Pennsylvania *Magazine of History*, 1888.

appointment, and Hayne wrote a remonstrance against his action, arguing that the administration ought to be as fair as the state rights party in South Carolina, which placed union men in state office regardless of their politics. Jackson replied frankly that he did not believe a state could nullify a law of congress and that he would be highly blamable if he appointed a man to execute the laws of the union who openly avowed that one of those laws could not be executed in the state in which he lived. It was a considerate letter, and it expressed great personal consideration for many of the nullifiers. It must have been the result of careful consideration; for on the back of Hayne's letter he wrote in terms less cautious: "Note — I draw a wide difference between State Rights and the advocates of them, and a nullifier. One will preserve the union of the States. The other will dissolve the union by destroying the Constitution by acts unauthorized in it."[1] This comment has logical defects, but the letter to Hayne must have left no doubt in that gentleman's mind in regard to the attitude of the President.

Having lost hope of Jackson's aid, the nullifiers now proceeded, as Calhoun indicated in January,[2] to organize that forceful protest which was to run so close to disunion. Even after the publication of the pamphlet in regard to the breach with the President, Calhoun thought it best to say little about Jackson and to concentrate the opposition on Van Buren,[3] his purpose being, evidently, not to give the former a pretext to take decided part in the controversy. But this was soon seen to be impossible. May 19th, a dinner was given to McDuffie in Charleston, at which the most extreme nullification sentiment was avowed. Even this did not arouse Calhoun. He saw the tendency it would have to commit the state, but he favored moderation for the present, believing it necessary to give the thinking portion of

[1] Jackson to Hayne, February 6, 1831; Hayne to Jackson, February 4, 1831, Jackson Mss.
[2] See above, II. 557.
[3] Calhoun, *Correspondence* (Jameson, Editor), 289, 290.

the democratic party time to rally to him, after his exposure of Van Buren.[1] His hesitation lasted until July 26th, when he came definitely forward as the avowed champion of the nullifiers. His challenge was expressed in the *Address on the relations which the States and General Government Bear to Each Other*, a restatement of the arguments of the *Exposition* of 1828. From that time he was the open and preëminent leader of the South Carolina movement, giving it a powerful impetus and making it clear that the people of the state could no longer avoid a choice between union and nullification.

When the *Address* was given to the public, Jackson's position was made equally clear. July 4th, both sides in Charleston made elaborate preparations to celebrate the holiday. There were speeches by the respective leaders, and the unionists read publicly with great pride a letter from Jackson announcing complete opposition to nullification, an opinion, he said, "which I have neither interest nor inclination to conceal."[2] This letter was dated June 14th, the day before Berrien, the last opposition member, left the cabinet and several days before the angry controversy between Eaton and Ingham incensed both sides. It seems that in this step Jackson acted deliberately: the alliance with Calhoun was repudiated, friends of Calhoun were thrust out of the cabinet, and now the administration was ranged against nullification. The democratic party had cast off the semblance of nationalism which internal improvements had implied, it was about to crush that extreme form of state rights which came to a head in South Carolina.

In the following winter, the tariff was again before congress. A new bill was passed, the chief purpose of which was to remove the inequalities which won for the bill of 1828 the name, "Tariff of Abominations." It was much like the bill of 1824, and was

---

[1] Calhoun *Correspondence*, 294; Niles, *Register*, XL., 236
[2] Niles, *Register*, XL., 351.

still strongly protective. It did not satisfy the South, and the nullifiers, whose aim was to threaten so loudly that the majority would abandon some of their numerical advantage, decided that the contest should go on.

The tariff passed in July. South Carolina found it exceedingly objectionable and the nullifiers raised loud cries in the campaign then waging and demanded a convention to consider the state's relation to the new law. The results at the polls were favorable and the governor, an ardent nullifier, called a meeting of the legislature, which quickly ordered an election for a convention to meet on November 19th. This precipitancy was employed in order that the intended programme might be completed before the meeting of congress in December, 1832. Now appeared the effects of the powerful efforts of Calhoun. Nearly the whole state turned to his doctrine, and, November 24th, the convention passed the famous nullification ordinance. This instrument declared the tariff laws of 1828 and 1832 unconstitutional and not binding on the state, it prohibited appeals to the supreme court of the United States in cases arising under this ordinance, it ordered all state officials except members of the legislature to take an oath to obey the ordinance, and it fixed February 1, 1833, as the day when it would go into operation. It closed with a threat that an attempt of the federal government to oppose its enforcement would absolve South Carolina from allegiance to the union and leave it a separate sovereign state.[1]

Three days later the state legislature met in regular session and passed laws to meet contingencies likely to arise. It enacted a replevin law and other bills to enable a person who refused to pay duties to recover damages from federal customs officers, who might seize his goods, it passed a law looking to armed resistance, and finally adopted a test for ridding the state of officials who would not accept nullification. Thus panoplied

---

[1]Houston, *Nullification in South Carolina*, 106-111.

South Carolina marched to the contest with the nation, at whose head was Andrew Jackson, keenly alive to the situation.

September 11, 1832, before the South Carolina elections were held, Jackson, fully alive to the progress of nullification, sent a warning to Woodbury, secretary of the navy. Efforts were being made, he said, to win naval and army officers in Charleston from their loyalty to the union, and this must be prevented. There were plans, he asserted, to gain possession of the forts there in order to prevent a blockade of the place, and he directed that the naval authorities at Norfolk, Virginia, be in readiness to despatch a squadron if it were needed.[1] October 29th, he ordered the commanders of the forts in Charleston harbor to double their vigilance and defend their posts against any persons whatsover.[2]

Early in November, he sent George Breathit to South Carolina ostensibly as an agent of the post-office department, but he carried letters to Poinsett and was instructed to visit various parts of the state observing the temper, purposes, and military strength of the nullifiers. "The duty of the Executive is a plain one," said Jackson, "the laws will be executed and the Union preserved by all the constitutional and legal means he is invested with, and I rely with great confidence on the support of every honest patriot in South Carolina."[3]

When Jackson heard the news from South Carolina, he wrote in his fragmentary journal:

South Carolina has passed her ordinance of nullification and secession. As soon as it can be had in authentic form, meet it with a proclamation. Nullification has taken deep root in Virginia, it must be arrested by the good sense of the people, and by a full appeal to them by proclamation, the absurdity of nullification strongly repudiated as a constitutional and peaceful measure, and the principles of our govt. fully set forth, as a government based on the confederation of perpetual union

[1] Jackson to Woodbury, September 11, 1832, Jackson Mss.
[2] Jackson to secretary of war, October 29, 1832, Jackson Mss.
[3] Jackson to Poinsett, November 7, 1832, Poinsett Papers, Stillée's sketch reprinted, 61.

made more perfect by the present constitution, which is the act of the people so far as powers are granted by them in the federal constitution.[1]

Here we have the germ of the nullification proclamation. The ideas are not as clear as in that famous paper, but the note shows that he was on his own initiative thoroughly opposed to secession.

The position of the executive, however, had some serious difficulties. Legally he might interfere forcefully in state matters in two events: 1. If the governor of the state requested him to suppress an insurrection; but under existing circumstances in South Carolina this was not to be expected. 2. To enforce the laws of congress; but the laws provided no clear procedure for such intervention when the law was violated by a state. It was contemplated that in an ordinary case a federal officer could summon a *posse comitatus*, as a state officer might do, to aid him in his duty; but this could hardly be done against a whole people. It was an unforseen contingency, and the executive branch of government must find a way to meet it. Jackson realized the deficiency and asked congress to enact a law to remedy it; but until that could be done, he fell back on the theory of the *posse*. He encouraged Poinsett and his friends to be ready to be summoned on such duty, he placed arms at convenient and safe places, some of them across the North Carolina border, and he promised that if necessary, he would march to the aid of the defenders of the union at the head of a large force from other states, itself a kind of augmented *posse comitatus*.

Such was Jackson's feeling: in practice, he could not go so far. Nullification, until the adoption of the ordinance of November 24th, was closely bound up with the general Southern opposition to the tariff, and the administration hesitated to press it lest the whole South should become nullifiers. The

[1] Jackson Mss.

South Carolinians played earnestly for this wider cause, and sought particularly to win Virginia. To that end, they stressed the connection between nullification and the Virginia and Kentucky Resolutions, trying to convert the regular republicans in that state. But the old antipathy was too strong: Virginia republicans of the Crawford school disliked Calhoun and all he stood for too much to follow him into his new vagaries. All this did not appear on the surface, and when in July, 1832, Senator Tazewell, an extreme state rights doctrinaire, suddenly resigned his seat in the United States senate, it caused much apprehension in administrative circles[1] which desired to avoid taking the initiative in a policy of repression.

But vigilance was not relaxed. Seven revenue cutters and the *Natchez* a ship of war, were sent to Charleston with orders to be ready for instant action. They took position where their guns could sweep the "Battery," the fashionable water front, on which dwelt the most prominent families in the place. Troops were ordered from Fortress Monroe to reinforce the garrison, and General Scott was directed to take chief command of the defenses and to strengthen them as he found necessary. There was to be no relaxation of the customs regulations, and in all things the authority of the government must be unimpaired. But it was not desired to irritate the inhabitants, and the commander was directed to surrender all state property claimed of him, even to arms and military supplies.

November 18th Jackson pronounced the movement of the nullifiers a bubble, but admitted their recklessness might lead to worse. In the forthcoming message, he said, he would refer to the affair as something to be checked by existing law. He would only ask that the revenue laws be changed so that in states where the legislature sought to defeat them, the collector might demand duties in cash. By ceasing to give bonds to

[1] Jackson to Poinsett, December 9, 1832, Poinsett Papers, in Stillé's reprint, page 64.

secure deferred payments, the payer of duties could not bring suit in which he disputed the legality of the duty. "This," declared Jackson, "is all that we want peacefully to nullify the nullifyers."[1]

The quick and vigorous action of the nullifiers in the succeeding fortnight made him change his mind. In his annual message, December 4th, 1832, he referred to the danger which threatened, expressed the hope that the laws would prove sufficient for the crisis, and promised to communicate further information on the subject if it should be necessary.[2] These words disappointed most friends of the union, and his opponents openly expressed their horror. "The message," said Adams, "goes to dissolve the the Union into its original elements and is in substance a complete surrender to the nullifiers." Jackson was much embarrassed by the situation. The party was alarmed at the prospect of a contest which might involve the whole South. When the message was written, some days before it went to congress, he was not convinced that extreme measures would be necessary.

About this time he received a letter from Poinsett, written November 29th, which showed how dangerous the situation had become in the disaffected state. Sixteen thousand citizens, said the writer, were deprived of their rights by the recent action of the legislature and left without other source of help than the national government. Some unionists, Colonel Drayton among them, thought congress would acquiesce and let South Carolina go in peace: some despairing ones even talked of leaving the state for other homes. But Poinsett protested that he would remain and fight it out, whatever the consequences. Such a letter was calculated to arouse the deepest emotions in a man like Jackson, who on December 2nd, said in a letter of his own, "Nullification means insurrection and war; and the other States have a right to

---

[1] Jackson to [Van Buren], November 18, 1832, Jackson Mss.
[2] Richardson, *Messages and Papers of the Presidents*, II., 599.

put it down." December 9th, he announced that congress would sustain him in a programme of force against nullification. "I will meet it," he said, "at the threshold and have the leaders arrested and arraigned for treason. I am only waiting to be furnished with the acts of your Legislature to make a communication to Congress, asking the means necessary to carry my proclamation into complete effect, and by an exemplary punishment of those leaders for treason so unprovoked, put down this rebellion and strengthen our happy Government both at home and abroad. . . . The wicked madness and folly of the leaders, the delusion of their followers, in the attempt to destroy themselves and our Union has not its parallel in the history of the world. The Union will be preserved. The safety of the republic, the supreme law, which will be promptly obeyed by me."[1]

The proclamation, which he issued the day after he sent this message of support to the union men in South Carolina, was a warning to the nullifiers, an appeal to the patriotism of the nation, and a constitutional argument against the doctrines of Calhoun. The doctrine of state veto on laws of congress, said the proclamation, is constitutionally absurd, and if allowed it would have dissolved the union when Pennsylvania objected to the excise law, when Virginia resented the carriage tax, or when New England objected to the War of 1812. A law thus nullified by one state must be void for all; so that one state could repeal an act of congress for the whole union by merely declaring it unconstitutional. Through the whole document, ran a strong vein of nationalistic philosophy, supporting the right of congress to establish protection, denying that the constitution is a compact of sovereign states, and announcing that a state has no right to secede. The proclamation closed with a fervid appeal to the "fellow-citizens of my native state" not to incur the penalty of the laws by following blindly "men who are either de-

---

[1] Jackson to Poinsett, December 2 and 9, 1832, Poinsett Mss.

ceived themselves or wish to deceive you." "The laws of the United States must be executed," said the President, "I have no discretionary power on the subject; my duty is emphatically pronounced in the Constitution. Those who told you that you might peaceably prevent their execution, deceived you; they could not have been deceived themselves. They know that a forcible opposition could alone prevent the execution of the laws, and they know that such opposition must be repelled. Their object is disunion. But be not deceived by names. Disunion by armed force is *treason*. Are you ready to incur its guilt?"[1]

The nullification proclamation is written with a charm of logic and nicety of expression worthy of John Marshall. There is a persistent and widely accepted tradition that it was the work of Edward Livingston, who as secretary of state signed it with Jackson. Both its literary quality and its subtlety of reasoning show that at least the part relating to constitutional matters was not the work of the President. The closing part — the appeal to the South Carolinians — has much of his fire and suggests that he wrote it originally, but that its style was remodeled by him who wrote the former part. As a whole, the proclamation is one of the best papers of an American President and compares favorably with the inaugural addresses of Lincoln.

A letter to General Coffee, written December 14th, gives Jackson's views without Livingston's charm of statement. In it is the following:

Can any one of common sense believe the absurdity that a faction of any state, or a state, has a right to secede and destroy this union and the liberty of our country with it, or nullify the laws of the Union; then indeed is our constitution a rope of sand; under such I would not live. . . . This more perfect union made by the whole people of the United States, granted the general government certain powers, and retained others; but

[1]Richardson, *Messages and Papers of the Presidents*, II., 640.

nowhere can it be found where the right to nullify a law, or to secede from this union has been retained by the state. No' amendment can be made to the instrument, constitutionally, but in the mode pointed out in the constitution itself, every mode else is revolution or rebellion. The people are the sovereigns, they can alter and amend, and the people alone in the mode pointed out by themselves can dissolve this union peaceably. The right of resisting oppression is a natural right, and when oppression comes, the right of resistance and revolution are justifiable, but the moral obligations is binding upon all to fulfil the obligations as long as the compact is executed agreeable to the terms of the agreement. Therefore, when a faction in a state attempts to nullify a constitutional law of congress, or to destroy the union, the balance of the people composing this union have a perfect right to coerce them to obedience. This is my creed, which you will read in the proclamation which I sent you the other day. No man will go farther than I will to preserve every right reserved to the people, or the states; nor no man will go farther to sustain the acts of congress passed according to the express grants to congress. The union must be preserved, and it will now be tested, by the support I get by the people. I will die for the union."[1]

In this letter we find no mental subtlety and but the simplest ideas of constitutional law; but in strength of will and devotion to the union it is splendid.

The response of the states,[2] about which he was anxious, was soon seen to be all that could be desired. One after another they sent assurances of support, and later came resolutions from states north and south condemning nullification as a doctrine and as an expedient. There could be no doubt that if the matter came to the worst, ample forces would be ready to suppress the nullifiers. In forty days, Jackson said, he could throw fifty

---

[1] *American Historical Magazine* (Nashville), IV., 236.
[2] For responses of the states and other documents on this subject, see Ames, *State Documents on Federal Relations*, 164-190.

thousand men into South Carolina and forty days thereafter as many more.[1]

The attention of both the administration and South Carolina was especially directed toward Georgia and Virginia. Between the position of the former in regard to the Indians[2] and that of the nullifiers there was much in common. Jackson feared that she would go over to the new heresy and foresaw that if he had a clash with her on that account, she would be ranged on the side of South Carolina in the larger quarrel. He urged the Georgia congressman and ex-Governor Troup to do all they could to avoid a clash and to Governor Lumpkins wrote, "My great desire is that you should do no act that would give to the Federal Court a legal jurisdiction, over a case that might arise with the Cherokee Indians;" and he begged Lumpkins to believe in "my continued confidence and respect, in which, you may always confide, until you hear otherwise from my own lips, all rumors to the contrary notwithstanding."[3] Under the circumstances, Georgia owed it to Jackson to remain quiet, and her attitude in the crisis of the winter was all that could be expected. Her legislature was content to pass resolutions calling for a convention of the states to amend the constitution in regard to the point in question.

Virginia was important on account of her influence. To the earnest entreaties of South Carolina her reply was resolutions in which she professed entire loyalty to the resolves of 1798 and 1799, and the dispatch of an agent, B. W. Leigh, to urge the nullifiers to suspend their ordinance until congress adjourned. He arrived after February 1st, but what he asked had been done before that time. A group of prominent nullifiers, acting informally, in Charleston, on January 21st, approved certain resolutions advising the officers of government that it would not be well to enforce the ordinance at present and pledging themselves

[1]Jackson to Poinsett, December 9, 1832, Poinsett Mss.
[2]Jackson to Lumpkins, June 22, 1832, Jackson Mss.
[3]See below, pages 684–692

to fulfil the program of nullification if at the end of a reasonable time the demands of the state were not granted. The resolutions were extra legal, sensible, and effective. February 1st came and went without conflict, and the federal officers continued to collect duties in the Charleston custom-house without opposition.

Meantime, the state was greatly excited. The unionists were actively preparing for an encounter, though careful to do all in their power to prevent one through some rash deed. The nullifiers were equally self-restrained in regard to actual fighting. But each side prepared arms and ammunition, drilled its supporters, and kept watch on its antagonist. Jackson was kept informed of all that was done and was keen for a struggle. His fighting blood was up, and he threw aside all that caution which he displayed earlier in the movement. "The moment they are in hostile array in opposition to the execution of the laws," he wrote, "let it be certified to me, by the atty. for the District or the *Judge*, and I will forthwith order the leaders prosecuted and arrested. If the Marshall is resisted by twelve thousand bayonets, I will have a possee of twenty-four thousand."[1] While the "force bill" was before congress, he wrote: "Should congress fail to act on the bill and I should be informed of the illegal assemblage of an armed force with the intention to oppose the execution of the revenue laws under the late ordinance of So. Carolina, I stand prepared forthwith to issue my proclamation warning them to disperse. Should they fail to comply with the proclamation, I will forthwith call into the field such a force as will overawe resistance, put treason and rebellion down without blood, and arrest and hand over to the judiciary for trial and punishment the leaders, exciters and promoters of this rebellion and treason." He had a tender of volunteers from every state in the union and could bring two hundred thousand into the field within forty days. Should the governor of Virginia, he

[1] Jackson to Poinsett, January 16, 1833, Poinsett Mss.

said, have the folly to forbid the passage of troops through his state to the scene of treason "I would arrest him at the head of his troops and hand him over to the civil authority for trial. The voluntiers of his own state would enable me to do this." [1]

When Jackson sent his proclamation to Poinsett in December, he said he was only waiting for certified copies of the acts of the South Carolina legislature putting nullification into force in order to ask congress for power to enforce the proclamation and punish the leaders of the rebellion. [2] This information did not come, and unwilling to wait longer than January 16th, he sent to congress on that day, a special message asking for authority to alter or abolish certain ports of entry, to use force to execute the revenue law, and to try in the federal courts cases which might arise in the present contingency. Five days later, a bill in accord with these requests was introduced in the senate by Wilkins, of Pennsylvania. It was popularly called the "force bill," but the nullifiers expressed their horror by styling it the "bloody bill." There was much opposition to it; for many who were not nullifiers, were unwilling to coerce a state.

The situation brought genuine alarm to the managers of the Jacksonian democracy. It was not possible to tell how much the Calhoun defection would weaken the party. The last stages of the fight against the bank were approaching when the administration would need all its resources. Moreover, the tariff wave was receding. It had been partly due to the enthusiasm of the rural North and West for "the American system" through which, it was believed, cities, better transportation, and rich and prosperous farming communities would soon spring up. This was an unwarranted expectation, and the moment of elation was passing. Many politicians of the old republican school yielded to the tariff unwillingly and at the first intimation of recession

---

[1] Jackson to Poinsett, January 24, 1833, Poinsett Mss.
[2] *Ibid* to *Ibid*, December 9, 1832, Poinsett Mss.

supported the reaction.   From all these causes the time favored compromise.

Before congress met the administration was prepared to take a milder position on the tariff.   The approaching extinction of the public debt, which would give a surplus, made revision seem necessary.   December 13th, in a letter in the Richmond *Inquirer*, a close friend of the government, probably Cass, secretary of war, suggested that Virginia propose a reduction of the tariff.   This was better than a suggestion in the annual message, since such a course would tend to turn from the President the protectionist group.   December 27th, the house committee of ways and means, through its chairman, Verplanck, of New York, introduced a new tariff bill, reducing the duties in two years to about half of the former rates.   It was prepared by Cass, Verplanck, and other administration friends, but was especially supported by the New York school, who following suggestions from South Carolina, were willing to have their favorite appear as "pacificator."[1]   Its appearance aroused strong hostility from the protectionists, and not all the New York democrats could be got to vote for it.   It was too drastic a reduction for the circumstances, and it stuck in the house so long that Van Buren's opponents had the opportunity to pass a bill less injurious to the manufacturers; and in doing so, they gave the honor of the compromise to another than he.

Clay came into the senate in December, 1831: early in January 1833, Calhoun, resigning the vice-presidency, took the seat in that body made vacant by the election of Hayne to the governorship of his native state.   Each new senator smarted from defeat at Jackson's hands, each felt that Jackson was leading the country to misfortune, and each was bent on impeding the course of the destroyer.   Early in the year it was noised abroad that they were in alliance against the administration.   In regard to the

---

[1]Cambreleng to Van Buren, December 29, 1832, and February 5, 1833, Van Buren Mss.

"force bill" the Kentuckian was chiefly silent. He would not fight the battles of the state rights advocates, not even to embarrass Jackson, nor would he help suppress nullification. In the final vote on the bill, he did not respond on either side. His energy was saved for the tariff.

But Calhoun was deeply engaged as soon as the "force bill" appeared in the senate. He offered resolutions in support of his theory of government, and when the senate brushed them aside, he plunged into the acrid debate with all his energy. In the beginning it was evident that the extreme state right democrats found the bill very disagreeable. Jackson was forced to see a division in his own ranks. "There are more nullifiers here," he said, "than dare openly avow it," but he did not doubt they would be good Jackson men at home.[1]

If his enemies had combined with the disaffected in his own party the bill might have been defeated. But they could no more combine in this way than the radical state rights men could support a bill to give the President the authority to suppress a state. Webster has been praised for coming to the defense of the bill. It would have been entirely captious for him to oppose it. He could hardly break down Hayne's nullification arguments in 1830 and refuse in 1833 to create the means necessary to put his own views into execution. But his aid was splendidly rendered and most effective. He brought the anti-Jacksonians with him, and these, with the loyal Jackson followers, made the bill safe in the senate.

Before it could pass Calhoun withdrew his opposition in consequence of Clay's concession on the tariff. February 12th the father of the "American system," while Verplanck's bill was still in the house, arose in the senate and offered a compromise tariff of his own. It proposed that for all articles which paid more than 20 per cent. duty the surplus above that rate

---

[1] Jackson to Cryer, February 20, 1833. *American Historical Magazine* (Nashville), IV., 237.

should be gradually reduced until in 1842 it should entirely disappear. Verplanck would have reduced duties within two years by half: Clay would do it in ten years to a 20 per cent. basis. The latter plan was less violent than the former and was preferred by the manufacturers, if either must be taken. This was all that South Carolina contended for. Nullification was the club with which she sought to ward off a danger, and that danger gone she willingly threw the club away: she protested from the first that she disliked to use it. When the vote on the "force bill" was taken Calhoun and his followers left the chamber. Obstinate John Tyler would not run away, and he loved state rights too much to support the bill. He, therefore, remained in his seat and cast the only negative against thirty-two affirmative votes. In the house the bill passed in much the same manner, John Quincy Adams leading the anti-Jackson party in favor of the measure.

Clay's part of the compromise was adroitly played. His bill was opposed in the senate because it was unconstitutional for a revenue bill to originate in that chamber. He then arranged through much quiet work to have it substituted for the Verplanck bill in the other house, which through the opposition of the tariff party was not likely to pass at that session. February 25th, in the afternoon as the house was about to adjourn for dinner, Letcher, of Kentucky, Clay's fast friend, arose and moved the substitution of bills. After a short debate the change was made and the bill ordered engrossed for the third reading by a vote of one hundred and five to seventy-one. The tariff men were surprised, but the administration party were previously informed of the plan. They rallied to the proposition as part of the compromise by which the South Carolina crisis was to be removed from the stage of action. The thing was done so quickly, said Benton, that the hot dinners of the representatives were eaten before the food became cold.[1]

[1] Benton, *View*, I., 309-312.

Van Buren's friends were shocked. All the honor of pacification to which they looked through the Verplanck bill were suddenly snatched away by Clay. They thought a trick was played on them and Cambreleng complained that everybody seemed to be against New York.[1] He was nearly right: except for Jackson himself, very few of the leaders in Washington seemed to care to help the New Yorker to the goal of his ambition.

Although the South Carolinians resisted the passage of the "force bill" to their uttermost, they accepted the compromise. Their convention reassembled March 11th to consider the situation. It repealed the ordinance nullifying the tariff laws of the union and passed another nullifying the "force bill." The latter step was ridiculous, but it saved the face of the nullifying party and enabled it to claim complete victory. No one, within the state or out of it, was disposed to deny them this comfort. Most people were glad to be rid of an unpromising situation — the politicians because they had other affairs to arrange, and the people because they loved peace and feared disunion.

Jackson alone of his party seems to have looked beyond the political significance of the situation. In spite of his latent feeling of protest, he temporized along with the others until the nullification ordinance was passed. This action he took as a challenge, and leading his unwilling followers he committed his party to the cause of union. His letters to Poinsett and the replies to them show well the conditions in South Carolina. But the Van Buren correspondence at this period — the letters of party lieutenants to Van Buren and those which passed between him and Jackson — show the political side.

The nullification proclamation, as it was the first note of Jackson's more energetic programme, was the first sign for dissatisfaction among his followers. They disliked its national tone

[1]Cambreleng to Van Buren, February 5, 1833, Van Buren Mss.

which Cambreleng pronounced "the metaphysics of the Montesquieu of the Cabinet." To the mass of people, he said, this would make no difference; they would see only an endangered union, whereas "the speculations are left for refinements of those who are only capable of transferring the special pleading of chancery into the councils of statesmen." [1]

The listlessness of the party in the face of disunion is another illustration of the divergence between its attitude and that of the President. The day before the date of the proclamation Michael Hoffman, a New York congressman, described the situation to Van Buren. He thought the ways and means committee would be satisfactory on every bank question, and that on the tariff it would not adopt South Carolina's equalizing ultimatum; but "meanwhile South Carolina will rush on *in furorem*. The President will march against her, civil war will rage, and the poor fools who can see no danger now, will be frightened out, not of their wits, for they have none, but out of their folly. How they will behave then I cannot anticipate, for when their folly is gone, there will be nothing left of them." He added that General Scott thought the situation very 'delicate. [2]

A week later so valiant a person as Benton wrote that everybody was concerned to prevent the beginning of bloodshed in South Carolina, that there was talk of an extra session of congress in the spring, and that all agreed peace would come if Jackson's suggestion in his message of a more moderate tariff were adopted, but the existing congress would not support this. [3] This idea found support in Cambreleng's terse forecast: "We shall do nothing," he wrote "but project tariffs this winter — while the Legislature will talk of a convention of states. We shall have some riots in Charleston, some bloodshed perhaps; some stormy debating in congress in February and the new congress will

[1]Cambreleng to Van Buren, December 10, 1832, Van Buren Mss.
[2]Hoffman to Van Buren, December 9, 1832, Van Buren Mss.
[3]Benton to Van Buren, December 16, 1832, Van Buren Mss.

have to act and supersede the necessity of a convention."[1] In no letter in either the Jackson or Van Buren correspondence is there evidence that any other leader in his party felt the same impulse that Jackson felt to crush resistance and enforce the authority of the union.

These alarms were poured into the ear of Van Buren, who as vice-president-elect remained decently at Albany until March 4th. With characteristic, and probably necessary, caution he approached Jackson on the subject. Our people are restive, he said, because the opposition try to interpret some parts of the proclamation as a condemnation of the state rights doctrine of the West and South. They find difficulty in holding meetings, and there is a disposition to say harsh things, which is unfortunate. Great discretion is necessary in New York on account of the diversity of tariff opinion and of feelings engendered in the late election. This he said in substance, closing with the assurance that he would do what he could to keep things on the right course.[2]

Jackson's reply took little notice of Van Buren's warning but dwelt on the imminence of armed force. The moment the nullifiers raised an army, he said, he would issue a proclamation telling them to disperse and give the marshal troops enough to suppress them. He would arrest the leaders and turn them over to the United States courts for trial. He referred to Virginia's late reassertion of the doctrine of 1798, saying:

The absurdity of the Virginia doctrine is too plain to need much comment. If they would say, that the state had a right to fight, and if she has the power, to revolution, it would be right but at the same time it must be acknowledged, that the other states have equal rights, and the right to preserve the union. The preservation of the union is the supreme law. To shew the

---

[1] Cambreleng to Van Buren, December 9, 1832, Van Buren Mss.

[2] Van Buren to Jackson, December 22, 1832, Van Buren Mss.

absurdity — Congress have the right to admit new states. When territories the[y] are subject to the laws of the union; The day after admission they have the right to secede and dissolve it. We gave five millions for Louisiana. We admitted her into the union. She too has the right to secede, close the commerce of six states, and levy contributions both upon exports and imports. A state cannot come into the union without the consent of congress, but it can go out when it pleases. Such a union as this would be like a bag of sand with both ends open — the least pressure and it runs out at both ends. It is an insult to the understanding of the sages who formed it, to believe that such a union was ever intended. It could not last a month. It is a confederated perpetual union, first made by the people in their sovereign state capacities, upon which we the people of these United States made a more perfect union, which can only be dissolved by the people who formed it, and in the way pointed out in the instrument, or by revolution.[1]

Van Buren's anxiety was not allayed by this vigorous utterance and he wrote again. He agreed that there should be no faltering now, but warned his friend that merely passing an act to raise a military force was not treason and that constructive treason was unpopular in the United States. He advised Jackson to ask only for force to execute the laws. He knew the latter would say that this was the writer's old trick of saying, " 'caution, caution'; but my dear sir, I have always thought that considering our respective temperaments, there is no way perhaps in which I could better render you that service which I owe you as well from a sense of deep gratitude as public duty." He added that Virginia was much concerned over the proclamation that he did not think South Carolina would secede but if such a thing happened Virginia would desire the remaining states to decide whether they would form a new union without

[1] Jackson to Van Buren, December 25, 1832, Van Buren Mss.

the seceder or wage war to retain her in the union. The best solution he saw was the modification of the tariff.[1]

Other letters followed from the same writer, but a fortnight passed before they were answered by the busy Jackson. This reply showed unexpected self-control. It was necessary, he said, to protect good citizens and federal officers in South Carolina who might fall under the state's laws of vengeance; and as to the tariff, it was necessary to think of both ends of the union; for New England, protected by the tariff, might be as willing to secede if protection was abandoned as the South if it was not abandoned. Nullification and secession must be put down once for all: he must give congress full notice of the danger so that it could act before February 1st, or he would be chargeable with neglect of duty. "I will meet all things with deliberate firmness and forbearance, but wo to those nullifiers who shed the first blood. The moment I am prepared with proof I will direct prosecution for treason to be instituted against the leaders, and if they are surrounded with 12,000 bayonets our marshal shall be aided by 24,000 and arrest them in the midst thereof. Nothing must be permitted to weaken our government at home or abroad. Virginia, except a few nullifiers and politicians, is true to the core. I could march from that State 40,000 men in forty days. Nay they are ready in North Carolina, in Tennessee, in all western States, and from good old democratic Pennsylvania I have a tender of upwards of 50,000; and from the borders of South Carolina in North Carolina I have a tender of one entire Regiment. The union shall be preserved."[2]

On the day Jackson wrote this determined letter, Silas Wright wrote in another strain to Van Buren. Everything, he said, was at stake, even the union as well as "our most favorite political hopes and prospects." For the time he seems to have forgot-

[1] Van Buren to Jackson, December 27, 1832, Van Buren Mss.

[2] Jackson to Van Buren, January 13, 1833, and Cambreleng to Van Buren, December 26, 1832, Van Buren Mss.

ten that all his hope consisted in sticking close to that leader who alone could carry into safety the head of the New York group. In consternation he demanded that Van Buren tell him how to vote on the Verplanck bill, he admitted that he had never voted from conviction on the tariff question, but from expediency, and declared himself willing to do it again. As to others, "the President is very well and cool, calm, and collected, but very firm and decided as to the use of force. As to the sustention of his position that a state cannot secede he is very sensitive, and even abuses mildly Mr. Ritchie." The secretary of war was "highly excited" and McLane in the treasury department, "is much more so." [1]

Jackson's keen observation of the situation did not relax and for the next month the politicians tried to find a way out of the labyrinth. The postponement of the execution of the nullification ordinance seemed only to delay the day when he must strike rebellion. By this time he had lost most of his interest in the attempt to settle the tariff question; and when Clay's compromise was introduced he was quick to resent the prospect that it should take precedence of the "force bill." "I am just informed," he wrote hastily to Grundy on the night of April 13th, "that there will be another move to lay the judiciary ['force'] bill on the table until Mr. Clay's tariff bill is discussed. Surely you and all my friends will push that bill through the senate. This is due the country, it is due to me, and to the safety of this union and surely you and others of the committee who reported it will never let it slumber one day until it passes the senate. Lay all delicacy on this subject aside and compel every man's name to appear upon the journals that the nullifiers may *all* be distinguished from those who are in support of the laws, and the union." [2] His efforts were not successful. His

[1] Wright to Van Buren, January 13, 1833, Van Buren Mss.
[2] Jackson to Grundy, February 13, 1833, *American Historical Magazine*, (Nashville), V., 137.

bill—in the letter to Grundy he calls it "my bill" — passed the senate before Clay's compromise tariff bill, but they both reached Jackson for signature on the same day. It must have made him feel that it was worth little to provide a means of checking the pretensions of a wilful state while giving it at the same time the object for which its wilfulness was exerted. Nullification was South Carolina's weapon. Using it successfully in 1833 showed how it could be used and established her prestige in the practice. Had the desires of Jackson been supported by a less timid group of politicians state rights might now have been broken and a sterner struggle in the succeeding generation might have been avoided.

It is difficult to give Clay and Calhoun their just places in this affair, so well are mingled selfish and apparently sincere motives; it is easier to praise Webster, although when he fought for the union he but stood where he stood before; but as regards the President there can be no such hesitation. He forsook his old position, cast aside the formulas of his party, and declared for the union when it was in danger. His political philosophy was a simple one, when put to the test. It embraced obedience to his authority, hatred of monopoly, and courage to carry out his purposes. The first and the third united to shape his course on nullification: the second and third united to direct it in the next great crisis of his career, the struggle against the Second United States Bank.

CHAPTER XXVII

So FAR this account of Jackson's administration has been chiefly concerned with the evolution of the Jacksonian party. In 1824, one man's popularity boldly utilized, drew together a vast number of voters. To them were joined the groups by Crawford, Calhoun, and Clinton, each fully supplied with politicians of all grades. When the party came into power it was a group of factions which slowly became an organic unit. The alignment of interests into the Calhoun and Van Buren groups, the exclusion of the opponents of Van Buren from the cabinet, the identification of the New Yorker with the original Tennessee following, the formation of a cabinet devoted to this faction, the clever elimination of Calhoun until he was forced into party rebellion, and finally the escape from a struggle with the South at the instance of South Carolina whereby the party might be rent in twain; these were the chief steps in the process of unification, and each has been explained at length.

At the head of this array stood Jackson, probably stronger through his forceful personality than any other American since Washington. He was no economist, no financier, no intelligent seeker after wise and just ideals, and his temper and judgment were bad; but his will was the coherent force of a party organization more complicated, and yet better adjusted, than existed before that time in our government. Courage, knowledge of the people, simplicity of manner, the common man's ideal of honesty and patriotism, and a willingness to discipline his sub-

584

ordinates when necessary were the qualities which kept the party oganization effective. "Jackson's popularity will stand anything," said his friends in expressing their confidence in his leadership. His opponents said he was drunk with power. Popular hero or tyrant he was now, in the years 1832 and 1833, come to the supreme test of his strength, the open fight against the bank.

The Second Bank of the United States was chartered in 1816, to continue for twenty years with one year more to close its affairs. The capital was thirty-five millions, one fifth subscribed by the government. This subscription was paid in a note at 5 per cent. interest, and it was believed that the dividends and the rise in the value of the stock would bring the public treasury a good profit on the transaction. A board of twenty-five directors, one fifth appointed by the President of the United States, selected the bank's administrative officers, created branches with local boards of directors, invested the bank's funds, and provided for its other business. Foreign stockholders were not to vote for directors and frequent reports must be made by the bank to the secretary of the treasury.

The most important other features of the charter were as follows: (1) The bank might issue notes without restriction, but they must all be signed by the president of the institution and must be redeemed in specie under penalty of paying 12 per cent. interest per annum on notes for which specie was refused. (2) Its notes were receivable for government dues, a privilege extended to notes of state banks only when they were redeemed in specie. (3) It kept the public deposits without interest, a valuable privilege in the prosperous years during which the charter ran. (4) It was to pay a bonus of one and a half millions and to transfer public funds without cost to the government. (5) The secretary of the treasury might remove the deposits from the bank, but he should "immediately lay before congress, if in session, and if not, immediately after the commencement of the next session, the reasons for such order or direction." But was congress then to pass on the reasons submitted? And would the deposits be restored if it did not approve? On this point the charter was not so clear that it escaped much later controversy.[1]

The size and privileges of the bank gave it power over other banks, and such was the intention of congress. It received large quantities of state bank-notes and by presenting them for redemption forced the banks of issue to maintain adequate specie reserves and to refrain from overissue. No single state bank or possible combination of them was able to exercise the same influence over the great bank, which was thus able to appropriate to itself much of the volume of new bank-notes which the business of the country demanded. This, probably, was its most pronounced monopolistic feature.

The bank inevitably had the opposition of the state banks, and since the latter were connected with local politics it became an issue in state politics. Bad management and the panic of 1819 made it necessary to take over large quantities of real estate, especially in the West, and when this was later sold at an advance the former owners gnashed their teeth. "I know towns, yea cities, . . . where the bank," said Benton in 1831, "already appears as an engrossing proprietor." Out of this hostility of the people and the politicians grew state legislation intended to check or destroy the federal incorporated institution. The bank was saved by the interference of the supreme court. In two cases, McCulloch vs. Maryland (1819) and Osborn vs. the Bank (1824), it was held that a state had no power over a bank incorporated by congress. Thus baffled, popular hostility receded but did not die. It survived in local differences, and when Jackson raised his voice against the bank it came to

---

[1] For the charter, see United States Statutes at Large, III., 266.

his aid. Some of his strongest supporters, as Amos Kendall and Frank P. Blair, of Kentucky, were warm in the early fight to restrain that institution.

Nicholas Biddle was president of the bank when it completed this victory. He graduated at Princeton, became a lawyer, dabbled in literature, and at length was secretary of legation in London and Paris. In 1819, through political influence, he was appointed government director of the bank. He knew something of political economy and now gave himself to the study of banking, of which his active mind soon achieved the mastery. He was a man of personal power, came to dominate the board of directors, and in 1823 was elected president to succeed Langdon Cheves. He quickly became the controling force in the institution.

When Cheves became president in 1819 bankruptcy was imminent. He adopted a severe policy, curtailed loans, collected debts without regard to persons, and brought affairs again to a safe condition. But he made himself unpopular and his resignation gave pleasure to the bank's patrons. Biddle profited by the reaction. He increased loans moderately, enlarged the note issues, and made some slight concessions to the state banks. Business generally was good, and results justified his liberality. He reorganized the branches, got better directors as opportunity offered, and adopted better banking methods. Dividends increased and the bank's stock became more valuable.

Besides having many sober qualities Biddle was bold and imaginative. In the beginning he restrained these impulses, but as success came he gave them freer play. Holding down the issues of state banks as much as his favored position permitted, he enlarged his own circulation from four and a half millions in 1823 to twenty-one millions in 1832. This caused dissatisfaction on the part of the competing banks, but it was not like him to turn aside on account of his opponents. He had much latent pride, he loved his own power, and soon became the chief force in the administration of the bank. He was allowed to control the selection of the private directors, the appointment of the committees, and thus he became, as was inevitable with a strong man, the centre of the bank's policy as truly as Jackson was the dominant force in the national government. When his will was limited by his opponents his resourcefulness was apt to find some way to circumvent them, as was shown in the case of the branch drafts.

These drafts came into existence in the following manner: In developing his policy of restraining overissue of state banks he wished to put out large amounts of his own notes. But the charter provided that he and his cashier must sign all such notes, and it was a severe tax on his physical strength to sign as many as were needed. Four times before his term of office the bank asked that this feature of the charter be amended, but congress always refused, probably because they desired to use this peculiarity of the law to restrain the issue of the bank. Biddle construed it as an act of pique. A cautious man would have yielded, but not he. He invented the branch draft, in size, design, and coloring so much like a bank-note that the average man took it for one. It was drawn by the branch on the mother bank in Philadelphia and made payable to some subordinate of the branch, or order. The subordinate endorsed it, and it became transferable. These drafts were received without question by the bank and the public and until 1835 by the government itself. They were not illegal and they were all redeemed by the bank; but they were a subterfuge and the anti-bank group declared that they were a practical violation of the charter.

Biddle could not have kept the bank out of politics, and he probably did not expect to do it. The fact that its charter must be renewed made the question a political one. The general revival of state rights theories had its bearing, and the personnel of the bank's management had an influence on the question; for men of dignity and wealth, as were the directors and officers, naturally opposed Jackson's election. On the other hand, wherever the anti-bank party existed it as naturally turned to Jackson. In Kentucky and New Hampshire this was particularly true. Biddle understood the situation, but observing that the opposition came from the less intelligent portion of the Jackson supporters, he hoped he could by reasonable methods carry his cause through congress. He could count on all the Adams men and on the followers of Calhoun. His chief trouble would come from old-school followers of Crawford and from the Jacksonian democrats, not a very formidable combination. Biddle looked upon it as a group inspired by ignorance and prejudice, and he felt that it would yield before the intelligence which he could bring to bear on the matter. His expectations would in all probability have been accomplished but for the opposition of Andrew Jackson.

We know little of Jackson's early attitude on the subject, but all we know marks him for an opponent in one way or another. In 1817 "the aristocracy at Nashville," as he later called it, tried to secure the establishment of a branch in the town. They encountered a state law forbidding a bank without a state charter, but got it repealed in spite of the opposition of Jackson and many others.[1] Later in the same year he refused on constitutional grounds to sign a memorial for such a branch; but he was willing to recommend certain men for officers in the branch, not as an endorsement of the institution but as a testimonial of the character of the persons.[2]

In New Orleans in 1821 when about to assume the office of governor of Florida he asked the branch in that city to cash a draft on the state department for ten or fifteen thousand dollars

---

[1] The date of this recommendation was formerly given as 1827, but Catterall correctly places it as 1817; See *Second Bank of the United States*, 183.
[2] Jackson to Benton, November 29, 1837, Jackson Mss

and was refused because at that time the parent bank had ordered that drafts should not be cashed. The incident annoyed him. He could have got the money by selling a draft to brokers in the city, but he said he would never discount his government's bills, "and more particularly to the branch bank of the United States, in which is deposited all the revenue of the government received in this place."[1]

In 1821, while governor of Florida, he forwarded a petition for a branch at Pensacola. Opponents later took this to indicate that he then favored the bank; but he replied with evident truthfulness that in sending the petition he merely acted for others and was not committed to support the request. There is no evidence to show that his bank views changed after his election. On the contrary such facts as we have go to support his plain assertion made in 1837: "My position now is, and has ever been since I have been able to form an opinion on this subject, that Congress has no power to charter a Bank, and that the states are prohibited from issuing bills of credit, or granting a charter by which such bills can be issued by any corporation or order."[2]

During the six years throughout which Jackson was before the country as presidential candidate nothing happened to show his views on this question. But the increasing certainty that he would be President made him an object of interest to the bank. In 1827 a branch was created at Nashville and thither came Gen. Thomas Cadwalader, of Philadelphia, agent of the bank, to supervise its establishment. He became acquainted with Jackson, and the two corresponded after the agent's return to Philadelphia. Cadwalader's letters are filled with insinuating friendliness. In one he regrets that he cannot settle in Nashville, and he extends a warm invitation for Jackson and Mrs. Jackson

---

[1]Jackson to Adams, April 24, 1821; *American State Papers, Foreign,* IV., 756.
[2]Jackson to Benton, November 29, 1837, Jackson Mss.

to visit Philadelphia. "Mrs. Cadwalader," he concludes, "desires me to say that no endeavor will be spared to supply to Mrs. J. the places of those warm friends whom she will leave behind her."[1]

Election day had not quite arrived when he wrote in a pean of glorification that the Philadelphia contest went "right" and that Sergeant was defeated. Coming to the bank he said: "Having had a particular agency in selecting the first list of Directors of the office of the Bank in your Quarter, I feel very anxious to know how far public opinion approves of the administration." Complaint had come to him that the men were unpopular, that the president was selfish and had no influence out of his office, that relatives of the president were given unwarranted favors in borrowing, that G. W. Campbell was the only proper man on the board, and that under pretext of getting business men in office "our friend Major Lewis is removed in order to make way for a man recently accused and convicted (in public opinion) of fraud for a series of years by the use of false weights at his cotton gin." He closed by saying he should be grateful if Jackson would convey any useful information on this subject to him, either personally or as a director in the parent bank.[2]

Nothing could be plainer than this offer to hand the Nashville branch over to the Jackson party; the reply was creditable to the writer of it. "Never having been," said Jackson with dignity, "in any manner, connected with Banks, and having very little to do with the one here, I feel myself unable to give you any satisfaction about it." The directors, he added, were reputed honest men, most of them were Europeans who had recently settled in the neighborhood, and some were young men who were under obligations to the president of the branch. He had heard complaints but could not say whether they were true or not, but "if it is any part of the policy of the mother bank to conciliate

[1] Cadwalader to Jackson, June 21, 1828, Jackson Mss.
[2] Cadwalader to Jackson, October 15, 1828, Jackson Mss.

the states and make their Branches acceptable to the people, then I think a portion of their board at least, should have been composed of men better known, and possessing more extensive influence than most of the directory of the Bank at Nashville do."[1]   Here were both dignity and policy.

Polk assures us that in the winter before the first inauguration Jackson talked freely to his friends at the "Hermitage" about his opposition to the bank.   The President's own recollection of the matter supported Polk in the assertion that a declaration against the bank was incorporated in the first draft of the inaugural address, probably an early, rough draft, from which the intended matter was dropped at the suggestion of friends.[2]

Soon after the inauguration Jackson returned to the subject, writing to Grundy in regard to a national bank scheme.   The latter had long been interested in banks, being the author of the Tennessee law of 1820 creating a loan office.[3]   What he said to Grundy is not preserved, but the latter said in his reply: "On the subject of the National Bank you have in view — I admire the project and believe that the president of the U. States, who shall accomplish it, will have achieved more for his country, than has ever been effected by any act of legislation, since the foundation of the government.   I will furnish as early as I can my views at large on that subject, agreeably to your request."

Five months later Grundy sent an outline plan of a bank with a capital stock of forty millions based on the national revenues, half of the capital to be owned by the states in proportion to population, the rest to be owned by the federal government, and the central directors to be elected by congress. The plan had little influence, perhaps not as much as a suggestion of John Randolph's which probably reached Jackson about the

---

[1]Jackson to Cadwalader, November 16, 1828, Jackson Mss.
[2]See above, II., 430.,   See also *Congressional Debates*, X., Part II., 2263.
[3]Sumner, *Life of Jackson* (edition 1899), 158, 159.
[4]Grundy to Jackson, May 22, 1829, Jackson Mss.

end of December, 1829. In 1811, said he, he prepared a plan of a bank to take the place of the first bank: it was to be attached to the customs of the government and the great custom-houses were to be branches to keep and pay out funds.[1]

While Jackson thus thought of the bank from the standpoint of principles, some of his party managers considered it from a practical side. They charged, and they probably believed, that it took active part in politics in several states in the election of 1828. The charge seems to have been true to some extent in Kentucky. The victors were hardly in the saddle before they began to talk openly about their wrongs. They may have intended to frighten the bank, with the object of lessening its partiality for the opposition and of getting members of their own party appointed directors. The result showed that Biddle was not proof against their designs.

The incident which best served them was the charges against strong-willed Jeremiah Mason, president of the Portsmouth, N. H., branch, and friend of Daniel Webster. Isaac Hill, leader of the rural wing of the Jackson party there, charged that Mason discriminated against administration men in making loans, that he was cold in his manner and generally unpopular. The complaint was made to Ingham, secretary of the treasury, in June, 1829, and he sent it to Biddle. About the same time Biddle received complaints directly from Senator Woodbury with other protests of the same nature, and he concluded the situation demanded serious consideration. But he made the initial mistake of getting angry. He wrote two letters on the same day, July 18, 1829, explaining in one of them the situation in Portsmouth. This was calmly stated and made a good showing for Mason. But in the other he undertook to defend the bank from the imputation of partisanship. There were not, he thought, another five hundred persons in the country so free

[1] Randolph to J. H. Burton, December 12, 1829, Jackson Mss.

from politics as those who directed the affairs of the bank and its branches. He was confident of his position, and as for the demands of those enemies he made by refusing credit, he felt that "even in the worst event, it is better to encounter hostility, than appease it by unworthy sacrifices of duty."

It was indiscreet to open this phase of the affair; for it gave Ingham an opportunity to shift the correspondence from the facts and to rest it where he could appeal to party feeling. In his reply he nearly ignored the first of the two letters but turned to the other eagerly. He said:

While I would scrupulously forbear to assume any fact derogatory to the character of your board or those of the branches, it is not deemed incompatible with the most rigid justice, to suppose that any body of five hundred men, not selected by an Omniscient eye, cannot be fairly entitled to the unqualified testimony which you have been pleased to offer in their behalf. It is morally impossible that the character of all the acts of the directors of the branches, much less their motives, could be known to the parent board; hence, the declaration that "no loan was ever granted to, or withheld from an individual, on account of political partiality or hostility," must be received rather as evidence of your own feelings, than as conclusive proof of the fact so confidently vouched for.

In closing Ingham reiterated his right to keep an eye on the bank's relation to politics, said he knew this would be attributed to false motives, but that he should do his duty as an officer of the government.

Before Biddle replied to this the Portsmouth investigation was ended in Mason's favor. Reporting this, he added, as though he could not resist the temptation to argue:

Your predecessors, Mr. Morris, General Hamilton, Mr. Wolcott, Mr. Gallatin, Mr. Campbell, Mr. Dallas, Mr. Crawford, and Mr. Rush, were gentlemen of acknowledged intelligence and fidelity to their duty. Yet, neither during the existence of the first Bank of the United States, even when there were no government directors, nor since the existence of the present bank, nor in the interval between them, does it seem even to have occurred to them that it formed any part of their duties to enquire into the political opinions of officers of the banks in which public funds were deposited.

Analyzing and construing the secretary's letter he alleged that it contained three false assumptions: (1) that the treasury could influence the election of bank officials, (2) that there was "some unexplained but authorized action of the government on the bank" of which the secretary was the proper agent, and (3) that he could and should make suggestions in regard to the attitude of the bank toward political matters.

This letter was undiplomatic. Aggression was not Biddle's cue, but he did not know it. Like most of his class, he had contempt for these new politicians who rode into power under cover of popular enthusiasm for a war-lord. He believed they dared not attack so powerful an institution as the bank. He did not realize until too late the immense strength of popular feeling as embodied in the new party.

Ingham showed a better comprehension of the situation. He denied flatly the first and third of his correspondent's assertions but assented to the second. The relation of the bank to the currency, the credit, and the political life of the country gave him, he said, the right to enquire into the actions of the institution. And he added significantly, speaking of himself as the secretary of the treasury:

Before he can be tempted to exercise the authority with which Congress have invested him, to withdraw the public deposites, he will do as he has done, submit directly to your board whatever imputation may be made, and respectfully, resolutely, and confidently ask, nay demand, the fullest examination; and he trusts that he may not be misconceived when he adds, that nothing could, in his opinion, more imperatively exact this energetic movement than a well formulated conviction of the bank's being, as was said of its predecessor, an engine of political party.

He also said, and it was with clearer political wisdom than Biddle's:

I must premise, notwithstanding the peculiar incredulity shown to similar [previous] assurances, that no wish is, or ever has been, felt by me, to convert or attach the influence of the bank to any political party, but, on the contrary, speaking with "unreserved freedom," although in the joint discharge of public functions, comity and co-operation cannot be too much cultivated; in the arena of party conflict which you almost tempt me to believe unavoidable, the hostility of the bank, as a political engine, would be preferable to its amity.

Biddle submitted this letter, like the others, to his board of directors. They evidently realized to what a state of irritation the affair was tending and at their behest he wrote that as the secretary disclaimed the views attributed to him they were satisfied, and he withdrew their protest against those views.[1]

This ended the incident. In it the administration showed its teeth, probably all it intended to do in the beginning. Biddle showed, also, his method of opposition: it was incautious, over-sanguine, and liable to underestimate the strength of popular feeling against the bank. But reflection lessened pugnacity, and before the correspondence closed various administration men were appointed directors in the branches. For all his strong words Biddle bent easily to necessity; and not persistence so much as bad judgment accomplished his defeat.

[1] This controversy is described, and the correspondence is published, in *Reports of Committees*, 1st session 22nd congress, Volume IV., 437, *et seq.*

Jackson took no part in this affair, although he must have watched it keenly. An extract from Biddle's letter of September 15th, was sent to him and on the back we read in Jackson's hand: "Biddle's letter. Repeats their good feelings to the administration and their great aid offered to it in the payment of the late sum of the public debt? Why this so often mentioned? Answer for political effect — and newspaper slang &c.?. . . The act of Congress their guide — true, but if that charter is violated is there no power in the government to inquire and correct if true. . . . See answer. The reply as to the purity of the Branch directors *well said.*"[1] This endorsement in Jackson's own hand shows that in the autumn of 1829 he was keenly alive to the political activity of the bank and on the whole suspicious and hostile.

Biddle knew not Jackson's feelings and was already planning to make the administration his friend. October 14th, while his correspondence with Ingham was in progress, Biddle was writing to Lewis, on whom he relied for influence with the administration, seeking to establish an understanding with the President. He desired his letter shown to Jackson, which was done. Lewis, who was friendly to the bank, replied hopefully, asserting that the latter had high esteem for Biddle personally and saying that politics should not enter into the management of the institution. Biddle also sent friends to Washington to assure the head of the government that reports of political discrimination in the branches were exaggerated. By this means and by placing Jackson men on the directorates of some of the branches he felt that this danger was passed. He even asked Lewis to induce the President to speak favorably in the annual message of the aid the bank had given in redeeming $ 8,710,000 of the debt in the preceding July. The assistance in that transaction was

[1] Jackson Mss.

really considerable and Jackson readily promised to do what was desired, and kept his promise, as his message shows.[1] At that time he had no specific grudge against the bank, although he was generally opposed to it. Lewis, leaning as usual to the institution, made more of this concession than the facts warranted and deceived the over-sanguine bank president. "I think you will find," he wrote, "the *old fellow* will do justice to the Bank."

Biddle, pleased with this success, determined to move for re-charter. He conceived a plan by which through the operations of the bank he would pay the remaining national debt by January 8, 1833, knowing well how quickly Jackson would catch at the idea of making the anniversary of the battle of New Orleans the time for achieving an object so much in his heart. The idea, suggested through the faithful Lewis, pleased the President, who asked for particulars. They were as follows: For a new charter and for the government's seven millions of stock in the bank and cash equal to one half the par value of the thirteen millions two hundred and ninety-six thousand of 3 per cent. revolutionary debt still unpaid, Biddle would give the seven million dollars certificate of indebtedness, bearing interest at 5 per cent., which the government owed for its stock and assume all of the 3 per cents. The remaining debt, a little more than thirty-seven millions, he thought might be redeemed from the surplus revenue in the time specified. It is true that about nine millions of this was not due until the years 1833-1836, but there would be enough surplus revenue to meet this, and if the government would pay the money to the bank he would also assume that. He even suggested that he would agree to give in addition a bonus of one and a half millions.

By this offer the bank seemed to be willing to assume twenty millions of debt in exchange for six millions six hundred and forty-eight thousand dollars to meet half the revolutionary

[1] Richardson, *Messages and Papers of the Presidents*, II., 451.

3 per cents. and for the government's bank stock, a total of little more than thirteen millions par value. But it was not really so advantageous to the national treasury. The 3 per cents. were then worth less than par and the bank stock was worth one hundred and twenty-five and with a new charter would probably be worth one hundred and fifty. Professor Catterall justly observes that the property the government was asked to transfer was worth to the bank under the proposed conditions as much as seventeen millions, so that Biddle would be giving for the new charter, bonus included, only four and a half millions, and not the seven and a half millions which on its face the offer seemed to imply. This plan was communicated to Lewis, November 15, 1829.[1]

For all this the propostition was a good one, and Jackson was impressed by it; but it did not overcome his constitutional scruples, and he said as much. Biddle went to Washington, had a conversation with the President, and carried away the conviction that he would at last overcome all objections and get what he wanted. He has left the following memorandum in his own hand which gives the distinct idea that Jackson in the interview made no definite promises but bore himself with dignity and self-restraint:

Mr. Biddle, I was very thankful to you for your plan of paying off the debt sent to Major Lewis.

[Biddle replied:] I thought it my duty to submit it to you.

I would have no difficulty in recommending it to Congress, but I think it right to be perfectly frank with you. I do not think that the power of Congress extends to charter a Bank ought [out] of the ten miles square.

I do not dislike your Bank any more than all banks. But ever since I read the history of the South Sea bubble I have been afraid of Banks. I have read the opinion of John Marshall who I believe was a great and pure mind — and could not agree

---

[1]Catterall, *Second Bank*, 188-194, has well described this incident.

with him — though if he had said, that as it was necessary for the purposes of the national government there ought to be a national bank I should have been disposed to concur. But I do not think the congress has a right to create a corporation out of the ten miles square. I feel very sensibly the services rendered by the Bank at the last payment of the national debt and shall take an opportunity of declaring it publicly in my message to congress. That is my own feeling to the Bank — and Mr. Ingham's also — He and you got into a difficulty thro' the foolishness — if I may use the term of Mr. Hill.

Observing he was a little embarrassed I, [Biddle] said "Oh, that has all passed now." He said with the Parent Board and myself he had ever reason to be satisfied— that he had heard complaints and then mentioned a case at Louisville of which he promised to give me the particulars.

I said "Well I am very much gratified at this frank explanation. We shall all be proud of any kind mention in the message — for we should feel like soldiers after an action commenced by their General." "Sir," said he, "it would be only an act of justice to mention it."[1]

Biddle probably did not appreciate Jackson, whom popular opinion thought easily influenced. He doubtless knew that the majority of the cabinet were for the bank, he counted strongly on Lewis, and he said that some other advisers, meaning members of the "Kitchen Cabinet" had become friendly. He could not have included among them Amos Kendall who never favored the bank. Later he was surprised at the annual message and thought Jackson had deceived him; but without more specific information than he gave it is hard to believe this of a man whose nature was admittedly frank to the point of rashness. It is easier to think that the bank president counted too much on his own manipulations. However that may be, he was in no position to complain that the question of recharter was prematurely opened.

[1]Catterall, *Second Bank*, 179, 184, 192, thinks this document an unsigned letter from Jackson to Biddle. But the handwriting is Biddle's and its content is only explainable as above.

The first annual message, December 8, 1829, was expected with keen interest. Near the close of the document was the following:

The charter of the Bank of the United States expires in 1836, and its stockholders will most probably apply for a renewal of their privileges. In order to avoid the evils resulting from precipitancy in a measure involving such important principles and such deep pecuniary interests, I feel that I cannot, in justice to the parties interested, too soon present it to the deliberate consideration of the legislature and the people. Both the constitutionality and the expediency of the law creating this bank are well questioned by a large portion of our fellow-citizens, and it must be admitted by all that it has failed in the great end of establishing a uniform and sound currency.

Under these circumstances, if such an institution is deemed essential to the fiscal operations of the Government, I submit to the wisdom of the Legislature whether a national one, founded upon the credit of the Government and its revenues, might not be devised which would avoid all constitutional difficulties and at the same time secure all the advantages to the Government and country that were expected to result from the present bank.

Remonstrance came at once from the friends of the bank, and the Adams men echoed the protest. To say that the bank had not given the country a uniform and sound currency was undoubtedly an error and indicates the superficiality of his ideas of finance. He probably meant that the bank failed in the purpose for which it was established because the country had a variety of depreciated state bank-notes, but a good financier would have known that the bank measurably restrained such issues and prevented far worse conditions than existed.

The message was also criticized because it raised at this early date a question which must be settled after the end of the term for which he was elected. But on that point he stood on better

---

[1]Richardson, *Messages and Papers of the Presidents*, II., 462.

ground.   There was an educational value in an early consideration of the matter; for if the bank ought not to be rechartered
the people ought to have their attention called to it soon enough
to form an opinion.   If financial evils should come from such
a precipitation of the question, that was an evil inherent in the
system by which financial interests were made dependent on
political connections.

The reference to the bank pleased all who supported the school
of revived state rights as well as that vast democratic mass whose
political consciousness Jackson was then calling into existence,
men who resented the privileges of a great monied corporation.
Business interests and persons generally who did not distrust
wealth found it ill advised, and the politicians who followed Clay
and Adams stimulated their opposition.   But Jackson did not
falter; he wrote on December 19th:

I was aware the bank question would be disapproved by all
the sordid and interested who prize self-interest more than the
perpetuity of our liberty, and the blessings of a free republican
government. . . .   The confidence reposed by my country
dictated to my conscience that now was the proper time, and,
although I disliked to act contrary to the opinion of so great a
majority of my cabinet, I could not shrink from a duty so imperious to the safety and purity of our free institutions as I considered this to be.   I have brought it before the people, and I
have confidence that they will do their duty. [1]

And he took up at once the formulation of a plan for a bank
to replace the one then in existence.   He had talked over his
idea with the facile Hamilton; and he now asked him to work
out the details in two plans, one for a bank subordinate to the
treasury department, which would receive deposits, transfer
the public money, and establish a sound and uniform currency;
"the other of a mixed character which may fulfil all the purposes

[1]Hamilton, *Reminiscences*, 151.

of a bank, and be free from the infringement of state rights and our Constitution." Two weeks earlier Hamilton was informed in confidence that in a certain contingency he would become secretary of state, and he applied himself to the task now required with such industry that on January 4, 1830, he sent the President a scheme for the creation of five "offices of deposit" to receive, collect and disburse the national funds.[1] But nothing came of Jackson's efforts at that time. Congress was soon considering his suggestions with such an unfavorable attitude as to preclude further development of his ideas.

But they were continually in his mind, and in a letter of July 17th, he stated them in a way which, though not very explicit, leaves no doubt of the spring of his aversion to the institution then existing. He wrote:

I have not time to go into the Bank question at present, can only observe, that my own opinion is, that it should be merely a *National Bank of Deposit*, with power in time of war to issue its bills bearing a moderate rate of interest, and payable at the close of the war, which being guaranteed by the national faith pledged, and based upon our revenue would be sought after by the monied capitalists, and do away, in time of war, [with] the necessity of *loans*. This is all the kind of a bank that a republic should have. But if to be made a bank of discount as well as deposit, I would frame its charter upon the checks of our government, attach it to, and make a part of the revenue, and expose its situation as part thereof annually to the nation, and the property of which would then enure to the whole people, instead of a *few monied capitalists*, who are trading upon our revenue, and enjoy the benefit of it, to the exclusion of the many. The Bank of deposit, and even of discount would steer clear of the constitutional objections to the present Bank, and all the profits arising would accrue and be disposable as other revenue for the benefit of the nation.[2]

---

[1] Hamilton *Reminiscences*, 151 (2).
[2] Jackson to ———. July 17, 1830, Jackson Mss.

Jackson preserved a letter from Alfred Balch, a Nashville supporter, which voices the ordinary complaints against the bank, complaints which sunk deeply into Jackson's mind. Balch writes:

Old Mr. Crutcher told me a few days ago, that he had a check on the Bank of the U. States last week, drawn by a public officer, payable at sight at Phila. He went to the office here and wished cash for it. They charged him one per cent. for advancing the money. Notes payable at the office at Boston are thrown in here. If you wish to receive silver for them you must pay two and one-half per cent. Instead of loaning money here at 6 per ct., they will buy a bill on the office at New Orleans, charge you $1\frac{1}{2}$ per cent. premium and 6 per ct., all payable in advance and the office at New Orleans will charge you $1\frac{1}{2}$ per cent. for accepting it there. So that the object of this immense institution is to make money, to secure a large dividend for the benefit of the great stock-holders on the other side of the Atlantic. As to the effects of the office here, they must in the end prove in the last degree calamitous. Those who borrow are encouraged in their extravagant modes of dressing and living which are far greater than their means will justify. Many are building little palaces, furnishing them in very expensive style, and the children of many are dressed as though they were the sons and daughters of princes. What may remain of the wrecks produced by these splendid follies will after a few years be seized on by this Mammoth Bank. [1]

The writer was a man of note in Tennessee, a politician of influence, and a supporter of Van Buren. His opinion was not worse than that of the average man in the country; and it was this average opinion, which resented the bank as a great and devouring monopoly, that gave the ultimate stroke to what Jackson repeatedly called "the hydra of corruption."

That part of the message which related to the bank was referred

---

[1] Balch to Jackson, January 7, 1830, Jackson Mss.

in the senate to the committee on finance and in the house to the committee of ways and means. Biddle welcomed this as an opportunity to get endorsement for the bank, since he knew that each house was now in its favor. He wrote the report of the former committee almost verbatim[1] and furnished the facts on which the latter rested. When these reports were accepted in the two houses he scattered them broadcast throughout the country. He said he was anxious lest this activity and the opposition of congress should irritate the president.[2] That he could have the least doubt on the point shows that he knew not Jackson.

The bank situation at this time derived a peculiar significance from its connection with Calhoun, who in May of this year came to a definite, but not yet announced breach with the President. McDuffie, Calhoun's representative in the house, was chairman of the ways and means committee, whose report not only supported the bank of the United States, but contemptuously declared that the proposed substitute was fraught with danger. It would increase the patronage, become an engine of tyranny, and fail to give needed banking facilities. Perhaps the Calhoun wing of the party thought it time to show that they were not identified with Western ideals. Van Buren also played his part. He professed strict state rights theories, which showed Jackson that his heart was right, while to his friends he said — with an eye on the financial influence of New York — that with Madison he thought that doubts of the power of congress to create the bank were settled by the decisions of the supreme court and by the acquiescence of the people.[3] Every little helped, and the upshot was that the McDuffie report awakened Jackson's wrath. He called on J. A. Hamilton to write a crushing reply and got willing compliance, but with

[1] Catterall, *Second Bank*, 198, note 3.
[2] Catterall, *Second Bank*, 199, note 5.
[3] Hamilton, *Reminiscences*, 150.

admirable calmness he returned the paper with the request that Calhoun's name be stricken from it.

"From a correspondence lately between him and myself," he continued, "in which I was obliged to use the language of Cæsar, 'Et tu, Brute?' it might be thought to arise from personal feeling, and arouse the sympathy of the people in his favor. You know an experienced general always keeps a strong reserve, and hereafter it may become necessary to pass in review the rise and progress of this hydra of corruption, when it will be proper to expose its founders and supporters by name. Then, and then only, can his name be brought with advantage and propriety before the nation. I return it for this correction, which, when made, and two following numbers forwarded with it, I will have them published in the *Telegraph*. This is the paper, for more reasons than one."[1]

It was good politics to make Green publish the piece; for it would tend to weaken McDuffie as the exponent of the Calhoun faction, and Jackson did not feel strong enough in the party to try to go alone. But he foresaw the open breach and was determined to have a new editor.[2]

To sum up, he opposed a bank in the hands of individual capitalists, Eastern men and foreigners, who might and probably did have a large political influence through a series of powerful lobbies as well as through participation in nominations if not in actual elections. He believed that a bank attached to the treasury would give all necessary banking services. His plan would build up a patronage quite as dangerous as the influence of the present institution, but he was honestly unconscious of danger from that source. He knew that Biddle was striving for re-charter, that he circulated thousands of documents favorable to the bank, that he employed Gallatin and others to write for

---

[1] Hamilton, *Reminiscences*, 168.
[2] Jackson to Lewis, June 26, 1830, Mss. New York Public Library.

it, that Webster was a member of the central board of directors, and that all its influence would be brought to bear on members of congress to get a new charter. At this time the Calhoun controversy, the Eaton affair, and the cabinet dissensions embarrassed the party, and it took a great deal of courage to drive the quarrel with the bank into the midst of this complex political situation. But he did not hesitate. No other man then in public life, says Van Buren, equaled him in confidence that the people would support one who labored with sincerity for their interests.[1]

During the autumn of 1830 Biddle induced many bank supporters to urge Jackson to change his views. They found him calm but reticent. They got the impression, and it became a certainty with Biddle himself, that while the President preferred his own bank plan he would not veto a new charter if congress took the responsibility of passing it. The moment seemed propitious, and the bank's president determined to ask for a charter at the coming session. His hopes were transitory; for the second message, December 6, 1830, repeated the declarations of the first and amplified the President's scheme for a bank.

Some autograph notes prepared in anticipation of this occasion indicate that the plan incorporated in the message was essentially Jackson's. They have this other advantage that they show what he at that time really thought of the existing bank. The corporation, he said, had two disadvantages. (1) It was unconstitutional because congress had no power to create a corporation, because it withdrew capital from the control of the state, because it bought real estate without the consent of a state, which the federal government itself could not do; and (2) It was dangerous to liberty because through its officers, loans, and participation in politics it could build up or pull down parties or men, because it created a monopoly of the money power, because much of the

---

[1]Van Buren, *Autobiography*, VI., 36, Van Buren Mss.

stock was owned by foreigners, because it would always support him who supported it, and because it weakened the state and strengthened the general government. Two things about these reasons are notable: nothing is said about the failure of the bank to give a good currency, and the institution is not pronounced unsafe. On the contrary, much is said for the bank. "This Bank," says the memorandum, "renders important services to the Government and country. It cheapens and facilitates all the fiscal operations of the Government. It tends in some degree to equalize domestic exchange, and produce a sound and uniform currency." It was not to be destroyed but a substitute provided "which shall yield all its benefits, and be obnoxious to none of its objections." There is every reason to believe that at this time Jackson's attitude toward the institution was reasonable and well meaning.

The bank party were discouraged. Their newspapers found the proposed substitute unworthy of serious notice. But the situation was not alarming. Lewis gave Biddle private assurances of peace,[1] and he well might do so; for as yet the chief members of the administration circle were for the bank. The policy of opposition was distinctly Jackson's, and he was not disposed to push his ideas for the present. No bill to re-charter was introduced in the winter of 1830-'31, congress adjourned in March, the cabinet was reorganized in May and June, and harmony reigned in the party. Most of the new cabinet were friendly to the bank, but none would oppose the President openly on what was now a fixed policy with him. McLane, secretary of the treasury, an old federalist, favored the bank, but the President liked him personally and each was disposed to overlook the conviction of the other on this crucial point. Livingston was for temporizing, but Taney, who became attorney-general was a resolute state rights man and gave a vigorous mind with

[1]Catterall, *Second Bank*, 204, note 1.

a vast capacity for work to the destruction of the bank, which he disliked as much as Kendall or Jackson, himself. Cambreleng pronounced him "the only efficient man of sound principles in the Cabinet."[1] Outside of it Blair gave powerful aid with the *Globe* and Kendall planned unceasingly. Van Buren, whose hand in the conflict was usually conceded, was sent to England, but his New York supporters followed Jackson faithfully.

Thus throughout the first congress under Jackson the bank controversy was precipitated, but neither side ventured to carry it to the final stage. Each made a definite appeal to public opinion, Jackson by his statements that the objects for which the institution was founded were not accomplished, that it was, in fact, a menace to good government, and by his proposition that its functions be given to a bank in the profits of which the capitalists of the country should not share. The bank was now put on the defensive, although the time was coming when it must assume the initiative and ask for its object or pass out of existence. Newspaper comment on each side was acrimonious and the people were taking sides with more passion than judgment. The twenty-second congress, which met December 5, 1831, saw the conflict fought to its legislative close.

---

[1]Cambreleng to Van Buren, February 5, 1832, Van Buren Mss, Jackson to Blair, January 17, 1843, Jackson Mss.

CHAPTER XXVIII

THE ATTEMPT TO RE-CHARTER THE BANK

As THE beginning of the new congress approached Biddle became alive to the situation. He was already in communication with McLane and Livingston, both of whom favored a new charter. The former went to Philadelphia in October and pledged the administration to a more pacific policy. He said that since Jackson knew he could not get his own bank scheme adopted he would accept the old charter with certain modifications. It was agreed that McLane, as secretary of the treasury, should advocate re-charter in his own report and that the President in the message should say that having brought the matter before congress he would leave it with them. Both features of the agreement were kept, McLane's literally but Jackson's with a modification which gave uneasiness to the bank. He said in the message, December 6, 1831, that he still held "the opinions heretofore expressed in relation to the Bank as at present organized," but that he would "leave it for the present to the investigation of an enlightened people and their representatives." [1] Reasserting his previous opinions and speaking about the approval of the people were matters not considered in the secret conference in Philadelphia.

It seems likely that McLane misjudged Jackson. Knowing his inexperience and mistaking the import of his cordiality in personal relations, he based his assurances not merely on what Jackson said but on what he thought he could induce him to say. We know not what Jackson told him, since no first hand

[1]Richardson, *Messages and Papers of the Presidents*, II., 558.

evidence survives on the point. All our information comes from Biddle, who had it from McLane and others equally biased toward the bank. They were all striving to influence the President, especially the secretary of the treasury, who would gain in public esteem if he could take the party safely through this perplexing situation. Jackson probably was carried further by this assault than he realized. He liked McLane's frank way of dealing with him and forgave him the contrary report on the bank. "It is an honest difference of opinion," he said, "and in his report he acts fairly by leaving me free and uncommitted. This I will be on this subject." [1]

The growing ascendency of McLane dismayed the anti-bank men. They began to say Jackson had surrendered, and they never forgave the secretary for what they considered a treacherous and selfish policy. [2] When the President knew of their suspicions he denied the imputation of shifting, saying: "Mr. McLane and myself understand each other, and have not the slightest disagreement about the principles, which will be a *sine qua non* in my assent to a bill rechartering the bank." [3]

The situation favored wire-pulling. A group of New York democrats sought to advance their own interests by getting a charter for a bank to replace the existing institution, but the scheme was weak politically and financially and did not go far. The bank democrats sought to reconcile the President's oft-mentioned bank plan with something the present bank would accept as a modification of their charter. They used all their power of persuasion on him, and he probably gave up something for the sake of the party; but he talked little and we cannot say what he relinquished. Divided as the party was, it was evident

---

[1] Jackson to Van Buren, December 6, 1831, W. Lowrie to *ibid*, February 27, 1832; Van Ness to *ibed* March 9, 1832; Van Buren Mss.
[2] J. A. Hamilton to Van Buren, December 7, 1831, Van Buren Mss.
[3] Jackson to Hamilton, December 12, 1831, *Reminiscences*, 234.

that the bank question ought to be deferred until after the coming election: on this point all democrats were agreed.

The anti-bank men were alarmed at these developments. J. A. Hamilton spoke in dismay of making a flying trip to London to talk over the matter with Van Buren. Cambreleng wrote, January 4, 1832, that Jackson stood entirely alone, and that McLane, Livingston, Cass, Lewis, Campbell, were for the bank. "Woodbury," he said, "keeps snug and plays out of all the corners of his eyes. Taney, strange as it may seem, is the best Democrat among us. He is with Kendall, Hill, Blair, etc. Barry, I presume, I should have put with the President, or else in the last list. McLane has burnished all his satellites with the Bank gold and silver. Somehow or other they all begin to think the Bank must be re-chartered." Neither Hamilton nor Cambreleng would say that Jackson had entirely surrendered.[1]

John Randolph, also, wrote to remonstrate. On his opposition to "the Chestnut Street Monster," he said, rested his support of the administration; for he considered this the overshadowing issue. If Jackson disappointed him in this respect he would still support him against Clay, Webster, Calhoun, and Adams — "the best of the set" — but his vote would be delivered with forceps.[2] Jackson replied at once. Reports that he was for the bank were not true, he said: he believed it unconstitutional and "on the score of mere expediency dangerous to liberty, and therefore, worthy of the denunciation which it has received from the disciples of the old Republican school." He believed it had failed to serve the country as was expected and would never give it his official sanction; and as to McLane's report, that was a matter of individual opinion over which he, Jackson, had no control. When Randolph got this letter he was very ill but managed to send a reply worthy of his wit. "I see," he wrote,

[1]Hamilton to Van Buren, December 23, 1831; Cambreleng to Van Buren, January 4, 1832; Van Buren Mss.
[2]Randolph to Jackson, December 19, 1831, Jackson Mss.

"that with your arch enemy the grand Nullifier working in the Senate with the Coalition and his *clientèle* dependent upholding the Bank in the other House and all working against you that you have Sysiphean labor to perform. I wish I were able to help you roll up the stone, but I cannot. I am finished." On this letter Jackson endorsed as directions for his secretary; "Regret his indisposition and never fear the triumph of the U. S. Bank while I am here."[1]

Nor was McLane himself sure of his ground with the President; he told the bank it ought to be satisfied with the message, that it showed Jackson was wavering, and that if time were given him, he would become convinced of his error. Both McLane and Lewis urged that in the meantime the President ought not to be pressed. Every party consideration demanded that he veto a charter introduced in the coming session of congress but they put their advice on other grounds. He would, they thought, take a charter now as a challenge and veto it, even if he thought it would mean defeat in the next election.[2]

Clay's followers, the national republicans, were dismayed at the apparent agreement between the President and the bank. They considered the bank controversy their chief asset; and Clay was in no mood to let McLane's clever manipulation withdraw it from their hands. In their national nominating convention in December, 1831, they championed the bank, arraigned Jackson for his hostility to it, and asked the people not "to destroy one of their most valuable establishments, to gratify the caprice of a chief magistrate, who reasons and advises upon a subject, with the details of which he is evidently unacquainted, in direct contradiction to the opinion of his own official counsellors. . . . He is fully and three times over pledged to the people to negative any bill that may be passed for re-chartering

---

[1]Jackson to Randolph, December 22, 1831; Randolph to Jackson, January 3, 1831, 1832; Jackson Mss.
[2]Catterall, *Second Bank*, 218, 219, notes 1, 2 and 4.

the bank, and there is little doubt that the additional influence which he would acquire by reëlection, would be employed to carry through Congress the extraordinary substitute which he has repeatedly proposed." [1]

In congress the leading national republicans urged an aggressive policy. They believed a veto would leave them in good fighting shape in the coming campaign, and even if Jackson were reëlected they expected such a majority in the two houses that the charter could be carried over a veto. Let the bank but act boldly, they said, and the world should see.

For a brief time Biddle was courted by two parties, the supporters of Clay and the democratic faction which followed McLane. He hesitated and considered, seeking to get the best results for the institution over which he presided. To proceed now meant a veto: everybody told him that. Should he take McLane at his word, keep the bank out of the coming campaign, and trust Jackson not to veto it afterward? What assurance had he from Jackson himself that he could rely on democratic friendship? Was the party not afraid of the election and merely seeking for time? For if the bank did not ask for a charter now it must do so in Jackson's next term. It could not escape Jackson's veto, if he were determined to give it. Thus Biddle pondered, weighing the arguments on each side. He himself was a national republican. His friend, John Sergeant, who was long a trusted standing counsel for the bank, was candidate for vice-president on that ticket. Webster, another retained counsel and a member of the central directorate, was a leader in that party, and the whole financial connection was trained with it. It was the side to which he would eventually turn if necessary, and in the absence of definite assurances from Jackson himself it was probably considerations like these that weighed most with him.

[1] Niles, *Register*, XLI., 310.

January 6th he forwarded to Dallas, democratic senator from Pennsylvania, the memorial of the bank asking for a new charter, and on the ninth it was presented in each house. In the senate it was referred to a select committee of which Dallas was chairman. In the house it was sent to the committee on ways and means, McDuffie, chairman. Four and a half months it lay untouched while each side gave itself to the task of arousing the country to the situation. Petitions were secured in large numbers, the most notable being from banks and business organizations in favor of the bank. But that which commanded most attention, after the congressional investigation,[1] was a memorial passed by the Pennsylvania legislature with nearly a unanimous vote in favor of the charter. It was believed that Jackson could not be reëlected without the vote of this critical state.[2]

McLane was discouraged by the introduction of the bank's memorial. Four days before it appeared he protested to Biddle, saying that if his advice to defer action were not taken he could do nothing further for the bank. He now became indifferent, but Livingston took up the work his colleague let fall. An intimation was given that a charter might not be vetoed, and Biddle caught at the hint. A new negotiation began in which he declared of Jackson: "Let him write the whole charter with his own hands. I am sure that we would agree to his modifications; and then let him and his friends pass it. It will then be his work. He will then disarm his adversaries." With these instructions, Ingersoll, Biddle's agent, approached Livingston, who now claimed to speak for the administration. February 22d, they drew up a plan with the following new features: (1) The government to own no stock but to appoint directors on the parent board and one on the branch directorates. (2) States to tax the bank's property as they taxed other property within their

---

[1]See below, p. 617.
[2]Catterall, *Second Bank*, 221-223.

borders. (3) The bank to hold no more real estate than it needed for its own use. (4) A portion of the stock in the bank to be opened to new subscriptions. (5) The directors to name two or three of their number one of whom the President of the United States would appoint president of the bank. The first three of these features were offered as Jackson's terms, the others as coming from other persons in the administration circle. Biddle approved all but the last, which he passed over in silence.[1]

Professor Catterall thinks that here Livingston spoke truly for the President, but it seems more probable that the secretary misjudged his superior. Jackson's strong assurances to Randolph show that up to this time he played a game, concealing his real purpose from the bank democrats and working for party harmony. It ought to require stronger evidence than the general assertion of the enthusiastic and impractical Livingston to show that Jackson was now willing to retreat after the combat was joined. Two months earlier he said of Livingston, "He knows nothing of mankind. He lacks in this respect that judgment which you [Van Buren] possess, in so eminent a degree, his memory is somewhat failing him."[2] Is it likely that Jackson would now have revealed himself to one of whom he spoke such things? Moreover, Livingston later told Parton that Jackson would have accepted a charter if the bank had been a little complaisant.[3] This was in opposition to Livingston's position in 1832, when he said Jackson had agreed to accept a charter and when the bank was entirely complaisant. It adds a shade of doubt to Livingston's credibility as a witness of Jackson's intentions in February 1832.

During all this time the anti-bank democrats had been as quiet as Jackson himself. But now they came forward with a

---

[1]Catterall, *Second Bank*, 224-228.
[2]Jackson to Van Buren, December 17, 1831, Jackson Mss. See also Van Buren, *Autobiography*, VI., 186, Van Buren Mss.
[3]*Life of Jackson*, III., 395.

play that checked all attempts at compromise. It was such a simple thing that we must think it was held back for just such an emergency. Benton has the credit of originating the idea. At his suggestion Clayton, in the house, moved an investigation into the affairs of the bank. Since that institution was applying for re-charter it could not oppose the investigation, nor could it hurry the charter through until the inquiry was made. A committee was appointed, the majority democrats, with Clayton for chairman. For six weeks it gave itself to the task, taking evidence in Washington and Philadelphia. At the end it submitted three reports, one by the majority against the bank, one by the minority in support of the bank, and an individual report by John Quincy Adams, concurred in by one other member of the committee. The last was a scathing denunciation of the whole movement against the bank.[1] The findings of the majority have not received much respect from posterity, so far as they involve principles of finance; but they displayed certain weak points in the bank's conduct which appealed strongly to the popular mind when the report became an important campaign document. They had little influence on the fight within congress, where members' minds were already made up.

The bank sent its shrewdest lobbyists to Washington to watch the situation. Horace Binney, reputed one of the best lawyers in the country, appeared soon after the memorial was introduced; Cadwalader did what he could, and Samuel Smith, of Baltimore, was nearly as energetic; but on May 20th, as the debates were about to begin, Biddle himself went to Washington and took personal charge of the fight outside of congress. Three days later the bill was taken up in the senate, June 11th it passed by a vote of twenty-eight to twenty and was sent to the house, where it passed July 3rd by one hundred and seven votes to eighty-five.

Jackson's veto came promptly, prepared probably by Taney,

---

[1] These three reports are in *Congressional Debates*, VIII., part III., Appendix, 33-73.

who wrote many of his papers in connection with the bank affair. It attacked the bill on grounds of constitutionality and expediency. It was written with an eye to the coming campaign, and the most important features were the following:[1]

The bank was a monopoly extended for fifteen years beyond its existing term for which the proposed bonus of three million dollars was not adequate payment. With re-charter the stock would undoubtedly be worth one hundred and fifty dollars a share, and instead of continuing to have the old bank "why should not the government sell out the whole stock and thus secure to the people the full market value of the privileges granted?" Moreover, other citizens than the present shareholders — who were foreigners and a few wealthy Eastern capitalists — had asked to be allowed to subscribe for a part of the stock, and their rights should not have been ignored: they would have given more than the bonus provided in this bill. But it is said that closing up the bank would make a pressure in business: this was not true in any just sense, since the time was ample for easy adjustment to new conditions, and any pressure resulting must be due solely to the deliberate action of the bank.

The charter by obliging the bank to furnish lists of stockholders made it possible for the states to tax the shares, but this became a blemish in the eyes of the President, since in the West and South, where the bank realized a large part of its profits, there were few shareholders. For example, there were none in Alabama, yet the Mobile branch made ninety-five thousand dollars of profit the preceding year, all taken out of the state, much of it for foreigners, and the state not allowed to tax it one penny.

By the new charter the notes of a branch were to be redeemed by any branch without discount when offered by a state bank. This was very well so far as the state banks were concerned,

---

[1]For the veto see Richardson, *Messages and Papers*, II., 576.

said the veto, but why discriminate against the individual holders of branch notes?

Foreign stockholders were not to vote, and as the stock went abroad the holders of it at home would have an increasing share of power until the bank was at last controlled by a small clique of our own bankers. But if war occurred with the nation in which the foreign holders lived their position would give them a great advantage over us. The American officers of the bank would be subservient to the foreign shareholders, "and all its operations within would be in aid of the hostile fleets and armies without. Controlling our currency, receiving our public moneys, and holding thousands of our citizens in dependence, it would be more formidable and dangerous than the naval and military power of the enemy." The writer of the paper thus found no difficulty in making the foreign shareholders powerless in times of peace and predominantly powerful in times of war.

There was much like this, five pages of it at the beginning and three at the end, but in between these two parts was an argument on constitutionality which could have come from no other member of the anti-bank coterie than Taney. It was in itself a veto message and repeated some of the things which went before or came after it. It was expressed in concise, legal style, in contrast to the loose illogic of the rest of the document. It is as if it were furnished to the President as a message proper, was deemed too cold for popular reading, and was lengthened at each end by some such purveyor of balderdash as Isaac Hill or Amos Kendall.

In this interior, more argumentative, part the writer laid down the President's view of his relation to the supreme court. This tribunal, said the message, "ought not to control the co-ordinate authorities of this government. . . . Each public officer who takes an oath to support the Constitution swears that he will support it as he understands it, and not as it is understood by others. . . . The opinion of the judges has no more authority over Congress than the opinion of Congress has over the judges, and on that point the President is independent of both. The authority of the supreme court must not, therefore, be permitted to control the Congress or the Executive when acting in their legislative capacities, but to have only such influence as the force of their reasoning may deserve." This statement has often been quoted without the last sentence in it. Such an omission does injustice to Jackson, so far as the sentiment can be said to be his.

The bank men received the veto message with shouts of delight. They believed it would make converts for their side and ordered thirty thousand copies printed for distribution. Biddle said of it: "It has all the fury of a chained panther, biting the bars of his cage. It is really a manifesto of anarchy."[1] This utterance shows how much the head of the bank party was carried away by the ardor of combat. The message contained neither fury nor anarchy. There was ignorance of finance in it, but it was shrewdly planned to reach a class of people whom Biddle and the important men who dealt in banking understood no more than Jackson understood the bankers. For every respectable citizen whom the message disgusted there were many average men who believed that the accumulation of great wealth in the hands of one corporation threatened liberty and to these its reasoning was satisfactory.

The veto drew party lines for the democrats, some of whom voted for re-charter with misgivings. But they must now stand for Jackson or against him. The very rejoicing of the national republicans hardened the allegiance of democrats to their own party. While many politicians nearer home sent assurances of support, James Buchanan, in St. Petersburg, sent in his submission. Till now, he said, he was for the bank, but the veto

---
[1]Clay, *Correspondence*, 341.

converted him; he would support his leader. More interesting still is the course of Senator Dallas, whom the bank selected to lead its fight in the senate. The first evidence of Jackson's wrath filled him with dismay, and before the end of the session he was talking to his intimates about repudiating the bank. Arrived at home he fulfilled his threat. He said:

A few days satisfied me, that my friend, The Bank, was, either with or without its own consent and connivance, taking a somewhat too ostensible part in the political canvass. The institution, as an useful agent of government, is one thing — its directors or managers, or partizans, are quite another thing — both united are not worth the cause which depends on the re-election of Jackson. On the very day of my arrival, I passed by a large Town-meeting convened to denounce the Veto and uphold the bank — and the sight of it roused me into an immediate effort to procure a counteracting assemblage on the same spot, that day week. Some very kind friends strove to throw cold water upon my ardor by hinting that my votes and speeches in the Senate were recent and well remembered — that my position would be awkward, if I did not fall into the ranks of those who at least condemned the Veto, etc. I took counsel of my conscience and judgment — and being perfectly self-convinced that I might be both a true and constant friend of the Institution, and at the same time an unflinching adherent to Democracy and the re-election of Jackson, I attended the meeting — made my speech — and felt instantly relieved from what seemed to me, before, might be thought an undecided and equivocal attitude. The truth is, as you know, that altho solicitous to save the corporation by a re-charter, I never conceived it to be of the immense and essential importance described by my Senatorial neighbor on the left and rear — I was always for the sentiment which is now hoisted most high — Jackson, bank or no bank.[1]

In applying for a charter and throwing himself into the hands

---

[1] G. M. Dallas to Bedford Brown, no date but in 1832, probably late in the summer. See *Trinity College (North Carolina) Historical Papers*, VI, 68.

of the national republicans Biddle made the bank the chief question of the presidential contest, and the stumps throughout the
country rang with cries for and against until the November
election was held. Jackson's two hundred and nineteen votes
to Clay's forty-nine can only be considered as the nation's verdict.
The President ever claimed that Biddle ought to have accepted
the result as final, and that if he had done so the later evils in
the situation would have been avoided. It is certain that Biddle
did not think the fight ended. He hoped by some turn to wrest
victory from the situation. Foreseeing the distress which must
attend the closing of the bank, he hoped that it would be enough
to show the American people the folly of 1832, and to induce
them to reverse their verdict.

During the campaign of 1832, and in the controversy over the
removal of the deposits in 1833, many charges were made against
the bank. Some were true, some partly true, and some false.
It seems well to deal with them here.[1]

1. It was charged that directors, especially in the branches,
were appointed from political motives. The charge was partly
true. From the beginning directors were selected with the
intention of favoring the party in power. Biddle found the
system in force when he took office but disapproved of it and
did something to check it. It existed when Jackson became
President of the United States. Directors were usually taken
from the merchant class, most of whom opposed him. From the
victors came a demand for representation on the boards. Biddle
was too practical to resist absolutely. He threw the Nashville
branch entirely into Lewis's hands and held back only when he
saw that this prince of spoilsmen was bent on getting control
of all the branches in the West. The trouble here lay with the
system, not with Biddle. Americans were hot partisans: there

---

[1] These charges have been so well summed up in Professor Catterall's eleventh chapter (pages 243-284)
that I have been left no choice but to follow his treatment with little addition of new facts.— The Author.

was no neutral class from whom strictly non-partisan directors could be supplied.

2. The bank was said to lobby in its own behalf. It never denied the assertion; but it declared that it used no corrupt methods, and proof to the contrary was not produced. Jackson claimed that it bribed its way in congress, but this was the vaporing of partisan anger. Nevertheless the wealth of the bank, its able direction, and its extended influence gave it great power through the use of what may be termed legitimate lobbying. It is a question if merely in this kind of activity it could be pronounced a harmless participant in public life.

3. There were frequent charges of using money at the polls. The charge was repeated most forcefully and with most details in regard to the Kentucky branches. It was alleged that in 1828, two hundred and fifty dollars of the bank's money were used outright in treating at the polls and in hiring hacks to take voters to the voting places. Worden Pope, connected with the Louisville branch, denied this charge. He was the man accused in it and said that the "new court" party had spent money in politics and he merely "beat them with their own dirty stick," but that all the money he used was his own and he spent it of his own volition.[1] Reliable evidence on such a point is difficult to obtain, but when the officers individually avowed the practice, the public was naturally sensitive about the action of the bank.

4. Biddle was accused of giving special favors to congressmen, such as lending money on insufficient security, transferring money for them without charge, and paying their salaries in drafts on distant cities without cost, favors which he did not extend to private persons. Facts to prove these assertions were adduced, although the occurrences were not so common as the professed terror of the democrats implied. He also

---

[1] Jackson to Ingham, December 20, 1830; R. Desha to Jackson, December 5, 1828; W. Pope to Jackson, June 19, 1831; Jackson Mss.

advanced the money for congressmen's salaries in anticipation of the passage of the general appropriations bill and without interest. By loss of such interest and of exchange on drafts the bank gave to members of congress several thousand dollars a year. Biddle's philosophy on matters like these is expressed in the following words:

The existence of this institution must depend on the opinion entertained of it by those who will before long be asked to continue its Charter and altho' I would sacrifice nothing of right or of duty to please them or to please anybody, still if a proper occasion presents itself of rendering service to the interior proving the usefulness of the Bank, so as to convert enemies into friends, we owe it to ourselves and to the stockholders not to omit that occasion.[1]

5. Another charge was subsidizing the press. It was persistently made and widely believed. Biddle, it was thought, lent money readily to newspapers and made them his tools, and only those were considered honest which did not wear his collar. Yet his avowed policy was otherwise. When Webster advised him to help Gales and Seaton, publishers of the *Intelligencer*, on the ground that their influence was useful, he refused pointedly, saying that it would be a just reproach to the bank to undertake to lend its funds under such conditions. This he said in 1828, when the question of re-charter was not up; but three or four years later he made large loans to editors, some of them the most important defenders of the bank in the profession, and others opposed to it. The *Intelligencer* now got over forty-four thousand dollars and Duff Green of the *Telegraph*, since Calhoun's defection a friend of the bank, got twenty thousand. Biddle declared that all these loans were made as mere business propositions, and it was pertinently asked if editors alone should be denied accommodation — as pertinently as Jackson asked if

---

[1] Biddle to Webster, December 2, 1828, quoted by Catterall, *Second Bank*, 257.

editors alone should be denied appointments to office. The matter is perplexing; for we cannot know how much a loan to a supporter was an inducement to defend the bank, or how much one to an opponent was given because a refusal would be heralded as an act of oppression. It was only one of the unfortunate complications arising from the connection of the bank with politics.

But in one loan Biddle was not clear of wrong-doing. The *Courier and Enquirer*, of New York, was one of the most important papers in the country. Its editors were J. Watson Webb, James Gordon Bennett and Major M. M. Noah. Webb was for Adams, but his associates were for Jackson and fixed the policy of the paper. In 1831 they formed a scheme against the bank, as Bennett described it. Through the aid of Silas E. Burrows, a merchant with a shifty political connection, they got fifteen thousand dollars from Biddle, in Philadelphia, giving in exchange Noah's note endorsed by Webb for eighteen months. The note was payable to Burrows, who transferred it to Biddle and from him personally received the money, and it was only some months later that the President entered it on the books of the parent bank; but as soon as it was given the journal changed its policy and began to advocate re-charter. In February, 1832, when an investigation of the bank was moved in the house of representatives, Burrows appeared in Philadelphia, borrowed fifteen thousand dollars of the bank, and with it took up the tell-tale note, thus transferring the debt from the editors to himself. In the same year Noah left the paper and it came out for Clay. In August Webb borrowed twenty thousand and in December fifteen thousand more. With accrued interest his debt amounted to a little less than fifty-three thousand dollars. A part of it, eighteen thousand six hundred dollars, was protested in 1833, and two years later he offered to settle it at ten cents on the dollar. Webb claimed that when the debt was made the paper was ample security for its repayment. But the devious manner in which the first loan was secured, the fact that the time allowed amounted to five years — which was against the rule of short loans for ordinary patrons — and the efforts to conceal it from the investigating committee show that it was not an ordinary business transaction.

6. The liberal circulation of speeches, pamphlets, and magazine articles was considered an evil by Biddle's enemies. His own point of view was irreproachable. The first bank, he thought, was destroyed in 1811 because the people did not understand its services. "I saw the manner in which the small demagogues of that day deceived the community," he said — "and I mean to try to prevent the small demagogues of this day repeating the same delusions."[1] He threw himself into the task of enlightenment with his usual energy, and he soon had the appearance of trying to carry the popular mind by storm. To the democrats it seemed that he identified himself with the propaganda of their enemies. They complained that a semi-public institution should use its money against them. When the investigations showed that in 1831 the directors in Philadelphia gave the bank's president power to spend money for necessary purposes without vouchers and without reporting the purpose of expenditure, the democrats made bitter complaint. The authority was excessive: it witnessed the confidence of the directors in Biddle but it ought not to have been granted.

7. Biddle's power was really autocratic, and it was alleged that he used it improperly. By the rules he was a member of each committee of the directors, and by the rules of 1833 he named every committee but one. The most important committees in the transaction of business were those on discounts, which met twice a week, and on exchange, which met daily. His strong personality dominated each group, as, indeed it dominated

---

[1] Biddle to Gales, March 2, 1832; quoted by Catterall, *Second Bank*, 266, note 1.

the board and even the shareholders. At meetings of the latter he usually held individually or jointly with others a majority of the proxies, and from the time he showed himself successful in the management of the institution his word was decisive in annual meetings. He was of the type frequent enough in the financial world, a strong willed man who takes the initiative and whose assumption of authority is approved on account of his success.

8. The charge which attracted most attention was in connection with] the redemption of the 3 per cents., the facts of which were as follows: In March, 1832, the government notified the bank that in July it would pay half of the thirteen millions of this debt still outstanding. The moment was inopportune for Biddle: the government had recently paid a large amount of its debt for which the bank furnished the money out of the deposits, and it was not able to furnish six and a half millions more in specie on such short notice. But he himself was to blame. He knew the policy of Jackson was to pay the debt as fast as possible, and he could well have assumed that all the surplus which was accumulating in the treasury would be used for that purpose. Instead of reserving it in his vaults, he had incautiously lent it to the investing public, and it could not quickly be called in. Lending had been too liberal in the past year, and six months earlier he gave orders to lend no more unless it was necessary to support the vital business of the country. Time and again he repeated this warning, but the branches were lax, or the impetus of speculation was irresistible, and discounts went on increasing at the rate of ten millions in six months.[1]

The only other thing was to postpone the payment of the debt. Biddle appealed to the government with that in view and was given an extension of three months. Within this addi-

---

[1] Catterall, *Second Bank*, 146.

tional time the bank could not hope to withdraw the necessary money from the business of the country, especially as it soon got notice that on January 1, 1833, the government would pay the other half of the 3 per cents. Then Biddle conceived, with the aid of Cadwalader, the plan of postponing a large part of the installment by a deal with its holders. Cadwalader was sent to London to offer the foreign bondholders the obligations of the bank at one year's time with interest at 3 per cent. for these bonds to the amount of five millions. Bonds thus secured were to be turned over to the government, which would relieve itself from all responsibility by cancelling them. Thus the bank would take the place of the government for this much of the debt, which it would be able to extend one year.

Some of the foreigners gave approval to the scheme, but anticipating that some would be slow to accept it, Cadwalader arranged that the Barings, of London, should buy for the bank the rest of the required amount and withhold the certificates from the government. Now the charter of 1816 forbade the Bank of the United States to buy government stock. The scheme as arranged by Biddle was no violation of this law, but Cadwalader's modification of it was quite another thing. Moreover, it involved delay in the payment of the debt, which would certainly give offense in Washington. Cadwalader seems to have desired to keep the affair secret, but it was known at once in London and soon after in New York. It was reported to Biddle in two letters, the first informally and a few days later in the written agreement with the Barings. The latter was received in Philadelphia, October 12th, after its substance was published in New York. The president of the bank at once repudiated it; but his enemies said he did not repudiate the informal agreement and only rejected the formal one because he found the matter had become public.

The affair caused much comment. Cadwalader took all the

blame on his own head, and the bank managed to get the money for the 3 per cents. No one could justify the purchase of bonds in violation of the charter; but Biddle did not think the attempt to interfere with the government's plan to pay the debt unjustifiable. "Supposing that the certificates are delayed for a few months," he said, "what harm does that do to anybody? The interest has stopped — the money remains in the Treasury; so that instead of depriving the Government of the use of its funds, directly the reverse is true, for the Government retains the funds and pays no interest."

The various charges against Biddle were greatly exaggerated by his enemies. He was painted as drunk with the power which money gives, and the denunciation was so extravagant that he benefited by the reaction. But he is not to go scot free. He did not buy votes to control elections, but he appointed partisan directors when he thought it necessary; he did not really subsidize the press, but he was unquestionably entangled with Noah and Webb in an unjustifiable manner: he did not bribe legislators, but he employed a strong lobby, gave favors to members of congress, and by circulating their speeches identified himself with party propaganda: he did not improperly lend the bank's money to friends, but he took the authority into his own hands and against its own rules until he had the power to do so: he did not authorize the purchase of the 3 per cents., but he showed himself defiant of the will of government in trying to postpone payment in order to get out of a situation into which his own carelessness had brought him.

We ought not to forget that Biddle's difficulties were great. The nation was not wise enough to exercise political oversight over so large a machine as the bank. It had a feeling that a corporation as powerful as this was dangerous to liberty, and it would not be shown otherwise. Biddle's well-meant efforts to enlighten the people were thought to be attempts to hide his own errors. Jackson frequently declared for "a complete divorce of the government from all banks": if there is no other reason for this, it would be enough that the separation he established has prevented the recurrence of the painful scenes and controversies which were precipitated by an enraged people about the Bank of the United States in the days of its destruction.

CHAPTER XXIX

THE presidential election was now over, and the veto was sustained. Many people hoped that the question would be dropped and the bank allowed to die peacefully when the charter expired, but not Jackson. He believed that the bank by calling in its loans could distress the people until they demanded re-charter. He believed, also, that congressmen were not proof against the wiles of the bank and that a democratic majority might, in the face of strong business pressure and by means of bribes, be induced to pass a charter over his veto. He decided to remove the deposits at once, and thus to cripple the bank's fighting power, to settle the question before the election of 1836, and to avoid jeopardizing the public deposits at the time when the last fight for re-charter must come up.

Van Buren, who was opposed to the bank on constitutional grounds, wished to see the question settled before the next election. He suggested that congress be asked to establish a bank such as Jackson would approve in the District of Columbia, with branches only by the consent of the states concerned.[1] It was believed that congress could not be induced to take this step, and Van Buren then supported removal. But he feared its influence on his following in the North, and by common consent he was allowed to remain as much as possible in the background in the contest about to begin.

Nothing was to be expected from the congress which in the recent session passed the charter. If a blow was struck it must

[1] Van Buren to Jackson, November 18, 1832, Van Buren Mss.

be by the executive itself; and the long vacation beginning March 4, 1833, afforded the opportunity for such action.   Up to that time nullification and the tariff compromise occupied the attention of the politicians.   Everybody, Jackson included, was willing to let the bank question lie till those matters were disposed of; but their program was made out and only awaited the adjournment of congress to be put into force.   This was in spite of the fact that in the preceding December, Henry Toland, appointed by Secretary McLane to investigate the condition of the bank, reported that the institution was perfectly sound, and in spite of the plainer fact that the house of representatives on March 2nd by a large majority declared that the deposits were safe in its custody.

The anti-bank democrats were prepared to ignore Toland and congress, but they could not ignore the secretary of the treasury, since he alone could give the order for removal.   McLane was so strong a man that he could not easily be dismissed, and some other way must be found to dispose of him.   It was discovered that Rives desired to return from Paris and that Livingston wished to have his place.   It was accordingly arranged to make the transfer and to give McLane the secretaryship of state which Livingston would relinquish.   For the vacant treasury a New York man was first thought of, probably because the Van Buren men could be counted on; but the idea was rejected, and a Pennsylvanian was taken.   William J. Duane was the man, suggested, it seems, by McLane.'   He was the son of the former republican editor, ancient enemy of Gallatin, Dallas, and the whole conservative republican faction.   The old man was the leader of the masses, whose support was essential to carry the state against the bank, and it seemed a good thing to have the son deal the blow which was now meditated.

Duane was not an able man.   Henry Lee, when he turned

---

¹Jackson to Van Buren, September 15, 1832, Van Buren, *Autobiography*, V., 180-195, Van Buren Mss.

against Jackson, described him as "that other Darling whom you fished up from the desk of a dead miser, and the bottom of the Philadelphia Bar, to put in the seat which was once filled by Alexander Hamilton."[1]   The offer was made by McLane in behalf of the President, and after hesitating for two months Duane accepted January 30, 1833.   It was not the plan to change the cabinet until after the tariff muddle was cleared up, and so it was not until June 1st that the new secretary took his place.

Jackson was now in constant consultation with Kendall, Blair and Taney, the most active enemies of the bank.   To accomplish their purpose would deprive the government of a safe place of deposit and lessen the volume of sound currency in the country.   To meet the objections on these accounts they urged that state banks of undoubted soundness could be got to keep the deposits, and as for the currency, the country would be better off if only hard money was used.

But they were more immediately concerned with the political phase of the question.   As a manifesto on this side Amos Kendall prepared a letter to the secretary of the treasury giving reasons for removal.   He mentioned the insecurity of the funds, but dwelt on the political aspects of the matter.   The bank, he said, was as much of an enemy as it could be and removing the deposits would not increase its hostility.   On the other hand, the state banks, now intimidated by the great corporation, would become friends of the government as soon as they knew the public money was taken away from that corporation.   Removal would please the South and West and have the support of the banks of New York, always jealous of Philadelphia's preëminence in financial affairs.   Pennsylvania, he admitted, would be dissatisfied, but New England cared little for the bank and could be ignored.   Re-charter, thought Kendall, was likely if nothing was done.   Congress was full of doubt and the bank would

[1]Lee to Jackson, December 27, 1833, Jackson Mss.

corrupt enough members at the next session to have its way. But vigorous action now would commit the friends of the administration, show that the banks were unnecessary, and answer the complaint of many Jackson men that "it is useless to buffet the bank with our left hand as long as we feed it with our right."[1]

Three days after his lieutenant delivered this manifesto Jackson submitted five questions to his cabinet. He asked: (1) Has anything happened since congress met last to justify a new charter? (2) is the bank reliable and faithful to its duties? (3) should there be a new bank, and if so with what privileges? (4) should re-charter be allowed with modifications? and (5) what should be done in the future with the deposits? Commenting on his own questions Jackson indicated that he was against the continuation of the deposits.

It was about this time, a little earlier or later, that he took the advice of the cabinet as to whether it would be wiser to proceed against the bank by a writ of *scire facias* or to remove the deposits. They all agreed that a writ would be unwise: it would come at last to the supreme court, and no one could doubt how Marshall would decide it.

The President soon knew the attitudes of the secretaries. Livingston and Cass were for the bank, Barry and Taney were outspoken against it, Woodbury was not clear in his reply to the questions asked, but believed that if the bank continued it ought to have new directors and stockholders on the principle that the old set had received the benefits of it long enough. McLane took two months to write a long reply to each question. He thought the bank safe, the deposits in no danger, and he opposed removal. "The winding up of [the bank's] concerns without embarrassment to the country," he said, "is under the most favorable circumstances rather to be hoped than expected.

[1]Kendall to McLane, March 16, 1833, Jackson Mss.

It is not for the Government to add to the inherent difficulties of the task, but rather to aid in obviating them; *not for the sake of the bank, but rather that of the community.*" On the report Jackson endorsed, "There are some strong points in this report all ably discussed.— A. J."[1]

It is hard to reconcile this outward appearance of deliberation with his inward suspicion and irritation. To intimates he spoke of a newly discovered combination between Clay and Calhoun which secured the recent tariff law in order that the revenues should be large and remain on deposit for the benefit of the bank. These utterances throw so much light on his intellectual quality that one of them is given at length:

This combination wields the U. States Bank, and with its corrupting influence they calculate to carry everything, even its re-charter by two thirds of Congress, against the veto of the executive, if they can do this they calculate with certainty to put Clay or Calhoun in the Presidency — and I have no hesitation to say, if they can re-charter the Bank, with this hydra of corruption they will rule the nation, and its charter will be perpetual, and its corrupting influence destroy the liberty of our country. When I came into the administration it was said, and believed that I had a majority of seventy-five. Since then, it is now believed it has been bought over by loans, discounts &c., &c., until at the close of last session, it was said, there was two thirds for re-chartering it. It is believed that in the last two years, that it has loaned to members of congress and subsidized presses, at least half a million of dollars, the greater part of which will be lost to the Bank, and the stockholders,— and if such corruption exists in the green tree, what will be in the dry?

Such has been the scenes of corruption in our last congress, that I loath the corruption of human nature and long for retirement, and repose on the Hermitage. But until I can strangle this hydra of corruption, the Bank, I will not shrink from my

---

[1]McLane to Jackson, May 20, 1833, Jackson Mss.

duty, or my part. I think a system may be arranged with the State Banks, with all the purposes of deposits, and facilities of the government in its fiscal concerns, which if it can, will withdraw the corrupting influence now exercised over congress by this monied institution which will have a healthy effect upon the legislation of congress and its morals, and prevent the continued drain of our specie from the western states to the East, and to Europe to pay the dividends. I am now engaged in this investigation, and I trust that a kind superintending providence will aid my deliberations and efforts.[1]

Jackson had real doubts about the disposal of the deposits if they were removed. He asked several friends if they would be safe in the state banks. Kendall urged their entire security, and other advisers wrote to the same effect. Hugh L. White, of Tennessee, approved of the state banks and suggested that all the funds be deposited in one state bank — one of those in Virginia would serve — and let this bank distribute the money among other institutions and become responsible to the government for its safety. As to the time of removal, that ought to have been when the bank failed to call in the 3 per cents., but the opportunity having passed and congress having declared the institution solvent, public opinion would not now support removal. He advised that the matter be submitted to congress at its next session.[2]

An appeal to congress was not the purpose of Jackson, and it was decided early in May to proceed with his plans. It was time for action, if the matter was to be accomplished before congress met in December. First, the cabinet was reorganized. Livingston went to Paris, scandalizing his friends by borrowing eighteen thousand dollars from the wicked bank before his departure. McLane took the state department, and Duane

---

[1]Jackson to Cryer, April 7, 1833, *American Historical Magazine*, (Nashville,) IV., 239.
[2]White to Jackson, April 11, 1833; Thomas Ellicott to Jackson, April 6, 1833; Powhatan Ellis to Jackson July 2, 1833, Jackson Mss.

on June 1st became secretary of the treasury. The President was now ready to proceed. He desired to set things going before June 6th, when he was to leave on a visit to New England.

Duane was not told beforehand what was expected of him, but he was stupid if he did not have a pretty clear knowledge of the situation. For three months and a half he carried on a game of fence the object of which was to defer action. Jackson at first pressed him gently, showing for once forbearance and self-control. In the beginning he merely stated what was wanted, and when Duane demurred told him to take time and report on the matter when the trip to the North was over. Meanwhile he promised to send the secretary a statement of his views.

The day he began his journey Jackson wrote Van Buren as follows:

I want relaxation from business and rest, but where can I get rest; I fear not on this earth. When I see you I have much to say to you   The Bank and change of deposits, have engrossed my mind much, is a perplexing subject, and I wish your opinion before I finally act. This is the only difficulty I see now on our way. I must meet it fearlessly, as soon as I can digest a system that will insure a solvent currency.[1]

Three days later Kendall also wrote to Van Buren. Jackson, he said, was decided about the necessity of removal, but was still debating as to the time and the new method of keeping the deposits. In anticipation of this visit Kendall sent Van Buren the following outline of a plan of procedure with reasons for action: Place the deposits with two banks in New York and with one each in Boston, Philadelphia, and Baltimore, and possibly in Norfolk, Charleston, Savannah, Mobile, and New Orleans, with the understanding that these banks should collectively guarantee the safety of the funds, though they should place some

---

[1]Jackson to Van Buren, June 6, 1833, Van Buren Mss.

of the money in such other banks as they should select with the approval of the treasury. This, it will be seen, was an amplification of White's suggestion.

Kendall further suggested the gradual withdrawal of funds then in the Bank of the United States. This, he said, ought to be done "soon enough to take the last dollar out of the United States Bank and present a new machine in complete operation before the next session of Congress" and it ought to begin before September at least. The bank, which had hitherto been on the defensive, would thus yield the advantage of that position to the government; the state banks, liberated from their fears of the "great Mammoth," would become friends of the government; and these facts, with the popularity of Jackson, would carry the country.

In New York the President and vice-president went over the matter, and June 26th the former sent his decision to the secretary of the treasury. He outlined a plan for removal with the essential features of Kendall's plan and inclosed a long exposition of the whole question, evidently from the pen of Kendall. He gave little more time to his journey. Illness prostrated him in Boston, and in a very feeble condition he set out northward but not until he attended Harvard commencement, where the president and corporation conferred upon him the honorary degree of doctor of laws. The honor was lost on its recipient, who cared nothing for such a compliment, and it angered his opponents, especially John Quincy Adams, who after that referred to him as "Doctor Andrew Jackson." At Concord, N. H., the traveler became so ill that he gave up the journey and returned to Washington as quickly as possible, arriving there July 4th.

He soon invited Duane to an interview. The latter was recovering from a severe illness and arrived very weak and pale. Jackson met him warmly, took both his hands in his own, reproved him for coming out in such an enfeebled condition, and told him to defer the interview until strength returned.[1] Duane willingly complied, and July 12th he delivered in person a long letter summarizing his reasons for not removing the deposits until the matter was referred to congress.   On the fifteenth there was a conference in which the two men came no nearer together, but they preserved their good temper, Jackson protesting his admiration for the frankness of his secretary.   But Duane was not really frank; for he still hesitated to say whether or not he would do what was expected of him.

Several interviews followed,[2] in which neither man convinced the other; but Duane was induced to appoint Kendall special agent to interview state banks and report on their availability as places of deposit.   He did this reluctantly, but said that if when he considered the report he was unable to order the removal of the deposits he would retire from the administration.   This was the first real satisfaction Jackson got from the secretary, and shortly afterward he went to the Rip Raps, in Hampton Roads, for a month's rest.   He was accompanied by Blair, and the two had daily conferences about the political situation. Kendall meanwhile industriously visited the bankers of the cities to the northward.

It was a critical period in the conflict.   Duane was fighting for time; McLane and most of the cabinet supported him; and Van Buren himself, bound to his leader by every possible interest, could not bring himself to favor immediate action.   It was at best but little time that could be gained before congress met: why not let it pass?   Many persons, whigs and democrats, felt that an order for removal would but make plainer the incompetence and passions of the President and in that way make surer the fight for ultimate re-charter.   Would Jackson yield before

[1]Van Buren, *Autobiography*, V., 202, Van Buren Mss.

[2]For the facts in the Duane controversy reliance has been had chiefly on Duane's *Narrative*, where the letters are given on both sides.

the fears of his friends or the evident glee of his opponents? The bank men were extremely busy. Biddle exerted himself to send to Jackson an avalanche of petitions in favor of the bank. They came from all kinds of business organizations and reflected the general apprehension of disaster if the centre of the banking function were struck down. McLane was also active. He was in close touch with Duane, so that some men said he was the real head of two departments. He conceived a compromise, which about the middle of August he laid before Van Buren. He proposed that Jackson should assert executive control over the deposits, order their removal on January 1, 1834, and announce it in his message to congress. He would thus avoid the imputation of ignoring congress. Kendall heard of the scheme on his travels and said he would accept it if McLane, Duane, and the bank democrats would agree to use their influence to remove the deposits when congress met; otherwise he feared a two thirds majority would order the continuation of the bank.[1]

About this time Jackson appealed to Van Buren for advice. That cautious gentleman was in a difficult position. His well-known support of McLane in general caused him to be considered persistently friendly to the bank democrats, and so good a judge of events as James Gordon Bennett thought the plan to remove the deposits was hatched by Kendall to kill Van Buren along with the bank.[2] Appealed to directly, the vice-president sought to avoid the responsibility of a direct answer. He knew nobody, he said in reply, whose opinion on such a matter was worth so much as that of Silas Wright, whom he had sent for; and later he would write more definitely.

"This bank matter," he added, "is to be the great finale of your public life, and I feel on that account a degree of solicitude

---

[1] Kendall to Jackson, August 11 and 14, 1833, Jackson Mss.
[2] Bennett to Van Buren, September 25 (2), 1833, Van Buren Mss.

about it but little less than that which is inspired by the public considerations connected with it. I hope that we shall in the end see the matter in precisely the same light; but be that as it may, inasmuch as I know no man in the purity of whose intention as it respects the public I have greater, if as great, confidence as I have in yours, and as I cannot but look upon you as incomparably the most faithful, efficient, and disinterested friend I have ever had, so I go with you against the world, whether it respects men or things."[1]

Wright duly reported that three of the leading democrats in Albany favored immediate removal, one advised waiting on congress, while he himself was for the plan suggested by McLane. Van Buren supported his friend's recommendation. Let all arrangements be made at once, he said, and especially the selection of the state banks of deposit, three of which ought to be in New York, and it would be better to have four there; for "those engaged in them, like the rest of their Fellow Creatures are very much governed by their own interests."[2]

To this Jackson replied in mild surprise that Van Buren had accepted the plan of McLane. It brought real alarm into the breast of the New Yorker, who, in company with Washington Irving, was then about to set out on a four weeks' trip to the Dutch settlements on the North River and Long Island. He wrote hastily to explain that he and Wright were not understood, that they gave their advice thinking that January 1st began the fiscal year, but since they learned that October 1st served for that purpose they were not so decided. In fact, they only preferred New Year's Day, but would yield to the wisdom of the President.

And then came to Van Buren a more disquieting message. Jackson, beset by doubts, wanted his best lieutenant with him and asked him to come to Washington. It was a rude interruption of the carefully planned visit to the Dutch. Van Buren

[1]Van Buren to Jackson, August 19, 1833, Jackson Mss.
[2]Silas Wright to Van Buren, August 28th; Van Buren to Jackson, September 4, 1833; Jackson Mss.

wanted to keep himself as free as possible from the commotion at the capital. His letter declining the suggestion also contains other interesting matter:

"I shall be governed in that matter," he wrote, "altogether by your wishes. You know that the game of the opposition is to relieve the question, as far as they can, from the influence of your well-deserved popularity with the people, by attributing the removal of the Deposits to the solicitations of myself, and the monied junto in N. York, and as it is not your habit to play into the enemies hands you will not I know request me to come down unless there is some adequate inducement for my so doing. With this consideration in view, you have only to suggest the time when you wish me to come down, and I will come forthwith. . . . And always remember that I think it an honor to share any portion of responsibility in this affair.

"Allow me to say a word to you in regard to our friend McLane. He and I differ *toto coelo* about the Bank, and I regret to find that upon almost all public questions the bias of his early feelings is apt to lead us in different directions. Still I entertain the strongest attachment for him, and have been so long in the habit of interceding in his behalf that I cannot think of giving it up, as long as I believe it in my power to serve him, and his. From what passed between us at Washington, I think it possible, that he may, (if Mr. Duane resigns) think himself obliged to tender his resignation also, which if accepted would inevitably ruin him. Your friends would be obliged to give him up politically and when stript of his influence his former Federalist friends would assuredly visit their [illegible] mortifications at his success upon him in the shape of exultations at his fall. I am quite sure that if ever he tenders his resignation he will nevertheless be anxious to remain if he can do so with honor, and if you should say in reply — that you will accept his resignation if he insists upon it but that you confide in him &c., notwithstanding the difference between you upon this point, and that if he could consistently remain in the administration you would be gratified, I think he would be induced to withdraw it."[1]

[1]Van Buren to Jackson, September 7, 11, 14, 1833, Jackson Mss.

Jackson at this time was much influenced by a report from the government directors in Philadelphia. Before the bill to recharter was introduced, when final action was still doubtful, Biddle was courteous to these directors, but afterward his attitude changed. In the beginning of 1833, when new committees were made up, no government director was appointed to a standing committee, although later in the year two found places on minor committees. Saner men like Webster advised against this policy, but Biddle's attitude was thorough.[1] Early in April Kendall communicated to the government directors Jackson's desire that they should report on the condition of the bank. They replied that the books were not open to directors generally and that they could do nothing unless the secretary of the treasury gave them authority to inspect individual accounts.[2] But April 22nd they sent a report showing that Gales and Seaton had borrowed a large sum on the security of a contract to print the *Congressional Debates*, for which the money was not yet appropriated, but which would without doubt be paid. The loan was technically irregular, but it was reasonably safe.

This report did not warrant action, but August 19th the directors, four of them now coöperating, sent another report. They at last had access to the expense account and reported a large increase in recent years, chiefly for printing pamphlets and other articles in defence of the bank. They cited a resolution of the board, March 11,1831, authorizing Biddle to print what he chose to defend the bank, and under which many items were charged without vouchers. This, as the directors said, enabled the bank's president to use the whole press of the country to aid him in his fight, and without accountability, if he chose to go that far. As a matter of fact Biddle spent in this way without vouchers until the end of 1834, twenty-nine thousand and

1Catterall, *Second Bank*, 309.
2Sullivan, Wager and Gilpin to Jackson, April 8, 1833, Jackson Mss.

six hundred dollars, a sum which seemed very large to the people of the day. It made a deep impression on the President, as his paper read in the cabinet on September 18th[1] shows.

Early in September Jackson was back in Washington pressing Duane for final action; and as the secretary still held that congress should be consulted the President hesitated no longer. Before going southward he told Taney to be prepared to take the treasury department, and he now proceeded with his plans.[2]

While at the Rip Raps he dictated his reasons for removing the deposits and sent the paper to Taney for revision. Under his hand it became a proper state paper and not a "combattive Bulletin," as Van Buren pronounced the first draft.[3] September 17th the President took the opinion of the cabinet; it was as in the preceding March, except that Woodbury came over definitely to the President. Next day they were summoned to hear the statement of his reasons for removal. It became known as "The Paper read to the Cabinet on the Eighteenth of September" and contained the assertion that the deposits ought to be removed on October 1st. Duane must now determine what he would do, since Jackson's position amounted to an order. He took a night to consider and announced that he would not order the transfer or resign. He preferred dismissal, thinking he would stand better with the country and thought himself justified in ignoring his promise to resign. Through five days Jackson sought to change the decision of the secretary, displaying at the same time the greatest personal consideration for his feelings. Nothing shook Duane's decision, and September 23rd he received a formal note of dismissal, the draft of which exists in Taney's handwrit-

---

[1]The reports of the directors, April 22nd and August 19th, are in *Congressional Debates*, Volume X., part 4, pages 69-74.

[2]Taney to Jackson, August 5, 1833, Jackson Mss.

[3]Van Buren, *Autobiography*, V., 216.

ing.[1] On the same day the attorney-general was authorized to take charge of the treasury.

Administration friends were now concerned lest McLane and Cass should feel compelled to resign also. They dreaded another explosion in the cabinet, and when they were discussing Taney's copy of the paper read to the cabinet they suggested as much to Jackson, who said he cared not; they could do no mischief; but that he was willing to assume the responsibility, and he added a clause to that effect to the paper before him. This, says Blair, is the origin of the oft-mentioned responsibility clause. When Taney read it later he was puzzled to know how it got in and, when Blair told of its origin, he said: "This has saved Cass and McLane; but for it they would have gone out and been ruined. As it is, they will remain and do us much mischief."

When McLane and Cass consulted Jackson on the 24th he said they ought to be satisfied with his assumption of responsibility unless they wished to go into opposition. They gave no definite answer for some days and in the meantime he cast about for their successors. He desired, as he said, men who did not think they had "a right to transact the business of the departments adversely to what the Executive believes to be the good of the country. . . . I hope for the best; but let what will come, the sun will continue to rise in the East and set in the West, and I trust in a kind Providence to guide and direct me and in a virtuous people's support."[3]

Taney's apprehensions were groundless. September 26th he ordered that government funds henceforth be deposited in specified state banks, and immediately came such an outpouring of wrath that democrats generally, bank and anti-bank men, were driven into solid formation. McLane and Cass offered their resignations and Jackson, in the words suggested by Van

[1]Jackson Mss.
[2]Van Buren, *Autobiography*, VI., 3, Van Buren Mss.
[3]Jackson to Van Buren, September 24, 1833, Mss. Library of Congress.

Buren, refused to accept them. Benjamin F. Butler, intimate friend and law partner of the vice-president, according to a plan previously formed by that far-seeing adviser, was given the vacant attorney-generalship.[1]

The meeting of congress, December 2nd, saw the beginning of an angry struggle. The message pronounced the bank "a permanent electioneering engine" which sought "to control public opinion through the distress of some and the fears of others." Biddle, it said, was curtailing discounts as the public funds were withdrawn, and this was done in order to force restoration of the deposits and ultimate re-charter. The message acknowledged that the President in regard to the bank did not agree with the recent session of congress, for whose opinions generally it protested respect; and it left the issue to the judgment of the members of congress fresh from the people. The style of the message was like that of Taney.

The secretary of the treasury reported at length his reasons for removing the deposits. He was the ablest man in the anti-bank faction, and his report is in pleasing contrast with the loose reiterations of suspicions and assumptions which came so plentifully from his colleagues. He clearly ignored Jackson's contention that the deposits were not safe in the bank but justified removal on grounds of expediency. By the sixteenth section of the charter he had full discretion to act as he saw fit. He must report his reasons to congress, but that body was not given the right to pass on them. The power to order restoration with the consent of the President was, however, implied in the general control of congress over the public funds.

The whigs and the bank, now thoroughly united, struck back at Jackson as they could. They believed public opinion was outraged by removing the deposits and felt warranted in

---

[1]Van Buren to Jackson, September 14, 1833, Jackson Mss. See also above, II., and Parton, *Life of Jackson*, III., 501-503.

adopting a policy of minor restrictions which were, in fact, but expressions of their anger.   By a vote of twenty-five to twenty they refused to confirm the renomination of the government directors, whom the bank party called spies.   Biddle used his influence to secure this rejection,[1] but Jackson renominated the directors, and they were again rejected.   The senate showed its displeasure further by repudiating Taney's nomination as secretary, and in 1835 they refused to confirm his nomination to a seat on the supreme bench, although in March, 1836, when the administration was somewhat stronger in the senate, he was by a strictly party vote confirmed as chief justice in succession to John Marshall.   It was Taney's fortune to take an unpopular side in two important crises, but his mental acumen cannot be denied.   During the rest of the administration he was the President's chief adviser and wrote for him many state papers, among them the *Farewell Address*.

The session of congress beginning in December, 1833, was a stormy one.   In the house Jackson had a majority; in the senate he was in the minority, and his opponents embraced Clay, Calhoun, and Webster.   Over six hundred petitions, chiefly from the trading and manufacturing towns of the seaboard, were sent to congress in reference to existing business distress. Most of them admitted that distress existed.   Those prepared by the whigs claimed it was due to the removal of the deposits, and those which the democrats forwarded said that it came through the designs of Biddle.   There can be no doubt that the politicians' pictures of distress increased the feeling of panic beyond its natural limits.

As deputation after deputation came to ask Jackson to restore the deposits he lost his temper.   Let them go to Biddle, he said, and ask him to stop contraction.   As for Jackson, he would never consent to re-charter the "mammoth of corruption";

---

[1]Catterall, *Second Bank*, 309.

he had his foot on it and would not relinquish his advantage; sooner than favor restoration of the deposits or re-charter he would suffer ten Spanish inquisitions. Returning delegations reported much like this in reply to their requests. The tone was enough like his private letters to make it seem very probable, and after a while, probably by the advice of friends, he denied himself to all petitioners. Announcement of his furious replies produced disgust among thoughtful people, but such persons were arrayed against Jackson long before that. It pleased the masses to know that their hero would not relax his hold on the bank.

Early in the session Clay, accepted leader of the bank men, got the senate to call for the paper read before the cabinet on September 18th. Jackson refused on the ground that the senate had no right to call for a paper submitted to the cabinet. He meant no disrespect to the senate, he said, whose functions he would ever respect, but he would preserve the independence of the executive as a coördinate branch of the government.[1] It was a very firm reply, as dignified as the request itself, and it left Clay without ground of protest. The criticism that it was the act of a despot is baseless, since Jackson acted clearly within his constitutional rights. Nor is there force in the charge that he violated the secrecy of the cabinet in publishing the document. The President is not bound to keep secret his own utterances to the cabinet, especially in the case under consideration, where the utterance was a general defense of an action vitally interesting to the public.

December 26, 1833, Clay introduced two resolutions, one against Jackson's and the other against Taney's part in removing the deposits. After much debate they were amended and passed in the following form: "Resolved, (1) That the President, in the late executive proceedings in relation to the public

---

[1] Richardson, *Messages and Papers of the Presidents*, III., 36.

revenue, has assumed upon himself authority and power not conferred by the Constitution and the laws, but in derogation of both. (2) That the reasons assigned by the Secretary for the removal are unsatisfactory and insufficient." They were passed, the latter on February 5th, by a vote of twenty-eight to eighteen, the former on March 28th, the vote being twenty-six to twenty.

The resolution against Taney was to be expected, but how could that against Jackson be justified? Clay fell back on the phraseology of the law of 1789 creating the treasury department, in which congress, desiring to keep within its own hands the finances of the nation, assigned to the secretary specific duties and required him to report to congress, and not to the President, as other secretaries reported. Clay, therefore, held that the secretary of the treasury was the agent of congress, that under congress he had sole control of the deposits, and that the President's interference was unwarranted. The argument was weak because the President had power to remove the secretary of the treasury and congress knew it when it gave the latter the power to withdraw the deposits. The secretary, therefore, must exercise his control over the deposits subject to the power of the President to remove him, and congress must have intended this to be, or it would have provided otherwise in the charter.

To this attack Jackson sent a protest[1] in which he pronounced the senate's resolution unconstitutional. It was, he said, really a judicial act analagous to impeachment, for which the constitution provided a procedure. The argument was not convincing, but it served to introduce a long defense of all the President had done in the matter of removal, and it contained bodily copies of state resolutions approving his course. It was designed for an appeal to the people. The senate refused to enter it on the records, which gave his friends an opportunity to say he was

[1] Richardson, *Messages and Papers*, III., 69-94.

not only condemned without a hearing, but his protest in defense of his conduct was treated with contempt.

The composition of this protest illustrates Jackson's method of using his assistants. Butler worked on the legal side of it, Taney was worn out with other cares and probably did little, and to Kendall was assigned the task of presenting arguments of a political nature. But neither subordinate was left unaided. Jackson worked out each phase of the protest and sent it to the proper man for review and suggestion.[1]

When these resolutions passed the senate it seemed to many that Jackson's defeat was sure. Some of his friends were doubtful and his enemies were jubilant. But he did not falter. He looked to the approval of the people, whose feelings he understood, because he was their representative. Although arguments were made on each side of the controversy then waging, it was a battle of passions, and in it his strong spirit was at its best. Every charge of calamity from the course he had pursued could be turned by ingenious statement into a charge of evils due to the bank; and the public mind was not sober enough to weigh the nice points in the case.

Jackson was not blindly guessing when he expressed confidence in the people. The election of 1832 showed how much they trusted him. As Van Buren said many years afterward, nothing but his popularity could have carried the people in the contest against the strongly intrenched bank. The congress which met in December, 1833, showed the effect. Although the senate, less responsive to popular will, was for the bank, the house was strongly against it. It showed its temper by reëlecting Stevenson, a thorough Jackson man, speaker, and by substituting James Knox Polk, equally committed to Jackson, as chairman of the ways and means committee, for McDuffie, Calhoun's devoted agent. Removing the deposits completely identified the issue with Jackson, and Polk's aggressive policy forced members to support it or appear before the people as opponents of the President. Thus, while the senate passed a resolution for restoring the deposits, Polk was able to carry in the house four resolutions reported from his committee to the following purport: (1) That the bank should not be re-chartered, carried by a vote of one hundred and thirty-two to eighty-two; (2) that the deposits should not be restored, one hundred and eighteen to one hundred and three; (3) that state banks should keep the public funds, one hundred and seventeen to one hundred and five; and (4) that a select committee be appointed on the bank and on the commercial crisis, one hundred and seventy-one to forty-two. The margin of safety was not large, but it showed a great change in sentiment since 1832, when the charter passed the house by a vote of one hundred and seven to eighty-five.

Meanwhile the advocates of the bank showed weak points. In the first place, their opposition was partly factious. When the commercial panic became acute the bank held tightly to its funds, although it was evident that they were not immediately needed. A mild spirit at the time would have done it much credit in the public eye. Some of its friends took this as evidence that it had too much power. Biddle, who was cautious and rash by turns, now meant that the country should have enough of Jackson's financiering. "The relief," he said," to be useful and permanent, must come from congress and from congress alone. If that body will do its duty, relief will come — if not, the bank feels no vocation to redress the wrongs inflicted by these miserable people. Rely upon that. This worthy President thinks that because he has scalped Indians and imprisoned judges he is to have his way with the bank. He is mistaken."[1] This was in February, 1834.

---

[1] Catterall, *The Second Bank*, 339. The course of the bank in this connection is discussed in Catterall's chapter XIII.

Moreover, the senate majority was rent by dissension. Clay, Calhoun, and Webster each had his own plan of action. The last mentioned introduced a bill to extend the charter six years. Calhoun, thinking the time too short, moved to extend twelve years, but Clay would accept neither, and forced the others to inactivity in order to prevent open dissension. He was determined to lead or oppose the combination.

His triumph in the resolutions to censure Jackson was a barren victory. Already the country was going against the bank. People were getting accustomed to the financial distress and the poignancy of suffering was passing.[1] February 26th, Governor Wolf, of Pennsylvania, a consistent democrat, formerly friendly to the bank, sent a message to the legislature charging the bank with producing the pressure in the money market "to accomplish certain objects indispensable to its existence."[2] The party in that state came to his support to the dismay of Biddle. In New York at Governor Marcy's suggestion the state issued six millions of stock to be loaned to the banks to relieve their embarrassment.[3]

At this point Biddle was face to face with a revolt by the merchants, especially in New York. They formed a committee which said that if he did not resume discounts they would publish their conviction that he ought to do so. He hesitated, but at the end of March announced that loans would be resumed for a month. Immediately the public declared that this action showed that contraction had not been necessary, and the bank was never able to meet the charge. Men thought, all but the outspoken bank men, that Biddle had gone into a conflict with Andrew Jackson using for weapon his ability to create a money pressure, and they concluded that abandoning the weapon indicated his defeat.

[1] Catterall, *Second Bank*, 336-337.
[2] Niles, *Register*, XLVI., 26.
[3] Hammond, *History of New York*, II., 441; Alexander, *Political History of New York*, I., 400.

The courage of the anti-bank men was admirable, their general-ship was excellent, but their methods were not always commend-able. Prejudice, ignorance, and selfishness abounded rather more than on the other side. For example, after denouncing the bank for creating distress, they declared when it resumed discounting that this was only done to create another oppor-tunity to inflict a pressure.[1] Of the same nature was the plan early in 1834 of some old bank men and some of Jackson's supporters in New York to have a new bank for their own advantage. Van Buren would not countenance the scheme. It would have been unwise to crush one bank to build up another in which administration favorites had part, and popular indigna-tion over such a thing must have fallen heavily on the vice-president, since his immediate supporters were in the scheme.[2]

The congressional elections of 1834 were made to turn on the bank question. The most excited feeling prevailed in the country; and Biddle, fearing personal violence, filled his house with armed men as the election approached. He was not molested, but the election went against him by a large majority, and the fate of the bank was sealed. The institution was so dead that some whig politicians began to rejoice that they would not again have to carry its weight of unpopularity. Its later history is not a part of this story.[3]

The shifting of public opinion was utilized by the administra-tion leaders in the fight for the expunging resolutions. When Clay's motion of censure passed, Benton gave notice that he would move to expunge it and in the following session redeemed his promise. Clay charged Jackson with assuming power illegally, and Benton moved to expunge on the ground that the charge was false, unjust, and passed without giving the accused

[1]Polk to Jackson, August 23, 1834, Jackson Mss.

[2]Van Buren to Thomas Jefferson (of New York), January 15, 1834; J. Hoyt to Van Buren, January 29, February 4, 1834, Van Buren Mss.

[3]For an account of the closing of the bank, see Catterall, *Second Bank*, chapter XV.

an opportunity to be heard. The resolution was, therefore, an indictment of the senatorial majority, the court of trial being the people. The only overt act to be alleged in support of Clay's charge was the dismissal of Duane, which was not unconstitutional. Benton's indictment, therefore, was essentially true, and Clay's impetuosity had placed his party in a bad position. The democrats made an issue of redressing the wrongs against Jackson, the people were rallied, state legislatures voted instructions to senators, and senators gave place to others who came fresh from the convinced people until the complexion of the senate was changed. As Benton said in announcing his purpose to keep the matter before the people until the expunging resolutions were passed, the decision was with the American people.

He thought he was beginning a contest of several years, but opinion developed so fast that victory came in less than three. December 26, 1836, the third anniversary of the day on which the condemnatory resolutions were introduced, he announced that retribution was about to be taken. After reading an exulting preamble he moved that black lines be drawn around the entry in the journal of the obnoxious resolutions and across it written the words, "Expunged by order of the Senate." The motion came up for adoption on January 16th. Foreseeing a long night session he provided in a committee room an abundance of hams, turkeys, roast beef, wines, coffee, and other food to sustain his friends through the struggle. His own friends said little, but Calhoun, Clay, and Webster in mournful speeches protested against what was about to be done. It was, they said, in violation of the constitution, which required a correct journal of the senate's proceedings. The resolution was carried by a vote of twenty-four to nineteen.[1]

Benton's florid language does not hide the true meaning of the fight. Clay's initiative was wrong: he sought to crush Jackson

---

[1] Benton, *Thirty Years' View*, I., 524-550, 545-549, 717-727.

and thought it would discredit a man to have the majority of the senate pronounce him guilty. The time had come when the people did not follow a senate vote blindly. Benton made them see the personal feeling in the attack of Clay, Webster, and Calhoun. Although his appeal contained both passion and misstatement, it rested on truth. The old school of politicians, Clay among them, were apt to think too little of the average man's ability to understand their real motives.

The expunging resolutions chiefly concerned the welfare of the party. For Jackson they were important as representing the end of his bank war. The revived nationalism of 1815-1820 expressed itself in the tariff, the movement for internal improvements, and the Second Bank. They were now all checked, and, besides that, the erratic desire for decentralization in South Carolina was suppressed, and the tendency to aristocratic institutions in the hands of the conservative republicans was replaced by a vigorous and well-organized democratic party. All these were the achievements of Jackson and the few men who supported him. They were the chief results of his administration. Probably no other President in time of peace has effected such important steps in our political history. But they are not Jackson's only achievements. The period of his power is also marked by notable events in foreign affairs and by such domestic actions as his Indian and land policies, all of which are yet to be examined.

CHAPTER XXX

AMERICAN DIPLOMACY UNDER JACKSON

THE phases of Jackson's administration thus far discussed relate to domestic politics. Of the other phases the most important is foreign affairs; and in this field it will be necessary to observe his dealings with Great Britian, France, and Mexico.

The West India Trade: When Jackson became President England persisted in her ancient policy of exploiting trade with her colonies for the benefit of her own merchants. The West India trade, closed to the United States when they became an independent nation, was still denied to them after much negotiating. In the treaty of Ghent, 1814, no relaxation was secured, nor were concessions obtained during Monroe's administrations. John Quincy Adams, secretary of state, whose vigorous policy served well against a nation as weak as Spain, could wring nothing from the mistress of the seas. The situation was not improved when he became President with the aggressive Clay for secretary of state. Retaliation succeeded here no better than in the days of Jefferson.

The development of this controversy was as follows: After due efforts at a diplomatic settlement Monroe in 1818 resorted to retaliation. At his suggestion congress closed American ports to British ships coming from the ports not regularly open to American ships. We thus meant to put England in our ports on the same footing in regard to the West India trade as she insisted on allowing us in the island ports. It was a hardship to the planters in the islands, for they found it convenient to give themselves chiefly to sugar raising and to rely on the United States for their food supply.

Great Britain was anxious to save the planters and opened Halifax to American ships. This, she thought, would draw to that place the American products which had formerly gone to the islands and that they would be shipped thence to their former destination in her own ships. We met her move by tightening our own system. We forbade the exportation of our products to the West Indies in British ships and the importation of products from that place unless they came directly. These regulations, it must be remembered, did not concern our direct trade with England, which was not affected on either side.

In announcing the latter restriction our minister said we would modify it if England would make reciprocal concessions; but the British ministry treated the proposition with indifference. They soon had reason to change their views. The West Indian planters depended on the United States for certain supplies; and if they could not have them legally they would have them illegally. Smuggling, ever an attendant on the navigation laws, now became worse than before, and the British government could not stop it. Law-abiding planters protested against the situation, and in 1822 restrictions were made somewhat lighter. We were allowed to carry certain products to certain West India ports on paying colonial tariffs there plus 10 per cent. discriminating duty in favor of the Canadian and other British ports northeast of us.

In reply Monroe opened our ports to British ships bringing West India products, but he imposed on them a differential tonnage duty of one dollar a ton and a differential impost of 10 per cent. This concession did not concern our trade with the colonies on our northeast. The restrictions Monroe retained were thought to equalize those England retained, but to England they seemed excessive and she issued an order to collect a differential tonnage duty of four shillings sixpence on American ships in the West Indies.   Thus the evidences of a relaxing policy in 1822 disappeared in 1823, and the contest went on as formerly.   Each side stuck to its position, and although attempts were made at a settlement through diplomacy the situation was unchanged for two years.

Finally, July 5, 1825, Parliament passed a new act which was a still further concession.   Adams pronounced it ambiguous, but it offered us the same rights in the West Indies that we gave to English vessels in our waters, provided we accepted the offer in one year.[1]   Congress failed to meet this offer, partly because the opposition flouted anything the administration was supposed to desire, and partly because the rising spirit of protection was instinctively against any suggestion of lower rates.

The President thought the affair could be settled by negotiation and sent Gallatin to London to see what could be done.   He arrived after the year of grace expired and was met with news of a recent order to exclude our ships from the West Indies.   By no persuasion could he get Canning, now Foreign Secretary, to open the door again which some months earlier we might have freely entered.[2]

British politics were then in a state of change, and the law of 1825 grew out of a wave of reform.   The years 1822-1825 were very prosperous ones: revenues increased, taxes were reduced and made more logical, trade expanded, and the merchants were too well pleased to be intolerant of change.   Behind the reforms of the day was a group of liberal men led by Huskisson and Robinson.   They planned large things, but in December, 1825, the bubble of prosperity burst, the buoyancy of reform receded, and hope of changing the country's colonial trade relations went

---

[1] For documents connected with this phase of the controversy, see *American State Papers, Foreign*, VI.; 84, 214-247.   See also, Richardson, *Messages and Papers of the Presidents*, II., 184.

[2] *American State Papers, Foreign*, VI., 246-266, 294; Adams, *Life of Gallatin*, 615-620.

with it. Canning, who relished a policy of force if he thought it justifiable, remained obdurate until his death in 1827.[1]

The position of Adams was characteristic. It was, also, just that which his father, minister to England in 1785, took when the West India trade first became a matter of negotiation after the revolution. He would convince England that her navigation laws were unwise; and England would not be convinced. He would make her see her true interests: Canning thought it humiliating in the mistress of the seas to be instructed by America. Loyalty to the national dignity and a willingness to hector his opponents came naturally to the rigid New Englander. We are not surprised that he closed his account of the affair by saying: "It becomes not the self-respect of the United States either to solicit gratuitous favors or to accept as the grant of a favor that for which an ample equivalent is exacted."[1] They were fine words, but they were not exactly applicable to the situation.

In the campaign of 1828 Adams was reproached for his failure to accept England's offer, and his successor felt obliged to try to undo the wrong which was alleged to have been done. Mc-Lane, minister to England, was impressed with the opportunity he had to achieve important results. He was very ambitious and saw in the business the pathway to the highest hopes. His instructions gave him every incentive to boldness. After reviewing the progress of the affair since 1815 Van Buren said plainly we had made three mistakes: one in denying that England should levy protecting duties in her colonies, another in requiring that British ships from the colonies to the United States should return thither, whereas England allowed our ships leaving her colonies to go anywhere, and another in failing to accept the offer

---

[1]Walpole, *History of England*, II., 151-161, 168, 181-193.
[2]Richardson, *Messages and Papers of the Presidents*, II., 383.

of 1825. McLane was to communicate as much of this to British minister as he saw fit.[1]

We must not criticise Van Buren too severely for this attitude. The three errors he named are taken strictly from three which Gallatin announced in one of his first despatches from England in 1826.[2] Later on Gallatin added other reasons for the unhappy feeling over the question, but he thought the errors of our government very important. Van Buren, therefore, was only acknowledging openly what another had admitted in confidence to his superior.

But Van Buren's greatest departure from conventional methods of negotiating was his way of assuring England that his offer was reliable and justified. Our former policy, he said, had been submitted to the American people and by them rejected; and the present government now spoke with authority. "It should be sufficient," he added, "that the claims set up by them, and which caused the interruption of the trade in question, have been explicitly abandoned by those who first asserted them, and are not revived by their successors."

Van Buren's diplomacy was direct, that of his predecessor was formal. He undoubtedly violated the dignified conventions of the service, but he gave a clear and sensible turn to the business in hand. His practicality is shown in the form in which he would have the settlement embodied. The former administration had preferred to act through diplomacy and a treaty, he said; and the English government had stood for an act of the legislature. But he was willing to use either method, as was thought most convenient. He says that McLane himself, looking through the case before his departure for England, concluded that the only way to re-open it after England's summary decision in 1826 was to urge a change in American opinion

---

[1]McLane's correspondence went to Congress, January 3, 1831, and was published in *Executive Documents*, 21st congress, 2nd session, number 24, page 64.

[2]Adams, *Life of Gallatin*, 617.

and asked permission to proceed on that basis. Jackson consented and McLane wrote his own instructions to that intent.[1]

The British government received the American advance cordially, but Canada protested loudly. She had advantages in the West Indies which would be destroyed by the proposed agreement. Her protest delayed action several months, but Van Buren had private assurances that matters went well. Jackson's first annual message also helped to make yielding easy. "With Great Britain, alike distinguished in peace and war," said the message, "we may look forward to years of peaceful, honorable and elevated competition. Everything in the condition and history of the two nations is calculated to inspire sentiments of mutual respect and to carry conviction to the minds of both that it is their policy to preserve the most cordial relations."[2]

But the American position was not altogether conciliating. While it abandoned the contention of the past, it announced a positive attitude for the future. "Whatever be the disposition which His Majesty's government may now be pleased to make of this subject," said McLane to Lord Aberdeen, "it must necessarily be final, and indicative of the policy to which it will be necessary, in future, to adapt the commercial relations of each country." One who knew Jackson could not doubt the meaning of these words.

Waiting without results at last began to exhaust the President's patience, and April 10, 1830, he wrote Van Buren as follows:

We ought to be prepared to act promptly in case of a failure. We have held out terms of reconciling our differences with that nation of the most frank and fair terms. Terms which, if England really had a wish to harmonize, and act fairly towards us, ought to have been met in that spirit of frankness and candor

[1]Van Buren, *Autobiography*, V., 61, Van Buren Mss.
[2]Richardson, *Messages and Papers of the Presidents*, II., 443.

and friendship with which we proposed them. These terms being rejected our national character and honor requires, that we should now act with that promptness and energy due to our national character. Therefore let a communication be prepared for Congress recommending a non-intercourse law between the United States and Canady, and a sufficient number of cutters commanded by our naval officers and our own midshipmen made revenue officers and a double set on every vessel &c., &c. This adopted and carried into effect forthwith and in six months both Canady and the West India Islands will feel, and sorely feel, the effects of their folly in urging their government to adhere to our exclusion from the West India trade. Will Mr. Van Buren think of these suggestions and see me early on Monday to confer upon this subject? [1]

April 6, 1830, after six months of waiting, McLane hinted to Van Buren that an act of congress might pave the way for success, and May 29th such a law was passed. It authorized the President to grant the necessary privileges to British ships as soon as he knew that England would give us similar terms.[2] This was followed by complete success in London. The British restrictions were removed, and October 5, 1830, Jackson issued a proclamation opening the trade with the islands.[3]

The arrangement merely opened the American and West India ports respectively to the ships of the other nations without restriction as to tonnage or place of departure. It did not lessen the right of either nation to lay imposts in the islands or at home. Under this feature of the case the British government imposed such duties that the American trade suffered greatly, and opponents of Jackson declared that the boasted diplomatic triumph of the administration was as nothing. But we never could hope to prevent another nation from collecting duties, most of all when we were committed to our own tariff policy;

[1] Jackson Mss.
[2] Peters, *United States Statutes at Large*, III., 419.
[3] Richardson, *Messages and Papers of the Presidents*, II., 497.

and we had removed an unpleasant source of international irritation.

Opponents of Jackson have said that it was the failure of the British colonial policy more than diplomatic ability that won the settlement of 1830. On the other hand, the British ministry was more disposed to relax in 1825 than in 1830. This was partly due to the strong movement for economic reform in the former year. In the latter the whole kingdom was still alive for reform, but of a political kind. So far as the break-up of the old system of restriction was concerned, all was done in 1825 that was done later. The task was to remove from the minds of the ministry the determination to resent the tone of American diplomacy, and that was done by the direct and practical methods under Jackson's direction.

The French Spoliation Claims. Since 1815 American citizens had claims against France for destruction of property under Napoleon. Like the matter of West India trade, they long encumbered our diplomacy, and it was wise to have them settled. W. C. Rives, of Virginia, who went to France as minister, was instructed to settle the claims if possible. European nations had similar claims in 1815, but they were soon paid: Americans felt the sting which their own position thus involved.

Rives arrived in Paris in the autumn of 1829, just after the Martignac ministry was replaced by the reactionary Polignac, a change which he thought unpropitious for his hopes. Polignac's first position was that France could not pay for Napoleon's spoliations, but when reminded that she paid other similar claims and that the United States should insist that the nation was responsible for the acts of the *de facto* government he promised to look into the matter.

Rives pressed the subject steadily, and two months later the ministry agreed that they ought to pay for American property destroyed at sea, but were not liable for seizures under the Berlin and Milan decrees. Rives took this for a favorable sign, but soon learned that the minister was bent on delay. A reference in Jackson's first annual message to a possible "collision" with France was construed as offensive, and it took much patience on Rives's part to smooth matters. Finally, on February 12, 1830, Polignac admitted that the Berlin and Milan decrees grossly violated the law of nations, but said it would bankrupt the country to pay all the damages from Napoleon's violations of that law. Under the pressure of Rives's continued demands he agreed that he might be willing to pay for the seizures at sea and for some of those under the offensive decrees. Rives disclaimed any special desire to establish his theory and said he would be satisfied with payment for losses, whatever ground it was placed on. It was agreed that a project be submitted to the king and ministry for a commission to consider the claims specifically, and a few days later it was announced that the plan was approved.

At this point the chambers met in the beginning of March. They were bitterly opposed to the king for many illegal actions; paying the American claims was unpopular because it would necessitate increased taxes; and the opposition used the occasion to weaken the government with the people of France. Rives, deeply alarmed, called on Lafayette, still a firm friend of America, who by his influence was able to secure the silence or moderation of several important newspapers, and thus the danger was alleviated.

But immediately another obstacle appeared in certain counter claims France brought forward. The eighth article of the Louisiana purchase treaty provided that French ships should have the privileges of the most favored nation in American ports, and damages were now asked because losses were incurred in the troublous times of Jefferson and Madison. It was a strained interpretation, but Rives saw it would embarrass the negotiations and wrote to Van Buren for permission to offer to meet it by reducing the duty on French wines imported into America. The request was granted, and May 20th he mentioned it to Polignac, whose willingness to conciliate the commercial interests of his country prompted him to receive it gladly. Hope again revived, only to be dashed to the ground when on June 8th an investigating committee reported against the claims on the ground that Napoleon himself would not have paid them. The despairing and disgusted Rives expressed his feelings in a private letter in which he said: "In the diplomacy of this government nothing is certain but what is past and irrevocable. Indeed, in my transactions with them I have almost come to adopt the vulgar rule of interpreting dreams, and from what is said to conclude that the precise contrary will be done."

A week later affairs brightened without apparent cause. Polignac became amiable and proposed a commercial treaty in which should be included the concession on wines. It was about to be consummated, when the revolution of July 26-30 drove Charles X into exile and placed Louis Philippe on the throne. Negotiations now ceased; and the unwillingness of the new government to increase the taxes left little hope that the business would soon be resumed.

Yet on September 9th Rives took it up again, only to be met by a refusal. Molé, the new foreign minister, said the claims were just, but the government needed money too badly to think of assuming their payment. Rives, however, persisted and secured a commission to examine them specifically. On it served G. W. Lafayette, son of the Revolutionary hero. The king interested himself in the matter, professing his sympathy for our claims, and urging us to have patience.

Matters were really progressing; and added promise came from a handsome allusion to the king which Jackson, at Rives's suggestion, incorporated in his second annual message.

Finally the commission concluded its labors late in March, 1831. The majority would not allow the claims under the decrees, but were willing to pay ten million francs for other losses. The minority — G. W. Lafayette and Pinchon — admitted both kinds of claims and fixed the damages at thirty million francs.

Subsequently Sebastiani, then the foreign minister, communicated the decision to Rives and said the ministry, willing to be liberal, would pay fifteen millions. Rives was indignant and said it was mockery to talk of that sum and if the offer was definitive the negotiation was at an end. Sebastiani said it was not definitive but told him to reflect on it. A fortnight later he offered twenty-four millions, when Rives said he would settle for forty millions. After some other higgling they compromised on twenty-five million francs, and it was agreed that we should pay France one and a half millions for seizures on our own part, and the reduction of wine duties was to be made as an offset for the claims under the eighth article of the Louisiana treaty. These terms were embodied in a treaty which was duly signed July 4, 1831. It was a notable triumph for which Rives's energy, tact, and patience were mostly responsible. It pleased the American people, who saw in it another illustration of Jackson's just but vigorous methods of clearing our diplomacy of old issues.[1]

The treaty, ratified February 2, 1832, provided for payment in six annual instalments, the first a year after ratification. But no money could be paid until it was voted by the chambers, and as French public opinion thought the amount agreed upon too large the chambers were loath to execute the treaty. It was not until they were about to adjourn after an eight months' session that the matter was taken up, and then it was dismissed without action. In the meantime, the secretary of the treasury

---

[1] The facts for this narrative of the French negotiation are taken from the records in the office of the secretary of state in Washington, *France*, volumes 24-27. For the treaty of 1831, see Haswell, *Treaties and Conventions*, 345.

drew a draft on the French government for the first instalment, which, forwarded through the United States Bank, was duly protested for lack of funds. On this transaction Biddle demanded the usual protest charges amounting to nearly one hundred and seventy thousand dollars. One hundred and thirty-five thousand dollars of this sum were for damages, the rest for protest cost, interest, and re-exchange. The administration was willing to pay all but the item for damages. The demand was within the meaning of the law, but to Jackson and to most people it seemed unfair for the rich bank to exact the last pound of flesh, especially since it handled so large a portion of surplus government funds without paying interest on them. This was in May, 1833, and had something to do with the determination to remove the deposits. Jackson took refuge behind the government's immunity from a suit and refused to pay the bill. When in July, 1834, Biddle deducted the amount from the government's dividend as a stockholder in the bank the wrath of the administration was unbounded.

In September, 1833, Livingston, succeeding Rives, arrived in Paris and addressed himself to the problem of getting the treaty executed. The king and ministry professed themselves ready to pay, but the chambers were obdurate, and with them Livingston could have no relations. He concluded that nothing but a show of force would reach the ears of the French people, long accustomed to despise us. He hinted at such a course to the ministry and broadly suggested to Jackson that the coming annual message take a firm tone.

The suggestion was so quickly seized that it may be doubted if it was necessary. In fact, June 6th Jackson ordered the navy to be ready for service.[1] October 5th he said, "There is nothing now left for me but a recommendation of strong measures." Van Buren, now a close adviser in all things, gave his approval

[1] Jackson to the Secretary of the Navy, June 6, 1834, Jackson Mss.

of an energetic policy. "Your past forbearance," he wrote, "will now come to our aid, and the opposition will, I trust, before winter be whipt."

The message bore witness to the President's earnestness. It recounted the efforts to induce France to execute the treaty, gave the king credit for his intention to urge the chamber at its next session to vote the money, and declared that the President had exhausted his resources. If congress wished to await the action of the French chambers, nothing need be attempted during its coming short session; but if from the omission of the chambers in five sessions to provide for the execution of a solemn treaty it should doubt their intention to execute it, congress must determine for itself what course should be followed. "Our institutions are essentially pacific," said he in dismissing the subject. "Peace and friendly intercourse with all nations are as much the desire of our government as they are the interests of our people. But these objects are not to be permanently secured by surrendering the rights, or permitting the solemn treaties for their indemnity in cases of flagrant wrong, to be abrogated or set aside." He dismissed the subject by recommending that if France did not pay we seize enough French property, public or private, to satisfy the claim.[1]

The message reached France early in January and raised a storm of anger. But it also showed the people they faced a crisis and made the world see that the supineness of American diplomacy was past. Livingston reported that the higher respect for our government was discernible in the attitude of his fellow ministers in Paris.

The French ministry dared not acquiesce in the position taken by Jackson. They held that the national faith was impeached, and after five days informed Livingston that they had recalled their minister in Washington and added that Livingston's

[1]Richardson, *Messages and Papers of the Presidents*, III., 100-106.

passport was at his disposal. But our representative was not willing to leave his post without a more definite dismissal. He held on for awhile and received instruction as to his conduct. If the chambers did not pass a law then before them to pay the money Livingston would close the legation and leave Paris; if they passed it he might leave the legation in the hands of a *chargé d'affaires* and retire to a neighboring country.

The law referred to was not defeated. It hung fire a long time and finally passed with the proviso that the money should not be paid until satisfactory explanation was made of the language of the annual message. Livingston at once left affairs in the hands of Barton, *charge*, and sailed for home on the *Constitution*, which by orders awaited his departure at Havre. He protested as he went that France had no right to require explanation of words in the President's message, a paper solely for the information of congress.

The law in question was sent to Pageot, *charge* in Washington, who offered to read it to Forsyth, now secretary of state. But Jackson forbade such recognition, saying: "We would not permit any foreign nation to discuss such a subject. Nor would we permit any or all foreign nations to interfere with our domestic concerns, or to arrogate to themselves the right to take offence at the mode, manner, or phraseology of the President's message or any official communication between the different co-ordinate or other branches of our government."[1]

Barton, in Paris, was at the same time instructed[2] that he must not discuss the message or give any explanation of it. He was directed to inform the French ministry that the Rothschilds were our agents to receive the money due. If it was not paid in three days he was to make a last formal demand for it: if it was not then paid within five days more, he was to demand his passports,

---

[1] Jackson to Livingston, September 9th; *ibid* to Forsyth, September 6, 1835, Jackson Mss.
[2] Jackson to Barton, instructions, draft in Jackson's hand, September 6, 1835, Jackson Mss.

close the legation, and come home. He complied with instructions, but the only reply of the ministry was that they were ready to pay the money as soon as the United States would declare that they "did not intend to call in question the good faith of His Majesty's government." Barton could make no such concession. November 8th he asked for his passports, and three weeks later left Paris, closing the legation until the appearance of Cass, December 1, 1836.[1]

When in September, 1835, Pageot offered to communicate to Forsyth the French law disposing of the matter he read, also informally, a letter in explanation of the case. Forsyth refused to receive it or to take a copy, but it contained the French defense. It admitted that the law to pay the money was thrice presented to the chamber and once rejected, and that it was not presented to the short session of August, 1835; but this was because the king felt that it would be rejected at that session. It declared what seemed to be true, that the ministry sincerely desired to execute the treaty. As to Jackson's contention that a foreign government could no more notice a President's message than a committee report or a speech in congress, the reply was that France did not demand a categorical denial, but only assumed that a disclaimer would be made and suspended action until it came. In view of assurances to Barton, this feature of the explanation was merely a quibble.

The French complication had its influence on political conditions. In the senate Clay introduced resolutions which passed unanimously, declaring that legislative action ought not to be taken. In France they were cited in debate to show that Jackson was not supported in congress. The house was less hostile. It resolved that the treaty ought to be executed and that steps should be taken to meet any probable emergency.

[1] Livingston's and Barton's reports are in *Letters from Ministers*, state department, *France*, volume 27. Their instructions are in *Instruction, France*, volume for 1829-1844. See also, Richardson, *Messages and Papers of the Presidents*, III., 130-132, 135-145, 178-185, 193-197.

This happened in January and February, 1835. As the months passed public opinion sobered. There was little real apprehension of war, but the whigs affected to believe that it might come through the rashness of an irascible old man. The message of 1834 was, in fact, needlessly strong. Members of the President's own party urged him to be moderate in the next annual message.[1] They had some effect, although they did not seriously modify his private views. If France were an honorable nation, he said privately, she would pay the money and demand an apology afterward; that was what Napoleon would have done. But from Maine to Florida came the voice, "No apology, no explanation — my heart cordially responds to that voice."[2]

The message of 1835 showed careful treatment. There was a long review of the French affair justifying what had been done, but expressed in terms of restraint; there was also a specific denial of any intention "to menace or insult" France, and the case was closed in these words:

France having now through all the branches of her government acknowledged the validity of our claims and the obligation of the treaty of 1831, and there really existing no adequate cause for further delay, will at length, it may be hoped, adopt the course which the interest of both nations, not less than the principles of justice, so imperiously require. The treaty being once executed on her part, little will remain to disturb the friendly relations of the two countries — nothing, indeed which will not yield to the suggestions of a pacific and enlightened policy and to the influence of that mutual good will and of those generous recollections which we may confidently expect will then be revived in all their ancient force. In any event, however, the principle involved in the new aspect which has been given to the controversy is so vitally important to the independent administration of the Government that it can

[1] Gooch to Jackson, November 28, 1835, Jackson Mss; Ritchie to Van Buren, November 28, 1835; J. A. Hamilton to Van Buren, January 20, 1836, Van Buren Mss.

[2] An undated draft, destination not given, in Jackson's handwriting, Jackson Mss.

neither be surrendered nor compromitted without national degradation. I hope it is unnecessary for me to say that such a sacrifice will not be made through any agency of mine. The honor of my country shall never be stained by an apology from me for the statement of truth and the performance of duty."[1]

It is not difficult to guess what parts of this paragraph were in Jackson's original draft.

By this time it was evident that neither nation desired war, and France accepted the pacific utterances in the message as sufficient disclaimer. Before this was known in Washington Barton arrived with news of the last acts of his residence in Paris. Jackson sent another message, January 15, 1836, softened probably through the efforts of Livingston, in which he firmly insisted on his position and suggested that if the money was not paid we should exclude French ships and goods from our ports. Before it could be known in France a settlement was practically arranged. January 27th, Bankhead, British *chargé* in Washington, offered the services of his nation to mediate the dispute and each side accepted. He next announced that France was satisfied with the message of December, 1835, and would pay the money. All trouble disappeared quickly, and May 10th Jackson sent a gracious message announcing that four of the six instalments were already paid and cordial relations with France were reëstablished.[2]

One characteristic touch closed the incident: February 16th Livingston wrote inclosing a letter from Baron de Rothschild intimating that France would receive a minister and that Livingston's reappointment would be agreeable. Livingston closed his letter by admitting that he had a "desire of enjoying on the spot the triumph of your firm and energetic measures."[3]

---

[1] Richardson, *Messages and Papers of the Presidents*, III., 160.

[2] Hunt, *Life of Livingston*, 428; Richardson, *Messages and Papers of the Presidents*, III., 188-193, 213, 215-222, 227.

[3] Jackson Mss.

Such flattery was supposed to be most effective with Jackson, but here it had no power. Cass got the appointment to Paris, and Livingston retired to private life.

Relations with Mexico: In the treaty with Spain, 1819, the United States gave up their claim to Texas in order to make sure of Florida. Many people, some of them politicians of influence, like John Quincy Adams, hoped to purchase what the treaty relinquished. Jackson, who consented to the treaty because at the time he thought more of Florida than of Texas, had the general Southwestern feeling for Texas, but he refused the offer to be our first minister to Mexico after that nation became independent.[1] Ninian Edwards, to whom the place was next offered, was recalled before he reached his destination; and Poinsett, dispatched early in Adams's administration, first took up the task of arranging a commercial treaty between the two powers. Acting on instructions from Clay, he tried to get the new republic to accept the Rio Grande, or some other point south of the Sabine, for our boundary. Mexico took this as an attempt to profit by her weakness, her suspicions of our motives were aroused, and she steadily refused to yield to our plans. Poinsett was then directed to offer one million dollars for Texas, but he concluded that to do so would only enrage that power, and did not mention the offer. Instead, he concluded a commercial treaty in 1828 in which the Sabine was declared the boundary.

When Jackson became President this treaty was not ratified. He suspended action upon it and sought to reopen negotiations for the purchase of Texas. Expressing himself confidentially to Van Buren he said that he thought two million dollars would serve to amend the Mexican constitution so as to allow a sale of a part of the domain, and he was willing to give five millions to get Texas to the "great prarrarie or desert." He believed we

---

[1] Jackson to Adams, March 15, 1823, Mss. in state department.

ought to have this region, because a foreign power ought not to have the tributaries of the Mississippi and because "the God of the universe had intended this great valley to belong to one nation."[1]

Next day he outlined Poinsett's instructions and sent them to Van Buren. He pointed out the following advantages to Mexico if she sold us Texas: the boundary would be a natural one, the money would enable Mexico to maintain herself against Spain, the danger of a conflict between her citizens and ours would vanish, the difficulty of managing the Texans be obviated, and finally by surrendering the territory as a mark of esteem for a sister republic she would show herself "worthy of that reciprocal spirit of friendship which should forever characterize the feelings of the two governments toward each other."

Our objects in getting Texas were: the safety of New Orleans and the Mississippi valley, the need of new territory for the Indians who must be moved from the East, and the acquisition of a natural boundary. He thought the middle of the great desert would be such a boundary, and if that could be obtained he would pay not more than five millions.[2]

Meanwhile Poinsett was in trouble in Mexico. He took the side of the party favoring a democratic government, aroused the anger of an opposing faction which made capital out of the suggestion that the domain was about to be divided, and resolutions were passed against him in the legislature of one of the confederated states. He was no longer useful, and Jackson recalled him, but in doing so sought to save his feelings in all possible particulars. He even protested against the resolutions concerning Poinsett.

Poinsett was succeeded by Col. Anthony Butler, a former military comrade of Jackson, whose diplomacy proved to be

---

[1] Jackson to Van Buren, August 12, 1829, Van Buren Mss.
[2] The draft is preserved in the Jackson Mss. and also in the Van Buren Mss. See also, Reeves, *Diplomacy under Tyler and Polk*, 65, note 11.

bad. The years during which he directed our affairs in Mexico are pronounced by Professor Reeves "a seven years' period of cheap trickery."[1] He led Jackson to think that Texas could be purchased by proper negotiation and he produced on the Mexican government and people the worst opinion of our aim and honesty. His chief object seems to have been to prolong his period of employment and to overcast his failure by deluding the administration with false hopes. He wrote many personal letters to Jackson in which he promised everything but fulfilled nothing.[2] In April, 1831, he confirmed Poinsett's commercial treaty of 1828 and in a separate agreement accepted the boundary of 1819. Both were ratified and promulgated by the American government in 1832.[3]

Buying Texas, the greatest object of his mission, was thus left to further negotiation. As no direct offer moved the Mexicans, Butler tried indirection. He referred to Jackson a plan to pay five million dollars, part to Mexico and part to the adventurers who had acquired vast land grants in Texas. The scheme contained great possibility of fraud. Jackson said in reply that we would not take Texas subject to any land grant except Austin's, that we would pay the money to Mexico, and cared nothing about what she did with it, but that Butler must take the greatest care to avoid "the imputation of corruption."

This was not encouraging, and in 1835 Butler appeared in Washington to urge in person a still more doubtful scheme. He brought a letter purporting to be from Hernandez, a priest in Santa Anna's household, saying that for a bribe of half a million to be distributed where needed the sale could be made for five million dollars. On it Jackson endorsed the following:

---

[1]Reeves, *Diplomacy under Tyler and Polk*, 69.

[2]The Jackson Mss. contain many private letters from Butler to Jackson, with replies of the former. See February 27, 1832, October 28, 1833, February 6, March 7 and October 2, 1834: of the latter, see April 19, 1832, and November 27, 1833, with endorsements on Butler's letters.

[3]Reeves, *Diplomacy under Tyler and Polk*, 69-74; see also, Adams, *Memoirs*, XI., 343. The Hernandez letter is in the Jackson Mss. under date March 22, 1835.

Nothing will be countenanced by the Executive to bring the Government under the remotest imputation of being engaged in corruption or bribery. We have no concern in the application of the consideration to be given. The public functionary of Mexico may apply it as they deem proper to extinguish *private claims* and give us the cession clear of all incumbrances except the grants which have been complied with. A. J. June 22-35.

The reader will give his own interpretation to these words. To the writer they seem to show that Jackson was a practical man among other practical men, and that he was not shocked at the idea of bribery, but was careful that he should not commit it. That he did not dismiss Butler indicates a dull conscience on the point. But he was not willing to tolerate dallying. Butler was alarmed at the tone taken toward him and protested that he could finish the business if given another chance. He was sent off to his post with the information that something must be done before the annual message was prepared. His renewed despatches were, however, in the old tone of apology and delay, and December 16th he was recalled. Powhatan Ellis, his successor, quickly realized the true situation of affairs in Mexico and gave up the plans for purchasing Texas.

Later Butler's proposition became known to the public, and he sought to justify himself by saying that in a private conversation Jackson gave it his approval. He said he was authorized to distribute eight hundred thousand dollars of the purchase money where it would be useful and that Santa Anna was to get one fourth of the amount.[1] Jackson denied the charge and pronounced its maker a liar. It is a point of veracity which defies certainty. Butler's course as minister leaves us little disposition to accept his word; and Jackson's memory on points of controversy was apt to be bad. His memorandum quoted above probably expresses his real attitude at the time.

[1] A. Butler to Jackson, July 28, 1834, Jackson Mss.   Jackson's denial is endorsed on this letter also.

ANDREW JACKSON IN 1835.   AGE 68

From a painting by Major R. E. W. Earl who lived with Jackson in the White House and had
orders for many portraits.   Political opponents called him the "King's Painter."   In
this picture the posture is characteristic, but the expression of the mouth
is like that of most of the portraits by Earl, and was considered unsatisfactory by the friends of Jackson

By this time the province was in the throes of revolution, and Mexican diplomacy took another turn. A large number of claims of American citizens against Mexico were taken up vigorously. Ellis was ordered to press their adjustment and if not successful to demand his passport. He followed instructions faithfully, met a refusal, and December 16, 1836, left Mexico, where we had no other minister for three years.[1]

One of the severest charges against Jackson in connection with Texas was aiding the revolutionists. It grew partly out of his desire for the province and more particularly out of his friendship for Samuel Houston, Texan leader. The first thing in connection with this charge is a note in his own handwriting in a fragmentary journal which he kept for a time after he became President. It reads:

May 21, 1829 — recd from Genl. Duff Green an extract of a letter (Doctor Marable to Genl. G) containing declarations of Gov. Houston, late of Tennessee, that he would conquer Mexico or Texas, and be worth two millions in two years, &c. Believing this to be the efusions of a distempered brain, but as a precautionary measure I directed the Secretary of War to write and inclose to Mr. Pope, Govr of Arkansas, the extract, and instruct him if such illegal project should be discovered to exist to adopt prompt measures to put it down and give the government the earliest intelligence of such illegal enterprise with the names of all those who may be concerned therein.[2]

Of similar significance is the following: In the year 1830, Houston was in Washington, where he fell in with a Dr. Robert Mayo. He spoke about his plans and Mayo revealed them to Jackson in a long letter. The latter endorsed the letter and ordered that William Fulton, secretary of Arkansas Territory, be informed of the report. Such a letter was written to Fulton

[1]Reeves, *Diplomacy under Tyler and Polk*, 76.
[2]Jackson Mss.

stating that the allegation was probably erroneous, but that careful watch should be made for attacks on Texas, and if such should be probable to communicate with the President. A copy of this letter was placed with Mayo's and they remained in Jackson's possession until he was about to leave Washington. Then they were both sent to Mayo, who placed them in the hands of John Quincy Adams. Jackson's Fulton letter was then read in the house of representatives by the New Englander as evidence that Jackson favored Houston's designs. Jackson did not know he returned the copy of the letter to Fulton with Mayo's and persisted in thinking that it was stolen from his files. He made, also, some bitter remarks about Adams for his supposed part in the transaction. But his treatment of Mayo's letter is like that of Marable's, and the two incidents show pretty clearly that he proposed to preserve neutrality, at least outwardly, which, in view of American feeling, was about all that could be expected.

Nor can it be held that he desired Texas in order to increase slave territory. As a slaveholder he probably sympathized with the feeling that the institution should have a normal field for growth, but he wanted the province beyond the Sabine for national reasons. When President Burnet of Texas sent him a letter justifying annexation on sectional and political grounds, he repudiated the argument, saying that nationality was the only sufficient basis for such a policy.[1]

In the beginning of the revolution Jackson ordered the district attorneys to prosecute violators of neutrality "when indications warranted,"[2] but the instructions were generally disregarded. Agents openly collected bands of "emigrants" for Texas who made no secret that they would fight for the revolutionists. Without their help Texas could not have defeated Mexico. It

---

[1]From copy of a letter in Van Buren Mss., without date, endorsed by Van Buren, "President's Letter."
[2]Richardson, *Messages and Papers of the Presidents*, III., 151.

is said that most of them returned to their former homes after the war. Public opinion supported them, and it would have been difficult for the government to detain them had it been more serious in its efforts to do so.

Fighting began in October, 1835; and in the following January, General Gaines, commanding the Western department, was ordered to the Louisiana border to protect it from Indian attacks, no signs of which were visible. He was ordered to cross the Sabine if necessary as far as Nacogdoches, fifty miles within the province of Texas. He was given the 6th regiment and called on each of the governors of four neighboring states for one thousand mounted riflemen. When the Texans won their victory at San Jacinto, April 21st, he was twenty-five miles north of the boundary waiting for the riflemen. He now concluded they would not be needed and suspended the call. It was afterward pointed out that at this time it was generally believed in Texas that the war was over. But a few weeks later it was known that Mexico was preparing to renew the struggle. About the same time two white men were killed by Caddo Indians near Nacogdoches, and some white women and children were taken prisoners. Gaines declared these Indians must be overawed and in June, 1836, threw two hundred men into that place and with the rest of his force encamped on the Sabine.[1] There was no real danger from the Indians, and it is hard to believe that Gaines's movements were not made with an eye on the development in Texas.[1]

When Gaines decided to occupy Nacogdoches he called out the militia the second time. Jackson was at the "Hermitage" when news of it came to Tennessee. The governor responded with eagerness and asked Jackson if he might send more men than were required of him. He was told in reply that Gaines's

---

[1] Report of secretary of war, *Congressional Debates*, XIII., part 2, page 23; correspondence of Gorostiza with Forsyth and Dickins: *ibid*, XIV., part 2, 178.

call was overruled as unnecessary and that no troops were to be sent unless orders came direct from the war department. To the governor of Kentucky he sent the same directions. This seems to have been on Jackson's own initiative. A few days later he received a letter from Kendall in Washington saying that Gaines's advance was ill-advised and ought to be retraced. September 4, 1836, he ordered that general to observe strict neutrality, not to enter Texas unless the Mexicans failed to restrain the Indians, and to hold no correspondence with either Texas or Mexican leaders.

As soon as the Texans began to fight they appealed to Jackson for recognition of independence or annexation. While Houston was fleeing before the advancing Santa Anna, six days before San Jacinto, Stephen Austin sent an earnest appeal. "Oh, my countrymen," he cried, "the warm-hearted, chivalrous, impulsive West and South are *up* and *moving* in favor of Texas. The calculating and more prudent, tho' not less noble-minded North are aroused. . . . Will you turn a deaf ear?"[1] This appeal came as a letter to the President, cabinet, and congress. On the back of it Jackson wrote: "The writer does not reflect that we have a treaty with Mexico, and that our national faith is pledged to support it. The Texans before they took the step to declare themselves Independent which has aroused and united all Mexico against them ought to have pondered well. It was a rash and premature act, our neutrality must be faithfully maintained. A. J."[2]

The victory at San Jacinto changed the aspect of affairs. Commissioners came now to ask for annexation, on the following terms: (1) confirmation of the Texan laws, (2) assumption of Texan debts, (3) guarantee of land titles to *bona fide* settlers, (4) the recognition of slavery, and (5) liberal appropriation of

[1]Cannon to Jackson, August 4 ; Jackson to Cannon, August 5th; *ibid* to Governor of Kentucky, August 7th; Kendall to Jackson, August 3rd; Jackson to Gaines, September 4, 1836; Jackson Mss.
[2]Jackson Mss

land to education.[1] The indorsement on Austin's letter indicates that Jackson was not entirely enthusiastic for the strugglers. His action in the summer in regard to recognition and annexation confirms the view. June 6th the house of representatives resolved to recognize the independence of the province as soon as it had an established government. He accordingly sent a confidential agent beyond the Sabine to report on conditions there, and to the Texans he would promise nothing until he had definite information. He was following the example of Monroe in recognizing the South American states. The reports from the agent, Morfit, were adverse to Texas. The inhabitants, he said, were few and widely distributed, and probably not able to maintain themselves against their enemies. In a private letter to Jackson, Houston confessed that the new state could not sustain itself and appealed to his old friend to save it.[2] December 21st the President in a special message recommended that recognition of independence be deferred.[3] It was believed that Van Buren inspired it.[4] Certainly on December 8th Jackson was willing to let congress act.[5]

The Texans were greatly disappointed, but they soon found grounds to hope for better things. Sentiment in the country developed, and talk of action by congress was heard. February 2, 1837, Jackson took up the matter with the chairman of the house committee on foreign affairs. He had come to think that England was about to recognize Texas.[6] March 1st the senate resolved to extend recognition and the house voted to pay the expenses of a minister to the republic if the President saw fit to appoint one.

[1]Forsyth to Jackson, July 15, 1836, Jackson Mss.
[2]Houston to Jackson, November 20, 1836; see Miss Ethel Z. Rather, *The Annexation of Texas*, published in the *Quarterly* of the Historical Association of Texas, 1910.
[3]Richardson, *Messages and Papers of the Presidents*, III., 265; for some of Morfit's reports see *Congressional Debates*, XIII., part 2, page 82.
[4]Van Buren to John Van Buren, December 22, 1835; W. Irving to Van Buren, February 24, 1836; Van Buren Mss.
[5]Jackson to Kendall, December 8, 1836, Cincinnati *Commercial*, February 4, 1879.
[6]Jackson to Howard, February 2, 1837, Jackson Mss.

When this matter came up the presidential election of 1836 was approaching. The bank was dead legally, but the whigs openly declared their purpose to restore it. Jackson was extremely anxious to avoid anything which would weaken Van Buren's chances in the election or divide the democrats in congress. He and the New York group must have seen that the administration could not afford to identify itself too far with Texas. It was, said he to congress, a very delicate matter. The delicateness of it lay in the fact that Americans of the South and Southwest had revolutionized the province, Gaines standing conveniently by as an apparent resource in time of trouble. Hastily to recognize Texan independence would have the air of an indorsement by the administration, and that would imperil Van Buren's chances and threaten the continuation of Jackson's policies.

In the summer Jackson received a letter from captive Santa Anna proposing American interposition between Mexico and the resisting Texans. He replied that he would be pleased to extend the good offices of his country when he knew that Mexico desired them. He permitted the proposer to go to Washington to try to make some arrangement of a pacific nature. Santa Anna arrived early in 1837. He was well received and set out for his home in February, promising to use his efforts for peace. In Mexico his influence was superseded by a rival, and he retired to his estate until a new revolution gave him an opportunity to regain power. Jackson thought Santa Anna a true friend of Texas.[1]

The only surviving evidence of his relations with Jackson in Washington is an undated memorandum in Jackson's hand which seems to refer to this period. It relates to a communication with Santa Anna and contains an offer of three and a half millions for Texas, not as a purchase but as a concession

---

[1] Lewis to Houston, Oct. 27, 1836, Mss. in New York Public Library.

on our part, the boundary to be the Rio Grande to thirty degrees latitude and thence west to the Pacific. Santa Anna, for his part, agreed to use his influence for peace.[1]

Jackson's diplomacy satisfied the nation. What it lacked in dignity it gained in strength. It secured American interests in the West India trade, the French claims, and the Texas matter. In regard to the last his course was moderate and national. Had he taken the view of either extreme he must have driven the other to desperation. As he said repeatedly in the close of his administration, he chiefly desired to repress the growing sectionalism which came from the efforts of designing men. Both his principles and his desire to make Van Buren President were in support of this feeling.

Abroad Jackson's diplomacy was well respected. Foreigners thought less than we about his diplomatic form. They saw chiefly the results of his forceful will. He brought a greater respect for American rights into their minds than any man since Washington. Van Buren reporting a conversation with Palmerston writes: "He said that a very strong impression had been made here (in London) of the dangers which this country had to apprehend from your elevation, but that they had experienced better treatment at your hands than they had done from any of your predecessors."[2]

---

[1]Jackson Mss. The correspondence of Jackson and Santa Anna is also in the Jackson Mss., July 4 and September 4, 1836. See also Richardson, *Messages and Papers of the Presidents*, III., 274-276.

[2]Van Buren to Jackson, September 28, 1831; Van Buren, *Autobiography*, III., 94.

CHAPTER XXXI

MINOR PROBLEMS OF THE TWO ADMINISTRATIONS

BESIDES the matter already considered, Jackson had to deal with certain important minor affairs, some of which he inherited from the preceding administration, and some others which were created in his own time. Of the former class was the task of removing the Indians from the region north of the Gulf of Mexico and east of the Mississippi in order to open this land to white settlers.

When the stream of population ran into the wilderness it followed the Ohio in general, filling the land on each side and down the Mississippi to its mouth. In the North, another stream ran along the lake shores and, carrying the Indians of the old Northwest before it, gradually swept them back into the great plains of the newer Northwest. But the extension of settlements down to the Gulf made impossible such a riddance of the red men of the South. It left surrounded by a zone of white population the Cherokees, Creeks, Choctaws, and Chickasaws, together numbering in 1825 as many as fifty-three thousand six hundred souls; and they occupied tribal lands aggregating more than thirty-three million acres. They could not be pushed gradually back as in the Northwest: they must be exterminated or induced by one means or another to remove to the plains, where the problem of contact with the whites would be postponed to a remote generation. The other alternative, peaceful residence among the whites, was not considered possible for any large body of Indians, North or South. The only thing which people thought feasible was to remove them bodily: and as this was a task for the national government its execution devolved on the President.

Of the four Southwestern tribes the position of the Cherokees was severest, and by following the story of this nation in some detail we may understand the experience of the others.   Although they held lands in both Alabama and Tennessee, their chief holding, more than five million acres, was in Georgia, and the land was very fertile.   In 1802 Georgia made a general agreement with the United States, one feature of which was that the latter should extinguish the title of the Indian lands within the state's bounds "as early as the same can be peaceably obtained on reasonable terms."   At that time the Cherokees and Creeks owned twenty-five million acres in the state.   By 1825 the amount had been reduced by several treaties to nine million acres.   But the spread of cotton cultivation made their land seem necessary for settlement, and Georgia became eager that the federal government should execute the promise of 1802. It did not appease her to say that the Indian title could not be quieted either "peaceably" or "on reasonable terms," which was all that was promised.   She saw herself threatened permanently with the presence of an inferior people, with a government of their own planted solidly within the state limits and claiming immunity from the state laws.   Such a situation could not have been contemplated in the formation of the union; and Georgia found much sympathy with her desire to overthrow it, although her methods of dealing with it were neither reasonable nor becoming.

The Cherokees also deserve our sympathy.   They were the most civilized of the Southern tribes, they had passed far into the agricultural stage, and removal was sure to bring economic loss and social disorganization.   They were specifically protected in their rights by treaties with the United States.   There was in the beginning a feeling that an Indian treaty was not fully a treaty and that it was not, therefore, the supreme law of the land. The supreme court, in a case which arose in this controversy, decided to the contrary;[1] but at that time public opinion was so much excited in Georgia that it was not modified by the decision. In fact, there was something illogical in the idea that an Indian tribe, which had no sovereignty, could make a treaty, usually a mark of sovereignty; and congress recognized it in 1871 when it ordered that in the future *agreements* and not *treaties* be made with the Indians. The Cherokees had good advice in all phases of the controversy. In 1824 they declared in tribal council that they would not sell a foot of land and sent commissioners to Washington to ask that the agreement of 1802 be rescinded. Calhoun, secretary of war, told them in reply that the agreement must be kept and the Indians must remove or give up their tribal authority and be absorbed with the citizens of Georgia. They, on their part, refused to budge, and thus the matter was left to simmer for five years. Meanwhile the state threatened the Indians and denounced the national government, but it did not precipitate civil war by an actual resort to force.

Jackson entered the presidency when this matter was still unsettled. Adams showed a certain amount of sympathy for the constitutional position of a state threatened with division of its power by creating a separate authority within its border; but he was for legal methods and would not tolerate violence on the part of Georgia. Jackson, however, had a Western man's view of the Indian question. He showed it by a determination to appoint a Westerner secretary of war. Eaton, who filled the office, soon gave the Cherokees to understand that the government would not support them in opposition to the laws of Georgia. The Georgians were counting much on just this stand, but in order to be certain they waited for the first annual message.

[1] Cherokee Nation *vs* Georgia, 5 Peters, 17.

It gave them all they required. It not only referred to affairs in Georgia, but it laid down a general Indian policy at variance with that previously followed and in every respect essentially favorable to their purposes.

The old idea, it said, was to civilize the savages; but by purchasing their lands piecemeal we have kept them moving westward so constantly that they could not absorb civilization, and thus the government's object was defeated. A portion of the Southern Indians, however, with a fair prospect of civilization, were in conflict with the states of Georgia and Alabama, which claimed sovereignty respectively over everybody within their limits. Now the constitution guarantees that no new state be can formed within another state without the consent of the latter. Does it not follow that no independent state could be formed within those limits? Would such a thing be tolerated in Maine or in New York? Jackson reported, therefore, that he had told the Indians they would not be supported in their attempt to establish independent governments within state lines and that he adviced them to settle beyond the Mississippi. He also recommended that congress set apart an ample region in the Far West to which the Indians might remove and live without conflict with the whites. A few weeks later a bill was introduced and passed by a party vote to set aside a Western region and to appropriate money to aid the removal of those Indians who chose to accept the offer.

This boded ill for the Cherokees. Anticipating the action of congress, their legislative council ordered that all who accepted lands in the West and settled on them should lose tribal membership, that those who sold their property to emigrate should be whipped, and that those who voted to sell a part or all of the tribal possessions should be put to death. It was their reply to the attempt to lure them away.

On the Georgians the effect of Jackson's announced view was

equally decisive. December 22, 1829, the legislature passed a law to extend its authority over the Creeks and Cherokees on June 1, 1830, with provisions to make it difficult for the savages to evade its enforcement. They knew definitely that there was now a President who would not interfere with their plans. Alabama and Mississippi legislatures followed the example of Georgia.

On the appointed day the governor of Georgia proclaimed this law throughout the state. Soon afterward a clash occurred between state officers and the United States troops in Georgia, and the governor asked the President to order the withdrawal of the troops. The request was readily granted. It emphasized Jackson's position that Georgia might exercise sovereignty within her borders.

The Cherokees had friends and advisers among the whites, and all persons opposed to state rights were naturally drawn to their side. They rested their case on the sanctity of their treaties. An Indian tribe, they contended, was a state, a foreign sovereign state, and a treaty with it was a part of the supreme law of the land. When Georgia was about to execute her law of December 22, 1829, they applied to the United States supreme court through their counsel, William Wirt, for an injunction to restrain such action. The case was argued in the January, 1831, term, Georgia ignoring it entirely on the ground of no jurisdiction. Marshall gave the decision, taking up first the question of jurisdiction. By the constitution the United States courts are open to states, citizens of states, foreign states, and citizens of foreign states. Manifestly an Indian tribe to come within the meaning of the constitution, must be either a state as a state within the union, or a foreign state. Marshall held that it was neither, that it occupied a peculiar position and was, in fact, a "domestic dependent nation" with a relation to the United States analogous to that of a ward to a guardian. A tribe, therefore, could not sue in the United States courts, and the injunction prayed for could not be granted. While the Cherokees lost the case in point, they were pronounced a state—that is, a definite civil power, and this was in opposition to Georgia's purpose to treat them as a mass of individuals over whom she might assert authority. The point would be worth something in resisting the state's pretensions.[1]

Meantime the case of Corn Tassel came up. This brave had killed a fellow Cherokee, for which he was tried and condemned in a state court. He appealed to the federal supreme court, alleging no jurisdiction in the Georgia tribunal. Although Wirt hurried to trial the injunction case, which was then pending, Georgia would not stay sentence, and Corn Tassel was executed before the highest court in the land could consider his fate. This utter defiance of the court could not have happened if the executive department had been disposed to protect the court. The case of the Cherokee Nation *vs.* Georgia, just described, lost some of its strength in view of this situation. It was decided a few days after Corn Tassel was hanged.

Another case showed even more plainly the attitude of the President. By the Georgia law whites might not reside with the Indians without state licenses. This was intended to exclude from the tribes those white friends who encouraged them not to sell their lands. Among these people were a number of Northern missionaries, who trusted to the United States law. Eleven of them were arrested for violating the state statute; nine yielded rather than remain in prison, but two, Worcester and Butler, appealed to the United States supreme court. Again Georgia denied jurisdiction and refused to appear, and again Marshall decided against her. In an opinion whose positive tone seems to proceed from a feeling of indignity that he was already ignored, Marshall held that Georgia was

---

[1] 5 Peters, 1-80.

wrong at every point. "The Cherokees," he said, "were a nation, they were so recognized by the government and by Georgia herself until recent years, their laws were not to fall before a state, and the United States had the authority to protect them. The sentence of the missionaries was pronounced null.[1] Georgia disregarded the verdict utterly, kept the missionaries in prison more than a year to vindicate her authority, and finally pardoned them.

Jackson's refusal to execute the decree of the court displeased the friends of the missionaries, particularly the Methodists and Friends, and votes were lost in the election of 1832. Van Buren said the defection from this cause was eight thousand in western New York alone.[2] It produced a more permanent impression on persons interested in constitutional interpretation. The President justified himself on the ground that the executive, coördinate in authority with the judiciary, was not bound to interpret the constitution as the supreme court interpreted it. He could hardly have known his own mind on this point, for he put his defense on more than one ground. To Cass he wrote that it must rest on the principles in Johnston vs. McIntosh.[3] He said in explanation of his general position: "No feature in the Federal Constitution is more prominent than that the general powers conferred on Congress, can only be enforced, or executed upon the people of the Union. This is a Government of the people."[4] This position was nearly opposite to that he assumed in reference to nullification within a year. To his friend Coffee he wrote that the difficulty was weakness of the government. "The decision of the Supreme Court," he said in allusion to the case of the missionaries, "has fallen still from the Government, not strong enough to protect them in

---

[1] 6 Peters, 515-596.
[2] Van Buren, *Autobiography*, III., 119-120, Van Buren Mss.
[3] 8 Wheaton, 543-605.
[4] Draft in Jackson's handwriting, no date, Jackson Mss.

case of a collision with Georgia."[1] It seems at this time not to have occurred to him that the government was weak or strong as the executive willed.

The fundamental explanation of Jackson's argument on this matter was his sympathy with Georgia. He believed that the Indians should not remain permanently within the borders of a state. Of removal as a fact Van Buren observes: "That great work was emphatically the fruit of his own exertions. It was his judgment, his experience, his indomitable vigor and unrelenting activity that secured success. There was no measure in the whole course of his administration of which he was more exclusively the author than this." It was a policy conceived in a spirit of humanity. February 22, 1831, it was formulated in a special message to congress.[2] A real friend of the Indians, said he, would urge them to remove. If they remained within state limits there would ever be trouble, and liberal aid ought to be given them in settling new homes. No one regretted the hardships incidental to the process more than he; but they were ills which must be endured.

The conflict with the supreme court brought him into opposition to Chief Justice Marshall. A popular tradition, first printed so far as I know by Horace Greeley, represented Jackson as saying after the decision in the case of the missionaries: "John Marshall has made his decision. Now let him enforce it."[3] It is not sure that these words were actually uttered, but it is certain from Jackson's views and temperament that they might have been spoken. His antipathy for the chief justice was so strong that in 1835 he refused to attend a memorial meeting in his honor. He avowed high appreciation of Marshall's "learning, talents, and patriotism," but as one who did not agree with the ideas of constitutional law held by the deceased

[1]April 7, 1832, copy in Dyas Collection, Library of Congress.
[2]Richardson, *Messages and Papers of the Presidents*, II., 536.
[3]Greeley, *The American Conflict*, I., 106.

jurist he could not unite in honoring him with those who did so agree.[1]

Jackson's refusal to execute the judgment of the supreme court left the Cherokees at the mercy of Georgia. They realized that they must lose in the long run, and a party of them, led by John Ringe, advocated removal, while another, led by John Ross, were for staying in Georgia. In 1835 the former party agreed to the cession of the remaining tribal lands to the United States for five million dollars and land beyond the Mississippi. The Ross faction held out until 1838, when United States troops under General Scott forcibly expelled them. They went to Indian Territory, created by a law of 1834, when they received lands near those of the Creeks, Chickasaws, and Choctaws, who had before that time accepted the terms of the government. These other tribes had all looked to the Cherokee case for an intimation of what would be done and made terms accordingly.[2]

The payment of the public debt was another measure which appealed to Jackson's political sense. Scrupulous in paying his own obligations, he thought it equally desirable that the government should owe nothing. His first message held out hope of the early accomplishment of his desire — privately, he thought it might be done within his first term of office. The revenues from imports and land sales were large and yielded a yearly surplus which was used for this purpose. In 1834 the last of the debt was discharged. His message to congress in that year expressed his gratification, but he added the caution that the situation be not made the excuse for future extravagance.

Extravagance was, in fact, a menace, as it ever is when there is a large surplus. Plans were made by various interests looking to the dissipation of the surplus. Internal improve-

[1] Jackson to Chandler and Williams, September 18, 1835, Jackson Mss.
[2] For important documents on the controversy with Georgia, see Ames, *State Documents on Federal Relations* 113-132.

ments would have been a ready preventive of government hoarding, but the Maysville veto had too well disposed of them to warrant the hope that they could be carried. The most probable course was one suggested from several sources, and very popular in the West, for distributing the surplus among the states after the debt was paid. The anti-tariff men declared that it was supported by the tariff party, lest an accumulating surplus should lead men to think that the tariff ought to be reduced.

Early in his presidency Jackson believed in distributing the surplus among the states according to representation in congress. He said as much in the first draft of his inaugural address and he repeated it in his first annual message. If it could not legally be done, he said, it would be wise to amend the constitution so as to allow it; and he made it a point against Calhoun that he opposed distributing the surplus. Jackson's view was in opposition to the state rights school, and as this group came into prominence in his party he veered away from distribution. There was as little reason that he should favor it as that he should support internal improvements, and he must have seen it. In his second annual message he returned to the subject as a means of providing internal improvements. The surplus, he said, should be given to the states according to representation in congress; for they could best assign it to the ends contemplated. By the time he wrote the third message his opinion had undergone a change. He then recommended that the tariff be so adjusted that after the debt was paid no more money should be taken from the people than was necessary for the expenses of the government.[1]

The ground thus left unoccupied was seized upon by Clay — not at first through design on his part, but through the manipulation of his enemies. By a trick he was forced in 1832 to take

[1]Richardson, *Messages and Papers of the Presidents*, II., 451, 514, 556.

a stand on the land question.[1] After deliberating he moved to distribute among the states the proceeds of the sale of public lands. He took pains to say that it was unconstitutional to distribute the revenue, but that the proceeds of land sales was another matter. The bill got through the senate, to fail in the house. Clay brought it forward again in December, 1832. It was then passed and went to Jackson in the last days of the congress. He applied the "pocket veto" and sent congress when it convened in the following December his reasons therefor. Clay argued that the lands were a guarantee for the payment of the national debt, and that inasmuch as this was about paid the further proceeds should be distributed. Jackson denied the first proposition, held that no distinction was to be made as to the source of revenue, and objected to the method of distribution provided in the bill. He also found it at variance with the doctrine of the Maysville veto, which of itself was enough to insure rejection. In the veto Jackson took occasion to say, as he said in the message of 1832, that the proper way to deal with a surplus from the sale of the lands was to reduce the price to or near the expense of sales.[2] In this he put himself in line with the general Western land policy, dear to the heart of Benton and of many another Jackson leader from the newer states.

But the strongest argument against approving the bill was its tendency to make the states look to the federal government for benefactions. The object of the bill was to distribute not the surplus of the land sales, but all the proceeds from such sales, while the expenses of the land offices were made a charge on the general revenue. This was a bill to create a surplus and once adopted might lead to vast extravagances of a similar nature. "It appears to me," said Jackson, "that a more direct

---

[1]Sargent, *Public Men and Events*, I., 205-208.
[2]Richardson, *Messages and Papers of the Presidents*, III., 56-69.

road to consolidation can not be devised. Money is power, and in the Government which pays all the public officers of the states will all political power be substantially concentrated. . . . However willing I might be that any unavoidable surplus in the Treasury should be returned to the people through their State governments, I cannot assent to the principle that a surplus may be created for the purpose of distribution." Many of Clay's policies seem to have been adopted without definite conviction of their soundness. In seeking an exit from a perilous position he had hit upon a measure which he thought very popular; but most thinking people must have found it an unhealthy symptom of a feverish state of public morals. There was abroad a strong desire for assistance from the central government. Clay was willing to stimulate and profit by it politically: Jackson did not hesitate to attack it and to seek to check it.

The veto of 1833 did not dispose of the question. The actual accumulation of a surplus strengthened the demand for distribution. By 1836 the surplus was more than thirty millions, and the abstraction of so much money from business channels was an economic evil. Clay, therefore, returned to his plan for relief, which he vainly sought to get adopted in the session of 1833–1834. Another bill introduced late in 1835 was much like that which Jackson vetoed in 1833 It proposed to distribute the net proceeds of the land sales during the years 1833 to 1837 inclusive. Fifteen per cent. of the sales in the new states was to go to those states and the remainder was to be divided in proportion to federal population, the new states sharing in this allotment also. Clay put the net amount for 1833–1835 at twenty-one million. He pushed the bill with his usual skill and early in May it passed the senate.

But other plans were formed. In the house a bill was now introduced to distribute the surplus from whatever source. It was called "An act to regulate the deposits of the public money." Some of its sections, when it took final shape, provided more careful regulations for the banks of deposits. Others provided that the surplus funds of the government above five million dollars should be deposited with the states, according to federal population. It soon became known in congress that Jackson would approve this bill but would veto Clay's. Administration men were evidently alarmed at the trend of opinion for distribution and took this means of meeting it. They were pleased that the President would not longer resist what they considered the inevitable and carried the bill through the house with enthusiasm by a vote of 155 to 38. In the senate it was also passed, and Jackson approved it June 23, 1836. It provided that all the money in the treasury January 1, 1837, above five million dollars, should be deposited with the states in four equal payments on the first days of January, April, July, and October. In return the states were to give negotiable certificates of deposit, without interest until negotiated, payable to the secretary of the treasury on demand. This preserved the form of a true deposit, by which many who voted for it made themselves believe the law constitutional. Jackson himself in his last annual message spoke as though he believed this, and he deprecated the habit of speaking of the distribution as though it were a loan. But practical men thought the payments would never be demanded.

Jackson himself had doubts about the correctness of his approval and turned to Taney, then his mentor in constitutional matters. The chief justice replied that the precedent was bad; for if congress might collect money to deposit with the states it might do anything; that the money could not practically be recovered from the states; and that most democrats regretted the passage of the bill. But he added that he thought Jackson did well to approve it under the circumstances.[1] Probably

---

[1] Taney to Jackson, June 20, 1836, Jackson Mss.

the impelling cause of approval was the necessity of helping
Van Buren in the campaign then in progress.

By December, when congress met, Jackson's ideas were more
definite; and he spoke severely in his annual message of the law
just enacted.   Adverting to the fact that the deposits were real
deposits and not to be considered as gifts, he opened the whole
discussion again.   He pointed out with a clearness that suggests
the pen of Taney the evils likely to come from the policy inaugurated, and he urged that the best way of preventing them
was to collect smaller taxes.   "To require the people," he
said, "to pay taxes to the Government merely that they may be
paid back again is sporting with the substantial interests of the
country."   The paragraphs on the subject closed with a strong
argument for economy and self-control in the government's
financial policy.[1]   Events about to come reinforced it, and,
with the panic of 1837 at hand, the further distribution of the
surplus ceased to be a problem for the statesman.

In the same message Jackson discussed the state of the currency.   He came out for specie as the money of the constitution,
and spoke at length of the bank-note system then in use and
much abused.   He realized the danger to the country from the
issue of notes in large excess of good business principles and he
brought out in more than legitimate relief the bearing of the
point on the bank controversy.

This warning was well timed; for the accumulation of the
large surplus in the deposit banks had led to the overissue of
their notes.   With it went a wave of speculation which called
out a vast amount of paper from banks whose soundness was
questionable.   This was especially true in the West, where
speculation, chiefly in land, was most prevalent.   So evident
was it that the currency was bad that Jackson issued, July 11,
1836, through the secretary of the treasury, the celebrated

---

[1]Richardson, *Messages and Papers of the Presidents*, III., 239-246.

Specie Circular, by which lands must be paid for in specie. The occasion for this order was evident.

In the West a distinct kind of currency had become abundant known as "land-office money." This was the notes of the deposit banks and those of such other banks as the deposit banks would receive. They were legally receivable for lands and were paid in for that purpose at the land offices, to be deposited in the banks, where they were lent to land speculators, who again paid them in for lands. The ease with which this could be done stimulated a great amount of speculation. Land sales before 1834 were less than four million dollars a year; in 1835 they were nearly fifteen millions, and in 1836 more than twenty-four millions. For these large sales the government had chiefly the credits of the banks in which the funds were deposited, and the soundness of those banks was jeopardized by their large loans to the speculators. Nor did the lands sold represent settlements. They were largely held by speculators, great and small, and the actual settlers must buy of them at an advance or take inferior lands or lands remote from the zone of settlement. The situation was altogether unhealthy both from a fiscal, a business, and an agrarian standpoint; and Jackson's determination to check it before worse evils followed was a wise move. The Specie Circular caused distress among the speculators, it started a specie movement toward the West, and it helped to accentuate the panicky trend of 1837; but it was a healthy antidote to the situation of 1836 and enabled business men to take some precautions against danger before the storm actually burst. Jackson in the annual message of 1836 summed up its benefits as follows:

It checked the career of the Western banks and gave them additional strength in anticipation of the pressure which has since pervaded our Eastern as well as the European commercial cities. By preventing the extension of the credit system it measurably cut off the means of speculation and retarded its progress in monopolizing the most valuable of the public lands. It has tended to save the new states from a non-resident proprietorship, one of the greatest obstacles to the advancement of a new country and the prosperity of an old one.

The Specie Circular was by Jackson's own admission inspired chiefly by the desire to restrain the land speculators. Van Buren justly said the people would approve it on this account. In this respect it was like most of his other measures relating to business interests. His policies toward the bank, the currency, the sale of land, internal improvements, and the distribution of the surplus had this thing in common: they were all aimed at what he considered an abuse of privilege. While each of these measures had its specific economic significance, each had, also, a common relation to the anti-monopolistic spirit which came as a reaction against the rapid growth of the speculative class. In all these matters he voiced the people's cry against their own exploitation. Crude as some of his ideas were, they were founded on some of the most permanent principles of equality. It cannot be doubted that he checked tendencies essentially dangerous in the day of over-confidence, when men forgot ancient principles and looked mostly to the present advantage. He espoused the interest, as he thought, of the average man, and the average man approved it.

CHAPTER XXXII

PERSONAL CHARACTERISTICS

AT THIS point we turn from Jackson's conflicts and problems and consider the man himself. His enemies hated him and rarely saw his good qualities; his friends loved him and reluctantly admitted his failings; and in a sense each was right. Some of the good things he did are excellent and some of the bad things are wretched. His puzzling personality defies clear analysis, but we must admit that he was a remarkable man. He lacked much through the want of an education, and he acquired much through apparent accident, but it was only his strong character which turned deficiency and opportunity alike to his purpose and made his will the strongest influence in his country in his time.

The secret of his power was his adjustment to the period in which he lived. Other men excelled him in experience, wisdom, and balanced judgment; but the American democrats of the day admired neither of these qualities. They honored courage, strength, and directness. They could tolerate ignorance but not hesitancy. Jackson was the best embodiment of their desires from the beginning of the national government to his own day.

. Jackson accepted democracy with relentless logic. Some others believed that wise leaders could best determine the policies of government, but he more than any one else of his day threw the task of judging upon the common man. And this he did without cant and in entire sincerity. No passionate dreamer of the past was more willing than he to test his principles to the uttermost. "You know I never despair," he said; "I have confidence in the virtue and good sense of the people. God is just, and while we act faithfully to the Constitution, he will smile upon and prosper our exertions."[1]

Mere military glory will not explain his hold on the nation. It undoubtedly had much to do with his introduction into national politics, but it soon gave place to a popularity resting on other qualities. In fact, his peculiar character shone behind his military fame and recommended him to the people. They liked his promptness in invading Florida in 1818 and his abrupt bridling of the dallying Callava in 1821 as much as his victory at New Orleans. Other generals won victories in the war, but they did not become political forces through them. To the people the old government seemed weak and unequal, and Jackson, the man who solved difficulties, was elected to reform it. When the process of reform began his capacity as a political leader showed itself. Probably he could have been reëlected in 1832 independently of his war record.

Much has been said about his honesty. The historical critic and the moralist know this for a common virtue. Most of Jackson's contemporaries were as honest as he, but he excelled them in candor, which is frequently pronounced honesty. He was apt to speak his mind clearly, although he could on occasion, as has been seen, be as diplomatic as a delicate case demanded. Van Buren said in apparent sincerity that he believed "an honester or in any sense a better man was never placed at the head of the Government."[2]

Many citations and incidents in the preceding pages witness Jackson's lack of restraint and fair judgment. They seem to suggest habitual errors of mind; but we are assured that such was not the case. Even Calhoun, in the bitterness of the final

---

[1]Jackson to Van Buren, November 1, 1830, Van Buren Mss.
[2]Van Buren to John Randolph, April 13, 1831, Van Buren Mss.

quarrel, admitted that in ordinary matters and when not irritated by some unusual thing he was fair and reasonable. The explosions of anger for which he was noted were incident to a tense natural temperament; and they were apt to come when he was off his guard. In dangers which were anticipated he was extremely cool. Thus at New Orleans he broke into violent rage when he saw the column on the west bank falling back, although when the lines were assailed two hours earlier he was complete master of himself. In the long struggles against his political enemies he was never surprised into some rash explosion, although many efforts were made by opponents to lead him into such a situation. "He was," says Van Buren, "in times of peculiar difficulty and danger, calm and equable in his carriage and always master of his passions." [1]

But Van Buren would not claim that he was fair toward an opponent. "The conciliation of individuals," he said, "formed the smallest, perhaps too small a part of his policy. His strength lay with the masses, and he knew it. He first, and at last in all public questions, always tried to be right, and when he felt that he was so he apprehended little, sometimes too little, from the opposition of prominent and powerful men, and it must now be admitted that he seldom overestimated the strength he derived from the confidence and favor of the people." [2]

In England Van Buren came into contact with the Duke of Wellington, then a leader of the conservatives there; and he made the following comparison between the Duke and Jackson:

There were many points in which he and General Jackson resembled each other. In moral and physical courage, in indifference to personal consequences, and in promptness of action there was little if any difference in their characters. The Duke was better educated and had received the instruction of

[1] *Autobiography*, V., 84, Van Buren Mss.
[2] *Ibid*, III., 52.

experience upon a larger scale, but the General in native intellect had, I think, been more richly endowed.[1]

But there was a marked dissimilarity which Van Buren overlooked. The Englishman was cautious, steady, and persistent; the American was aggressive, incautious, and disposed to throw all his strength into a frontal attack. Wellington was a conservative by nature, Jackson was a radical; Wellington in politics led the party of privilege, Jackson led the party of equality. Neither could have performed the task of the other. When Jackson became President it was expected that he would fall under the influence of favorites. His inexperience in national affairs made it essential that he should take advice freely, and he himself was conscious of it. But he was never a tool. In all his important measures he was the dominant figure. The Maysville veto was, perhaps, the affair in which another had most part, but even here Van Buren, who suggested the measure, was careful to base it on Jackson's known opposition to the invasion of state rights and to the exploitation of the public treasury by private parties. He approached the matter most cautiously and used his best tact to conceal his purpose.

Other Presidents were dependent on advice, but they usually consulted their cabinet. Jackson, when a general, rarely held military councils; when President he rarely held cabinet meetings. A formal cabinet decision limited him; he preferred to consult whom he wished, informally and without responsibility. Out of such conditions grew the "Kitchen Cabinet." This group did not control him outright; all its members approached him with great caution, and they accomplished their ends only by tact and insinuating appeals to his feelings.

If his policies were his own his documents were usually prepared by others. He was not a master of writing or argumen-

---

[1] *Autobiography*, IV., 167, Van Buren Mss.

tation, but he knew well what he would fight for. His private letters show crude reasoning to support objects which are dictated by common sense. His best documents are his military proclamations, where there is room for the play of such strong feelings as courage, endurance, and loyalty — qualities in which he was at his best.

His lack of political knowledge made him in cases where knowledge was essential a bad judge of men. In 1834 he expressed a desire to appoint Cuthbert, of Georgia, to the supreme bench, upon which Van Buren observed that there were two Cuthberts in Georgia, Alfred, of whom he had never heard that he was a lawyer, and John, whom he did not think equal to the position.[1] Jackson took the rebuke in good spirit, and appointed another man.

Van Buren's anxiety to escape blame for participating in the removal of the deposits has been alluded to;[2] but we are hardly prepared for the following audacious utterance made the day after the order to remove went into effect:

You will see by the inclosed, that the opposition have commenced the game I anticipated. They have found by experience that their abuse of you is labour lost, and they conclude wisely that if they could succeed in shifting the Bank question from your shoulders to mine, they would be better able to serve the Mammon than they are at present. Now, although I cannot grumble at the service they are rendering me with the people, by identifying me with you in this matter, it will not do for us to expose the great measure to prejudice by doing anything that would tend in the slightest degree to withdraw from it the protection of your name.[3]

The object of this peculiarly insidious flattery probably never

[1] Jackson to Van Buren, October 27th; Van Buren to Jackson, November 5, 1834, Van Buren Mss.
[2] See above, II., 640-642.
[3] Van Buren to Jackson, October 2, 1833, Van Buren Mss.

suspected its nature. To the faults of a friend he was singularly blind.

Of associates other than Van Buren, Lewis seems to have had influence chiefly in personal affairs. He was at home in the Eaton intrigue, the exclusion of Calhoun, and the nomination of Van Buren in 1832. He lived in the President's house and encouraged the impression that he held the key to his favor. He was able by this means to exert a wide influence among the office-seekers. Jackson used him freely in matters high and low. At one time he wants him to stay in Washington to keep an eye on the situation during the President's absence: at another he gives him all kinds of minor commissions, as writing papers and selling cotton.[1] Kendall had more to do with policies, but his influence came comparatively late. He was powerful in the bank controversy, a strong supporter of Jackson's anti-bank views, and after that war was won his influence survived in general matters. Blair, who came into touch with the administration in 1830, became after a while a warm personal associate; but he was not a man of creative power. He loved Jackson and fought faithfully for him, but the many letters which passed between them show no evidence that he sought to modify the President's political life.

But Blair gave a rich friendship. He had the homely virtues of the West. His home on Pennsylvania Avenue opposite the President's house was presided over by a wife who to a larger culture added the reliable virtues of Mrs. Jackson. It was a haven of comfort to the tired spirit and body of the harassed and pain-racked Jackson, and he made touching references to it as long as he lived. To Mrs. Blair on the eve of his departure from Washington he wrote the following characteristic words:

I cannot leave this city without presenting you my grateful

---

[1] Illustrations are found in the Ford Mss. See calendar in *Bulletin of New York Public Library*, IV., 295-302.

thanks for the great kindness you have extended to me and my family whilst here. When sick you visited us and extended to me and our dear little ones all comforts within your power. We all part with you and your dear husband and amiable family with sincere regret; but I trust in a kind providence that I may reach home and be spared until I have the pleasure of seeing you and Mr. Blair and your dear Eliza at the Hermitage. You will receive a good welcome. I beg you to accept as a memento of my regard a heifer raised by me since my second election. She will bring you in mind of my fondness for good milk, and how I was gratified in this fondness from your liberal hands.[1]

If he had the failings of suspiciousness, narrowness, and vindictiveness, he had also the calmer virtues of domesticity and personal honor. He was peculiarly gentle with the weak. Women were pleased with his protecting chivalry. They admired his grave dignity and warm emotions. For children he had a tender heart, and the cry of an infant aroused his warm sympathy. His letters contain many expressions of pride in the developments of the children of his adopted son and of distress over their suffering. Into his relations with his relatives storms rarely entered. To them he was the clan leader and defender.

With true Southern feeling he took every woman seriously. In 1833 a New Haven spinster appealed to Van Buren to introduce her to Jackson, so that she might win his affection and become his wife. Her letter was forwarded to Jackson, who wrote in the finest possible strain, and with his own hand: "Whatever may be her virtues, I could make but one answer to any partiality they could form for me, and that is, my heart is in the grave of my dear departed wife, from which sacred spot no living being can recall it. In the cultivation of the sentiments of friendship, which are perhaps rendered more active by the loss I have sustained, I trust I shall always be able to produce

[1] March 6, 1837, Jackson Mss.

suitable returns for the favor of my acquaintances; and if therefore I ever meet this lady I shall hope to satisfy her that I appreciate as I ought her kindness, tho' I cannot for a moment entertain the proposition it has led her to make."[1]

Much of the affection of his old age centred in the family and person of his adopted son, a man whose business failures brought much sorrow. For the son's wife, Sarah York Jackson, the father had a strong affection which was well deserved by her calm and faithful care of his old age. His fatherly instinct was marked. It appears with many other virtues, in the following letter to Andrew Jackson, Jr., written from Washington, March 9, 1834, after paying many of the young man's debts:

My dear son, I recd yesterday your letter of the 16th ultimo, and have read with attention, and am more than pleased that you have taken a just view of that fatherly advice I have been constantly pressing upon you, believing as I do, that unless you adopt them you cannot possibly get well thro life and provide for an increasing family which it is now your duty to do, and have the means of giving them such education as your duty to them as a parent requires, and their standing in society, merits.

My dear son, It is enough for me that you acknowledge your error, it is the error of youth and inexperience, and my son I fully forgive them. You have my advice, it is that of a tender and affectionate father given to you for your benefit and that of your dear and amiable family, and I pray you to adhere to it in all respects and it will give peace and plenty thro life and that of your amiable Sarah and her dear little ones. Keep clear of Banks and indebtedness, and you live a freeman, and die in independence and leave your family so.

Before this reaches you, you will have received my letter enclosing Mr. Hubbs note, cancelled; and as soon as you furnish me with the full amount of the debts due by the farm, with any you may have contracted in Tennessee, and the contract with Mr. Hill for the land purchased, I will, if my means are

[1]Van Buren to Jackson, July 22nd; Jackson to Van Buren, July 25, 1833; Van Buren Mss.

equal to the object, free you from debt and the farm, when the farm with the aid of your own industry and economy must support us, and after I am gone, you and your family. Hence it is, and was, that I was and am so solicitous to be furnished with the full information on all the points required of you. Those who do not settle all their accounts at the end of the year, cannot know what means he really possesses, for the next; and remember, my son, that honesty and justice to all men require that we should always live within our own means, and not on those of others, when it may be, that those to whom we are indebted are relying on what we owe them, for their own support. Therefore it is unjust to live on any but our own means honestly and justly acquired. Follow this rule and a wise and just providence will smile upon your honest endeavours, and surround you with plenty, so long as you deserve it by your just and charitable conduct to all others.[1]

In 1829 many persons thought that a democratic President would rob the office of its dignity. Their fears were only partially realized; for although the new party gave a touch of crudeness to life in Washington generally, the manners of the democratic President on formal occasions were all that could be desired. Francis Lieber, who visited him, spoke admiringly of his "noble, expressive countenance," and said: "He has the appearance of a venerable old man, his features by no means plain; on the contrary, he made the best impression on me."

Tyrone Power, the actor, gives this account:

As viewed on horseback, the General is a fine, soldierly, well-preserved old gentleman, with a pale, wrinkled countenance, and a keen clear eye, restless and searching. His seat is an uncommonly good one, his hand apparently light, and his carriage easy and horseman-like; circumstances though trifling in themselves, not so general here as to escape observation. . . . Both the wife and sister of an English officer of high rank,

[1] Jackson Mss.
[2] Perry, *Life of Lieber*, 92, 93.

themselves women of remarkable refinement of mind and manners, observed to me, in speaking of the President, that they had seldom met a person possessed of more native courtesy, or a more dignified deportment.[1]

A more critical and less friendly observer was Nathaniel Sargent, who said: "In any promiscuous assembly of a thousand men he would have been pointed out above all the others as a man 'born to command,' and who would, in any dangerous emergency, be at once placed in command. Ordinarily, he had the peculiar, rough, independent, free and easy ways of the backwoodsman; but at the same time he had, whenever occasion required, and especially when in the society of ladies, very urbane and graceful manners."[2]

John Fairfield, congressman from Maine, said of him: "He is a warm-hearted, honest old man as ever lived, and possesses talents too of the first order, notwithstanding what many of our Northern folk think of him. He talks about all matters freely and fearlessly without any disguise, and in a straightforward honesty and simplicity of style and manner which you would expect from what I have before said of him. I wish some of our good folks North could hear him talk upon a subject in which he is interested, say the French question, which he talked about on Monday evening. I think their opinions would undergo a change."[3]

Life in the President's house now lost something of the good form of the Virginia régime, but it lost nothing of the air of domesticity. Throughout most of the two administrations the household was directed by Mrs. A. J. Donelson, a woman of firm and refined character whom the people of Washington greatly respected. Her husband, a private secretary of more

---

[1]Power, *Impressions of America* (London), 1836, I., 279, 281.

[2]Sargent, *Public Men and Events*, I., 35, 246.

[3]John Fairfield to his wife, December 9, 1835; Fairfield Mss. in the possession of Miss Martha Fairfield, Saco, Me.

than ordinary ability, was related to Mrs. Jackson. Their presence in the White House gave something of the "Hermitage" feeling to the place. Politicians came and went as freely in office hours as in any exterior public office in the city. Intimates like Van Buren, Eaton, and Blair dropped in at any time, before breakfast, or in the evening, as inclination prompted; and the industrious Lewis for a large part of the administrations lived in the house. Ordinarily the President and his family made one group in the evenings. If a cabinet member, or other official, appeared to talk about public business, he read his documents or otherwise consulted with Jackson in one part of the room, the ladies sewing or chatting and the children playing meanwhile in another part.[1]

The levees were as republican as Jefferson could wish. George Bancroft thus describes one he attended in 1831:

The old man stood in the centre of a little circle, about large enough for a cotillion, and shook hands with everybody that offered. The number of ladies who attended was small; nor were they brilliant. But to compensate for it there was a throng of apprentices, boys of all ages, men not civilized enough to walk about the room with their hats off; the vilest promiscuous medley that ever was congregated in a decent house; many of the lowest gathering round the doors, pouncing with avidity upon the wine and refreshments, tearing the cake with the ravenous keenness of intense hunger; starvelings, and fellows with dirty faces and dirty manners; all the refuse that Washington could turn forth from its workshops and stables. In one part of the room it became necessary to use a rattan.[2]

Bancroft was ever a precise gentleman and in his own day in the capital his entertainments were models of propriety, but we cannot doubt that the people at the levee he attended were absolutely rude. Fortunately he was at a select reception and his

---

[1]For Van Buren's praise of Jackson's love of family, see *Autobiography*, IV., 82, Van Buren Mss.
[2]Howe, *Life of Bancroft*, I., 196.

impressions of it were better. "The old gentleman," he said, "received us as civilly as any private individual could have done; he had me introduced to all the ladies of the family, and such was the perfect ease and good breeding that prevailed there, they talked to me as though I had been an acquaintance of ten years' standing. . . . I received a very favorable impression of the President's personal character; I gave him credit for great firmness in his attachments, for sincere kindness of heart, for a great deal of philanthropy and genuine good feeling; but touching his qualifications for President, avast there — Sparta hath many a wiser than he."[1]

Of a reception at the President's, December 24, 1835, we have this description: More than 300 guests were invited, and there was on this evening much scurrying of the innumerable hacks on Pennsylvania Avenue to take guests to the mansion. Entering the door we leave our wraps, cross a large empty room, pass another door to a room in which Jackson meets his guests. He receives his company by shaking hands with each, which is done in a very kind, courteous and gentlemanly manner, and sometimes with friendly warmth, according to the personage." We may loiter in this room if we will, but we probably pass on to the "blue room," whose light is so trying to the complexion that few ladies will linger a moment in it. Beyond that is the brilliantly lighted "east room," in which the guests promenade, and it fills with people intermingling informally, a lively "scene of bowing, talking, laughing, ogling, squinting, squeezing, etc." In the room are many of the notables of the city, congressmen with their wives, senators, army and naval officers with swords and uniforms, and persons of distinction. The ladies are handsome, or not, as nature made them, but they are uniformly dressed with elegance, mostly in satin gowns with here and there a mantle of rich silk and velvet. Ices, jellies, wine, and lemonade are passed continually among the guests; and at eleven o'clock

[1] *Ibid.* I., 192.

supper is served. Into a large dining-room enter the guests. A table, or counter, surrounds the space set so as to allow the company to sit outside of its perimeter, next the wall. Within this square is a smaller table from which food and drink are served. Of each sort there is an abundance. "I can't describe this supper," says our informant; "I am not capable of it. I can only say it surpassed everything of the kind I ever saw before, and that we had *everything*. This party could not have cost the President much short of $1,500."[1]

Jackson's dinners were generous and in good form. Gen. Robert Patterson, of Philadelphia, gives us this impression of one he attended: "At 4 o'clock, we went to the President's. The party was small, comprising only the General's family and ourselves. The dinner was very neat and served in excellent taste, while the wines were of the choicest qualities. The President himself dined on the simplest fare; bread, milk and vegetables. After dinner took a walk through the grounds about the 'White House' which are laid out with much neatness and order, and filled with a number of shrubs and flowers."[2]

The following items from his personal accounts of 1834 will show how amply his table was spread: October 1st, he had twelve pounds of veal, forty-nine of beef, and nineteen cents' worth of hog's fat. October 2nd, he had eight pounds of mutton, forty pounds of beef, and twenty-five cents' worth of sausages. October 3rd, it was twenty-two pounds of mutton and twenty pounds of beef. October 4th, he had six pounds of sweetbreads, sixteen pounds of mutton, three pounds of lard, $1.10 worth of beef, and twenty-five cents' worth of veal. For drink he was charged on October 13th, with one barrel of ale and half a barrel of beer, and on the 31st, with another barrel of ale. October 1st, he bought three gallons of brandy, two gallons of Holland gin,

[1] John Fairfield to his wife, December 25, 1835, from the Fairfield Mss. in the possession of Miss Martha Fairfield, Saco, Me.

[2] General Patterson's diary, in possession of Mr. Lindsay Patterson, Winston-Salem, N. C.

and one gallon of Jamaica spirits. October 13th, he bought
three bottles of Chateau Margeaux, a like quantity of Chateau
Lafitte, and a dozen bottles of London porter. October 22nd,
he had two gallons each of brandy, Jamaica spirits, and Holland
gin.[1]

Some idea of the furnishing of the President's House under
Jackson may be had from an inventory made March 24, 1825.
The contents of each room appear in faithful description and
are here reproduced because I know of no other such reliable
account. In the entrance hall were four mahogany settees, two
marble consul tables, two elegant brass fenders, one oilcloth
carpet, one thermometer and barometer, and one "lamp with
branches wants repair." In the large levee room were four
large mahogany sofas and twenty-four large mahogany arm-
chairs — all "unfinished," — eight pine tables, one door screen,
one paper screen partition, one mahogany map-stand, one
"common" wash-stand, basin and ewer, one pine clothes-press,
and a book case in three sections. In the "Elliptical Drawing
Room" were one "large glass and gilt chandelier, elegant," two
gilt brown mirrors, one gilt consul table, marble top, two china
vases, one elegant gilt French mantel clock, four bronze and
gilt candelabras with eagle heads, pair of bronze and gilt andirons,
two sofas — gilt and satin — with twenty-four chairs, four settees
and five footstools to match a large French carpet, double silk
window curtains with gilt-eagle cornices and six small curtain
pins, and with two fire screens in gilt and satin, two bronze
candlesticks, and shovel and tongs. Beside the two rooms
mentioned, there were on the first floor a "Yellow Drawing
Room," a "Green Drawing Room," large and small dining-
rooms, a china closet, a pantry, and a porter's room. There
were a "first service" of two hundred and seventy pieces of
French china, a "second service, dessert," of 157 pieces of crim-

[1]Jackson Mss.

son and gilt china, a service of white and gilt china of 232 pieces, a white and gilt French china tea service containing 156 pieces, a blue china dinner service of 66 pieces. The solid silver consisted of 28 dishes in three sizes, one coffee pot, two teapots, one urn, two large tureens with buckskin cases, one sugar dish, eight castor rolls, one set of castors, five nut crackers, with spoons, forks, fish knives, etc. Among these was one large chest with 167 pieces, most of which were solid silver. Another case had 150 pieces of French plate, and there was a French gilt dessert set of 140 pieces. In the basement were the kitchens, the steward's rooms, the servants' hall, servants' rooms with the scantiest furniture, this being a sample: "No. 1, one cot, worn out, one mattress, worn out, one short bench." On the second floor were the family sleeping quarters with six furnished bedrooms, and private drawing and dressing rooms. No mention is made of bath rooms, and the illumination of the house was by candles and lamps.[1]

Jackson was never a careful spender, and through this trait as well as by an abundant hospitality he used all his presidential salary, $25,000 a year. When he left Washington he was poorer than he entered it. "I returned," he said, "with barely ninety dollars in my pockets, Beacon for my family and corn and oats for the stock to buy, the new roof on my house just rebuilt leaking and to be repaired. I carried $5,000 when I went to Washington: it took of my cotton crop $2,250, with my salary, to bring me home. The burning of my house and furniture has left me poor."[2] The "Hermitage" with its contents was burned in 1834.[3] He ordered it rebuilt, according to the old plans. His receipts from his farm during his absence were very small.

As his administration progressed Jackson became deeply

[1]See inventory in the House of Representatives Library, of Congress.
[2]See endorsement on Rev. A. D. Campbell to Jackson, March 17, 1837, Jackson Mss.
[3]Jackson to Van Buren, October 27, 1834, Van Buren Mss.

engrossed in its controversies. Visitors were liable to have from him hot outbursts of wrath against Biddle, Clay, or Calhoun. His particular friends learned to ignore such displays, but other persons found them disagreeable. A caller who alluded to contemporary politics might have a harangue on the decay of liberty.[1] It soon dawned on the public that the President was feeling the effects of the strain on him. Victor as he was, sorrow pressed him down, and he was much alone. Defiantly he watched his beaten foes, who dared not renew the battle as long as he was in power.

The two terms of the presidency brought him continued ill health. Chronic indigestion made it necessary to diet strictly, and but for an iron will he could hardly have lived through the period. Beside this, he suffered continually from the wounds he received in the Benton and Dickinson duels. For his most distressing attacks his favorite remedy was bleeding, and he insisted on using it even when he could ill afford the weakening effects. The winter of 1832-33 was very trying; and in the following spring and summer its difficulties were increased by the death of Overton and Coffee, two of his oldest and best loved friends. More than this, the period saw the culmination of the nullification movement and the opening of the controversy over the removal of the deposits. Together they brought great depression. "I want relaxation from business, and rest," he said, "but where can I get rest? I fear not on this earth."[2] Of Coffee's death he said: "I mourn his loss with the feelings of David for his son [sic] Jonathan. It is useless to mourn. He is gone the way of all the earth and I will soon follow him. Peace to his manes."[3]

It was May 6th of this year that Robert B. Randolph, a lieutenant of the navy, discharged for irregularities in his ac-

[1]Sargent, *Public Men and Events*, II., 21; Howe, *Life of Bancroft*, I., 193.
[2]Jackson to Van Buren, January 6, 1833, Van Buren Mss.
[3]*Ibid* to *ibid*, July 24, 1833, Van Buren Mss.

counts, assaulted Jackson in the cabin of a steamboat at the Alexandria dock. Randolph felt aggrieved for some words in the President's letter approving the dismissal. He found the object of his wrath seated at a table; and when Jackson, who did not know him, rose, Randolph thrust out his hand with the intention, as he later asserted, of pulling the President's nose. Bystanders interfered and bore the irate lieutenant to the shore. Newspapers of both parties deplored the affair. Jackson saw in it a plot to humiliate him and believed that Duff Green was privy to it.[1] The affair brought from him an outburst of his old-time indignation which he expressed in the following words to Van Buren:

If this had been done [*i. e.*, if he had been told that Randolph approached], I would have been prepared and upon my feet, when he never would have moved with life from his tracks he stood in. Still more do I regret that when I got to my feet, and extricated from the bunks, and tables, that my friends interposed, closed the passage to the door, and held me, until I was obliged to tell them if they did not open a passage I would open it with my cane. In the meantime, the villain, surrounded by his friends, had got out of the boat, crying they were carrying him to the civil authority. Thus again I was halted at the warf. Solomon says, "there's a time for all things under the sun," and if the dastard will only present himself to me, I will freely pardon him, after the interview, for every act or thing done to me, or he may thereafter do to me.[2]

This interview, so interestingly conceived, was never brought into reality.

The protest of Southerners in 1835 against circulating abolition literature in the South also was a disturbing factor. Kendall, since 1835, postmaster-general, was asked to exclude such matter from the mails on the ground that it was incendiary: he dared

[1]Jackson to Van Buren, May 19, 1833, Van Buren Mss; Niles, *Register*, XLIV., 170.
[2]*Ibid* to *ibid*, May 12, 1833, Van Buren Mss.

not arouse the North by complying. His decision was in the spirit of the Missouri Compromise, which gave each section what it asked within its own limits. He decided that abolition literature might be mailed in the North but need not be delivered in the South. Jackson seems to have taken little interest in the compromise, but it affected him politically. The extreme Southerners, most of them followers of Calhoun, held meetings which could have no other object than to commit the Southern people to resentment. No man in Southern politics dared oppose the meetings; for to urge that the abolitionists be tolerated was political suicide in that section. The bolder of the leaders went so far as to say that Jackson was blamable because he let this menace develop in the nation.[1]

Jackson deprecated the alarm of the South and thought that the agitation there was unwise, not only because it imperiled his own policies through party dissension, but also because it threatened disunion. John Randolph, old but undiminished in his opposition to Calhoun, realized how much Jackson meant for the preservation of nationality. "I can compare him to nothing," said the Virginian in his last illness, "but a sticking-plaster. As soon as he leaves the Government all the impurities existing in the country will cause a disruption, but while he sticks the union will last."[2]

In 1836 the forces of sectionalism were not strong enough to affect the elections. Neither did Clay, Jackson's arch foe, feel strong enough to defeat him. He withheld his hand and trusted those democrats who objected to the elevation of Van Buren to produce enough disorganization to defeat the favorite. The defection showed first in Tennessee, where Van Buren was identified with the friends of Eaton and Lewis. Both these men were unpopular in the state, and Eaton's foes formed

---

[1] Cf. Judge R. E. Parker to Van Buren, August 12, 1835, Van Buren Mss.
[2] Abram Van Buren to Martin Van Buren, June 3 (or 5), 1833, Van Buren Mss.

an efficient organization when, under Grundy's able leadership, they defeated his hopes of the senate in 1833. Governor Carroll gave the New Yorker fair warning that if he wished the state he should conciliate Grundy.[1]

The threatened disruption took shape in December, 1834, when a majority of the Tennessee members of the national house of representatives endorsed Judge White for President. Jackson was so greatly surprised at this evidence of division that he refused at first to believe his old friend would forsake him. Other states followed the lead of Tennessee. White's boom seemed propitiously launched, but it gained no force in the North and Northwest, where it was not desired to see another Tennessee President. Harrison, of Indiana, and Webster got endorsement in their respective sections, and the opponents of Van Buren began to hope they could throw the election into the house. But they could not shake the hold of the strong machine which the Jackson managers had built up. The results showed 170 votes for Van Buren and 124 for all his opponents. It was a party triumph, but with it was a drop of bitterness: Tennessee went for White and with it went Georgia, on which Jackson lavished all his care in the matter of the Cherokees. Harrison's vote was chiefly in the Northwest and Webster's in New England. South Carolina threw her vote away on Mangum, a Southern whig, but the Jackson organization maintained its hold on North Carolina, Virginia, Pennsylvania, and New York, all old republican states, who together cast 110 of the 148 electoral votes necessary to a choice.

From the election in November events hurried on to the meeting of congress in December. The last annual message, December 5th, was in a tone of triumph. Of the issues before the country in 1829, all had been settled to Jackson's satisfaction. Internal improvements were relegated to the background, the

---

[1] Wm. Carroll to Van Buren, March 11, 1833, Van Buren Mss.

tariff was compromised and the "American system" was checked, the Bank of the United States was closing up its affairs, nullification was laid low, foreign affairs were on a satisfactory basis and our prestige was heightened, the national debt was discharged and revenues were abundant beyond expectation, the irritating situation in Georgia was pacified, and above all the party organization was established on a splendid popular basis. This totality of achievement was so great that it was hardly discredited by the anxiety that came from the Mexican situation and from the uncertain state of the currency. The panic of the following year was not yet discernible. The message closed with an expression of gratitude "to the great body of my fellow-citizens, in whose partiality and indulgence I have found encouragement and support in many difficult and trying scenes through which it has been my lot to pass during my political career. . . . All that has occurred during my administration is calculated to inspire me with increased confidence in the stability of our institutions."[1]

When this message was written he had taken steps for a more formal farewell. The idea was in his mind in 1831, before he decided to stand for reëlection.[2] He recurred to it in 1836, and October 13th wrote to Taney, now his chief agent in preparing such papers, asking for assistance. The subjects he wished to treat, he said, were the glorious union and the schemes of dissatisfied men to dissolve it, the drift toward monopolies, the attempts to "adulterate the currency" with paper money, the rage for speculation and stock-jobbing, and all other things which tended to corrupt the simple virtue which was left us by the fathers. The danger he foresaw for the spirit of union especially alarmed him. "How to impress the public," he said, "with an adequate aversion to the sectional

[1]Richardson, *Messages and Papers of the Presidents*, III., 259.
[2]Jackson to Van Buren, December 17, 1831, Van Buren Mss.

jealousies, the sectional parties, and sectional preferences which centring on mischievous and intriguing individuals, give them power to disturb and shake our happy confederacy, is a matter which has occupied my own thought greatly." He asked Taney to "throw on paper" his ideas on these subjects. Taney willingly complied and promised to bring the result with him when he came to Washington about New Year's to open the regular term of the supreme court.[1] The *Farewell Address*, issued March 4, 1837, follows closely the copy which is preserved in Taney's handwriting in the Jackson manuscripts.

The whigs declared it presumptuous and self-conceited for this ignorant old man, as they called him, to send out a farewell address in imitation of Washington. The extravagance of their criticism discredited their argument and, as in other cases, brought sympathy to its object. Jackson as the leader of a great party might with propriety assume to give them advice. But his advice in itself was not remarkable. The appeal for union was well conceived, but it was overcast by the other points in the document, points which were after all but the re-stated argument of a thousand democratic stumps in the preceding campaign. But the address pleased the democrats, and many a copy on white satin was laid away as a valuable memento of the time.

Ere the people of Washington read the address they crowded the famous "Avenue" to see its author, pale and trembling from disease, ride up to the place at which he laid down his office. The scene gratified his soul. The oath was administered by Chief Justice Taney, twice rejected by the senate but now in office through an awakening of popular opinion: it was taken by Van Buren, who also had been made to feel the effects of the senate's ire. The plaudits of the great multitude were chiefly for the outgoing President. The polite and unruffled Van Buren

---

[1] Jackson to Taney, October 13th; Taney to Jackson, October 15 and 27, 1836, Jackson Mss.

aroused little enthusiasm; but the frank, convinced, and hard-hitting man at his side had either the love or the hatred of men. For weeks before his exit from office he was overwhelmed by visitors, delegations, and addresses from organizations to express approval of his course and good will for his future. When he left Washington on March 7th, his journey was impeded by the demonstrations of his friends. Eighteen days later he arrived in Nashville.

Writing to his successor he characterized his term of office as follows: "The approbation I have received from the people everywhere on my return home on the close of my official life, has been a source of much gratification to me. I have been met at every point by numerous democratic-republican friends, and many repenting whigs, with a hearty welcome and expressions of 'well done thou faithful servant.' This is truly the patriot's reward, the summit of my gratification, and will be my solace to my grave. When I review the arduous administration through which I have passed, the formidable opposition, to its very close, of the combined talents, wealth and power of the whole aristocracy of the United States, aided as it is, by the monied monopolies of the whole country with their corrupting influence, with which we had to contend, I am truly thankful to my God for this happy result. . . . It displays the virtue and power of the sovereign people, and that all must bow to their will. But it was the voice of this sovereign will that so nobly sustained us against this formidable power and enabled me to pass through my administration so as to meet its approbation." No words of the author could characterize Jackson better than these from his own pen. They give a sincere and faithful explanation of his inner self, and they are unconscious of their own egotism.

[1]Jackson to Van Buren, March 30, 1837, Van Buren Mss.

CHAPTER XXXIII

CLOSING YEARS

THE eight years of Jackson's retirement, ending with his death on June 8, 1845, brought him little of the rest he desired. With keen eyes on public affairs he found abundant cause for harassment in the panic of 1837, the long drawn out fight for the sub-treasury, the whig triumph of 1840, the quarrels of Tyler, the obtrusion of the slavery controversy, the question of Texan annexation, the restoration of the New Orleans fine, and the eclipse of Van Buren in 1844. In each of these questions he took the greatest interest, sometimes giving advice that could not be taken, and scolding because it was not followed, but usually contending for a vigorous prosecution of his former policies.

In private affairs he had much anxiety. Bad health, which is particularly distressful to a man of seventy, continued to harass him. Probably it was only his strong will that kept him alive most of these years. His business entanglements had to be cleared by the sale of outlying lands so that to be free of debt he brought his holdings down to the "Hermitage" tract alone, on which with his 150 slaves he must support himself, the family of his son, and the slaves themselves. His house was the object of pilgrimage for many travelers, some of them attached friends and some merely curious strangers. All were received with hearty demonstrations of welcome. Family, slaves, and visitors taxed the resources of the fertile farm to its utmost.

His reception by his neighbors on his return was most cordial. They met him as he neared the "Hermitage," forced him to alight from his carriage, and read him addresses of welcome. A youth speaking for the children said the descendants of his old soldiers and friends hailed him and would serve under his banner. Children and loyalty ever aroused his deep interest, and hearing this speech he bowed his head on his cane, while tears rained from his eyes and from those of the bystanders.

He fell easily into the old life. Neighbors respected him even if they opposed him politically. His family pleased him greatly: the children of his son appealed to his heart: and old friends were received with the utmost graciousness. For his slaves he ever had the patriarch's care and authority. In 1839, when four of them were arrested on a charge of murder, he thought they were persecuted by his enemies through spite and spent much time and money in acquitting them.[1] His manner of life was now sober as became his age and station. Cock-fighting, tall swearing, and other youthful laxities were forgotten. He retained his love of a good horse, and gave himself earnestly to the welfare of his colts, but not with the enthusiasm of former years.

He was hardly at home before the panic of 1837 was upon the country. The Specie Circular of July, 1836, which drew money from the East to pay for Western lands, and the distribution of the surplus revenue, by which nearly nine millions must be transferred quarterly from locality to locality were undoubtedly two immediate causes. But behind both was a long series of land speculation, Western booming, extravagant expenditures, with general over-confidence and some disastrous crop failures. All the New York banks but three suspended specie payment on May 10th, and the banks elsewhere immediately followed their example. Since by law the government could receive only specie and the notes of specie-paying banks, and since the small amount of specie was largely in hiding, the govern-

---

[1] Jackson to Blair, February 20, 1839, Jackson Mss.

ment, though out of debt through Jackson's rigid policy, had not enough money to transact its business. Much of what it had on hand was locked up in banks which could not withstand the tide of depression. A further embarrassment was due to the fact that government funds could legally be deposited only in banks which paid specie for their notes, and the administration was thus forced to care for its funds, since none of the banks met this requirement. Whigs declared the Specie Circular responsible for the evil of the day and began the old trick of sending committees to Washington to ask the President for relief. So strong was the tide that many democrats began to say that the circular ought to be rescinded at least temporarily. Van Buren withstood the demand, much to the gratification of Jackson, who watched him closely. Business men turned to the expedient of private money. Various public and private corporations issued their tokens of credit; and one of the striking resources was several kinds of copper medals the size of a cent which passed as such generally. They had mottoes of political significance. One with the inscription, "Executive Financiering" depicts a strong box inscribed "subtreasury" being carried off on the back of a tortoise, while on the reverse is shown a very lively mule with the legend, "I follow in the steps of my illustrious predecessor." Another design is favorable to the democrats; on one side is the ship *Constitution* with the words, "Van Buren, Metallic Currency," and on the other is shown a strong box above which rises Jackson, sword in hand, evidently guarding the treasure. Around the design are the words, "I take the responsibility."

Though Van Buren would not rescind the Specie Circular, he called congress in extra session for the first Monday in September. It seemed a good opportunity to adopt Jackson's cherished policy of a "complete divorce of the Government from all banks," both as to currency and as to the deposit function. He recommended, therefore, the issue of ten millions of interest-bearing treasury notes, to be receivable with specie for government dues, and he also suggested the creation of a series of sub-treasury offices to hold and pay out public funds without recourse to banks. The first suggestion was enacted into law. It was an emergency measure, but something like it was necessary. The second was incorporated in the first sub-treasury bill, generally known as the "divorce bill," and failed in the house after passing the senate. The democrats controlled the house, but they were not united in their ideas on this subject, and Van Buren was not masterful enough to force them to do his will.

These matters could not but interest Jackson deeply. At the first suggestion of trouble he urged Van Buren to be firm. "You may rest assured," he said, "that nineteen-twentieths of the whole people approve it [the Specie Circular] — all except the speculators and their secret associates and partners."[1] Referring to conditions in Mississippi, where slaves were selling for one third of the former prices, and state bank-notes were 15 per cent. below par, he said that the government would have been in a wretched condition if it had continued to receive for its lands the notes of banks which depended on such conditions. "Let the President," he observed, "take care of the currency or the administration will be shook to the centre." As to the panic, it "will pass away as soon as all the overtraders, gamblers in stock and lands, are broke. Hundreds are yet to fail." And again, "You know I hate the paper system, and believe all banks to be corruptly administered. Their whole object is to make money and like the aristocratic merchants, if money can be made all's well."[2]

His letters to Van Buren and Blair were read by many of his

[1] Jackson to Van Buren, March 22, 1837, Van Buren Mss.
[2] Jackson to Blair, April 2, 18, 24, June 5, 1837, Jackson Mss.

Washington friends and continually gave advice, insistently, as his nature was, but with such continued expressions of affection that no one could have suspected him of dictation. Some former democrats left the party when the sub-treasury was proposed, and this gave him real pain. When some of the deserters set up a so-called democratic paper called the *Madisonian*, he pronounced it a "Trojan Horse, intended to cut the Republican wall into the citadel, and by dividing yield to the federal shin-plaster party, the entire Republican fortress." When he saw indications that Calhoun was coming back to the party he exclaimed, "Be careful of Catiline!"[1]

The year 1838 brought severe illness. There was a swelling in the head, with delirium, after which came sores. For a time his life was despaired of, but with the spring he recovered and "had hope," as he said, "to live to see the Government divorced, a mensa and thora, from all Banks."[2]

By this time Van Buren had returned to the sub-treasury, urging its establishment and a metallic currency in his regular annual message in December, 1837. The senate took up the matter, passing a sub-treasury bill after a long debate. The democrats were in a majority in the house, but were not united. They would not pass the senate bill and nothing was done on the subject.

When this happened the crisis of the panic was past. By August 13th, most of the banks had resumed specie payment and business was approaching normal conditions. But the arguments of the whigs made a strong impression on the public, and the congressional elections showed democratic reverses. That party did not lose the house, but its majority was reduced to eight with seven seats contested. By seizing these doubtful additions the democrats made themselves safe on party measures,

---

[1] Jackson to Blair, September 27, 1837, Jackson Mss.
[2] *Ibid* to *ibid*, March 26, 1838, Jackson Mss.

although they laid themselves open to the charge of partisanship. But their forces were united on the sub-treasury. In January, 1840, the senate passed the bill hastily and sent it to the house, where the whigs managed to delay the vote till the end of June, but not to defeat it ultimately. They sought to affect the elections. They predicted that the results in November would favor their cause, and events showed how well they calculated. The sub-treasury, from which the democrats hoped so much, and which eventually proved a serviceable piece of machinery, went into operation on July 4th, which was not long enough before the election to change results.

The long delay in the house was due to the lack of united effort in the democrats. Van Buren was not the man to force a majority to do his will; and Jackson became keenly alive to the weakness of the situation. When he noticed that although the party had a clear majority it took two months to organize the house, he exclaimed: "It has truly sickened me to see the disgraceful proceedings of Congress by the opposition and the want of unity in the Republican party to check and put such disgraceful proceedings to our country down." June 27th, when the struggle was near the end he urged that party discipline be employed and that the bill be forced through. What would one think, he asked, of a general who gave furloughs to his soldiers when the enemy was drawn up before him in line of battle? If members were absent without permission let them be brought back by the sergeant-at-arms; for "it is no time for the Democratic party to use delicacy or usual comity to those who have combined to destroy our Government."[1] But the ultimate triumph of the "divorce bill" gave him much pleasure, although it was soon offset by the chagrin which the whig victory produced. That event surprised him greatly. In October, 1838, he predicted that Clay would

[1] Jackson to Blair, February 15 and June 27, 1840, Jackson Mss.

not run as the candidate of his party and that Van Buren would not have opposition, unless the whigs put up Harrison, who "will be scarcely a feather, as Ohio is lost to him."[1]

About this time he was asked to get a *nol pros* entered in the indictment of Randolph, who assaulted him in 1833.[2] He refused to interfere on the ground that he had not indicted Randolph, and he disdained to redress wrong in such a manner. "I have to this old age," he said, "complied with my mother's advice to indict no man for assault and battery or sue him for slander."[3] But he added that he hoped Randolph, if convicted, would be pardoned.

The September days brought a visit from Mrs. Blair and her daughter, and about the same time came Kendall to examine the large collection of papers Jackson had preserved for the historian. He was about to begin a life of the hero, a work destined to abandonment before it reached a vital stage in the life of its subject. In the same autumn died Colonel Earl, the painter, whose chief occupation during the last ten years of his life was to paint portraits of Jackson. He was not an industrious worker. Many of his orders came from political admirers of the President, who thought thus doubly to recommend themselves to favor, both through flattering Jackson and through the personal influence of the artist over him. Many of these orders were unfilled when the painter died. He lived with the general for years and was his constant companion, a genial and confiding personage in whom Jackson took great delight. He was shocked by Earl's death and wrote to his other friend, Blair: "I am taught to submit to what Providence chooses, with humble submission. He giveth and he taketh away, and blessed be his name, for he doeth all things well."[4]

[1] Jackson to Van Buren, October 22, 1838, Van Buren Mss.
[2] See above, II., page 715.
[3] Jackson to Van Buren, December 4, 1838, Van Buren Mss.
[4] Jackson to Blair, October 22, 1838, Jackson Mss.

At times his letters become reminiscent. Thanking Blair for past loyalty, he said: "The aid you gave me in my administration, in the most trying times, will not be soon forgotten by me — not whilst I live. There was no temporizing with either; trusting as we did to the virtue of the people, *the real people*, not the politicians and demagogues, we passed through the most responsible and trying scenes, sustained by the bone and sinew of the nation, *the laborers of the land*, where alone, in these days of Bank rule, and ragocrat[1] corruption, real virtue and love of liberty is to be found. May there be no temporizing by the present, no *hotchpotch* with the Banks, and the same people, will be found nobly supporting the present — esto perpetuam."

There was a gleam of the old fire of self-assertion in 1839. Van Buren, mindful of his chances in the following year, planned a tour throughout the Southwest. He spoke of visiting Jackson, but Polk feared that the opposition in Tennessee would take this as outside dictation. The question was referred to Jackson for decision. He replied with bluntness. The apprehensions, he said, were groundless. He wanted to see Van Buren, the democrats of the state wanted to see him, and he himself would meet the visitor at Memphis and conduct him to Nashville. "My course," he told his friend, "has been always to put my enemies at defiance, and pursue my own course."[2] Van Buren's projected tour was abandoned, and that ended the doubts which had been raised.

Richard Rush sent from England a letter on duelling by the Earl of Clarendon. Jackson endorsed on it, "The views of the Earle are those of a Christian but unless some mode is adopted to frown down by society the slanderer, who is worse than the murderer, all attempts to put down duelling will be vain. The murderer only takes the life of the parent and leaves his character

[1] An allusion to " rag-money."
[2] *Ibid* to *ibid*, January 29, 1839, Jackson Mss.
[3] Jackson to Blair, February 20, 1839, Jackson Mss; Jackson to Van Buren, March 4, 1839, Van Buren Mss.

as a goodly heritage to his children, whilst the slanderer takes away his good reputation and leaves him a living monument to his children's disgrace.— A. J."[1]

To Blair he wrote:

I sincerely thank you for the correction of that unwarrantable statement on oath of old Ringgold. There never was more gross falsehoods than he has stated. Governor had my deposition taken. But as it did not suit him and give the negative to all which it appears Ringgold has deposed to, Mr. Butler writes me the Governur would not produce it. What a set of villains we were surrounded with in Washington. Foes exterior with daggers in their hearts. No wonder then that the confiding Barry fell a victim to their treachery and dishonesty. Even Mayo, that the secretary of war and myself kept literally from starving, under the assurance of friendship, purloined my confidential letter, handed it to Adams to do me an injury. This will recoil upon these confederate scamps heads, I hope. Say to my friend Key to spare them not as the receiver of stolen goods is as bad as the thief.[2]

Mayo, it should be said, was suing Blair for saying in the *Globe* that the letter alluded to was stolen, and Francis Scott Key, with whom Jackson had friendly relations while President, was Blair's counsel. Gouverneur was Monroe's son-in-law.

The campaign of 1840 opened gloomily for Van Buren. The confused state of the finances, the growing power of the abolitionists in close Northern states, and the general desire to repudiate a man who had no real strength aside from that of his predecessor all contributed to his weakness. He was a relentless politician and in his rise to power had pushed aside so many of that class that he had no deep hold on them. Unlike Jackson, he had none of that boldness which charms the people. And yet he was the embodiment of the Jacksonian

[1] Rush to Jackson, August 12, 1837, Jackson Mss.
[2] Jackson to Blair, June 5, 1839, Jackson Mss.

policies, which the whigs were trying to reverse, and he must be kept at the head of his party.

His opponents were in several groups, some of them Clay whigs and some of them democrats who would not accept Clay's leadership. These groups disliked one another too much to march under the banner of Clay, the old line whig, and it was seen that Van Buren could be defeated only under the leadership of a man against whom there were not so many inveterate enemies. It thus happened that the whig convention nominated Harrison, of Ohio, with Tyler for vice-president, a state-rights Virginian who repudiated Jackson partly on the doctrine of anti-nullification and partly because he felt that the President assumed too much power in ordering the removal of the deposits. The democrats esteemed Harrison slightly and made the mistake of saying so in terms of undisguised contempt. He was a prosperous farmer of simple taste and the opposing papers exaggerating his poverty made him a man of no account. A disappointed Clay supporter was heard to say that if the candidate were given a pension of $2,000 a year, plenty of hard cider, a log cabin, and a coon, he would give up all pretension to the presidency. A democratic correspondent sent this gleefully to a democratic paper: other papers of the same party took it up, enlarging on the idea. One of them represented the ladies of the District of Columbia as raising money "to supply the 'war-worn hero' with a suit of clothes. If you have any old shoes, old boots, old hats, or old stockings, send them on and they will be forwarded to the 'Hero of North Bend.'"[1] The whigs accepted the issue on this basis and the famous hard-cider campaign was the result. It became so potent that in 1841 Polk was defeated for governor of Tennessee by a man of no ability whose chief performance on the stump was to arise with the most comical manner, draw from

---

[1] Quoted by McMaster, *History of the United States*, VI., 386, Harrison lived at North Bend, O.

his pocket a whig coonskin, gently stroke it with his hand, and say, "Did you ever see such fine fur?"[1] The democrats had shown how to appeal to the masses in one way, but their opponents now found a more successful way in seeking to arouse popular enthusiasm for a plain farmer candidate. Their success disgusted Jackson, who spoke with contempt of "the Logg Cabin, hard cider, and Coon humbuggery."

Although the democrats had no trouble to select their candidate for President, they had the greatest embarrassment in regard to the candidate for vice-president. R. M. Johnson, the incumbent, who in 1837 was only carried by a vote in the senate, desired reëlection. Jackson and his particular following desired Polk for the place. So strong a contest appeared likely that the nominating convention decided to name no one, trusting the issue again to the senate, where the party was safe. Jackson heard of the plan before it was adopted and opposed it in several letters as strongly as he could. It subjected the party, he said with entire honesty and good sense, to the same criticism that it used so effectively against its opponents in 1836 — that as neither candidate could be elected nobody need vote for them.[2]

During the campaign Calhoun and Van Buren drew closer together, and it was then that Jackson sent the latter the letter, already quoted[3] in which he acquitted him of stimulating the quarrel of 1830. It was written more to serve Van Buren than to relieve Calhoun. The latter was coming into his own. The passing of Jackson and of his protégé removed the barrier by which the South Carolinian was shut out of the democratic party. Tyler's administration, the Texas question, and the growth of sectionalism in the South gave him the chance to dis-

[1]Garrett and Goodpasture, *History of Tennessee*, 190.
[2]Jackson to Blair, February 15 and April 3, 1840, Jackson Mss.
[3]Jackson to Van Buren, July 31, 1840, Van Buren Mss. See above, II., 514

solve his alliance with Clay and become again a leader of the democrats.

To the old man at the "Hermitage," racked by disease and disappointed in many ways, the opening events of the new administration seemed ominous. He expected the whigs would pass a bank bill and urged that the democrats give notice as soon as it passed that they would fight for its repeal. He characterized Clay, without apparent occasion, as "always a swaggering, unprincipled demogogue, boldly stepping into difficulties, but meanly sneaking out."[1] He expressed his opinion of Harrison's military ability in the exclamation, "May the Lord have mercy upon us, if we have a war during his Presidency." General Scott he called "a pompous nullity."

The death of Harrison gave him pleasure, which he did not attempt to disguise from his friend Blair. "I anticipated this result," he said, "from the causes you have named. He had not sufficient energy to drive from him the office hunters, and he was obliged to take stimulants to keep up the system. This with fatigue brought on the complaint which carried him hence. A kind and overruling providence has interferred to prolong our glorious union and happy republican system which Genl. Harrison and his cabinet was preparing to destroy under the direction of the profligate demogogue Henry Clay. . . . The Lord ruleth, let the people rejoice."[2] He did not believe Tyler would surrender himself to Clay.

The following observation, also, is interesting, coming from Jackson: "The Genl. [Harrison] had not sufficient energy to say to his heads of departments you shall not dismiss officers without my approbation, not remove any without a fair hearing. . . . Had he removed the first member of his cabinet, as I should have done, who attempted it without his orders, he

[1] Jackson to Van Buren, March 31, 1841, Van Buren Mss.
[2] Jackson to Blair, April 19, 1841, Jackson Mss.

would have been spared by providence."[1] Some allowance must be made for the irritation of a man old and ill, but that done, he still remains in such utterances as this — and his letters at this stage are full of them — a capricious man, whose anger overrides his sense of justice as well as his intellectual consistency.

When Tyler quarreled with Clay in the summer of 1841 he drew near to the democrats, who received him gladly. Jackson thought to facilitate the approach by a letter congratulating the President on his position in relation to a bank. The Virginian replied unctuously. He was pleased, he said, "that the plaudits of the multitude have received the endorsement of the sage in his closet."[2]

But the purposes of Jackson and Tyler were widely apart. Signs of the times indicated that the enthusiasm of 1840 was passing, and the democrats began to have hopes for 1844. Jackson intended that Van Buren should have the nomination for vindication and as the logical candidate. Tyler hoped that he would be able to appear as the regular democratic candidate. It was preposterous that he who defeated the democrats in 1840 should aspire to lead them four years later, but Tyler was capable of illogical plans. Some democrats encouraged his hopes, but Jackson put his veto on them. He was willing, he said, to receive Tyler as a penitent, but not to make him head of the democratic church until he did penance for the sins of 1840.[3] He was then most earnest for Van Buren and said that if that gentleman were elected he would go to Washington in his old "Constitution" carriage and himself escort his friend to the capitol to take the oath of office.[4]

But Calhoun had also to be dealt with. He had no love for

---

[1]Jackson to S. J. Hays, May 4, 1841, Transcripts in Library of Congress.
[2]Tyler to Jackson, September 20, 1842, Jackson Mss.
[3]Jackson to Blair, August 18, 1843, Jackson Mss.
[4]Jackson to Blair, November 25, 1842, Jackson Mss.

Van Buren, although he was now a loyal party man. He led a convinced Southern group who talked of nominating him for President when the democratic convention met in Baltimore in May, 1844. They probably knew this could not be done, but they were in a position to make trouble for other candidates, and they insisted that the interests of the South be respected. That they might accomplish their purposes the better they urged the annexation of Texas with great vigor. It was the kind of question to develop their strength in the South, and they cared little about the effects elsewhere. It was an ominous affair for any candidate who relied on support in both sections of the country.

Jackson was now warmly in favor of annexation. He seems to have forgotten that there was as much likelihood that bringing up the question now would damage Van Buren's chances as in 1836. Perhaps the difference lay in the fact that in 1836 he was better advised. He let his opinion be known; and the enemies of his favorite took advantage of it. They began to urge annexation, and Aaron V. Brown, a Tennessee congressman, wrote him early in 1843 to know his views on the matter. His reply was full and positive. Texas was ours, he said, by the Louisiana purchase; and although he consented to the Florida purchase in 1819 as the best that could be done under the circumstances, he now censured Monroe's government for throwing away an opportunity to increase the national domain, and he attributed that action to Northern jealousy of the rising power of the South and West. Jackson said his change of opinion came when, after he was President, he discovered from Erving's correspondence that Spain would have given up Texas in 1819. He caused to be made a series of extracts to that purport, and they survive among his papers. John Quincy Adams with accustomed vigor attacked him in a speech, and Jackson burst forth in an unbecomingly angry reply in the form of a letter to Gen.

Robert Armstrong.[1] Perhaps the public took little interest in this renewal of an old conflict.

It was a day when prominent politicians were not above playing tricks on one another, and Van Buren's opponents concealed the letter to Brown nearly a year, and in March, 1844, gave it to the public with the date changed to 1844. They had recently seen some cautious utterances of the New Yorker against immediate annexation, and they thus hoped to show that Jackson and his protégé were at variance on the important question. When the Van Burenites saw the situation they hurried one of their number to the "Hermitage" to lay the whole case before its master; and in due time came a second letter from Jackson on annexation. He repeated all his former arguments, but added a strong endorsement of Van Buren, who, it was said, could be trusted to do what ought to be done in the situation.

It is doubtful on which side the advantage now lay, had not the affair been given a decided turn by two letters, one from Clay and the other from Van Buren. The Kentuckian wrote April 17, 1844, a letter from Raleigh, N. C., in which he said: "I consider the annexation of Texas at the present time as a measure compromising the national character, involving us certainly in a war with Mexico, probably with other foreign powers, dangerous to the integrity of the Union, inexpedient in the present financial condition of the country, and not called for by any general expression of public opinion." This letter pleased the North, but that advantage was later undone by a second letter in which he tried to please his Southern followers.

A little earlier than this W. H. Hammett, an unpledged Mississippi delegate to the democratic nominating convention, asked Van Buren's views on the same question. The New

[1]Parton, *Life of Jackson*, III., 662.

Yorker was suspicious of the request, and got Silas Wright to
talk with the questioner. Hammett protested good faith and
said he was informed that Van Buren was for annexation.
He was assured he should have an answer, and Van Buren, somewhat unwillingly, as it seems, wrote a very good letter, in which
he gave reasons why Texas should not be annexed at present.
He urged our neutral obligations, and evils coming from a lust
for power, and said that if there came a real probability that
Texas would fall into English hands the American people would
rise unanimously against it. He also said that if the question
should be forced on him as President he would follow the will
of the American people as expressed in congress. The fact
that these two letters, so similar in sentiment, came so nearly
at the same time has given rise to the suspicion that there was
an agreement between the writers that if it were necessary to
speak they would speak as they did. Van Buren's letter was
sent to Wright, who gave it to Hammett in Washington. Both
men, with some others true to the leader, considered it a fine
stroke and had it printed at once.[1]

The country at large was of a decidedly contrary opinion.
Jackson gives us a graphic picture of how the news came to
Nashville, and it may serve for an illustration of the effect in
other Southern communities. May 4th, the democrats in the
town called a meeting to endorse annexation. The place was
full of people of both parties; for neither whigs nor democrats
dared openly oppose this policy. Early in the day came a
mail with papers containing Clay's letter. It was received
with chagrin by his friends and with joy by his opponents.
Later in the day came another mail, and Van Buren's letter
was in it. Gloom now settled on the faces of the democrats.
The meeting dissolved with little demonstration on either side.

[1]Wright to Van Buren, April 11 and 29, 1844, Van Buren Mss. The letters are summarized by McMaster, *History of the United States*, VII., 328-330.

Jackson was so deeply grieved that he became ill. "I would to God I had been at Mr. V. B. elbow when he closed his letter," he wrote to Blair. "I would have brought to his view *the proper conclusion*. We are all in sackcloth and ashes." By the proper conclusion he meant that although the writer's views were as stated, yet in a case of supreme necessity he would favor annexation. Jackson became convinced that Benton induced Van Buren to write the letter, but he gave no reason for the opinion.[1] A few days showed the seriousness of the situation. Advices from the states south of Tennessee began to come suggesting Polk for the candidate and inquiring for a good Northern man to run with him. "My heart bleeds to hear them, but the die is cast I fear," said Jackson; and he closed a fourth long letter to Blair on this subject in saying: "I write you now, fearful that my complaint, if not checked, may soon deprive me of the strength. I hope for the best, but with calm resignation say 'The Lord's will be done.'"[2] Thus it happened that Van Buren's promising hopes came to an end and the Baltimore convention named Polk for its candidate.

There was much intrigue behind the defeat of Van Buren, and he himself attributed his misfortune to that fact. "If I could think with him" [Jackson], he wrote to Blair, "that my Texas letter controlled the proceedings at Baltimore, I would have a much better opinion of the actors in them. But this I could abundantly show was not the case, if the play were worth the candle. How much like the old man it is to be so entirely engrossed with a single idea, and that always a pregnant one. But whilst he is fighting the British and Mexicans, we will fight the Whigs."[3]

In the meantime Texan annexation came before the senate. Tyler favored this policy as much as Calhoun, and he lent himself

[1] Jackson to Polk, June 27, 1844, Polk Papers, Library of Congress.
[2] Jackson to Blair, May 7, 11 (2 letters), and 18, 1844, Jackson Mss.
[3] Van Buren to Blair, October 5, 1844; Mss., Library of Congress.

to the plans of the Southerners. A small party of abolitionists in Texas in communication with brethren of the same opinion in England formed a plan by which the British government was to be asked to pay for the slaves then in that state on condition that Texas should declare for emancipation. Such a move would give England a strong hold on the country, and it was believed would lead to British occupation. Tyler was informed of the project, and although the British ministry disclaimed any purpose to support the plan, he would not believe that it was no menace to American hopes.

The Texans desired American annexation, but they were not willing to seem to press it. Van Zandt, their agent in Washington, in the winter of 1843–1844 suggested that Texas would ask for annexation if assured that two thirds of the senate would favor a treaty for that purpose. He proposed, also, that Jackson write to President Houston, of Texas, making the offer. Judge Catron, of the supreme court, a Tennessecan, inquired and satisfied himself that the senate was favorable, reported the fact to Jackson, who wrote at once to Houston. A week later Catron became convinced he was mistaken and so informed Jackson, who declined to communicate that information to Houston, saying that the treaty ought to be offered any way and that if this was done American opinion would demand that the rich province be secured. Jackson added that he would close his eyes in peace if Texas were ours.[1]

Jackson got Houston's reply by the hand of W. D. Miller, Houston's private secretary, authorized to talk to the venerable ex-President with the utmost freedom. The result was a letter to a prominent man in Washington, probably Catron, in which Jackson said: "The present golden moment to obtain Texas must not be lost, or Texas must, from necessity, be thrown into

[1]Catron to Jackson, March 9, 1845. Catron puts the date 1833 or 1834, but he evidently meant to say 1843 or 1844. For this phase of the Texas question, see *Executive Documents*, 28th congress, 1st session, volume VI., No. 271. The Jackson letter is at page 109.

the arms of England, and be forever lost to the United States."
He based his opinion on the assurance of Houston that Texas
having offered annexation three times would, if now rejected,
never agree to it again.

Houston did what was expected, writing Jackson a long letter
in which he urged reasons for securing Texas at once. Tyler,
acting through his secretaries of state, Upshur and later Calhoun,
pushed on the preparation of a treaty, and presented it to the
senate April 22, 1844. By this time the extreme Southerners
were vigorously demanding its approval, and the abolitionists
in the North as vigorously urging its rejection. It cannot
be doubted that each side looked chiefly at the bearing of the
matter on the slavery question. So strong was the protest
against it that the moderate men in each party were opposed
to the treaty, and it was rejected by a vote of thirty-five to
sixteen. But neither Tyler nor his followers thought that the
matter was settled.

Jackson's letters at this time were full of annexation. One
of them was to the President, who replied to it on April 14th,
with the assurance that the treaty of annexation was about to
go to the senate. What that body would do he would not say,
but the question was so powerful that it must sooner or later
break down opposition. Tyler added: "For the part, my
dear sir, that you have taken in this great matter, you have
only added another claim to the gratitude of the country. God
grant that you may live many years to enjoy the gratitude
incident to the reflections on a well-spent life."[1]

Benton's attitude toward annexation is interesting. January
16th, when it was newly urged, he wrote to Jackson in haste
and confidence, supporting it warmly. "I think the annexation
of Texas depends *on you*," he said; and he wanted Jackson to
get Houston to authorize the submission of a treaty. "It is now

---

[1]Tyler to Jackson, April 14, 1844, Jackson Mss.

more than twenty years," he continued, "since I had the honor to present your name, for the presidency, to the *first* Democratic meeting in the union, and I have supported you from that day to this, and as I grow older, I feel every day, increased and increasing confidence, in the wisdom of the great measures of your administration."[1]

But Benton soon realized the hand of Calhoun, for whom he ever had distrust; and he refused to vote for the treaty when it appeared. He placed his opposition on the ground that it meant war with Mexico, and he made a three days' speech to that effect. He pronounced the treaty, with its wide boundaries for Texas, an outrage on a neutral power and a selfish scheme to advance the presidential aspirations of Calhoun, the secretary of state, under whose supervision it was prepared. Writing to Jackson a few days later he said that his speech would show all his objections to the treaty but one, and that it concealed a plan for "the dissolution of the union and the formation of a Southern confederacy to include California. We are in a bad way here [in Washington] about as we were in 1824-25. . . . Since the meeting of Congress a nest of members of Congress have been at work to nullify the will of the people in the person of Mr. Van Buren, and now they [are] at work to nullify the convention, and break it up without a nomination, or with the nomination of some one whom the people have rejected. Offices, one hundred millions of Texas lands, ten millions of Texas stock, are making fearful havoc among our public men."[2]

Benton's outspoken words led to a bitter encounter in the senate with McDuffie, who spoke for Calhoun; and the papers told how after it was over the old Jacksonian encountered John Quincy Adams, holding out his hand and saying: "We are

[1] Benton to Jackson, January 10, 1844, Jackson Mss.
[2] Benton to Jackson, May 28, 1844, Jackson Mss. See also Meigs, *Life of Benton* 344-349

both old men, we must now unite and save the Constitution." When Jackson saw these words in the newspapers he wrote: "Do my dear Mr. Blair inform me if this can be true. If it is I want no better proof of his derangement, and it politically prostrates him."

When Benton made the charge that politicians held Texas land, he could not have known that Jackson himself held such property. A. J. Donelson, now Minister to Mexico, writing to his old patron, said, December 24, 1844, that W. D. Miller, Houston's private secretary, was looking after Jackson's land claims in Texas and that they were located about eighty miles from the town of Washington, in that state. Miller made a visit to the "Hermitage" early in 1844.[1] Whether Jackson acquired these claims by purchase or by gift does not appear; but he could not have had them before this question came up, since there are in his letters several references to his property, and nothing is said there about possessions in Texas before 1844.[2]

Tyler's attitude toward the whig program brought Jackson to think well of him, and his position on annexation made the two men friends. As the campaign of 1844 progressed it became of increasing importance that the Virginian should give up his pretensions to the Presidency; and at Polk's request Jackson undertook to persuade him to that step. He gave such a request through Major Lewis, and Tyler acceded to it in a letter to Jackson. He made no conditions, but suggested that his followers be received by the democrats with consideration. He was particularly anxious that Blair and Benton be induced to cease denouncing him and his supporters.[3] He continued to show his favor to Jackson, who was now of great importance to the cause of annexation. In the autumn he

---

[1] Jackson to Blair, June 24, 1844, Jackson Mss.
[2] A. J. Donelson to Jackson, December 24, 1844, Jackson Mss.
[3] Tyler to Jackson, August 18th, September 17th, Polk to Jackson, July 23, 1844, Jackson Mss.

appointed A. J. Donelson, Jackson's former private secretary, minister to Mexico. He was bent on securing Texas in the coming session of congress. Every effort was made to keep the Texans in a frame of mind favorable to annexation, a task probably not so difficult as appeared, and when congress early in 1845 passed the joint resolution for that purpose, he signed it on March 1st, with much pleasure. Jackson also considered it a great achievement; Polk was pleased that a vexatious affair was not left over for his administration. It was the last matter of public interest with which Jackson was prominently connected.

In their private relations the years of Jackson's retirement were not happy. A few of his friends still loved him, among them Blair, Van Buren, and Lewis. But many others forgot him as soon as he ceased to be the commander of a political army, with the power to make himself obeyed and the ability to give rewards. As man after man turned against Van Buren, he took the desertions as personal injuries to himself.

His relation with Major Lewis, which was clouded by the latter's attitude toward the bank controversy, was strained for some time after March 4, 1837. Van Buren did not remove Lewis from his auditorship, but left him without influence. Jackson advised his friend to return to his estate in Tennessee, but the suggestion was not followed. Lewis did not gain in favor with the new administration, and finally, in 1839, Jackson hinted that he had better resign before he was forced out in obedience to the principle of rotation in office. This brought a long protest from the neglected auditor. He admitted that he was out of favor, but it was due to his enemies who poisoned the minds of those who should be grateful. Shortly after Van Buren's inauguration he called on the President and tried to converse with him in the "frank and unreserved manner we had been in the habit of doing before our intercourse had been embarrassed and clouded with distrust." But Van Buren's cold manner satisfied the caller that his alienation was complete. Lewis thought this ingratitude; for no one had stood by the New Yorker when he needed a friend more steadily than he. Let Jackson say if Van Buren had followed "the precept of our divine Saviour, which teaches us to do unto others as we would they should do unto us. The coldest heart would scarcely be incompetent to appreciate my feelings when I first discovered the petrifying change in the deportment toward me, on the part of one for whom I had labored night and day, and on account of whom I had drawn on my devoted head the opposition's fiercest lightning."[1] We can feel for Lewis. He was a tool, but a faithful one. He had served Van Buren well in 1832 and earlier. But his day was past and he was cast aside. In his letter he used some sharp reproaches for Jackson, whom also he thought ungrateful; but these brought a reply equally outspoken.[2] The upshot of this stage of the matter was rather to clear the atmosphere; and after that the two men returned to something of their old intimacy. They exchanged letters at regular intervals as long as Jackson lived.

The years of retirement brought financial embarrassment, the announcement of which gave grim joy to his enemies. It was fit, they said, that he should suffer in the catyclasm he himself brought on others. But his troubles were not due to himself. Unwise management by his son, Andrew, Jr., brought an accumulation of debt. Jackson said most characteristically that it came from the machinations of his enemies,[3] but he determined to pay the indebtedness, although to do so would leave him shorn of all his property except the "Hermitage" tract. He sought to borrow in various places, but there was little money to be had in the West, and from recent experi-

---

[1]Lewis to Jackson, August 30th; Jackson to Lewis, August 13, 1839, Mss. in New York Public Library.

[2]Jackson to Lewis, September 9, October 19, 1839, Mss. in New York Public Library. Many other letters which passed between the two men are in the same collection.

[3]Jackson to Kendall, May, 23, 1842, *Cincinnati Commercial*, February 5, 1879.

ences the Eastern capitalists would not lend in that section. He secured $6,000 from his old friend, Plauché, of New Orleans, but $10,000 more was needed. One day Blair heard Lewis say that the general needed to borrow. He wrote at once to offer $10,000 to be forwarded as soon as the appropriation bill passed. He perhaps saw the fitness of lending to his old patron some of the profits on the fat printing contracts which he got through that patron's favor. The loan was arranged at 6 per cent. interest, although Jackson offered 7 per cent.; and it was to be repaid in three annual instalments. Blair's partner, Rives, insisted on sharing the honor of making the loan. They generously made the accommodation as much like a gift as possible, and extended it when the first payment was not met. It was still unpaid in 1855. In his gratitude to Blair, Jackson sent him a filly out of one of his blooded mares, calling her "Miss Emuckfau," after one of his battles against the Creeks.[1]

March 10, 1842, Senator Linn, of Missouri, introduced a bill to remit the fine of $1,000 laid on Jackson for contempt of Judge Hall in New Orleans, in 1815. It aroused bitter opposition from the whigs. They made it a point of civil polity to refuse, and Jackson made it a point of personal honor to insist as a means of vindication. The discussion was prolonged for two years, Linn dying in the interval. It was ably continued under the leadership of C. J. Ingersoll, who ten years earlier was a leading lawyer for Biddle in the bank controversy. Stephen A. Douglas, then a young member of the house, made a speech in favor of the bill.[2] At last the fine was remitted by a law approved on February 16, 1844. The fine with interest amounted to $2,732; and Jackson sent $620 of it to Blair, $600 to pay interest on the loan and $20, and he playfully said, for the

---

[1] Blair to Jackson, January 18, Jackson Mss. Jackson to Lewis, February 28, March 30, 31, April 2, 23, June 2, 1842, Mss. in New York Public Library.
[2] Johnson, *Life of Douglas*, 69-72.

"outfit of Miss Emuckfau," who was with foal by Priam. The debate on the fine gave him great concern. "My dear Blair," he wrote while it progressed, "I can say to you confidently, unless relieved from some of my afflictions under which I now labor I cannot remain long here. If providence will spare me to hear of your election [as printer to congress], and to see the result of the vote in congress on the subject of the fine imposed by Judge Hall I will be thankful. I hope my friends will press it to a final vote."[1]

During the period of retirement Jackson was an object of veneration to many people. Admirers named their children for him, asked for his autograph, and so many wrote to request a lock of his hair that he adopted the custom of keeping the clippings when he had it cut. A South Carolinian writing for a lock proposed to put it in a thousand-dollar locket and pass it down to his son as a valuable heirloom. A Philadelphia gentleman wrote from his Walnut Street residence in a similar strain, and thanked God as well as Jackson that he owned so great a treasure. John Y. Mason, secretary of the navy, was another who expressed gratitude for a lock of the general's hair.

The approach of Polk's inauguration revived the old man's interest in politics. Judge Catron said that Jackson was responsible for the election because it was he who secured the withdrawal of Tyler.[2] In securing that action, he undoubtedly brought the two wings of the party together, pledging Polk to reasonableness and securing through Tyler the coöperation of the extreme Southerners. The latter now desired Calhoun for the cabinet, but Jackson urged that it should not be granted them. "You could not get on with him," he said. "England is the place for him, there to combat with my Lord Aberdeen,

---

[1]November 22, 1843, Jackson Mss.
[2]Catron to Jackson, November 13, 1844, Jackson Mss.

ANDREW JACKSON IN 1845.   AGE 78

From a daguerreotype by Dan. Adams, of Nashville.   Taken a few weeks before Jackson died.
In the background are seen the pillows on which was propped the invalid's
body when the picture was made

the abolition question." He also suggested that Silas Wright be not offered a cabinet position for the present.[1]

Office-seekers sought his intercession with the President-elect, among them Kendall, in financial straits. He wanted the Spanish mission, then filled by Irving. He wrote Jackson for his influence, saying it would be necessary to remove G. W. Irvine [*sic*]. Jackson was complaisant and wrote Polk as desired. "There can be no delicacy in recalling Erwin," he said, "he is only fit to write a book and scarcely that, and he has become a good Whig."[2] G. W. Erving was minister to Spain when Jackson invaded Florida in 1818; and it seems that the general was not quite clear in his mind as to the difference between the two men.

The state of affairs in regard to Oregon aroused his keenest anticipations. When he knew of England's demands, all his spirit rose in protest. May 2nd, five weeks before he died, he wrote to urge Polk to be firm, saying: "This bold avowal by Peele and Russel of perfect claim to Oregon, must be met as boldly, by a denial of their right, and confidence in our own — that we view it too plain a case of right on our side to hesitate a moment upon the subject of extending our laws over it, and populating it with our people. Permit me to remind you that during the canvass I gave a thousand pledges for your courage and firmness, both in *war* and in *peace*, to carry on the administration of our government. This subject is intended to try your energy. Dash from your lips the councils of the timid on this question, should there be any in your council. No temporizing with Britain on this subject now — temporizing will not do."[3]

Some of his enemies said that Jackson's mind weakened in

[1] Jackson to Polk, December 16, 1844, *Polk Papers*, Library of Congress.
[2] Jackson to Polk, December 13, 1844; Kendall to Jackson, December 2, 1844; *Polk Papers*, Library of Congress.
[3] Jackson to Polk, May 2, 1845, *Polk Papers*, Library of Congress.

old age. His letters on ordinary topics show that he lost something of the power of sustained energy, but on each matter which interested him the outcome of his mental activity was clear and positive; and the words just quoted show that on a subject which appealed deeply he thought as vigorously as in his palmiest days. His ringing call to Polk has, in fact, all the Napoleonic fire of his early military proclamations.

In Jackson's old age he fulfilled the promise he had long since made to his wife to join the Presbyterian church. This he did early in the year 1839 at the end of a series of revival services and with the usual manifestations of conversion. For thirty-five years before he became President, he said, he was accustomed to read at least three chapters of the Bible daily.[1] Such a man could not have been at any time indifferent to religion as an intellectual fact, however little it may have affected his outward conduct. While President he attended the Presbyterian church regularly. Mrs. Calhoun, mother-in-law of the distinguished South Carolinian, once said that if Jackson were elected President in 1824, she would spend the following winter in Washington, in order to see a President who would go to church. Of her, it was once said that she and Jackson were "the only independent characters" in Washington.[2] In the passages in this book quoted from his letters are abundant evidences of a pious attitude in bearing sorrow and of dependence on God in times of great danger. These feelings increased with old age and with the approach of death: they do not seem to have been more frequent after the date of his conversion. Nor is there any noticeable decrease after that date in the angry epithets he hurled at his opponents. Clay and Adams to the day of his death were unforgiven, and some of his last utterances were to pronounce them falsifiers. Religion was only one of his emotions.

---

[1]Parton, *Life of Jackson*, III., 633.   See also, B. F. Butler to Jackson, March 16, 1839, Jackson Mss.
[2]Rev. E. S. Ely to Jackson, January 28, 1829, Jackson Mss.

Next to his devotion to his wife Jackson's best friendship was with Blair. From the beginning of his retirement to the end of his life he wrote regularly to his friend in Washington. Hardly a week passed without a letter. In 1842 both Blair and Lewis visited the "Hermitage," and Van Buren came also on his tour in the South. The visits brought cheerfulness for a time; but the progress of disease prevented real happiness. Eyes failed, dizziness and weakness became more notable, and at last in the winter of 1844–45 came dropsical symptoms. To the doctors it indicated a failure of functions which precedes the end. They knew not how to control them, and the dropsy developed throughout the spring.

The letters to Blair witness in many ways the advance of the disease. The patient, who knew the significance of his symptoms, reported faithfully all that bore on them. His handwriting, bold and large in ordinary times, now shows his advancing weakness. The characters never lose their size, but they get a greater slant, the loops run down and up to a point, and the lines are made with a fine waver which leaves its zigzag throughout their entire course. But for all that, every detail to the crossing of t's and dotting of i's is complete, except that now and then a word is inadvertently omitted.

The last letter of the series is dated May 26th, two weeks before he died. It contains some information for C. J. Ingersoll, in regard to the invasion of Florida, and after that comes to his health. Describing it he says: "This is my situation, and in what it may result God only knows. I am resting patiently under the visitations of providence, calmly resigned to his will. It would be a miracle should I be restored to health under all these afflictions. The Lord's will be done."

June 8, 1845, he died peacefully and two days later was buried by the side of his wife in the "Hermitage" garden. The long illness had attracted the attention of the whole country, and many friends came to say farewell. By his own wish the funeral was as simple as possible. An Oriental sarcophagus popularly said to have once contained the bones of Alexander Severus, the Roman emperor, was offered him in March, 1845, for his own body. He refused it, saying: "My republican feelings and principles forbid it, the simplicity of our system of government forbids it." Memorial services were held by his friends in many cities. Some bitter partisans would not attend them, even as he himself would not attend a similar meeting in honor of John Marshall. But with the majority of the people his death was a genuine sorrow. To them he was a real hero — a personification of a great cause, and the passing of his influence was a national loss.

Time has softened some of the asperities of the epoch in which he lived. The American who now knows how to estimate the life of the Jacksonian era will take something from the pretensions of his enemies and add something to the virtues hitherto accorded his partisans. Jackson's lack of education, his crude judgments in many affairs, his occasional outbreaks of passion, his habitual hatred of those enemies with whom he had not made friends for party purposes, and his crude ideas of some political policies — all lose some of their infelicity in the face of his brave, frank, masterly leadership of the democratic movement which then established itself in our life. This was his task: he was adapted to it; he did it faithfully, conscientiously, ably. Few American Presidents have better lived up to the demands of the movement which brought them into power.

INDEX

INDEX

A

Printed in the United States of America.

DATE DUE

Demco, Inc. 38-293